Fakes, Forgeries,
and
Fictions

Fakes, Forgeries,
and
Fictions

Writing Ancient and Modern Christian Apocrypha

PROCEEDINGS FROM THE 2015 YORK UNIVERSITY
CHRISTIAN APOCRYPHA SYMPOSIUM

Edited by
TONY BURKE

Foreword by
ANDREW GREGORY

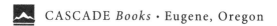 CASCADE *Books* · Eugene, Oregon

FAKES, FORGERIES, AND FICTIONS
Writing Ancient and Modern Christian Apocrypha
Proceedings from the 2015 York University Christian Apocrypha Symposium

Cascade Books
An Imprint of Wipf and Stock Publishers
199 W. 8th Ave., Suite 3
Eugene, OR 97401

www.wipfandstock.com

PAPERBACK ISBN: 978-1-5326-0373-0
HARDCOVER ISBN: 978-1-5326-0375-4
EBOOK ISBN: 978-1-5326-0374-7

Cataloging-in-Publication data:

Names: Burke, Tony, 1968-, editor | Gregory, Andrew F., foreword.

Title: Fakes, forgeries, and fictions : writing ancient and modern Christian apocrypha : proceedings from the 2015 York University Christian apocrypha symposium / edited by Tony Burke ; foreword by Andrew Gregory.

Description: Eugene, OR: Cascade Books | Includes bibliographical references and indexes.

Identifiers: ISBN: 978-1-5326-0373-0 (paperback) | ISBN: 978-1-5326-0375-4 (hardcover) | ISBN: 978-1-5326-0374-7 (ebook).

Subjects: Apocryphal books (New Testament) | Apocryphal Gospels | Jesus Christ—Biography—History and criticism | Church history—Primitive and early church, ca. 30-600.

Classification: BS2850 F21 2017 (print) | BS2850 (ebook).

Manufactured in the U.S.A.

To Éric Junod and Pierluigi Piovanelli,
whose work on broadening the definition of Christian apocrypha made
the 2015 York Symposium possible.

Contents

Illustrations and Tables

Foreword

— Andrew Gregory —

THIS IS THE THIRD and final volume of printed proceedings of the York University Christian Apocrypha Symposium, from the meeting that took place in 2015, so it seems appropriate to make some comments about the previous two collections in addition to the present book.[1] My brief is to bring a self-consciously European perspective, if that is possible. That seems particularly poignant, as I write this foreword in a week in which I and many others who identify ourselves as both British and European are still struggling to come to terms with the United Kingdom's vote to leave the European Union. Many colleagues (especially scientists) in the University of Oxford, where I work, and in other British universities, are uncertain how this will impact upon co-operation at an institutional level between universities in the UK and elsewhere in Europe, and we face the future with some trepidation. But none of us is in any doubt that scholarly research takes place in an international context, and that the modern equivalent of the Transatlantic Republic of Letters will continue to provide a forum for scholarship and research regardless of how exactly one small cluster of islands to the west of mainland Europe relates to its continental neighbours.

This brings me to the self-consciously North American perspective of the York Symposia and their proceedings, which their editor Tony Burke established out of a desire to raise the profile of scholarship in Canada and in the United States on Christian apocrypha. He notes this in the preface to the first volume,[2] and explains in the introduction that all those who were invited were resident in those two countries.[3] As it happened, their

---

1. The previous volumes were published as Burke, ed., *Ancient Gospel*; and Burke, ed., *Forbidden Texts*.

2. Burke, ed., *Ancient Gospel*, xxiv; echoed in the present volume on p. xix.

3. Burke, "Introduction," 20.

sole focus was on a debate that took place most keenly in North America about the authenticity of the *Longer Gospel of Mark*, since most of the key contributors were based there—a debate that continues in this volume in chapters by Scott Brown (ch. 6), one of the key protagonists, and by Tony Burke (ch. 12). That volume made a significant contribution to clarifying what exactly were the key questions to be addressed, as Burke claims in his preface,[4] and ought to be taken into account in any further discussion of the topic, whether in North America or elsewhere. But what it did not do was to offer any reflection on why the debate was apparently of more interest to North Americans than to Europeans, or how it might have been shaped by a distinctively North American context and perspective. Did European or other scholars simply assume that the debate was closed, and that the *Longer Gospel of Mark* was demonstrably a forgery? Or was it the more Christian culture of the United States (as opposed to a more secular Canada and Europe) that made it a particularly fertile ground for debates about a text that some read (or misread) as portraying Jesus in a homoerotic encounter with a young disciple?

The second volume, however, provided an opportunity for scholars resident in the United States and Canada to reflect on what it might mean to speak of a particularly North American perspective. Some contributions addressed the topic only obliquely, or in passing, and focussed variously on a range of apocryphal texts or on specific issues in the study of those texts, and perhaps approached them in ways that others might see as shaped by their authors' social and intellectual context. Others, however addressed the issue head on, noting not only how North American scholars have built on and were influenced by the work of previous generations of European scholars, as well as by their European contemporaries, but also how the North American context has shaped the work of Europeans working there along with American and Canadian colleagues.

Turning to the present volume, there is much less emphasis on articulating a distinctively North American approach to the study of Christian apocrypha in general, but the range and vigour of work being pursued in Canada and in the United States is evident throughout the volume. In his introduction Burke repeats the point that the collection, like its two predecessors, is intended to showcase the work of North American scholars (p. xix), but he does not labour the point, perhaps because their contribution can now hardly be in doubt, if indeed it ever were. Most contributors do not draw attention to anything distinctively North American in their approach, although Janet Spittler (ch. 18) offers a fascinating account of the notion of

4. Burke, ed., *Ancient Gospel*, xxiii.

a married Jesus in American religiosity, with particular reference to Mormon thought and anti-Mormon propaganda, but noting also the influence of *The Da Vinci Code*, and the responses that it has elicited from American authors. Bart Ehrman, by contrast, notes how many colleagues in North America and elsewhere have neglected important scholarship published in German on the topic of forgery (p. 44), thus reminding us all of the need for an international perspective.

The volume contains much that is of interest, but I limit myself to three observations about its content. First, in its focus on forgery, and on its discussion of the debate about the now certainly forged text referred to as the *Gospel of Jesus' Wife*, it picks up on some issues that were prominent in the first of these three volumes. Scott Brown's contribution to this volume shows that there is more to be said in the debate about the authenticity of the *Longer Gospel of Mark*, as does Tony Burke's, whereas those who survey the debate about the *Gospel of Jesus' Wife* (chs. 15–18 and, in part, ch. 12) show that there are good grounds on which to prove that certain texts are modern forgeries—a conclusion that now seems certain, thanks not only to careful scholarly analysis of the fragmentary Coptic text, but also to the work of a particularly determined and resourceful investigative journalist who seems to have established beyond doubt the identity of the author and the provenance of the text.[5] Thus the greatest value of their contribution lies in their sophisticated analysis of how much of the debate was conducted, rather than in their contribution to the debate itself. As they show, digital technology allowed the process of peer review to take place both quickly and publicly, and reached a conclusion through the application of proven methods in the humanities rather than through scientific analysis of the papyrus and ink, but could not overcome (and may indeed have exacerbated) the limitations of the gendered ways in which scholarship and research is often still conducted in the field of Early Christian Studies, which remains disproportionately populated and often dominated by men. As Caroline T. Schroeder notes, "As scholarship becomes more digital, as our work is increasingly conducted online, our awareness of our own political and ideological commitments—and how they matter—becomes increasingly important" (p. 305). For, as Janet Spittler observes, although the *Gospel of Jesus' Wife* tells us nothing about the historical Jesus or early Christianity, it tells us something about ourselves—"about both our moment in religious history and our moment as an academic field" (p. 373)—and it may tell us things that many of us may find not only difficult to hear, but also difficult to respond to in ways that will help to address the structural discrimination

---

5. Sabar, "Unbelievable Tale."

embedded not only in human society as a whole but also in the academic
fields of Biblical and Early Christian Studies.

Yet the *Gospel of Jesus' Wife*, as we now know, is but one example of
a modern forgery, and stands in a long succession of ancient and modern
texts whose authors have written them with the purpose of deceiving their
readers. Forgery was a form of literary deceit, as noted by Bart Ehrman in
his useful summary of his much longer monograph on this topic (ch. 2), and
it existed in various forms, whether its author included an explicit claim to
be someone else, usually a well-known and authoritative person, or simply
changed or expanded—and thus forged—the work of another author. The
phenomenon, as Ehrman observes, was both widely practiced and widely
condemned (p. 44), and he gives a number of examples of what he considers canonical as well as apocryphal forgeries, as also does Tony Burke in
his survey of forgeries in antiquity, in the Renaissance, and in the modern
world (ch. 1). The history of Christian apocrypha, he notes, is intertwined
with the phenomenon of forgeries, since by their very nature most Christian
apocrypha contain false attributions. But his reminder that they appear to
have been written to satisfy the needs of different communities at different
times (p. 15), reflected also in Piovanelli's claim that "*religious* pseudepigraphy is *more often than not* far removed from forgery" (p. 60), perhaps serves
to problematize the sense of moral clarity that Ehrman finds embedded in
ancient attitudes to pseudepigraphic and other forged texts, even if it does
not directly address or counter his central claims.

Second, we may note the wide range of primary sources that the various contributors to the volume address. These include not only ancient texts
in their ancient contexts, but also later works. Brandon Hawk (ch. 11), for
example, discusses the Latin *Gospel of Pseudo-Matthew*, possibly written
in the early seventh century, and drawing on earlier apocryphal traditions.
Tony Burke (ch. 12) discusses a number of forged gospels from the nineteenth century, one of which Bradley Rice (ch. 13) considers in more detail,
and Eric Vanden Eykel (ch. 14) brings us even closer to the present with
his discussion of novels by living authors. Recent collections of apocryphal
texts produced in Europe, most notably the two Pléiade volumes edited by
François Bovon, Pierre Geoltrain, and Jean-Daniel Kaestli,[6] and the recent
German collection, edited by Christoph Markschies and Jens Schröter,[7]
have already accepted the point that the definition of Christian apocrypha
cannot be restricted to the more limited range of texts previously defended
by Schneemelcher and others, and reflected in earlier collections such as

---

6. Bovon, et al., eds., *Écrits apocryphes chrétiens*.

7. Markschies and Schröter, eds., *Antike christliche Apokryphen*.

that of J. Keith Elliott,[8] or Wilhelm Schneemelcher's most recent revision of Hennecke's *Neuetestamentliche Apokryphen*;[9] but the contributors to this volume ask if the corpus can be extended further still.

Burke, for example, argues that a number of nineteenth-century "lost gospels" are little different from other apocryphal texts created throughout Christian history: "They all claim to be written either by an esteemed early Christian figure or their disciple, they all draw upon canonical Christian Scripture (variously reinterpreting and augmenting it), and they all seek to speak to contemporary situations in ways that the canonical texts do not" (p. 263). Vanden Eykel goes further still, when he suggests that the apocryphal corpus might be expanded even more widely to include twenty-first century novels about Jesus, none of which was written with the goal of deceiving their readers into thinking that they are ancient, and all of which were written as fiction under the name of their actual authors (p. 283). Thus his claim is boldest not because the texts that it seeks to include as Christian apocrypha are contemporary but because they are unambiguously works of modern fiction (i.e., not forgeries, and perhaps in some ways comparable to the ancient texts that Ehrman describes as literary fictions; pp. 46–47) even if they show certain parallels with ancient or medieval apocrypha in terms of style, form, and subject matter. It would be a bold move, he concedes, to remove from Junod's influential definition of Christian apocrypha the requirement that they not only show some connection with events narrated in biblical texts but are also "anonymous or pseudepigraphical texts of Christian origin," but he makes an appealing if playful case for doing so that other scholars (or even Vanden Eykel himself) may wish to develop elsewhere, just as others will surely wish to challenge it.

So what of the future? This is the third and final volume of proceedings of the York University Christian Apocrypha Symposium, as the meeting will no longer take place. But that is because it has given rise to the newly-established NASSCAL, the North American Society for the Study of Christian Apocryphal Literature, which will establish a new open access digital journal, and will lend its weight to a number of projects that seek to encourage or showcase ongoing work on these texts, among them an online bibliography of research, the *More New Testament Apocrypha* volumes, to be published by Eerdmans, and the editions of apocryphal texts published by Polebridge Press, together with a new series, Studies in Christian Apocrypha, also published by Polebridge Press.[10] This is an exciting development,

---

8. Elliott, ed. and trans., *Apocryphal New Testament*.

9. Schneemelcher, ed., *New Testament Apocrypha*.

10. For further details, see http://www.nasscal.com.

and it clearly invites comparisons with the work of a similar European-based organisation, L'Association pour l'étude de la littérature apocryphe chrétienne (AELAC), founded in 1981, whose history and ongoing contribution Jean-Michel Roessli surveyed in the previous volume of proceedings. Some North Americans, among them contributors to these three volumes and associated programmes, are already members of AELAC. It is to be hoped that scholars based in Europe will be able to join members of NASSCAL in their stated aim of furthering work on Christian apocrypha, and that together we can give them the attention that they deserve as valuable windows onto the way in which Christian piety and belief developed in different places at different times. As Ehrman observes, "All of us who labor in the fields of early Christian apocrypha know they are white for harvest" (p. 33), so it is good for the labourers to work together whenever and wherever they can.

Preface

THE PAPERS IN THIS volume were presented at the York University Christian Apocrypha Symposium, "Fakes, Forgeries, and Fictions: Writing Ancient and Modern Christian Apocrypha," held September 25–26, 2015 at York University in Toronto, Canada. The goals of the Symposia Series from its inception was to provide a forum for North American Christian apocrypha scholars to gather, to discuss possible collaborative projects, and to raise awareness of the results of their investigations. Previous symposia in 2011 and the 2013 were critical successes. The 2011 event gathered together experts on the controversial *Secret Gospel of Mark*, a text that many scholars consider a modern forgery. The papers from that event were published in early 2013 as *Ancient Gospel or Modern Forgery? The Secret Gospel of Mark in Debate*. The 2013 symposium featured over 20 Canadian and U.S. scholars to reflect on the North American approaches to Christian apocrypha. The papers from that event were published in 2015 as *Forbidden Texts on the Western Frontier: The Christian Apocrypha in North American Perspectives*.

As in 2013, the 2015 Symposium was organized with Brent Landau and in collaboration with Janet Spittler. My thanks to both of them for all of their work to make the event a success. Also contributing to the event were Joe Oryshak, Peter Dunn, and Richard Last, who volunteered to chauffeur our presenters to and from the airport. Most of all, I want to thank all of the presenters, particularly Caroline Schroeder and Janet Spittler for some last-minute consultation on the discussion of the *Gospel of Jesus' Wife* that occurred in July 2016. Early in the planning process I was informed that our application for government funding, which we enjoyed for the 2013 Symposium, had been denied. Rather than cancel the event, I asked the presenters to help out by funding their own travel. To my surprise, virtually everyone was able to do so. It was gratifying to see such support for the Symposium. Of course, we were not completely without financial support. Several funding bodies within York University came through for us, so we

xix

wish to thank Martin Lockshin and Savitri Ramjattan in the Department of the Humanities, the Office of the Vice-President Research and Innovation, Office of the Vice-President Academic and Provost, the Faculty of Graduate Studies, the Faculty of Liberal Arts and Professional Studies, and the Office of the Master of Vanier College. Particular thanks go to Janet Friskney, Research Officer for the Faculty of Liberal Arts and Professional Studies, who provided vital support throughout the grant-writing process and the pursuit of alternate funding.

We are grateful also to all those who attended the Symposium and participated in the discussions that arose. Special appreciation goes to Andrew Gregory who brings an international voice to the project with his foreword, to to K. C. Hanson and Matthew Wimer at Wipf and Stock Publishers for their continued support of the Symposium, and to Ian Creeger at Wipf and Stock for his patience and diligence throughout the proofing and indexing stages of publication.

As I mention at the end of the introduction to this volume, the YCAS Series is now concluded. Future North American gatherings will take place under the banner of the North American Society for the Study of Christian Apocryphal Literature (NASSCAL). Watch for news of these events on the society's web site (nasscal.com). This brings to an end my role as convener of YCAS. It is gratifying to see how successful the series has been. It has allowed me the opportunity to meet and collaborate with some top-rate scholars, many of whom are also fine people. My thanks go out to all those who have participated in the symposia over the years.

Tony Burke
August 2016

Abbreviations

1 Clem.	*1 Clement*
3 Cor.	*3 Corinthians*
Acts Paul	*Acts of Paul*
Acts Pet.	*Acts of Peter*

Augustine

Haer.	*De haeresibus*

Aulus Gellius

Nocte. att.	*Noctes Atticae*

Clement of Alexandria

Exc.	*Excerpta ex Theodoto*
Paed.	*Paedagogus*
Protr.	*Protrepticus*
Quis div.	*Quis dives salvetur*
Strom.	*Stromata*

Diogenes Laertius

Vit. phil.	*Lives of Philosophers*

Disc. Seth   *Second Discourse of Great Seth*
Ep. Pet. Phil. *Letter of Peter to Philip*

Eusebius of Caesarea

Hist. eccl.   *Historia ecclesiastica*

Herodotus

Hist.   *Historiae*

Ignatius

Eph.   *To the Ephesians*
Magn.   *To the Magnesians*
Pol.   *To Polycarp*
Rom.   *To the Romans*
Smyrn.   *To the Smyrnaeans*
Trall.   *To the Trallians*

Irenaeus

Haer.   *Adversus haereses*

Josephus

Ant.   *Antiquities*
J.W.   *Jewish War*

Keph.   *Kephalaia*

Life Issa   *Life of Saint Issa*

Mart.   Martial

Mart. Pol.   *Martyrdom of Polycarp*

Origen

Comm. Jo.   *Commentarii in evangelium Joannis*

Pass. Andr.   *Passion of Andrew*

Philo

Abr.	*De Abrahamo*
Cher.	*De cherubim*
Leg.	*Legum allegoriae*
Migr.	*De migratione Abrahami*
Sacr.	*De sacrificiis Abelis et Caini*
Somn.	*De somniis*

Plato

Ep.	*Epistulae*
Leg.	*Leges*
Phaedr.	*Phaedrus*
Symp.	*Symposium*
Theaet.	*Theaetetus*

Plutarch

Cam.	*Camillus*
Mor.	*Moralia*
Rom.	*Romulus*

Polycarp

Phil.   *To the Philippians*

Ps.-Mt.   *Gospel of Pseudo-Matthew*

Rev. Magi   *Revelation of the Magi*

Tertullian

Bapt.   *De baptismo*
Marc.   *Adversus Marcionem*
Scorp.   *Scorpiace*

MODERN

ABRL   Anchor Bible Reference Library
AJP   *American Journal of Philology*
APF   *Archiv für Papyrusforschung*
BCNH   Bibliothèque Copte de Nag Hammadi
BHG   *Bibliotheca Hagiographica Graeca.* Edited by François Halkin.
          3 vols. 3rd ed. Brussels: Société des Bollandistes, 1957
BHL   *Bibliotheca Hagiographica Latina Antiquae et Mediae Aetatis.*
          Edited by Société des Bollandistes. 2 vols. Brussels: Société des
          Bollandistes, 1898.
BibInt   *Biblical Interpretation*
BibIntSer Biblical Interpretation Series
BSOR   *Bulletin for the Study of Religion*
CANT   *Clavis Apocryphorum Novi Testamenti.* Edited by Maurits
          Geerard. Turnhout: Brepols, 1992.
CBQ   *Catholic Biblical Quarterly*
CCSA   Corpus Christianorum: Series apocryphorum
CCSL   Corpus Christianorum: Series latina
CHJ   *Cambridge History of Judaism.* Edited by William D. Davies
          and Louis Finkelstein. 4 vols. Cambridge: Cambridge Univer-
          sity Press, 1984–2006
DOP   *Dumbarton Oaks Papers*
ESCJ   Studies in Christianity and Judaism/Études sur le christian-
          isme et le judaïsme
ETR   Études théologiques et religieuses
ExpTim   *Expository Times*
FCNTECW Feminist Companion to the New Testament and Early Chris-
          tian Writings
GCS   Die griechische christliche Schriftsteller der ersten [drei]
          Jahrhunderte

HTR	*Harvard Theological Review*
HTS	Harvard Theological Studies
HUT	Hermeneutische Untersuchungen zur Theologie
ITQ	*Irish Theological Quarterly*
JAAR	*Journal of the American Academy of Religion*
JAC	*Jahrbuch für Antike und Christentum*
JBL	*Journal of Biblical Literature*
JCSCS	*Journal of the Canadian Society for Coptic Studies*
JE	*The Jewish Encyclopedia*
JECS	*Journal of Early Christian Studies*
JES	*Journal of Ecumenical Studies*
JETS	*Journal of the Evangelical Theological Society*
JGRChJ	*Journal of Greco-Roman Christianity and Judaism*
JQR	*Jewish Quarterly Review*
JRS	*Journal of Roman Studies*
JSJ	*Journal for the Study of Judaism*
JSNT	*Journal for the Study of the New Testament*
JSNTSup	Journal for the Study of the New Testament Supplement Series
JSOT	*Journal for the Study of the Old Testament*
JTS	*Journal of Theological Studies*
LNTS	Library of New Testament Studies
LCL	Loeb Classical Library
MAAR	Memoirs of the American Academy in Rome
MH	*Museum Helveticum*
MRTS	Medieval and Renaissance Texts and Studies
MS	*Mediaeval Studies*
NedTT	*Nederlands theologisch tijdschrift*
N.F.	Neue Folge
NHMS	Nag Hammadi and Manichean Studies
NHS	Nag Hammadi Studies
NovT	*Novum Testamentum*
NovTSup	Novum Testamentum Supplements
n.s.	new series
NTOA	Novum Testamentum et orbis Antiquus
NTS	*New Testament Studies*

NTTS	New Testament Tools and Studies
NTTSD	New Testament Tools, Studies, and Documents
OECT	Oxford Early Christian Texts
RBén	*Revue Bénédictine*
RelStTh	*Religious Studies and Theology*
RSR	*Recherches de science religeuse*
SBL	Society of Biblical Literature
SBLTT	Society of Biblical Literature Texts and Translations
SBLSymS	Society of Biblical Literature Symposium Series
SBS	Stuttgarter Bibelstudien
SC	Sources chrétiennes
SHR	Studies in the History of Religions (supplement to *Numen*)
SNTSMS	Society for New Testament Studies Monograph Series
SPAW	*Sitzungsberichte der preussischen Akademie der Wissenschaften*
SR	*Studies in Religion/Sciences Religieuses*
StBibLit	Studies in Biblical Literature
StPatr	*Studia patristica*
SUNT	Studien zur Umwelt des Neuen Testaments
SVC	Supplements to Vigiliae Christianae
TENTS	Texts and Editions for New Testament Study
TSAJ	Texte und Studien zum antiken Judentum
TU	Texte und Untersuchungen
TUGAL	Texte und Untersuchungen zur Geschichte der altchristlichen Literatur
VC	*Vigiliae christianae*
VCSup	Supplements to *Vigiliae Christianae*
WGRW	Writings from the Greco-Roman World
WUNT	Wissenschaftliche Untersuchungen zum Neuen Testament
ZKT	*Zeitschrift für katholische Theologie*
ZPE	*Zeitschrift für Papyrologie und Epigraphik*

Contributors

Scott G. Brown is an independent scholar living in Toronto, Ontario.

Tony Burke is Associate Professor of Early Christianity at York University in Toronto, Ontario.

Bart D. Ehrman is James A. Gray Distinguished Professor of Religious Studies at the University of North Carolina at Chapel Hill.

Gregory Peter Fewster is a PhD Candidate in the Department for the Study of Religion at the University of Toronto.

Mark Goodacre is Professor of Religion at Duke University in Durham, North Carolina.

Andrew Gregory is Chaplain and Fellow of University College, Oxford.

Brandon W. Hawk is Assistant Professor in the Department of English at Rhode Island College.

Brent Landau is Lecturer in Religious Studies at the University of Texas at Austin.

James F. McGrath is Clarence L. Goodwin Chair of New Testament Language and Literature at Butler University, Indianapolis.

Anne Moore is Associate Professor in the Department of Classics and Religion at the University of Calgary.

Pamela Mullins Reaves is Assistant Professor in the Department of Religion at Colorado College.

Timothy Pettipiece is Instructor in the Department of Classics and Religious Studies at the University of Ottawa and in the College of Humanities at Carleton University.

Pierluigi Piovanelli is Professor of Second Temple Judaism and Early Christianity in the Department of Classics and Religious Studies at the University of Ottawa.

Stanley E. Porter is Professor of New Testament (and President and Dean) at McMaster Divinity College.

Bradley N. Rice is a PhD Candidate in the Department of Religious Studies at McGill University.

Caroline T. Schroeder is Professor in the Department of Religious and Classical Studies at the University of the Pacific.

Janet E. Spittler is Assistant Professor of Religious Studies at the University of Virginia.

Eric M. Vanden Eykel is Assistant Professor of Religion at Ferrum College.

— 1 —

Introduction

— Tony Burke —

SINCE THEIR ORIGINS, THE texts that came to be categorized as Christian apocrypha have been maligned by critics. Today also, many modern writers consider them inferior—whether theologically or stylistically—to their canonical counterparts; some writers even try to discourage their readers from seeking them out, worrying that their heretical contents will lead Christians away from orthodoxy. In my short introduction to Christian apocrypha, *Secret Scriptures Revealed*, I describe the efforts of these modern apologists: "They characterize the Apocrypha as late texts, not early; written to destroy Christianity—to promote error, not truth. They are fakes, forgeries, and fictions."[1] Pleased by my alliteration, I advocated using the phrase as the title for the third York University Christian Apocrypha Symposium: "Fakes, Forgeries, and Fictions: Writing Ancient and Modern Christian Apocrypha." The plan was to build the symposium around recent discussion of the *Gospel of Jesus' Wife* (GJW), a recently published apocryphon that according to the emerging scholarly consensus, is a modern "forgery."[2]

1. Burke, *Secret Scriptures Revealed*, 3.

2. The term "forgery," notoriously difficult to define, is used throughout this paper in a general sense for a text written to deceive its intended readers as to its true origins. Other terms used for some of the material here include hoax, mystification (both of which imply the intention of a practical joke), fake, and counterfeit. Defined in the legal sense, forgery has to do specifically with texts. See Russett, *Fictions and Fakes*, 6–8. Bart Ehrman (*Forgery*, 31), for his part, defines "forgery" simply as "books with false authorial claims," and thus includes within it such phenomena as pseudonymity and pseudepigraphy. His definition, however, does not apply well to modern apocrypha

Such a classification is problematic in the study of religion. Pseudepig-raphy is *de rigeour* in religious literature, since most texts were composed long after the events they report. Writing under the name of an illustrious figure from the past bridges the gap in history and lends the texts much-needed authority, and creating new stories of the religion's founders enables contemporary writers to justify developments in the thought and practice of the community. Much of the world's scriptures, then, are forgeries. The phenomenon is even more acute with apocryphal texts, which are excluded from Scripture precisely on the grounds that they are "fakes" or "fictions."

The goal of the symposium, then, was to place GJW and other apocry-phal texts within the larger context of the creation of religious literature. The meeting brought together nineteen Canadian and U.S. scholars to examine the possible motivations behind the production of Christian apocrypha from antiquity until the present day. Authors of these texts may have in-tended to deceive others about the true origins of their writings but it is questionable that they did so in a way distinctly different from the authors of canonical texts. Indeed, what would phrases like "intended to deceive" or "true origins" even mean in various historical and cultural contexts? This question invites examination of our own context, of how scholars within both Biblical Studies and Christian Apocrypha Studies have reacted to the publication of GJW. Just as ancient and medieval texts provide us with a window into the circumstances of their creation and reception, GJW, if it is indeed a modern production, reveals much about interests of the twenty-first century, particularly about the prejudices and proclivities of the schol-ars who have examined it.

But GJW is not the first apocryphal text to be declared a forgery, nor even the first modern text to be so labelled. The nineteenth and twentieth centuries saw the creation of such texts as the *Life of Saint Issa*, the *Letter of Benan*, and the *Essene Gospel of Peace*, each said to have been found in ancient manuscripts. But the creation of apocrypha did not leap over the Middle Ages, nor skip the Renaissance. This phenomenon is intertwined with the history of Christian literature and particularly with efforts of Renaissance-era scholars to reconstruct the past using texts of their own creation.

since several, including the fragmentary GJW, do not include claims of authorship.

BIBLICAL AND CLASSICAL FORGERY:
FROM ANTIQUITY TO THE RENAISSANCE

If lying is as old as language,[3] then forgery must be as old as writing. One of the earliest examples from the classical world is the trick played by the fourth-century BCE historian Anaximenes of Lampsacus, who composed a text insulting Athens, Thebes, and Sparta and attributed it to his rival Theopompus; he then sent copies of the text to each of these cities.[4] Another trick was played on Heraclides of Pontus by Dionysius "the Renegade" around the same time. Dionysius created a tragedy entitled Parthenopaeus and attributed it to Sophocles. Heraclides quoted it as genuine only to find out later that an acrostic in the text spelled out "Heraclides is ignorant of letters."[5] Forgery was commonplace, though not tolerated, throughout antiquity, and biblical writers were not immune to it.[6]

The Bible and contemporaneous Jewish and Christian literature is replete with examples of pseudonymous attributions—some perpetrated by copyists and compilers (biblical texts associated with Moses, David, and Solomon; the New Testament Gospels), some by the authors themselves (Daniel, the *Letter of Aristeas*, the Pastoral and Catholic Epistles, and a wide assortment of apocryphal Christian and Jewish texts). The practice continued into the Middle Ages, primarily occurring in church decretals, hagiography, and legal documents; the phenomenon is so widespread, Anthony Grafton writes, that "perhaps half the legal documents we possess from Merovingian times, and perhaps two-thirds of all documents issued to ecclesiastics before A.D. 1100, are fakes."[7]

The practice of what I prefer to call scholarly forgery—the contemporary creation of a text with the attendant claim of its discovery in an ancient manuscript—begins in the Renaissance, when the search for texts and inscriptions from the classical world brought a flood of material to the

3. According to linguistic theorist Edgar H. Sturtevant (*Introduction to Linguistic Science*, 48–49), language was created out of the desire to deceive.

4. Cited in Metzger, "Literary Forgeries," 6–7. Grafton (*Forgers and Critics*, 8) begins his overview of forgery a little earlier with examples from Middle Kingdom Egypt (2000–1700 BCE) and ancient Israel (the finding of Deuteronomy by the seventh-century BCE King Josiah as narrated in 2 Kings 22). A full range of Ancient Near Eastern and Greco-Roman forgeries are surveyed in Speyer, *Die literarische Fälschung*, 109–49, and briefly in Brox, *Falsche Verfasserangaben*, 45–48.

5. Grafton, *Forgers and Critics*, 3–4. See also Ehrman, *Forgery*, 11–14.

6. Grafton, *Forgers and Critics*, 12–13. Grafton notes ancient terms for forgery and steps taken to prove and prevent its practice. See also Ehrman, *Forgery*, 31–32.

7. Grafton, *Forgers and Critics*, 24.

West "heavily polluted by streams of fraudulent matter."[8] Fragmentary inscriptions were filled in by their discoverers and entirely new texts were
invented to recreate a past "even more to the taste of modern readers and
scholars than was the real antiquity uncovered by technical scholarship."[9]
This became such a problem that the sixteenth-century Spanish jurist Antonio Augustin wrote an essay on telling true inscriptions from false and said
"reasonable men agreed that texts should not be cited until they had been
tested for genuineness and value."[10] Among the literary creations of the time
are: letters of Marcus Aurelius fabricated by Antoine Guevara, archbishop
of Montenedo, in 1529;[11] the Will of Julius Caesar retooled from a Ravenna
manuscript in the sixteenth century by French calligrapher Pierre Hamon,
who was executed for forgery in 1569;[12] 17 treatises by 11 different writers
(including Philo and Cato the Censor) found, according to Giovanni Nanni,
on a journey to Mantua in the fifteenth century;[13] a number of unsubstanti-
ated manuscripts of genuine, extant classical texts published by Simeo Bosius
in the sixteenth century;[14] *De Consolatione* of Cicero, otherwise known only
in fragments, published by Carlo Sigonio of Modena in 1583;[15] a fragment
of Petronius' *Satyricon*, said to have been found in a library at Trau in Dal-
matia around 1645, published by Marinus Statileus;[16] and the complete text
of the *Satyricon* published by François Nodot in 1693 from a manuscript he
said was given to him from somewhere in Belgrade.[17] Spurious discoveries
continued into the eighteenth and nineteenth centuries: in 1784 Gieuseppe
Francesco Meyranesio published 24 new texts;[18] someone writing under the

8. Ibid., 26. Chambers (*History and Motives*, 36, see also 20) remarks that the
interests of forgers changes with the times: "When, as in the Renaissance, men's minds
are bent on the classics, he produces classical imitations; when, as at the end of the last
century, they turn to primitive and forgotten literatures, these become to him a new
source of inspiration."

9. Grafton, *Forgers and Critics*, 26.

10. Ibid., 30.

11. Chambers, *History and Motives*, 21.

12. Grafton, *Forgers and Critics*, 28; see further Delisle, "Cujas déchiffreur de
papyrus."

13. Grafton, *Forgers and Critics*, 28 and 54–55; Farrer, *Literary Forgeries*, 67–81;
Chambers, *History and Motives*, 20.

14. Grafton, *Forgers and Critics*, 32; see further Pasquali, *Storia della tradizione*,
94–95

15. Grafton, *Forgers and Critics*, 45–48; Farrer, *Literary Forgeries*, 5–10; Chambers,
History and Motives, 20–21.

16. Farrer, *Literary Forgeries*, 12–21.

17. Ibid., 23–24.

18. Grafton, *Forgers and Critics*, 32.

pen name P. Seraphinus published an otherwise-unknown, and decidedly Christian, fourth book of Cicero's *De Natura Deorum* in 1811;[19] yet another portion of the *Satyricon*, this time from a manuscript in the monastery of St. Gallen in Switzerland, was published in 1800 by Joseph Marchena, who also claimed to have found in Herculaneum 40 unpublished verses of Catullus;[20] between 1789 and 1794 the Abbé Joseph Vella claimed to have found an Arabic version of the lost books of Livy;[21] Philo Byblius's lost translation of *Sanchoniathon* (a history of Pheonicia) was published by Friedrich Wagenfeld in 1835;[22] and in the nineteenth century Vrain-Denis Lucas fabricated 27,320 letters from such figures as Plato and Seneca as well as some of the apostles, including a letter of Mary Magdalene to Lazarus, and another from Lazarus to Peter, all of which he sold to Michel Chasles, a geometrician and astronomer.[23] In almost all of these cases, no manuscript of the text could be produced when requested—the exceptions being Hamon's Will of Julius Caesar and Statileus's *Satyricon* fragment, both of which bear tell-tale signs of forgery[24]—though it must be said that the early Humanists, at least, were not careful about preserving manuscripts once they had been carefully copied and formally published.[25]

In response to these supposed finds, scholars became quite adept at detecting contemporary forgeries. This happened first with "forged" ancient and medieval texts, such as the Epistles of Phalaris, a Sicilian tyrant of the sixth century BCE, first published in 1470 but determined by Richard Bentley in 1697–1698 to have been written in the second century CE.[26] Bentley's work began a new wave of historical pyrrhonism;[27] indeed, according to Jacob Tunstall, after Bentley, the highest aim of classical criticism became "the distinguishing of what is genuine and what is spurious, in the several writings which are come down to us under ancient and celebrated names."[28] Bentley's two *Dissertations on the Epistles of Phalaris* (1698 and 1699), writ-

19. Farrer, *Literary Forgeries*, 10–12.

20. Ibid., 24–25. Chambers, *History and Motives*, 31–32 mentions two other contemporary forgeries of Catullus.

21. Chambers, *History and Motives*, 32.

22. Farrer, *Literary Forgeries*, 191–201; Chambers, *History and Motives*, 35.

23. Farrer, *Literary Forgeries*, 202–14; Sparrow, *Great Forgers*, 139–49.

24. Farrer, *Literary Forgeries*, 19–20.

25. See Reynolds and Wilson, *Scribes and Scoundrels*, 139–40.

26. Chambers, *History and Motives*, 11–12; Baines, *House of Forgery*, 34–35; Levine, "'Et Tu Brute?'," 72–74; on Bentley's wider career see Reynolds and Wilson, *Scribes and Scholars*, 184–88.

27. A connection made by Levine, "'Et Tu Brute?'," 71.

28. Cited in Baines, *House of Forgery*, 35.

ten to prove the epistles forgeries, is a treasure trove of information on ancient and medieval forgeries. Several other writers of the time got in on the
act by presenting their peers with outlines of the methods in development
for determining the true authorship of texts.[29] The skepticism reached such
a peak that Jean Hardouin, librarian of the Lycee Louis-le-Grand in Paris,
advanced a theory in 1693 that only a handful of ancient works (Cicero,
Pliny's *Natural History*, Virgil's *Georgics*, and Horace's *Epistles* and *Satires*)
are genuine; all others were created in the thirteenth-century. Hardouin
argued also that the Latin Vulgate was the original New Testament and that
the Greek manuscripts, becoming popular at the time in text criticism of the
Bible, were inaccurate translations of the Latin.[30]

Hardouin's interest in the origins of both biblical and classical texts
demonstrates what Bains calls "a strong connection between the two critical
arts in the period,"[31] and how issues of authorship and forgery impacted
them both. The Reformation opened up questions about the authorship
of biblical texts, though these questions were particularly aimed at texts
undervalued by Protestants: the Epistle to the Hebrews and the Catholic
Epistles. Efforts were made to establish the original text of the Bible, employing Hebrew and Greek manuscripts, and several of the classicists,
including Richard Bentley, were involved in that process. Medieval texts,
particularly those that figured in contemporary ecclesiastical debates, also
came under scrutiny. The *Donation of Constantine*, in which Constantine
bequeaths a large part of the Roman Empire to Sylvester, Bishop of Rome
was shown by Lorenzo Valla in 1440 to be a creation of the eighth century;[32]
the *Decretals* attributed to Isidore of Seville proved to be products of the
ninth, not the seventh century;[33] and the genuine Epistles of Ignatius were
separated, thanks in part to the work of Isaac Voss in 1646, from the larger
corpus of the letters, which includes six pseudo-Ignatian epistles created in
the fourth century.[34]

Just as classicists investigated both ancient and contemporary forgeries, scholars of Christianity also were presented with newly-created
texts. Erasmus, known for his work on the Greek New Testament and for

29. See Jones, *New and Full Method*, which discusses and prints many of the texts,
and Lenglet du Fresnoy, *New Method for Studying History*, 1:304–15.

30. Chambers, *History and Motives*, 4; Love, *Attributing Authorship*, 186–87.

31. Baines, *House of Forgery*, 34.

32. Grafton, *Forgers and Critics*, 24 and 30; Chambers, *History and Motives*, 15–16;
Reynolds and Wilson, *Scribes and Scoundrels*, 142–43. For further details on Valla see
Coleman, *Treatise of Lorenzo Valla*.

33. For detailed discussion see Chambers, *History and Motives*, 131–44.

34. Voss, *Epistulae genuinae*. For more on Ps.-Ignatius see Ehrman, *Forgery*, 460–80.

determining true writings of Jerome from the spurious and misattributed,[35] apparently created a forgery of his own. In 1530 he included in his fourth edition of the works of Cyprian a text called *De duplici martyrio* ("On the Two Forms of Martyrdom") which he claimed to have found in an ancient library; yet the Latin is much like Erasmus's style, the contents agree with his own views of martyrdom, and no copy of the text has ever been found.[36] Christoph Matthäus Pfaff claimed in 1712 to have found four fragments of Irenaeus of Lyons and a few years later published them with an extensive commentary. Again, the manuscript, said by Pfaff to reside in Turin, could not be located.[37] Then there is the strange case of Constantin Simonides in the nineteenth century.[38] Simonides sold biblical and classical manuscripts to museums and collectors; some of these are genuine but many are believed to be forgeries, including portions of the *Shepherd of Hermas*. Simonides was associated also with the Mayer Papyri, a collection of biblical manuscripts that included fragments of James, Jude, Genesis, and a manuscript of Matthew that includes a prologue stating that the text was dictated to Nicolaus the Deacon in the fifteenth year after the ascension.[39] Most interesting of all is Simonides' claim to have created Codex Sinaiticus, a claim made in an apparent vendetta against Constantin Tischendorf, who had exposed Simonides as a forger in 1856.[40] The nineteenth century also saw one of the few examples of a forgery related to the Hebrew Bible. In 1883 Moses Shapira, a Jerusalem antiquities dealer, made efforts to sell fragments of a Deuteronomy scroll written in Moabite script and containing an eleventh commandment ("Thou shalt not hate thy brother in thy heart: I am GOD, thy GOD"). This so-called "Shapira Scroll" was determined to be a forgery by Charles Clermont-Ganneau and David Ginsburg who argued that the text was written on strips taken from the lower margin of a disused synagogue roll and then treated with chemicals to look ancient.[41]

---

35. Discussion in Love, *Attributing Authorship*, 19–22.

36. Grafton, *Forgers and Critics*, 44–45.

37. Ibid., 32; also summarized in Carlson, *Gospel Hoax*, 16. Pfaff's discovery was countered by Scipio Maffei in his own time but was effectively settled by Adolph von Harnack (*Pfaff'schen Irenäus-Fragmente*) in 1900.

38. Examined in detail in Elliott, *Codex Sinaiticus*; Schaper, *Odyssee des Fälschers*; and somewhat sympathetically in Farrer, *Literary Forgeries*, 39–66. Brief discussion in the context of GJW in Jones, "Jesus' Wife Papyrus," 370–71.

39. On the Mayer Papyri—published as Simonides, *Fac-similes*—see Farrer, *Literary Forgeries*, 53–59.

40. Farrer, *Literary Forgeries*, 59–66.

41. Chambers, *History and Motives*, 35. For further discussion see Rabinowicz, "Shapira Scroll"; and Press, "'Lying Pen of Scribes.'"

As knowledge of the ancient world increases, it becomes easier to find anachronisms, stylistic inconsistencies, and other blunders in supposedly forged texts. But better knowledge of the ancient world and ancient authors also has led to re-evaluations of the charge of forgery. The Croatian manuscript of Petronius' *Cena Trimalchionis* ("Dinner with Trimalchio"), first published in 1664, is now considered genuine, as are the Artemidorus papyrus[42] and the letters of Brutus and Cicero.[43] Some have argued even for a re-evaluation of the Shapira Scroll in light of the subsequent discovery of the Dead Sea Scrolls.[44] Curiously, many of the arguments advanced for forgery at the time—the unlikelihood of sheepskin surviving for 3000 years, the confusion of certain letters by the scribe, the size of the strips—are no longer valid, since the same phenomena are observable in some of the scrolls. The only certain piece of evidence that remains is Shapira himself, who had been exposed earlier as a forger of artefacts.[45]

As Anthony Grafton states, just as a forger's work often bears the stamp of his time period, critics also are influenced by their time: "Many ancient and some later documents have fallen criticism only to rise again when the critic's notion of what can and cannot be 'classical' or 'medieval' reveals its limitations."[46] It is noteworthy also that many critics of forgery were themselves forgers, and sometimes critics who could detect forgeries "showed far less critical discrimination when they dealt with texts that coincided with their assumptions and desires."[47] Care must be taken, therefore, in evaluating the arguments for forgery, particularly since the motivations of those who make the accusations are not much different from those of the forgers—as the Simonides case demonstrates, false charges can result from vendettas, and scholarly careers can be advanced just as much by an investigation of a forgery as by its creation.[48] In the words of Paul Baines, "the discovery of forgery was never neutral."[49] As scholars became more adept at uncovering forgeries and more rigorous about the proper care and cataloging of manuscripts, the forgers had to become more sophisticated

42. Listed, along with several artifacts, in Jones, "Jesus' Wife Papyrus," 368.

43. Levine, "'Et Tu Brute?,'" 89.

44. See Allegro, *Shapira Affair*.

45. For a summary of the early arguments for forgery and their current value see Press, "'Lying Pen of Scribes,'" 146–47.

46. Grafton, *Forgers and Critics*, 125–26.

47. Ibid., 95.

48. In this context, Sari Kivistö ("Crime and its Punishment," 153) discusses the unfounded accusations of dishonesty made against sixteenth-century humanists Giovanni Gioviano Pontano and Angelo Poliziano in the crafting of their critical editions.

49. Baines, *House of Forgery*, 31.

in their craft. Simonides and Shapira, for example, rose to the challenge by fabricating manuscripts using ancient papyrus, duplicating ancient ink recipes, and imitating forms of script.[50] But critics have kept up the pace, employing complex methods of scientific investigation to test the validity of the evidence.

FORGERY AND CHRISTIAN APOCRYPHA

While biblical scholars have been hesitant to use the term "forgery" to describe biblical pseudepigrapha (often preferring to label them "pious frauds"),[51] they have been far less timid in their assessment of noncanonical pseudepigrapha, particularly texts written in late antique or medieval times.[52] From as early as the late second century, texts not accepted by the Roman church have been characterized using the terminology of forgery: *nothōn, pseudos, falsa,* and, of course, *apokryphōs* (Irenaeus, *Haer.* 1.13.1; 1.20.1; 5.21.2; Tertullian, *Pud.* 10.12; *Res.* 63; Eusebius, *Hist. eccl.* 2.23.24; 3.3; 3.25; 4.11.8; 4.22.9; Athanasius, *Ep.* 39).[53] But few of these texts actually bear false attributions—some, like the canonical Gospels, were originally anonymous and acquired apostolic credentials late in the manuscript transmission; others are written *about* early Christian figures, not *by* them. They are "false" principally because the early Roman church did not like their contents, not because of their claims of authorship.[54] That said, some apocryphal texts have at times approached the canonical in estimation. For example, *3 Corinthians*, though not valued in the West, was canonical in Eastern churches for centuries; Paul's *Epistle to the Laodiceans* appears in over 100 Vulgate manuscripts;[55] Eusebius, an authority on canon

---

50. For suspicious qualities about Simonides' manuscripts see Farrer, *Literary Forgeries,* 48–49, 55–56; on the Shapira Scroll, see Rabinowicz, "Shapria Scroll," 9–10, 14–15

51. Metzger, "Literary Forgeries," 15–19 surveys some of the literature; see also Ehrman, *Forgery,* 35–43.

52. On forgery and apocrypha see Chambers, *History and Motives,* 12–14; Frarrer, *Literary Forgeries,* 126–44; and inter alia Ehrman, *Forgery.*

53. For a comprehensive discussion of the terminology as applied to Christian apocrypha, see Tóth, "Way Out of the Tunnel?" 50–63; also Speyer, *Die literarische Fälschung,* 185–86. Speyer incorporates a variety of early Christian apocrypha in his study but particularly noteworthy is his excursus on apocryphal acts (ibid., 210–18). Brox (*Falsche Verfasserangaben,* 26–36) surveys a range of examples of pseudepigraphy in Christian apocrypha and church orders, focusing, like Speyer on the motives for attribution and noting that in some cases, attributions are due to secondary efforts to determine authorship rather than an intention to deceive.

54. See Metzger, "Literary Forgeries," 14–15.

55. The manuscript sources are provided in Berger, *Histoire de la Vulgate.*

in the fourth century, considered the *Abgar Correspondence* to be authentic (*Hist. eccl.* 1.13); and Jerome (*Vir. ill.* 12) and Augustine (*Ep.* 153.14) felt the same about the *Epistles of Paul and Seneca.* Apocrypha clearly created in the medieval period, such as the thirteenth-century *Epistle of Lentulus* and the sixth-century *Epistle of Christ from Heaven*, are frequently dismissed and neglected by scholars as "recent forgeries" and thus unworthy of study, despite their popularity and impact over the centuries.[56] The *Gospel of Barnabas*, too, is often called a forgery, though here at least the deception is more acute, since its Muslim author portrays Jesus uttering prophecies about the coming of Muhammad.

Within Christian apocrypha are three examples, often cited, of texts whose true authorship was discovered in antiquity. In the late second century, Tertullian (*Bapt.* 17) revealed that a certain elder in the church of Asia Minor was removed from office when it was discovered that he had written the *Acts of Paul*. An anti-Christian "Acts of Pilate" of the fourth century is accredited to Theotecnus, an apostate from Christianity and a persecutor of the church at Antioch (Eusebius, *Hist. eccl.* 1.9.3–4; 9.2–5; 9.7.1). And the *Epistle of Pseudo-Titus* was proven by Bishop Salonius to be written by Salvian, a priest of Marseilles.[57] These examples only add to the perception of Christian apocrypha as "forgeries" though, in many respects, they differ little from the similarly-pseudonymous texts contained within the New Testament. Perhaps the situation would be different if the identities of the true authors of the disputed canonical texts were discovered.

The rediscovery of Christian apocrypha in the Renaissance naturally was attended by concern for and accusations of forgery. When Guillaume Postel introduced Western readers to the *Protevengelium of James*,[58] Henri Estienne, the well-known printer of Paris, accused him of creating the text: "Quant au contenu, il est certain qu'il a été forgé par un tel esprit que celui dudit Postel, si d'aventure lui-même n'en est l'auteur, en dérision de la religion chrétienne." He said also that "le diable s'est evidemment mocqué de la chrestienté" in publishing this text.[59] Perhaps Estienne was offended more

56. Beskow, *Strange Tales*, 25–30 and Goodspeed, *Strange New Gospels*, 96–108; *New Chapters*, 191–96; *Modern Apocrypha*, 70–75 include the *Epistle of Christ from Heaven* in their discussions of modern apocrypha; Goodspeed, *Strange New Gospels*, 88–91 includes also the *Epistle of Lentulus*, which Charlesworth (*Authentic Apocrypha*, 5–16) calls "an obvious fake" (5) and "inauthentic" (16).

57. For a discussion of *Ps.-Titus* in this context see Ehrman, *Forgery*, 94–96; see also Speyer, *Die literarische Fälschung*, 31; Brox, *Falsche Verfasserangaben*, 74–75.

58. Postel, *Protevangelion*.

59. Estienne, *Traité préparatif à l'apologie pour Hérodote* (1566) quoted in Amann, *Protévangile de Jacques*, 166.

by Postel's theory on the text—that *Prot. Jas.* was the lost prologue to the Gospel of Mark—than the text itself. It did not help that Postel published only a Latin translation, not the original Greek text, and did not name the manuscript that he used. The publication of a Greek manuscript by Michael Neander fifteen years later,[60] followed by many, many more over subsequent centuries, have made it clear that *Prot. Jas.* is not a Renaissance-era forgery.

Turnabout, as they say, is fair play, and Estienne later was implicated by J. M. Cotterill in an elaborate forgery plot that involved several noncanonical works. In an 1877 article for the *Church Quarterly Review*, Cotterill questioned the authenticity of the *Epistle to Diognetus*, published first by Estienne in 1592 from a now-lost manuscript.[61] His theory is developed further in an 1879 monograph in which he charges that Estienne was knowingly involved in the dissemination of thirteen texts forged between the eighth and thirteenth centuries; these texts included *Ep. Diog.* along with *1* and *2 Clement*, and the *Infancy Gospel of Thomas*.[62] If true, this would mean that the Codex Alexandrinus, one of the principal witnesses for *1* and *2 Clement*, is a Renaissance forgery. Also putting strain on the theory is that, even in Cotterill's time, five Greek manuscripts of *Inf. Gos. Thom.* were known to scholars, along with another in Syriac dating to the sixth century; since Cotterill, the number of witnesses to the text has multiplied to include additional Greek and Syriac manuscripts, as well as Latin, Georgian, Ethiopic, Slavonic, and Irish. Cotterill's theory was never taken seriously. One reviewer at the time called it "a work of great erudition sadly misapplied."[63] Another said that Cotterill's monograph has no "sense of a coherent statement of the case with beginning, middle, and end."[64] The best antidote to such theories, it seems, is new manuscript discoveries that render the possibility of forgery impossible.

---

60. Michael Neander, *Catechesis Martini Lutheri.*

61. The manuscript, *Codex Argentoratensis Graecus* 9 (13th/14th cent.) was burned in a German attack on Strasbourg in 1870. Before its destruction, three transcripts of the text were made: one by Estienne for his edition, one by B. Haus, and another by J. J. Breuer. Estienne's and Haus's still exist but Breuer's is lost. See further Foster, "*Epistle to Diognetus*," 147. James Donaldson, after examining the peculiarities of the text, also speculated that Estienne had created it, but said it was "more likely" that it was created "as to write a good declamation in the old style" by Greeks fleeing to Italy from the Turks (Donaldson, *Critical History*, 2:126–42, esp. 142).

62. Cotterill, *Peregrinus Proteus*. In an 1884 rejoinder to his critics (*Modern Criticism*), Cotterill added Clement's *Epistles to Virgins* to the list of Estienne and co.'s forgeries.

63. In an uncredited review in *The Dublin Review* 3rd ser. 10 (1883) 226–27.

64. Simcox, Review of Cotterill, *Peregrinus Proteus*, 205.

The creation of modern apocrypha began in the late nineteenth century and continued sporadically into subsequent centuries. Their production seems to have been inspired by two activities in biblical scholarship: the publication of manuscripts of legitimate ancient apocrypha and biblical texts, particularly those found in high-profile archeological discoveries, and the romanticism about Eastern religions occasioned by the work of the Religionsgeschichtliche Schule. Add to these activities the broader discussion in the academy about the authenticity and reliability of the Bible and the search for the historical Jesus, filter it all through the perspectives of nineteenth-century occultist movements such as the Theosophical Society and the result is a steady crop of newly discovered gospels presenting Jesus as everything from an Essene to a Buddhist to a vegetarian.[65] An anxious public, their faith eroded by attacks on the biblical Gospels and their interest peaked by reports of lost gospels recovered from the Egyptian sands, provided an eager market for these new texts. As Philip Jenkins remarks, the nonspecialist public "had no reliable way of telling whether the new offerings represented genuine archeological discoveries scrupulously edited by conscientious scholars, or spurious fictions."[66]

Modern apocrypha have attracted little interest from scholars, likely due to the widespread sense that once proven not to be ancient, they deserve little attention. M. R. James, the great English compiler of apocryphal texts, mentions several of them (the *Life of Saint Issa*, the *Book of Mormon*, and the *Book of Jasher*, along with the apparently-forged fragments of Constantine Simonides) in a lighthearted review of the *Archko Volume*, which he calls "an extremely bad book," for the *Guardian Church Newspaper* in 1900.[67] He returned to the texts (this time mentioning also the *Letter of Benan* and Mendès/Greene's the *Childhood of Christ*) in his 1823 collection *The Apocryphal New Testament*, "more to show my consciousness of their existence than because they are at all interesting."[68] The first systematic treatment of the texts came in 1931 with Edgar J. Goodspeed's *Strange New Gospels*. The volume covers seven of the most well-known nineteenth-century texts (including the *Life of Saint Issa* and one "revealed" text: the *Aquarian Gospel*) and one medieval (the *Epistle of Christ from Heaven*). Though Goodspeed was serious in his efforts to examine these texts, he was candid about the

65. Jenkins, *Hidden Gospels*, 43–53 captures well this spirit of the times but see Maffly-Kipp, *American Scriptures*, vii–xxi for a more sympathetic view.

66. Jenkins, *Hidden Gospels*, 47. See also Goodspeed, *Strange New Gospels*, 1–9.

67. James, "Mare's Nest."

68. James, *Apocryphal New Testament*, 89. Other apocrypha collectors have been similarly dismissive of modern apocrypha; see, for example, the comments made by Schneemelcher in *New Testament Apocrypha*, 1:83–85.

fact that his treatment of the material is not deep nor comprehensive. "I did not seek these curious pieces out," he wrote, "they were brought to me by students and others who had come across them and wished information about them."[69] The goal of the survey was to provide "a useful service . . . by describing them together, and pointing out their failure to meet the simple and familiar tests of antiquity and genuineness."[70] Goodspeed returned to the texts in 1937 in a chapter of his *New Chapters in New Testament Study,*[71] adding to his earlier survey the *Gospel of Josephus,* the *Book of Jasher,* and a critical discussion of *The Lost Books of the Bible,* a poorly constructed collection of apocrypha based on earlier compendia by William Hone and Jeremiah Jones. Finally, Goodspeed revised *Strange New Gospels* in 1956 under the title *Modern Apocrypha* and added to his previous efforts introductions to the *Death Warrant of Jesus,* the *Long-Lost Second Book of Acts, OAHSPE,* the *Nazarene Gospel,* and the medieval *Epistle of Lentulus.*[72]

Shortly after, Bruce Metzger took interest in one particular modern apocryphon: Paul R. Coleman-Norton's "amusing *agraphon,*" published in a 1950 article for *Catholic Biblical Quarterly.* The agraphon, said by Coleman-Norton to have been found in a fragment of the *Opus imperfectum in Matthaeum,* is an expansion of Matthew 24:51, which continues in the fragment with a question from the disciples about how those who are toothless can "gnash their teeth" at the judgement. Metzger proved the saying to be Coleman-Norton's creation by noting that Coleman-Norton knew its contents before his alleged discovery.[73]

A treatment similar to Goodspeed's multiple works was provided in 1953 by Per Beskow's *Strange Tales about Jesus.*[74] Beskow envisioned his edition as an update of Goodspeed, adding texts that had appeared in the interim and with a more European focus.[75] The most significant of these additions, for our purposes, are the *Gospel of the Holy Twelve,* the *Essene Gospel of Peace,* and *Secret Mark.* Beskow included *Secret Mark* because he suspected it to be a modern forgery and insinuated that Morton Smith created the text. Smith was so incensed by the accusation, that he threatened to sue the publisher; as a result, the edition was withdrawn and then reissued

69. Goodspeed, *Strange New Gospels,* vii.

70. Ibid., viii.

71. Goodspeed, *New Chapters,* 189–219.

72. Reprinted in 1968 as *Famous Biblical Hoaxes.*

73. Metzger, "Literary Forgeries," 3–4 (see also Metzger, *Reminiscences of an Octogenarian,* 136–39).

74. Originally published in Swedish in 1979.

75. Beskow, *Strange Tales,* viii. Page references are to the 1983 edition.

in 1985 with a rewritten chapter on *Secret Mark*.[76] The strength of Beskow's collection is its investigation into the pre-history of those texts that proved to be transformations of works of fiction (*A Correct Transcript of Pilate's Court*, and the *Crucifixion of Jesus, by an Eyewitness*).[77] Beskow also contributed a study of legends about Jesus in India—*Jesus i Kasmir* from 1981—and most recently a 2011 survey essay of "Modern Mystifications of Jesus," by which he means "unverified speculations about Jesus."[78] Under this umbrella term he includes, once again, Jesus in India, descendants of Jesus and Mary Magdalene, Mary Magdalene as a feminist symbol, and an indictment of American scholarship for its willingness to embrace these ideas.

No one within Christian Apocrypha Studies has embraced Goodspeed's and Beskow's work more than Pierluigi Piovanelli, though he does not share with them the need to prove the texts "inauthentic." Piovanelli has criticized modern collectors of apocrypha for their dismissive attitudes to these texts. He sees their production as little different from the production of antique or medieval apocrypha, all of which were created to reinterpret Christian mythology for a new era: "the apocryphal reinvention of the origins is, in my opinion, an almost universal phenomenon that can contribute to save a living tradition from the oblivion that is in store for it, constantly reactualizing and re-legitimizing such a tradition as time goes by."[79] Even modern fiction—such as Nikos Kazantsakis' *The Last Temptation of Christ*[80]—can function the same way. Focusing specifically on the *Aquarian Gospel*, Piovanelli seeks to show that not every modern apocryphon was written by "unscrupulous swindlers"; instead he considers this text a thoughtful work of piety.[81] The same sympathetic attitude to the literature lies behind Piovanelli's call for a third volume to the well-regarded Pleiades series *Écrits apocryphes chrétiens*, this one compiling a variety of modern apocrypha.[82] Something like Piovanelli's proposed volume is available in Laurie Maffly-Kipp's *American Scriptures*. The 2010 compilation includes excerpts from both "scholarly" (the *Life of Saint Issa*, the *Archko Volume*)

76. Beskow, "Mystifications," 459–60 looks back at the threat of suit and its consequences.

77. Beskow, *Strange Tales*, 47, 53–54. See the discussion of these texts in ch. 12 of this volume.

78. Beskow, "Modern Mystifications," 460–61.

79. Piovanelli, "What is a Christian Apocryphal Text?," 39. Much of Piovanelli's remarks on modern apocrypha are contained also in Piovanelli, "Que'est-ce qu'un 'écrit apocryph chétien'?" 178–86.

80. Piovanelli, "What is a Christian Apocryphal Text?," 37–38.

81. Ibid., 34–36.

82. Piovanelli, "Que'est-ce qu'un 'écrit apocryph chétien'?" 186.

and "revealed" texts (the *Book of Mormon*, the *Occult Life of Jesus of Nazareth*, and others) with brief introductions.

Piovanelli would find Maffly-Kipp's sympathetic approach to the literature congenial; she says of the texts, "These works are compelling and historically valuable because they represent the wide range of popular writings catalyzed by the democratization of religious life in the decades after the American Revolution, an era when men and women, African Americans and whites, and elites and nonelites felt empowered to enact and even design their own scriptural traditions."[83] It is no surprise that scholars most sympathetic toward modern apocrypha are found in the same land that produced the *Book of Mormon*. Beskow thinks this is because North American scholars are more fanciful in their theories, motivated, at least in part, by the "constant pressure . . . to demonstrate their academic efficiency," whereas European scholars focus their attentions on real manuscripts of real texts.[84] Beskow's generalization is easily challenged—Piovanelli, for one, advocates serious study of modern apocrypha but also works on establishing critical editions of late antique apocrypha—and describing the texts simply to dismiss them as "inauthentic" is no help for understanding the phenomenon of apocryphicity, ancient or modern.

Forgery and Christian apocrypha are old, constant friends. By their very nature (i.e., they contain false attributions), most Christian apocrypha *are* forgeries, created to satisfy the ever-changing needs of Christian communities. Throughout the Middle Ages, ecclesiastical voices tried to discredit noncanonical texts by declaring them false. When Enlightenment historians in the West were introduced to new texts from the East, Christian apocrypha were found among them; and when some of these same scholars created texts to fill in the gaps of history, Christian apocrypha were created also. When fiction writers took up the age-old motif of presenting their work as if it were from a lost text found in a newly discovered manuscript, new, fictional gospels also came to light. The motif became part of nonfiction when archeologists and manuscript hunters reported finding legitimate lost gospels, each featuring remarkable new tellings of the lives of Jesus and his contemporaries; suddenly early Christian history was up for grabs, and everyone wanted to create a Jesus that was meaningful to them. And the Christian apocrypha figured also in battles waged by scholars over the authenticity of texts. Just as with classical texts, certain Christian apocrypha have been targeted by scholars simply because of objections to the contents

83. Maffly-Kipp, *American Scriptures*, x.

84. Beskow, "Modern Mystifications," 470–71. A similar distinction between European and American scholarship, particularly when it comes to Christian apocrypha, is made by Roessli, "North American Approaches," 32.

of the texts, and careers were created and destroyed in the process. Christian apocrypha research, particularly in North America, has focused primarily on texts written in the first four centuries, though there is a vigorous effort now to broaden the scope of study to late antique and medieval texts. Little attention has been paid to Renaissance and modern apocrypha, and even the small amount of scholarship available on these texts has seen its goal as to demonstrate that they are forgeries rather than to understand them as products of their time, just like ancient and medieval apocrypha and, indeed, all forms of literature. The 2015 York University Christian Apocrypha Symposium aimed to address this lacuna in the field by examining the means and motives for composing Christian apocrypha at various points throughout history, including our own time.

THE 2015 SYMPOSIUM

The papers collected here represent much of the content of the 2015 Symposium, though they do not appear in the order in which they were presented. Shifts in the contributors' schedules led to numerous rearrangements of the programme, leading at times to awkward combinations of presenters. It was decided that a thematic arrangement of the published papers would be of more benefit to readers. Two of the papers, by Ross Ponder and Dominique Côté, are not included in the volume as the authors were not able to revise their papers in time for publication. The following account of the event is drawn from my reports posted on the blog Apocryphicity; additional overviews of the Symposium have been published in print and online by James McGrath, Timo Paananen, and Bradley Rice.[85]

The first day of the Symposium looked at the composing of apocrypha at several key points in Christian history. The morning session, "Writing Early Christian Apocrypha," began with Stanley Porter's look at our earliest material evidence of apocryphal texts: "Lessons from the Papyri: What Apocryphal Gospel Fragments Reveal about the Textual Development of Early Christianity." Porter's expertise in NT text criticism and the editing of early papyrus fragments is widely acknowledged. Particularly notable with regards to apocryphal texts is his work on the unidentified text of P. Oxy. 210.[86] Porter mentions in his paper that it is difficult to identify the precise nature of apocryphal "gospel fragments"—are they pieces of lengthy

---

85. McGrath's play-by-play of the Symposium starts with his post "#YCAS2015 Begins"; Paananen, "York Christian Apocrypha Symposium"; Rice, "Chronique."

86. Landau and Porter, "Papyrus Oxyrhynchus 210"; Porter, "POxy II 210"; Porter, "Der Papyrus Oxyrhynchus II 210."

"gospel" texts? homilies? canonical gospel harmonies? or are they the remains of apotropaic texts (i.e., magical amulets)? The answer may come
closer to within our reach when the fragments are treated to complete critical editions based on new, in-person evaluation of the manuscripts, tools
that Porter thinks are long overdue. Also still undetermined, Porter states, is
how the texts were used by early Christian communities; "if these fragmentary gospels were used in a liturgical fashion," he writes in his paper, "they
do not appear to have been used in the same way as scriptural readings
of texts. They were perhaps supplementary episodes, read for edification
and further elaboration, but not as the scriptural text itself or as a substitute for it" (p. 72). The statement seems to impose a hierarchy upon the
evidence, with NT Gospels necessarily occupying a superior place in the
early period than noncanonical texts. This viewpoint reflects assumptions
about early Christian literature that are somewhat at variance from those of
the majority of the Symposium's participants—for example, he believes the
canonical Gospels were all composed prior to the Jewish War. This confessional approach may lie behind his argument that the fragments "reinforce
a relatively stable text of the Greek New Testament by the time of their composition." Audience members at the Symposium, including Bart Ehrman,
found Porter's statement somewhat puzzling—there is no "Greek New Testament" to speak of in the first few centuries, and the gospel fragments only
show contact with the NT gospels, not the entire NT. Porter's finished paper
clarifies the issue somewhat with its substitution of "canonical Gospels" for
"Greek New Testament" (see p. 77).

Some of the questions posed by Porter about the nature of the apocryphal gospel papyri were answered, at least in part, by Ross Ponder, the
first of three student presenters at this year's Symposium. His draft paper,
"Reconsidering P. Oxy. 5072: Creation and Reception, Visual and Physical
Features," examines a gospel fragment that contains a version of the story of
the Gadarene demoniac and a conversation between Jesus and his disciples.
Ponder notes the presence in the manuscript of several reader's aids (*para-
graphos* marker, diaieresis, and slashes) which, Ponder writes, "could mean
that it was intended for liturgical/public reading."[87] This text, then, could
have been held in just as high an esteem as those that were later deemed
canonical, a determination that challenges Porter's canonical/noncanonical
dichotomy. After Ponder's presentation, Bart Ehrman again joined in the
discussion, remarking to Stanley Porter that the contents of P. Oxy. 5072
demonstrated the fluidity of the "Greek New Testament," not its stability.

---

87. For more on Ponder's thoughts on these aids see Ponder, "Papyrus Oxyrhynchus
5072."

The third paper in the session was delivered by Brent Landau, the co-convenor of the Symposium. The paper, "Under the Influence (of the Magi): Did Hallucinogens Play a Role in the Inspired Composition of the Pseudepigraphic *Revelation of the Magi*?," directly addresses the issue of composition, suggesting that the contents of *Rev. Magi* may have originated in visions. Landau argues that the text contains "references to visionary experiences that some group of early Christians underwent" (pp. 79–80) and that the star-food mentioned in the text "is best explained by positing that the early Christians behind *Rev. Magi* had ingested, quite possibly in a ritual manner, a hallucinogenic substance of some sort" (p. 80). The theory places Landau among "entheogenists," a group of scholars studying hallucinogens in religious ritual. The group's theories have not been taken very seriously by Biblical Studies scholars, and Landau goes to great pains to defend some aspects of their work; he is helped in this by Jim Davila, who has presented a set of criteria for determining whether certain actions in ancient religious texts can be identified as evidence for ritual practices.[88]

The session concluded with a contribution from third-time Symposium presenter Pierluigi Piovanelli. His paper, "What Has Pseudepigraphy to Do with Forgery? Reflections on the Cases of the *Acts of Paul*, the *Apocalypse of Paul*, and the *Zohar*," touches on a number of topics that were revisited in later discussions over the course of the Symposium. First, he notes that accusations of forgery, such as Tertullian's indictment of a certain presbyter for the creation of the *Acts of Paul*, result from the accuser's distaste of the text's contents. In Tertullian's case, he branded the text a forgery because he objected to its support of women performing baptism and teaching. Second, Piovanelli draws attention to a medieval forgery: the *Zohar*, attributed to Rabbi Aquiva, but apparently composed in the fourteenth century by Moses de Léon. Piovanelli uses Gershom Scholem's defense of de Léon's deception to excuse the practice of pseudepigraphy as being "far removed from forgery" and "a legitimate category of religious literature of the highest moral order."[89] Leading the response to Piovanelli's paper, Bart Ehrman asked, "are you saying that the writers of texts like the *Acts of Paul* are not trying to deceive?" To which Piovanelli replied, "No, they see themselves as inspired" and writing in the "school of thought" of the person whose name appears as author of the text. Ehrman and Piovanelli then discussed the "we" section in the canonical Acts, which Piovanelli explained as a "historiographical device, not a mark of forgery." Ehrman ended the exchange saying, "We have a lot to disagree about."

88. Davila, "Ritual in the Jewish Pseudepigrapha."
89. Scholem, *Major Trends*, 204.

The afternoon began with the session "Reusing and Recycling Christian Apocrypha," which moved the discussion away from the origins of texts to their transformation and transmission in new contexts. Brandon W. Hawk spoke first with "'Cherries at Command': Preaching the *Gospel of Pseudo-Matthew* in Anglo-Saxon England." The paper examines the use of *Ps.-Mt.* in two medieval sources. The first is an Old English sermon designated Vercelli 6 (created ca. 959–988), which contains an enumeration of miracles heralding Jesus' birth (including golden rings around the sun and the Roman emperor forgiving all people) followed by excerpts from *Ps.-Mt.* on Jesus' birth, the slaughter of the innocents, and the flight to Egypt. The second source is the eleventh-century Sacramentary of Robert Jumièges, which contains 13 illuminations, two of which feature iconography related to *Ps.-Mt.* Hawk's paper effectively demonstrates the ongoing integration of canonical and noncanonical traditions in the life of the church. Timothy Pettipiece followed Hawk with "Manichaean Redaction of the *Secret Book of John.*" In his paper, Pettipiece laments the neglect in scholarship of the Manichean codices found at Medinet Madi in 1929; compared to the similar discovery at Nag Hammadi, Pettipiece writes, the "editing and publication of these manuscripts has proceeded at a somewhat glacial pace" (p. 195). The *Secret Book of John*, he states, "reveals substantial evidence of both Manichean reception and redaction" (p. 195), including the presentation of "the First Man" accompanied by five powers. Similar evidence is found, he says, in other Codex II texts, such as *On the Origin of the World* and the *Hypostasis of the Archons*, but he cautions that some Nag Hammadi texts contain anti-Manichean statements. Pettipiece promises to investigate these phenomena further in additional papers on Manichaean readings of the Nag Hammadi texts.

Session three focused on apocrypha written, or believed to have been written, in the last few centuries. I started the session with "Apocrypha and Forgeries: Lessons from the 'Lost Gospels' of the Nineteenth Century." The paper grew out of an interest in the theories of forgery advanced for *Secret Mark*. I wondered how evidence for the text would stack up against other texts considered to be modern creations, asking what proof led scholars of these other texts to declare them forgeries and how does evidence for *Secret Mark* compare? The recent publication of the *Gospel of Jesus' Wife* added a second contested apocryphon to the discussion. By the time of the mounting of the Symposium it seemed quite clear that GJW was indeed a modern, not ancient, text but I conclude in my paper that both *Secret Mark* and GJW urge us to question our motivations in debunking these texts, to "ask what these accusations say about our own assumptions about antiquity, and how much the need to declare a text a forgery—or even 'apocryphal'—is motivated not so much by a desire to understand its origins as by a distaste for its contents" (p. 264). In the discussion that followed, Stanley Porter asked about Richard J. Arthur's theory that the *Gospel of Judas* is a modern forgery created by members of the National Geographic team who prepared the first critical edition of the text. He wondered why this theory did not catch on since, as I describe in the paper, Arthur invokes the same kind of evidence against this text as used against *Secret Mark* and GJW: suspicious knowledge of a known copy of a text from antiquity, an awareness of modern issues in Christianity, and it reads like a patchwork assembly of other texts. I can only assume it did not receive support because of the solid reputations of the National Geographic team—there was no Morton Smith among them.

Bradley Rice, our second student presenter, followed with a look at one particular modern apocryphon in his paper, "The Apocryphal Tale of Jesus' Journey to India: Nicolas Notovitch and the *Life of Saint Issa* Revisited." One of the qualities of the text highlighted in Rice's discussion is its rejection of Jewish culpability in Jesus' death and Rice connects this modern viewpoint to the Jewish experience of late nineteenth-century Russia, thus reinforcing the notion that modern apocrypha have much to tell us about their time of composition. Rice concludes, "As we continue to investigate modern apocrypha in the years to come, perhaps the question ought not be 'What do they say about Jesus?' but 'What do they say about us?'" (p. 284).

Eric Vanden Eykel followed Rice with "Expanding the Apocryphal Corpus: Some 'Novel' Suggestions." His paper looks at four works of fiction (Bruce Longenecker's *The Lost Letters of Pergamum*, Christopher Moore's *Lamb: The Gospel according to Biff*, Colm Tóibín's *The Testament of Mary*, and Naomi Alderman's *The Liar's Gospel*) that share some things in common with ancient apocrypha. Vanden Eykel's excerpts from the novels, particularly Moore's comedic *Lamb*, were well-received, coming as they were near the end of a long day of presentations. He declared at the time that studying the novels is "boring" since there is little mystery as to their authors' identities, the novels' sources, etc. (see p. 301 in the finished paper). But the novels are still valuable because, despite being clearly fictional, they affect one's understanding of Jesus and early Christian history. Vanden Eykel wonders if reading ancient apocrypha had the same affect on early Christians—indeed, that is precisely the fear of such early heresy hunters as Irenaeus and Epiphanius.

The session ended with Scott Brown's "Behind the Seven Veils, II: Assessing Clement of Alexandria's Knowledge of the Mystic Gospel of Mark," a sequel to his paper from the 2011 symposium. Brown is one of the leading scholars on *Secret Mark* but he has grown weary of defending the authenticity of the text. He began his presentation stating, "this is probably my last paper on *Secret Mark.*" The paper gives thought to the interpretation of *Secret Mark* that Clement promises to deliver at the end of his letter to Theodore. Brown draws upon Clement's unchallenged works to see how Clement would have interpreted the longer version of Mark's gospel. "If this is not possible," Brown says, "then we have reason to doubt that Clement read and expounded this story himself, and, by extension, that he authored the letter" (p. 97). Brown finds that "the richness and consistency of the resulting spiritual interpretation and its concordance with both every facet of Clement's program of perfection and the life setting for the mystic gospel described in the letter . . . satisfy any reasonable standard of proof that Clement knew the mystic gospel and therefore wrote the *Letter to Theodore*" (p. 127). Brown asked the audience at the Symposium if they felt his arguments were convincing; no one equivocally responded yes or no, but the silence was due likely to the fact that few of us have Brown's facility with Clement's writings. Discussion turned to other arguments for authenticity, with Stanley Porter commenting that he spoke to Morton Smith once about the response to his work on the text and Smith voiced "disbelief" about the mounting accusations of forgery.

Following in the tradition of previous York Symposia, the first day concluded with a keynote address. Once Brent and I settled on the theme of the 2015 event ("Facts, Fictions, Forgeries"), Bart Ehrman seemed to us the perfect fit as our keynote speaker, since he had recently published two books on forgery in antiquity: his scholarly monograph *Forgery and Counterforgery: The Use of Literary Deceit in Early Christian Polemics* (in 2013) and its popular-market counterpart, *Forged: Writing in the Name of God—Why the Bible's Authors Are Not Who We Think They Are* (in 2011). Ehrman is often criticized for his popular work, both by conservatives who object to his positions on the instability of the text of the New Testament and his support of the Bauer Thesis , and by liberals who object to his simplification of complex issues. Nevertheless, he commands a certain amount of respect and awe, and his presence at the Symposium brought palpable energy to the entire event. Ehrman's address is reproduced in this volume in much the way it was presented—i.e., it reflects his conversational tone and is supplemented with a minimum of bibliographical references. The aim of his talk is to discount the widely-held view that plagiarism did not exist in antiquity. He proposes a universal taxonomy of forgery, ranging from falsification (including additions to texts, such as Luke's bloody sweat), to fabrication (representing historical events that are fictions), to literary fictions (pseudonymity, pseudepigraphy, and forgery). Ehrman's key point, as stated in *Forgery and Counterforgery*, is that "Forgery was not an acceptable practice in the ancient world, any more than other forms of lying and deception were acceptable practices."[90] This point is restated at the end of his paper: "Deceit comes in many guises, and we do well to recognize it for what it is and not to call it something that it is not" (p. 49). Ehrman said at the start of his talk that he was pleased to be among scholars for a change instead of the often-hostile audiences that attend his debates. But scholars too are passionate about their views, and several members of the audience took issue with Ehrman's views on forgery. Philip Harland (of York University) questioned Ehrman's "value-laden" terminology; in calling the texts "lies" and "deceptions," he said, Ehrman was not acting as a responsible historian. In response, Ehrman said that he was not attaching value to the terminology at all—a lie can be told for good reason, but it is still a lie, and a writer putting someone else's name on a text is certainly deceptive. He countered also that he can find no one in antiquity who writes in support of the practice, including Christian writers. Pierluigi Piovanelli, continuing his exchange with Ehrman from earlier in the day, raised another objection to Ehrman's typology by citing inspiration—i.e., the writers do not see themselves as being deceptive, instead they believe they are inspired to write in others' names. Even so, Ehrman's argument that pseudepigraphy was universally condemned in antiquity cannot be denied.

Day two of the Symposium began with a thematically-fluid session entitled, "Reimagining the Past in Christian Apocrypha." Gregory Fewster, the third of our student presenters, began the session with "Paul as Letter Writer and the Success of Pseudepigraphy: Constructing an Authorial Paul in the Apocryphal Corinthian Correspondence." The paper is a response to Alberto D'Anna's argument that discrepancies between 3 Corinthanians and other Pauline letters "reduces a lot . . . the possibility of success for the fiction."[91] But, as Fewster demonstrates, 3 Corinthians actually was successful, so much that it was included in some NT canons, even the occasional Latin codex. It seems that constructing a believable Pauline pseudepigraphon was relatively easy, given that even in the second century Paul was known more for his letter-writing practice than for the contents of his letters. So, despite the discrepancies, Fewster says, "one could thus believe that Paul wrote this response letter because Paul is the type of person who would have written this letter" (p. 175).

Attention shifted from Paul to Peter in a paper by Pamela Mullins Reaves (Colorado College): "Pseudo-Peter and Persecution: (Counter-) Evaluations of Suffering in the Coptic Apocalypse of Peter (NHC VII,3) and

90. Ehrman, Forgery, 132.
91. D'Anna, "Third Epistle," 142.

the *Letter of Peter to Philip* (NHC VIII,2)." Reaves focuses much of her paper on *Apoc. Peter*, noting how it reflects intra-Christian conflict over suffering. But both works recognize in Peter a figure associated with martyrdom and use him, not as a spokesperson for a particular Christian group or theology, as we have come to expect in apocryphal texts, but as a site for debate over suffering. This use of an apostle's legacy is similar in some ways to the teachings of Paul in *3 Corinthians*, which, like Paul's canonical letters, articulates views on resurrection.

After a short break, our lone Francophone presenter, Dominique Côté, presented a draft of his paper, "In the Name of James and Clement: The Brother of Jesus in the *Pseudo-Clementines*." Côté has worked extensively over the years on the *Pseudo-Clementines*. In this presentation he focused on how the entire novel is presented as a lengthy letter to be sent to James and wonders why it was necessary to use the epistolary motif to circulate the novel. He concluded that James is used in the Pseudo-Clementine *Homilies* (here seen as representing well the sources used by both the *Homilies* and the *Recognition*) in an effort to harmonize Christianity with Judaism. The same motivation is attributed to Rufinus, the Latin translator of the *Recognitions*, though for different reasons: "to affirm the continuity between the church of Jerusalem, founded by James and appointed bishop by Jesus himself, and the church of Rome, founded by Peter, designated as the foundation of the church by Jesus himself." Rufinus, however, was intent on showing continuity in church leadership, not on allying Christianity with Jewish thought and praxis.

The morning session concluded with Anne Moore's paper, "'Days of Our Lives': Destructive Homemakers in the *Passion of Andrew*." The first three papers of the session are somewhat cohesive, each focusing on a certain pillar of the church and how the figure is used by writers of apocrypha. But Moore's paper is quite different. It focuses on the *Passion of Andrew* and characterizes the text as having a similar setting, plot, and characterization as a modern soap opera. The acts and soaps also share a similar social function. "The [Apocryphal Acts] offer an alternative to the traditional roles of wife and mother," Moore writes. "Analogously, the soap operas provided women of the 1960s (and thereafter) with an alternative to the traditional role of housewife and mother" (p. 179). The *Passion of Andrew* features the type of household typical of soap operas, with characters vying with one another for sexual dalliances and thus threatening the honor of the family. Moore's paper focuses on the minor characters of the narrative, the slaves Iphidama and Euclia, and how they play out the role-sets expected of them in the Roman *domus*. Iphidama introduces her mistress Maximilla to Andrew, which leads to the breakdown of the household and the loss of the family's honor. Euclia is tasked by Maximilla to have sex with her husband Aegeates. Euclia is thus fulfilling one of the roles of a female slave, but the mistress of the house is usually presented in contemporary literature as trying to limit these interactions; instead, Maximilla "is assuming the role of a pimp providing her husband with sexual release" (p. 189). This could lead to an additional challenge to the family honor: the creation of a non-elite heir. Clearly, Moore's paper stands out not only from the papers in the morning session, but also from the Symposium on the whole. But this difference worked to Moore's benefit, as the audience responded to her paper very positively, so much that it became one of the highlights of the event.

The final session of the day was devoted to the controversial *Gospel of Jesus' Wife*. Given the text's exposure in the media—during the planning of the Symposium and then reinvigorated in the final days leading up to the event—it seemed wise to incorporate it into the program as a way to draw the attention of non-scholars to the Symposium. But we wanted to avoid arguments of authenticity, in part because that was the focus of other gatherings on the text and because with a year between planning and mounting the Symposium, there was no telling where the discussion on authenticity would go. We decided to focus instead on the reception of the text in scholarship, in particular the role of bibliobloggers in the study of the text.

After a brief introduction from Brent Landau, the session began with Caroline Schroeder's presentation, "Gender and the Academy Online: The Authentic Revelations of the *Gospel of Jesus' Wife*." She drew attention to several "markers of authenticity" related to the text, including: the privileging of scientific studies of the manuscript over traditional humanistic ones; issues of provenance and the resulting political and ethical ramifications of working with unprovenanced materials; issues of status, gender, and identity and how these affect the academic production of knowledge; and attitudes in the field toward digital scholarship and digital publishing. Schroeder juxtaposed traditional publishing methods (typically slow to release results and employed by higher-status scholars like Karen King through print publications such as *Harvard Theological Review*) vs. digital publishing/blogging (with speedy dissemination and featuring the voices of independent scholars and scholars at less high-profile institutions). Regarding gender, Schroeder noted that women are discouraged from online scholarship because of intimidation and rape threats and that there are fundamental barriers to the presence of women's voices in the field, including the problem of the "leaky pipeline" (very few women complete their PhDs). Furthermore, she criticized Harvard University for helping to create the hostile environment surrounding discussion of the text; "Harvard bears no small amount of responsibility in this controversy," Schroeder writes in the finished paper, "for winding it up and exposing King to the resulting maelstrom" (p. 324). But Schroeder also criticized King for agreeing to keep the identity of the owner of the text a secret (though admitting that, in similar circumstances, she may have done the same) and urged scholars to consider carefully the ramifications of working with unprovenanced texts: "As we move forward as a scholarly community, we need to apply self-scrutiny when we use the 'pursuit of knowledge' to rationalize what we now know to be ethically murky work" (p. 313). Schroeder finished with a defense of social media and digital publishing as genuine scholarship and urged female scholars to become more involved online, despite the risks, though she called for other scholars, particular senior scholars, to support female colleagues online.

James McGrath followed Schroeder with "Slow Scholarship: Do Bloggers Rush in Where Jesus' Wife Would Fear to Tread?" McGrath had positive things to say about the speed of online scholarship on GJW and, echoing Schroeder, about how the Internet democratizes scholarship by allowing in voices of non-experts. That said, among the 27 bloggers who commented on the text, McGrath was most interested in the number of well-known scholars in the group and called this embrace of digital media "a noteworthy moment in the history of scholarship" (pp. 331–32). But McGrath also had plenty of criticism of online scholarship. He noted that the consensus that emerged on GJW as a forgery is likely correct, but was wary about the nature of the consensus. First, the bloggers who argued for forgery may have been right but they were right before the evidence was presented that proved it so. "Within *three days* (and in some cases significantly less)," McGrath writes in his finished paper, "there were scholars who felt that they were in a position to comment with confidence on a question pertaining to a papyrus which had not been subjected to scientific testing, which they had not studied in person, and about which experts in papyrology had expressed a range of opinions" (p. 330). McGrath is not calling for a "slow scholarship movement," rather he urges bloggers to work "as scholars" using appropriate scholarly methodology, "to move as quickly as we can while still being *careful*" (p. 336). The second point McGrath made about the consensus was that it may not be fully representative of the opinions in the field, in part because bloggers "tend to have views that are a minority stance in the guild," and because "consensus building takes time" (p. 336). And third, McGrath drew attention once again to the tone of the discussion online; because blog posts are written typically in a more relaxed style than traditional scholarship, snide or offensive remarks slipped into the articles.

Mark Goodacre took a step back with his presentation "Jesus' Wife, the Media, and *The Da Vinci Code*," looking for the "perfect storm" environment in popular culture that could have given rise to the creation of

GJW. He presented an overview of Mary Magdalene in Jesus films, noting a significant change in her portrayal after the publication of Dan Brown's *The Da Vinci Code* in 2003—going from a prostitute to a prominent disciple. Goodacre threw a jab also at his frequent sparring partner Simcha Jacobovici who has appealed to GJW for support of his contention that Jesus was married (as seen in his work on the excavation of the Talpiot Tomb and in his controversial interpretation of *Joseph and Aseneth* in his book *The Lost Gospel*). Goodacre responded also to Jacobovici's characterization of his critics as "underwear bloggers," described as "people that I imagine sitting in their underwear, eating out of pizza boxes and spending their days and nights attacking me and others personally."[92] Goodacre finished his presentation with the conclusion that "It is *The Da Vinci Code* that gives GJW its frisson, its cultural significance, its media clout," though he stopped short of declaring that GJW's appearance in the post-*Da Vinci Code* world necessarily means it is a forgery, since life often imitates art purely by coincidence.

The discussion of the GJW presentations began with a response by Janet Spittler, who also had a hand in organizing the panel. The response was at once entertaining and scathing in its criticism of attitudes toward GJW, of the fallacy of feminist support of a married Jesus, and of treatment of women online. Spittler stated she was in agreement with much of Schroeder's presentation and said that the "positive, heartwarming" message from her discussion was that humanities methods were more effective in determining authenticity than scientific studies. On Goodacre's presentation, Spittler noted that a married Jesus goes as far back as the mid-nineteenth century in Mormon circles, though this view was not sanctioned in the church. She then turned to the connection between *The Da Vinci Code* and Jesus' marital status as a feminist issue. Though Brown's novel claims that Jesus was the first feminist, Spittler's comic reading of the excessive "mansplaining" from ch. 58 of the novel illustrates that Brown is no feminist himself. Spittler added that the belief that feminists want a married Jesus is a "weird notion"—"that's right, guys," she said, "we want to marry you" (see pp. 363–66) in the finished paper). Regarding McGrath's presentation, Spittler agreed with his calls for improvement in the level of scholarship and discourse on blogs, noting also that of McGrath's list of 27 bloggers who contributed to discussion on the text, only one is a woman. "The chatter on blogs is openly misogynist," she said, "so it is not a pool I want to jump into."

Before taking questions from the audience, the presenters were invited to respond to Spittler's comments. At this point Goodacre mentioned that he had copied Christian Askeland's joke (calling the Lycopolitan manuscript

---

92. Jacobovici, "Underwear Bloggers."

of John an "ugly sister-in-law" to the GJW fragment on his own blog think-ing it was funny; once he realized that it was offensive, he apologized online for repeating the joke. He added that he was grateful for the openness of the conversation on the panel. He said also in regards to *Secret Mark* that, as a forgery proponent, the association of arguments for forgery with homopho-bia made him "uncomfortable." Spittler responded that you cannot ignore that connection, given that the accusation of forgery is so tied to Smith's sexuality—a gay gospel created by a gay man must be a fake, though no one ever accuses straight men of creating texts that feature a straight Jesus; and similarly, some commentators saw something suspicious in a female scholar editing a text that featured a married Jesus. From there the audience turned from GJW to a lengthy discussion of Schroeder's comments on the acad-emy's "leaky pipeline" and the difficulties that female scholars experience in the guild. This conversation about how scholars treat one another may be the most positive outcome of the whole GJW controversy.

The 2015 Symposium came to a close with a small reception officially launching NASSCAL, the North American Society for the Study of Chris-tian Apocryphal Literature, an association founded with the goal of foster-ing collaboration between North American scholars of Christian apocrypha as well as scholars of cognate disciplines. The origins of NASSCAL go back to a discussion at the end of the 2013 Symposium of how we might more effectively work together. The intervening time was spent establishing a founding board, selecting an executive, and creating a website (nasscal. com) to enable interested scholars to join the group. One of the outcomes of creating the society is that the York Christian Apocrypha Symposium will now transform into a bi-annual NASSCAL meeting to take place at various locations in the U.S. and Canada.

But the story of GJW is not over. Just a month before this volume went to press, Ariel Sabar revealed the identity of the owner, and perhaps creator, of the fragment in an article for *The Atlantic*.[93] Sabar had followed the story of GJW from the beginning, interviewing King in 2012 in preparation for an article in the *Smithsonian*, and accompanying her to Rome to cover her announcement of the text. He returned to the story last year to investigate suspicions he had about the ownership documentation accompanying the fragment and used it to track down the man who brought GJW to King: Walter Fritz, a German expatriot now living in Florida. Earlier in life, Fritz was a Master's student at the Free University of Berlin and for a short time the head of the Stasi Museum in East Berlin. In interviews with Sabar, Fritz

93. Sabar, "Unbelievable Tale."

admitted to being the owner but not the creator of the fragment. Sabar was not convinced:

> By every indication, Fritz had the skills and knowledge to forge the Jesus's-wife papyrus. He was the missing link between all the players in the provenance story. He'd proved adept at deciphering enigmatic Egyptian text. He had a salesman's silver tongue, which kept Laukamp and possibly others in his thrall. Perhaps most important, he'd studied Coptic but had never been very good at it—which could explain the "combination of bumbling and sophistication" that King had deemed "extremely unlikely" in a forger.[94]

But what would be Fritz's motive? Fritz and his wife, Anitra Williams-Fritz, have an interest in esoterica: she claims to channel the voices of angels, which she recorded in a self-published book titled *Spiritual Evolution Universal Truths*, and Fritz confessed to Sabar an interest in gnostic gospels, stating, "The Gnostic texts that allow women a discipleship and see Jesus more as a spiritual person and not as a demigod—these texts are probably the more relevant ones." Fritz even tried to convince Sabar to collaborate with him on a religious thriller with a plot very much like Dan Brown's *The Da Vinci Code*. And in 2009 Williams-Fritz's online business Cute Art World was selling pendants containing scraps of papyrus she claimed originated in the second century. The Fritzes seemed to have been in it simply for the money. Before publishing his story, Sabar approached Karen King for her reaction to his investigation. At first she was hesitant to comment, but after the article appeared, she declared that the evidence "tips the balance towards forgery" and that she felt she had been deceived by Fritz.[95]

Reaction to Sabar's article was swift. Within two weeks of its publication, nine scholarly bloggers—including Caroline Schroeder, Mark Goodacre, Christian Askeland, and Roberta Mazza—had posted comments.[96] Several of these were of the "I told you so" vein, with Askeland stating that he and several other scholars were aware of Fritz since October 2015 when Owen Jarus consulted with Askeland for an article written for *Live Science*.[97]

94. Ibid.

95. Sabar, "Karen King Responds." Of interest also is an article in *The North Port Sun*, Fritz's home-town newspaper, in which Fritz responds to his portrayal in Sabar's *Atlantic* article. See Lawson, "Jesus' Wife Evidence."

96. For overviews see Grondin, "Jesus' Wife Fragment 2016"; and Goodacre, "Last Chapter."

97. Askeland, "More on the Gospel of Jesus' Wife"; Jarus, "Origins." Jarus does not mention Fritz in the article as he had not yet confirmed Fritz was the owner of the fragment. After Sabar's piece appeared, Jarus wrote a second piece ("Likely a Fake")

Reportedly, Jarus was close to publicly associating Fritz with the text but Sabar beat him to the scoop. Several early commentators, and their readers, remarked that King was targeted by Fritz specifically for her interest in apocryphal texts as well as, in their view, her "feminist interests."[98] The delicate issue of so-called "feminist criticism" observable in early discussion of the text (see Schroeder's and Spittler's comments in this volume, pp. 318–19, 363) is misrepresented by the recent commentators, with Charlotte Allen stating "once the fragment's authenticity was questioned, a wagon-circling by feminist scholars . . . shielded her from criticism by accusing the critics of sexism,"[99] and Timothy Pettipiece remarking that "accusations of sexism were brought forward to silence critics"—a statement later changed in response to criticism to "accusations of sexism further complicated the discussion."[100] In fact, the accusations of sexism were directed at objectionable, gendered language used by a select few commentators and were not raised in defense of King or GJW authenticity. The juxtaposition of feminist critics and GJW authenticity on one hand and critical text critics and forgery on the other is a false dichotomy that makes for a sensational narrative of scholarly conflict, but it is not an accurate depiction of the nuances involved in the discussion. By far the most outrageous comment generated by Sabar's investigation was made by Leo Depuydt who, in an interview for the *Boston Globe*, suggested that King should lose her job for her role in the affair: "I see that King is still at Harvard. Unbelievable."[101]

The participants in the York Symposium who added their voices to the discussion primarily reiterated points they made in their presentations on the text. Interviewed on CBN (Christian Broadcasting Network) News, Goodacre mentioned his skepticism about the text in light of interest in a married Jesus sparked by the publication of *The Da Vinci Code*. When asked about the biases of scholars who argued for the authenticity of the text, he remarked that "the owner of this fragment wanted to give it to somebody who would be really interested in the contents of the fragment" and that the choice of King was "a natural decision on the owner's front." Goodacre also expressed surprise at details about Fritz revealed in Sabar's article: "The

revealing the full extent of his own investigative work.

98. See e.g., Allen, "Jesus' Wife?," who attributes King's "downfall" to "an ideological commitment to those theories about suppressed early Christian voices that clearly trumped objective assessment of the 'Jesus' wife' fragment."

99. Ibid.

100. Pettipiece, "Publish or Perish."

101. Wangsness, "Papyrus Likely Fake."

guy that turns out to be the owner of this fragment is a pornographer; he's someone that is clearly involved in shady dealings of all sorts."[102]

Timothy Pettipiece focuses his comments on the issue of academic prestige, noting the apparent dismissal of scholars critiquing the text online: "Predictably, the academic establishment dug in its heels. After all, who were a bunch of precariously employed adjuncts and bloggers to question the tenured wisdom of the Ivy League?"[103] He also comments on the current emphasis being placed upon academic partnership with sensationalist media and the harm that results: "The oft-repeated cliché used to be *publish or perish*. Today, it seems to me, this has been replaced by a new imperative—*publicity or perish* . . . In this age of academic celebrity and infotainment, a CV without at least a *History Channel* appearance or a *National Geographic* special seems second rate and decidedly lacking in scholarly star-power."[104]

Academic prestige is revisited also in a series of posts by Caroline Schroeder.[105] She takes issue particularly with Fritz's scornful comments about critics of the text (Sabar says he derided them as "'county level' scholars from the 'University of Eastern Pee-Pee Land'").[106] And after a few days of reading bloggers' comments on the Fritzes' titillating sexual proclivities, Schroeder cautioned scholars to resist the temptation of "imprint[ing] upon the fragment whatever 'sketchiness' or 'skeeviness' we attribute to the owner. Does the fact that the owner was involved in pornography necessarily mean the fragment is inauthentic?"[107] At Schroeder's request, and with the consent of our publisher, I made her article in this volume available for viewing on the NASSCAL website and this led to additional discussion online, culminating in Schroeder's third and final post on the text. Here Schroeder expands on her discussions about the value of academic blogging, the role played by humanities methods in determining the authenticity of the text, the ethics of working with unprovenanced texts and artifacts, and the need for scholars to "assert control over our digital identities." In this regard Schroeder notes that the Harvard Divinity School website on GJW, having languished since 2014, was finally updated on June 21 with a statement from HDS Dean David N. Hempton acknowledging Sabar's article and stating that "the preponderance of the evidence now presses in that direction"

102. The interview is available online at http://www1.cbn.com/cbnnews/world/2016/june/debunking-the-myth-of-jesus-wife.

103. Pettipiece, "Publish or Perish."

104. Ibid.

105. Schroeder, "Provenance"; Schroeder, "More on Social Networks"; and Schroeder, "On Institutional Responsibilities."

106. Sabar, "Unbelievable Tale."

107. Schroeder, "More on Social Networks."

(i.e., towards forgery).[108] Schroeder criticises Harvard for their silence on scholarship (primarily appearing online) in the intervening years, stating "through omission, the institution misrepresented the state of the field rather than publish notice of research that contradicts their faculty. Arguably, as of this writing, it continues to do so by addressing only the Sabar piece." The danger in this for scholars is that an institution's efforts to publicize research can reflect upon the work and practices of scholars; thus Schroeder warns "Individual academics need to consider how much their own personal identity and reputation will be wrapped up in their university's media exposure. While we may want personal exposure, it may come at a price."

In the end, GJW's lasting impact may be in what it has taught scholars about the importance of provenance. King has been criticized for not using basic electronic research tools to learn more about Fritz. When confronted by Sabar with his discoveries she declared, "I haven't engaged the provenance questions at all,"[109] and in her response to Sabar's article she told the author, "Your article has helped me see that provenance can be investigated."[110] Roberta Mazza remarks that King's comments "demonstrate a shocking unawareness of the importance of verifying the collection history of an object before publication."[111] Ideally, all material related to a text or artefact's history should be made public. But, as Malcolm Choat points out, King is not alone in not following this practice—along with general comments about museum policies, he cites two recent examples, one by Dirk Obbink in 2014 and another by Geoffrey Smith in 2015, of scholars guaranteeing manuscript owners anonymity.[112] Indeed, Choat says that King provides more information in her *HTR* article than is usual and notes that supporting documents typically are not revealed until or unless authenticity is challenged.

Finally, perhaps we all have one more thing to learn from GJW, something directly related to the contributions to this volume, which focus more on the reception of the text than its origins or content. Choat expresses this lesson well, in the concluding words to his assessment of Sabar's investigation:

> Finally, among the disquieting aspects of this affair was the tone evident in some of the discussion: language that was variously

108. The HDS web site dedicated to GJW can be found at http://gospelofjesuswife. hds.harvard.edu/introduction/.

109. Sabar, "Unbelievable Tale."

110. Sabar, "Karen King Responds."

111. Mazza, "End of Story?"

112. Choat, "Lessons."

unfortunately chosen, polemical, hyperbolic, sexist, loaded, and sometimes wholly unnecessarily vicious was used on all sides of the debate. Not always, certainly, and assuredly not by everyone: but with noticeable frequency. The motives, backgrounds, affiliation (in academic, confessional, and socio-political terms) of some of the scholars involved in the debate was subject to imputation, implication, and worse . . . In part, this tone was a result of the debate playing out across the media and the Internet, when anonymous commenting and the ability to say whatever comes into one's head allow a far less regulated discussion . . . Much of this democratisation of discussion is for the better; but this does not mean that the manner in which this debate was often conducted should model future such discussions.

— 2 —

Apocryphal Forgeries
The Logic of Literary Deceit

— Bart D. Ehrman —

ALL OF US WHO labor in the fields of early Christian apocrypha know they
are white for harvest. But even as significant advances are made in producing critical editions, new translations, and significant studies, there are still
some preliminaries that require our attention.[1] One of them involves devising and agreeing upon a sensible taxonomy of literary deceit, a set of discrete terms to refer to the wide range of literary phenomena confronting us
when we deal with deceitful or potentially deceitful literary practices.[2] The
problems of recognition, definition, description, and delineation should be
clear to all of us at this symposium, and if not, I'd at least like to explain why
they are clear to me.

For openers, many scholars simply don't recognize the various ancient phenomena for what they are, and others don't agree on what to call
the phenomena once they identify them. As an example of the former, I
cite a popular publication of the Jesus Seminar, which proclaimed with

---

1. Caveat lector: this paper was delivered as the keynote address of the symposium. I have not revised the paper out of an oral into a literary form, but have simply
adding documentation as necessary. It stills bears all the marks of a public presentation.

2. I provide a much fuller discussion in Ehrman, *Forgery and Counterforgery*, 29–
67, esp. 43–67.

characteristic boldness that: "The concept of plagiarism was unknown in the ancient world."[3] That claim, as many of you know, and as I'll be stressing later, is quite demonstrably false. Our good colleagues in the Jesus Seminar simply didn't know this because they weren't familiar with ancient, explicit discussions of the phenomenon.[4]

I would group the concept of forgery itself among those that scholars sometimes deny to antiquity, at least to Christian antiquity, or at least to early Christian antiquity, or at least to New Testament antiquity. But truth be told, the letter allegedly written *to* Titus in the New Testament is just as much a forgery as the letter allegedly written *by* Titus that shows up in later times. A forgery is a forgery. But what is a forgery?

That's my second point. Not only do many scholars not recognize the various ancient phenomena for what they are, others—including many of us here—simply don't agree on how to differentiate among and label these phenomena. We are lacking a universally agreed-upon taxonomy. Just as one example, it is sometimes pointed out that one of our earliest explicit discussions of forgery occurs in that famous passage of Tertullian, *On Baptism* 17:

> But if the writings which wrongly go under Paul's name claim Thecla's example as a license for women's teaching and baptizing, let them know that, in Asia, the presbyter who composed that writing . . . after being convicted, and confessing that he had done it from love of Paul, was removed from his office (trans. Thelwall, 677).[5]

If, as I think most plausible, Tertullian is speaking of the *Acts of Thecla*, or at least an early form of the *Acts of Thecla*, he is not stating that their author was accused of falsely writing a literary work in the name of Paul (which, as I will argue, is what we should call forgery). The *Acts of Thecla* is not an account that Paul is alleged to have written. Paul is the subject of these writings, not their reputed author. At least as they have been handed down to us, assuming that what we have is what Tertullian is referring to—the *Acts of Thecla* are anonymous. The presbyter is being faulted, then, for making up stories about Paul that are not historically accurate. That's not literary forgery; that's fabrication.

I will define those two terms more closely soon enough. For now I simply want to stress that they refer to different phenomena, one in which an author makes a false authorial claim, stating in writing that he is an

---

3. Funk, ed., *Five Gospels*, 22.

4. On plagiarism, see my discussion in Ehrman, *Forgery and Counterforgery*, 52–55.

5. See my discussion in ibid., 59–60.

otherwise well-known person even though he is not, the other in which an author invents an ostensibly historical narrative that is, in fact, his or her own fiction. Whether anyone agrees with the taxonomy that I will be urging in this talk, or whether, instead, some other taxonomy is deemed better, my overarching point is that we ought to *have* a taxonomy, one that we all agree on.

And so let me lay out for you a group of related categories, some of them comprising works that are clear literary deceits and others that can at least be construed in many instances as literary deceits. Some of my categories are actually subcategories. Together they include the following: falsification, fabrication, pseudonymity, pen names, pseudepigraphy, false attribution, forgery, redacted forgery, embedded forgery, and non-pseude-pigraphic forgery. I'll start, then, with falsification.[6]

I first became interested in the field of apocrypha and Christian literary forgery about twenty-five years ago, when I was principally obsessed with New Testament textual criticism. Almost everyone else at the time who was also obsessed with textual criticism was principally obsessed with one question only: how do we establish the original text of the New Testament? I too, at the time, was largely interested in that question, but I realized as well that the reality is that we are not ever likely to get closer to the authorial texts of the New Testament than we already are, barring some amazing discoveries (such as the autographs) or some astounding transformations of method. And so I became interested in a different area of research to which had been paid but scant attention. I was intrigued with the textual variants in our tradition not as chaff to be discarded as we tried to find the wheat of the original text, but as important in and of themselves as literary productions of the scribes who created, or at least preserved them.[7]

The first textual variant I discussed in print was the famous passage of the so-called bloody sweat in Luke 22:43–44.[8] In this passage, Jesus is shown to be in prayer prior to his betrayal by Judas Iscariot and his arrest. Jesus tells his disciples to pray so as not to enter into temptation; he leaves them to pray in private, and he begins to pray. As he prays, he falls into deep agony, his sweat becomes like great drops of blood falling to the ground, and an angel comes to minister to him. He finishes his prayer, returns to the disciples, and again tells them to pray so as not to enter into temptation. At

6. See Ehrman, *Forgery and Counterforgery*, 61–67.

7. This resulted in my book, Ehrman, *Orthodox Corruption of Scripture*.

8. Ehrman and Plunkett, "Angel and the Agony." I returned to the discussion in Ehrman, *Orthodox Corruption of Scripture*, 187–94.

that point Judas arrives with the troops, Jesus is arrested, and the passion narrative proceeds to its inevitable climax.

As widely noted, it is a passion narrative without much passion. Jesus does not seem to suffer much in Luke's version of the events. He is calm and in control the entire time, up until he breathes his last. His only agony appears to occur during his prayer before his arrest, sweating great drops as if of blood. But there is a textual problem at just this point. The two verses that discuss the agonizing sweat and the ministering angel are missing from some of our oldest and best manuscripts of the Gospel of Luke. And in fact there are compelling reasons, which I am happy to provide to anyone who is interested, for thinking that they were not found in the oldest version of the Gospel of Luke. They were added by a scribe.

Here, then, is the key point I want to make: when a scribe added these words, he was, in a sense, putting words on the pen of an author who did not write them. He was, in effect, making a false authorial claim, claiming that the words that he produced were written by another author. As I will argue more fully, the term "forgery" is best reserved for literary deceits that involve false authorial claims, for when an author claims that his words were written by someone else. And in a sense, that is just what scribes did when they altered the texts they were copying—at least if they changed or added words to the text.

One could argue that since the Third Gospel is anonymous, the scribe was not forging a small piece of text in the name of another author, since the text's author has no name. About that I would make two points. The first is that the scribe would be passing off his own words as if they were another's, even if the other is not named. In that case he would be implicitly claiming that his words were the words of the unnamed author of this Gospel. That is what I would call a non-pseudepigraphic forgery, a text forged as if it were written by a different, unnamed author. But second, if the scribe made this falsification at a time when it was thought in his community that Luke was the author of the Third Gospel, then more directly he would have been putting his words on the pen of another allegedly known writer: Luke, the companion of Paul.

Some people might object that the term falsification is too negative and that ancient Christians (and ancient others) did not ascribe motive to this kind of textual change and did not look askance at it. Anyone who thinks that, in my view, should simply see what ancient writers say about the alteration of texts by scribes who copy them. Judgments against those who modify the texts they copy are common and harsh, and involve such pleasant wishes as that the guilty parties roast in hell forever. I use "falsification," then, not to offend post-modern sensibilities but as an emic term, to convey the ancient sense of scandal at intentional alterations of the text away from what an author wrote. I should stress I am *not* saying that these altered texts are more false in their truth claims than any other text. And I'm not saying that such changes were always made with the intent to deceive a reader. They may often have been that; they may often have not been that. Some of these changes could even be seen as purely accidental. That's not the issue I am trying to address. I'm simply saying that they represent alterations of older forms of the text.

There are, of course, hundreds of such alterations in the textual tradition of the New Testament, far more by a vast margin than in any other literature that has come down to us from antiquity. But there are also plenty of alterations in the apocryphal texts that many of us work on. Indeed, it may be practically impossible and theoretically naïve for us to talk about an original text in any of these cases but it is possible to say that a scribe has altered a text in this, that, or the other place, and any such alteration, by the term I'm suggesting, is a falsification of what the scribe inherited from his predecessors. On another level these scribal changes are also sometimes something else. The story of Jesus' bloody sweat is also an ostensibly historical narrative that in fact someone simply made up. In that sense, it is also a "fabrication."

This then is my second term. A fabrication, as I'm using it, is a narrative or collection of narratives that implicitly claims to represent historical events when it is, in reality, a fiction.[9] I should repeat that when I earlier used the term falsification it was not in order to contrast an alteration with the "truth" found in the untouched original text; it was simply used to refer to an alteration of a text. So too with fabrication: I'm not saying that the episode of the bloody sweat was made up in contrast to the rest of the narrative. It's not that Luke's Gospel is necessarily historically reliable otherwise. It too, at least in my judgment, is largely made up of fabrications: history-like stories that in fact never happened. So the insertion of the bloody sweat could well be seen as a fabrication within a fabrication.

Again, it would be practically impossible and theoretically naïve to say that we can point a finger at a culprit who is guilty for devising this, that, or the other false historical tale and say that this author is the fabricator. False stories—by which I mean stories that narrate events that did not really happen (which, one could well argue, is true of all stories)—are made up all the time, and not always with the intention to deceive. Whoever came up with the bloody sweat may well have thought that it was something that happened. So too, in theory, the person who devised the tales of Paul and

---

9. See my discussion in Ehrman, *Forgery and Counterforgery*, 55–61.

Thecla may have thought that they, or something very close to them really happened. Maybe he heard such stories from someone who heard them from someone who heard them from someone who, and so on. So, who knows who made them up? But wherever they came from, they are almost certainly history-like tales with implicit claims to historicity that are, by contrast, either pure or relatively pure fiction. That too is the case with the tale of Paul and the baptized lion, or the tale of the infant Jesus withering a playmate, or the tale of the healing of King Abgar, or the tale of the converted Pontius Pilate, or—well, pick your apocryphal tale. We have to call these stories something; they are not history. If someone in antiquity were charged with making up such stories that did not happen, they would typically be maligned for it. Since such stories have been made up, I call them fabrications. I will not go here into our modern-day question of whether all history writing, in a deeper sense, is also made up.

It is important to note that "falsifications" entail an inherent false authorial claim, whether the book into which they were inserted was anonymous, pseudonymous, or orthonymous. Fabrications do not necessarily make any such claim. If they do implicitly or explicitly make such a claim, then they are more than fabrications: they are also pseudepigraphic. This would be true, for example, of the *Acts of Pilate*, known also in its Latin form as the *Gospel of Nicodemus*. As everyone here knows, this is a text filled with wonderful, entertaining, and even glorious tales that didn't happen (fabrications, in my term): from the standards that bow before Jesus when he enters, twice, into Pilate's presence, to the tale of Joseph of Arimathea's wrongful imprisonment and miraculous escape, to the account found in Tischendorf's B text of the harrowing of hell.[10]

But among the striking literary features of the *Acts of Pilate* is that it not only contains fabricated accounts, like, for example, the *Acts of Thecla*, but, unlike the *Acts of Thecla*, it makes a false authorial claim. In fact, it makes a double-false authorial claim. The first-person narrator of the text is allegedly a man named Ananias who was a member of the procurator's body guard, writing in the year 424–425 CE. It seems unlikely that the name Ananias was meant to mean anything in particular to its reader, so this would not be a forgery in the way I am using the term; it would be a pseudonymous work written under a pen name. At the same time, Ananias falsely claims that he is not composing this work but is translating into Greek a text written originally in Hebrew by none other than Jesus' follower Nicodemus. That's different from a writing produced under a pen name.

---

10. For the Greek text and a new translation, see Ehrman and Pleše, *Apocryphal Gospels*, 419–63.

Here we are getting into terminological complications. It is easy enough to differentiate between falsifications and fabrications, but now that we are into authorial claims we are dipping into muddy waters. There are a range of related phenomena when it comes to authorial claims, and I would propose that we differentiate between them clearly in our heads and in our writings. Here is the taxonomy I prefer. It involves the differentiation among the terms pseudonymity, pseudepigraphy, pen names, false attributions, and forgery—with several kinds of forgery being possible.

By way of ground-clearing I should say that there should be no real ambiguity (even if there are sometimes practical problems) with the terms orthonymity, homonymity, and anonymity. An orthonymous writing is a work that really was written by the person who claims to have written it. The practical problems usually involve establishing if the claim is true; but if it is so established, the work is orthonymous. Hermas really wrote the *Shepherd*, Irenaeus really wrote *Against the Heresies*, Augustine really wrote the *Confessions*, and so on.

Homonymous writings are those that are written in the name of an author who shares the name with someone else who, unlike the writer, is well-known.[11] That appears to be the case, for example, with the New Testament book of Revelation. It quite plainly claims to be written by a prophet named John. But we aren't told which John it was. John, of course, was a very popular name, and one of the persons who bore it was John the son of Zebedee, one of Jesus' disciples. It was a much-disputed point in some learned circles in the early church whether the John of Revelation was *that* John, as noted most memorably by Eusebius in his discussion of the writings of Dionysius of Alexandria, who argued—in convincing fashion—that whoever wrote Revelation, it was not the author of the Gospel of John (Eusebius, *Hist. eccl.* 7.25). That much is true. Dionysius, however, went on to argue—sensibly in his own context—that therefore Revelation was not written by John the son of Zebedee, the author of the Fourth Gospel. That is an unfortunate leap in logic, at least for modern critical scholars, since John the son of Zebedee almost certainly did not write the Gospel, given the fact that as an uneducated, Aramaic-speaking peasant from the rural backwaters of Galilee, John could almost certainly not write anything, let alone an extended narrative in cultured Greek. But still, the point should be taken. The John who wrote Revelation may well have simply been someone named John; later church leaders came to think, Dionysius's arguments notwithstanding, that this John was John the son of Zebedee. It is a case of mistaken identity, or, when speaking of literary authorship, a case of homonymity.

11. For fuller discussion see Ehrman, *Forgery and Counterforgery*, 47–49.

Homonymity was a surprisingly wide-spread phenomenon in antiquity; or perhaps it is not so surprising given naming practices. But widespread
it was, as anyone who has spent a quality afternoon perusing Diogenes
Laertius knows. No one took the problem more seriously than Demetrius
of Magnesia, who, as Diogenes tells us (*Vit. phil.* 1.38.79; 1.73.169), devoted
an entire book to the issue, not only to differentiate among homonymous
writers but also to tell anecdotes about them.

Finally, anonymous writings are simply works that have no authorial
name attached to them.[12] Such writings might be falsely attributed to someone who didn't write them; or they might, as I will argue, make implicit false
authorial claims—but technically speaking no name is attached. I should
add that rarely did anonymous writings remain anonymous, since authorial
names almost invariably came to be attached to works that were originally
put in circulation under the cloak of anonymity. But that process almost
never was the author's fault, and so clearly there was no deceit involved at
least on his part, even if there could conceivably have been deceit involved
on the part of the one making the false attribution. I see that as an important distinction. When such attributions were made, I would say that these
works were not merely anonymous but also falsely attributed. And so one
might contrast the *Epistle to Diognetus*, which remained anonymous until
discovered in the fifteenth century, possibly because it didn't circulate at *all*,
or relatively not at all, and the *Epistle of Barnabas*, which was attributed to
Paul's apostolic companion as far back as we have a record of its existence.
In sum, there should be no problems, in theory at least, with the terms orthonymous, homonymous, and anonymous.

With the other terms I have mentioned, there are greater complications, occasioned in no small part by the fact that scholars use them in different ways. And so now I would like to discuss the terms pseudonymity,
pseudepigraphy, and forgery, along with several related terms. I start with
pseudonymity. I prefer to use this as the broadest umbrella term we have
for works circulating under a false name. By false name I mean the name of
an author who in fact did not write it. Let me stress that I am now speaking
of literary texts that *circulate* under names of authors who did not actually
write them. In some instances, the author does not actually make a false
authorial claim, as we have just seen with the *Epistle of Barnabas*; in other
instances, she or he does. It is important to keep the distinction clear.

As I use the term, there are two broad kinds of pseudonymity: there
are works that are written by someone using a pen name and there are other
words that circulate under the name of a well-known person who did not

12. See ibid., 49–50.

write them, whether the person is well-known widely or only locally. The use of a pen name sometimes functions simply to keep an author's identity secret, or a thinly disguised secret, as when Samuel Clemens wrote as Mark Twain. Sometimes there are more profound reasons, as when Mary Ann Evans wrote as George Eliot, in part, at least, in order to get published in an otherwise rigidly patriarchal literary culture. So too in antiquity, motives could have been complicated, or not. Ronald Syme has shown that the six purported authors of the *Historia Augusta* were in fact pen names of a single learned but somewhat mischievous scholar from around 400 CE, who fabricated a good deal of information, much of it for his personal enjoyment. And he was remarkably successful in his endeavor to cover up his identity: up to the end of the nineteenth century his work was held to be authentic and basically reliable.[13] Sometimes a pen name serves a fairly obvious purpose, as when Xenophon wrote his *Anabasis* in the name of Themistogenes, an alleged general of Syracuse; Plutarch (*Moralia* 345E) points out that Xenophon was able to give himself greater credence and glory by discussing his own military activities in the third person by a purported outsider who would be particularly well positioned to know what had taken place. At other times the choice of a name is a real puzzle, as when Iamblichus wrote *On the Mysteries* as Abamon.[14] In any event, pen names are not an overwhelming concern for those working on early Christian apocryphal texts, as the names authors choose when writing pseudonymously are by a wide margin those of well-known figures, almost always figures of the apostolic past.

At this point I need to make one of the fundamental categorical differentiations between what I am calling pseudonymity and what I am calling pseudepigraphy. In German circles these two terms are sometimes differentiated by making the former, pseudonymity, refer to pen names, and the latter, pseudepigraphy, refer to the false use of the name of a well-known person. I do not like that particular usage, because it seems to me that pseudepigraphic writings—literally writings that are falsely inscribed, or inscribed with a lie—are also pseudonymous, that is, literally, they go under a false name. And so I prefer to use pseudonymity as a broad umbrella term, referring to any work that circulates under a name other than the name of the actual author (whether a pen name or a known name), and pseudepigraphy to be a sub-category of pseudonymous writings. Thus a pseudonymous writing could be produced under a pen name, or it could circulate under the

---

13. Syme, *Emperors and Biography*, 1–16.
14. I discuss some of the options in Ehrman, *Forgery and Counterforgery*, 46.

name of a known person who was not its actual author. The latter is, for me, a pseudepigraphical writing.

Either to complicate or clarify things further, there are also two sub-categories of pseudepigrapha. Some pseudepigraphical writings—that is, writings circulating under the name of a famous person who did not in fact write them—are anonymous writings that have been falsely attributed, as I have already discussed. Other writings are produced by people making an explicit false authorial claim. Those are two very different phenomena, and as I said, I think it is highly important to differentiate between them.

The discussion of false attributions goes back in antiquity almost as far as we have any critical literary discourse at all.[15] Already in the fifth century BCE Herodotus (*Hist.* 2.117; 4.32) expressed his doubts concerning the attribution of the Cyprian poems to Homer, based on their material discrepancies with the Homeric epics themselves. Sometimes false attributions were simply somebody's best guess as to whom the author was. This is probably the case for the assignation of *Against All Heresies* to Tertullian or the anonymous treatises the *Exhortation to the Greeks* and the *Oration to the Greeks* to Justin. Hundreds of sermons came to be attributed to Chrysostom, most of them wrongly. In other instances, however, the attributions were not at all innocent. Whoever assigned the five books of the Torah to Moses, or the four Gospels to Matthew, Mark, Luke, and John, were not simply picking names out of a hat. With respect to the Gospels, it is no accident that two of them are attributed to Jesus' earthly disciples, and the other two to close companions of the chief apostles Peter and Paul. The logic for the latter choice is somewhat unwittingly expressed by Tertullian, who tells us that, "that which Mark produced is stated to be Peter's, whose interpreter Mark was. Luke's narrative also they usually attribute to Paul. It is permissible for the works which disciples published to be regarded as belonging to their masters" (*Marc.* 4.5.3–4; trans. Evans, 271).

As a side note I should clarify what Tertullian is saying, since this passage is often misquoted by those who want to see literary forgery as an innocent undertaking in antiquity, or at least in Christian antiquity. Tertullian is not—he is decidedly not—saying that it was acceptable for a disciple to write a treatise in the name of his teacher. That is a common claim, a claim that many of us were fed in graduate school when we were learning that Paul did not really write the Pastoral Epistles, but that that was not a problem, because it was a common practice for disciples to write in the name of their teachers, with complete impunity. As it turns out, that claim is demonstrably false: ancient authors who wrote in the names of their

15. See ibid., 50–52.

teachers who were found out were not treated with impunity, but just the opposite.[16] But in any event, the quotation from Tertullian has nothing to do with the matter. Tertullian is not saying that Mark could write as Peter and Luke as Paul. He is saying that these authors represent the views of their teachers. Mark's Gospel, however, was not called the Gospel according to Peter and Luke's was not called the Gospel according to Paul. The authors did not write in the names of their teachers. According to Tertullian they wrote their own accounts with the *authority* of their teachers. That's a different matter altogether. When we are dealing with issues of pseudepigraphy, we are concerned with authorial claims.

In any event, to return to my point, sometimes those authorial claims are not made by the authors themselves, but by later readers and writers who assign anonymous works to this or that famous person. And sometimes such false attributions were not made innocently but in order to provide greater authority for the work in question. One could make the argument that this is ultimately what lay behind the aforementioned assignment of the *Epistle of Barnabas* to Paul's apostolic companion. The attribution happened at least by the time of Clement of Alexandria, and so some time in the late second century. As we all know, that was a key time for all sorts of Christian debates, including one central to the thematic interests of the letter: the status of the Old Testament. Barnabas's understanding of the Old Testament was hugely different from that of other figures from roughly the same time, including Marcion and some leaders of various gnostic groups. Like the proto-orthodox, Marcion claimed Paul as an ultimate authority for his views, but unlike the proto-orthodox he maintained that the Jewish Bible was a book only for the Jews, not for the Christians. Not so for the *Epistle of Barnabas*. Even though the book is vitriolic toward contemporary Jews and historical Judaism, it is not at all opposed to the Old Testament. The problem, as this author presents it, is that the Jews have always misinterpreted the Old Testament. For him, the Old Testament is not a Jewish book and never has been. It is a Christian book. And so, given this dispute over the status of the Old Testament, a dispute for which the writings of Paul were being invoked on all sides, it can scarcely be surprising that this anonymous letter came to be attributed, at the very height of the debate, to one of Paul's closest companions, Barnabas. Here, again, the disciple is representing the view of his teacher, but now that disciple is named as the book's author.

And so, to repeat myself in the faint hopes of clarity: "pseudonymous" writings can involve either a pen name or the circulation of a writing under the name of someone who is well known. "Pseudepigrapha," in

---

16. Examples scattered throughout ibid., e.g., ch. 2.

my terminology, are specifically pseudonymous writings circulated under a well-known name. But further, pseudepigrapha come in two varieties: falsely attributed writings and writings that make a false authorial claim. It is this latter kind of pseudepigraphon that I am calling forgery. A forgery is a writing that falsely claims to be written by a well-known person, whether he is well known broadly or simply within a small community.

I have already pointed out that many of us learned in graduate school, and have heard repeatedly since then, that the use of someone else's name was not a condemned practice in antiquity. My view is that anyone who makes that claim simply hasn't read either what ancient sources have to say about the practice or what modern scholars have uncovered about it.[17] No-one can read the great classic works of Wolfgang Speyer and Norbert Brox, or the more recent works of someone such as Armin Baum, and come away with any such conclusion.[18] We could spend the entire evening looking at the evidence, but there is no need. The English term "forgery" is no more or no less derogatory than the ancient terms used to describe the same phenomenon, the three most common Greek terms being ψεῦδος (lie), νόθος (bastard), and κίβδηλος (counterfeit). And modern condemnations and punishments for literary forgery are no more severe than those one can readily find in the ancient sources. Forgery was a form of literary deceit. It was condemned as lying. It was not socially acceptable. The fact that it was widely practiced has no bearing on whether it was widely approved, any more than widely practiced iniquitous activities today are socially approved (use your own imagination to think of examples; you might start with either the Internal Revenue Service or Ashley Madison).

And so the activity was condemned, but it was practiced. Hence our disciplinary field, where we consider gospels allegedly written by Peter, Thomas, and Philip; letters allegedly written by Paul, Abgar, and Seneca; apocalypses allegedly written by Peter and Paul; and, well you know the list as well as I do. In these instances someone other than the alleged author wrote a book claiming to be the alleged author, almost certainly in order to deceive his readers into thinking that he was the alleged author. If a book does not make such a false authorial claim, whatever you might think of other deceitful schemes the author had in mind, it is not a forgery.

Under this category of forgery though—which is itself a subcategory of pseudepigrapha, which is a subcategory of pseudonymous writings—I

17. See ibid., *passim*, and esp. 128–37.

18. Of course, most English-speaking scholars, even those who write on the topic, have *not* read them. Still, the classic is Speyer, *Die literarische Fälschung*; penetrating as well, but much briefer, is Brox, *Falsche Verfasserangabe*; most recent is Baum, *Pseudepigraphie und literarische Fälschung*.

want to point out that further differentiations need to be made. There are three kinds of forgery other than the one I just described, where an author makes an explicit authorial claim. These three kinds of forgery have rarely been identified, but I think it is helpful to bear them in mind as discrete phenomena. These are what I am calling embedded forgeries, redactional forgeries, and non-pseudepigraphic forgeries.

1. Embedded forgeries.[19] Some writings do not make the explicit claim to be authored by a well-known person, but instead embed first-person narratives—or other self-identifying devices—in the course of their discussions, without differentiating the first person from the author. In these instances the reader naturally assumes that the person speaking in the first person is actually the writer of the account. A good example occurs in the *Ascension of Isaiah*, whose author does not self-identify at the outset, but instead sets out an anonymous historical framework, written to sound very much like the prose narrative sections of the book of Isaiah itself. Part way through the narrative, however, and at key points throughout, the revelation given through Isaiah begins to be delivered in the first person. The author of the account does not indicate that he is now quoting someone else, making the reader assume that the author has now begun speaking about what he himself experienced. This provides an unimpeachable authority for the account—it is revealed by none other than Isaiah.

This kind of embedding strategy shows how blurry the lines of distinction can be between forgery and other kinds of writing. In many ways an embedded forgery is comparable to the use of speeches invented by historians and placed on the lips of their protagonists; but in those cases it is clear that the author has moved from narrative description to an (alleged) speech—even though the speech is invented. In an embedded forgery the narrator simply slips into a different guise and becomes the authenticating figure. In another sense this kind of forgery is not so very different from fabrications of sayings that an authoritative figure is reported to have said, but which are actually the inventions of the author or of the unknown tradents who have passed them along in the oral tradition—such as many of the sayings of the *Gospel of Thomas* or later (or earlier) gospel materials. But there again the sayings are attributed to another person and are presented by a narrator who is distinct from the speaker, unlike what happens in the embedded forgery. So such materials may entail fabrication, but not forgery. For an embedded text, the narrator becomes the speaker (or participant in the action of the narrative). The *Ascension of Isaiah*, then, is a kind of

19. See Ehrman, *Forgery and Counterforgery*, 264–65.

forgery; the speaker who describes his experiences to the scribe recording the account is allegedly none other than Isaiah of Jerusalem himself.

2. Redactional forgeries.[20] There are a number of instances in which a book was originally circulated as an anonymous work, and was known in that form for some time, before a later editor and/or scribe altered the text to make it present an authorial claim. The book is not, then, a forgery from its inception, but it becomes a forgery in the course of its transmission—not in the sense that the (original) author made a false authorial claim but in the sense that a later redactor reworded the text in such a way as to make the author (unwittingly) make such a claim. This is the case for example with the *Infancy Gospel of Thomas*. In the oldest parts of the textual tradition, this account of Jesus the mischievous wunderkind is simply narrated apart from any authorial claim. Only in later manuscripts is the name Thomas attached to it. Presumably this Thomas is to be taken as Jesus' twin brother Judas Didymus, a particularly qualified authority to recount the miraculous childhood of the Son of God. But as Stephen Gero has argued, the attribution is late, probably from the middle ages.[21] The author himself made no authenticating claims.

3. Non-pseudepigraphic forgeries.[22] There are other instances in which a book makes clear, but false, authorial claims without actually naming an author. This is true of one of the forgeries of the Hebrew Bible, the book of Ecclesiastes, which is allegedly authored by the "son of David," who is ruling as the king in Jerusalem, a man both inestimably rich and wise. Obviously the author means his readers to take him to be Solomon; but he never calls himself by name. This, then, creates an ironic situation: the author claims to be a famous person without actually naming himself. And so the book is a forgery (Solomon did not actually write it) but it is not, technically speaking, pseudepigraphic, since it is not inscribed with the false name. A similar situation obtains much later in Christian circles in a book such as the *Martyrdom of Marian and James*, whose author claims, falsely, to have been a personal companion of these two estimable martyrs, but never identifies himself by name.

Before bringing this paper to a close, I want to speak about two other literary phenomena that are related to the literary deceits I have been describing but require distinct categories of their own.

1. Literary Fictions. It is widely recognized by scholars today, as it evidently was in antiquity, that *some* writings that make false authorial claims

20. See ibid., 34–35.

21. Gero, "Infancy Gospel of Thomas," esp. 59.

22. See Ehrman, *Forgery and Counterforgery*, 35.

were not meant as deceptions but as literary fictions.[23] This is particularly the case in certain letter collections and epistolary novels written in the names of well-known figures—especially philosophers—but probably as rhetorical exercises rather than attempts to deceive a reading public. In many instances, however, it is difficult to tell whether deception was part of the intent. As Patricia Rosenmeyer points out in her thorough and illuminating study, verisimilitudes were typically part of the exercise, as these letters speak about the mechanics of writing, sending, sealing, receiving, and so on, for one major reason: to make the letter sound more convincing.[24] But that makes it difficult to draw a very clear line in some instances between the attempt at verisimilitude and pure literary deception.

One might consider, for example, the two sets of Socratic epistles, one connected with Antisthenes, which urges a rigorous life-style, and the other with Aristippus, which supports hedonism. Both advocate their own perspective and inveigh against the other. And why is that? It is because, in Rosenmeyer's own words, "a treatise on the subject would be rejected as just another (mis)interpretation of the philosopher; but a letter in the voice of the great man himself, or in that of his most highly-regarded disciple, would be hard to refute."[25] That is exactly right; but it is also the reason that some of these fictions may be seen as going a step further in wanting their readers really to believe them to be actual letters written by the philosopher himself. It is at least possible, that is, that some of these works were produced not simply as rhetorical exercises but in order to perpetrate a literary deceit. However one judges that issue, fictions of this kind were difficult to keep in check. In any event, with only one or two possible exceptions—possibly the letters of Paul and Seneca?—there are probably no literary fictions among the early Christian writings produced simply as rhetorical exercises.

2. Plagiarism. As I noted at the outset of this paper, it is sometimes erroneously stated that plagiarism was either non-existent or non-problematic in Greek and Roman antiquity. In reality, plagiarism (usually discussed in terms of literary "theft") was known, discussed, and condemned in ancient sources. There is, for example, the case of the fourth-century-BCE Heraclides Ponticus, who, according to Diogenes Laertius (*Vit. phil.* 5.92–93), not only published extensively works of his own but also occasionally published works of others as if he had written them. This was plagiarism by a man who, strikingly, wrote two separate treatises περὶ ἀρετῆς. Or consider his Athenian predecessor Aeschines, who stole dialogues of Socrates after

23. See ibid., 43–45.

24. Rosenmeyer, *Ancient Epistolary Fictions*.

25. Ibid., 202.

the great man's death and was calumniated for it on more than one occasion (*Vit. phil.* 2.60). At other times authors complained about writers who plagiarized their own work, none more memorably than Martial: "You mistake, you greedy thief of my works, who think you can become a poet at no more than the cost of a transcript and a cheap papyrus roll. Applause is not acquired for six or ten sesterces" (Mart. 1.66; trans. Ker).

When plagiarism was detected in antiquity, it often had actual social repercussions. Thus we learn of the expulsion of Empedocles from the school of Pythagoras, on the grounds of plagiarism (Diogenes Laertius, *Vit. phil.* 8.54). At other times the perpetrator was subject to harsh condemnation, as one explicitly finds in the writings of Polybius, Vitruvius, and Pliny the Elder, who in his *Natural History* discusses his own practices of citation in contrast to those who are "of a perverted mind and a bad disposition" (Pref. 20–23; trans. Rackham) and steal the work of others to pass off as their own.

The ancient discourse on plagiarism is relevant to the "unacknowledged borrowings" found throughout early Christian literature. For the Neutestamentlers among us, let me refer to a canonical instance. Assuming the Two-source Hypothesis, Matthew and Luke both acquired considerable amounts of their material—often verbatim—from Mark and Q, and used it without acknowledgment. But if plagiarism is defined as taking over the work of another and claiming it as one's own, possibly the charge does not apply in these cases, as all the writings in question are anonymous. That is to say, the later Synoptic authors are not claiming anything as their own, as they do not even name themselves. The same would apply to the extensive and often verbatim reproduction of the *Protevangelium of James* in such later texts as the *Gospel of Pseudo-Matthew*, in that the later author does not claim the earlier work as his own, since he is, in fact, writing pseudonymously. A comparable situation obtains in the wholesale incorporation of the *Didascalia Apostolorum*, the *Didache*, and the *Apostolic Traditions* in the fourth-century *Apostolic Constitutions*. But here the situation is somewhat more complex. Two of these earlier works are anonymous, making it difficult to give credit where credit is due. The *Didascalia*, on the other hand, was inherited as a forgery—it falsely claims to be written by the apostles— and is itself embedded in another work that is also a forgery, also allegedly written by the apostles. Why would a forger need to credit an earlier work that he allegedly (but in fact did not) write?

In all these instances we are dealing with complex literary relations that do not neatly line up in taxonomies of fraudulence, either ancient or modern. But taxonomies we must have, as I have been urging in this paper. If we can agree on the terms we use, we will make our task easier and more efficient. I am arguing for a variety of forms of literary deception, some of it intended and some of it probably not. Among the kinds of false claims that may not be deceptive are literary fictions and false attributions. But both of these may, in some other instances, in fact involve intentional deception. So too may pen names. I would argue that forgery itself, in almost every instance, involves an intent to deceive. This deception either comes through an explicit authorial claim to be someone other than who one actually is, or through embedding devices designed to make the read think the author is someone else, or through redactional activities in which an editor changes the wording of a text in order to make the finished form make authorial claims not found in the text that the redactor inherited. This latter kind of editorial activity can only be distinguished with difficulty from the scribal practice of falsification; if push came to shove, I would say that redaction tends to be a more thorough form of editing, and falsification tends to be a more piecemeal and occasional alteration of a text. All of these activities may involve, but in most instances do not involve, the fabrication of historical narratives, a practice that can be deceptive on its own terms.

Although it may be a challenge to keep these categories straight—the difference between pseudonymity, pseudepigraphy, forgery, embedded forgery, redacted forgery, non-pseudonymous forgery and the like—it does seem to be a useful procedure to devise such categories and to be clear in our heads what we are talking about when we are discussing individual cases of literary deceit. Deceit comes in many guises, and we do well to recognize it for what it is and not to call it something that it is not.[26]

26. On the morality of deceit within the early Christian tradition, see Ehrman, *Forgery and Counterforgery*, ch. 16.

— 3 —

What Has Pseudepigraphy to Do with Forgery?

Reflections on the Cases of the *Acts of Paul*, the *Apocalypse of Paul*, and the *Zohar*

— Pierluigi Piovanelli —

EVERY STUDENT OF APOCRYPHAL literature is probably familiar with Tertullian's offhand dismissal of the *Acts of Paul*. In his treatise *On Baptism*, written ca. 198–200 or 200–206 CE (in any case, before his Montanist radicalization), the hot-tempered North African apologist claims that a presbyter was convicted in Asia of having compiled the document and that he had done this out of his love for Paul (17.5). Such amazing information is provided at the end of a chapter dealing with those Christians who are authorized, in Tertullian's opinion, to administer baptism.

> **17.1** Superest ad concludendam materiolam de observatione quoque dandi et accipiendi baptismi commonefacere. dandi quidem summum habet ius summus sacerdos, si qui est episcopus: dehinc presbyteri et diaconi, non tamen sine episcopi auctoritate, propter ecclesiae honorem quo salvo salva pax est. **2** . . . episcopatus aemulatio schismatum mater est. omnia licere dixit sanctissimus apostolus sed non omnia expedire. **3** sufficit

scilicet in necessitatibus [ut] utaris sicubi aut loci aut temporis aut personae condicio compellit: tunc enim constantia succurrentis excipitur cum urguetur circumstantia periclitantis, quoniam reus erit perditi hominis si supersederit praestare quod libere potuit. **4** petulantia autem mulieris quae usurpavit docere utique non etiam tinguendi ius sibi rapiet, nisi si quae nova bestia venerit similis pristinae, ut quemadmodum illa baptismum auferebat ita aliqua per se [eum] conferat. **5** quod si quae Acta Pauli, quae perperam scripta sunt, exemplum Theclae ad licentiam mulierum docendi tinguendique defendant, sciant in Asia presbyterum qui eam scripturam construxit, quasi titulo Pauli de suo cumulans, convictum atque confessum id se amore Pauli fecisse loco decessisse. quam enim fidei proximum videtur ut is docendi et tinguendi daret feminae potestatem qui ne discere quidem constanter mulieri permisit? Taceant, inquit, et domi viros suos consulant. (ed. Evans)

17.1 To round off our slight treatment of this subject it remains for me to advise you of the rules to be observed in giving and receiving baptism. The supreme right of giving it (i.e. baptism) belongs to the high priest, which is the bishop: after him, to the presbyters and deacons, yet not without commission from the bishop, on account of the church's dignity: for when this is safe, peace is safe. **2** (. . .) Opposition to the episcopate is the mother of schisms. The holy apostle has said that all things are lawful but all things are not expedient (1 Cor. 6:12): **3** which means it is enough that you should use <this right> in emergencies, if ever conditions of place or time or person demand it. The boldness of a rescuer is acceptable when he is constrained to it by the necessities of the man in peril, since he will be guilty of a man's destruction if he forbears to give the help he is free and able to give. **4** But the impudence of that woman who assumed the right to teach is evidently not going to arrogate to her the right to baptize as well—unless perhaps some new serpent appears, like that original one, so that as that woman abolished baptism, some other should of her own authority confer it. **5** But if certain Acts of Paul, which are falsely so named, claim the example of Thecla for allowing women to teach and to baptize, let men know that in Asia the presbyter who compiled that document, thinking to add of his own to Paul's reputation, was found out, and though he professed he had done it for love of Paul, was deposed from his position. How could we believe that Paul should give a female power to teach and to baptize, when he did not allow a woman even to learn by her own right? *Let them keep*

silence, he says, *and ask their husbands at home* (1 Cor. 14:35).
(trans. Evans)

As Ernest Evans aptly summarizes, Tertullian's point of view is that,
"[t]he right of administering baptism belongs to the bishop: priests and deacons may baptize, but only with the bishop's license; laymen baptize only in
urgent necessity; women not at all."[1] Contravening this rule amounts to disturbing *ecclesiae honorem*, "the church's dignity," the preservation of which
is essential to ensure the peace of the Christian community (*quo salvo salva
pax est*). Actually, every threat to the bishop's authority is an open door to
heresy; in Tertullian's words, *episcopatus aemulatio schismatum mater est*,
"jealousy towards (better than 'opposition to') the episcopate is the mother
of schisms." In exceptional cases, however, the Carthaginian Father is ready
to justify the right of male non-ordained Christians to baptize, for example,
when the life of the fellow who should receive the sacrament is in danger. To
the *constantia succurrentis*, the "firmness of character of a (male) rescuer,"
Tertullian opposes the *petulantia . . . mulieris*, the "impudence of a woman"
who, having already assumed the right to teach, claims now the right to
baptize as well. He remarks also that while, ironically enough, on the one
hand the anonymous heterodox (?) woman who provoked the writing of his
treatise—*quaedam de caina haeresi vipera venenatissima*, "a certain female
viper from the Cainite sect," at least if we accept Adolf von Harnack's conjecture and read *caina* instead of *canina* of Codex Trecensis 523 and *gaiana* of
Martin Mesnart's 1545 Parisian *editio princeps*—wished to abolish baptism
(more probably, she denied that baptism could wash away the sins of the
soul),[2] on the other hand another woman (a "straw woman"?) now wishes
to administer it.

---

1. Tertullian, *Tertullian's Homily on Baptism* (ed. Evans), 97.

2. 1.2 atque, adeo nuper conversata istic quaedam de caina haeresi vipera venenatissima doctrina sua plerosque rapuit, imprimis baptismum destruens. plane secundum naturam: nam fere viperae et aspides ipsique reguli serpentes arida et inaquosa
sectantur. 3 sed nos pisciculi secundum ἰχθὺν nostrum Iesum Christum in aqua nas-
cimur, nec aliter quam in aqua permanendo salvi sumus. itaque illa monstrosissima, cui
nec integre quidem docendi ius erat, optime norat necare pisciculos de aqua auferens.
"And in fact a certain female viper from the Cainite sect, who recently spent some time
here, carried off a good number with her exceptionally pestilential doctrine, making
a particular point of demolishing baptism. Evidently in this according to nature: for
vipers and asps as a rule, and even basilisks, frequent dry and waterless places. But we,
being little fishes, as Jesus Christ is our great Fish, begin our life in the water, and only
while we abide in the water are we safe and sound. Thus it was that that portent of a
woman, who had no right to teach even correctly (1 Tim. 2:12), knew very well how to
kill the little fishes by taking them out of the water" (ed. and trans. Evans).

It is at this point that mention is made of Thecla's exemplary role in the *Acts of Paul*. Let's read again this difficult passage, recently reexamined by Anthony Hilhorst.[3]

> But if certain Acts of Paul (*quae Acta Pauli*), which are falsely so named, claim the example of Thecla for allowing women to teach and to baptize, let them know that in Asia the presbyter who compiled that document, thinking to add of his own to Paul's reputation (*quasi titulo Pauli de suo cumulans*), was convicted and having confessed that he had done it for love of Paul (*id se amore Pauli fecisse*), was deposed from his position.

Beside discussing some difficult interpretations—should we read "But if certain Acts of Paul (. . .) claim the example of Thecla" and "thinking to add of his own to Paul's reputation," with Ernest Evans, or "But if certain women (*quae* for *aliquae mulieres*) refer to the Acts of Paul (. . .) and claim the example of Thecla" and "thinking to add Paul's reputation to his own," with François Refoulé and Maurice Drouzy?[4]—Hilhorst makes a compelling case for completing the textual dossier of this passage with the help of an (apparently) faithful quotation of it found in Jerome's *Lives of Illustrious Men* 7.

> Igitur περίοδοι Pauli et Theclae et totam baptizati Leonis fabulam inter scripturas apocryphas computemus. Quale enim est ut indiuiduus comes apostoli inter ceteras eius res hoc solum ignorauerit? Sed et Tertullianus, uicinus illorum temporum, refert presbyterum quemdam in Asia, σπουδαστὴν apostoli Pauli, conuictum apud Ioannem quod auctor esset libri et confessum se hoc Pauli amore fecisse, loco excidisse. (ed. Ceresa-Gastaldo)

> Therefore the *Acts of Paul* and all the fable about the lion baptized by him we reckon among the apocryphal writings, for how is it possible that the inseparable companion of the apostle in his other affairs, alone should have been ignorant of this thing. Moreover Tertullian who lived near those times, mentions a certain presbyter in Asia, an adherent of the apostle Paul, who was convicted by John of having been the author of the book, and who, confessing that he did this for love of Paul, resigned his office of presbyter. (trans. Richardson)

3. Hilhorst, "Tertullian on the Acts of Paul." See also Davies, "Women, Tertullian, and the *Acts of Paul*"; Mackay, "Response [to S. Davies]"; Rordorf, "Tertullien et les *Actes de Paul*"; Barrier, *Acts of Paul and Thecla*, 21–24; Ehrman, *Forgery and Counterforgery*, 59–60, 84, 132–33, 379–80 and 383; Pervo, *Acts of Paul*, 43, 50–51, 58–59, 61 and 70–71; Nogueira, "Tertuliano e os Atos de Paulo e Tecla."

4. Tertullian, *Traité du baptême* (ed. Refoulé), 89–91.

Surprisingly enough, in Jerome's reading of Tertullian's text, the Asian presbyter guilty of having fabricated the *Acts of Paul* was *conuictum apud Ioannem*, "convicted by John" or "before John." Such a detail, perhaps originally part of the poorly-preserved text of Tertullian's treatise, could possibly shed some light on the literary source of information, if any, available to a Carthaginian author writing at some 1500 kilometers away from the shores of Asia Minor, a piece of evidence that appears to have been absolutely unknown to other early Christian authors. The mention of an Asian presbyter partisan of Paul in the days of John—either the apostle or a homonymous elder—seems to me to point to an early Christian author who claimed to be familiar with many elders who had known John and other disciples of Jesus; I mean Papias of Hierapolis, the author of the now lost *Exposition of the Sayings of the Lord* written in Greek between ca. 95 and 120 CE.[5] With this in mind, we should not forget that Tertullian was able not only to read but also to write Greek, and that the very language of his treatise *On Baptism* is heavily influenced by Greek terminology (e.g., the Grecism *amartia* at 18.1) and thought.[6]

Be that as it may, even if we imagine that Tertullian had had privileged access to Papias's work, a highly speculative suggestion such as this does not solve the essential question that lies behind his report on the fabrication of the *Acts of Paul*—namely, how can we trust the testimony of a rhetorician who, according to the leading specialists of his work,

> in every instance . . . wrote to win arguments. He did not describe, he advocated. It was his overall position about which he was passionate; everything else was merely there to prove the point. . . . So he could advance arguments that, in the context, helped his case but which were ones he personally would have found difficult to swallow.[7]

In other words, Tertullian was so determined to deny Christian women the right to teach or baptize that any scriptural text that would support this kind of claim would necessarily be, in his opinion, false, a forgery perpetrated by a poorly-advised and deceitful author.

5. Since Irenaeus of Lyon, Papias is generally considered to have been one of John's "auditors," with the only exception of Eusebius, followed by Jerome, who prefers to associate Papias with an Asian presbyter also named John. For a critical assessment, see Norelli, *Papia di Hierapolis*, 40–45.

6. See Tertullian, *Traité du baptême* (ed. Refoulé), 55–56.

7. Dunn, *Tertullian*, 29 (based on Timothy David Barnes's conclusions on Tertullian's rhetorical proclivities).

Almost two and a half centuries later, in the continuation of his *Ecclesiastical History* written around 440–443 and covering the period from the conversion of Constantine (312) to the accession of Valentinian III (425), the church historian Sozomen declares that a certain Cilician, an aged presbyter from Tarsus, had told him that the story of the discovery of the *Apocalypse of Paul* buried in the apostle's house was completely false (7.19).

19.9 Καὶ εὐχαῖς δὲ καὶ ψαλμῳδίαις ταῖς αὐταῖς ἢ ἀναγνώσμασι κατὰ τὸν αὐτὸν καιρὸν οὐ πάντας εὑρεῖν ἔστι κεχρημένους. Οὕτω γοῦν τὴν καλουμένην Ἀποκάλυψιν Πέτρου, ὡς νόθον παντελῶς πρὸς τῶν ἀρχαίων δοκιμασθεῖσαν, ἔν τισιν ἐκκλησίαις τῆς Παλαιστίνης εἰσέτι νῦν ἅπαξ ἑκάστου ἔτους ἀναγινωσκομένην ἔγνων ἐν τῇ ἡμέρᾳ τῆς παρασκευῆς, ἣν εὐλαβῶς ἅπας ὁ λαὸς νηστεύει ἐπὶ ἀναμνήσει τοῦ σωτηρίου πάθους. **10** Τὴν δὲ νῦν ὡς Ἀποκάλυψιν Παύλου τοῦ ἀποστόλου φερομένην, ἣν οὐδεὶς ἀρχαίων οἶδε, πλεῖστοι μοναχῶν ἐπαινοῦσιν. Ἐπὶ ταύτης δὲ τῆς βασιλείας ἰσχυρίζονταί τινες ταύτην ηὑρῆσθαι τὴν βίβλον. Λέγουσι γὰρ ἐκ θείας ἐπιφανείας ἐν Ταρσῷ τῆς Κιλικίας κατὰ τὴν οἰκίαν Παύλου μαρμαρίνην λάρνακα ὑπὸ γῆν εὑρεθῆναι καὶ ἐν αὐτῇ τὴν βίβλον εἶναι. **11** Ἐρωμένῳ δέ μοι περὶ τούτου ψεῦδος ἔφεσεν εἶναι Κίλιξ πρεσβύτερος τῆς ἐν Ταρσῷ ἐκκλησίας· γεγονέναι μὲν γὰρ πολλῶν ἐτῶν καὶ ἡ πολιὰ τὸν ἄνδρα ἐδείκνυ· ἔλεγε δὲ μηδὲν τοιοῦτον ἐπίστασθαι παρ' αὐτοῖς συμβάν, θαυμάζειν τε εἰ μὴ τάδε πρὸς αἱρετικῶν ἀναπέπλασται. Ἀλλὰ περὶ μὲν τούτου τάδε. (ed. Sabbah et al.)

19.9 The same prayers and psalms are not recited nor the same lections read on the same occasions in all churches. Thus the book entitled the "Apocalypse of Peter," which was considered altogether spurious by the ancients, is still read in some of the churches of Palestine, on the day of preparation, when the people observe a fast in memory of the passion of the Savior. **10** So the work entitled the "Apocalypse of the Apostle Paul," though unrecognized by the ancients, is still esteemed by most of the monks. Some persons affirm that the book was found during this (i.e., Theodosius the Great's) reign, by Divine revelation, in a marble box, buried beneath the soil in the house of Paul at Tarsus in Cilicia. **11** I have been informed that this report is false by *a Cilician*, a presbyter of the church in Tarsus, a man of very advanced age, as is indicated by his gray hairs, who says that no such occurrence is known among them, and wonders if the heretics did not invent the story. What I have said upon this subject must now suffice. (trans. Hartranft, modified)

Sozomen's testimony is a real goldmine of information about the launching of the "orthodox" *Apocalypse of Paul* (to distinguish it from the homonymous text from Nag Hammadi, NHC V,2, probably a Valentinian apocryphon). To begin with, the church historian contrasts the case of the old *Apocalypse of Peter*, "which was considered altogether spurious (νόθον παντελῶς) by the ancients" and is still read on Good Friday, but only in a few Palestinian churches, with the situation of the new *Apocalypse of Paul*, presently in circulation and greatly appreciated by the majority of the monks in spite of the fact that it was "unrecognized by the ancients." He confirms also that the readers of the *Apocalypse of Paul* took seriously the story of its discovery as told in the prologue that still survives in some of its manuscripts and versions:

> **1:1** At what time was it (i.e., the *Apocalypse of Paul*) made public? In the consulship of Theodosius, the pious king, and of the very illustrious Cynegius (i.e., 388 CE), a very honored man was then living in the city of Tarsus, in the house of Saint Paul the apostle. **1:2** An angel of the Lord appeared to him in a dream, saying: "Destroy the foundations of this house and take out what you will find." But he thought it was a hallucination. **2:1** The angel then returned and, a third time, obliged him to destroy the foundations. While digging, he found a small marble chest with an inscription engraved on the sides, which contained this Apocalypse and the sandals that Paul would wear when he taught the word of God. **2:2** Afraid of opening the chest, he carried it to the magistrate of the city. The magistrate saw that it was sealed with lead, and, fearing that it was something else, he sent it to Theodosius. **2:3** When the king had received it, he opened it and found the Apocalypse of Saint Paul; he had it copied and sent the original to Jerusalem. This is what is written there. (my own trans.)[8]

In this connection, Sozomen is particularly adamant about the time when the book was discovered, the precision "during this reign" (ἐπὶ ταύτης δὲ τῆς βασιλείας, 7.19.10) referring to the reign of the emperor under discussion in the second part of Book 7 of his *Ecclesiastical History*—i.e., Theodosius I, the Great (379–395), not his grandson Theodosius II, the Younger (408–450).[9] Therefore the need to emphasize that the anonymous, yet still more than respectable, Cilician presbyter from Tarsus he had interrogated—not "Cilix (*sic*), the venerable presbyter of Tarsus," with whom Sozomen was, according

8. Concerning the prologue's narrative function, see Piovanelli, "Miraculous Discovery."

9. As incorrectly suggested by Silverstein, "Date of the 'Apocalypse of Paul,'" 342–44.

to Chester D. Hartranft, "on good terms"—was old enough to have been, in his younger days (before 395), a credible witness to the events mentioned in the prologue. Having thus demonstrated not so much the falseness of the *Apocalypse of Paul* in itself, but the implausibility of the conditions of its late discovery, Sozomen was probably content to imply that given the circumstances, it was impossible to validate the authenticity of such a new relic, if it was not, as the presbyter said, the invention of some heretics.

To these early examples of vague and polemical accusations, rhetorically constructed to invalidate the appearance of embarrassing new scriptural texts, we could add the much later case of the equally questionable unmasking, based on rumors attributed to his widow, of Moses de León (ca. 1250–1305) as the true author of the *Zohar*, the famous and impressive esoteric commentary (ca. 1700 printed pages!)[10] of the Pentateuch, the Book of Ruth, and the Song of Songs, written in Aramaic and attributed to Rabbi Shimon bar Yohai (Rashbi), a disciple of Rabbi Aqiva.

At the beginning of the fourteenth century the rumor spread among cabbalists that a new text, the *Zohar*, had been discovered in a Galilean cave where it had been hidden for more than 1000 years, that the philosopher and cabbalist Nahmanides (Ramban, 1194–1270) himself had sent the original manuscript from Jerusalem to his son in Spain, and that Rabbi Moses de León had finally obtained it and was copying it on behalf of his associates. Puzzled by this, the young cabbalist Isaac of Acre, possibly one of Nahmanides' students, went to Spain to personally inquire about the whereabouts of the manuscript. He met Moses de León in Valladolid, where Moses promised to show the manuscript to him, but he unhappily died a few days later. Nevertheless, no-one in Avila (Moses de León's Castillan hometown) was able to find a trace of it and both his widow and his daughter confessed, so Isaac was told, that no such manuscript had ever existed: the only reason why Moses de León had crafted it was to deceive his audience in order to get more attention and to better sell his book!

> Isaac left his home when he was still a young student after the conquest of Acre by the Moslems (1291), apparently for Italy where he also seems to have heard of the Zohar, and finally went to Spain in 1305, where he began to take an interest in the circumstances under which the book was published. His diary, of which a few other parts have also been preserved in manuscript, gives a rather naive account of the information he gathered on the subject. We are told that he met Moses in Valladolid and was informed under oath that he (Moses de Leon) was in possession

10. See now Matt, *Zohar.*

of "the ancient book written by Simeon ben Yohai" and would
show it to him in his house at Avila. Subsequently, when after
Moses de Leon's death he came to Avila, he was told that a rich
citizen of the town, Joseph de Avila, had offered to marry his
son to the daughter of the deceased in exchange for the original
manuscript of the Zohar, said to be ancient as well as authentic,
from which Moses de Leon was supposed to have copied, but
that both the widow of the deceased and his daughter had denied the existence of such an original. According to them, Moses
de Leon had written the Zohar all by himself, and, to his wife's
question why he did not claim the authorship of the work, had
replied: "If I told people that I am the author, they would pay no
attention nor spend a farthing on the book, for they would say
that these are but the workings of my own imagination. But now
that they hear that I am copying from the book Zohar which
Simeon ben Yohai wrote under the inspiration of the holy spirit,
they are paying a high price for it as you know." Isaac of Acre,
who did not himself speak to Moses de Leon's widow but relates
all this as second, or rather third hand information, also speaks
of further researches, but unfortunately his account, as quoted
by a later chronicler of the fifteenth century, breaks off at the
very point where he proposes to disclose what he was told under
solemn oath by a pupil of Moses de Leon about "the book Zohar
which was written by Rabbi Simeon ben Yohai."[11]

Not so surprisingly, this anecdotal evidence has been taken by every
rationalist philosopher, critic, or historian of Judaism, from Leon of Modena
(1571–1648)[12] to Heinrich Graetz (1817–1891), as definitive confirmation
that the Zohar is but a medieval forgery. As Yeshayahu Leibowitz ironized,
"It is clear that the Zohar was written by de Leon as it is clear that Theodor
Herzl wrote Medinat ha-Yehudim ('The Jewish State')."[13] The relevance of
Isaac of Acre's report was questioned, however, by one of the greatest specialists of Jewish mysticism, Gershom Scholem, who concluded the fifth
lecture of his epochal Major Trends in Jewish Mysticism, originally delivered
at the Jewish Institute of Religion in New York in 1938, with the evocation

---

11. This is Scholem's summary (Major Trends, 190–91) of Abraham Zacuto's Sefer
Yuḥasin, "Book of the Genealogies," quoting Isaac of Acre's key passages published by
Neubauer, "Bahir and the Zohar," 361–65.

12. See Dweck, Scandal of Kabbalah, 95–100.

13. This statement is attributed to Leibowitz in Wikipedia's entry on the Zohar.
However, I was not able to locate it in any of his writings—e.g., Judaism, Human Values,
and the Jewish State—available to me.

of an eloquent passage from the *Sefer Mishkan ha-ʿEduth*, one of Moses de
León's works written under his own name.

> I looked at the ways of the children of the world and saw how in
> all that concerns these [theological] matters, they are enmeshed
> in foreign ideas and false, extraneous [or heretical] notions. One
> generation passes away and another generation comes, but the
> errors and falsehoods abide forever. And no one sees and no one
> hears and no one awakens, for they are all asleep, for a deep sleep
> from God has fallen upon them, so that they do not question
> and do not read and do not search out. *And when I saw all this
> I found myself constrained to write and to conceal and to ponder,
> in order to reveal it to all thinking men,* and to make known all
> these things with which the holy sages of old concerned them-
> selves all their lives. For they are scattered in the Talmud and
> in their [other] words and secret sayings, precious and hidden
> better even than pearls. And they [the sages] have closed and
> locked the door behind their words and hidden all their mysti-
> cal books, because they saw that the time had not come to reveal
> and publish them. Even as the wise king has said to us: "Speak
> not in the ears of a fool." Yet I have come to recognize that it
> would be a meritorious deed to bring out to light what was in
> the dark and to make known the secret matters which they have
> hidden. (trans. Scholem, emphasis added)[14]

These days, it has become customary to qualify Scholem's approach to the
study of Jewish mysticism as "aggressively advanced" or as "scholarship . . .
not meant to nurture people's religious lives."[15] However, when I read what
Scholem has to say on Moses de León's decision to place his cabbalistic masterpiece under the authority of Rabbi Shimon bar Yohai, I must confess that
I still find it, at the same time, extremely sensitive and enlightening.

> Pseudepigraphy is far removed from forgery. The mark of im-
> morality, which is inseparable from falsehood, does not stain it,
> and for this reason it has always been admitted as a legitimate
> category of religious literature of the highest moral order. The
> historian of religion in particular has no cause to express moral
> condemnation of the pseudepigraphist. The Quest for Truth
> knows of adventures that are all its own, and in a vast number
> of cases has arrayed itself in pseudepigraphic garb. The further a
> man progresses along his own road in this Quest for Truth, the

14. This text has just been published for the first time: Moses de Leon, *Sefer Mishkan ha-Edut* (ed. Bar Asher).

15. Thus Myers, "Kabbalah," 178–79.

more he might become convinced that his own road must have already been trodden by others, ages before him. To the streak of adventurousness which was in Moses de Leon, no less than to his genius, we owe one of the most remarkable works of Jewish literature and of the literature of mysticism in general.[16]

"The Quest for Truth knows of adventures that are all its own, and in a vast number of cases has arrayed itself in pseudepigraphic garb"—yes, indeed, in an impressive number of cases, if we take into account the many Jewish pseudepigrapha discovered among the Dead Sea Scrolls or those subsequently rewritten by Christian authors,[17] not to mention the countless texts attributed to Pythagoras, Orpheus, Hermes Trismegistus, and other illustrious founders of religious or philosophical movements. Were the "real" authors of these writings moved exclusively by trivial purposes or were they sincerely convinced that they were inspired by, and speaking on behalf of, Enoch, Moses, Jesus, Paul, Shimon bar Yohai, and various other heroes of their memorial traditions? Paraphrasing Scholem, I would say that *religious* pseudepigraphy is *more often than not* far removed from forgery. Perhaps the time has come to put into critical perspective the testimonies of the church fathers and to reconsider the phenomenon of early Christian pseudepigraphy with the eyes not of a theologian but of a historian, yes, of religion.

16. Scholem, *Major Trends*, 204. For the ongoing debate on the *Zohar's* origins, see Green, "Introduction," in Matt, *Zohar*, 1:liv–lviii.

17. On the long-term aspects of the phenomenon of apocryphicity, see now Jenkins, *Many Faces of Christ*.

— 4 —

Lessons from the Papyri

What Apocryphal Gospel Fragments Reveal about the Textual Development of Early Christianity

— Stanley E. Porter —

THE FIRST GREEK APOCRYPHAL gospel (=GAG) fragment discovered and published was the so-called Fayyum fragment (P. Vindob. G 2325), part of the collection bought by Archduke Rainer and donated to the Austrian Emperor Frans Joseph. It was published in 1885, with an official edition appearing in 1887, followed by a number of editions up to the early years of the twentieth century.[1] This discovery came at the advent of the discovery and subsequent publication of thousands of papyri—both documentary and literary (including semi-literary)—from the sands of Egypt and nearby, including Palestine. It was quickly followed by the publication of P. Cair. 10759 (the Akhmim Fragment of the *Gospel of Peter*) in 1892,[2] and then the "Logia of Jesus" from Oxyrhynchus in 1897 (official publication in 1898 as P. Oxy. I 1).[3] Since then, a number of other Greek papyri with supposed gospel-like texts have been published, although the exact number is hard to

1. See Bickell, "Papyrusfragment," 498–504; Bickell, "Nichtkanonische Evangelien-Fragment."
2. Bouriant, *Fragments du texte grec*.
3. Grenfell and Hunt, *Logia Iesou*; Grenfell and Hunt, *Oxyrhynchus Papyri I*, 1–3.

quantify. Some that were originally nameless were subsequently identified, such as P. Oxy. I 1, along with P. Oxy. IV 654 and 655,[4] which are early Greek versions of the *Gospel of Thomas*, while others were identified only recently as apocryphal gospels, such as P. Oxy. II 210. The publication of such GAG fragments continues, most recently with P. Oxy. LXXVI 5072, which contains an episode of Jesus exorcizing and another of Jesus in dialogue. Altogether, there are probably roughly around fifteen such fragments that are usually discussed, constituting perhaps ten different gospel-like texts. Building upon previous work that I have done on these documents, in this paper I wish to explore what these apocryphal gospel-like texts reveal about the textual development of early Christianity. After 150 years of such discovery and publication, it is appropriate that we ask ourselves what we have learned from these documents and what we still do not know, especially as they (among the other Christian apocrypha) have not been given their rightful place in tracing the origins and developments of early Christianity. In this paper, I explore what we can learn from the GAG fragments within the literary and textual development of the early Christian movement. Hence, I divide my paper into two parts, the first concerned with what we have learned and the second with what we still do not know.

WHAT WE HAVE LEARNED

Over the course of 150 years of discussion there are a number of important things that we have learned regarding these apocryphal gospel fragments, and what they have to offer our knowledge of the textual development of early Christianity. Here are a few that I would note. I would not pretend that this list is inclusive.

1. We Need Critical Editions of the Apocryphal Gospel Fragments

In 1997, I published an article in the conference papers from the 1995 Berlin papyrological congress entitled "The Greek Apocryphal Gospels Papyri: The Need for a Critical Edition." In that paper I argue that there were three major reasons that justify a critical edition of these fragmentary apocryphal gospels. The first is that there were problems in the standard critical editions and that these problems have consequences. I note the varying standards for their editing and how the standards have changed over the years—especially

---

4. Grenfell and Hunt, *Oxyrhynchus Papyri IV*, 1–28; see also Grenfell and Hunt, *New Sayings of Jesus*.

as the history of knowledge of the GAG fragments spans the entire field of papyrological studies, from its advent to the present. The first edition of P. Vindob. G 2325 actually preceded publication of the first series of papyrological texts, which originated in Vienna. Since then we know much more about the field of papyrology, if for no other reason than having the experience of discovering and publishing additional documents, including other gospel fragments. The second reason I offered was that, at the time, there was no complete edition of all the identified texts, each with a full critical apparatus. In 1997 there had been a number of compilations, but they were not full critical editions. To find critical editions one had to gather together a variety of disparate publications, with editions constructed to varying levels in varied ways. As an example, one can compare the relatively sparse editorial practice of the original publication of P. Vindob. G 2325 and the rather fulsome annotations of the recently published (2011) P. Oxy. LXXVI 5072. The third reason I gave was that the GAG fragments are important for study of the New Testament and of early Christianity, and need to be made much more widely known. I will discuss this importance further below.

I am pleased to see that since the publication of my article, there have been a number of publications that attempt to extend the scope of accessible editions of these texts, although none of them is the kind of critical text that one might desire, and we still do not have the kind of critical text that I envisioned. To be a true critical edition, I believe that the edition must be based upon actual examination of the document. Few can make this claim, even partially. In 2000, Dieter Lührmann and Egbert Schlarb published an edition of apocryphal gospel fragments in Greek and Latin, as a first effort in this regard.[5] However, I believe that their edition was made not on the basis of first-hand examination of the fragments, but by utilizing previous editions. Better in this regard is Andrew Bernhard's edition from 2007, for which he personally examined about half of the documents that he includes in his collection.[6] The collection by Bart Ehrman and Zlatko Pleše at least does not pretend to provide critical editions, as they admit that they have used the editions of others, and simply provide facing-page translations.[7] Thomas Wayment has fairly recently published a collection of the Christian apocrypha found in Greek manuscripts up to the fifth century, but his editions are not based on examination of the actual manuscripts (he apparently relies exclusively upon photographs) and does not include evidence for all

5. Lührmann and Schlarb, *Fragmente Apokryph.*
6. Bernhard, *Other Early Christian Gospels.*
7. Ehrman and Pleše, *Apocryphal Gospels.*

of the apocryphal gospels (e.g., P. Cair. 10759, because of its date).[8] There have been better efforts made with individual documents, including new editions of P. Vindob. G 2325 by Stanley Porter and Wendy Porter[9] and another by Thomas Kraus,[10] P. Oxy. II 210 by Stanley Porter,[11] P. Oxy. V 840 (called by its most recent major editor the "Gospel of the Savior") by Michael Kruger (twice),[12] and P. Oxy I 1, IV 654 and 655 by Simon Gathercole as part of a commentary on the *Gospel of Thomas*;[13] to be fair, neither Thomas Kraus and Tobias Nicklas nor Paul Foster could make such an examination for the *Gospel of Peter*, as the main manuscript, P. Cair. 10759, appears to have disappeared, leaving us only with photographs.[14] Unfortunately, it is difficult to know how many of the originals were examined for a number of other editions including some of those in *Gospel Fragments* by Thomas J. Kraus and Tobias Nicklas.

For a number of years, we have had collections of Christian apocrypha in translation, including German, Spanish, Dutch, Italian, and French, besides of course English. The best known in English are by M. R. James and J. K. Elliott, along with the translation of the Hennecke-Schneemelcher volumes.[15] It is hard to know how many of the sections devoted to the GAG fragments are based upon first-hand examination, but the number does not appear to be high, if any. I know that reliance upon previously published editions does cause problems. In his translation of P. Vindob. G 2325 for the recent standard English edition, Elliott translates a text that relies upon several previously-published editions, none of them apart from Bickell's apparently based on direct examination of the manuscript, and he ends up producing a translation of a conglomerate text that has never existed in any of the previous editions, and does not match the original text.[16] The situa-

8. Wayment, *Text of the New Testament Apocrypha*.

9. Porter and Porter, *New Testament Greek Papyri*, no. 62, 1:291–94.

10. Kraus, "*P.Vindob.G* 2325," 69–94; see also Kraus, "Other Gospel Fragments," 219–27; and discussions in Kraus, "Fayum Gospel," 150–56; and Kraus, "Das sogenannte Faijumfragment."

11. Porter, "POxy II 210," 1095–1108; see also Landau and Porter, "Papyrus Oxyrhynchus 210."

12. Kruger, *Gospel of the Savior*; Kruger, "Papyrus Oxyrhynchus 840" (from Foster, ed., *Non-Canonical Gospels*) and discussion in Kruger, "*Papyrus Oxyrhynchus 840*" (from Kraus et al., *Gospel Fragments*).

13. Gathercole, *Gospel of Thomas*.

14. Kraus and Nicklas, eds., *Petrusevangelium und die Petrusapokalypse*; Foster, *Gospel of Peter*.

15. James, *Apocryphal New Testament*; Elliott, *Apocryphal New Testament*; Schneemelcher, ed., *New Testament Apocrypha*.

16. See Porter, "Greek Apocryphal Gospels Papyri," 796–97.

tion is better for the recent translations provided in the revised Hennecke-Schneemelcher collection of Christoph Markschies and Jens Schröter.[17] In at least seven of eleven instances these translations had access to first-hand examination or transcriptions of the manuscripts; one document, however, is no longer available for examination so far as I know.

Thus, regarding this first point, we do indeed know that we need a complete critical edition of these GAG fragments—but we have not yet achieved that goal. We are still relying upon either previous editions or photographs. This current situation is of course much easier than taking the trouble to go see the originals, especially if they are located in difficult or distant places, but I can attest from first-hand experience that there is no substitute for actually seeing the original manuscript before creating an edition. I must confess that with access and transportation what they are today, I find it astounding that so many purported editions—which by definition cannot be critical editions—continue to be produced, when opportunity to examine the manuscripts themselves is greater than ever before.

2. The Apocryphal Gospel Fragments are Worth Studying in Their Own Right

From what we do know about these apocryphal gospel fragments, we know that they are worth studying in their own right, first for their own intrinsic value as simply more examples of non-documentary texts from the ancient world. They are not literary texts as usually defined, because they do not appear to be texts of established ancient literary authors. They are often called semi-literary—which is probably a misnomer—simply because they represent forms of early Christian texts rather than texts by classical and similar authors. If we discover more of them and find more interconnections among them, perhaps we will be able to say more about the literary nature of these texts. In the meantime, we can study them as examples of a type of literary text that does not fit within the established canons of ancient literary authors. As such, they can give insight into this kind of popular literature of the ancient world, especially popular religious literature. These manuscripts show that there was a variety of types of Christian documents produced in the ancient world, besides those documents that were accepted as canonical (I will return to this point below). These manuscripts offer examples of some of the writing conventions used in the ancient world, such as the development of handwriting types and the use of *nomina sacra* or "sacred names"—the shortened and highlighted forms used with a relatively

17. See Markschies and Schröter, eds., *Antike christliche Apokryphen*, 357–89.

small number of names in Christian texts—and related phenomena sometimes cited as parallels. There is divided scholarly opinion on the origins of the *nomina sacra*—whether they derive from Jewish practice or secular practice, whether they constitute simply a convention for abbreviation, or whether they indicate some kind of textual highlighting. Nevertheless, the GAG fragments are worth studying to see how the use of *nomina sacra* developed in noncanonical documents and how their use spread to other types of texts, as well as how the convention itself expanded over time.[18]

Several examples will help to illustrate the value of the GAG fragments. P. Egerton 2 (by which I also include P. Köln VI 255) is probably the most well-known of the GAG documents, not least because it is one of the largest and has a relatively clear narrative.[19] However, of the four episodes that it conveys, there is one that stands out as it is not paralleled in the canonical Gospels. This episode depicts Jesus as standing on the edge of the Jordan River and stretching out his right hand and sprinkling something on the water, which brings forth fruit. We do not have this episode in the canonical Gospels, even though it still seems to reflect the kind of language of the Gospels. I do note that the reference to producing fruit seems to be a common idea in the GAG fragments; it is also found in P. Oxy. II 210 and in P. Merton II 51.[20] In all of these texts there is some apparent reference to fruit, such as in the parable of producing good or bad fruit (Matt 7:15–20// Luke 6:43–45). We again see that this is reflective of language within the canonical Gospels, but it seems like it is disproportionately represented in the GAG fragments.

P. Egerton 2 has a large number of *nomina sacra*, so far as we can tell from reconstructing the manuscript. These include Jesus (used five times), Moses (four times), God (twice), Lord (twice), father (once), prophets (once), kings (once), and Isaiah (once).[21] This distribution of *nomina sacra* provokes some interesting ideas, even if we must recognize that our knowledge is constrained by the limited extent of the manuscript. Nevertheless, we can certainly understand why P. Egerton 2 is called an apocryphal gospel fragment, when we see that "Jesus" is its most frequent *nomen sacrum*. We might also be surprised that Moses is the next most frequent *nomen sacrum*. Is this because of the subject matter of the particular episode in which it appears?—Jesus tells lawyers to search the Scriptures, in which not Jesus but

---

18. See Porter, "What Do We Know," 41–70, esp. 64–66. See also Hurtado, *Earliest Christian Artifacts*, 95–134.

19. For an introduction, see Nicklas, "Papyrus Egerton 2," 139–49.

20. See Porter, *How We Got the New Testament*, 104–105.

21. I use the edition by Nicklas, "'Unknown Gospel.'"

Moses accuses them—or is it because this text reflects a Christian group that found its identity in some way in relationship to Moses, and hence probably Judaism? If Moses is the one who condemns, then there is the possibility that the Christians responsible for this text were opposing a type of Judaism that emphasized the Mosaic law. This might constitute another form of Judaizing (although Abraham does not appear in P. Egerton 2, as one might expect in a document fashioned in relation to Judaism).

The GAG fragments, though they are fragmentary, have both literary integrity and historical significance that makes their further study important. There have been a number of efforts in this respect, although there is much more that can be done.

3. The Apocryphal Gospel Fragments Give Insights into Early Christianity and Its Creative Processes

The discussion of the possible relationship of the Christians associated with P. Egerton 2 and Judaism leads to the third consideration regarding what we have already learned as a result of the apocryphal gospel fragments: they tell us about the creative processes of early Christianity.

The history of discussion of the GAG fragments, often in conjunction with other apocryphal documents, is an intriguing one. When these fragmentary gospel documents were first discovered, they were welcomed with some fanfare. For example, P. Vindob. G 2325 was published in the first volume (the combined issue of fascicles 3 and 4) of the *Mitteilungen* series, which continues to today. Similarly, P. Oxy. I 1, with the "Logia of Jesus," was the first text published in the newly-inaugurated Oxyrhynchus Papyri series in 1898, fifty years before it was identified as the *Gospel of Thomas*. However, these discoveries were examined within the context of their being derivative of the New Testament documents. It was clear to those who discovered them, for example, that P. Vindob. G 2325 was an edited conflation of Mark 14:26–30 and Matt 26:30–34, not an earlier tradition from which Mark and Matthew derived their accounts of Peter and the cock crowing. In 1935, when P. Egerton 2 was published,[22] it was seen as an intriguing text that probably drew heavily upon John's Gospel (as well as upon the Synoptic Gospels), rather than as the tradition from which John's Gospel got its material, although the original editors recognized the possibility. Only within more recent times did the climate shift so that some began to emphasize that earlier traditions could be found within apocryphal texts, such as P. Egerton 2.

22. Bell and Skeat, eds., *Fragments of an Unknown Gospel*, 1–41.

I believe that examination of the GAG fragments within the wider scope of the history and transmission of early Christian texts indicates that these fragments played a part in the development of early Christianity. First of all, they are indicators that early Christianity was a culturally literate movement. I distinguish between being formally illiterate and being culturally literate. What I mean is that even though many, probably the vast majority, of those in the ancient Greco-Roman world were formally illiterate, they were part of a larger culturally-literate society that depended upon written documents. There was a literate culture of the ancient world that demanded that a person, whether formally illiterate or not, had access to writing, whether first or second hand. The result was that even those who could not read or write were participants in literate culture. Christian documents are part of that literate culture. Early on, Christianity recorded its traditions in written form and then transmitted them from generation to generation. These documents included both those texts that took on recognizable canonical status and those that did not. Nevertheless, all of these documents are part of the literate culture. This includes the GAG fragments, all of which have been found in Egypt, so far as I know. We know that Egypt was a complex multilingual literate culture, in which written documents played a crucial role in socio-religious construction, including the early church. Apocryphal gospels were part of that construction. As indicated in some of the features that we have learned from studying the documents, the apocryphal gospel fragments give us an idea of the development of early Christianity around its written documents. The canonical documents seem to have provided the core traditional material, and the noncanonical documents provided literate expansion and commentary upon that core.[23]

The second and related insight for early Christianity is that it was a creative and literarily generative community that produced a surprisingly wide range of important early documents. These include many letters, histories, and biographies, among others. I believe that the early Christian canonical books, in this case the Gospels, were possibly all written before 70 CE, and so provided the core material that was developed further by later Christian writers.[24] These writers, as the GAG fragments indicate, primarily drew upon the Gospel texts and traditions, as well as other material. I have already mentioned the apparent literary creativity of P. Egerton 2. A further example is P. Oxy. V 840. This small parchment codex does not explicitly cite any biblical text, but it contains allusions to Gospel traditions. The fragment begins with a statement about punishing evildoers and then turns to a

23. Porter, "What Do We Know," 45–50.
24. Ibid., 50–60.

scene where the "Savior" speaks of purification, holy vessels, and the temple. The other side continues the dialogue with the Savior questioning the purity of his dialogue partners. This text appears to draw upon Luke 11:37–52; Matt 23:13–22; John 7:1–52; John 13:10; and Mark 7:1–23.[25]

The third insight is not just that the early Christians were literarily creative but that they were a reflective and interpretive theological community. P. Oxy. II 210 provides an interesting example of an apocryphal gospel that combines material from the Gospels and the Pauline letters. The recto of this document contains material regarding something that is good, something about angels, and something being spoken or given as a sign (all of this is fairly hypothetical based on the fragmentary nature of the document). This reflects material in Matthew 1:24 and Luke 2:10, 12. The verso again seems to mention several times things that are good, plants, the father (*nomen sacrum*), and God (*nomen sacrum*); it uses "I am" language, and discusses the image and form of God. This language reflects wording similar to Mark 10:17–22 par., as well as Matthew 7:17–19//Luke 6:43–44, and Johannine expressions. It is also worth observing that the recto seems to reflect 1 Corinthians 1:26–27 on wisdom and the flesh, and the verso 2 Corinthians 4:4 and Colossians 1:15, as well as Philippians 2:6, and possibly some other biblical texts.[26] P. Oxy. II 210 brings together Gospel language and then explicates it christologically by drawing upon the Pauline epistles. More could be said in this regard about each one of the apocryphal gospel fragments.

WHAT WE STILL DO NOT KNOW

We have learned much from the GAG fragments, and I expect that we will learn more in the years to come, whether we discover any more of them or not (I think that we will discover more, as we find and publish more papyri). However, there are also a number of areas where there are still lessons to be learned from the apocryphal gospel fragments. I identify three of these areas.

25. See Kruger, *Gospel of the Savior*, 161–88.
26. See Porter, "POxy II 210."

1. We Do not Know What Constitutes
a Fragmentary Greek Gospel

The major question that still haunts study of the GAG fragments is that we do not have firm criteria for defining them. Andrew Bernhard defines a gospel for his collection as follows: "a label for any written text that is primarily focused on recounting the teachings and/or activities of Jesus during his adult life."[27] As a result of this definition, he does not include P. Cair. 10735, P. Oxy. L 3525, P. Ryl. III 463, and P. Oxy. VIII 1081 (he did not know P. Oxy. LXXVI 5072, which probably would have been included). P. Ryl. III 463 and P. Oxy. L 3525 are portions of the *Gospel of Mary* and so are no longer to be considered among the unidentified fragmentary gospels (and it is not a gospel of Jesus in any event), and P. Oxy. VIII 1081 is part of the *Sophia Jesus Christ*, not an apocryphal gospel.[28] Kraus, however, includes P. Cair. 10735. Bernhard disqualifies the text because it does not speak of the adult Jesus, but it does speak of the annunciation of Mary and the angel commanding Joseph to take Mary to Egypt, reflecting episodes in Luke 1:36 and Matt 2:13. It would appear that Bernhard's definition is too narrow. Andrew Gregory and Christopher Tuckett differentiate three means of identifying a gospel: essentialist, nominalist, and pragmatic. The essentialist method looks for what constitutes the essence of a genuine gospel. This definition is clearly unworkable, as scholars have not been able to decide on an essential definition of what constitutes a GAG (or many other similar categories) and it would probably be too restrictive, especially if some kind of essential Christian doctrine being discussed or depicted was also required. The nominalist method requires use of the word "gospel" in its title or reference to the text as a gospel by others. None of the apocryphal documents being considered uses the word "gospel," so far as I can tell; but this may be asking too much of these fragmentary documents, as Gregory and Tuckett recognize. The pragmatic method, which they utilize, is that the text is not one of the other kinds of texts in the New Testament (such as an epistle), and that a gospel makes "at least some claim to give direct reports of the life and/or teachings of Jesus, but taking 'life and teaching' broadly enough to include accounts purporting to give teaching given by Jesus after his resurrection."[29] Even this definition may be problematic, as it encounters some of the same definitional problems as attend the canonical Gospels (Matthew and Luke), which include teaching by Jesus after his

---

27. Bernhard, *Other Early Christian Gospels*, 2.

28. Kraus, "Introduction," 5–6.

29. Gregory and Tuckett, "Series Preface," vii.

resurrection. Even if we agree that the pragmatic definition is most useful, there are still problems. When Kraus handles the fragmentary Gospels, he includes P. Oxy. X 1224, P. Vindob. G 2325, P. Cair. 10735, P. Berol. 11710, and P. Merton II 51 (P. Egerton 2 and P. Oxy. V 840 are included but handled elsewhere in the volume), as well as now presumably P. Oxy. LXXVI 5072 if he had known it. He excludes P. Aberd. 3, which is an ostracon, prob-ably because it is a fragmentary narrative of John's baptism of Jesus; P. Oxy. XI 1384, which is not a narrative but at best a quotation; and P. Gen. 125, which is also a citation.[30] He should also probably exclude P. Berol. 11710, which is an amulet, not a narrative. P. Merton II 51 may also be a homily or commentary. However, Kraus does not include P. Ryl. III 464, which Wendy Porter and I introduced into the latest German collection of apocryphal gospels.[31] It is highly fragmentary, but it does appear to include a narrative that involves Jesus (there is a *nomen sacrum* for Jesus) and his teaching, with reference to God (probably another *nomen sacrum*). Nor does Kraus include P. Oxy. II 210, already described above, nor PSI XI 1200bis, which contains the *nomen sacrum* for God (twice), a reference to "first" and "last," and to "finding" and "doing."[32]

I have differentiated many of the gospels that are found elsewhere and possibly linked to other streams of early Christianity, such as gnostic docu-ments, and have eliminated those that are not narratives, but have included those that narrate any episode or teaching of Jesus that is paralleled in the canonical Gospels. Nevertheless, we are assuming that these relatively short fragmentary gospels—the only two that are of any significance in length are P. Egerton 2 and P. Cair. 10759—are more than the brief fragments that they are, and that if we were to discover more of any given text that this would confirm its status. In the case of the *Gospel of Peter*, additional fragments have been found (P. Oxy. XLI 2949 and LX 4009), but there is debate over whether they should truly be assigned to this text.[33] There clearly is more work to be done on determining whether a GAG fragment is indeed a gospel.

2. We Do not Know What Specific Function These Fragmentary Greek Apocryphal Gospels Served

Even though we may know that the GAG fragments are worth studying and that they provide some insights into the origins of Christianity as a

30. Kraus, "Introduction," 5–6.

31. Porter and Porter, "Rylands Apokryphes Evangelium (?)," 377–78.

32. See Lührmann and Schlarb, *Fragmente Apokryph*, 178–79.

33. See Porter, "Early Apocryphal Gospels," esp. 353 n. 6.

literate, creative, and even theologically-aware religious movement, we still do not know the specific function that the apocryphal gospels—if in fact they were such a thing—really performed. Were they simply auxiliary documents designed to reflect the creativity of early Christianity? Were they the kind of natural creative response of early Christianity written simply for personal use or did they have a wider function? We know that early Christians did feel free to comment upon their early texts. This is indicated in the Johannine *hermeneia* manuscripts.[34] These manuscripts contain Johannine Gospel text with some type of interpretive comment or remarks underneath, probably Christian theological reflection upon the biblical text. The question is whether these apocryphal Gospel fragments were part of this interpretive tradition.[35] If they were, they commented in a different way, as they intermix similar accounts, paraphrases, and citations of New Testament texts—mostly the Gospels but probably other texts as well—into their short continuous narrative. If they had a wider function, what was that wider function? Were they used as part of early Christian worship or liturgy? We know that early Christians did use their manuscripts, especially biblical manuscripts, for worship. We have a variety of manuscripts that are marked with various types of developing ekphonetic notation. What begins with simple marks to indicate how the text is to be intoned becomes a full-blown system of intonation, with individual pericopes within the biblical text being marked for suitable liturgical use.[36] The GAG fragments, however, do not have any of these markings.

If these fragmentary gospels were used in a liturgical fashion, they do not appear to have been used in the same way as scriptural readings or texts. They were perhaps supplementary episodes, read for edification and further elaboration, but not as the scriptural text itself or as a substitute for it. We do have an account in Eusebius of the use of the *Gospel of Peter* in Antioch. This is the well-known Serapion episode. Eusebius says that it was being read in churches, apparently as a gospel text, although this is not entirely clear (Eusebius, *Hist. eccl.* 6.12.4). In any case, on the basis of the gospel not being by Peter, and the fact that it had heterodox teaching, its reading was immediately discontinued. The question of whether such a gospel could be used for other purposes is not addressed.

The fact that we have so few apocryphal gospel fragments so far discovered poses its own set of interesting questions. We might well wonder

34. See Porter, "What Do We Know," 60–63.

35. See Watson, *Gospel Writing*, who argues for a model of the textual development of early Christianity in which canonical formation included intertextual interpretation of what later came to be known as canonical and noncanonical texts.

36. Porter, "What Do We Know," 66–69.

why there are not more of them and more of the ones we have, if they were part of a literate, creative, and even theological development within early Christianity. Once the *Gospel of Peter* was condemned, did this have a stultifying effect on the use of others and account for their shortage? Were they mostly the product of an early period in Christian history, which came to an end in the fourth century with the institutionalization of Constantine, and the more absolute fixity of the biblical canon that not only firmly defined the borders of the canon but called into question the use of other texts even if not for scriptural purposes? We know that the vast majority of the GAG fragments date to pre-Constantinian times. This would apply to P. Egerton 2, P. Vindob. G 2325, P. Merton II 51, P. Oxy. II 210, P. Ryl. III 464, P. Oxy. LXXVI 5072, and PSI XI 1200bis, and possibly P. Oxy. V 840 and P. Oxy. X 1224. It would not apply, however, to the *Gospel of Peter* (P. Cair. 10759), P. Cair. 10735, or P. Berol. 11710, unless it can be shown that these reflect significantly earlier textual traditions.[37]

In other words, with all that we know about the GAG fragments, there is an awful lot that we do not know about their specific use within early Christianity.

3. We Do Not Know How to Use the Greek Apocryphal Gospel Fragments in New Testament Research

Because we do not know the function of the GAG fragments within early Christianity, it has been difficult to know how to use them in New Testament research. Besides the broad use as witnesses to the creative literary and theological development of early Christianity, there are several other uses to which they might be put.

One of these uses is as sources for the Synoptic Gospels or John's Gospel, as already mentioned above. I take P. Egerton 2 as an example, as it is the largest of the GAG fragments worth considering and one that has been dated to the second century (the turn of the second and third centuries at the latest). It was first proposed by Goro Mayeda in his dissertation published just after World War II that P. Egerton 2 was independent of the canonical Gospels.[38] This has been taken up by a few scholars since, including most notably Helmut Koester, but also Jon Daniels, most recently (and similarly) Francis Watson, and possibly others.[39] Koester's argument is that,

---

37. See Porter, "What Do We Know," 54–59; Lührmann and Schlarb, *Fragmente Apokryph*, 170–79.

38. Mayeda, *Das Leben-Jesu-Fragment Papyrus Egerton 2*.

39. Daniels, "Egerton Gospel"; Koester, *Ancient Christian Gospels*, 205–16; and

by examination of the four major pericopes of P. Egerton 2 in comparison to supposed canonical Gospel parallels, he can establish the presumption that P. Egerton 2 reflects pre-Johannine and pre-Synoptic tradition, as if these were separate traditions that P. Egerton 2 had access to before they were taken up by their respective Gospel authors. If this is the case, then this certainly would provide a means for using P. Egerton 2 in New Testament studies. Close examination of P. Egerton 2, and perhaps other GAG fragments, would give us access to the earliest traditions upon which our canonical Gospels are based, and perhaps even earlier forms of other writings that are used within some of them. This would provide a tremendous insight into the origins of Christianity, its traditions regarding Jesus, and the traditions that were used by the Gospel writers. This would indeed be a major use within New Testament Studies.

The problem with such a solution is that Koester's and others' arguments are generally unconvincing. Koester hedges his statements at a number of places, only to draw the conclusion that P. Egerton 2, if independent (I note that he does at least use the conditional structure), "is an important witness to an earlier stage of the development of the dialogues of the Fourth Gospel."[40] I find it interesting that he does not draw the same explicit conclusion regarding the Synoptic Gospels. However, he does hedge his statements all along the way leading up to this point. A closer examination of the arguments that he makes offers little to support such a conclusion. He claims, for example, that the episode of the lawyer and Jesus regarding Moses reflects language that is not as "Johannine" as the Gospel itself.[41] The only substantive example he cites is P. Egerton 2's use of "life" rather than John's "eternal life," claiming that "eternal life" is more typically Johannine. In fact, John's Gospel uses the word "life" 36 times, with 17 of these coupled with "eternal"—so, "eternal life" is hardly more Johannine than "life" alone. Watson also appears to base his initial argument on a questionable interpretation. He argues that at one point P. Egerton 2 should read "our fathers," rather than "your fathers," thus, in Watson's view, not indicating separation between early Jewish and Christian communities. He says that this is "a

---

Watson, *Gospel Writing*, 286–340. Watson is no more convincing than is Koester (see below). He questionably argues on the basis of six passages that priority of P. Egerton 2 is more plausible than that of John. He uses this to reconstruct a Johannine Christianity separate from Judaism and asserting a high Johannine Christology. Watson also relies upon a number of questionable arguments, including a textual reconstruction of P. Egerton 2 on the basis of a photograph.

40. Koester, *Ancient Christian Gospels*, 215.

41. Cf. Watson, *Gospel Writing*, 304–309.

totally un-Johannine usage on the lips of Jesus."[42] He fails to note that in fact Jesus uses the wording "our fathers" in John 4:20 and 6:31. Another un-Johannine phrase, "answered and said," is pointed out by Koester. He first claims that "rulers of the people" is the only Synoptic feature of the passage, but then notes that "answered and said" "is frequent in the Synoptic Gospels"[43] and used in a place with no parallel in John; also, it uses "unbelief," another non-Johannine word. It appears that there are more Synoptic features than Koester has noticed or is willing to admit. Koester then reconstructs the original text that was taken up and distributed in various ways in John's Gospel. This text makes far less sense than if the author of P. Egerton 2 had taken John's Gospel and combined it with some Synoptic features. As for these Synoptic features, Koester strains to make the "hour had not yet come" phrasing in the episode on the attempt to arrest Jesus appear to be more Synoptic-like than it is (the parallel simply with "hour" in Mark 14:35 is not adequate).[44] And in the healing of the leper, Koester contends that "redactional additions" found in Mark 1:43 and 44a indicate that P. Egerton 2 is earlier.[45] However, he also admits that Matthew and Luke do not include these elements either, which argues against his conclusion and for Mark's account being earlier. The use in P. Egerton 2 of "Master Jesus" to address Jesus also indicates later usage, whereas Mark has no such address (even though Koester tries to wish it into existence). In the final episode concerning paying taxes, Koester admits that this is a difficult episode. It is indeed difficult for his hypothesis, as it appears to be a composite from both Mark 12:13–15 and Mark 7:6–7//Matt 15:7–9 as well as Luke 6:46 and John 3:2. Koester's defense is that there "are no analogies to this kind of gospel composition."[46] That may well be true in the canonical Gospels, but that is in fact what appears to have happened in P. Egerton 2, with the Markan source being drawn on in two instances, with some interspersion of Luke and John. The use of "teacher Jesus" in P. Egerton 2, when Mark has "teacher" and John "rabbi," look more like conflation and christological exaltation rather than the reverse.[47] The reference in P. Egerton 2 to "kings," where Mark has

---

42. Ibid., 295.

43. Koester, *Ancient Christian Gospels*, 209.

44. Ibid., 211. Cf. Watson, *Gospel Writing*, 315–20, but where he engages in the same kind of speculation regarding lines of dependence of which he accuses C. H. Dodd.

45. Cf. Watson, *Gospel Writing*, 321–25, but where he distances the Synoptics from the Johannine/P. Egerton 2 accounts.

46. Koester, *Ancient Christian Gospels*, 215.

47. Contra Watson, *Gospel Writing*, 330–40, who sees John as establishing the high Christology as part of its interpretation of its sources, including P. Egerton 2.

Caesar, seems to indicate a wider (and later) application of the teaching. Koester contends that this episode is both pre-Johannine and pre-Synoptic, when a better explanation is that it is dependent upon both.

If we cannot use the GAG fragments as indicators of sources for the New Testament writings (I am not categorically excluding this, but have not found suitable evidence), another proposal is to use them in textual criticism as indicators of developments within the textual tradition and, possibly in some instances, as indicating or pointing in the direction of the better reading. I have made such an attempt on two previous occasions.[48] I noted previously that the major issues in using the GAG fragments in textual criticism are several: establishing which fragments are to be used, a topic that I have been discussing throughout this essay; establishing their dates; establishing a critical text for each one so that it can prove to be a reliable textual witness in such discussion (hence the need for a critical edition); and, finally, developing an appropriate methodology for their use, as prima facie they do not, according to the canons of New Testament textual criticism, qualify for use as they are not canonical texts.

If we were to use such manuscripts in textual criticism, then we would need an apparatus for doing so. I have suggested elsewhere, and suggest again here, the creation of two levels of manuscript types for consideration.[49] The first level consists of those texts that are continuous texts of the New Testament. Within our currently existing body of designated New Testament manuscripts, there are a number that do not fit this criterion, as they are so fragmentary as to be indeterminate with regard to their being continuous text. Once the list is sifted down to its appropriate size, that body of manuscripts becomes the basis of textual criticism. The other manuscripts—those that are not continuous as well as those that we already have identified as lectionaries and liturgical texts, miniature codices and magical papyri or amulets, commentaries, excerpts, and unknown works—can be placed in a second category along with apocryphal texts such as the GAG fragments.[50] This second group of manuscripts is used in relation to the first list to determine the development of the New Testament text-critical tradition. This proposal allows for these non-continuous texts that have discernable features of the New Testament text to be used in textual criticism, even if they are not the primary texts relied upon in such a task.

48. Porter, "Apocryphal Gospels and the Text of the New Testament," esp. 237–41; and "Early Apocryphal Gospels."

49. For the latest statement, see Porter, How We Got the New Testament, 141–46. For the most recent reaction to my proposal, which arrived too late for my response, see Jones, New Testament Texts, 15–18.

50. Porter, How We Got the New Testament, 142–46.

Even without development of a second list, I have examined those texts that appear to be most suitable for textual criticism of the New Testament— P. Egerton 2, P. Cair. 10759, P. Vindob. G 2325, P. Merton II 51, P. Oxy. X 1224, and the Greek *Gospel of Thomas* fragments (P. Oxy. I 1, IV 654 and 655), and reached the following three conclusions.[51] The first conclusion is that the direct textual evidence in the GAG fragments for the canonical Gospels (and occasionally other books found in the New Testament) is not as great as one might think. Most of these works contain relatively few close parallels to the Gospels, and some none at all. The only two texts that do appear to cite the New Testament with any frequency are P. Egerton 2 and the P. Cair. 10759. The second conclusion is that there are a number of competing factors that must be considered when comparing the apocryphal and canonical gospels. However, my research indicates that the general tendency—and I realize that this is a debatable point—is for the apocryphal gospel to modify and/or improve the canonical source, often conflating several Gospel accounts when not following just one account and then switching to another. In such instances, John's Gospel and the Synoptics seem to have been used side-by-side. Whatever one thinks of the relationship of John's Gospel and the Synoptics regarding their dates of composition, it appears that apocryphal authors used both alongside each other. The third conclusion is that the apocryphal gospel texts reinforce a relatively stable text of the canonical Gospels by the time of their composition.[52] I believe that P. Egerton 2 was probably created in the middle of the second century, perhaps reflecting a text originally written in the early to middle part of the century, with the other GAG fragments written later.[53] This indicates that the Greek text of the New Testament was relatively well-established and fixed by the time of the second and certainly the third centuries. Those places indicating transmissional change in the vast majority of instances indicate that the apocryphal gospels have drawn upon the canonical texts, not only in individual wordings but in the structuring and sequencing of events (as in P. Egerton 2).

There may well be other uses to which these texts can be put, but so far the return on knowledge of them has tended to confirm what we already knew. This leaves many areas of new exploration still unexamined.

---

51. See Porter, "Apocryphal Gospels and the Text of the New Testament," 242–58; and Porter, "Early Apocryphal Gospels," 352–66. I did not use P. Oxy. LXXVI 5072 in such studies, because it was published after I had written my articles.

52. Porter, "Early Apocryphal Gospels," 369.

53. Porter, "Recent Efforts," esp. 84. Cf. Porter, *How We Got the New Testament*, 86–87 n. 24.

CONCLUSION

We have learned many lessons from the GAG fragments. As a result we have gained a significant amount of knowledge from them that helps us to understand the textual development of early Christianity, but there is much more to be done in attempting to understand them. We must acknowledge their importance and that they merit further examination, and we have some knowledge that they indicate several features of the development of early Christianity. However, there also remain several tasks that have not yet been successfully undertaken but that are necessary if we are going to push our knowledge further. Whereas we have produced a number of various types of editions, we still lack the kind of critical, first-hand edition that reasonably encompasses all of the pertinent texts. This is greatly to be desired, so that we can perform the kinds of close textual examination that is needed. In the meantime, even though we have some rough idea of their usefulness for the area of textual criticism, we still have a relatively limited idea of how these texts were used in the early church and the role that they played within the developing Christian community. Even in the area of textual criticism, where they have played some role, their function has been limited because there is not currently a place for them within New Testament textual criticism. Even if such a role were developed, however, so far the results indicate that they will serve more to reinforce traditional understanding of the text of the New Testament rather than call for any radical rethinking of our knowledge of the Greek New Testament.

— 5 —

Under the Influence (of the Magi)

Did Hallucinogens Play a Role in the Inspired Composition of the Pseudepigraphic *Revelation of the Magi*?

— Brent Landau —

THE *REVELATION OF THE Magi* (*Rev. Magi*) presents itself as a first-person description of Christ's coming by the Magi of the Gospel of Matthew's infancy narrative. According to *Rev. Magi*, the star that guides the Magi to Bethlehem is none other than Christ himself, who alternates in this narrative between human and celestial form. As Christ guides the Magi in the form of a star, he causes their food supplies to multiply. When the Magi arrive back in their homeland at the end of the journey, they show the inhabitants of their country the abundance of food that the star has created. The Magi tell the people that they too can experience the amazing visions and revelations that they experienced under the guidance of the star—all the people need to do is eat of the food that the star has multiplied. As soon as the people eat the food, they immediately begin to see visions of the different stages of Jesus' life.

In seeking to understand the significance of this very strange episode in *Rev. Magi*, I propose the following. First, I argue that *Rev. Magi* contains references to visionary experiences that some group of early Christians underwent, experiences that then were attributed, pseudepigraphically, to the biblical figures of Matthew's Magi. In arguing this, I am following recent work by other specialists in ancient religion, particularly those specializing in the Jewish pseudepigrapha, who have suggested that some pseudepigraphical texts have preserved the religious experiences of the individuals who composed them. Second, I argue that the strange incident of the star-food that produces visions of Jesus is best explained by positing that the early Christians behind *Rev. Magi* had ingested, quite possibly in a ritual manner, a hallucinogenic substance of some sort, even if *Rev. Magi* is too vague in its description to offer any clear idea of precisely what substance this might have been. In making this argument, I am the most recent in a rather long line of authors and scholars to suggest that a hallucinogen lies behind some ancient religious practice or textual reference. However, most of these claims about the ancient use of hallucinogens have been advanced on the basis of evidence that is quite limited and highly ambiguous. To put the matter another way, such writers have sought to find hallucinogenic practices by "reading in-between the lines" to detect veiled references to such substances; in contrast, I suggest that *Rev. Magi* presents us with the description of a substance whose hallucinogenic effects could not possibly be stated more clearly—even if the exact substance remains unspecified.

The first section of this paper provides some orienting information about *Rev. Magi*, since it is still quite poorly known. Then I will discuss how an interpreter can be justified, methodologically, in using a pseudepigraphical Jewish or Christian text as evidence for a "real world" practice by a community or individual. In the third section, I will apply this methodology to those passages from *Rev. Magi* that refer to the miraculous food produced by the star. But prior to this, I will contextualize this star-food among other practices in *Rev. Magi* that seem also to have been part of the ritual system of a group of early Christians. I do this in order to demonstrate that *Rev. Magi* has embedded within it far more than just an isolated reference to some hallucinogenic substance, but potentially also other traces of rituals and experiences undertaken by these Christians. My logic is that if *Rev. Magi* presents us with a number of instances in which it is reasonable to conclude that a "real world" religious practice is being referenced, then it becomes more plausible that the hallucinogenic star-food also corresponds to an actual practice in the life of the early Christians that produced this text. These rituals include immersion, ascent of a sacred mountain, the communal reading of prophetic books, and silent prayer. Fourth and finally, I will situate my interpretation of *Rev. Magi* within the broader trend of seeking to uncover references to hallucinogens in ancient texts and rituals, with an eye to demonstrating that *Rev. Magi* offers far stronger evidence for the use of hallucinogens than those advanced for other texts.

THE *REVELATION OF THE MAGI* AS AN ANCIENT CHRISTIAN APOCRYPHON

Among ancient Christian writings, *Rev. Magi* is by far the longest and most complex apocryphal text devoted to the Magi.[1] Furthermore, almost the entire narrative is told from the perspective of the Magi themselves, so it is a pseudepigraphon. In *Rev. Magi*, the Magi are descendants of Seth living in the far-eastern land of Shir, a semi-mythical place that seems to have been roughly equivalent to China, based on comments about the land in other Greek, Latin, and Syriac authors (2:4–6).[2] The etymology of the name "Magi," the text informs us, is related to their distinctive practice of silent prayer (1:2; 2:1), about which more will be said later. The Magi have been entrusted with the guardianship of Seth's books of revelation, the first books ever written. These books contain a prophecy of a coming star that will herald the birth of God in human form (4:1–10). The Magi have waited for the fulfillment of this prophecy for thousands of years, passing down the prophecy from generation to generation. In anticipation of the star's appearance, every month the Magi gather at their country's most sacred mountain, the "Mountain of Victories." They immerse themselves in a spring at the mountain's foothills, and ascend to the summit of the mountain. They pray in silence, and then finally enter a cave atop the mountain's summit, called the "Cave of Treasures of Hidden Mysteries," in which Seth's books of revelation are housed. The Magi practice this ritual throughout the generations, with new Magi taking the place of the deceased (5:1–11).

Finally, the star appears in the sky, so bright that the sun seems as faint as the daytime moon (11:5–7), yet it can only be seen by the Magi themselves. It descends to the Magi, and transforms itself into "a small and humble human being" (13:1). This being, who is Christ despite never actually being named as such, tells the Magi to follow him to Bethlehem

---

1. For more information on *Rev. Magi* see my 2008 dissertation, "The Sages and the Star-Child," available also online at http://www.academia.edu/207910/The_Sages_and_the_Star-Child_An_Introduction_to_the_Revelation_of_the_Magi_An_Ancient_Christian_Apocryphon. The text can be read also in a translation and introduction aimed at a general audience (Landau, *Revelation of the Magi*) and a summary of the text, along with a more detailed introduction, is included in the *New Testament Apocrypha: More Noncanonical Scriptures* collection (Landau, "Revelation of the Magi").

2. See Reinink, "Das Land 'Seiris.'"

to witness his birth. This seemingly long and strenuous journey is accomplished in an impossibly short period of time, during which the star's light relieves the Magi of their fatigue and causes the food brought by the Magi to multiply (16:1–7). At Bethlehem, the Magi witness their star transform into a luminous, talking infant, who commissions them to return to the land of Shir to proclaim his gospel to their fellow countryfolk (18:1—21:12). When the Magi return to Shir with the star, the people of Shir gather together to hear about their journey. The Magi's provisions of food are now overflowing from the power of the star, and they invite the people to eat of them so that they can share in what the Magi have experienced. As soon as they do, the people of Shir immediately start seeing visions of the heavenly and earthly Jesus, and convert gladly to the faith that the Magi proclaim (27:1—28:6). Finally, after many years have passed, the apostle Judas Thomas arrives in the Magi's homeland and after being told of the revelation of Christ that they experienced, he baptizes them and commissions them to preach throughout the entire world (29:1—32:4).

This rich and strange narrative is preserved only in Syriac, probably the language in which it was originally composed, and is extant in a single eighth-century manuscript, housed at the Vatican Library (*Vat. Syr. 162*). The manuscript in its entirety is a Syriac world-chronicle known either as the *Chronicle of Zuqnin*, or, less accurately, as the *Chronicle of Pseudo-Dionysius of Tell-Mahre*, into which a number of previously independent literary sources have been incorporated without changes, including *Rev. Magi*.[3] The same basic narrative of *Rev. Magi* is briefly summarized in the *Opus imperfectum in Matthaeum*, a fifth-century anonymous Latin commentary on Matthew's Gospel. Some Syriac version of the text, therefore, must have existed no later than the fifth century, and had probably been translated into Greek or Latin as well.[4] To further date *Rev. Magi* with any confidence, one must rely on the internal evidence of the text. As I argue in my 2008 dissertation, the ending featuring the apostle Judas Thomas is most likely a later addition.[5] Two of the strongest pieces of evidence for this theory are the sudden and inartful switch from the first-person narration of the Magi to third-person narration, and also the gratuitous use of the familiar name "our Lord Jesus Christ," which the first-person part of the narrative seems to have carefully avoided. An epiclesis spoken by Thomas at the baptism of the

3. See Witakowski, *Syriac Chronicle of Pseudo-Dionysius*, 124–36.

4. See van Banning, *Opus Imperfectum*, for an overview of this text and its manuscript situation. For English translations of the *Opus Imperfectum*'s summary of *Rev. Magi* see Landau, *Revelation of the Magi*, 97–98; Kellerman, *Incomplete Commentary*, 1:32; and Toepel, "Apocryphon of Seth."

5. Landau, "Sages and the Star-Child," 176–201.

Magi strongly resembles other such prayers found in the apocryphal *Acts of Thomas*, so it seems probable that this new ending for *Rev. Magi* originated in approximately the same time and place as the *Acts of Thomas*—namely, eastern Syria in the third century. How much earlier than this the original first-person portion of *Rev. Magi* was composed is difficult to determine, but it shows an intriguing number of parallels with the content of an archaic but little-known infancy gospel preserved in Latin and Irish witnesses.[6]

EXTRACTING RITUAL PRACTICES AND VISIONARY EXPERIENCES FROM THE REVELATION OF THE MAGI

It is my contention that in *Rev. Magi* some early Christian community or individual has used the personae of the Magi in order to communicate mystical practices and experiences that they themselves have undergone. But how do we know that everything described in the *Rev. Magi* is not simply "made up" or freely invented by a gifted and imaginative author? James Davila, in his article "Ritual in the Jewish Pseudepigrapha," articulates eight criteria that could be used for detecting "real world" practices embedded within a small group of pseudepigraphic texts that he considered to be incontrovertibly Jewish.[7] Although Davila crafted some of these criteria for the purpose of identifying specifically Jewish (as opposed to Christian) practices, three of them are sufficiently general that they could potentially work well for the examination of Christian pseudepigraphic texts.

As his first criterion, Davila states that "greatest weight will be given to descriptions of rituals that are actually prescribed for the reader or implicitly presented as normative. We can reasonably assume that these formed part of the writer's ritual repertoire."[8] His second criterion is also potentially quite relevant for *Rev. Magi*:

> I shall make special note of rituals carried out by actors in the narratives when those rituals do not correspond to events or acts described in a biblical story. This perhaps indicates indirectly that the author approved of at least some of them, although many amount to the filling out of obvious details or to the grafting of details from elsewhere in the Bible, and some are obviously made up. It is reasonable to keep the possibility open that some of these rituals were also realities in the ritual life of

6. For more on this infancy gospel see Kaestli, "Liber de Nativitate Salvatoris." On its connection to *Rev. Magi* see Landau, "Sages and the Star-Child," 202–14.

7. Davila, "Ritual in the Jewish Pseudepigrapha," 162–63.

8. Ibid., 162.

the author or the author's community, especially if a ritual appears repeatedly in one or more texts.[9]

In his fifth criterion, Davila points out that in order for something in a text to qualify as a ritual, it needs to include physical action in some way. This would mean that experiences are not to be counted as rituals unless "the experience is generated by deliberate actions: visions and dreams are not rituals unless explicitly preceded by vision quests or incubations."[10]

In what follows, I will attempt to apply Davila's criteria first to one ritual (or set of rituals, rather) and then to one experience from *Rev. Magi.* The ritual in question is, in fact, the Magi's elaborate ritual system as a whole. This quite complex set of practices, which takes place every month, involves purification in a spring, ascent of a sacred mountain, prayer in silence at the summit of the mountain, and the reading of Seth's books of revelation in a cave atop the mountain. The experience is the people of Shir's eating of the Magi's food that was multiplied by the star's light, an action that immediately produces visions of Jesus for the people of Shir.

Rev. Magi 5 describes a detailed monthly ritual that has been carried out by the Magi for thousands of years in expectation of the coming of the star. They travel from their respective dwelling-places and assemble at the foothills of the Mountain of Victories (5:2). On the twenty-fifth day of each month, the Magi bathe in a spring on the foothills of the mountain called the Spring of Purification (5:3). Around this spring stands a remarkable combination of seven trees: an olive, vine, myrtle, cypress, orange, cedar, and juniper (5:4). Moreover, we are told that the mountain itself smells of sweet spices (5:5). When it becomes the first of the month—we are not told how many days there were between the twenty-fifth and the first—the Magi ascend to the peak of the mountain (5:6). At the mouth of the Cave of Treasures of Hidden Mysteries atop the mountain's summit, they kneel, stretch forth their hands, and pray to God in silence (5:7). On the third day of the month, they enter the cave, view the gifts that are being kept for the star, and read from Seth's books of revelation (5:8). They then descend from the mountain and teach their mysteries to both their families and any other of their compatriots who wish to participate (5:9–11).

This ritual does seem to fit Davila's first and second criteria (the fifth criterion being more relevant for the experience discussed below). It is normatively presented as the Magi's ancestral custom, and the other inhabitants of Shir are enjoined to participate in the ritual as well (5:11). Moreover, there is no hint of such a ritual in Matthew's story of the Magi, although

9. Ibid.
10. Ibid.

Matthew 2:1–12 is notoriously brief and cryptic. But neither does a ritual comprised of all (or even most of) these actions appear anywhere else in the Hebrew Bible or New Testament, which seems to rule out the possibility that the author of *Rev. Magi* has based the Magi's ritual system on a precedent found in Scripture. Yet even if this ritual system coheres with Davila's first and second criteria, it is difficult to know how to evaluate ritual actions that are quite widespread in antiquity—rites of purification, adoration, and instruction, in this case—but occur in a fantastical setting. The Magi's monthly ritual takes place in an idealized sacred landscape, complete with a spring, a grove of trees whose co-existence within a single ecosystem is impossible, a mountain so holy that it smells of incense, and a cave. Are the Magi's ritual actions to be considered any more "real" than this landscape in which they take place? Based on the application of Davila's criteria, I believe that the answer is probably yes, though with some caveats. To be sure, it not terribly difficult to imagine an early Christian group that immersed itself once a month, ascended a mountain to pray in silence, and read from writings—quite possibly the products of inspired writing by members of the group—that they claimed were authored by Seth. The fantastical environmental features of the land of Shir could therefore perhaps be set aside as embellishments on the part of the author of *Rev. Magi*.

What proves much more difficult is finding any existing Christian group sharing all of these traits. It is, of course, entirely possible that the circle or community in which *Rev. Magi* was produced is simply not discussed in any other extant Christian literature. Nevertheless, if the ritual system described in *Rev. Magi* did indeed correspond to one that took place in the life of some early Christians, then it is striking how poorly attested most of the elements of this ritual system are elsewhere in early Christian literature. Whereas baptism is generally treated in early Christianity as a one-time event, in *Rev. Magi* ritual immersion takes place once a month in preparation for the ascent of their sacred mountain. Ritual immersions are certainly attested in ancient Jewish and Jewish-Christian communities, but in most cases they happen much more frequently than once a month, often every day.[11]

Although many religious traditions have mountains that are set aside as especially sacred, there is relatively little evidence for early Christians regarding one particular mountain or another as sacred and routinely ascending it. One could certainly mention Mount Sinai or Mount Tabor, traditionally identified as the mountain of the Transfiguration, as places for Christian ritual and pilgrimage, although there has been, to my knowledge,

---

11. See Rudolph, "Baptist Sects."

almost no work done on the place of mountains in early Christian religious practice.[12] There is also, however, the fact that many early Christians—in particular Syriac Christians—depicted Paradise as a mountain instead of a garden,[13] and it is possible that *Rev. Magi* has freely invented the "Mountain of Victories" as a sort of Paradise-like environment.

The silent prayer practiced by the Magi is a particularly interesting and challenging case in and of itself. *Rev. Magi* indeed regards silent prayer as an integral part of the Magi's identity, mentioning it again and again throughout the text. At its very beginning, we are told twice (1:2; 2:1) that the Magi were called by this name in the language of their country because they prayed in silence, thus seeming to posit an etymological relationship between the words "Magi," "silence," and/or "prayer." However, it is nearly impossible to make sense of this word derivation, since there is no linguistic similarity between these words in any of the obvious early Christian languages of transmission (Greek, Latin, Coptic, or Syriac). So this relationship between the name Magi and silent prayer may very well be completely imaginary, and is perhaps in part a strategy to distance these Magi from both the Zoroastrian religion and from magical practices. Even so, this in no way explains why *Rev. Magi* would choose to emphasize this particular religious practice in the construction of the Magi's identity. Indeed, as Pieter van der Horst has demonstrated, silent prayer was extremely unusual in the ancient Mediterranean,[14] even though today it is a very common practice in many Christian communities. Silent prayer until quite late in antiquity tended to be viewed with a fair amount of suspicion; since most prayers were spoken out loud, those who prayed silently were usually thought to be seeking some evil (or at least embarrassing) outcome. Van der Horst attributes the origins of silent prayer as a regular practice to Middle and Neoplatonist circles that regarded God as completely beyond the human capacities of expression. This Platonic concept was utilized by Philo and perhaps also by gnostic Christian forms of spirituality.[15] Nevertheless, silent prayer only became a truly influential practice in Christianity with the growth of monasticism in the fourth century and later. Yet even in this context, we often see it being prescribed not for theological reasons, but for practical ones—for example, so as to not disturb the prayers of one's fellow monks.[16]

12. One exception is Hilhorst, "Mountain of Transfiguration."

13. See Anderson, "Cosmic Mountain."

14. Van der Horst, "Silent Prayer."

15. Ibid., 10–12.

16. Ibid., 20.

Thus *Rev. Magi*, by repeatedly characterizing the Magi as practitioners of silent prayer, is very likely attempting to mark them out as an unusual group in terms of their religiosity. Of course, the perspective of the narrative is that their silent prayer is wholly positive, and is not meant to camouflage some sort of maleficent activity; nevertheless, there is still evidence in the text that the silent prayer of the Magi was controversial and/or objectionable to some potential adherents. In 5:11, which unfortunately is rather garbled and may be corrupt, it seems to be stated that some inhabitants of Shir rejected membership in the order of the Magi because of their practice of silent prayer. It is certainly tempting to suppose that this rejection experienced by the Magi corresponds to real-world rejection of the authors of *Rev. Magi* for their own practice of praying in silence, since 5:11 does nothing to move the narrative forward and the negative sentiments of some inhabitants of Shir are never mentioned again.

The question of why the community that produced *Rev. Magi* practiced silent prayer is difficult to answer, though some of van der Horst's observations are pertinent in this regard. Although there is some limited evidence for silent prayer in gnostic Christianity, there is very little in *Rev. Magi* to suggest any knowledge or acceptance of the full-blown gnostic mythology that appears, for example, in the *Apocryphon of John*. Yet given that *Rev. Magi* states on several occasions that God is completely beyond the human capacity to experience or describe (e.g., 1:3–4), this appears to be an obvious link to the justification for silent prayer proposed in Middle and Late Platonic texts. It must be cautioned that *Rev. Magi* never explicitly states that the reason the Magi practice silent prayer is because of the ineffability of God, but the combination of the practice of silent prayer with a belief in God's ineffability is certainly suggestive of Platonic influence. Though the evidence is sparse, it is tempting to speculate that the Christian group in which *Rev. Magi* was produced had silent prayer as one of their distinctive marks, and when *Rev. Magi* was composed, this distinctive practice was then transferred onto the Magi as one of the marks of their own religiosity. This would explain, for example, why there is no obvious etymological relationship between the words "Magi" and "silent" and/or "prayer": because there was no tradition of the biblical Magi practicing silent prayer until this practice was invented for them by the authors of *Rev. Magi*.

The components of the Magi's ritual just described are, either all or in part, quite plausible as the religious practices of some early Christian group. The second incident from *Rev. Magi*, however, is more challenging and more controversial for the interpretation of this text. According to *Rev. Magi*, the light of the star (which, it must be remembered, is Christ himself in nonhuman form) generates a kind of food that when ingested by the people of Shir near the end of the narrative, produces visions of Christ. The Magi pack this food, always described ambiguously as "provisions" (*zwd'*), in preparation for their presumably lengthy journey to Bethlehem (16:2). During the course of this miraculous journey, we learn that these provisions at no time decreased, but instead increased whenever the star's light came to rest over them (16:5). The provisions are next mentioned during the Magi's return trip to Shir, when they notice with great awe that their provisions are even more full than when they left their country (26:5)—something that should not be a surprise to them since it was already stated earlier that the star was multiplying their provisions. At any rate, they eat of the provisions and have marvelous visions throughout the night (26:6), though it is not explicitly said that the provisions are the cause of their visions, and the Magi have already experienced a number of visions through their interaction with the star in which the provisions have played no apparent role. The pivotal event regarding these provisions is when the Magi return to their homeland and tell their countryfolk of their experiences. The Magi show the people the bags of provisions, which now sit overflowing before them, and invite them to eat of them so that they may share in the Magi's experience (27:9–11). As soon as the people of Shir eat them, they immediately see visions of the heavenly and earthly Jesus at different times in his life (28:1–4). The fact that the provisions are the cause of these visions for the people of Shir is made abundantly clear: the first inhabitant of Shir to describe his vision states that it began "[a]t the moment I ate of these provisions" (28:1). It is again stated in 28:4 that only those people who partook of the provisions were describing their visions. Therefore, what *Rev. Magi* presents us with is one or more incidents in which the consumption of a certain food, miraculously altered by the star in both quantity and quality, directly leads to visions of Jesus. This direct causal connection will be very important when we consider below whether this is likely a reference to some sort of hallucinogenic substance.

If we consider Davila's criteria, this event fits two of the three we have singled out rather easily. First of all, taking into account his fifth point, it is legitimate to consider the visionary experience of the people of Shir as a sort of ritual because it is immediately preceded by the ingesting of a sort of sacred food. Concerning his first point, the activity is certainly regarded as normative by the author of the text, since *Rev. Magi*'s protagonists encourage the people to partake of the food and the food brings them to faith in Christ. The most complicated question is whether this event might be modeled upon a pre-existing biblical or even non-biblical incident. If it were, then this could potentially decrease the likelihood that it refers to something that happened in the life of an early Christian community. There are a number of stories in the Bible that share some similarities with this incident from *Rev. Magi*. The fact that Christ causes the Magi's food to increase certainly echoes Jesus' miracle of the feeding of the multitudes (Mark 6:30–44 par; Mark 8:1–10 par; John 6:1–15). It also evokes God's providing of the mysterious manna for the Israelites in the desert (Exod 16; Num 11). So *Rev. Magi* does share with these texts the belief in God's or Christ's ability to produce food miraculously in times of need, either creating it out of nothing or multiplying existing food. However, in these biblical texts visionary experiences do not appear to be linked with this miraculous food production. The scrolls that are eaten by the prophet Ezekiel (Ezek 3:1) and John of Patmos (Rev 10:8–10) are inextricably tied to the prophecies they are about to impart, though it should be noted that in both of these cases there is no suggestion that it is the eating of the scroll that facilitates the visionary experience. As for ancient Jewish extrabiblical texts, in *4 Ezra*, the prophet eats flowers prior to the transcribing of revelatory books that takes place (9:23–26; 12:51), though there is not an explicit causal connection wherein the flowers themselves somehow produce the revelations. Even more intriguing, in *Joseph and Aseneth* 16 an angel visits Aseneth prior to her marriage to Joseph and miraculously creates a honeycomb that continues to regenerate itself when eaten. Again, there is no explicit mention of visionary experience, even though Aseneth is subsequently surrounded by a great swarm of bees that do not harm her. Finally, in the *Martyrdom of Perpetua and Felicitas* 1.3, Perpetua receives cheese from a shepherd in the course of a vision, and immediately following this vision, she knows that she is going to be martyred. Thus in all three of these texts, there are hints that the consumption of certain substances may produce visionary experiences, but this connection is only hinted at in these works. Finally, we should not overlook the basic functional parallel between this incident in *Rev. Magi* and the early Christian celebration of the Eucharist, since in both cases we have to do with an event that brings its participants into some sort of relationship or union with Jesus himself.

None of these biblical or extrabiblical parallels demonstrate the close causal connection between the ingesting of a substance and visionary experience.[17] Therefore, it is entirely reasonable to consider the possibility that

17. It is important to mention here that another vision in *4 Ezra* may be a clearer case of what Meredith Warren terms a "hierophagy"—an eating of heavenly food that effects an immediate change in the eater. In *4 Ezra* 14:38–41, Ezra is given a "fiery cup" from which to drink, which allows him finally to understand the content of the divine revelations he has received. Warren, however, chooses not to speculate about whether this incident was based on the consumption of an actual hallucinogenic substance, and further research would be necessary to determine whether such an interpretation is warranted. See Warren, "'My Heart Poured Forth Understanding.'"

the "star food" of the Magi corresponds to a hallucinogen that was deployed by an early Christian group in a ritual of some kind to facilitate visionary experience. Indeed, I do not believe that it takes an overactive imagination to see the parallels between this event in *Rev. Magi* and other religious rituals using hallucinogens, and I would argue that no other case from early Jewish or Christian literature presents such an obvious causal link between consumption and vision. The visions happen immediately after the people eat from the Magi's provisions, and the first of the people to speak says that his vision commenced at the moment he ate from the provisions. Moreover, the application of Davila's criteria seems to strengthen the likelihood that this was something practiced in the community that produced *Rev. Magi*. The much more difficult question to answer is whether *Rev. Magi* gives us enough information to discern what this hallucinogenic substance might have been.

HALLUCINOGENS, ENTHEOGENS, AND THE STUDY OF LATE ANTIQUE RELIGION

The possible use of hallucinogens by religious communities in late antiquity has received little scholarly attention, though it has not been altogether marginalized by scholars of religion. Indeed, particularly within the subfield of the anthropology of religion, much well-regarded work has been done on the contemporary use of hallucinogens by indigenous religious groups in South America, North America, and Africa.[18] But in such studies, it is important to point out, there is no doubt that hallucinogens are being consumed by the ritual actors; botanists have identified the specific plants in use, chemists have isolated the specific chemical compounds that are psychoactive in such plants, and neuroscientists have described the particular ways these compounds affect the cognitive function of the brain. In sum, because anthropologists can actually participate in these indigenous rituals and study the specific substances being employed, there is absolutely no doubt that the substances in question are hallucinogens.

This straightforward situation changes, however, when the religious groups being studied are long dead. In the case of late antique Mediterranean religions, the question of hallucinogenic use is far more contentious among scholars. Or, to describe the situation more accurately, there really is no ongoing debate about this issue: there is instead a small group of scholars and authors who posit the presence of hallucinogens in a number of ancient religious rituals, and the claims of these scholars are, with a few exceptions,

18. See, for example, Shanon, *Antipodes of the Mind*.

generally ignored by the rest of the academy. For the sake of convenience, we will designate these scholars, in particular R. Gordon Wasson, Carl Ruck, Dan Merkur, David C. A. Hillman, and John Marco Allegro, as the "entheogenists," based on their preference for the terminology of "entheogen" instead of "hallucinogen." In fact, the term "entheogen" was first coined by a group of scholars and writers that included Wasson and Ruck.[19] This term is composed of three separate Greek etymologies: "en" (meaning "in" or "within"), "theo" ("god" or "divine"), and "gen" ("to create" or "to beget"). Therefore, the term roughly means something like "generating the divine within." Thus it implies that hallucinogens, far from creating illusory images that have no correspondence to reality, actually serve as portals to the realm of the divine. They are, for the entheogenists, generative of authentic religious experience. It is not simply a descriptive term, but is instead highly prescriptive and value-laden. It is more value-laden, I would suggest, than "hallucinogen," which means something that causes the mind to wander or travel off its normally traversed pathways—in other words, a substance that produces an altered state of consciousness.[20]

The reasons for the rejection or silence that usually follow the claims of entheogenists are complex. It is not simply that the arguments of entheogenists are totally without merit, since some prominent scholars have been convinced by their theses—this would not be the case if their work were mere pseudoscience. Nor is it that scholars of antiquity are uniformly puritan about investigating problematic or controversial aspects of ancient society. It is probably the case, as a number of the entheogenists have alleged, that some scholars who study ancient religions are squeamish about the idea of their theological or cultural forebears partaking of substances that are today illegal and stigmatized, particularly if said substances may have played a role in their thought or the revelations they claimed to receive. But the larger share of the blame is to be placed with the entheogenists for several reasons.

19. See Ruck et al., "Entheogens."

20. As Elisa Guerra-Doce discusses, the term "entheogens" has been met with controversy: "Thus, it seemed inappropriate to refer to these plants using certain terms with pejorative connotations or others that are also applied to the synthetic substances associated with the counterculture of the 1960s. In 1979, a group of ethnobotanists and scholars of religion therefore coined the neologism *entheogen* to refer to those vision-producing drugs that figure in shamanic or religious rites, although in a looser sense the term can be applied to other drugs, both natural and artificial, that induce alterations of consciousness similar to those documented for ritual ingestion of traditional entheogens (Ruck et al., "Entheogens"). The objections and misinterpretations of this neologism compelled J. Ott, one of the coiners, to explain it at length: entheogen thus means literally 'becoming divine within,' not 'generating the divine within' (Ott 1996, 205)." See Guerra-Doce, "Psychoactive Substances," 102; it is not clear to me how different "becoming divine within" is from "generating the divine within."

First of all, in most cases the evidence, usually textual but sometimes icono-graphical, for the use of hallucinogenic substances in ancient religions is extremely sparse. Almost no texts state overtly that a substance that was consumed facilitated visionary experience, and so entheogenists have been forced to piece together their hypotheses with very little direct evidence and a great deal of inference. This certainly characterizes Merkur's identification of the biblical manna as the hallucinogenic grain fungus ergot.[21] This thesis was quite fairly demolished in the few academic reviews of Merkur's book,[22] despite the fact that Merkur has done other work that has been quite well-received by scholars of ancient Jewish mysticism.[23] Second, entheogenists sometimes seem to view every major ancient religious ritual as an instance of hallucinogenic use. Such is the case for Boston University classicist Carl Ruck, who has authored or co-authored a series of books in which, one by one, the Eleusinian mysteries,[24] the Christian Eucharist,[25] and the Mithraic sacrifice,[26] are all regarded as occasions where, somewhat predictably, hal-lucinogens were consumed. A more nuanced position would seem to be that, just as present-day religious rituals oftentimes involve the consump-tion of food that is *not* hallucinogenic, ancient religions probably often did so as well. Third, in many cases the work of entheogenists has tended to adopt a rhetoric of persecution where they state again and again that the evidence for hallucinogenic use is patently obvious and that their critics are willfully oblivious. As a chief example, David C. A. Hillman's book, *The Chemical Muse: Drug Use and the Roots of Western Civilization*, though con-taining some truly intriguing primary source material that would benefit from closer study, presents itself very early on as a reaction against members of his dissertation committee who requested that the chapter on Roman recreational drug use be expunged from his thesis on medicinal substances in the Roman Republic.[27] One reviewer voiced significant frustration with Hillman's book, which despite its excellent bibliography, was nevertheless filled with inaccuracies and bitterness.[28] As a whole, the products of this impassioned rhetoric, unfortunately, often are poorly organized and fail to

21. See Merkur, *Mystery of Manna*.

22. See, for example, Hodges, review of Merkur, *Mystery of Manna*.

23. See, for example, Merkur, "Visionary Practices."

24. Ruck, *Sacred Mushrooms of the Goddess*.

25. Ruck et al., *Apples of Apollo*.

26. Ruck et al., *Mushrooms, Myth, and Mithras*.

27. Hillman, *Chemical Muse*, 1–3.

28. Charlier, review of Hillman, *Chemical Muse*. Charlier writes, "Enfin, la lecture de cet ouvrage se révèle particulièrement éreintante, le lecteur étant sans cesse freiné par les inexactitudes et les remarques noyées d'aigreur ponctuant chacune des 243 pages."

produce the necessary textual and bibliographical information needed to support their arguments, and thus tend to be published by fringe presses well outside of the realm of careful peer-review.[29]

Despite the claims of the entheogenists, I would suggest that the reasons that their arguments are not taken very seriously have much more to do with their weaknesses of method and presentation, and very little to do with some widespread conspiracy among Religious Studies scholars to ignore, deny, or suppress the evidence they put forth. However, scholars should not automatically dismiss any proposal about the use of hallucinogens in ancient Mediterranean religions simply because of the fact that the entheogenists have given this avenue of study a rather bad name. If there is indeed compelling evidence to be found for the use of hallucinogens, it should receive a fair hearing.

That is, to a certain degree, what happened with R. Gordon Wasson's original argument for the identification of soma in the Veda and haoma in the Avesta as a hallucinogen.[30] Even if not all scholars agreed with Wasson's precise identification of soma as the fly agaric mushroom, there now seems to be little doubt that Wasson was correct in recognizing the use of a hallucinogenic substance in the ritual, given the description of soma in the Vedic hymns as a plant. Furthermore, the book on the Eleusinian mysteries that Wasson co-wrote with Carl Ruck was reviewed very positively by the late eminent classicist Georg Luck of Johns Hopkins University.[31] This praise of two of Wasson's works is quite ironic, given the fact that, of all of the entheogenists I have mentioned, Wasson had practically no formal training in Religious Studies, Classics, or mycology. He spent most of his career as a vice president for the J. P. Morgan Company before turning his attention to the study of hallucinogenic mushrooms. It is a rather amusing career transformation, but I believe it does give the lie to the belief of some of the most strident entheogenists that scholars simply refuse to give credence to their theories out of principle. In the case of Wasson, at least, some of his interpretations of religious rituals have been accepted by prominent scholars, which suggests that his arguments have some merit.

29. Though not focused exclusively on the Greek and Roman world, a very solid overview of the evidence pertaining to ancient evidence for the use of hallucinogens is Merlin, "Archaeological Evidence."

30. Wasson, *Soma*.

31. Luck, review of Wasson et al., *Road to Eleusis*.

CONCLUSION

I am hesitant to claim that the hallucinogen described in *Rev. Magi* can be identified with any degree of certainty, since the text only uses the vague term "provisions" to describe this substance. But if pressed, I think that a hallucinogenic mushroom is a plausible candidate. The most distinguishing characteristic of *Rev. Magi*'s miraculous food is that it multiplies when the light of the star shines upon it, and it is possible to read this as an opaque reference to the well-known phenomenon of mushrooms appearing to grow quite rapidly in the overnight hours. However, this is simply a preliminary guess on the basis of very limited data. To my mind, the more important and persuasive conclusion is that some early Christian group in which the strange text known as *Rev. Magi* was produced, seems to have used a hallucinogenic substance ritually to produce visionary experiences. If I am correct in this, then alongside of all the other unique interpretations of the Magi and their star in this text, *Rev. Magi* also contains the only clear reference to a hallucinogen in ancient Christian or Jewish texts.

– 6 –

Behind the Seven Veils, II
Assessing Clement of Alexandria's Knowledge of the Mystic Gospel of Mark

— Scott G. Brown —

THE LETTER TO THEODORE, attributed to Clement of Alexandria, quotes from a "mystic gospel" that the evangelist Mark reportedly composed in Alexandria following Peter's death. This "more spiritual gospel" consists of the original version, which Mark created in Rome for catechumens, plus additional materials "suitable to those studies which make for progress toward knowledge," which Mark selected from "his own notes and those of Peter." Upon his death, Mark "left his composition to the church in Alexandria, where it even yet is [very securely kept], being read only to those who are being initiated into the great mysteries."[1] It might have disappeared from history altogether had not "the foul demons" conspired with Carpocrates

---

1. Translations of the Letter to Theodore are from Smith, Clement of Alexandria, 446–47. The translation of the mystic gospel is my own. Except where indicated, translations of Quis dives salvetur? and the Protrepticus are by George William Butterworth in LCL 92; translations of the Paedagogus and the Stromateis are by William Wilson in ANF 2. Translations of the Bible are from the NRSV. My revisions to these translations appear in brackets and my explanatory additions in parentheses. The translations by Roy Kotansky were prepared collaboratively for Part I of this paper.

to create a falsification of this gospel, some troubling passages of which Theodore had heard and enquired about.

In the course of setting the record straight, the *Letter to Theodore* quotes the real wording of one of the adulterated narratives: a short and distinctly Markan variant of the raising of Lazarus. Within the expanded text of Mark, this story, according to the letter, occurs in two parts, the first appearing before the request of James and John for positions of power (Mark 10:35–45), the second, immediately after (within Mark 10:46). I shall refer to these verses as LGM 1 (Longer Gospel of Mark 1) and LGM 2:

> [LGM 1] **1** And they come to Bethany. And a certain woman was there whose brother had died. **2** And coming, she prostrated before Jesus and says to him, "Son of David have mercy on me." **3** But the disciples rebuked her. **4** And having become angry Jesus went away with her into the garden where the tomb was. **5** And immediately a great cry was heard from the tomb. **6** And approaching, Jesus rolled the stone from the door of the tomb, **7** and going in immediately where the young man was, he stretched out the hand and raised him, having grasped the hand. **8** But the young man, having looked upon him loved him and began to beg him that he might be with him. **9** And going out from the tomb they went into the house of the young man; for he was rich. **10** And after six days Jesus gave charge to him; **11** and when it was evening the young man comes to him wearing a linen sheet over his naked body, **12** and he remained with him that night; for Jesus was teaching him the mystery of the kingdom of God. **13** Now rising, he returned from there to the other side of the Jordan. (then comes Mark 10:35–45 and 10:46a)

> [LGM 2] (And he comes to Jericho.) **1** And the sister of the young man whom Jesus loved and his mother and Salome were there, **2** and Jesus did not receive them. (And as he and his disciples and a large crowd were leaving Jericho, Bartimaeus son of Timaeus, . . .)

The only direct evidence we possess for both this letter of Clement and the gospel that it quotes is one eighteenth-century Greek manuscript, which Morton Smith catalogued at Mar Saba in 1958. This fact has made it especially difficult to assess the letter's ascriptions of authorship. The conventional approach, which I pursued in Part I of this paper and other earlier studies, is to apply our current knowledge of Clement and Mark to the letter and its excerpts in order to determine what they mean and whether they make sense as works of those authors.[2] The results of that analysis were

2. Brown, *Mark's Other Gospel*, 28–34, 59–73, 121–53, 215–19 (on Clement);

positive. The letter makes good sense as a work of Clement and agrees with his statements about the way Alexandrian teachers privately transmitted a secret unwritten tradition ("the great mysteries") to spiritually mature students through mystical (i.e., allegorical) exegesis of inspired texts; likewise, the Markan literary techniques employed in the gospel excerpts (esp. intercalation, frame stories, and verbal echoes) reveal that the story about the young man indeed has a figurative ("mystic") level of meaning that accords with, and elucidates, the theology of the Gospel of Mark.

A second and much less obvious approach was pursued by Alain Le Boulluec in a paper published in 1996. Le Boulluec examined whether Clement's exposition in *Quis dives salvetur?* of the story of the rich man of Mark 10:17–22 and Jesus' subsequent discussion of the perils of riches in 10:23–31 offers indirect evidence of Clement's acquaintance with the story of Jesus raising and instructing a rich young man found in the mystic Gospel of Mark.[3] Le Boulluec's findings were likewise positive, but he did not consider the concordance that he demonstrated between the subplot involving the young man in the mystic Gospel of Mark and Clement's interpretation of Mark 10:17–31 to constitute sufficient proof that the longer text is authentic.

Le Boulleuc's approach is quite sensible. If Clement himself heard the mystic gospel expounded in the course of his own initiation into the great mysteries of the Alexandrian church, it follows that the interpretations he heard from his teacher Pantaenus and later expounded to his own students would have influenced his reading of scriptural passages that share the same themes and story elements. Yet Clement's exegeses of relevant scriptural texts are by no means confined to *Quis dives salvetur?* So a promising way to test the likelihood that Clement really wrote this letter is to consider whether the allegorical meanings that he ascribed to these elements in other texts that he treated as scriptural make some degree of sense when applied in sequence to the two known passages from the mystic gospel.[4] Can we, by doing this, gain some notion of the "true interpretation" promised in the last sentence of the letter, where the text breaks off in midsentence? If this is not possible, then we have reason to doubt that Clement read and expounded this story himself, and, by extension, that he authored the letter. But if this is possible, then we have a good reason to accept the letter's authenticity.

75–111, 153–62, 165–230 (on Mark); Brown, "*Letter to Theodore*"; Brown, "Behind the Seven Veils, I."

3. Le Boulluec, "Lettre sur L'Évangile secret' de Marc."

4. By "scriptural," I mean any text or part of a text that Clement treated as inspired by the Logos and therefore containing a hidden and more profound level of meaning.

Indeed, that conclusion would be unavoidable if these parallels combine perfectly to form a coherent and detailed allegorical interpretation.

The results of this study are surprising. Although I could find no significant parallels to the parts of the story that do not mention the young man (LGM 1:2–6, 13), the verses in which he factors (LGM 1:1, 7–12; LGM 2) yielded an abundance of parallels, all of which pertain to Clement's program of advancement through the church—his "project of Christian perfection," as Ashwin-Siejkowski aptly describes it.[5] The parallels in LGM 1 involve being raised by Jesus from the dead, the phrase "for he was rich," a period of seven days, wearing a linen garment over the naked body, a special relationship of love, and the mystery of the kingdom of God; those in LGM 2 concern the necessity of leaving behind family and possessions, which is arguably the issue behind Jesus' refusal to meet with the young man's sister and mother (Salome's relation to these two women is not clear).[6]

Clement can be a difficult author to understand. For that reason, those who have not studied his writings likely will benefit from reading Part I of this paper first, or the more accessible summaries of my research that I published as a two-part article in *The Fourth R*.[7]

JESUS RAISING A PERSON FROM THE DEAD

In his *Protrepticus*, Clement alludes to Christ's capacity, as the one who exhorts the heathen to repentance, to raise from the dead those who live in the darkness of ignorance and error:

> Wherefore the blessed apostle says: "I testify in the Lord, that ye no longer walk as the Gentiles also walk, in the vanity of their mind, being darkened in their understanding and alienated from the life of God, because of the ignorance that is in them, because of the hardening of their heart, who being past feeling gave themselves up to lasciviousness, to work all uncleanness and greediness." (Eph 4:17–19) When such a witness reproves the folly of men and calls upon God to hear, what else remains for unbelievers but judgment and condemnation? Yet the Lord does not weary of admonishing, of terrifying, of exhorting, of arousing, of warning; no indeed, He awakes men from sleep, and those that have gone astray He causes to rise from the

5. Ashwin-Siejkowski, *Clement of Alexandria*.

6. See Brown, *Mark's Other Gospel*, 155.

7. Brown, "Mystical Gospel of Mark (Part One)"; and Brown, "Mystical Gospel of Mark (Part Two)."

darkness itself. "Awake, thou that sleepest," He cries, "and arise from the dead, and there shall shine upon thee Christ the Lord" (Eph 5:14), the sun of the resurrection, He that is begotten "before the morning star," He that dispenses life by His own rays. (*Protr.* 9.83.3—84.2)

Again in the *Paedagogus*, Clement uses Jesus' raising of Lazarus as a metaphor for how Christ, this time in his capacity as Instructor (meaning a tutor of young children), heals both body and soul through his exhortations and gifts:

> Our Instructor, the Word, therefore cures the unnatural passions of the soul by means of exhortations . . . But the good Instructor, the Wisdom, the Word of the Father, who made man, cares for the whole nature of His creature; the all-sufficient Physician of humanity, the Saviour, heals both body and soul. "Rise up," He said to the paralytic; "take the bed on which thou liest, and go away home"; and straightway the infirm man received strength. And to the dead He said, "Lazarus, go forth"; and the dead man issued from his coffin such as he was [before] he died, having undergone resurrection. Further, He heals the soul itself by precepts and gifts—by precepts indeed, in course of time, but being liberal in His gifts, He says to us sinners, "Thy sins be forgiven thee." (*Paed.* I.2.6.1–4)

For Clement, then, the image of Jesus raising the dead evokes his power to convey people from the darkness of a life driven by passions to the light of a discipline that heals the soul. These are the initial stages of Clement's path to perfection (conversion and the moderation of the passions), the subjects of Clement's *Protrepticus* and *Paedagogus*, which involve exhortations and threats directed at repentance followed by gifts (forgiveness and healing), admonitions, and, "in course of time," elementary instruction in precepts.

"FOR HE WAS RICH"

Much of what Clement wrote about wealth in *Quis dives salvetur?* is apropos to his understanding of the phrase "for he had many possessions" in Mark 10:22b, which parallels the statement "for he was rich" in LGM 1:9b. Two passages in particular summarize the most relevant points. In the first, *Quis div.* 20.3–6, Clement considers the meaning of "riches" in Jesus' saying, "How hard it is for those who have riches to enter the kingdom of God!" (Mark 10:23 par.), and reasons that since Jesus' disciples had already abandoned their meager possessions at the time of their calling, their astonished response, "Who can be saved?" implies that the riches in question must concern more than material wealth and therefore also have a figurative meaning: "riches" must also denote "the passions," the possession of which excludes a person from the heavens, "for salvation belongs to pure and passionless souls." Therefore, the disciples despaired in the same way as "that very rich man who clung desperately to his possession, which indeed he preferred to eternal life."

The second passage, *Quis div.* 15.6—16.2, adds some new elements, which indicate what the rich man must do before he can heed Jesus' call to follow him:

> In this way then the Lord admits the use of [material possessions], bidding us put away, not the means of living, but the things that use these badly; and these are, as we have seen, the infirmities and passions of the soul. Wealth of these brings death (θανατηφόρος) whenever it is present, but salvation when it is destroyed. Of this wealth a man must render his soul pure, that is, poor and bare (πτωχεύουσαν καὶ γυμνήν), and then only must he listen to the Saviour when He says, "Come, follow me." For He Himself now becomes a way (ὁδός) to the pure in heart; but into an impure soul God's grace does not steal. An impure soul is that which is rich in lusts and in travail with many worldly affections.

Throughout *Quis dives salvetur?* Clement resists the literal meaning of Jesus' command to the rich man to divest himself of all possessions, and offers a more practical, but equally strenuous, spiritual meaning relating to detachment from worldly things. Literal wealth is actually a good thing, in his view, *if it is shared wisely* (14.1–6). However, a wealth of passions and sicknesses in the soul "brings death" (a point reiterated in 18.2–6 and 25.6). Elsewhere, in the *Paedagogus*, Clement makes the same point: "how can you not think that vulgar extravagance is banished by the Lord's authority? About this also, 'Sell your possessions,' says the Lord, 'and give to the poor; and come, follow me' (Mark 10:21). Follow God, stripped (γυμνός) of pretentiousness, stripped (γυμνός) of fading display, possessed of that which is your own, that good which alone cannot be taken away—faith towards God, confession towards him who suffered, generosity towards other humans, which is the most precious of possessions" (*Paed.* II.3.36.1–2; trans. Brown). The implications of Clement's exegesis for the subsequent fate of the rich man of Mark 10 are clear: If he does nothing after he goes away sorrowful, he will die, but if he decides instead to follow Jesus, he must first strip away these passions and all outward display and thereby render his soul "poor and bare." Only then can he answer Jesus' challenge, "Come, follow me." The applicability of these ideas to the story of the young man in mystic Mark is not hard to envision. Whether or not Clement would have supposed that the two anonymous rich men were one and the same,[8] he might well have presumed that the young man in Bethany had died because he "clung desperately to his possession, which indeed he preferred to eternal life." Jesus can give him physical life and evoke a desire for conversion, but the young man cannot attain eternal life until he manages "to banish from the soul its opinions about riches, its attachment to them, its excessive desire, its morbid excitement over them, its anxious cares, the thorns of our earthly existence which choke the seed of the true life" (*Quis div.* 11.2; cf. Mark 4:18–19). Intent, therefore, to "follow" Jesus "stripped" (γυμνός) of materialism and fading display, he rids himself of his literal and metaphorical riches during the subsequent week and returns to Jesus "wearing a linen sheet over his naked body (ἐπὶ γυμνοῦ)" (LGM 1:11). In this passionless state, he leaves behind his home and family (LGM 2) and "follows with" Jesus (συνηκολούθει αὐτῷ) in Gethsemane, where he loses even this sheet (Mark 14:51–52).

In Clement's rhetoric, a person stripped of passions is metaphorically naked, whereas other people are physically clothed by their passions and excesses like cockles inside their thick rounded shells:

> It was from Moses that the chief of the Greeks drew these philosophical tenets. For he commands holocausts to be skinned and divided into parts. (Lev 1:6) For the gnostic soul must be consecrated to the light, stripped (γυμνήν) of the integuments of matter, devoid of the frivolousness of the body and of all the passions (*Phaedo* 67a), which are acquired through vain and lying opinions, and divested of the lusts of the flesh. But [most people], clothed with what is perishable, like cockles, and rolled all round in a ball in their excesses, like hedgehogs, entertain the same ideas of the blessed and incorruptible God as of themselves. (*Strom.* V.11.67.1—68.1)

Within this metaphorical framework a single sheet over the naked body could well represent a soul that has succeeded in eliminating its passions, which is the goal of the stages of education that follow baptism. As Le

---

8. I doubt that the author of mystic Mark made this identification (see Brown, *Mark's Other Gospel*, 102), but there is good reason to think that Clement would have done so (see Le Boulluec, "Lettre sur L'Évangile secret' de Marc," 35–37). That the two rich men are equated in mystic Mark itself is argued by Smith, *Clement of Alexandria*, 114, 172; Meyer, *Secret Gospels*, 122–23, 161, 178; and Koester, *From Jesus to the Gospels*, 50.

Boulluec put it, "The soul thus 'bare' is the gnostic soul, according to *Strom.* V.11.67.4."[9]

In Clement's writings, as in Philo's, the process of eliminating the passions involves two stages. The first stage is directed to catechumens and the simple faithful and involves a diminishing and controlling of the passions. The second stage applies to Christians who choose to strengthen their faith with gnosis; they must strive to purge the passions completely through the cultivation of reason and virtue (*Strom.* I.24.159.3). This stage constitutes the advanced ethics of what Clement calls the lesser mysteries. As Ashwin-Siejkowski notes, "Clement stresses the necessity of parallel development: on one level from πίστις to γνῶσις; on another from 'moderate desires' μετριοπάθεια to 'passionlessness' ἀπάθεια" (*Strom.* VI.9.71.1).[10] Detachment from the passions and the physical senses is what allows a Christian to focus on the supersensible realities of the noetic world, which is what Clement means by initiation into the great mysteries (*Strom.* V.11.67.1—68.1).

"THE MYSTERY OF THE KINGDOM OF GOD"

During the last night spent at the young man's house, Jesus, we are told, "was teaching him the mystery of the kingdom of God." This sentence reintroduces the theme in Mark 4:11–12, where Jesus explains to his disciples and closest followers why he speaks to the crowds in parables: "To you has been given [the mystery] of the kingdom of God, but for those outside, everything comes in parables; in order that 'they may indeed look, but not perceive, and may indeed listen, but not understand; so that they may not turn again and be forgiven.'" Mark himself is referring to a theological mystery about God's kingdom that Jesus communicates in a veiled form to prevent outsiders from understanding it. That Clement understood this saying in a similar way is evident from his hybrid quotation of Mark 4:11 and Matt 13:11:

> And was it not this which the prophet (Moses) meant, when he ordered unleavened cakes to be made (Exod 12:15, 39), intimating that the truly sacred mystic word, respecting the Unbegotten and His powers, ought to be concealed? In confirmation of these things, in the Epistle to the Corinthians the apostle plainly says: "Howbeit we speak wisdom among those who are perfect, but not the wisdom of this world, or of the princes of this world, that

9. Le Boulluec, "Lettre sur L'Évangile secret' de Marc," 38 (trans. Brown).

10. Ashwin-Siejkowski, *Clement of Alexandria*, 158. Lilla, *Clement of Alexandria*, 92–106, 112–14, offers a detailed discussion of the two stages in the elimination of the passions.

come to nought. But we speak the wisdom of God hidden in a mystery." (1 Cor 2:6–7) And again in another place he says: "To the acknowledgement of the mystery of God in Christ, in whom are hid all the treasures of wisdom and knowledge." (Col 2:2–3) These things the Saviour Himself seals when He says: "To you it is given to know the [mystery] of the kingdom of the [heavens]." (Mark 4:11; Matt 13:11) And again the Gospel says that [our] Saviour [spoke] to the apostles the word in a mystery. For prophecy says of Him: "He will open His mouth in parables, and will utter things kept secret from the foundation of the world." (Matt 13:35) And now, by the parable of the leaven, the Lord shows concealment; for He says, "The kingdom of [the heavens] is like leaven, which a woman took and hid in three measures of meal, till the whole was leavened" (Matt 13:33). (*Strom.* V.12.80.3–8)

This passage is characteristically obscure, but there are sufficient clues to figure it out. Clement associates "the mystery of the kingdom of the heavens" that Jesus consigned to "the apostles" with the apostle Paul's various references to a wisdom of God that he speaks "among those who are perfect" and Jesus' use of parables to conceal such wisdom. All of this is Clement's proof that Christ believed that "the truly sacred mystic word concerning the Unbegotten and his powers ought to be concealed." Thus the mystery of the kingdom of God is secret teaching concerning the Unbegotten and his powers. The question we need to answer, then, is what Clement meant by this particular circumlocution for God.

The answer is found in Clement's source. Clement borrowed this language from Philo, together with the mystic interpretation of the "unleavened cakes" that God commanded the Israelites to make in Exod 12:15, 39. In Philo, this mystic interpretation concerns the great mysteries:

> For the words of the scripture are, "To make secret cakes"; because the sacred and mystic statements about the one uncreated Being, and about his powers, ought to be kept secret; since it does not belong to everyone to keep the deposit of divine mysteries properly . . . Those persons appear to me to have come to a right decision who have been initiated in the lesser mysteries before learning anything of these greater ones. "For they baked their flour which they brought out of Egypt, baking secret cakes of unleavened bread." (Exod. 12:34) That is to say, they dealt with the untameable and savage passions, softening them with reason as they would knead bread; for they did not divulge the manner of their kneading and improving it, as it was derived from some divine system of preparation; but they treasured it

up in their secret stores, not being elated at the knowledge of the mystery, but yielding and being lowly as to their boasting. (*Sacr.* 15.60—16.62; trans. Yonge)

Philo reasoned that the secrets about God and his powers ought to be kept secret, being the proper and privileged possession of those who have first mastered "the untameable and savage passions . . . with reason," thereby completing the lesser mysteries.[11] Clement affirms Philo's point in his ensuing discussion of concealment, which continues the theme of the impossibility of conveying God's nature in words, the point on which Clement's prior discussion of the great mysteries in *Strom.* V.11 concludes. Thus, in Clement's interpretation, the expression "the mystery of the kingdom of the heavens" is another term for the great mysteries, the most esoteric teachings about the nature of God and of the realms of mind and spirit that lie outside the material cosmos. We can conclude, therefore, that if Clement read LGM 1:12 he would presume that Jesus was teaching the young man the great mysteries.

"AND AFTER SIX DAYS"

To this point we have considered the figurative significance of being raised from the dead and Clement's interpretations of canonical Gospel parallels to the two *gar*-clauses that mark off the time that Jesus and the young man spend inside the young man's house. Bringing these interpretations together, we can readily imagine Clement treating the young man's return to life in terms of Christ awaking in him a desire to repent and convert, and reading the clause "for he was rich" as establishing the young man's need to strip himself of all passion through the fostering of virtue and reason. By entering his house with Jesus, he has essentially entered the church. Further, we can picture Clement explaining the young man's strange attire "after six days" as representing his completion of the lesser mysteries, and the teaching activity on the final night as denoting his initiation in the great mysteries. In other words, the young man figuratively passes through the sequence of Christian education as Clement represents it in his major works. Since the mystic gospel presents this period inside the house as lasting one week and identifies three discrete intervals, specifically, "after six days" (= the seventh day), "when it was evening" (before sunset on the seventh day), and "that night" (the beginning of the eighth day, according to the Jewish reckoning

---

11. For discussion, see Goodenough, *By Light*, 206.

of time used in the Gospels),[12] we are naturally curious to examine Clement's allegorical interpretations of periods of time involving six, seven, and eight days.

In the narrative itself the notice that six days have elapsed is mentioned in passing; the focus is squarely on the seventh and eighth days. Clement, however, was apt to find symbolic significance even in incidental scriptural references to the elapsing of x number of days. The following passage is quite relevant:

> "Abraham, when he came to the place which God told him of on the third day, looking up, saw the place afar off." (Gen 22:3–4) For the first day is that which is constituted by the sight of good things; and the second is the soul's best desire; on the third, the mind perceives spiritual things, the eyes of the understanding being opened by the Teacher who rose on the third day. The three days may be the mystery of the seal, in which God is really believed. It is consequently afar off that he sees the place. For the region of God is hard to attain; which Plato called the region of ideas, having learned from Moses that it was a place which contained all things universally. But it is seen by Abraham afar off, rightly, because of his being in the realms of generation, and he is forthwith initiated by the angel. Thence says the apostle: "Now we see as through a glass, but then face to face" (1 Cor 13:12), by those sole pure and incorporeal applications of the intellect. In reasoning, it is possible to divine respecting God, if one attempt without any of the senses, by reason, to reach what is individual; and do not quit the sphere of existences, till, rising up to the things which transcend it, he apprehends by the intellect itself that which is good, moving in the very confines of the world of thought, according to Plato. (*Strom.* V.11.73.1–2)

In this passage, Clement takes an incidental scriptural reference to the passing of three days and associates it with baptism ("the mystery of the seal") and Christ's resurrection. Having made this connection, he then imagines the two preceding days individually, despite there being no description of these days in the text. He associates the first and second days with a catechumen's progression in belief. On the third day (i.e., through baptism), the eyes of understanding are opened (baptism as illumination), but they are impeded from seeing clearly the region of God/the Ideas (i.e., the noetic world) because Abraham (the Christian initiate) is still within the realms of

12. If perchance Clement imposed the Roman reckoning in which a day begins at midnight, he would still picture the transition to the eighth day occurring during "that night" of teaching.

generation (the material cosmos). However, he is "forthwith initiated by the angel," which evidently refers to the beginning of more advanced education. In the remainder of the passage, Clement concentrates on the intellectual skills necessary to see into the noetic world. So in this example an incidental reference to "the third day" becomes a marker in the path to transcending the material cosmos through an initiation comprising "incorporeal applications of the intellect."

When we turn to the numbers six, seven, and eight, we discover that they each have strong and distinct associations in Clement's writings. The number seven interested him the most. In fact, his exegesis of the commandment to keep the sabbath day holy contains a long demonstration of the special sanctity of the number seven (*Strom.* VI.16.137.4–145.7). He tends to associate this number with the sabbath rest, the seven heavens, and the seven stages of advancement that culminate in the consummate rest in the eighth heaven.

In *Strom.* IV.17.109.2 Clement introduces the notion of "the gnostic mystery of the seven and the eight" (lit. "the Hebdomad and the Ogdoad"), which he begins to explain in IV.25 and returns to in V.14 and VI.16.[13] The first of these three passages explains the significance of the seven days of purification for a corpse-contaminated priest (Ezek 44:25–27; cf. Lev 21:1–4).[14] Clement initially suggests that the seven days represent "the period in which creation was consummated. For on the seventh day the rest is celebrated" (*Strom.* IV.25.158.4). After discussing a special propitiation required on the eighth day for priests who have incurred corpse-defilement,[15] he suggests other referents for the seven days of purification: "Whether, then, the time be that which through the seven periods enumerated returns to the [consummate] rest,[16] or the seven heavens, which some reckon one above the other; or whether also the fixed sphere which borders on the intellectual

13. Kaye, *Some Account*, 417 n. 1. For discussions of the passages relating to this mystery, see Daniélou, *Gospel Message*, 451; Itter, *Esoteric Teaching*, 46–49, 156–62.

14. The seven days in Ezek 44:26 actually denote a period of exclusion from the temple *after* the seven-day period of corpse impurity (during which brief purification rites are performed only on the third and seventh days), but Clement takes it to mean, "they purify themselves seven days."

15. Again, the text of Ezek 44:27 does not say that the priest presents his sin offering (i.e., purification offering) *on the eighth day*, but this notion might be based on an analogy with Lev 15:13–15, 28–30.

16. Clement most likely has in mind the seven weeks of years (i.e., 49 years) that precede the yearlong Sabbath of the Jubilee year. The seven *enumerated* periods thus refers to the expression "and you shall count seven weeks of years" in Lev 25:8, which Clement used to interpret the similar expression in Ezek 44:26, "they shall count seven days."

world be called the eighth, the expression denotes that the Gnostic ought to rise out of the sphere of creation and of sin" (*Strom*. IV.25.159.2).

Similar ideas recur in his exegesis of what he deems Plato's prophetic reference to the Sabbath ("the Lord's day") in the *Republic* (616b):

> "And when seven days have passed to each of them in the mead-ow, on the eighth they are to set out and arrive in four days." By the meadow is to be understood the fixed sphere (of the stars), as being a mild and genial spot, and the locality of the pious; and by the seven days [is to be understood] each motion of the seven planets (ἑκάστην κίνησιν τῶν ἑπτά), and the whole practical art which speeds to [the goal of repose] (τέλος ἀναπαύσεως). But after the wandering orbs the journey leads to heaven (ἡ δὲ μετὰ τοὺς πλανωμένους πορεία ἐπὶ τὸν οὐρανὸν ἄγει), that is, to the eighth motion and day. And he says that souls are gone on the fourth day, pointing out the passage through the four elements. (*Strom*. V.14.106.2–4)

This passage compares the fixed sphere with Plato's meadow (the stars in the night sky resemble flowers of a meadow) and associates the seven planetary spheres with the stages of Christian instruction that lead to repose. Since the seven days represent both a progression through the seven planetary spheres and the period of time within the fixed sphere (which is a separate region above them), I assume that Clement is picturing the progression through the seven heavens toward the fixed sphere as it would appear to a person looking upwards at the sky—that is, as occurring against the back-drop of the stars and in that sense within the starry meadow itself, through which the planets appear to wander. The end of this progression, following four more days (perhaps symbolizing the passage through the veil of the cosmic temple),[17] is the repose of "the eighth day," which, as we will see, is a term Clement uses for the Ogdoad and the original or archetypal sabbath repose, which constitutes salvation for the Gnostic.

This is all rather dense and confusing, but we have learned thus far that Clement associates the seven days of purification with the six days of creation followed by the repose of the sabbath and with the seven heavens and the seven planets that occupy the realm between earth and the fixed sphere of the stars. The repose of the sabbath is a type of the consummate rest in the Ogdoad. These ideas, in turn, are associated with the "practical

17. Itter, *Esoteric Teaching*, 157, perceptively notes, "Clement equates the four days in which the soul travels [from the meadow] with the four elements, which [in *Strom*. V.6.32.3] represent the four coloured materials making up the inner and outer veils in Clement's account of the tabernacle." This implies that leaving the meadow (fixed sphere) corresponds to passing through a veil of the celestial temple.

art" or instruction that leads a Christian to the final repose. Two other passages from the *Stromateis* help clarify the interrelations:

> Again the Barbarian philosophy knows the world of thought and the world of sense—the former archetypal, and the latter the image of that which is called the model; and assigns the former to the Monad, as being perceived by the mind, and the world of sense to the number six. For six is called by the Pythagoreans marriage, as being the genital number; and he places in the Monad the invisible heaven and the [invisible] earth, and intellectual light. For "in the beginning," it is said, "God made the heaven and the earth; and the earth was invisible." And it is added, "And God said, Let there be light; and there was light." And in the material cosmogony He creates a solid heaven (and what is solid is capable of being perceived by sense),[18] and a visible earth, and a light that is seen. (V.14.93.4—94.1)

> (The fourth commandment) is that which intimates that the world was created by God, and that He gave us the seventh day as a rest, on account of the trouble that there is in life. For God is incapable of weariness, and suffering, and want. But we who bear flesh need rest. The seventh day, therefore, is proclaimed a rest—abstraction from ills—preparing for the Primal Day, our true [repose]; which, in truth, is the first creation of light, in which all things are viewed and possessed. From this day the first wisdom and knowledge illuminate us. For the light of truth—a light true, casting no shadow, is the Spirit [of the Lord] indivisibly divided to [those] who are sanctified by faith, holding the place of a luminary [unto] the knowledge of [true] existences.[19] By following him, therefore, through our whole life, we become [passionless] (ἀπαθεῖς); and this is to rest. (VI.16.137.4—138.3)

The latter passage associates the rest on the seventh day with the "true repose" of the Primal Day, the day when, according to the former passage, God created the intellectual world. This is the form of salvation reserved for the Gnostic; yet a Christian who strives to become like God (free from passions) through the whole course of life will at length participate in this

18. The explanation in parentheses here is Clement's and belongs to the original translation.

19. This illumination by the Spirit of the Lord (πνεῦμα κυρίου) unto the knowledge of true existences is, I assume, what is meant in the *Letter to Theodore* II.17–18: "But we are 'children of light,' having been illuminated by 'the dayspring' of the Spirit of the Lord 'from on high.'" That is, the implied author (Clement) is telling Theodore that he is not only sufficiently pure to hear the words of the mystic gospel but also sufficiently advanced in knowledge.

repose proleptically. The seventh day, then, denotes three basic things: assimilation to God (the goal of Clement's advanced ethics[20]); the last of the "mystic stages" of advancement,[21] corresponding to the seventh heaven in the soul's postmortem ascent; and a return to the beginning, to the true repose of the intellectual world (the eighth day, which is also the true or archetypal sabbath). This final stage of advancement thus constitutes a transition from the sensible world to the supersensible world above it (cf. VI.16.140.1), a mystical passage from the seventh heaven to the eighth through the fixed sphere of the stars. The mystery of the seven and the eight is in part the paradox that the repose is both the seventh day of the week (Saturday) and the eighth (i.e., Sunday, the first day of the next week) (VI.16.138.5).[22]

The former passage also clarifies the significance of the number six. As the number of days of creation, six signifies the world of sense, or the visible heaven and earth; and six signifies generation. The same ideas appear in the paragraph that follows the latter passage, where six is again associated with marriage and the days of creation but also with the period between the solstices (six months), during which plants bud and mature, and then wither and die, and with the period in which the human embryo is perfected (VI.16.138.6—139.3).

Accordingly, the seven days of purification from corpse contamination, the seven days in the meadow, the seven days in which creation was consummated, the seven enumerated periods (weeks of years) preceding the Jubilee year), the seven planets, and the seven heavens represent the same thing: the program of Christian education as a mystical path of initiation that takes a Christian through the lesser mysteries of the sensible world of generation and change to the great mysteries of the supersensible world beyond the stars.

Clement's association of the number six with the sphere of generation and his various attempts to associate the number seven with a Christian's progression out of the material cosmos indicate that a Clementine interpretation would treat the mystic gospel's "and after six days" allegorically as signifying the young man's mastery of the sensible world and the gnostic science of nature. By the evening of the seventh day, the young man

20. For discussion, see Lilla, *Clement of Alexandria*, 103–17.

21. The phrase "mystic stages" occurs in *Strom.* VII.10.57.1. Clement similarly compares these stages to the seven stones on the high priest's regular robe, which symbolizes the material cosmos (V.6.37.1, 3).

22. The Jubilee Sabbath year would also be an "eight" in the sense that it starts after the period of seven sevens has been completed. Clement goes on to add the number six into this mystery. See Sagnard, *La gnose Valentinienne*, 376–86; Schoedel, "Scripture," 124–25.

has arrived at the threshold of the intelligible world, which for Clement is symbolized both by "the second veil" of the tabernacle (*Exc.* 27.1–2), which separates the holy place from the holy of holies, and by the fixed sphere of the stars, which separates the material and visible cosmos (earth and the seven material heavens) from the immaterial cosmos. More precisely, the seven days inside the young man's house would likely suggest to Clement "the whole practical art which speeds to the goal of repose," and the evening of the seventh day and the beginning of the eighth, when the young man puts on the linen sheet and receives instruction in the mystery of the kingdom of God, would mark his mystical entry into (i.e., ability to perceive) the noetic world, prefiguring his postmortem attainment of the consummate rest in the eighth heaven. In mystic contemplation, the young man enters the immaterial cosmos through instruction in the great mysteries, which primarily concern the realities of the immaterial world.

THE LINEN SHEET

Prior to receiving instruction in the mystery of the kingdom of God, the young man wears a linen sheet over his naked body, the same clothing that he wears later in Gethsemane (Mark 14:51–52).[23] We have already considered how this slender attire could signify a soul stripped of its passions, but more can be said concerning the fabric itself. Given what the *Letter to Theodore* indicates about the mystic gospel's ability to lead its hearers into the innermost sanctuary of the sevenfold veiled truth (I.25–26), it is *prima facie* significant that Clement's exegesis of the Day of Atonement ritual (*Strom.* V.6; Lev 16:3–4, 23–24) focuses on a single linen garment that the high priest puts on before entering this innermost sanctuary of the tabernacle. As I explained at greater length in Part I of this paper, this sanctuary, the holy of holies, is for Clement a symbol for the immaterial cosmos (*Strom.* V.6.35.5, 36.3, 39.4) and the experience of *epopteia*, the vision of God that forms the climax of the great mysteries. The young man in the linen sheet would be entering this "space" mystically by receiving instruction in the great mysteries (the mystery of the kingdom of God). Clement's understanding of the symbolism of the high priest's linen tunic is relevant, therefore, to a Clementine reading of the young man's linen sheet.

23. The fact that he could wriggle out of this material while attempting to flee suggests that he had wrapped a plain rectangular sheet around himself in the form of a sleeveless cloak. See Jackson, "Youth."

Clement's Allegory of the Day of Atonement Ritual

Leviticus 16 describes how the high priest is to enter the holy of holies on the Day of Atonement and purify it with the blood of a goat (v. 15). The whole ritual is very elaborate, involving several sacrifices, immersion, change of clothing, and the use of a protective cloud of incense. Clement's exegesis, however, ignores the sacrifices and the purification of the sanctuary with blood and instead focuses mainly on the elements of water immersion and change of clothing. In Clement's conception, the holy of holies represents the noetic world of the eighth heaven, and the high priest represents the Gnostic (*Strom.* V.6.39.4). Clement observes that before entering the innermost sanctuary, the high priest/Gnostic, "having undressed from his consecrated garment, . . . washes himself and gets dressed in the other, so to speak, holy of holies garment, the one that goes with him into the innermost chambers" (39.3; trans. Kotansky); Clement later describes this special tunic as "the linen robe" (40.2). Although Lev 16:3–4 specifies that the high priest's holy of holies attire also consists of linen undergarments, a linen sash, and a linen turban, Clement focuses exclusively on the tunic, calling it both a tunic (χιτών: an undergarment) and a robe (στολή: an outer garment). It is as if the high priest in this allegory, like the young man in LGM 1:11 and Mark 14:51–52, puts on a single linen garment.[24]

Both the high priest's regular robe and his special holy of holies tunic have symbolic meaning for Clement. The regular robe is "the symbol of the world of sense," depicting aspects of the material cosmos such as the seven planets, the 360 (*sic*) days of the year, the sun and the moon, the zodiac and the four seasons (*Strom.* V.6.37.1, 4; 38.3–4). Like the six days of creation, the regular robe encapsulates "the (material) universe, and the creation in the universe" (39.3). The regular robe of the high priest is also what Christ (a second referent for the high priest) "puts on" during his incarnation (40.3). Hence this "robe prophesied the ministry in the flesh by which he was [made directly visible to the world]" (39.2; cf. 34.1). Accordingly, the regular robe represents both the material cosmos and the materiality of beings within it, whereas the linen tunic, being what Christ "takes off" upon entering the "world of sense" and what the Gnostic "puts on" when entering the immaterial cosmos, must represent the divine and immaterial nature of beings within the Ogdoad (cf. the symbolism attributed to the high priest's two robes in Philo, *Somn.* 1.229).

Clement's exegesis of Lev 16:3–4 accordingly complements and refines our previous inferences concerning how Clement would likely construe the

---

24. Priests worked barefoot in the temple, so we cannot presume that Clement's high priest would have something on his feet.

symbolism of the young man's wearing a linen sheet over his naked body. He has not only stripped away the layers of his materiality but has also put on divinity and become "equal to the angels" (ἰσάγγελος; *Strom.* VI.13.105.1; VII.10.57.5, 14.84.2; cf. *Paed.* I.6.36.6).

A SPECIAL RELATIONSHIP OF LOVE

A peculiar aspect of the mystic gospel's narrative of the raising and instruction of the young man is the emphasis on reciprocal love. We are told, first, that the young man's response after Jesus brought him back to life was to look upon Jesus and love him. The subsequent stay in the young man's house contains no reference to Jesus' love for the young man, but that fact is indicated in passing in LGM 2, which refers to this character as "the young man whom Jesus loved." The two statements recall Mark 10:21, where Jesus looks upon the rich man and loves him after learning that this man had obeyed the commandments since his youth. This detail in Mark 10:21 is actually the only place in the Synoptic Gospels where Jesus is said to love one particular person. The raising story in LGM 1 evidently builds on this conception in the direction taken in the Gospel of John's version of this miracle story, where Jesus' special love for Lazarus is emphasized (11:3, 36). As Marvin Meyer has shown, the young man in mystic Mark is essentially a Markan parallel to the Johannine "beloved disciple."[25]

Does Clement describe a special relationship of love between Jesus and a particular disciple? Essentially, yes. He frequently describes the true Gnostic's relationship to Christ in these terms. The most pertinent parallel occurs in one of his most explicit descriptions of the path to perfection, where this intimate relationship applies to the Christian who has succeeded in attaining equality with the angels, at the point when the Gnostic passes through the seventh day to the eighth (i.e., receives instruction in the great mysteries):

> And, in my opinion, the first saving change is that from heathenism (ἐθνῶν) to faith, as I said before; and the second, that from faith to knowledge. And knowledge crosses over to love; hence here loved with lover; what knows with what is known, stand side-by-side. And this being the case, one has already attained the condition of "being equal to the angels." Accordingly, after the highest eminence in the flesh, always changing for the better, he hastens to our father's court, through the holy seventh (day) to the Lord's own (day/dwelling); to be a light, abiding,

25. Meyer, *Secret Gospels*, 135–48.

and continuing eternally, altogether and in every way immutable. (*Strom.* VII.10.57.3–5; cf. 10.55.5—56.1; 11.68.3–5)[26]

Christ and the Gnostic "stand side-by-side" as "loved with lover; what knows with what is known" (εἰς ἀγάπην περαιουμένη, ἐνθένδε ἤδη φίλον φίλῳ τὸ γιγνῶσκον τῷ γιγνωσκομένῳ παρίστησιν). The imagery is surprising in Clement, but let us put it in context.

Clement speaks of love for Christ and God as a trait shared by all Christians. However, he also speaks of a perfect form of love that is a unique attainment of the Gnostic both on earth and in the afterlife. This is perhaps clearest in connection with Clement's allegorical interpretations of the high priest's entry into the holy of holies, where the high priest acquires a new status in relation to Christ as "son" and "friend." This reward is mentioned

26. As translated in Itter, *Esoteric Teaching*, 38, with some modification. Clement describes this transition as "hasten[ing] to our father's court, through the holy seventh (day) (διὰ τῆς ἁγίας ἑβδομάδος) to the Lord's own (day/dwelling) (ἐπὶ τὴν κυριακήν)." This wording seems deliberately ambiguous. The phrase τῆς ἁγίας ἑβδομάδος can also be translated "the holy Hebdomad," in reference to the seven heavens of the material cosmos. In that case, the expression could refer to the Gnostic soul's unimpeded ascent after death through the seven heavens to its allotted abode in the Ogdoad. This inference would explain how one can continue to improve after attaining the highest eminence "in the flesh" (i.e., the soul must separate from the flesh for improvement to continue). And the reference to the Gnostic becoming "a light, abiding, and continuing eternally, altogether and in every way immutable" evokes the heavenly resurrection of the martyr, described in Daniel as "the wise will shine like the brightness of the heavenly expanse. And those bringing many to righteousness will be like the stars forever and ever" (12:2–3). But Clement also ascribes this condition to the living Gnostic in reference to her or his positive effect on the world: "He, then, who has first moderated his passions and trained himself for impassibility, and developed to the beneficence of gnostic perfection, is here equal to the angels. Luminous already, and like the sun shining in the exercise of beneficence, he speeds by righteous knowledge through the love of God to the sacred abode, like as the apostles" (*Strom.* VI.13.105.1). And he speaks of the Gnostic's attainment of the seventh stage of advancement in this life in terms of the separation of the body from the soul. So a reference to the seventh stage or "day" in the education of the Gnostic is warranted too. Moreover, the translation "the holy seventh day" accords with Clement's use of ἑβδομάς and ὀγδοάς in *Strom.* VI.16.138.1–5 to denote the seventh and eighth days in his discussion of how both Saturday and Sunday (the Lord's Day) can qualify as the Sabbath. As Daniélou (*Gospel Message*, 451) notes, the word κυριακή in these passages "is primarily a term for the Lord's Day, but which, as the eighth day, is used to symbolize the eighth sphere, the Ogdoad, the dwelling of the Lord." Hence, with the ambiguous terms ἑβδομάς and κυριακή Clement is describing both the Gnostic's perfection in gnosis by his or her mystical experience of the sacred abode on the symbolic eighth day and the effect of this initiation on the soul's future translation to the highest heaven. As Daniélou puts it, "The soul of the Gnostic, having already passed through these [seven heavens] by its growth in holiness in this life, can now after death traverse them without halting and attain at once the contemplation of God" (ibid.).

only briefly in *Strom.* V.6: "having become son and friend, he is now replenished with insatiable contemplation face to face" (40.1). In the more esoteric description in *Excerpta ex Theodoto*, however, these same titles denote a status equal to the highest angels and are combined with imagery of marital union to denote an especially intimate relationship of love. Once the high priest (representing the true Gnostic after death) has entered the Ogdoad, set aside his spiritual body, and "comes to the knowledge and comprehension of realities . . . it (his soul) is no longer a bride but has become a Logos and rests with the bridegroom (i.e., Christ) together with the first-called and first-created, who are friends by love, sons by instruction and obedience, and brothers by community of origin" (27.5; trans. Casey).[27]

These images call to mind the Valentinian conception of the holy of holies/Ogdoad as a bridal chamber (e.g., *Exc.* 63.1—65.2; 68.1; *Gos. Phil.* 69.14—70.5, 84.14—85.21). Yet even before the Valentinians, this concept of marital union between the soul and the Logos within the immaterial cosmos was already part of the great mysteries in Alexandrian Judaism. According to Philo, the Logos, in its feminine form as Sophia, sows in the soul of higher initiates the seeds of God, which are the Forms, which give birth to virtue, wisdom, immortality, and supreme happiness (see esp. *Cher.* 13.43—14.50; *Abr.* 100-102). Philo saw this marital union of the Gnostic with Sophia as symbolized in the marriages of the patriarchs and their wives.[28] The result here, too, is a group that shares a special degree of friendship with God.[29]

On this matter Philo is close to Plato, who speaks of the visionary recognition of the form of Beauty in terms of seeing it "face to face," of "gaz[ing] upon it in true contemplation and consort[ing] with it (συνόντος αὐτῷ)," with the result "that a man gives birth (τίκτειν) not to the images of virtue (because it is not the image that he will touch) but to the true virtue, because he will touch the truth. And when he has given birth and reared this true virtue, he shall be called the friend of god (θεοφιλεῖ γενέσθαι), and if ever it is given to man to put on immortality, it shall be given to him" (*Symp.* 211d8—212a7).[30] A similar description occurs in Plato's *Rep.* 490a8-b7, on

27. The first-called and first-created (πρωτοκλῆτοι and πρωτόκτιστοι) are a group of seven angels that were created before the other angels and in a condition of perfection and mutual equality; they exist one level below Christ and contemplate him (as the face of God) unceasingly. For discussion, see Bucur, "Divine Face"; Bucur, *Angelomorphic Pneumatology*, 38–42, *passim*.

28. Goodenough, *By Light*, 22–23, 139–40, 147, 157–65, 173, 201–202, 230–31, 239, 249, 268–72. For the interchangeability of Logos and Sophia in Philo's thinking, see pp. 22–23, 158, 160–61.

29. Ibid., 172–73.

30. Finkelberg, "Plato's Language of Love," 244, citing the translation by Michael Joyce in Hamilton and Cairns, eds., *Collected Dialogues of Plato*, 563 (except for the

which Margalit Finkelberg writes: "The terminology of love (ἔρως), intercourse (μιγνύναι), giving birth (γεννᾶν), and travail (ὠδίς), leaves no doubt about Plato's meaning: the culminating point of the final revelation is the sexual union, the 'sacred marriage,' which casts the *erastes*, the philosopher, as the bride. As a result of this union, the *erastes* becomes pregnant with the truth that will be born in due course."[31] As Finkelberg notes, these ideas are what

> the *Symposium* describes as the "greater mysteries of love." Its main elements are: philosophical training accompanying gradual elevation to the knowledge of true being; sudden revelation of true being to the initiate at the climax of such training; and quasi-sexual union, or the "sacred marriage," in which the initiate plays the part of the female partner, as the form that this revelation takes. . . . Plato intended this "most serious" part of his teaching for the use of those few who "are capable of discovering the truth for themselves with a little guidance" (*Ep.* 7.341e.2–3).[32]

Such ideas might even have preceded Plato. It is possible, though uncertain, that Plato's inspiration for this notion was an aspect of the Eleusinian great mysteries, the enacting of a sacred marriage in which the initiates participated vicariously in a "mystical communion" with the goddess.[33] It is difficult to know what exactly occurred in these secret ceremonies, but it is clear that initiates in the great mysteries become beloved of the gods,[34] and the same held for Plato's reconception of *epopteia* as the experience of seeing a form.[35] So Clement's conception of the Gnostic soul's mystic union with Christ in the Ogdoad and attainment of a new quality of friendship and sonship characterized by love is ultimately rooted in the philosophical reconception of the great mysteries, in which the vision of God or *epopteia* involves a quasi-sexual union.

In view of the language of lover and loved in *Strom.* VII.10, we should consider the possibility that Clement is here alluding to Plato's conception of the mysteries in terms of the Ladder of Love. Plato used Eleusinian terms

last two, the Greek words in parentheses were added by Finkelberg; the English words belong to the original translation).

31. Finkelberg, "Plato's Language of Love," 245.

32. Ibid., 256.

33. Willoughby, *Pagan Regeneration*, 52–54 (the phrase "mystical communion" appears on p. 54).

34. Schefer, "Rhetoric," 176–77, 181.

35. See Farrell, "Plato's Use," 130. Also, Plato, *Leg.* 4.716c–d, which explains that one must become like God in order to become dear to God, because like is dear to like.

to describe the soul's ascent to contemplate the form of Beauty, a process by which attraction to particular (male) individuals is transcended in an abstract appreciation of beauty:

> Beginning from obvious beauties he must for the sake of that highest beauty be ever climbing aloft, as on the rungs of a ladder, from one to two, and from two to all beautiful bodies; from personal beauty he proceeds to beautiful observances, from observance to beautiful learning, and from learning at last to that particular study which is concerned with the beautiful itself and that alone; so that in the end he comes to know the very essence of beauty. (*Symp.* 211c–d [Lamb, LCL]; see also *Phaedr.* 253c2–6)

The Ladder of Love is Plato's most prominent analogy to illustrate the lesser and great mysteries of philosophy, and the philosophical context which it presupposes is that of an intimate relationship between a teacher and his student, the *erastēs* and *erōmenos*. As Piotr Ashwin-Siejkowski explains,

> the spiritual climax ... described [in *Strom.* VII.10] as φίλον φίλῳ τὸ γιγνῶσκον τῷ γιγνωσκομένῳ ... recalls the well-known Platonic theme of a particular understanding of friendship and love. This phrase recalls the meeting or even communion of the two: the lover (ἐραστής) with the loved one (ἐρώμενος). In Clement's understanding of friendship between the Gnostic and the divine Logos it is possible to recognize the classical topos ... Clement did not, however, incorporate the element of physical attraction in his project, which is important to Platonic theory.[36]

Clement's capacity to adapt Plato's Ladder of Love to Christian sensibilities is evident in *Strom.* IV.18.116.2: "For ... he who in chaste love looks on beauty, thinks not that the flesh is beautiful, but the spirit, admiring, as I judge, the body as an image, by whose beauty he transports himself to the Artist, and to the true beauty; exhibiting the sacred symbol, the bright impress of righteousness to the angels that wait on the ascension." Clement believes that a beautiful body can be appreciated in a nonsexual way as an image or copy of the form of Beauty, and that this recognition transports the admirer to the Logos, the Artist who fashioned all beautiful images and is "the only true Beauty."[37] Clement goes on to describe "the bright impress

36. Ashwin-Siejkowski, *Clement of Alexandria*, 184–85.

37. The implication that the Logos itself is true beauty is stated explicitly in *Paed.* III.7.37.1; cf. II.12.129.4, where the Logos reveals "the true beauty, 'which eye has not seen and ear has not heard,'" which is Clement's Pauline phrase for the pneumatic

of righteousness" (cf. the golden plate in *Exc.* 27) and the glory that shone from Moses' face as physically visible manifestations of inner goodness; his point is clearer in the *Paedagogus*, where he explains how only an excellent character is truly beautiful and how "excellence alone appears through the beautiful body, and blossoms out in the flesh, exhibiting the amiable comeliness of self-control, whenever the character like a beam of light gleams in the form" (II.12.121.3–4). Clement attributes this nonsexual physical beauty to Jesus:

> And that the Lord Himself was uncomely in aspect, the Spirit testifies [through Isaiah] (Isa 53:2): "And we saw Him, and he had [neither physique nor beauty] (οὐκ εἶχεν εἶδος οὐδὲ κάλλος), but his form was mean, inferior to men." Yet who was more admirable than the Lord? But it was not the beauty of the flesh visible to the eye, but the true beauty of both soul and body, which He exhibited, which in the former is beneficence; in the latter—that is, the flesh—immortality. (*Paed.* III.1.3.3)[38]

LGM 1 AND CLEMENT'S PROGRAM OF PERFECTION

At this point we can well appreciate how Clement's allegorical interpretations of scriptural parallels to phrases and images in LGM 1 readily combine to form an interpretation of this passage as illustrating, indeed justifying, his particular program of perfection. The young man's return to life and desire "to be with" Jesus would represent what Clement calls "the first saving change" from unbelief to faith. The weeklong stay in the young man's house would represent the second saving change, from faith to knowledge, including the crossing of knowledge over to love. Jesus and the young man enter his house "because he was rich," meaning, for Clement, because this man needed to purge his soul of its spiritual infirmities and passions through the cultivation of reason and virtue. The young man completes these lesser mysteries "after six days," attaining the state of passionlessness equivalent to an angel. In the real world, this was a lengthy process of divesting ("stripping")

realities above the noetic world (*Strom.* VI.8.68.1). Hence the specifically Christian aspects of the great mysteries of the immaterial realm replace Plato's epoptic vision of the form of Beauty as the top of the Ladder of Love.

38. Cf. Plato's description of the effect that the ugly Socrates's inner beauty had on some young men. As the character Alcibiades explains, once this beauty is glimpsed, the unattractive philosopher becomes so desirable to young men like himself (he lists several) that they actively pursue him, behaving more like an amorous lover than a beloved (*Symp.* 216e–218a). For discussion, see Finkelberg, "Plato's Language of Love," 240–41, 245–46.

the soul of all material attachments while studying the mysteries of the material cosmos through an encyclical education. The completion of this process is represented by the young man putting on the single linen garment, "the 'tunic of incorruptibility' of which the Pedagogue speaks (I.9.84.3)."[39] At this point, corresponding to the transition from the symbolic seventh day to the eighth, knowledge, says Clement, passes into love, and lover and beloved stand together. The young man's return to Jesus for private instruction in the evening of the seventh day could readily signify this transition for Clement, the last "rung" in his nonsexual conception of the Ladder of Love. Viewed from this perspective, the earlier phrase "looking upon him loved him" would represent the initial rung of this ladder, where the young man's ability to see Jesus' inner beauty through his appearance elicits a "chase love" that will eventually transport him to a mystic union with true Beauty, the Logos. The subsequent reference to this character as "the young man whom Jesus loved" in LGM 2:1 would reinforce this philosophical topos, conveying the unique status of friend and son that the Gnostic possesses.[40] Like the high priest when he dons a simple linen robe and enters the noetic realm of the holy of holies, the young man now receives instruction from Jesus in the mystery of the kingdom of God, which for Clement refers to the great mysteries of this realm.

THE BAPTISMAL CONNOTATIONS
OF THE LINEN SHEET

Now that we have finished examining the main parallels between LGM 1 and Clement's various allegorical interpretations, we may consider a less conspicuous yet remarkably precise parallel between the implicit baptismal symbolism of the young man's linen sheet in LGM, as I have described this in earlier works, and Clement's symbolic exposition of the high priest's immersion prior to putting on the linen tunic, which is conveyed in *Strom.* V.6.39.4—40.1:

> (The linen tunic represents), it seems to me, the Levite and Gnostic as a "ruler" over the other priests—those priests washed in water and dressed in faith alone and expecting their own abode—he himself distinguishing the noetic things from those of sense perception, (and), according to a hierarchical progression, hastening past the other priests to the entrance to the

39. Le Boulluec, "Lettre sur L'Évangile secret' de Marc," 39.

40. Cf. the saying "My mystery is for me and the sons of my house" in *Strom.* V.10.63.7, which Clement says comes from "a certain gospel."

noetic (world), to wash himself from the things here below—not in water, as he was previously cleansed on being enrolled in the tribe of Levi, but already by the gnostic Word. (trans. Kotansky)

On the literal level this passage contrasts two kinds of priests and two kinds of immersions: the ordinary Levite, who was washed in water at the time of his enrolment as a priest,[41] and the high priest, who formerly underwent this immersion but has since washed himself in another way. On the allegorical level, the Levite represents ordinary Christians, who have faith but not gnosis, and the high priest represents the Gnostic, who is "clothed" not only in faith but also in gnosis, having acquired the ability to perceive the higher archetypal realities (the Forms of the noetic world) that lie behind the objects of sense.

The key to Clement's comparison between these two types of priests lies in the appearance of the holy of holies attire. On ordinary days, the high priest wears a colourful and highly ornate robe that sets him apart from ordinary priests. But on this day his simple linen garment resembles the linen garment worn by the other priests.[42] It therefore "represents the Levite and Gnostic." The affinity between ordinary priest and high priest that Clement intends to underscore has to do with the connection between these linen tunics and immersion. Leviticus 8:6–13 describes Moses washing Aaron's sons in water and then putting the linen tunic on them at the time of their enrolment as priests. Leviticus 16:4 similarly describes the high priest putting on his special linen tunic after washing his body in water. The former act is a type of Christian baptism, whereas the latter signifies immersion in "the gnostic Word," a washing "in knowledge," as Clement later clarifies with reference to 1 Cor 6:11 (*Strom.* VII.14.86.5).[43] Since Clement preserves the original connection in Lev 8:6–13 between washing and clothing in the phrase "those priests washed in water and dressed in faith alone and expecting their own abode," we may suspect that Clement perceives a resemblance between this linen tunic and a garment put on after Christian baptism, although we have no unambiguous (i.e., non-metaphorical) evidence for Christians putting on a special garment following baptism prior to the fourth century.[44] Whatever the actual practice in Clement's church,

41. Not all Levites were priests, but Clement uses "Levite" to refer to priests in general. The Hebrew Scriptures are inconsistent on this point. See Berry, "Priests and Levites."

42. See Exod 28:40–43 and Ezek 44:17–18; cf. Lev 6:10.

43. Kovacs, "Concealment," 429 n. 75.

44. As noted, e.g., by Jeffery, *Secret Gospel of Mark Unveiled*, 116. We have plenty of *metaphorical* evidence for an early Christian practice of taking off old garments and putting on new garments to signify the change in status accomplished through baptism,

in this literary context the linen tunic is baptismal. With respect to the ordinary Christian, the tunic signifies simple faith and an inferior form of salvation within the Hebdomad (the holy place of the celestial temple, which is accessible only to Christians/priests), which is acquired through a literal baptism. With respect to the Gnostic, however, this tunic signifies faith perfected into gnosis and a superior form of salvation within the Ogdoad (the celestial holy of holies), which is acquired through *a metaphorical baptism.* Clement's point is that the "immersion" which precedes the high priest's entry into the innermost sanctuary is analogous to but also different from the church's rite of initiation: "not in water, as he was previously cleansed on being enrolled in the tribe of Levi, but already by the gnostic Word." In other words, for Clement the high priest's act of removing his regular attire, washing, and putting on a linen tunic recalls his earlier literal baptism in water but actually represents a metaphorical baptism "from the things here below" that is a prerequisite for entering the noetic world.

The Platonic Conception of This Metaphorical Baptism

Clement describes this metaphorical baptism in terms of the high priest "hastening past the other priests to the entrance to the noetic (world), to wash himself from the things here below." This imagery of hurrying from this world to the world of Ideas and the characterization of this escape from materiality as a purification have a strong Platonic flavour and are part of a related system of ideas upon which Clement founded his conception of the lesser mysteries. In Plato's *Phaedo* 64a—69e, for instance, Socrates describes philosophy as a purification of the soul that constitutes a flight from the world. As a purification, philosophy is "the separation (so far as is possible) of the soul from the body" (67b–c, 65e)—that is, the attempt to disconnect one's soul from the body's distractions (emotions, desires, ailments; 66b–c) and unreliable sense perceptions (66a). It is only by shedding these impediments to knowledge created by the body that the soul can become free to see reality as it truly is. Socrates' larger point in this argument is that this practice of separating the soul from the body is a form of dying (64a, 67d,

beginning with Paul: "as many of you as were baptized into Christ have put on Christ" (Gal 3:27). Clement uses this imagery in *Paed.* I.6.32.4: "Truly, then, are we the children of God, who have put aside the old man, and stripped off the garment of wickedness, and put on the immortality of Christ; that we may become a new, holy people by regeneration, and may keep the man undefiled." For an argument that Christian rituals for baptism were based on the Israelite rituals of priestly ordination and that baptized Christians, like newly ordained priests, put on white garments already in the first century, see Gieschen, "Baptismal Praxis."

e), and like the purifications of the Eleusinian mysteries, it allows the soul to rise upward and "dwell with gods" after death (69b–c).[45] Socrates also describes this flight from the world in Plato's *Theaetetus* 176a–b:

> Evils, Theodorus, can never be done away with, for the good must always have its contrary; nor have they any place in the divine world; but they must needs haunt this region of our mortal nature. That is why we should make all speed to take flight from this world to the other; and that means becoming like the divine so far as we can, and that again is to become righteous with the help of wisdom.[46]

Clement frequently appeals to these ideas. He cites the former speech later on in book V of the *Stromateis*: "And is not, on this account, philosophy rightly called by Socrates the practice of Death? For he who neither employs his eyes in the exercise of thought, nor draws [anything] from his other senses, but with pure mind itself applies to objects, practises the true philosophy" (*Strom.* V.11.67.1–2; see also II.7.34.2; III.3.17.3—18.1; IV.3.11.2, 12.5–6; VII.12.71.3). Clement paraphrases the latter speech in *Strom.* II.22.133.3: "And having in the *Theaetetus* admitted that evils make the circuit of mortal nature and of this spot, he adds: 'Wherefore we must try to flee hence as soon as possible. For flight is likeness to God as far as possible. And likeness is to become holy and just with wisdom.'" The main themes connected to this flight—purifying the soul of the impediments of the body, and assimilation to God—are the goals of the lesser mysteries as Clement understands them.[47]

That these ideas form the background to Clement's interpretation of the high priest's washing in gnosis is confirmed in Clement's subsequent reference to this washing in *Strom.* VII, where he interprets Paul's intention in 1 Cor 6:9–11. Referring to the words "But you were washed, you were sanctified, you were justified in the name of the Lord Jesus Christ and in the Spirit of our God" (v. 11), Clement wrote:

45. On this theme, see Reale, *Plato and Aristotle*, 157–59.

46. As translated in Cornford, *Plato's Theory of Knowledge*, 87.

47. On the practice of death in Clement, see Lilla, *Clement of Alexandria*, 164–68; Itter, *Esoteric Teaching*, 194–97. Cf. Philo, *Leg.* 3.15.54–56 ("the soul which loves God, having put off the body and the affections which are dear to it, and having fled a long way from them, chooses a foundation and a sure ground for its abode . . . On this account the high priest will not come into the holy of holies clad in a garment reaching his feet, but having put off the robe of opinion and vain fancy of the soul . . . will come forward naked."); 23.90–91; *Migr.* 2.7–9 ("Depart therefore from the earthly parts which envelop you, O my friend, fleeing from that base and polluted prison house of the body, and from the keepers as it were of the prison, its pleasures and appetites").

> "But you have been washed," not simply as the [others], but with
> knowledge; you have cast off the passions of the soul, in order to
> become assimilated, as far as possible, to the goodness of God's
> providence (cf. Plato, *Theaet.* 176b) by long-suffering, and by
> forgiveness "towards the just and the unjust" (Matt 5:45) . . .
> "But you have been sanctified." For he who has come to this state
> is in a condition to be holy, falling into none of the passions in
> any way, but as it were already disembodied (ἀσάρκῳ) and [hav-
> ing become, in this respect, above this earth in holiness] (καὶ
> ἄνω τῆσδε τῆς γῆς ἁγίῳ γεγονότι). (*Strom.* VII.14.86.5—87.1)

Further corroboration appears in Clement's other description of the high
priest's entry into the holy of holies in *Exc.* 27. Whereas *Strom.* V.6 envisions
the Gnostic's earthly efforts to surpass other Christians (priests) through
a washing in gnosis in preparation to apprehend the noetic world, *Exc.* 27
envisions the corresponding stages of the soul's progression in the afterlife, that is, its ascent through the Hebdomad and entry into the Ogdoad.
Clement describes the transition into "the noetic world" in terms of the
priest "laying aside" the body, which, while in the Hebdomad, "has become
pure and light in weight through the purification of the soul." The "naked"
(disembodied) soul then "passes into the pneumatic (realms) and becomes
now truly rational and high priestly" (trans. Kotansky). Thus, in *Exc.* 27 the
overarching theme of purifying the soul for its separation from the human
body is completely explicit.

Accordingly, we may conclude that Clement understood the high
priest's metaphorical baptism (the lesser mysteries) in terms of Plato's goal
of assimilation to God through the separation of the body from the soul. By
"putting off" his regular robe (materiality) and immersing (in gnosis), he is
allegorically purifying the soul of all bodily impediments to the truth (the
senses and the passions) so that he can perceive realities by the mind alone.
This purification results in the transition from the human and material to
the angelic and immaterial, which is represented by putting on the linen
robe. In reality, he is still a human living in the flesh, so what we are really
talking about is the condition that Clement calls "equal to the angels."

Although Clement's overall conception of the high priest's act of immersing before entering the holy of holies is Platonic, Clement nevertheless
Christianizes Plato's "practice of death" by equating it with the way of the
cross:

> He called the crowd with his disciples, and said to them, "If any
> want to become my followers, let them deny themselves and take
> up their cross and follow me. For those who want to save their

life will lose it; and those who lose their life for my sake, and for the sake of the gospel, will save it. For what does it profit them to gain the whole world and forfeit their life?" (Mark 8:34–36)

"For the minds of those even who are deemed grave, pleasure makes waxen," according to Plato; since "each pleasure and pain nails to the body the soul" of the man [who] does not sever and crucify himself from the passions. "He that loses his life," says the Lord, "shall save it"; either giving it up by exposing it to danger for the Lord's sake, as He did for us, or loosing it from fellowship with its habitual life. For if you would loose, and withdraw, and separate (for this is what the cross means) your soul from the delight and pleasure that is in this life, you will possess it, found and resting in the looked-for hope. And this would be the [practice] of death, if we would be content with those desires which are measured according to nature alone . . . (*Strom.* II.20.108.2—109.1)

And, in fine, the Lord's discipline draws the soul away gladly from the body, even if it wrench itself away in its removal. "For he that loveth his life shall lose it, and he that loseth his life shall find it," if we only join that which is mortal of us with the immortality of God. It is the will of God (that we should attain) the knowledge of God, which is the communication of immortality. He therefore, who, in accordance with the word of repentance, knows his life to be sinful will lose it—losing it from sin, from which it is wrenched; but losing it, will find it, according to the obedience which lives again to faith, but dies to sin. This, then, is what it is "to find one's life," "to know one's self." (*Strom.* IV.6.27.1–3)

In platonic language, the metaphorical baptism of *Strom.* V.6.39.4 is "that philosophic dying, by which alone the soul even after death is fitted for incorporeal existence."[48] In the language of the Gospel, it is the way of the cross.

The Mystic Gospel's Conception of the Linen Sheet

The specific baptismal significance that Clement attributes to the high priest's immersion and change of clothing presents a striking parallel to the significance of the linen sheet in LGM 1:11. As I argued in *Mark's Other Gospel*, this garment signifies baptism, but not a literal baptism in water.

48. Zeller, *Plato and the Older Academy*, 440.

In good Markan fashion, the juxtaposition created by the addition of LGM 1 and 2 around the story of James and John's request for places of honour implies that these two episodes are mutually interpretive; the significance of the young man's costume is conveyed indirectly by Jesus' question, "Are you able to drink the cup that I drink, or be baptized with the baptism that I am baptized with?" (Mark 10:38–39), which imparts a baptismal signifi-cance in the figurative sense of immersion in Jesus' sufferings and death. The numerous parallels between LGM 1 and the story of the discovery of the open tomb (Mark 16:1–8), moreover, indicate that the young man's linen sheet, like the one wrapped around Jesus' corpse in 15:46, is this man's former burial wrapping.[49] Thus, when he reappears in the same linen sheet in Gethsemane and attempts to "follow with" Jesus as Jesus is being led away under arrest (14:51–52), he is conveying his intention to be baptized with Jesus' baptism at the very point when Jesus has accepted "this cup" and is "betrayed into the hands of sinners" (14:32–42). In this way, the incident of the young man's flight is incorporated within the larger theme developed in Mark's central section that anyone who would follow (ἀκολουθεῖν) Jesus must deny one's self and take up his or her cross and follow him (8:34).[50] This is the true nature of the challenge that Jesus put to the rich man in 10:21. Thus in both Clement's tabernacle allegory and the mystic gospel, the linen garment is a baptismal garment used figuratively to symbolize the way of the cross. The difference is that for Clement the linen garment signifies the completion of this figurative baptism, whereas in mystic Mark the linen garment signifies the figurative baptism itself.

Clement's overly cerebral interpretation of this "way," which he terms "the gnostic martyrdom" (*Strom.* IV.4.15.4), does not exclude actual mar-tyrdom from the Gnostic's calling—he considers martyrdom the highest expression of love for Christ (IV.9); rather, his ideal is for physical death to occur as the culmination of a life spent separating the soul from the body and the world, a discipline that requires leaving behind "kindred, and wealth, and every possession, in order to lead a life free from passion" (IV.4.15.3–6). Le Boulluec reasons that Clement would read LGM 2 in terms of the true

49. These two incidents, which form a pair of frame stories around the passion narrative, share a linen sheet, a grouping of three women (the third of whom is Salome), a dead man buried in a rock-hewn tomb, a large stone that blocks the door of the tomb and is later rolled aside, a raising miracle involving both Jesus and an unnamed young man, and the verb "wearing" (περιβεβλημένος) to introduce the young man's unusual attire.

50. Brown, *Mark's Other Gospel*, esp. 145–46, 157–58, 165–75, 218; Brown, "Mys-tical Gospel of Mark (Part One)," 7–9.

Gnostic's need to abandon all worldly ties.[51] I agree, and I would add that Clement could make sense of the young man's naked flight in Gethsemane (Mark 14:50–52) and reappearance in the open tomb (16:5–7) within this framework as symbolizing the Gnostic's actual death through martyrdom and his special heavenly reward. Seized by the crowd while bravely attempting to follow Jesus after the other disciples have forsaken him, the young man "take[s] flight from this world to the other," abandoning his linen sheet, the symbol of his purity and "equality with the angels." "For flight is likeness to God as far as possible." His soul, "wrenched" from its body, departs "naked" of all attachments, only to become "a body of the power" within the Ogdoad (*Exc.* 27.3)—that is, an actual angel, which is signified by his reappearance as a divine messenger in a white robe.

CONCLUSIONS

When we consider how Clement, in his undisputed writings, interpreted scriptural phrases and story elements that also occur in LGM 1 and 2, the result is an internally consistent narrative in which this young man undergoes Clement's program of perfection.

In addition to the overall concordance between LGM 1 and 2 and Clement's soteriological scheme, there are several subtle parallels. Clement's unusual choice of the seven-day priestly rite of purification for corpse-defilement to illustrate his program of perfection is particularly intriguing given that both Jesus and the young man were exposed to this form of defilement by being inside a tomb (Num 19:11, 16).[52] If one imagines that they are following the regulations for purification, as their seclusion might suggest, then they would be pure again "when it is evening" on the seventh day, that is, when the young man returns wearing only a linen sheet. Similarly, the high priestly ritual that Clement uses to illustrate his program of perfection—disrobing, washing, putting on a linen tunic, entering the inner sanctuary—coincides in some subtle ways with the details of LGM 1. Not only does Clement focus on a single linen garment, ignoring three other garments mentioned in Lev 16:4, but he also associates the high priest's entry into the holy of holies with the transition from the Hebdomad to the Ogdoad, which precisely fits the timing of the nocturnal instruction in LGM 1. Finally, the linen garment in both LGM 1 and the *Stromateis* is a baptismal metaphor that symbolizes the way of the cross.

51. Le Boulluec, "Lettre sur L'Évangile secret' de Marc," 39–40.

52. Josephus, *Ant.* 3.11.3 indicates that Palestinian Jews in this condition would seclude themselves in a house during this period.

It is worth mentioning, too, that some of the passages that are most significant to this interpretation are themselves linked in Clement's thinking. His exposition of the seven days of purification for corpse-contaminated priests is connected to the Day of Atonement rite by his odd suggestion that the number seven could refer not just to the stages of salvation but also to "the time" which "through the seven periods enumerated returns to the [consummate] rest" (*Strom.* IV.25.159.2), that is, the seven weeks of years that precede the Jubilee year, a yearlong Sabbath rest. Leviticus describes these periods so:

> You shall count off seven weeks of years, seven times seven years, so that the period of seven weeks of years gives forty-nine years. Then you shall have the trumpet sounded loud; on the tenth day of the seventh month—on the day of atonement—you shall have the trumpet sounded throughout all your land. And you shall hallow the fiftieth year and you shall proclaim liberty throughout the land to all its inhabitants. It shall be a jubilee for you: you shall return, every one of you, to your property and every one of you to your family. That fiftieth year shall be a jubilee for you: you shall not sow, or reap the aftergrowth, or harvest the unpruned vines. (Lev 25:8–11)

By associating the seven days of purification with the 49 years, Clement equates the eighth day with the Day of Atonement rite that inaugurates the consummate repose, as if the former priestly rite culminates in the latter high priestly rite inside the holy of holies. Similarly, his description of how the appearance of beauty "transports" a Christian "to the Artist, to the true beauty" disjunctively concludes, "exhibiting the sacred symbol, the bright impress of righteousness to the angels that wait on the ascension," which alludes to his conception in *Exc.* 27.1 of how the aspiring Gnostic (as regular priest) progresses through the Hebdomad to the Ogdoad by displaying the lustre of his spiritual body (the golden plate worn by the high priest on his turban) to "the Heavenly Powers and the Authorities" that guard the ascent. In Clement's mind, the Ladder of Love is another way of envisioning the seven "days" of purification (in the church or the Hebdomad), which culminate in the high priest's entry into the holy of holies. If we suppose that Clement had spent time puzzling out the meaning of LGM 1 by interpreting it in relation to similar Scriptures, these strange exegetical choices and associations make sense.

The point of comparing the "spiritual" (allegorical) meanings that Clement ascribes to various elements that also occur in LGM 1 was to test how likely it is that he read and interpreted this text. I proposed at the outset that if the spiritual meanings that he ascribes to parallel elements in other Scriptures make little sense when applied to this story, it would be problematic to conclude that he knew this gospel and wrote this letter; but if these elements combine to convey some sense of the missing "true interpretation," it would be most reasonable to conclude that he did read this story and that it influenced his interpretations of those Scriptures. As it turns out, the richness and consistency of the resulting spiritual interpretation and its concordance with both every facet of Clement's program of perfection and the life-setting for the mystic gospel described in the letter (initiation in the great mysteries through exegesis that leads into "the innermost sanctuary of the sevenfold veiled truth") satisfy any reasonable standard of proof that Clement knew the mystic gospel and therefore wrote the *Letter to Theodore*.

ADDENDUM: MORTON SMITH'S THOUGHTS ON AN ALLEGORICAL READING OF LGM 1

Those who are familiar with Morton Smith's two books on the "secret" gospel know that he followed Cyril C. Richardson's suggestion in treating Mark 10:13–45 + LGM 1 as having a homiletic meaning relating to the baptism of neophytes. These books do not consider how one might read these passages allegorically, the way Clement's true Gnostic would, but Smith's desk copy of *Clement of Alexandria and a Secret Gospel of Mark*, which is preserved at the Jewish Theological Seminary, shows that that question eventually occurred to him. In the margin at the bottom of p. 169, where he was outlining this homiletic reading, he wrote a note to himself offering a suggestion for what an allegorical reading might look like (the portions in square brackets are my clarifications):

> How far is it safe to allegorize Mk. 10.17–34 + the resurrection story of the secret Gospel? I am tempted to say that when God revealed himself as lawgiver [= Mark 10:17–19] the Jews kept the Mosaic Law [= Mark 10:20]. Therefore God loved them [= Mark 10:21a] and revealed to them the deeper requirements of the Law—give all you have, follow me (cf. Mt. 5) [= Mark 10:21b]. This they refused to keep [= Mark 10:22] and therefore spiritually died [= LGM 1:1]. Accordingly God, because he loved them, descended into their tomb (the physical world) in human form (as Jesus) and took them by the hand and raised them from the dead [= LGM 1:1–7]. Therefore they now love him [= LGM 1:8], receive his mystery [= LGM 1:10–12], enter the kingdom, & are beyond the Law [= Smith's own theory

about LGM 1:10–12 representing a baptismal mystery rite that
results in freedom from the law].

Notice that he ignored LGM 2 altogether (which also did not fit into
his homiletic reading). These speculations show that Smith had no inkling
that Clement's writings contain the basis for a consistent allegorical reading
of LGM 1 + 2 and that this narrative could have served as the principal
scriptural basis for Clement's program of perfection. Indeed, there is nothing particularly Alexandrian or Clementine in Smith's speculation, and he
was not even sure whether a fully allegorical reading was warranted.

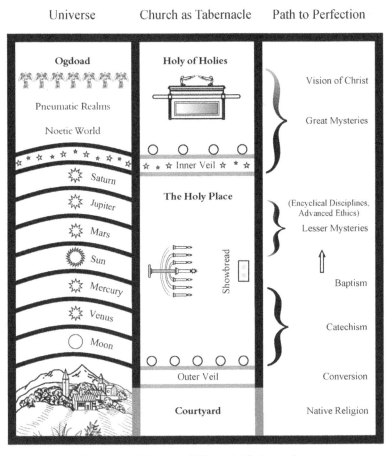

Figure 6.1: Clement of Alexandria's Cosmology

– 7 –

Pseudo-Peter and Persecution

(Counter-)Evaluations of Suffering in the *Coptic Apocalypse of Peter* (NHC VII,3) and the *Letter of Peter to Philip* (NHC VIII,2)

— Pamela Mullins Reaves —

IN WHAT FOLLOWS, I examine how concerns regarding persecution and suffering likely contributed to Peter's role as the pseudo-author of two early Christian texts: the Coptic *Apocalypse of Peter* (NHC VII,3) and the *Letter of Peter to Philip* (NHC VIII,2; Cod. Tch. 1.1—9.15). I show how both texts rely on and, to some extent, sustain the expectation of Christian suffering, but revise the nature and value of the experience. Peter's insights on suffering are achieved through each text's revelation regarding the crucifixion. These clarifications on the crucifixion diminish the relative value of physical suffering and, relatedly, martyrdom. Moreover, clues of intra-Christian discord within both texts, including *Apoc. Pet.*'s criticism of encouragement for martyrdom, also suggest that varied views on suffering are a key source of debate.

The selection of Peter as the pseudonymous recipient of Christ's revelation is thus especially relevant. I argue that this choice is guided by both his central role in proto-orthodox circles and his association with suffering in established traditions, including reports of his own martyrdom (Acts, 1

Pet, 1 Clem., Acts Pet.). Apoc. Pet. and Ep. Pet. Phil. counter these traditions and adapt others in seemingly deliberate attempts to redefine Peter's role as a key martyr, or witness, who receives and conveys special revelation. In doing so, these texts employ pseudonymity as a strategy for challenging alternative early Christian perspectives that value suffering and martyrdom.

To begin, I examine Apoc. Pet. more fully, due in part to its more extensive treatment of the relevant issues. I follow with a discussion of Ep. Pet. Phil., drawing on parallels with Apoc. Pet. as relevant. For both texts, I consider: 1. the nature and evaluation of suffering, both for Christ and his followers; and 2. how the role of pseudo-Peter, as the recipient of revelation, aligns with such perspectives on suffering, particularly in the context of intra-Christian discourse and debates.

THE COPTIC *APOCALYPSE OF PETER*

Apoc. Pet. depicts a situation of persecution within the early Christian community. Notes of oppression are, of course, typical of early Jewish and Christian apocalypses. What is striking in the case of Apoc. Pet. is the identity of the oppressor: fellow Christians, rather than Roman authorities, are the source of concern. The author's audience is cast as persecuted Christians; physical suffering, however, is not celebrated as part of their plight.

Still, the question of suffering dominates the apocalypse, beginning with Peter's initial visionary sequence. Apoc. Pet. opens with the Savior sitting in the temple alongside Peter, who is designated as the recipient of his special revelation (70.14—72.4).[1] Peter then sees priests, among others, rushing toward him and the Savior with stones (72.5-9). The prospect of physical harm, possibly death, disturbs Peter, but a correction by the Savior follows (72.9-21) as well as an additional vision of "new light" (72.23). Peter's initial understanding of his experience is flawed, prompting the Savior to offer further instruction, a pattern that continues throughout Apoc. Pet. As the value of persecution is sustained, the significance of suffering is challenged. The apocalyptic expectation of reward in the subsequent age encourages Peter and his cohort of "little ones" to persevere in their current situation. At the same time, there is no indication that a suffering death is the anticipated or celebrated outcome of the persecution.

---

1. The English translations of Apoc. Pet. are my own, in close consultation with the critical edition of Havelaar, *Coptic Apocalypse of Peter*. Additional critical editions consulted include the Coptic text and English translation of Brashler, "Apocalypse of Peter"; and Havelaar, "Apokalypse des Petrus"; and the English translation of Meyer, "Revelation of Peter."

This includes Peter's own death, which is not forecast. Rather, the author of *Apoc. Pet.* resituates Petrine traditions for his own purposes. One example of this strategy is an apparent allusion to Peter's threefold denial of Jesus (Mark 14:30 par; John 13:38). *Apoc. Pet.*'s version predicts that the Savior will *correct* Peter three times in the course of their night (71.34—72.4).[2] Peter's immediate response evokes the Gospel narratives. He expresses his fear of death, noting his vision of priests and others coming toward them with stones (72.5–9). Though the Gospel setting of pending persecution is maintained, the adaptation of the threefold denial at the beginning of the text shifts the focus to progressive instruction and its challenges in *Apoc. Pet.*

The Savior's instruction of Peter that follows emphasizes spiritual—or, in this case, sensory—awareness over bodily experience. The Savior directs Peter to cover his eyes in order to comprehend the "blindness" (*mentbelle*) of his opposition (72.13–17). By shielding his physical view, Peter ultimately gains clarification. He reports, "Fear with joy came to me, for I saw a new light greater than the light of day" (72.22–25). A comparable experience follows, in which the Savior instructs Peter to listen in an elevated way (73.6–8). The Savior's instruction thus conveys how Peter can, as Gerard P. Luttikhuizen puts it, "inwardly transcend visible reality," appropriately casting this experience as preparation for Peter's subsequent vision of the crucifixion.[3] But it also serves as a broader lesson, instructing the reader how to approach life as a Christian, which involves attention to one's spiritual development.[4] Peter's initial fear and anticipation of death symbolize his ignorance. The Savior responds with a reminder of the persecutor's error, rather than with any comment regarding Peter's own death.

The correction in the scene sets the stage for *Apoc. Pet.*'s critique of other Christians. The author highlights a range of misguided behaviors, which, I assert, includes physical martyrdom; those who encourage it are

2. Havelaar (*Coptic Apocalypse of Peter*, 83) doubts the connection with Peter's traditional Gospel betrayals, primarily based on the lack of consistent language. The commonalities, however, are sufficient to evoke the Gospel scene: in addition to the common setting, the presence of "three times" occurs alongside the reference to "this night." We should not expect the scene to have the traditional meaning for the author of *Apoc. Pet.*, since he often revises the Petrine tradition for his own purposes. Nicklas ("'Gnostic' Perspectives," 213) offers a useful reading of the Gospel revision. He writes that the denial "is not understood as a sign of weakness, but a sign that Peter does not want to know the fleshly Jesus, and so can be worthy of becoming chosen as the decisive recipient of revelation."

3. Luttikhuizen ("Suffering Jesus," 191) highlights the way Peter learns through the spiritual, rather than physical, side of his senses.

4. On this point, see also Schoenborn, *Diverbium Salutis*.

particular targets. The most substantial portion of *Apoc. Pet.* (73.10–81.3) is best characterized as a description of the emergence of error (73.26) within Christianity. Among the fellow Christians that the author of *Apoc. Pet.* criticizes are those who "cling to the name of a dead one (*refmoout*)" (74.13–14). While thinking that they will become "pure," they will, according to the author, in fact become "defiled" (74.15–16) and "will be ruled heretically (*mentheresis*)" (74.21–22). Divergent views on Christ are at least one element that fosters division among Christians. In this case, the dead one almost certainly refers to the crucified figure, whom the author of *Apoc. Pet.* emphasizes is not the Savior. This particular passage also implicates leaders in the division of the community. As part of the heretical rule, these misguided Christians will "lapse into a name of the error and into the hand of an evil schemer with a doctrine of many forms" (74.16–20). The key elements reflected in this passage—erroneous understandings of Christ, succumbing to error, and faulty leadership—recur throughout *Apoc. Pet.* and reflect intra-Christian conflict.

There have been a number of efforts to classify the opponents in *Apoc. Pet.*, but few attempts to offer a substantial explanation of the nature of this dispute. In one of the more thorough, recent discussions of group dynamics in *Apoc. Pet.*, Henriette Havelaar attributes the break in the community to "explicitly deviating beliefs," specifically divergent understandings of the Passion.[5] I agree that distinct interpretations of the crucifixion seem to relate, and possibly contribute, to the schism (as I discuss below). But there appear to be other factors involved as well, including the prospect of persecution. Divergent views about what it means to be a Christian, particularly in terms of practical matters—how one should behave and who holds authority—seem to have contributed significantly to the intra-Christian rift. Moreover, the doctrinal differences might have been extended as a product of the split, rather than its cause.[6]

The author of *Apoc. Pet.* expresses frustration over the efforts of other Christians, not only for their claims of exclusivity (79.14–16), but also for their capacity to mislead fellow Christians, with potentially dire consequences. One hazard of their misguidance appears to be the unnecessary suffering

5. She explains, "In the course of time a conflict concerning doctrine must have arisen, as a result of which the Petrine Christians were forced to leave the parent group" (Havelaar, *Coptic Apocalypse of Peter*, 201, 203–204).

6. One might deduce this based on *Apoc Pet.*'s reliance on canonical passion narratives. Though they appear in *Apoc. Pet.* as substantially altered, these proto-orthodox traditions also seem to have been valued by the author and his community at some point. I am not suggesting that differences in belief were not apparent early on; rather, such distinctions within the group likely became heightened and more significant over time.

of Christians, including exposure to persecution and physical martyrdom. Martyrdom itself is never explicitly referenced, somewhat surprising given that language of suffering permeates *Apoc. Pet.* Many scholars thus exhibit limited interest in *Apoc. Pet.*'s references to persecution,[7] but a few do recognize the threats of suffering as implicit indications of martyrdom.[8]

A series of passages, which I examine below, support the view that martyrdom and its celebration are problematic for the author of *Apoc. Pet.* The implicit nature of the references makes it difficult to identify martyrdom definitively as the key issue; still, the accumulation of evidence, read in the context of the apocalypse, persuasively points toward physical suffering as problematic. By establishing enthusiasm for martyrdom as a critical point of division in *Apoc. Pet.*, I set the stage for understanding Peter's particular role as a witness to the crucifixion and the Savior's related revelation.

7. For example, in his significant treatment of *Apoc. Pet.*, Koschorke (*Polemik der Gnostiker*, 134–37) does not mention martyrdom as a possible factor in the author's polemical criticism of other Christians; however, he does address martyrdom in gnostic traditions in general via an excursus in his chapter on the *Testimony of Truth*. Others more explicitly discount the language of persecution in *Apoc. Pet.* as metaphorical, an innate feature of apocalyptic literature, but with little to no basis in reality. For instance, Scholten, in his treatment of martyrdom in gnostic literature, rejects the idea that the language of persecution in *Apoc. Pet.* refers to an actual situation of suffering and/or martyrdom. Examples include threats of stoning, 72.4–9; 73.25—74.6; ruin, 80.2; oppression, 79.11–21; and Peter's fear of enemies, 84.6–10. Rather than take these references literally, Scholten claims that the use of "categories of physical suffering" derive from both the surrounding subject matter—the crucifixion narrative—and traditional eschatology (*Martyrium und Sophiamythos*, 80). As Moss (*Ancient Christian Martyrdom*, 3) reminds us, though, one can locate the concept of martyrdom in texts, even if they lack "martyr" language.

8. Pagels, for instance, reads the evidence of *Apoc. Pet.* literally. In her view, the author takes issue with early Christian coercion toward martyrdom, revealed by the references to "harsh fate" and "'the executioner,' under the illusion that by 'holding fast to the name of a dead man,' confessing the crucified one, 'they will become pure'" ("Gnostic and Orthodox Views," 274). The eagerness for suffering and "propaganda for martyrdom" are the issues for the author, according to Pagels. As her reading of *Apoc. Pet.* continues, however, Pagels also submits that "while the *Apocalypse of Peter* rejects the orthodox view of martyrdom, it does not reject martyrdom per se" (ibid., 274). She roots this claim in a reading of 78.32—79.2, which I revisit below. Tite ("Voluntary Martyrdom," 48–49) echoes Pagels's perspective and highlights "volunteerism" as the key issue, though he remains cautious about whether *Apoc. Pet.* actually addresses martyrdom, Ultimately, I find it difficult to envision the author as supportive of any sort of physical martyrdom. Havelaar (*Coptic Apocalypse of Peter*) also sees clues of persecution and possible martyrdom, given the author's resistance to those who celebrate suffering. In his translation, Meyer ("Revelation of Peter," 495) similarly understands this passage as a reference to martyrdom, indicated by his section heading to 78.31—79.31, which references "martyrs."

Apoc. Pet. 74.4–14

Following a reference to defection of certain Christians (73.23–28), the Savior informs Peter of the fate of those who stray. Referring back to "children of this aeon" (73.18), he explains, "those who associated with these will become their prisoners, since they are without perception (*anesthēton*)" (73.32—74.3).[9] Here, we discern at least two intersecting Christian groups with which the author takes issue. The initial "those" appears to reflect a group of misguided Christians, perhaps initially aligned with the author's community, but now swayed by the "children of this aeon" (73.18)—i.e., the second group ("these") involved with the misguidance. Though "prisoners" is likely not meant literally, the implication is that certain Christians are oppressed by others.[10] A lack of perception allows this situation, which Peter is ultimately tasked to resolve. This statement suggests that in the meantime, those lacking awareness might be unfavorably guided by other Christians, presumably those in relative positions of leadership.

As the apocalypse continues, we gain further understanding of what happens in the course of this imprisonment: "They deliver the pure (*akeraion*) and good one (*agathon*), who is without deceit (*atkrof*), to the executioner. And in their kingdom, Christ is glorified in a restoration, and the ones who lay down lies, who will succeed you, are glorified" (74.4–12). This passage suggests, first that those with power include Christians who advocate a resurrected Christ, and second that they are responsible for prompting a "pure and good one" toward death of some sort (literally, "the one who works for death"). Some interpreters understand the "pure one" as a christological reference.[11] An alternative is to understand the "pure one" as a general reference to Christians who are misled under the sway of other Christians.[12] The immediate context of the passage supports the view that this passage refers to intra-Christian conflict, with encouragement for martyrdom as a point of contention; immediately preceding this passage we

9. Havelaar observes, "The whole phrase (73.32—74.3) could be read as a reference to the transition of Petrine Gnostics to the hostile (orthodox Christian) side, formulated in terms that suggest struggle and oppression" (*Coptic Apocalypse of Peter*, 88).

10. Rather than suffer actual imprisonment and persecution from fellow Christians, it seems more reasonable to understand such experiences as occurring at the hands of Romans; the issue though is that certain Christians seems to prompt others toward this fate.

11. This possibility is explored by Havelaar, *Coptic Apocalypse of Peter*, 88.

12. Brashler (*Coptic Apocalypse of Peter*, 218) takes this perspective, considering this as a reference to hostile Christian interactions, potentially with actual executions. Evidence of the latter, though, is lacking.

find the description of the defection of certain Christians to the apparent proto-orthodox camp.

What follows this reference to executioners also supports an interpretation centered on martyrdom. First, if one considers a connection between the potential execution and the subsequent mention of glorification, this passage could reflect a situation of persecution and early Christian celebration of martyrs. The reference to "glorified" ones could well indicate martyrs, since among early Christians, they reflect the group most likely to be celebrated and praised. Second, the passage continues with the notice regarding allegiance to a "dead one" (74.13–14). Certainly, this statement reflects criticism of a christological focus on the crucified one,[13] but it also suggests a rejection of confession of this "dead one" and the related hope of purity.

Apoc. Pet. 77.33—78.6 / 78.7–15

As the polemic continues, Apoc. Pet. criticizes "messengers of error" (77.24–25) for, among other things, their belief that good and evil have a common origin (77.30–33). These "messengers" also represent a significant threat for the author and his community. The Savior says, "They do business with my word (pašaje). And they will establish a difficult fate from which the generation of the immortal souls will flee in vain, until my return (parousia)" (77.33—78.6). The accusation of misusing the Savior's "word" suggests a situation of competing Christian identities.[14] The allegiance to Christ is further associated with apparent persecution, which the "immortal souls" will try to avoid. The "difficult fate" involves a significant threat to the "immortal souls." It could refer simply to their general negative experience of suppression; however, the tenor of the passage combined with a subsequent reference to transgressions suggests that some more substantial action is meant.

The continuation of the passage also highlights the relative lack of boundaries among early Christian groups as well as the potential for error among those favored by Apoc. Pet. The Savior informs Peter, "They will remain among them. And I have forgiven the transgressions into which they fell through the adversaries. I accepted the ransom from their slavery, to give them freedom" (78.7–15). Given the context, the initial "they" likely

---

13. Havelaar (Coptic Apocalypse of Peter, 89) recognizes the reference to the "dead one" as a clear indication of the orthodox Christian belief in a crucified Jesus.

14. The beginning of this passage recalls 2 Cor 2:17, in which Paul likewise distinguishes his proper mission from those who are "peddlers of God's word," writing "we speak as persons of sincerity, as persons sent from God and standing in his presence."

refs to the immortal souls mentioned in the preceding lines. Here, *Apoc. Pet.* reiterates that even those favored by the Savior are not immune to error or, in this case, misguidance. The nature of the "transgressions" and the "ransom" is less apparent, making this a tricky passage to comprehend.[15] In my view, the reference to their "ransom from their slavery" is provocative. It could refer simply to escape from the body, but combined with the difficult fate encouraged by others, it could well indicate a martyr's death, one of the transgressions prompted by error and misguidance.

Apoc. Pet. 78.31—79.2 / 79.8–21

As the author of *Apoc. Pet.* continues to describe his adversaries, he explains the error of Christians who celebrate the value of suffering. The Savior explains to Peter their folly: "But others among them, because they endure suffering (*emkah*), think that they will fulfill the wisdom of the brotherhood that really exists" (78.31—79.2). Among the passages I examine, this one most clearly evokes the prospect of martyrdom.[16]

In the same section, presumably with the same opponents in mind, *Apoc. Pet.* continues,

> The similar generation of the sisterhood will appear as an imitation. These are the ones who oppress their brothers and sisters, saying to them, 'Through this our God has mercy, since salvation comes to us through this.' They do not know the punishment of those who rejoice in what has been done to the little ones whom they sought out and imprisoned. (79.8–21)

This passage reports that some within the community encourage others to take on a particular deed that reflects a mode of suppression and reportedly earns one salvation. Referring to 79.11-12, Havelaar suggests that "the

15. A subsequent reference to "Hermas, the first-born of unrighteousness" (78.18–19) leads Havelaar (*Coptic Apocalypse of Peter*, 96–97) to understand the transgressions as related to the concept of second penance. According to this understanding of the passage, the author of *Apoc. Pet.* takes issue with certain early Christian leaders' presumed ability to forgive sins repeatedly. Though this reading initially seems reasonable, it fails to take into account the harsh fate that is to be avoided as well as the Savior's forgiveness and acceptance of ransom. This reading also relies on the assumption that mention of Hermas is, in fact, a reference to the *Shepherd of Hermas*. As Brashler (*Coptic Apocalypse of Peter*, 232) notes, this is not self-evident, and there is reason to reject this reading. If one cannot assume the author has the *Shepherd of Hermas* in view here, then the importation of second penance as the issue is less persuasive.

16. Havelaar (*Coptic Apocalypse of Peter*, 98) and Pagels ("Gnostic and Orthodox Views," 274) both associate the "suffering" with physical martyrdom.

verb used to denote this suppression, *lōjeh*, may even point to a situation of persecution," but she does not explicitly connect the statement regarding salvation (79.14–16) to martyrdom; rather, she views it as a more general statement of orthodox salvation.[17] I see no convincing reason to be reticent in equating 79.11–21 with the early promotion of martyrdom, given the prior reference to suffering and the emphasis on a deed. In his brief notes on the text, Brashler states that this passage reflects "the author's rejection of the oppressors' motivation that they are promoting the salvation of the Gnostics by forcing orthodox doctrine upon them."[18] Rather than doctrine though, the passage makes an issue of some kind of practice. When one considers what sort of deed would fit here—one that causes others to rejoice, is reputed to earn mercy and salvation, and is associated with imprisonment—martyrdom stands as the most reasonable option.

Apoc. Pet. 79.32—80.7

At the conclusion of the Savior's overview of the rise of division, Peter expresses his concern over the situation with a statement symptomatic of his persistent lack of understanding. He confesses to the Savior, "I am afraid because of the things you have told me . . . there are many who will mislead many of the living ones, and they will be destroyed among them. And when they speak your name, they will be believed" (79.32—80.7). Peter's statement asserts that "living" Christians are being led astray by other Christians, with a destructive outcome. In addition, the final line in this passage suggests martyrdom as one possible threat. To "speak" the Savior's "name" as a means of encouraging belief (80.6–7) depicts a situation in which confession is central and public.

Collectively, this series of references to persecution suggests that promotion of a martyr's death was a key source of concern for the author of *Apoc. Pet.*, one that prompted conflict with other Christians. The critique of the promotion of martyrdom, as well as other faulty behaviors, appears rooted in an improper understanding of the nature of Christ; an extensive vision of the crucifixion narrative emphasizes that the Savior did not experience a suffering death, which, in turn, mitigates the value of a martyr's death. Here, Peter's position as the authoritative recipient of Christ's revelation—not only regarding Christian division but also the cross—becomes especially relevant.

17. Havelaar, *Coptic Apocalypse of Peter*, 98.
18. Brashler, "Apocalypse of Peter," 237.

Peter plays a central role in *Apoc. Pet.*'s distinctive portrait of the Passion (81.2—83.15); he serves as both a witness to the event and the recipient of special revelation. Peter experiences a series of three visions, each explained by the Savior. The progressive illumination highlights Peter's significant role in the narrative. Through these elements, the reader discovers a tripartite spiritual Savior who temporarily inhabits a fleshly body. Having departed this latter figure just prior to the crucifixion, the Savior stands by "laughing" (81.11; 15) as the authorities foolishly execute the irrelevant bodily remnant. *Apoc. Pet.*'s unique interpretation of the Passion thus illuminates the author's perspective on suffering.[19] Through the example of the Savior, the author rejects the glorification of physical plight, challenging those who advocate a suffering Savior. *Apoc. Pet.* makes it clear that the real Savior is only a bystander to the suffering, while those who persecute, like the false Christians, are blind and imperceptive (83.2–3). Moreover, Peter's role as an exclusive, proper witness to the crucifixion adds to his characterization as a different sort of martyr. As the Savior did not suffer, neither will Peter. In addition, Peter participates in conveying salvation to others by sharing his vision; in this manner, he further serves as a witness, in the term's more general sense. This special role of Peter also has implications for intra-Christian debate.

Following the Savior's description of erroneous Christians, Peter abruptly experiences a vision of the Savior's arrest and subsequent crucifixion: "After he had said these things, I saw him apparently being seized by them" (81.3–6). Peter then initiates a dialogue with the Savior to comprehend what he sees. He inquires, "What do I see, O Lord?' Is it really you whom they take? And are you grasping me? Who is this one glad and laughing above the cross? And is it another one whose feet and hands they are striking?" (81.7–14). Peter's initial observation of the crucifixion thus reflects the presence of (at least) two distinct figures: the hovering figure who laughs and the bodily figure hung upon the cross. At its core, *Apoc. Pet.*'s Christology appears dualistic, distinguishing the material from the spiritual. The latter, though, finds expression in multiple ways. The Savior explains, "The one you see above the cross, glad and laughing, is the living Jesus. But the one into whose hands and feet they are driving the nails is his fleshly part, the substitute. They put to shame the one who is in his likeness. But look at him and me" (81.15–24). This explication prompts a misunderstanding by Peter, who looks (81.25), notes that no one is watching the Savior, and thus suggests escaping the situation: "Lord, no one is looking at

19. There is a relative consensus regarding the essential Christology of *Apoc. Pet.*; in this discussion, my interest focuses more on what this information suggests about suffering and how it positions Peter in relation to it.

you. Let us flee this place" (81.26–28). The Savior's response suggests that Peter's proposed flight is absurd, since the persecutors do not reflect a real threat. He chastises Peter, "I have told you, 'Leave blind ones alone.' See how they do not know what they say. For they have put to shame the son of their glory, instead of my servant" (81.29—82.3). The persecutors are mocked for the pointless execution of one of their own. This passage also highlights Peter's particular role: he is instructed to be attentive to their lack of knowledge, rather than to any threat of physical persecution. The Savior thus refocuses Peter, and the primary lesson is to not worry about physical persecution.

The second part of Peter's vision further illuminates the nature of the Savior. Peter reports,

> And I saw someone approaching us who looked like him and like the one who was laughing above the cross. And he was woven with a holy spirit, and he was the Savior. And there was a great ineffable light surrounding them, and the multitude of ineffable and invisible angels blessing them. And it was I who saw that this one who glorifies was revealed. (82.4–16)

This passage details additional manifestations of the Savior. The approaching figure appears distinct from the laughing figure, but resembles the Savior already known to Peter. A third figure seems to be reflected by the presence of the "great ineffable light" as "one who glorifies." In addition, this passage reiterates Peter's distinctive role: he stresses that *he* is the key witness to the revelation.

Peter's position is further highlighted in the following lines, which convey additional details about the nature of the crucified one. The Savior instructs Peter, "Be strong (*čemčom*)! For you are the one to whom these mysteries have been given, to know through revelation that the one they crucified is the firstborn, the house of demons, and the stone vessel in which they dwell, belonging to Elohim and the cross that is under the law" (82.18–26). Here, *Apoc. Pet.* highlights Peter's role as recipient of the key mysteries surrounding the crucifixion—specifically, the actual identity of the one on the cross. The list of attributes makes it clear that this secondary figure reflects the material realm, the world associated with the law and the inferior, creator god. Moreover, it is apparent that other Christians have made this critical christological error. The themes of division and persecution, initially introduced in the central, polemical section, surface again in *Apoc. Pet.*'s portrait of the Passion (and are arguably central to it). The encouragement for Peter to remain strong suggests the tenuousness of his position; with uncertain parameters, Peter reflects the possibility for even "true" Christians to misunderstand and lapse.

The Savior continues with an explication of the figure standing by at the crucifixion scene:

> But the one who stands near him is the living Savior, the one who was initially in the one whom they seized, and he was released. He stands gladly, seeing that those who were violent toward him are divided among themselves. Therefore, he laughs at their inability to perceive, and he knows that they were born blind. (82.26—83.3)

A number of points in this passage are noteworthy.[20] First, the bystander is designated as "the living Savior," who inhabited the one who will be crucified. Prior to the punishment though, the spiritual form departs the distinct body.[21] Second, this passage reveals perspectives on persecution and suffering that correspond with the intra-Christian issues addressed previously in *Apoc. Pet.* The persecutors are mocked for their blindness, which presumably limits their ability to recognize the "true" identity of their prisoner; they err in their understanding of the situation. The laughing Savior highlights the futility of the persecution of one of their own. The persecutors are characterized also as internally divided. In *Apoc. Pet.*, the traditional persecutors associated with the Passion—Jews and Romans—serve as symbols of the author's contemporary Christian opponents. Both of these characteristics— lack of understanding and division—echo the author's critique of erroneous Christians in the preceding section of the apocalypse.[22]

The Savior goes on to detail the distinctions among the figures present in Peter's vision of the Passion scene: "Therefore, the suffering one must remain since the body is the substitute. But the one that was released was my bodiless body. I am the intellectual spirit filled with radiant light. The one you saw approaching me is our intellectual pleroma, which unites the perfect light with my holy spirit" (83.4–15). This passage distinguishes the physical body, which will suffer, from: 1. the Savior's "bodiless body," 2. the "intellectual spirit filled with radiant light" (the Savior's self-designation), and 3. the one Peter witnessed, "the intellectual pleroma." The latter three

20. A laughing Christ is also present at the crucifixion in *Disc. Seth* (VII,2) 56.19, in which Simon of Cyrene appears as the physical substitute on the cross. A similar perspective is attributed to Basilides by Irenaeus, *Haer.* 1.24.4.

21. Luttikhuizen ("Suffering Jesus," 194–95) ascribes this figure an intermediate role between Christ's intellectual spirit and the material body, comparable to an "ethereal soul-body" in a trichotomous concept of reality.

22. The recurrence of the lack of awareness and divisiveness reflects how these seemingly distinct sections of the apocalypse are actually intertwined.

appear to be related manifestations of the spiritual realm. The body that suffers is, on the other hand, purely physical; characterized as a "substitute (*šebiō*)," its role in the scheme seems to carry little to no value. In addition, it derives from a distinct, inferior cosmic realm. Combined with the negative associations noted above, the crucified one who suffers is not a figure to be glorified, as the author's critique of other Christians reveals.

No less significant than the christological reflections here are the recipient of the message and its purpose. The Savior's interpretation of events on Peter's behalf is immediately followed by a commission for the disciple to share what he has discovered. The Savior instructs Peter,

> You shall present these things that you have seen to those of another generation, who are not of this aeon. For there will be no honor in any one who is not immortal, but only for those who were chosen from an immortal substance, which demonstrates the ability to comprehend the one who gives his abundance. (83.15–26)[23]

Peter's delivery of the message is a significant task. Peter receives final encouragement: "You, therefore, be courageous and fear nothing. For I will be with you so that none of your enemies will prevail over you. Peace be with you. Be strong (*čᵉm nomte*)!" (84.6–11).

The depiction of the Passion in *Apoc. Pet.* thus reveals that physical suffering, including the actual crucifixion, is not to be celebrated. As Michel Desjardins concludes in his discussion of this crucifixion scene, "The author's main point . . . is that Jesus' external, physical form is not the one worth honoring."[24] This lack of enthusiasm corresponds with the author's apparent assessment of martyrdom. Nevertheless, the Passion scene itself makes up a significant part in the apocalypse. Rather than highlight suffering, though, it reveals the nature of the Savior and signals Peter's key role as the witness of this knowledge. This is apparent in the details the author chooses to highlight. The cross itself is secondary to the action of the scene from Peter's perspective. It also serves as a corrective to those who misunderstand the crucifixion and subscribe to a suffering Savior; Peter's vision of the crucifixion as well as the Savior's subsequent explanation of the scene and his nature demonstrate the futility of physical suffering and mock those who subscribe to it. The concluding instructions for Peter to share his

---

23. This passage recalls a preceding passage in *Apoc. Pet.* that describes the intended recipients of Peter's revelation. The Savior encourages Peter, "Now then, listen to the things that are being told to you in a mystery, and guard them. Do not tell them to the children of this age" (73.14–18).

24. Desjardins, "Apocalypse of Peter: Introduction," 206.

received knowledge also relate to the Savior's function—more specifically, his provision of salvation through his message.

As the pseudonymous author, Peter's role in *Apoc. Pet.* thus extends beyond that of the typical apocalyptic revealer.[25] In the context of intra-Christian debate, the choice of Peter as apocalyptic messenger is significant, given his prominent role in proto-orthodox tradition, the author's apparent opposition. Specifically, Peter's authoritative voice challenges the centrality of suffering for Christian identity and redefines his role as a proto-martyr or witness. Peter's progressive enlightenment, via the Savior, over the course of the apocalypse serves as a model for other Christians to imitate. His periodic misunderstandings reveal that his acquisition of awareness is not automatic. Through proper instruction and reflection they can participate in the immortal realm and become invulnerable to suffering. The encouragement to "be strong" (84.11) relates not to Peter's physical situation, but to his newfound understanding in the face of "persecution" by fellow Christians as he awaits the end of the present age.[26] Moreover, in depicting Peter as the original leader of a unified community (cf. 73.23–28), *Apoc. Pet.* offers hope that Peter will reclaim his authoritative role with the Savior's return. In the meantime, Peter is meant to await the Parousia (78.4–6), while bravely accepting his role in the midst of intra-Christian conflict (80.31—81.3).

Peter's portrait can thus be understood as a challenge to his traditional characterization as a dying witness, especially in light of the intra-Christian conflict in *Apoc. Pet.* By the time of its composition, the tradition of Peter as a key early martyr appears to have been well-entrenched.[27] Given Peter's martyr legacy and his expressions of fear in this text, it is all the more noteworthy that his own death is not forecast in *Apoc. Pet.* As with the crucifixion narrative, we find an adaptation of shared tradition in *Apoc. Pet.'s* portrait of the disciple: Peter admits fear, yet it is alleviated. Otherwise, his quest centers on perfection, a challenge posed by the Savior at the start of

25. Typical facets of Peter's role include his authoritative status as a figure close to the Savior and his ability to view "the future," given his experience in the historical past.

26. This contrasts Pagels's view of this final statement as encouragement for Peter to go on to confidently face his own suffering ("Gnostic and Orthodox Views," 275). Given the negative assessment of suffering in the text and the lack of reference to Peter's pending persecution, this reading does not seem entirely persuasive.

27. In *1 Clem.* 5, perhaps the earliest reference to the tradition of Peter's death as a martyr; note also the 'Quo Vadis' legacy of *Acts Pet.* 35–36; Origen, *Comm. Jo.* 20.12; and Eusebius's later reports, *Hist. eccl.* 3.1.2–3; 2.25.5–8. For a full account of the textual legacy, see Eastman, *Ancient Martyrdom Accounts*; for an account of Peter's role as a witness, see Perkins, "Peter, Witness and Martyr." Barnes, "'Another Shall Gird Thee'" offers a detailed discussion of evidence for Peter's death in Rome and related early traditions.

the apocalypse. He encourages, "Peter, become perfect, in accordance with your name, along with me, the one who has chosen you" (71.15–18).[28] In addition to highlighting Peter's special role, this opening also sets the Savior as an example for Peter to follow. The perfection involves attaining proper knowledge, particularly regarding the nature of the crucifixion (71.25–33).[29] The combination of a crucifixion without suffering and the call for Peter to imitate the Savior leads Brashler to consider this statement as a "subtle criticism of the orthodox view that martyrdom was the τελειότης of spiritual perfection."[30] One could also understand the moments of encouragement for Peter to "be strong" (71.22; 82.18; 84.11) and have courage (80.32–33; 84.7) as adaptations of typical support in the early martyr acts.[31] In this case, Peter's strength relates to his ability to perceive progressively through the course of the apocalypse. In the end, the indication that Peter "came to his senses" (84.12–13) reflects the awareness he achieves. If read as an allusion to Acts 12:11, in which Peter "came to himself" after a miraculous escape from prison, this final statement further implies Peter's ultimate distance from persecution.[32]

THE LETTER OF PETER TO PHILIP[33]

With this perspective on *Apoc. Pet.* in mind, let us turn to another pseudo-Petrine text, *Ep. Pet. Phil.* Less extensive than *Apoc. Pet.* in its depiction

28. It is somewhat unclear what is meant here by "in keeping with your name"; Havelaar (*Coptic Apocalypse of Peter,* 81) suggests a possible link between the Greek *telios* (71.16) and *petros*, noting that a rock might symbolize strength and perfection. The emphasis on the Savior's choice of Peter also recalls the tradition of Matt 16:18, in which Jesus casts Peter as the rock on which the church will be built. Baumeister also considers this apparent allusion, asserting that it positively shapes the subsequent revisions of the traditions regarding Peter's denial ("Rolle des Petrus," 7).

29. The author might have in mind the description of Peter as a "witness of the sufferings of Christ" in 1 Pet 5:1. See Smith, *Petrine Controversies,* 131.

30. Brashler, "Coptic Apocalypse of Peter," 209–10.

31. For example, in *Mart. Pol.* 9, a heavenly voice encourages the martyr in the arena, "Be strong, Polycarp, and be a man [*Or: be courageous*]" (trans. Ehrman).

32. Smith (*Petrine Controversies,* 126) mentions this parallel, though he does not discuss its potential significance in relation to *Apoc. Pet.*'s perspective on persecution and possible martyrdom.

33. *Ep. Pet. Phil.* appears as the second writing in Nag Hammadi Codex VIII; another version survives in Codex Tchacos, which suffers from considerable damage. In what follows, I rely primarily on the text from NHC VII, drawing on Wisse's English translation and the Coptic text in *Nag Hammadi Codex VIII* and consulting an additional English translation by Meyer in *Nag Hammadi Scriptures.* I also thank Lance Jenott for graciously sharing drafts of his Coptic transcriptions of *Ep. Pet. Phil.,* including a

of the crucifixion and its development of Peter, *Ep. Pet. Phil.* also suggests
intra-Christian debate, yet in limited and implicit ways. The primary hint
of competing Christian perspectives appears in the epistolary framework
of the text.[34] The actual "letter" of Peter to Philip, positioned at the start of
the text, places Peter as an intermediary between Christ and Philip; specifically, Christ encourages union among the apostles. Peter requests Philip's
return, but there are indications that this might not have been Philip's preference (133.1–5). Regardless, the request is happily met, and Philip rejoins
the other apostles, including Peter, for a post-resurrection encounter with
Christ. The separation, followed by reunion, of the apostles could be viewed
as indicative of division within the church, which the author hopes to correct; if so, it is admittedly a subtle, rather than overt, indication of Christian
discord. Regardless, the reunion does set the scene for Peter's role in relation
to the other apostles. They appear as a collective throughout much of *Ep.
Pet. Phil.*, but on significant occasions Peter distinguishes himself as a key
interpreter of Christ's revelation.

Like *Apoc. Pet.*, *Ep. Pet. Phil.* also regularly draws on existing traditions, primarily material from the canonical Gospels and Acts, to set the
scene for new revelation.[35] The author emphasizes the continuity between
the teachings received by Christ when he was "in the body (*sōma*)" (133.17;
138.3; 139.11) and those conveyed in the post-resurrection setting. At the
same time, the limits of the initial message are suggested, as the apostles
failed to fully comprehend it; therefore, they need to hear it again (135.5–8).
This suggests that the author valued existing traditions, but also saw a need
to extend and adapt them.[36] This strategy appears to reflect the author's in-

---

side-by-side comparison of the Nag Hammadi and Cod. Tch. texts.

34. The opening letter (132.12—133.8) essentially serves to preface the remainder
of the text, presented as a revelatory dialogue between the apostles and Christ, detailing
an abridged version of a gnostic myth, including the creation of humans and their current state of entrapment (134.24). The apostles, in particular, seek to understand how
to overcome this situation by learning how to battle opposing powers (134.26—135.2).
Kaler ("Letter of Peter to Philip") shows how the framing letter connects in clear, deliberate ways with the subsequent revelation.

35. The scene recalls John 20, Luke 24, and the early chapters of Acts. Smith (*Petrine
Controversies*, 122–23) outlines a series of parallels; Kaler ("Letter of Peter to Philip,"
269–73) also effectively demonstrates *Ep. Pet. Phil.*'s use of Acts 7–8—specifically, Acts
8 provides the basis for Philip's absence, and the martyrdom of Stephen in Acts 7 sets
the scene for the disciples' anticipation of suffering. He also notes that Philip of Acts 8
likely is conflated with Philip the apostle (Acts 1:13).

36. Kaler ("Letter of Peter to Philip," 273) highlights how *Ep. Pet. Phil.* reflects not
the typical gnostic "rewritten bible," but an "expanded bible." Providing the rationale
for such a move, Perkins observes, "the emphases of the narrative suggests that the
primary counter-arguments to the Gnostic preaching were founded on appeals to

terest in aligning his gnostic perspective with apostolic tradition, authority, and unity. The emphasis on suffering in the text, though, might signal an additional motivation: to problematize or counter what the author understood to be faulty views of suffering.

Ep. Pet. Phil. centers on the prospect of suffering, apparent in the apostles' initial prayer to Christ. En route to Jerusalem, they ask the Redeemer to "give us power, for they seek to kill us" (134.8–9).[37] Christ responds through a great light and in voice, inquiring, "Why are you asking me?," and calling upon the apostles to listen to his words (134.10–18). The concern regarding persecution and potential suffering thus initiates the dialogue with the Savior. The apostles then go on to ask about the "deficiency of the aeons and their pleroma" (134.21–22), their own situation in the world, as well as their departure. Recalling their role as "witnesses (*mentre*)" (135.5), Christ reminds the apostles of his prior teaching and admonishes them for their unbelief. The implication is that the apostles are not yet fully aware; Christ's response details their plight, outlining typical elements of a gnostic myth (135.8—137.4). Here, as in *Apoc. Pet.*, we find the initial threat of suffering reframed, shifting from the bodily concerns to spiritual realities.

Ep. Pet. Phil.'s attention to Christ's appearance in the body and the crucifixion also highlights the prospect of suffering. In this regard, both Christ and Peter reveal the proper insight. Noting his origins in the pleroma, Christ details,

> I am the one who was sent down in the body (*sōma*) because of the seed which had fallen away. And I came down into their mortal mold (*epeuplasma etmoout*). But they did not recognize me; they were thinking of me that I was a mortal human (*ourōme efmoout*). (136.16–22).

A few aspects of this revelation are worth noting. First, as Antti Marjanen observes, it "is possible but not inevitable" to read this as reflective of a docetic perspective. Alternatively, the notion of being "in the body" could simply convey "becoming subject to the predicament of earthly existence."[38] If one accepts the latter option, it still entails a consideration of whether suffering was part of earthly existence for *Ep. Pet. Phil.*'s Christ. Second, it is

canonical Scripture, particularly Acts, and to the unity of apostolic preaching. Concern to demonstrate the continuity of Gnostic teaching with Jesus' preaching and apostolic testimony leads the author to have all the disciples—not just their leader Peter—instructed in gnosis during the earthly ministry" (*Gnostic Dialogue*, 123).

37. Or, an alternative translation, noted by Kaler, "we are being sought after in order to be killed" ("Letter of Peter to Philip," 265).

38. Marjanen, "Suffering," 492.

worth considering who are those who fail to recognize Christ; *Ep. Pet. Phil.* does not make their identity clear. Luttikhuizen appropriately considers them as lower cosmic forces, representatives of the arrogant one.[39] But, as we have seen in *Apoc. Pet.*, such figures can simultaneously signal opposing Christians, those who similarly misperceive the realities of Christ's nature. In addition, the notion that they mistook Christ for a mere "mortal human" suggests that however one imagines his existence in the body, it was not typical.

Following Christ's explication of his identity, he associates the apostolic experience with his own: "you are being detained because you belong to me" (137.4–6). He encourages their particular path, which involves fighting against the archons. The apostles inquire again, this time regarding the prospect of their own suffering, and broadly, the nature of the apostolic mission (137.13—138.3). As in *Apoc. Pet.*, we find concern about possible persecution being redirected; instead, their struggle will be internal (137.20–22) and their proper mode of witnessing involves illumination of others (137.23–25).

Nevertheless, emphasis on potential suffering persists, both for Christ and for the apostles. As the dialogue continues, Peter emerges as a prominent voice, especially in relation to the other apostles. His responses appear as subtly corrective, perhaps reflecting tension between the author's view and that of other Christians. As the apostles venture back to Jerusalem following Christ's ascension, they inquire, "If he, our Lord, suffered (*afji mkah*), then how much must we suffer?" (138.15–16). Peter replies, "He suffered (*afji mkah*) on our behalf, and it is necessary for us too to suffer because of our smallness (*tenmentkoui*)" (138.18–20). Peter's reply emphasizes his position in relation to other apostles; he is part of the unified group, as the text suggests, but he also appears to have greater insight. The notion of smallness, not unusual in gnostic Christian writings, could indicate the experience of the human condition; this might then signal that the suffering that takes place is related to the entrapment of the spirit, or the light, in the earthly realm. The smallness could relate also to the relative position of the author's audience in relation to other Christians, similar to the minority experience portrayed in *Apoc. Pet.*

Peter's response to the apostles is echoed as *Ep Pet. Phil.* continues.[40] A voice (presumably of Christ) affirms, "I have often told you that it is necessary for you to suffer. It is necessary that they bring you to synagogues

39. Luttikhuizen, *Gnostic Revisions*, 154.

40. According to Smith, this "heavenly ratification" of Peter's message affirms that he is "the correct interpreter of the Savior's will" (*Petrine Controversies*, 123).

and governors, so that you will suffer" (138.22–27).[41] This passage certainly
appears, on the surface, to highlight the value of potential suffering, especially at the hands of authorities. Unfortunately, a lacuna of a series of lines
follows (139.1–3), prefaced with the distinction of one who will *not* suffer
(138.27–28).[42] In its current context then, it is difficult to develop any solid
understanding of this passage. Allowing for a bit of speculation, I wonder
whether what is missing might reflect a further inversion, or at least com-
plication, of the necessity of suffering; the distinction that precedes the gap,
as well as parallels in the canonical Gospels, suggest this possibility. The
reference to synagogues and governors recalls Synoptic sayings, specifically
Matt 10:17–18 and Luke 12:11–12; 21:12. Both Matthew and Luke emphasize the occasion before the authorities as an opportunity to testify through
the spirit (Matt 10:20; Luke 12:12); in addition, in these gospel scenes, Jesus
assures the disciples to "not be anxious" (Matt 10:19; Luke 12:11). The inclusion of the passage in *Ep. Pet. Phil.* appears to reflect this initial context—it
responds to apostolic concern and previews Peter's subsequent reception of
the spirit and related testimony.

As *Ep. Pet. Phil.* continues, Peter comes back into focus. He asks his
disciples, "Did our Lord Jesus, when he was in the body, show us everything? For he came down. My brothers, listen to my voice'" (139.10–13).
Peter becomes filled with the Holy Spirit (139,14) and affirms the crucifixion of Jesus:

> Our illuminator, Jesus, came down and was crucified. He wore
> a crown of thorns and put on a purple garment. And he was
> crucified on a tree and was buried in a tomb. And he rose from
> the dead. My brothers, Jesus is a stranger to this suffering. But
> we are the ones who have suffered (*pete anjiemkah*) through the
> transgression of the mother. And because of this, he did every-
> thing like us. (139.15–25)[43]

41. In the Cod. Tch. version, this segment (138.15–20; 138.22–27) of *Ep. Pet. Phil.*
includes language of death, rather than suffering; and "humanity" appears, rather than
"smallness." To the disciples, Peter replies, "He died (*entaf mou*) for us; we ourselves are
to die (*emou*) for humanity (*tmentpōme*)" (7.1–3); and similarly, the heavenly voice
explains, "I often told you, you are to die (*emou*), and you are to be brought into synagogues and before governors" (7.5–9). For discussion of a similar variant and its related
relevance, see below (n. 43).

42. The subsequent lines are also lost in the Cod. Tch. version.

43. Here again, we find an intriguing variant in Cod. Tch., one that highlights
death rather than suffering: "Jesus is a stranger to death (*mou*). But we are the ones
who have died (*nentamou*) through the transgression of our mother" (8.2–5). We do
not know which version of the text is earlier; so, one can only offer a tentative proposal
regarding the circumstances that could have encouraged each reading and the shift

Notably though, he does not affirm the suffering of Jesus; rather, he distinguishes Jesus from this particular facet of the experience and highlights his actions as *like* those of humans. I find Luttikhuizen's reading of this passage generally persuasive, specifically that it reflects a gnostic reinterpretation of the crucifixion tradition, one that revises the proto-orthodox perspective on the Savior's suffering.[44] In addition, through Peter's confession, the author positions the apostolic suffering as having already happened, perhaps with the implication that it will continue. Recalling the "transgression of the Mother" also situates the suffering of Peter and others in their essential, created human condition; as such, their suffering is not particular to nor does it signal their deaths.

In *Ep. Pet. Phil.*, the crucifixion is thus viewed as one moment in the fuller experience of what appears to be a limited incarnation; through the latter, Christ apparently suffers in taking on a human form, though in death he remains distant from suffering. Peter and the apostles progressively discern these matters over the course of their encounter with the risen Christ. Peter stands out as one who perceives these realities, offering explanations and subtle correctives to the perspective of the apostles. In addition, this particular perspective on the crucifixion, combined with the sense of suffering as involving more than physical harm, problematizes views of *Ep. Pet. Phil.* as a text that encourages martyrdom.[45]

---

from one to the other. I suggest that in the context of debates regarding the value of physical death, specifically martyrdom, among some early Christians, the "suffering" readings might have been preferred over the references to "death," particularly when "suffering" could be understood more broadly, as a scenario of persecution (not necessarily involving death) and/or an aspect of the human experience.

44. Luttikhuizen writes, "What we find here is that the contents of an early orthodox tradition testifying to the sufferings of Jesus are subsumed entirely into a Gnostic mythical thought pattern. In this mythical transformation, Christ is the illuminator from the transcendent world. The idea that he could suffer as a physical being is rejected explicitly. He is a stranger to this suffering" (*Gnostic Revisions*, 4). Van Os ("Role of the Apostles," 158) offers an alternative reading, one that diminishes the anti-orthodox perspective. He asserts that Peter's gnostic explanation does not necessarily replace the prior statement; rather, the two appear to work side-by-side in *Ep. Pet. Phil.* Given the letter's interest in unity, it is possible that the initial statement is validated, but only in a limited sense; the author's comment delivers the significant interpretation.

45. According to King, *Ep. Pet. Phil.* encourages missionary teaching which "requires suffering and death" ("Martyrdom," 29 n. 24). She considers the text, along with others in Cod. Tch., as "preparation for martyrdom," which involves, "articulat[ing] a set of practices aimed at training potential martyrs" (ibid., 25). King admits, though, that her understanding of martyrdom is broad; this is affirmed in her summary of the goals of this preparation: "people had to be trained well in the true teaching, learn to overcome fear, imitate laudable models from the past, and keep their eyes firmly fixed on the goal of salvation" (ibid., 26). I generally agree with King's discernment of these

Unlike *Apoc. Pet.*, which features Peter as an exclusive recipient of the Savior's revelation, *Ep. Pet. Phil.* links Peter's authority with the unified apostolic collective.[46] As we have seen though, moments in *Ep. Pet. Phil.* highlight Peter's leadership and elevated understanding, especially in relation to the apostles' consistent need for reinforced teachings.[47] This use of Peter suggests an interest in both affirming unity within the Christian message and prioritizing Peter.

As with *Apoc. Pet.*, it is possible that the choice of Peter as the pseudonymous author relates to his own association with traditions of suffering.[48] In this case, *Ep. Pet. Phil.*'s emphasis on apostolic ministry shifts the focus away from the apostles' trials and toward their message. Their mission involves becoming "illuminators in the midst of mortal humans," having themselves dismissed bodily corruptions (137.6–9). Their battle against the archons comes through unity and teaching salvation in the world (137.22–25). The conclusion of the letter further affirms their role—with the "power of Jesus" they scatter to share their message (140.23–27).

Considering *Ep. Pet. Phil.* alongside *Apoc. Pet.* also encourages us to consider whether similar intra-Christian negotiations regarding the value of suffering might be reflected in the former. It does not appear that its author or audience was entrenched in any considerable Christian dispute; still, the text appears to reflect emerging questions about the relative value of suffering.[49] Through pseudo-apostolic authority, particularly Peter's, the author expresses a need to recognize the "true" nature of suffering, one that

---

goals in *Ep. Pet. Phil,* though I do not find them to be exclusively connected with actual suffering and death; rather, these lessons could fit a range of early Christian texts.

46. See Perkins, *Gnostic Dialogue*, 122.

47. Perkins and Smith, among others, note how Peter's characterization draws on his portrait in the initial chapters of Acts, which appear to have significantly influenced the author of *Ep. Pet. Phil.* In addition, Nicklas highlights Peter's special role, as one who receives important revelation, brings the apostles together, and "speaks in accordance with the Lord" ("'Gnostic' Perspectives," 210).

48. Drawing on connections with Acts 9, Kaler discusses ways in which *Ep. Pet. Phil.* reflects Pauline, rather than specifically Petrine, tradition; he writes, "Peter is assimilated to Paul, in that the pivotal revelation that he and the other apostles share is in fact modeled formally on Paul's, and its content references Pauline writings" ("Letter of Peter to Philip," 285). If this "assimilation" is indeed the case, one should ask why the preference for Peter? Peter's role could make better sense, given the historical scenario of Acts, as Kaler suggests (ibid., 287). At the same time, the collapsing of Paul into Peter could also serve to claim the emerging authority of Peter within proto-orthodox circles.

49. There is no clear identification of the opposition, including those responsible for the pending persecution of the apostle. On this point, the comparison with *Apoc. Pet.* is suggestive. It is possible that other Christians are the source of the perceived persecution.

involves the body, but does not necessarily value the physical experience itself. His alignment with and leadership over the other apostles evokes apostolic unity.[50] *Ep. Pet. Phil.*'s special interest in unity among the apostles might be rooted in its use of Acts; at the same time though, it could operate as a means to dispel dissenting views within the church.[51] Van Os suggests that the apostolic unity of *Ep. Pet. Phil.* serves to mediate, rather than heighten, rifts between gnostic and proto-orthodox Christians, revealing the potential for multiple interpretations to co-exist.[52] I agree that we find an interest in unity among Christians in *Ep. Pet. Phil.*; but the interactions between the disciples and Peter also reveal an interest in *correcting* certain views, particularly regarding the prospect of suffering.

CONCLUSION

The inclination to correct potentially erroneous perspectives on suffering, apparent in both *Ep. Pet. Phil.* and *Apoc. Pet.*, signals related debates around the turn of the third century, a period in which expectations of persecution and martyrdom define proto-orthodox Christian identity.[53] In these texts, Peter, one reputed to have suffered himself, offers further enlightenment on the experience. Drawing on distinctive understandings of Christ, the bodily aspects of suffering are devalued in *Apoc. Pet.* and redefined in *Ep. Pet. Phil.* Given his emerging role as a martyr in proto-orthodox circles, Peter's appearance in both texts as the recipient of key revelation that offers alternative perspectives on suffering strikes me as strategic. His apostolic

50. Van Os ("Role of the Apostles," 158) notes how the initial reunion of the disciples reveals the necessity of apostolic unity prior to revelation; this distinguishes *Ep. Pet. Phil.* from other gnostic revelatory discourses, including *Apoc. Pet.*, that promote a single, exclusive recipient.

51. On this point, I find a middle ground between locating no evidence of intra-Christian conflict within the text (as suggested by Tite, "Voluntary Martyrdom," 43 n. 54) and positing a distinct social group of Christians, possibly associated with Philip; for the latter position, see Hartenstein, *Zweite Lehre*; and Matthews, *Philip*. Based on the evidence of the letter and our broader understanding of late second- and early third-century Christianity, it is quite possible that Christians within a single social group, reflecting diverse perspectives and practices, were debating a range of issues, some reflected discursively in texts like *Ep. Pet. Phil.*

52. According to van Os, the text advises, "it is better to stay in the mainstream or apostolic church, because one can interpret its scriptures, confession, and rituals in a Gnostic way" ("Role of the Apostles," 160, see also 158). He is responding, in part, to Luttihuizen (*Gnostic Revisions*, 119–29), who views *Ep. Pet. Phil.* as a more overt attack on proto-orthodox perspectives.

53. On this aspect of early Christian identity, see Perkins, *Suffering Self*, and Castelli, *Martyrdom and Memory*.

authority tempers opposing views, which appear to encourage martyrdom and celebrate bodily suffering. In this way, these pseudo-Peters exemplify how, as King writes, "Christians were variously (and polemically) engaging situations of persecution and violent death," in ways that do "not presume any particular predetermination of the meaning of Jesus' death or the deaths of his followers."[54] For *Apoc. Pet.* and *Ep. Pet. Phil.*, as I show, the deaths themselves are ultimately secondary, mitigating the appeal of martyrdom.

54. King, "Martyrdom," 24–25.

— 8 —

Paul as Letter Writer and the Success of Pseudepigraphy

Constructing an Authorial Paul in the Apocryphal Corinthian Correspondence[1]

— Gregory Peter Fewster —

IN A RECENT ARTICLE, Alberto D'Anna states that there are a number of discrepancies between 3 *Corinthians* and other Pauline letters that "reduces a lot . . . the possibility of success for the fiction."[2] This statement is predicated on the stated assumption that the use of Paul's name was an effort to assume the historical Paul's authority, and that discrepancies with authentic Pauline letters would make problematic the authoritative connection.[3] Yet, on a very basic level, 3 *Cor.* enjoyed some measure of success given its diverse textual history and periodic canonical status in the Armenian Church.

1. I am grateful to John Marshall and Benjamin White, who provided comments on a prepresentation draft of this paper.
2. D'Anna, "Third Epistle," 142. D'Anna does qualify this statement as a problem primarily for modern scholars.
3. Ibid., 135, 141. Several other studies assume that the use of Paul's name appeals to an associated authority. See Rist, "III Corinthians," 56; Snyder, *Acts of Paul*, 14. Judith Lieu ("Battle for Paul," 6) includes 3 *Cor.* among a selection of Pauline pseudepigraphy, which she claims were written to appropriate Paul's authority.

This tension between textual history and a lack of coherence with the letters of Paul raises questions about what it means to call a pseudepigraphon "successful" and how we can go about determining that success. Are we to understand success purely on the basis of coherence and a pseudepigraphon's ability to go on undetected as such? And how does such coherence depend upon scholars' own preconceived images of Paul? My objective in this paper is to engage the question of the success of Pauline pseudepigraphy, *3 Cor.* in particular, and propose why we might be able to consider it a "success" in spite of its apparent incoherence with the letters of Paul. I formulate the notion of success as a feature of reception history that consists of the interplay between images of Paul and strategies used in their textual reproduction. As such, I position the text of *3 Cor.* in comparison with the diversity of early images of Paul, while considering the textual history and codicological contexts of *3 Cor.* itself. By situating Pauline pseudepigraphy within the framework of the reception of Paul, I draw a connection between the production and circulation of pseudepigraphy and the reception of images of Paul. I propose that the success of *3 Cor.* operates on the basis of an emerging and compelling construction of Paul as a letter writer that pairs with an equally dynamic image of Paul in prison.

RECEPTIONS OF PAUL AND THE SUCCESS OF A PAULINE TEXT

Standard approaches to the reception of Paul rest upon a strong bifurcation between the thought and activities of the historical Paul and the interpretations and appropriations of that original by later writers. Interpretation and appropriation take a number of forms, including commentary and citations of portions of Pauline letters, descriptions of the character and activities of Paul by commentators and in Acts literature, and in the production of Pauline pseudepigraphy. Pseudepigraphy highlights the strange theoretical position held by the notion of "reception." In order for a pseudepigraphon to endure within the legacy of Paul, its coherence with the historical Paul had to become somewhat natural.[4] Reception necessarily represents the blurring of a material distinction between the historical Paul and the received Paul, yet this distinction is precisely what continues to propel studies in Pauline

---

4. Marguerat (*Paul in Acts*, 5) suggests that reception implies a "dialectic of identity and shift that characterizes the relationship between an original thought and it subsequent reception." This may take the form of imitation on one hand, or magnification, on the other. The difficulty with this formulation, however, is that processes of reception necessarily make the difference difficult to distinguish.

reception.[5] J. C. Beker, for example, distinguishes between the *traditum*, the original tradition stemming from Paul himself, and the *traditio*, subsequent adaptations to the tradition.[6] James Aageson argues that for the "person" of Paul to have achieved receptive status through, for example, the writing of the Pastorals, he was constructed into a "personage."[7] Martinus de Boer uses the term "image" to discuss the varied legacies of Paul in the late first century, a term that continues to hold traction.[8]

Images of Paul in the Second Century

From the perspective of this traditional framework, it seems reasonable to assert that since the historical Paul wrote letters, pseudepigraphal Pauline letters function as an imitative form of the reception of Paul.[9] For example, Richard Pervo advocates the view that the Pauline letters were foundational for the expansive production of other epistolary literature in early Christianity, in spite of the other literary genres available.[10] This is a tempting hypothesis, which immediately locates the production of pseudepigraphal letters in the context of Paul's own letter-writing activity and perhaps even in the context of a strong sense of a Pauline charisma. However, if we want to consider Pauline pseudepigraphy in the context of Pauline reception, we are immediately faced with the conspicuous lack of early memories of the image of Paul as a letter writer. The Acts of the Apostles, for example,

---

5. Attempts to place a higher value upon the early reception of Paul resists the older Pauline captivity narrative. This view, propagated especially by scholars like Harnack and Campenhausen, viewed Paul's legacy as hijacked by heretics and ignored by the proto-orthodox in the mid-second century so that it had to be reclaimed by later Christian apologists. This view was eventually resisted in the 1970s with some scholars promoting a widespread diversity of Pauline legends and images. For a critical overview of these two periods, see White, *Remembering Paul*, 20–69.

6. Beker, *Heirs of Paul*, 1–31.

7. Aageson, *Paul*, 8–9.

8. De Boer, "Images of Paul."

9. In this case, pseudepigraphy may function to interpret or clarify the letters of Paul, but with the appearance that it is self-authorized. See, for example, Merz, "Fictitious Self-Exposition"; Roose, "2 Thessalonians."

10. Pervo, *Making of Paul*, 119. He bases this argument on the common use of the epistle in early Christian literature in spite of alternative genres and frequent interaction with Pauline literature—both in admiration and in conflict. Similarly, J. L. White ("Saint Paul") argues that Paul's letters provide a formulaic model imitated by other "apostolic letters" in the New Testament. He does not elaborate on letters outside the New Testament. Interestingly, this opposes the view presented in the Muratorian Fragment (see below).

commemorates Paul as a traveller who spreads word of the resurrection of Christ in the synagogues and marketplaces of the Mediterranean. Luke imagines Paul as possessing a high level of scribal literacy[11]—he can quote lengthy passages of Jewish scripture and he can converse with philosophers in the Aeropagus—yet he is never recorded as writing a letter.[12] First Timothy and Titus, even though they exist in the form of the letter, are much more interested in positioning Paul as a figure who managed order among Christ groups and the flow of leadership.[13] Various other images were propagated as well. The Coptic *Apocalypse of Paul* apparently was interested in an apocalyptic Paul who enjoyed heavenly visions, expanding on the brief description provided in 2 Cor 12:2–4 and speculating on who Paul may have met during this experience.[14] Finally, Paul as a martyr at the hand of Nero is another image propagated outside the letters and the Acts of the Apostles. Paul's death is mentioned in texts such as *1 Clement*, is considered alongside the martyrdoms of other apostles (e.g., Tertullian, *Scorp.* 15.2), while an expanded story concludes the *Acts of Paul*.[15]

Under the conventional receptive framework of casting a simple divide between the historical Paul and the received legacy of Paul, there is

11. My understanding of scribal literacy derives primarily from Chris Keith's work on the literacy of Jesus (*Jesus' Literacy*, 71–116). Here literacy is placed on a spectrum between craftsman literacy and scribal literacy. The former end of the spectrum incorporates very basic reading and writing skills relevant to one's trade while scribal literacy implies a high level of education that would have included familiarity with authoritative bodies of literature and competency in composition. We must also acknowledge a difference between reading literacy and writing literacy, a separation particularly relevant for those who received an education in Judea, which emphasized Torah reading over compositional ability.

12. Kloppenborg ("Literate Media," 34) emphasizes the way in which representations of Paul valorized him as rhetorically and literarily sophisticated. Lukan literate valorization is a particular redactional technique also applied to Jesus. For example, Jesus' oral performance of the Isaiah scroll in Luke 4:16–30, diverges from Mark's and Matthew's depiction of Jesus as a builder (Mark 6:1–6//Matt 13:54–58), which Keith claims is a Lukan strategy to move "Jesus from the manual-labour class to the scribal-literate class" (*Jesus' Literacy*, 142–45).

13. I group 1 Timothy and Titus together without 2 Timothy on the basis of the increasingly common affirmation that the three Pastoral Epistles were not composed as a unit. See especially the discussion in Richards, *Difference and Distance*, 20–26; and Den Dulk, "I Permit No Woman."

14. Kaler ("Expanded Understanding") argues how consideration of this text widens our view of Nag Hammadi Paulinism in the second century. Where scholars have typically engaged the question of how Pauline theology is adapted by gnostic writers, Kaler argues that the *Apocalypse of Paul* bears witness to the construction of Paul as an apocalyptic hero.

15. See especially the comprehensive discussion of the legends of Paul's martyrdom in Tajra, *Martyrdom of St. Paul*; and Snyder, *Acts of Paul*, 24–65.

a strange disconnect between the fact that our primary access to Paul is his letters but there are a number of traditions that do not seem to put a lot of stock in that letter-writing activity itself.[16] Judith Lieu uses the title "the elusive Paul" to describe second-century impressions of Paul wherein these writers have only a passing and stilted knowledge of Paul and his teachings, resorting to formulaic applications and veiled allusions.[17] Lieu also cites the author of *1 Clement* and Ignatius as two writers who seem to know that Paul wrote letters, but their grasp of the content of these letters is somewhat lacking. She possibly overstates her case in some examples, but appropriately problematizes a direct connection between knowing Pauline letter content and remembering a Pauline letter-writing image. There is thus a difference between using and interpreting Paul's letters and considering him as scribal literate and a letter writer.[18] In the following examples we will see that commemoration of Paul as a letter writer does exist; however, this commemoration fits within the label "elusive Paul," since it does not often connect knowledge of Paul (or Pauline letter content) with reflection upon Paul's letter-writing activity.

Early Images of Paul as a Letter Writer

The first example comes from a Pauline letter itself. In 2 Cor 10:9–11, Paul attempts to mediate his authority and his opponents' accusations about his authority in a contrast between his bodily presence and absence; this absence is accommodated by writing a letter. It is taken for granted that the writing of a letter is used when the writer cannot physically be present. Paul thus constructs himself as someone who writes letters and has equivalent strength of authority both in his bodily presence and his absence.[19]

16. I here distinguish between letter-writing activity and the use of content from Paul's letters. For example, Irenaeus frequently engages Pauline letters both to defend his positions and to expose the misuse of Paul by opponents. See the helpful discussions in Norris, "Irenaeus' Use of Paul"; and White, "How to Read a Book." However, Irenaeus does not seem to explicitly discuss Paul's activity of letter writing, using verbs of speaking rather than verbs of writing. This observation was confirmed for me by Strawbridge, "'Preacher of the Truth.'"

17. See Lieu, "Battle for Paul," 11–13.

18. Keep in mind that remembering someone as scribal literate and as a letter writer are not equivalent. As in the example from Acts 17, Paul was remembered as scribal literate but not necessarily as a letter writer. With that said, I consider the construction of Paul as a letter writer part of a larger effort within early Christianity to represent themselves as literate and accordingly their early leaders as literate heroes. This project has been proposed in Kloppenborg, "Literate Media," 21–59.

19. Second Corinthians elsewhere foregrounds Paul's letter-writing activity and his

Two other examples of the construction of Paul as a letter writer occur within instances of verisimilitude, if indeed the letters in which they appear are both pseudepigraphal. Verisimilitude in pseudepigraphal letters refers to a fictitious self-reflexivity, with attempts to make the letter appear genuine through the inclusion of mundane detail and references to the act of writing the letter.[20] These instances are notable especially in contrast to other early Pauline pseudepigrapha (e.g., Ephesians, 1 Timothy, or Titus) that do not display the same kind of literary anxiety. Second Thessalonians famously includes an exaggerated signature at the end of the letter, which Paul supposedly appended to all of his letters.[21] Earlier in the letter, however, the author warns against being swayed by, among other things, "a letter as/supposedly from us" (ἐπιστολῆς ὡς δι' ἡμῶν) (2 Thess 2:2). However interpreted, this passage raises the letter-writing image of Paul by positioning him as someone whose letter-writing activity could be imitated.[22]

The author of 2 Timothy also makes a passing reference to writing materials near the end of his letter as he asks "Timothy" to bring with him the cloak he left in Troas as well as his books. There is some debate as to what τὰ βιβλία μάλιστα τὰς μεμβράνας (4:13) actually refers. This reference

absence from the Corinthians. See also 2 Cor 1:13–2:4; 3:1–4 (though metaphorical); 7:12; 9:1; 13:10. Note also Mitchell's suggestion ("New Testament Envoys," 641–43) that the sending of a letter, especially in the care of a designated letter carrier, could perform a mediatory function that Paul himself could not.

20. Donelson (*Pseudepigraphy*, 23–42) notes the tendency toward verisimilitude in the Pastorals and sets it in the context of analogous practices in Greco-Roman pseudepigraphy. See also Rosenmeyer (*Ancient Epistolary Fictions*, 204–209), who describes the pseudepigrapher's anxiety of producing a forgery, which frequently resulted in the inclusion of mundane biographical details and references to the act of writing.

21. According to the extant manuscripts, signatures do not appear at the end of all the Pauline letters. However, the signatures at 1 Cor 16:12; Gal 6:11; Col 4:18; Phlm 19 are other brief instances where Paul's letter-writing activity emerges from the background. The signature here thus invents the signer, so to speak, which Keith has argued is an attempt to foreground Paul's literate skill vis-à-vis the ability to sign his name and compose brief greetings. In the context of pseudepigraphy, the signature performs double duty, continuing to advocate for Paul's moderate literacy and implying that the letter came from Paul himself. See Keith, "'In My Own Hand'"; Fewster, "'Can I Have Your Autograph?,'" 34.

22. Most commentators who see 2 Thessalonians as pseudonymous take this to be a somewhat ironic warning against other Pauline pseudepigraphy, especially considering the signature at the end of the letter, which likely is there to authenticate the letter. E. Randolph Richards (*Secretary*, 174) suggests that the signature is meant to guard against forgery. Hanna Roose ("'A Letter as by Us'") appropriately notes the ambiguity of the ὡς, meaning either "supposedly" or "as," thus either referring to some pseudepigraphon or 1 Thessalonians, which she argues reflects the anxiety of the pseudepigrapher to construct a compelling pseudepigraphon. At the very least, this passage does seem to hint at Paul's letter-writing activity, even if in a roundabout way.

simply may construct Paul as someone who generally makes use of literature, but the books could also be blank scrolls that he would write on or
even collections of his own letters.[23] In an effort to avoid conflating scribal
literacy in general with letter-writing in particular, I will simply suggest that
it is possible that 2 Timothy hints at Paul's letter-writing activities, probably as a way of providing a sense of legitimacy to the pseudepigraphon as
well as self-reflexively referring to some aspect of literate practice within a
pseudepigraphal document. In both of these examples, verisimilitude is a
site where Paul's image as a letter writer can be constructed.

   1 Clement provides an early mention of Paul's letter-writing activity.[24]
The author recognizes continued factions in the Corinthian community
and using very bloated language tells his readers to take the blessed Paul's
letter (τὴν ἐπιστολὴν τοῦ μακαρίου Παύλου τοῦ ἀποστόλου),[25] asking them
to recall what he wrote (ἔγραψεν) to them, and that he wrote spiritually
(πνευματικῶς ἐπέστειλεν) about factions surrounding Peter and Apollos (*1
Clem.* 47.1–2; ed. Lightfoot). Clement thus seems to have a basic knowledge
of at least 1 Corinthians and elevates the image of Paul and his letter-writing
activity to a spiritual activity. Other instances of Pauline citations and allusions occur throughout; however, they are not explicitly paired with Paul's
letter-writing image.[26]

23. Donelson remarks that books and parchments are "particularly appropriate
materials for a travelling apostle who likes to write letters" (*Pseudepigraphy*, 56), and
Kloppenborg states that this reference "underscores the identity of Paul *as a writer*"
("Literate Media," 32–33, italics original).

24. *1 Clement* is usually dated to the mid-90s, though Gregory ("*1 Clement*: An Introduction") proposes the potential for an earlier date (70s–80s). The literary relationship between *1 Clement* and Polycarp establishes the composition of Polycarp's letter as
the latest possible date for *1 Clement*. See Berding, "Polycarp's Use of *1 Clement*," on the
relationship between Polycarp and *1 Clement*.

25. White (*Remembering Paul*, 79–81) identifies several early references, including
1 Clem. 47:1–7 along with 2 Pet 3:15–16; Ignatius, *Eph.* 12.2; and Polycarp, *Phil.* 3.2;
11.2–3, which "comingle honorific titles for Paul with reference to his letters." Calling
Paul "blessed" is particularly prominent. The brief account of the Scillitan Martyrs also
calls Paul a just man when the protagonists reveal that they have in their bag the books
and letters of Paul. See Musurillo, *Acts of the Christian Martyrs*, 12. It is probably the
case that the reference to the books and letters of Paul tells us less about the commemoration of Paul as a letter writer, and more about the relationship between early Christian
identity and the book as a cultural artifact. See Kloppenborg, "Literate Media," 30–31,
on this latter point.

26. Debate concerning the extent of *1 Clement*'s knowledge of Paul ranges. Downs
recently argued for Clement's knowledge of Romans, arguing that Clement's discussion
of justification follows Paul rhetorically, though their cosmology differs. Gregory takes a
fairly minimalist approach and limits *1 Clement*'s knowledge to Romans, 1 Corinthians,
Hebrews, as well as some Jesus tradition, while Hagner's study argues that *1 Clement*

The Muratorian Fragment articulates an interesting comparative account of Paul's letter-writing activity. While the date of the fragment remains a contested issue, the image of Paul that emerges in the fragment would not be entirely out of place in the second century.[27] The fragment states that Paul imitated John in writing to seven churches (Cum ipse beatus apostolus paulus sequens prodecessoris sui Iohannis ordine nonnisi comenati semptae eccleses scribat ordine tali, fol. ib.16–19; ed. Tregelles) and names each one.[28] Additionally, the fragment betrays knowledge that there are two letters written fictitiously in the name of Paul (Pauli nomine fincte, fol. iia.1–4; ed. Tregelles) to the Alexandrians and the Laodiceans.[29] Here, Paul's letter-writing activity is seen to be in continuity with other apostolic figures who also wrote letters and an activity that is subject to imitation. However, this information seems to proceed from basic inferences drawn from a 13-letter collection rather than from images of Paul circulating outside of the collection itself.

Polycarp contrasts his own writing of letters with Paul's writing of letters in *Phil.* 3.1–2. Polycarp seems to be very conscientious to mute his own status in comparison to the "blessed and glorious Paul" (τοῦ μακαρίου καὶ ἐνδόξου Παύλου; ed. Hartog). He insists that he did not write on his own accord but only responded to the Philippians' request, reasoning that he is unable to attain to the type of wisdom that Paul taught (ἐδίδαξεν).[30] While Polycarp first describes Paul's teaching in person (κατὰ πρόσωπον),

---

was familiar with all of Paul's letters except Philemon and 1 and 2 Thessalonians. See Downs, "Justification"; Gregory, "*1 Clement* and the Writings"; and Hagner, *Use of the Old and New Testament*, 236–37.

27. A late second-century date made up the early consensus. Sundberg's somewhat influential proposal, finally emerging in his 1973 article, proposed a fourth-century date, though this was forcefully rebutted by Ferguson (Sundberg Jr., "Canon Muratori"; cf. Ferguson, "Canon Muratori"). The more recent date has been argued even more vigorously in Hahneman's 1992 monograph, *Muratorian Fragment*. Recently, Armstrong ("Victorinus of Pettau") has argued for a third-century date by proposing Victorinus of Pettau as the author of the Fragment. For a more comprehensive survey of the issue of dating see Schnabel, "Muratorian Fragment." The list of Paul's letters itself creates problems for an early date, since there is no mention of Hebrews, whose Pauline attribution is well established in the late second century by its inclusion in P[46].

28. I have retained the incorrect spelling from the Fragment, rather than include editors' corrections.

29. Which letter to the Laodiceans the Fragment refers to is unclear. The text of the Fragment notes that these letters were written "ad he(re)sem marcionis" and Marcion includes an epistle to the Laodiceans in his list, though that reference is probably to Ephesians.

30. Cf. Lieu, "Battle for Paul," 11, who suggests that Polycarp simply follows in Paul's footsteps.

he adds that Paul wrote letters (ἔγραψεν ἐπιστολάς), which are able to continue building up the Philippians' faith.[31] Two implications arise from this assertion: Polycarp affirms the relationship between Paul's letter-writing and his bodily absence and he also affirms the continuing relevance of Paul's letter(s) long after his death. Berding notes that in Polycarp's letter, citations and allusions to Pauline texts cluster around the three occurrences of Paul's name.[32] However, only one of these instances mentions Paul's letter-writing activity (3.2) and two note Paul as a teacher (3.2; 11.2). This is similar to Ignatius, who in *Rom.* 4.3, differentiates himself from Paul and Peter—they are people with the authority to issue commands.[33] Even so, Paul's and Peter's ability to command are not necessarily predicated upon any letter-writing capability.

Both Polycarp and Ignatius function as witnesses to the early dissemination of at least some of Paul's letters.[34] But however provocative these citations and paraphrases are, references to Paul's letter-writing *activity* are somewhat pale in comparison to Ignatius's and Polycarp's reflection upon their own epistolary contribution. Ignatius makes frequent reference to his own acts of writing (using some form of γράφω), while only making the one passing reference to Paul's letters in *Eph.* 12.2, without mentioning the act of writing them.[35] In *Phil.* 13–14, Polycarp continues his final greetings,

31. Polycarp's use of the plural ἐπιστολάς is a contentious issue given that we currently possess only one letter that Paul wrote to the Philippians. Hartog (*Polycarp and the New Testament*, 223–26) suggests that the plural results from a combination of Polycarp referring to a multiple-letter collection of Paul's letters and the general notion that physical absence pairs with the writing of letters. Berding notes other solutions—Polycarp made a mistake, Polycarp knows other letters, he represents a single letter with the plural, he includes 1 and 2 Thessalonians or any Pauline letter is in view—but Berding sees no resolution to the problem (*Polycarp and Paul*, 62–63). Holmes ("Polycarp's *Letter to the Philippians*," 212) adds that this reference does not confirm a priori that Polycarp was aware of what we now recognize as Paul's letter to the Philippians.

32. Berding, *Polycarp and Paul*, 149–52; see also Holmes, "Polycarp's *Letter to the Philippians*," 201–18.

33. Paul is mentioned throughout Ignatius and, according to Foster ("Epistles of Ignatius"), the literary affinities between the two corpora confirm Ignatius's knowledge of the Pauline corpus. Ignatius, *Eph.* 12.2 makes explicit reference to Paul as someone who remembers the Ephesians in all his letters (ἐν πάσῃ ἐπιστολῇ). Curiously, the mention of the letters is replaced with "prayers" in the longer recension.

34. Holmes, for example, rightly notes that "*Philippians* is unquestionably an important early witness to Paul's written legacy" ("Polycarp and Paul," 58).

35. See Ignatius, *Eph.* 12.1; 20.1; *Magn.* 15.1; *Trall.* 3.3; 5.1; *Rom.* 4.1; 7.2 (2x); 10.1; *Smyrn.* 5.3; 12.1; *Pol.* 8.1 (2x, he also mentions the sending of letters). This count is higher than in Paul's letters themselves (see 1 Cor 16:21; 2 Cor 1:13; 9:1; 13:10; Phil 3:1; Col 4:18; 1 Thess 4:9; 2 Thess 3:17), not to mention that Paul (or the Pauline pseudepigrapher) mentions his own writing usually in the context of a signature/final greeting.

writing extensively about having received letters from the Philippians and from Ignatius, sending the letters of Ignatius to the Philippians appended to the present letter (and the benefit they will receive from them), and finally noting that he wrote the letter with the help of Crescens (*haec vobis scripsi per Crescentem*).[36] That Polycarp is able to write in some detail about epistolary correspondence between several parties while acknowledging his involvement in the collection and dissemination of Ignatius's letters implies a conscious awareness of literary practice that is only partially applied to Paul's activity. While it is true that Polycarp places his status (and particularly his own letter-writing activity) lower than Paul's, Polycarp's image of Paul as an active letter writer is not nearly as contoured as his own self-construction as a letter writer.

These descriptions of Paul's letter-writing activity are brief and, I suggest, do not provide nearly the depth of image construction that we see at play in biographical and apocalyptic modes of Pauline reception. First- and second-century writers are only able to invoke Pauline letter content and occasionally connect this letter content to letter-writing activity that was necessitated by Paul's absence and need to give commands. Second Peter 3:14–16 marks a later example that seems to assume a developing image of the beloved Paul as a letter writer, whose content is complex and able to be used in deceitful ways. However, it still does not attain to some of the later constructions we will see in the *3 Cor.* material. This brief account of images of Paul in early Pauline reception reveals a diversity and complexity of images and the genre choices made to propagate them. While the notion of image is a compelling feature of reception theory, it does not adequately address or explain a connection between developing images of Paul and the ways they were selected and deployed.

Challenges to the Traditional Reception Paradigm

Recent scholarship on the reception of Paul provides some more complex models that, while not without deficiency, present an excellent way forward. François Bovon divides the reception of Paul into two modes: he is received either as a *document* or as a *monument*.[37] The documentary Paul is a textual figure who is reproduced through pseudepigraphy or understood by interpreting his letters, while Paul as monument is admired and discussed because of his exploits. This paradigm would account for the data above by situating citation and allusion to Pauline letter content as documentary

36. See Hartog, *Polycarp's Epistle*, 94–95.

37. Bovon, *New Testament and Christian Apocrypha*, 305–17.

reception, while description of Paul's letter-writing activity would count as monumental reception—the former being stronger than the latter. Daniel Marguerat develops Bovon's model into a theory of Pauline reception that defines three poles or strategies that ancient writers invoked to negotiate the Pauline legacy. The significance of Marguerat's formulation rests in its attempt to cut through the strict comparison of Paul's epistolary self-disclosure and the portrayal of Paul in Acts, comparison that either must harmonize or emphasize historical or theological discrepancies.[38] These approaches privilege Paul's letters as the basis for reliable knowledge about Paul, to which Luke's Acts more or less adheres. Marguerat resists such privileging of Paul's letters by shifting them into a stream of reception in their own right and widening the possible sources for Acts' reception of Paul to include oral stories about him. Second-century writers deployed imagined features of a Pauline persona into three parallel streams of reception: the "biographical pole" instantiates Paul's activities and accomplishments, the "doctoral pole" pursues Pauline thought and authority through the penning of pseudepigraphal letters, and the "documentary pole" collects and preserves Paul's letters into a literary whole.[39]

According to Marguerat's model, the three poles are concurrent receptive strategies, but they are somewhat porous and interactive. Thus, images

---

38. See the discussion of these options also in Phillips, *Paul*. The literature on the historicity of Acts and its relationship to Paul's self-disclosure in his letters is extensive. Some studies see the portrait of Paul in Acts as completely irreconcilable with Paul's letters, such that Luke virtually invents his Paul (Mount, *Pauline Christianity*), or at least prefer to see Acts as of secondary value, especially regarding chronology (e.g., Jewett, *Chronology*; McLean, *Cursed Christ*, 148–64; cf. Riesner's argument [*Paul's Early Period*, 1–32] that the data of Acts cannot be completely abandoned and Paul's own autobiographical material must be critically scrutinized). Marguerat characterizes Porter's work (*Paul of Acts*, 187–206) as paradigmatic of conservative attempts at harmonization, though this is somewhat of a mischaracterization since Porter is more interested in Lukan characterization and literary and rhetorical variation within the Lukan portrait. Even so, when he finally treats the relationship between Acts and Paul's letters (*Paul of Acts*, ch. 9), he argues that the variation is not as significant as previous critical scholarship often portrays, and the types of variation are to be expected between two different and accomplished writers in that time. This sort of argument has also been taken up by Keener (*Acts*, 221–57), who emphasizes Luke's adherence to ancient historiographical standards. Still other treatments of Paul in Acts are primarily concerned with Luke's reconfigured portrait of Paul, and in the case of Lentz (*Luke's Portrait of Paul*), its potential reception by its second-century audience.

39. See Marguerat, *Paul in Acts*, 5–7. Holmes ("Polycarp and Paul," 58) claims to adapt Marguerat's poles in discussion of Paul and Polycarp, tracing Polycarp's treatment of Paul's letters, knowledge of Pauline biography, and the theological influence of Paul on Polycarp.

of Paul can shift and be influenced by adjacent streams.[40] The extent to which receptive strategies can remain distinct remains unclear. How might images of Paul propagate from one pole to another until the receptive strategy itself becomes undifferentiated? For example, treating Paul as a doctor of the church through the production of pseudepigraphy quickly folded into the treatment of Paul as a document through the inclusion of pseudepigraphy into the collection of Pauline letters. In spite of these remaining questions, Marguerat's notion of strategy will prove useful.

A second concern is brought to light in the recent work of Benjamin White, who advocates a thoroughgoing shift in theoretical approach to the reception of Paul. White argues that even provocative proposals, like that of Marguerat, continue to operate on the epistemologically problematic basis of a "real" Paul, which many scholars view as having been corrupted in the production of the Pauline legacy.[41] Instead of focusing on how the second-century writers "got Paul wrong," White is interested in basic images about the apostle that precede their deployment in commemorative texts.[42] From this perspective, White is able to argue that the interpretation of Paul is always mediated by conceptual images of the apostle. For example, both *3 Cor.* and Irenaeus of Lyons utilize an image of Paul as the defender of tradition against heresy, an image that they gained largely from the Pastorals.[43] White's model depends on articulating conceptual images that mediate subsequent Pauline interpretation and he demonstrates how different writers can employ the same image to similar effects, but with different compositional tactics.

Both White and Marguerat elaborate on features of a theory of reception that are important for my hypothesis. By elaborating on a theory of image construction, White warns us against evaluating later writers' constructions of Paul on the basis of "historical accuracy." With this

40. Marguerat (*Paul in Acts*, 5, 31) is adamant that "the canon of Pauline letters does not form the documentary basis, the backdrop for the apostles' reception," since that canon is itself a later production. What this means is that Paul's letters may still operate as origins for Pauline reception, but canonical understandings of Paul cannot.

41. See White, *Remembering Paul*, 1–7, 10–17. John Marshall observes similarly: "The appropriate question is not, Who in the second century understood Paul?, but rather, What axes of transformation and continuity characterize each reception of Paul?" ("Misunderstanding the New Paul," 27). Marguerat maintains the language of a "real Paul" that can be distinguished even from Paul received through the documentary pole.

42. White (*Remembering Paul*, 70–107) approaches this question through the use of social memory theory, which provides a social-scientific basis for how memories are formed and subsequently deployed.

43. Ibid., 108–69, esp. 166–69.

preoccupation set aside, I am able to investigate more closely the strategies and interests involved in producing a particular image of Paul from a shared cultural imagination. White recognizes that images are propagated through texts, thus narrowing his focus upon the function of images in the writing of novel texts while understanding these images as operating prediscursively for the writers of said texts.[44] However, there are two shortcomings of this formulation for the purposes of this essay. First, an interest primarily in the writing of new texts in the Pauline legacy diminishes our ability to account for lengthy and disruptive processes of textual transmission. Marguerat's notion of receptive strategies is a necessary contribution in order for us to appreciate the reception and reproduction of Pauline images through the material transmission of a single text. In particular, the doctoral pole provides a place to start thinking about Pauline pseudepigraphy as a feature of reception, within which we can analyze certain images of Paul.[45] Second, disconnecting the reception of Paul from the historical Paul reduces the need to speak of reception altogether. For example, Michael Kaler prefers to talk about the creation of a *Paulusbild* rather than the reception and passing on of Pauline images.[46] This returns us to the precise problem of harmonization vs. incompatibility that Marguerat sought to solve with his three poles of reception. However, questions of consistency and coherence between images of Paul exist between different images deployed in different texts, but also in reproductions of images in the history of a single text. This latter dimension is informative of the way we should think about the propagation of Pauline images, insofar as it positions difference in image construction within a discursive and textual trajectory and not grounded in a "real Paul." Thus, rather than considering images of Paul as prediscursive resources for the composers of Pauline pseudepigraphy, biography, etc., we may consider images of Paul as scholars' redescriptive attempts to trace variations in continuity and discontinuity across the field of Pauline reception.[47]

44. Ibid., 79–81. Recall White's treatment of some of the same examples I raised in the discussion of early memories of Paul as a letter writer.

45. I am sympathetic to Timothy Beal's criticism of a reception history that "priviledg[es] scriptural content over scriptural materiality" ("Reception History," 365–69). Textual transmission and the variation entailed by transmission is a feature of such materiality.

46. See Kaler, "Expanded Understanding," 306. Beal ("Reception History," 367) notes that "reception" implies an original to be received, a problematic notion with reference to the Bible, which has no original as such. He thus prefers to speak of a cultural history of the scriptures (ibid., 371).

47. This approach comes close to redeeming D'Anna's statement concerning the discontinuity between the authentic Paul and the Paul of 3 *Cor.*—i.e., discontinuity depends on scholars' expectations and constructions of the received Paul. This is precisely

As we saw above, the descriptions of Paul's letter-writing activity result in a pale but constructed image, from as early as 2 Corinthians and extending throughout a variety of early Christian literature. We also noticed that images do not occur on their own. In each example where Paul is pictured as a letter writer, there are other features that contribute to its portrait of Paul. The Paul who writes letters is also a Paul who is absent. The Paul who writes letters is also a Paul who gives advice. The Paul who writes letters is also an esteemed Paul with a great deal of wisdom. Early depictions of Paul as a letter writer are neither detailed nor programmatic, but are lost amid other concerns and images of Paul potentially more relevant to immediate concerns. It may be difficult to discern the effect that an image of Paul had on his reception, except insofar as it is materially constituted according to a particular strategy. This pairing of Pauline image, receptive strategy, and textual history is where we can begin to formulate a notion of success.

A document's success can be indicated by its textual history. Situating success within the framework of reception history provides a more robust way of assessing such success in spite of potential hindrances. First, success occurs through the propagation of an image or a cluster of images. And their validation relies upon previous instantiations and can be compared against future ones. A successful image is, in a sense, self-validating insofar as it recommends itself for future deployment. Second, authors use images according to strategies of reception, as initially proposed by Marguerat. Different writers may use a different strategy to deploy a given image and thus augment it compared to other uses of the same image. Third, the history of a single text, like *3 Cor.*, may reveal different receptive strategies, allowing for both the re-production and re-creation of a particular image or set of images of Paul.

PAUL IN *3 CORINTHIANS*

With this broad receptive framework in mind, I return to D'Anna's charge that the discrepancies in *3 Cor.* as compared to the letters of the historical Paul renders its success strange to the modern scholar. In what follows I will map out what I consider to be the relative success of *3 Cor.* on the basis of *image* and *strategy*, the two dimensions articulated above. On one hand, *3 Cor.* constructs a compelling image of Paul as a letter writer. This image is also dependent upon other relevant images at play in the Corinthian

---

the driving concept behind Marshall's reappraisal of Marcion's reception of Paul ("Misunderstanding the New Paul," 1–29). However, the discontinuity noted by D'Anna still revolves around the notion of a "real" Paul, a notion that has already been criticized.

Correspondence, especially Paul as prisoner.[48] On the other hand, the textual history of 3 Cor. sees what is initially a text within Marguerat's doctoral pole integrated into the documentary pole. In this textual history, the image of Paul as letter writer develops and expands. Further, the theological emphases of 3 Cor. are altered slightly because of its shifting codicological context, thus leaving the question of traction with the historical Paul irrelevant.

Paul as Letter Writer in 3 *Corinthians*

The shortest, and presumably earliest, text of 3 Cor. comes to us in Greek as one of several texts in the Bodmer Miscellaneous Codex.[49] This text is immediately striking compared to other familiar Pauline pseudepigrapha because it occurs as a correspondence: a letter from the Corinthians followed by Paul's response.[50] The Corinthians' letter claims to be sent by Stephanus and

48. Hovhanessian (*Third Corinthians*, 94–96) suggests that one of the pseudepigraphic techniques used by the writer of 3 Cor. is the creation of a fictive letter setting that plausibly maps onto well-known correspondence between Paul and believers in Corinth. He also notes the historical setting of Paul in prison but does not directly connect the two images closely.

49. The other texts include the *Protevangelium of James*, 11th *Ode of Solomon*, Jude, Melito's *Peri Pascha*, a fragment of a hymn, the *Apology of Phileas*, Psalms 33:2—34:1, 1 Peter, and 2 Peter. Brice Jones ("Bodmer 'Miscellaneous' Codex," 9; see also Wasserman, "Papyrus 72," 154) has argued that the Bodmer Codex should be considered a "composite codex" rather than a "miscellany" with no theme that unites the selection of texts, though possibilities for a unifying theme have been proposed by, e.g., Haines-Eitzen (*Guardians of Letters*, 96–104), who suggests the theme might be the body. Michel Testuz (*Papyrus Bodmer X–XII*, 9–45) provides the first edition of this third-/fourth-century manuscript. Scholars provide a range of dates for the original composition of 3 Cor., from the early first century to the early third. Snyder (*Acts of Paul*, 186–87) notes that determining the date is usually predicated upon determining the identity of the opponents. This range is suitable for my treatment of the letter-writing image. At the very least 3 Cor. was composed somewhat contemporaneous to 1 *Clement* and Polycarp, etc., though I would suggest that the inclusion of 3 Cor. in the composite codex mediates against its composition any later than the late second century. White ("Reclaiming Paul?," 517–20) proposes that the image of Paul at play in 3 Cor. bears such a resemblance to Irenaeus's that they must come from the same period—i.e., late second century.

50. Ehrman (*Forgery and Counterforgery*, 427) suggests that Paul's response may have been composed without the initial letter from the Corinthians, since Paul neither mentions the Corinthians' letter nor names the opponents. More importantly, v. 8 of the Corinthians' letter states that Paul was saved from the lawless one, whereas he is in prison when he writes the response. Compare this argument with Snyder (*Acts of Paul*, 155–68), who suggests that the Corinthians' letter was composed to set up the concerns addressed in Paul's "response." My hypothesis does not necessarily depend on the two letters being composed together or separately, though Ehrman's comments are

a group of elders, who are concerned with the arrival of Simon and Cleobius in Corinth and their disruptive teachings, which are listed in order.[51] Besides setting up "Paul" for a concise response to the "deviant views" (ἀστοχήμασι), this initial letter betrays a number of anxieties that are important to the production of the pseudepigraphon.[52] Benjamin White has already noted that one of the key images of Paul at play in the correspondence is Paul as defender of the faith against opponents.[53] However, there are a number of other details that play into the Pauline image construction in 3 Corinthians. First, the pseudepigrapher seems slightly anxious about the death of Paul. The voice of Stephanus is thankful that the Lord has shown mercy, insofar as Paul is still in the flesh and thus able to respond to their request or at least respond in writing (II.8).[54] This statement affirms the significance of "the flesh" in the scope of the pseudepigraphon by circumlocuting around Paul's continuing to be alive, but it also establishes the possibility for Paul to come to Corinth and respond to the teachings of Simon and Cleobius directly. Stephanus's final statement confirms this desire by asserting that Paul's prompt visit will save the Corinthians from foolishness and stumbling (II.16).

worth noting. In either case, Snyder's argument could be pushed to the benefit of my hypothesis. The necessity of Paul's letter-writing activity seems to play off the Corinthians' partial ignorance of Paul's situation, which is only heightened by their expectation that Paul is available to visit them and thus retroactively accentuating the fact that Paul responds with a letter rather than a visit.

51. Attempts to mirror-read opponents in this document have resulted in a fairly circumscribed set of conclusions. White ("Reclaiming Paul?," 499, 521–23) resists mirror reading for opponents altogether but suggests that 3 Cor. responds to opponents of "a generally 'gnostic' variety." A similar approach is advocated independently by Snyder (Acts of Paul, 155–68), who suggests that the opponents in the initial letter (usually the guide for scholars' reconstructions) are used as a rhetorical foil to set up Paul's doctrinal response. Previous interpreters have made more specific proposals including Marcionism (Rist, "III Corinthians," 49–58), Ophites (Hovhanessian, Third Corinthians, 126–31), Simon Magus (Klijn, "Apocryphal Correspondence," 22), Gnostics in general (Dunn, "Acts of Paul," 122–27, 190); or Gnostics, particularly Saturnilians (D'Anna, "Third Epistle," 143).

52. Scholars provide a variety of glosses for ἀστόχημα, including échecs, tribulations, afflictions, and failures. White's recent proposal ("Reclaiming Paul?," 501–503) that ἀστόχημα should be translated as "deviant views" is convincing.

53. White, "Reclaiming Paul?," 499–500, 505–10. White suggests that the image of Paul as the defender of the faith against deviant teachings is an image developed from the Pastorals.

54. That Paul is described as "in the flesh" rather than simply alive likely ties into the doctrinal anxiety of the pseudepigraphon. The numbering of the text follows that of Hovhanessian (Third Corinthians). See further n. 59 below.

In keeping with White's argument, Paul is immediately established as the type of person who defends against doctrinal deviance. Stephanus's letter also constructs Paul as the type of person who travels between cities in order to defend against those deviant views. However, the text of the Bodmer Miscellaneous Codex immediately mitigates against the prominence of that type of Paul, since he responds instead with a letter. The structure of the address appears to contain the usual Pauline elaborations, but rather than calling himself an apostle of Christ Jesus (cf. Rom 1:1; 1, 2 Cor 1:1; Gal 1:1; Eph 1:1; Phil 1:1; Col 1:1; 1, 2 Tim 1:1; Tit 1:1; *Ep. Lao.* 1), Paul refers to himself as a prisoner of Christ Jesus, a title only found elsewhere in the address of Philemon.[55] As the text unfolds, Paul responds to the Corinthians' listed concerns, reaffirming the birth of Jesus by Mary for the purpose of saving all flesh and providing arguments for the resurrection of the flesh with examples from nature and the Hebrew Bible.

Following the elaboration of his argument for the resurrection, Paul asserts his position as prisoner by describing the bonds on his hands and brands on his body (III.35). With this reiteration, the pseudepigrapher plays up the image of Paul as a prisoner. This Paul-as-prisoner image is critical to the successful construction of the composite image of Paul in *3 Cor.*, both in comparison to the more widespread reception of Pauline images and regarding the coherence of the Correspondence as a whole. The image of Paul as a prisoner occurs throughout Acts.[56] Paul is imprisoned with Silas in Philippi (Acts 16), then again in Jerusalem (Acts 21) and in Caesarea (Acts 25–26).[57] Paul as a prisoner is more commonly referenced in a number of authentic and pseudepigraphal letters. The most extensive description of Paul's imprisonment takes place in Phil 1:12–30, in which Paul describes his imprisonment by the Romans and his resignation to his inevitable death. As noted, Paul also calls himself a prisoner in Phlm 1 but he references his status as a prisoner in Phlm 9 and calls Epaphras a prisoner like himself in Phlm 23. This kind of co-prisoner language occurs also in Col 4:10 (regarding Aristarchus), while self-reflexive references to Paul's being a prisoner/ in chains appear in Colossians (4:18), Ephesians (3:1; 4:1; and 4:18), *Laodiceans* (v. 6), and 2 Timothy (1:8 and 2:9).

Paul as prisoner appears as a prominent image propagated within the early reception of Paul, especially in some pseudepigraphal letters. This

55. In Codex Claromontanus, both the Greek and Latin text read "Paul an apostle of Jesus Christ," with the Greek text adding "servant of Christ Jesus" in smaller letters at the end of the column, perhaps by the same hand.

56. This image also appears in *Acts Paul*, which will be treated in depth below.

57. In Acts 23:18 and 25:27 Paul is referred to as a prisoner by an opposing official (a centurion and by Herod Agrippa).

image provides for the *3 Cor.* correspondence a convincing scenario that explains why Paul wrote a letter rather than visiting the Corinthians in person, as they requested. As we already saw in 2 Corinthians, Polycarp's *Letter to the Philippians*, and possibly 2 Timothy, Paul's bodily absence pairs with his image as a letter writer. If bodily absence serves as a prerequisite for Paul's letter-writing activity, then Paul's imprisonment provides a reason for such absence. As *3 Cor.* takes up the Paul-in-prison image the picture of Paul as a letter writer is made more compelling. Within the Bodmer text, this image is not explicitly tied to any historical circumstance, thus allowing readers to imagine any number of imprisonments with which they may be familiar. In what follows, I will demonstrate the ways this image is developed in the life of the text of *3 Cor.*

The Success of *3 Corinthians* and Its Textual Instability

The Bodmer Miscellaneous Codex provides the earliest and shortest text of *3 Cor.*, though fourth-century attestation in the writings of Ephrem and Aphrahat reflects a diffusion of the text at least from Egypt to Persia to Syria.[58] The text appears in a variety of other witnesses, including Coptic, Armenian, and Latin, which collectively attest to four distinct portions of the text.[59] Sections II and IV contain the letters of the Corinthians and Paul

58. While the Bodmer Codex is the earliest and briefest manuscript of *3 Cor.*, it remains to be seen whether or not it represents the "original text." This designation of "original text" is itself a problematic category, now criticized on the basis of its diverse usage, material representation, and ideological content. See notably, Parker, *Living Text*, esp. 1–7; Epp, "Multivalence." Snyder (*Acts of Paul*, 152–53) suggests that the Bodmer Codex best represents the earliest recoverable text, though it may not be a good reflection of still earlier but now lost manuscripts. Based upon a suggestion from Eldon Epp, Snyder defends his qualification noting that P[72], a notoriously unreliable manuscript of 1–2 Peter and Jude, is collected in the same codex as *3 Cor.*, and thus may be similarly unreliable. This proposal must be modified somewhat, since the contents of the Bodmer Codex were copied by different scribes. However, it is generally agreed that the scribe of Jude and 1–2 Peter are the same as the scribe of *3 Cor.* and the majority of corrections were accomplished by the same scribe rather than another working with a different *Vorlage*. See Royse, *Scribal Habits*, 546–70; Wasserman, "Papyrus 72," 148–54; cf. Haines-Eitzen, *Guardians of Letters*, 96–104. In any case, given the problematic nature of the category of "original text," I am more comfortable considering the Bodmer manuscript of *3 Cor.* on the basis of its early and independent circulation as a useful point of comparison to other extant witnesses.

59. The enumeration and division of *3 Cor.* differ in the scholarship on the text. Roman numerals are the standard means of delineation, though the number of component sections are different. For example, Klijn ("Apocryphal Correspondence," 2) divides the text into three portions because he does not include the narrative introduction found in *Acts Paul*. Thus, his numbering begins at I, representing the Corinthians'

and appear in almost every witness, while sections I and III are spread out
through the various manuscripts and are quoted in the works of Ephrem
and Aphrahat.[60] These additional sections (I and III) and the variation with
which they appear in the manuscript tradition allow us to see how the images of Paul as letter writer and Paul the prisoner is important to the life
of *3 Cor.* as a text. Latin and Armenian versions incorporate *3 Cor.* into
the documentary reception of Paul, while its incorporation into *Acts Paul*
represent a biographical reflection of Paul's letter-writing activity.

Section III is a common addition to the correspondence, appearing in
most Armenian manuscripts and the Coptic version of *Acts Paul* (though
it is absent from the fourth-century Hamburg manuscript of *Acts Paul* and
from all but one of the Latin manuscripts), and it details the delivery of
the Corinthians' letter to Paul, Paul's reaction, and his decision to respond
with a letter.[61] The textual relationship between these versions is contentious. Schmidt argues that Armenian versions derive from the circulation
of the correspondence independently from its incorporation into *Acts Paul*,
whereas Luttikhuizen believes that the Eastern churches must have received
the correspondence and the narrative interlude from some version of *Acts
Paul*.[62] Despite the variation of contents and perhaps textual genealogy between the Armenian and Latin versions, they share a common feature: *3
Cor.* is included in biblical codices. This status is somewhat variable. On
one hand, the Syrian/Armenian tradition reflects early acceptance of *3 Cor.*
as authoritative—it is included right after 2 Corinthians and is treated as
authoritative by Ephrem and Aphrahat.[63] Most of these texts include the

letter. For the sake of consonance with recent studies I follow Hovhanessian's four-fold
division. Martin Rist ("III Corinthians," 49) also divides the text into four sections but
uses letters A–D.

60. The Latin manuscript Z lacks section IV, but does contain section III. Given
section III's description of Paul's decision to respond with a letter, De Bruyne ("Un
quatrième manuscrit Latin," 192) believes that section IV was originally present but has
been lost. See also Hovhanessian, *Third Corinthians*, 7–8.

61. See Klijn, "Apocryphal Correspondence," 2–4; Hovhanessian, *Third Corinthians*, 3–8.

62. Luttikhuizen, "Apocryphal Correspondence," 78–79. The presence of section
III in the Syriac/Armenian tradition may be best explained by influence of the *Acts
Paul* tradition. Though the absence of section I is slightly conspicuous, made more so
by the fact that Ephrem's commentary includes his own narrative introduction to the
correspondence.

63. Hovhanessian (*Third Corinthians*, 5) notes that in most Armenian manuscripts and Ephrem's commentary, *3 Cor.* comes after 2 Corinthians, though another
cluster of manuscripts includes it after Revelation. The commentary on and use of
3 Cor. in Ephrem's and Aphrahat's writings represent earlier treatments of *3 Cor.* as
somewhat authoritative and useful for their particular goals. See Walters, "Evidence for

narrative interlude, which suggests an interest, not just in the text of the letters themselves, but in the activity of Pauline correspondence. The Latin manuscript L (Codex Laon 45), on the other hand, is explicit that Paul's response to the Corinthians is not genuine and it is placed at the end of the codex.[64] The Latin traditions evince distinct interest in the pseudepigraphal constructions of Paul, highlighted by M's (Codex Ambrosianus E53 *infer*. X) inclusion of *Laodiceans* immediately after *3 Cor*. In both cases, *3 Cor*. enters into the documentary reception of Paul, where Paul's letters are collected and organized. This documentary reception occurs for some when Paul's letters are considered genuine, but for others even when they understand the authorship of the text to be spurious.

Section I is a brief and fragmentary introduction to the letter from Stephanus occurring only in the sixth-century Coptic version (P. Heid. Inv. Kopt. 300+301) of *Acts Paul*.[65] *Acts Paul* situates *3 Cor*. within Paul's visit to Philippi, prefixed to a narrative sequence that ends with Paul's martyrdom.[66] The narrative framing constructs a very different quality to the correspondence, which serves to emphasize the image of Paul as a letter writer.[67] This technique can be seen in other apostolic pseudepigrapha, like the *Letter of Peter to Philip*, which constructs what John Marshall has termed an "ethos of genre."[68] Narrative embedding shifts the letter characteristics

---

Citations," who provides a comprehensive treatment of citations and allusions to the text in Aphrahat.

64. See Hovhanessian, *Third Corinthians*, 6–7.

65. The Philippian episode, in which *3 Cor*. is embedded, is entirely absent from the Hamburg manuscript of *Acts Paul*; however, the top of p. 6 of P. Hamb. includes the heading ἀπὸ Φι[λί]ππων εἰς Κόρινθον (From Philippi to Corinth). See Schmidt and Schubart, *Act Pauli*, 44–45, 98–100. P. Hamburg is important to consider as it is perhaps two centuries earlier than P. Heidelberg and is Greek, rather than Coptic. Snyder argues (*Acts of Paul*, 196) that it is simplest to assume that the Hamburg compiler did not know the Philippian episode. If Snyder is correct, then it is difficult to know whether *3 Cor*. was embedded in the Philippian episode before or after that episode was incorporated into *Acts Paul* as a whole.

66. For an English translation of the Philippian episode, including *3 Cor*., see Schneemelcher, "Acts of Paul." Snyder has argued (*Acts of Paul*, 196–212, 254–56) that Paul's travel from Corinth to Rome was added early on to the *Martyrdom of Paul* in order to form a narrative sequence describing Paul's "passion," and forms a base for both the Hamburg and Heidelberg manuscripts. He goes on to argue that the Philippian episode is loosely connected to the passion narrative, as we now see reflected in the Heidelberg manuscript.

67. Thus, I modify Snyder's points that the image of "a Paul who was absent in the flesh but present in letter was reduced to one among many" (*Acts of Paul*, 189). My argument positions Paul's letter-writing image as becoming more prominent in relation to itself when it is embedded within other images significant to *Acts Paul*.

68. Marshall, "When You Make the Inside," 93. Marshall argues that the *Letter of*

from stereotyped formal features to foregrounded description of epistolary activity, including composition and delivery (i.e., sending and receiving letters). Section I describes the conflict in Corinth due to the arrival of Simon and Cleobius which instigates the Corinthians' letter. Two letter carriers are named (Threptus and Eutychus), who are to deliver the letter to Paul. Textual variation in P. Heid. also serves to foreground Paul's letter-writing activity. Whereas the Bodmer Miscellaneous Codex as well as the Armenian and Latin versions mention that Paul may reply to the Corinthians with a letter, the Heidelberg version simply requests that Paul visit.[69] This omission produces a strong juxtaposition between the Corinthians' request for Paul's visit and his reply by letter. That Paul may respond to doctrinal deviance by a letter is by now a perfectly natural and expected procedure. The *Acts Paul* version also includes section III, which, as we have seen, describes the delivery of the letter to Paul by letter carriers, Paul's distraught reception of the letter, and his decision to respond with a letter. This interlude participates in the narrative foregrounding of Paul's imprisonment and subsequent letter-writing activity. Unfortunately, the portion of the Philippian episode following Paul's letter is missing in P. Heid., though Paul apparently is released from prison and eventually is able to continue on to Corinth.

The inclusion of *3 Cor.* in *Acts Paul* bears witness to the continued play on the image of Paul as a letter writer and the interesting confluence of receptive poles. Play on Paul as a letter writer should not be surprising given its currency within the correspondence and since Paul's commemoration as literate and as a letter writer was, by the sixth century, well-established. A conflation of receptive poles occurs with *Acts Paul* insofar as the pseudepigraphal *3 Cor.* is simultaneously incorporated into a biographical construction of Paul and into a Pauline collection of sorts. Certainly, *Acts Paul* should be distinguished from Pauline letter collections of the first and second centuries or the inclusion of *3 Cor.* into the canonical collections of the

---

Peter to Philip's invented narrative frame is valuable for setting up the following narrative and for setting forth a particular ethical programme (ibid., 92). *Third Corinthians* is to be distinguished on this point given that it's narrative frame is a secondary editorial technique. Even so, when embedded in *Acts Paul*, the correspondence evokes the ethos of the letter genre similar to that in the *Letter of Peter to Philip*.

69. Schneemelcher reconstructs v. 7 as "do thou [write to us or] come to us." The inclusion of "write to us" in this location is evidently derivative of the Armenian and the Latin L, since Ephrem, M, and P. Bodm. X place the request for writing in v. 8. Schmidt makes the similar observation that the Latin and Armenian versions include the request that Paul visit or write. While lacunate, P. Heid. does not seem to have room for the conjecture that Schneemelcher seems to suggest. See Schmidt, *Acta Pauli*, 75, 40* and *Tafelband*, 46. See also Hovhanessian, *Third Corinthians*, 140, for a collation of the variants.

Latin and Armenian Bibles. However, comparison between the Hamburg and Heidelberg manuscripts, alongside the other independent portions of *Acts Paul* (e.g., the *Acts of Paul and Thecla*, the *Martyrdom of Paul*, and the *Ephesus Act*), indicate that a biographical collection of Paul took on a documentary flavour akin to that of Paul's letters.

How Pauline is *3 Corinthians* and Did It Matter?

To what extent can we call *3 Cor.* Pauline? The question of the traction of *3 Cor.* with the undisputed Pauline letters has occupied scholars for some time. The Correspondence quite evidently betrays some allusive connection with a wide variety of Pauline letters, although exact parallels are debated. Hovhanessian argues that using the name of Paul in a somewhat plausible historical circumstance is enough to reclaim Paul from those heretics who "captured" his persona.[70] Snyder argues that at least with regard to teaching about resurrection, flesh (σάρξ) in *3 Cor.* and body (σῶμα) in 1 Corinthians 15 are interchangeable, making the pseudepigraphal Paul look pretty "Pauline."[71] This proposal, however, neglects the extensive Pauline argument against σάρξ especially in Romans and completely ignores Benjamin L. White's argument that *3 Cor.* invokes the image of Paul as defender from the Pastorals so strongly that the Pauline teaching on the resurrection is able to be completely reformulated.[72] D'Anna likewise points out some significant discrepancies between *3 Cor.* and other Pauline texts, including shifts in the meaning of σάρξ, therefore questioning its success as a pseudepigraphon.[73]

There is little doubt that the Pastorals enact a powerful pivot for the reception of Pauline images.[74] In this case, White's formulation can be a

70. Hovhanessian (*Third Corinthians*, 82–87) is evidently still enticed by the Pauline captivity narrative.

71. Snyder, *Acts of Paul*, 173–85.

72. White, "Reclaiming Paul?," esp. 510–16.

73. D'Anna, "Third Epistle," 142–48. D'Anna also refers to some additional shifts in terminology and states that, while the pseudepigrapher esteems Paul and invokes his authority, Paul "was not assimilated in any deep way" (ibid., 143). This is interestingly reminiscent of Lieu's thesis of the "elusive Paul."

74. Aageson makes the instructive insight that the Pastorals function as hinge letters between the historical Paul and the Pauline legacy. The continued dispute over authorship operates on the basis of strained coherence with the undisputed Paulines, whereas a number of other studies have emerged investigating the reception of the Pastorals and the earliest interpreters of Paul. One's decision about authorship "simply moves the Pastorals from one side of that balance point to the other" (Aageson, *Paul*, 6–7). The effects of the Pastorals as opening hermeneutical opportunities for the Pauline legacy have been thoroughly explored in Merz, *Die fiktive Selbstauslegung,* and

compelling explanation for why *3 Cor.* was received as thoroughly Pauline in diffuse geographical and temporal locations. However, as *3 Cor.* is received and reproduced in various literary contexts, especially into *Acts Paul*, contradictions emerge that potentially confirm D'Anna's reservations. For example, in the Corinthian episode, Cleobius is cast as a prophetic figure who confirms Paul's impending martyrdom.[75] However, in the preceding Philippian episode, Cleobius is an agitator who stirs up trouble in Corinth, prompting the correspondence between Paul and the Corinthians. In both of these cases, Cleobius is an important constituent in the construction of Paul the letter writer and Paul the martyr in Rome in the compiled *Acts of Paul*. Yet, these differing images utilize very different portrayals of Cleobius How is it that the compiler of *Acts Paul* allowed for this kind of tension? We may also notice that different episodes reflect different relationships with the Pastorals. As White has shown, the relationship between *3 Cor.* and the Pastorals operates on the level of a shared imagination of Paul as a defender of tradition against heresy, as well as on the level of literary parallels.[76] Both the Pauline image and the literary parallels in particular derive from all three Pastoral Epistles, which possibly provide evidence for the writer's generally positive disposition toward the Pastorals as a unit. On the other hand, the *Acts of Paul and Thecla* diverge from the Pastorals, perhaps, as Den Dulk has argued, so that the *Acts of Paul and Thecla* uses 2 Timothy to argue against the socially conservative emphases of 1 Timothy and Titus.[77] This internal contradiction was already noticed by Tertullian, yet the Heidelberg manuscript includes both the Philippian episode (including *3 Cor.*) and *Paul and Thecla*, both of which reflect widely different productions of the image of Paul relative to shared literary sources.[78] It seems that by the time *3 Cor.* was incorporated into *Acts Paul*, the Pauline legend had little room for distinction between the historical Paul and the received Paul and even "hinge texts" like the Pastoral Epistles could be marshalled with vary-

---

Mitchell, "Corrective Composition."

75. See the translation of the Corinthians episode in Schneemelcher, "Acts of Paul," 257–58.

76. See the discussion and a helpful table in White, *Remembering Paul*, 116–21.

77. Den Dulk, "I Permit No Woman." The direction of influence between the Pastorals and *Acts Paul* is disputed, especially in MacDonald, *Legend and the Apostle*, 59–65. Both den Dulk ("I Permit No Woman," 192–95) and Ehrman (*Forgery and Counterforgery*, 379–84) effectively affirm the literary direction coming from the Pastorals to *Acts Paul*.

78. Tertullian argues against the right of women to teach and baptize in *De baptismo* 17, suggesting that some have appealed to Thecla's example in *Acts Paul*. Tertullian is adamant that this text is a forgery and does not represent the teaching of the real Paul, citing 1 Cor 14:35 for support.

ing effects in the reproductions of Pauline images. Likewise, the images of Paul as a letter writer and Paul as martyr seem to be more significant than the contradicting activities of what appears to be a single character.

Early forms of 3 *Cor.* contributed to the developing image of Paul as a letter writer, an image that seems to have enabled the continued production and use of pseudepigraphal Pauline texts. Further, for this image to be compelling, it required a close association with the image of Paul as a prisoner. Again, we see this briefly in early forms of the Correspondence, but increasingly, Paul as letter writer pairs with a more concrete image of a Pauline imprisonment associated with Philippi. Paul's letter to the Philippians is probably one reason why that image was propagated, but a Pauline imprisonment in Philippi is mentioned in the canonical Acts as well. In the Coptic *Acts of Paul*, a robust image of Paul's letter-writing activity fits naturally within an episode that places Paul in prison in the city of Philippi. As images of Paul were developed and naturalized into the imagination of Christians in late antiquity, a coherence operating between certain images enabled the reproduction of Pauline texts for which contradictions on other levels became less pronounced.

CONCLUSION

According to Alberto D'Anna's recent article, 3 *Cor.* uses a Pauline pseudonym because of a shared understanding of the authority of that name, yet D'Anna problematizes the success of the Correspondence on the basis of an incoherence of theology between the pseudepigraphon and the historical Paul's letters. In contrast to this hypothesis, I have considered the question of the success of a pseudepigraphal letter within the context of reception history. Building on the work especially of White and Marguerat, I have emphasized the interaction between Pauline image and the strategies used to deploy that image, with special attention to the textual history of 3 *Cor.* as a means of tracing the strategic deployment of Pauline images. In spite of muted early images of Paul as a letter writer, 3 *Cor.* makes use of and builds upon this image through the use of a fictive correspondence between Paul and the Corinthians—arguably a somewhat natural connection of image and genre. This particular strategy of constructing Paul as a letter writer in a pseudepigraphal correspondence (Marguerat's doctoral pole) invokes a certain logical circularity that recommends its success. One could thus believe that Paul wrote this response letter because Paul is the type of person who would have written this letter. *Third Corinthians* also relies upon pairing the image of Paul as a letter writer with the image of Paul in prison—an ideal context for letter-writing activity. Attention to the textual history of *3 Cor.* provides striking confirmation of this hypothesis as the image of Paul as letter writer is emphasized while the text of *3 Cor.* is enlarged using different receptive strategies. *Third Corinthians* enjoyed documentary reception as it was gathered with various other texts in the Bodmer Miscellaneous Codex and as it was added later to Paul's other letters in some Armenian and Latin Bibles. *Acts Paul* reflects Marguerat's biographical pole as it incorporates Paul's letter-writing activity into the narrative re-telling of his exploits. In fact, the Heidelberg manuscript of *Acts Paul* instantiates the convergence of all three of Marguerat's receptive strategies in the reproduction of the image of Paul as an imprisoned letter writer: a pseudepigraphal correspondence is placed in a narrative framework that consisted in the collection of several episodes detailing the exploits of Paul.

– 9 –

"Days of Our Lives"
Destructive Homemakers
in the *Passion of Andrew*

— Anne Moore —

ACCORDING TO KATE BOWES, the characteristics of soap operas include "an emphasis on family life, personal relationships, sexual dramas, emotional and moral conflicts; some coverage of topical issues; set in familiar domestic interiors with only occasional excursions into new locations."[1] Soap operas tend to follow the everyday activities and the personal relationships of a group of characters who, at least in the American and Canadian versions, are often glamorous, wealthy, and beautiful. The overlapping storylines of the different characters feature romance, duplicitous relationships, fraudulent pasts, deceitful characters, and extramarital affairs intersected with numerous and frequent plot twists featuring mysterious strangers. The *Passion of Andrew*,[2] specifically chs. 1–13, occurs in the domestic interiors of Aegeates' *domus*—specifically, the bedrooms of the wealthy Roman couple Aegeates and his beautiful wife Maximilla. The bedrooms are the sites for sexual dramas: developing, but hidden, relationships between Maximilla, her brother-

1. Bowles, "Soap Opera," 119.

2. Edition by Jean-Marc Prieur, *Acta Andreae*; and accessible English translation by MacDonald, *Acts of Andrew*.

in-law Stratocles, and the mysterious stranger Andrew, and the formulation of a deceitful arrangement intended to provide Aegeates with a "fake wife." The story features emotional and moral conflicts over the fulfillment of social obligations associated with the Roman elite family and the alternative lifestyle advocated by the apostle Andrew—an alternative that ultimately destroys Aegeates' household from within.

This comparison between soap operas and the *Passion of Andrew* may highlight some of the dramatic, even comedic, elements of the apocryphal text; however, the comparison also provides some insight into the classification of "gynocentric" genres and in turn, how scholarship has shifted towards a formulation of social roles as a means through which to comprehend both the characters within a text and the audience interpreting the text. This examination discusses this shift in soap opera scholarship in terms of understanding soap operas as a "gynocentric" genre and how this shift illuminates a similar transition in the classification of the *Passion of Andrew* as a "text for women." Further, the focus on social roles that is part of this scholarly shift will be presented and then utilized in the interpretation of the characters of Maximilla and the two female slaves, Iphidama and Euclia. Analyzing these female characters in terms of their social roles reveals the destructive impact of Maximilla's actions as she "brings down" the household she was obligated to protect and preserve.

SOAP OPERAS AS WOMEN'S TEXTS

Initial scholarship on soap operas classified these "TV texts" as illustrations of a "gynocentric" genre, a genre based in women's culture, focused on women's issues, and directed to women spectators. Within this academic discourse, Annette Kuhn raises a major issue in reference to the theoretical frameworks employed. According to Kuhn, early analysis of soap operas adopted a film theory framework, a framework drawn from the criticism-oriented tradition of literary studies.[3] Both film and literary frameworks, specifically in reference to gender, incorporate particular insights from psychoanalysis, resulting in an emphasis on "representation and feminine subjectivity."[4] Tania Modleski's analysis of soap opera provides an illustration of this "film theory" approach. According to Modleski, soap operas present various personal and domestic crises that are resolved with or through female skills. The narratives of crises and their resolutions appeal to female spectators because they are grounded in the female/domestic sphere,

3. Kuhn, "Women's Genres," 18–19.
4. Ibid., 19.

feature female protagonists, and challenge the patriarchal construction of the female subject.[5] "Modeleski's view," Kuhn says, "is that soaps not only address female spectators, but in so doing construct feminine subject positions which transcend patriarchal modes of subjectivity."[6] Soap operas are part of the process for the reconstruction of the female gender.

Modleski's observation about soap operas is analogous to some of the early scholarship on the apocryphal acts (AA).[7] Setting aside whether the texts were written by women, told and recorded/edited by men, or, like soap operas, drew upon tales of and about women that were reworked into a new narrative, there is the assumption that the AA were part of a specific process of gender construction. In fact, the narratives of both soap operas and the AA seem to function in a very similar way in that there are various crises in terms of relationships—both domestic and romantic—that are resolved through feminine cunning. And through this storyline, overlying systems of patriarchy are revealed and the potential for an alternative gender construction is provided. The AA served early Christian women who, especially through the adoption of a chaste ascetic lifestyle, could challenge and liberate themselves from some of the patriarchal structures of second-to fourth-century Roman/Christian society. The AA offer an alternative to the traditional roles of wife and mother. This is vividly the situation with Maximilla, who uses Euclia to play the role of the wife in bed with her husband, Aegeates. Maximilla is freed from her sexual duties and her obligation to ensure the continuation of her husband's house through the creation of a legitimate heir. Analogously, the soap operas provided women of the 1960s (and thereafter) with an alternative to the traditional role of housewife and mother; women could acknowledge both their sexuality as the sought-after "other woman" and their self-sufficiency as the divorced wife, both of whom function outside the male sphere of power.

This similarity between the possible function of soap operas and the AA confirms one of Kuhn's observations about the specific theoretical frameworks inherent in film/literary criticism and issues of gender. Kuhn notes that within these frameworks, gender is produced through representation found in the text. This construction of gender through representation tends towards the universal, rather than the specific.[8] The discussion is on how the texts are representing female gender and then how the spectator/

5. Modleski, *Loving with a Vengeance*; Modleski, "Search for Tomorrow."

6. Kuhn, "Women's Genres," 20.

7. Davies, *Revolt of the Widows*; MacDonald, *Legend and the Apostle*; Burrus, *Chastity as Autonomy*; and Solevag, *Birthing Salvation.*

8. Kuhn, "Women's Genres," 23.

reader engages and interacts with this textual representation as part of her own gender construction. Quoting Kuhn, the *"spectator,* for example, is a subject constituted in signification, interpellated by the film or TV text."[9] Now, Kuhn does not infer that the spectator/reader is solely a product of the text. Through her interaction with the text, the reader does bring into conversation with the text other discourses. Kuhn's point though is that there are certain proclivities within this literary/film theory framework that emphasizes: 1) gender as a product of representation; 2) the text as the significant focus, and 3) the spectator and/or reader as engaged with gender construction or re-positioning. These emphases tend to produce a more universalist presentation of gender, and results in the neglect of the cultural and social specifics inherent in the context of the text and the audience.

The early scholarship on the AA demonstrates similar proclivities; these similar proclivities are partly the product of a shared framework: the literary/film theory approach to the study of gender. Steven L. Davis, Dennis R. MacDonald, and Virginia Burrus—each advocating varying theories in terms of whether the texts were told by women, developed out of a stock of women's tales, or were written by women—all focus on how gender is represented in the AA and all assume the AA address the issue of re-positioning the female gender within an alternative lifestyle of chaste asceticism.[10] Stefaniw Blossom, for her part, brings into the discussion Galen's medical insights about the biology of sex; however, this is a supplement to the gender representations derived from the AA.[11] There is then the resulting depiction of a universalist "female" gender and the accompanying idea of women defying patriarchy through the adoption of Christian asceticism. This universalist view of gender has been challenged and criticized by Gillian Clark, Peter Brown, and Kate Cooper.[12] Quoting Gillian Clark, "There is no certainty that our own dissatisfaction was shared by women of the time, whose experience and expectation were to be different from our own."[13] Clark, Brown, and Cooper emphasize the social construction of gender; each society developed its own specific view of femaleness and maleness.

The other framework used in the analysis of soap opera is provided through TV theory, or what would now be termed Media Studies. The

9. Ibid., 23.

10. Davis, *Revolt of the Widows*; MacDonald, *Legend and the Apostle*; Burrus, "Chastity as Autonomy"; Burrus, *Chastity as Autonomy.*

11. Blossom, "Becoming Men, Staying Women."

12. Clark, *Women in Late Antiquity*, 4. See also Cooper, *Virgin and the Bride*, 67–72; and Brown, *Body and Society.*

13. Clark, *Women in Late Antiquity*, 4.

genealogy of Media Studies has family branches largely within the social sciences, specifically sociology, anthropology, and cultural studies. Within this framework, one of the major assumptions is a focus on the context. The medium is examined as a product created through and as part of a series of social processes and institutions. This attention towards context results in a shift in focus from spectator/reader to social audience. A social audience refers to a group formed of spectators who are in "the social act of consuming representations."[14] The shift to a social audience means one examines a group of spectators who already possess identities determined by class, social status, economics, and gender. The shift is evident in the various media studies that quantitatively and qualitatively examine the demographics of specific audiences. So, the contexts of the audience members become a significant focus.

Charlotte Brunsdon, in her analysis of a British soap opera, proposes a mediating position between the frameworks of film theory and TV theory.

> I should like to make a distinction between the subject positions that a text constructs, and the social subject who may or may not take these positions up. We can usefully analyze the 'you' or 'yous' that the text as discourse constructs, but we cannot assume that any individual will necessarily occupy these positions. The relation of the audience to the text will not be determined solely by that text, but by all positionalities in relation to a whole range of other discourses—discourses of motherhood, romance and sexuality, for example.[15]

First, implied in the 'you' or 'yous' constructed by a text's discourse is the variety and complexity of the social audience. The 'yous' represent the layered identities inherent within most groups. Second, the subject positions that the soap opera constructs derive significantly from the narrative's social setting and the characters' social interaction including: sexual relations, economic status, social class, and other familial connections.[16] In addition, the plotline of a soap opera does depend on the "twists and turns," the revelation of secrets and the discovery of deceit and forgeries; however, it is reliant on "constructing moral consensus about the conduct of personal life. There is an endless unsettling, discussion and resettling within the sphere of personal relationships."[17] In other words, the perennial soap opera question is what is the moral character of this person? This means

14. Kuhn, "Women's Genres," 23.
15. Brunsdon, "'Crossroads'" 32.
16. Kuhn, "Women's Genres," 34.
17. Ibid., 35.

that the text is focused on the construction of social identities, which are gendered; however, the emphasis remains on the social. The social audience, formed from a group of social subjects, is responding and interacting with these social identities. So, according to Brundson, the focus is not on the construction of the female gender; rather, it is the construction and interaction with the social position of the mother, which is gendered. Brundson, therefore, emphasizes that one of the competences required of the viewers of soap operas is "[c]ultural knowledge of the socially acceptable codes and conventions for the conduct of personal life."[18]

SOAP OPERA IN THE PASSION OF ANDREW

Continuing with the comparison, there was/is a shift within the study of the AA that focuses more on the social context—specifically "the socially acceptable codes and conventions for the conduct of personal life."[19]Andrew Jacobs places his discussion of the AA within the context of the emperor Augustus's reform of marriage and the subsequent development of conjugal ethics. Specifically, in the *Passion of Andrew*, conjugal ethics frame the expectations of the social roles of the husband and wife Aegeates and Maximilla. Aegeates addresses his wife through the language of *concordia*. "Sex for Aegeates," Jacobs writes, "represents a higher union in which female sexual submission becomes aristocratic, wifely 'fellowship' (as Plutarch might have described it)."[20] In following the apostle Andrew, Maximilla is choosing an alternative kinship; another family framed by a Christian ethos. Aegeates, rejected by his wife, dies without direct heirs and Stratocles rejects the brother's property. As Jacobs writes, "The marital union has failed on all counts—not even children were produced—and this failure signals the breakdown of a markedly upper-class *oikonomia* of status and gender relations."[21] In other words, Jacobs's analysis is focused on the text's construction of social positions—the elite wife and husband—and the expectations of conduct within the Roman household. However, both soap operas and the AA include a more expansive view of family. In particular, the Roman household, which is the focus of the AA, includes the slaves, freeborn and the extended biological family of the elite householders.[22] In

18. Brundson,"'Crossroads,'" 36.

19. Ibid., 36.

20. Jacobs, "'Her Own Proper Kinship,'" 37.

21. Ibid., 40.

22. Saller's review of the term *familia* ("*Familia, Domus*," 336–55), which, in legal discourse, consisted of slaves, the *mater* and children. In social discourse, *familia*

other words, there are additional social positions and relationships to be considered.

Rebecca Solevag in her recent work on the intersection of childbirthing and salvation discourse in early Christian texts addresses the social categories of class and gender; building upon some of Jacob's examinations, she discusses some of the social codes and conventions inherent within the Roman *familia*.[23] The competition between Aegeates and Andrew, for Solevag, is framed by role expectations inherent within exemplary portraits of Roman manhood. Aegeates has the necessary trappings of the *patria familias*: a high political position, wealth, authority within the community, and a high-born wife. However, he is unable to fulfill some of the major expectations associated with his social role such as: 1) the companionship of a submissive and obedient wife; 2) the presence of children to ensure his legacy; and 3) the loyalty of his slaves. In particular, he does not possess the self-control that is expected and required of all Roman male elites. He is defeated by Andrew, who as an exemplar of "philosopher masculinity," is the epitome of self-restraint and whose philosophical words win over Maximilla and produce an heir/child in the form of Stratocles, Aegeates' own brother. Solevag's analysis does illuminate various aspects of AA, especially in terms of the language surrounding birth and salvation, and the significance of Andrew's classification of Maximilla as an alternative Eve to his Adam. However, her examination focuses on Maximilla, Stratocles, and Aegeates. There is a lack of attention to the social sphere of the household, in all of its differing personal relationships and variety of roles. This is particularly apparent in the discussion of the slaves Iphidama and Euclia. They are reduced to stereotypes: "We may recognize this type/antitype in the *Acts*. Iphidama and Alcman are presented as 'faithful slaves'; whereas Euclia, on the other hand fits the stereotype of the 'enemy slave.'"[24] Euclia's character is reduced to the wanton woman, an uppity strumpet whose pride results in a very violent death. However, as any audience member of *Coronation Street* knows, or as Brundson would advocate, the minor characters in a soap opera are not mere stereotypes. The minor characters are social subjects and they are part of the social sphere of the family. They also contribute to the discussion and analysis surrounding the "socially acceptable codes and conventions for the conduct of personal life."[25] The relationships and

"usually meant only the slaves of the house, as distinct from the freeborn mother and children, or sometimes a lineage sharing a *nomen* or clan name" (Saller, "Symbols of Gender and Status," 87).

23. Solevag, *Birthing Salvation*, 137–97.

24. Ibid., 166.

25. Brundson, "'Crossroads," 36.

actions between Iphidama, Euclia and Maximilla reveal how corrupting and destructive Maximilla becomes in terms of her own husband's household.

To further aid in the reconstruction of the social roles and conventions of the Roman household, I draw upon insights provided by Sinclair Bell and others in an edited collection of essays entitled, *Role Models in the Roman World: Identity and Assimilation.* Bell proposes the adoption of the sociologist Robert Merton's understanding of role models and role sets as tools for understanding Roman society.[26] For Bell, the issue is to find an appropriate set of methodological tools for comprehending and analyzing Roman culture, a set of tools that reflect the predominant collectivist identity of the Romans rather than the individualism of the modern researcher. The scholarly consensus of the Roman world, as a highly competitive society in which behavior is governed by the public codes of honor and shame and determined by social class, necessitates a social understanding of identity. Bell thinks that Merton's idea of 'role-model' may be useful. Quoting Bell,

> Following Merton, an individual does not possess a single status and single role in society's structure; rather society is made up of interrelated statuses and roles. Status can be explained as one's particular position in society, while a role is the behavior expected of occupants of a particular status. One's roles are oriented toward "reference groups," the larger categories or groups of people in society to which individuals compare themselves (but to which they may not necessarily belong). So for any given status (e.g. parent, educator) one assumes an array of roles calibrated to meet the specific, individual set of expectations of the reference groups in his or her orbit (e.g. children, colleagues). This is the essence of Merton's theory of the "role-set": that an individual has a status to which is attached the role or patterns of behavior expected by his or her respective reference groups.[27]

Merton's idea of role-model and role-set coheres with Brundson's focus on social positions and the "codes and conventions" that would govern one's behavior. Brundson and Bell both acknowledge that the "codes and conventions" of family life and the role-sets for Romans are constructed from the various cultural texts of the society. They are found in more legal formats, conversations about the ideal, and other discourses about the family. For example, Maximilla has a "role-set" associated with her status as an elite wife of a proconsul. This role-set includes her relationships with her husband, slaves, brother-in-law, wandering tramps and/or philosophers, and

26. Bell, "Role Models," 1–39.
27. Ibid., 3.

other elite Romans, and her behavior associated with each of these roles differs. Her role as wife requires submission and obedience to her husband, while her role as *domina* requires authority and control. Bell's suggestion coincides with the expectations found in the Roman Empire. The various elaborations on household codes from which the New Testament letters (1 Timothy) and Clement of Alexandria (*Paedagogus*) drew their visions of the ideal household featured the common triad of husband and wife, father and son, and master and slave. Each element of this triad focuses on a specific relationship, which is governed by a set of codes of behavior that define the specific roles.

For this investigation, I will focus on Iphidama and Euclia and their role-set as slaves within Aegeates' *familia*. This attention to their role-set and the specific behaviors associated with these roles shows that they are more than stereotypes. Iphidama and Euclia are not merely representations of the "faithful" and "enemy" slaves;[28] rather, their behaviors contribute to the disruption, confrontation and destruction of the social codes and conventions governing an elite *domus* and the positioning of an alternative family in terms of Andrew's Christian ethos.

DESTRUCTIVE HOMEMAKERS

First, as a social institution, slavery was not merely economic; it was also an indication of the status and wealth of the *familia* and the slaves' behavior was tied to the family's honour.[29] This meant that the slaves, who functioned as majordomos, stewards, foremen, chamberlains, readers, secretaries, clerks, financial administrators, and priests, not only provided financial support, but the manner and skill with which they conducted their tasks reflected on their owners in terms of their ability to manage appropriately.[30] The Roman historians and the Greek novel *An Ethiopian Story* provide examples of serving slaves being dressed in elaborate and expensive costumes to visually display the wealth of their owners.[31] Generally, one of the standards used to judge both the *dominus* and *domina* were their ability to manage their *familia* of slaves. In other words, the codes governing slave behavior were a major part of the life of the *domus*.

---

28. Harrill, "Domestic Enemy," 232; see also Solevag, *Birthing Salvation*, 165–68.

29. Joshel, *Slavery in the Roman World*, 184–85.

30. Ibid., 179–83.

31. The sources are surveyed in Bradley, *Slavery and Society at Rome*, 87–88; Joshel, *Slavery in the Roman World*, 134–35.

Iphidama's role-set includes first and foremost her role as handmaiden or attending slave to her mistress, Maximilla. Specifically, she may be a *cubicularii* (bedroom servant), who performed some of the most intimate aspects of personal grooming and were also renowned as confidants.[32] Or, she may be an *ornatix* who was more equivalent to a personal maid who served her mistress both in public and private contexts.[33] Given that Iphidama is often tasked with errands and does accommodate her mistress in public places such as Andrew's prison, she is probably an *ornatix*. Within this role, as described by Solevag, Ipidama adheres to the expected set of behaviors. Iphidama performs her tasks faithfully; she follows her *domina's* instructions, and she is quiet, subservient.[34] Indeed, "Iphidama seems to be nothing but an extension of Maximilla."[35]

However, Iphidama's role-set is not strictly limited to fulfilling tasks for Maximilla. Attending slaves or handmaids, due to their intimate relationship with the *matrona*, become part of the *domus's* display of honor and status. A *matrona* was required to display her *prudentia* (prudence). This involved the wearing of appropriate garments and travelling "with a female slave attendant in public, preferably one unattractive enough not to attract inappropriate attention from male bystanders."[36] Cicero's speech *Pro Caelio* (2.7.3–4) confirms that the public behavior of a married woman included wearing a minimum of jewelry and being attended by preferably older companions. The handmaiden is one of the few slave roles that is displayed in funerary inscriptions and art. Marice Rose notes that "surviving evidence of the roles of domestic slave women comes from the first and second centuries C.E., when funerary inscriptions named individual slaves who were assigned to the caretaking of wardrobe and of specific objects, such as mirrors and jewelry."[37] Also in funerary art, and later in more elaborate representations such as the fourth-century silver Projecta Casket, the late fourth-/early fifth-century Sevso Casket, the fifth-century mosaic from the baths of the villa at Sidi Ghrib in Cathrage, and the late fourth-century Dominus Julius mosaic from Carthage, there are scenes depicting the *domina* attended by her slave(s) as she prepares herself for public viewing. These depictions are

32. Joshel, *Slavery in the Roman World*, 180.

33. Ibid.

34. Solevag, *Birthing Salvation*, 166.

35. Ibid., 167.

36. Perry, *Gender*, 11.

37. Rose, "Construction of Mistress and Slave," 41. Amy Richlin ("Making Up a Woman," 166–96) notes that Roman men, on the one hand, viewed a women's preparation as a preparation for love-making; however, they also understood it as a coverage for flaws and aging.

part of the visual rhetoric of the elite; the image of mistress with her symbols of wealth—jewelry, mirrors, and slaves—reinforces the social status of the woman and her household. These images also "idealize slaves' relationship with their mistresses."[38] Collectively, the image of mistress and handmaiden present the ideal behavior required of both within the household. In other words, Iphidama's role-set includes a set of behaviors expected in terms of maintaining or establishing the honor and status of the family, concerns that are predominantly associated with Aegeates as the *dominus*. There is an expectation that attending slaves or handmaidens protect the honor of the *familia*.[39]

Iphidama, in her role of protecting or maintaining the honor of the family, fails. As reported to Aegeates by one of the slaves, "My mistress, following Iphidama's lead, became acquainted with this stranger. She has so given way to desire for him that she loves no one more than him, including you I would say" (*Pass. Andr.* 25). The slave continues his report speaking about how the corruption of Aegeates' household includes his brother. In fact, as shown by Saundra Schwartz, the literary trope of the adulterous wife is evoked in the text.[40] Iphidama, whose role as handmaiden focuses on the presentation and protection of her mistress and thereby contributes to the family's honor and status, has facilitated adultery. She is the one who introduces Andrew to Maximilla; she is present in the bedroom when Andrew and Maximilla meet, and, as an attending slave, she probably assists Maximilla in her disguises. She certainly is key in maintaining Maximilla's contact with Andrew even while he is in prison. Solevag is correct that "Iphidama acts dutifully (πιστῶς, 28) and is called faithful (πιστοτάτη, 28)."[41] However, as Solevag also notes, this praise comes from Andrew, the other man in this strange love triangle. Therefore, in terms of Iphidama's role-set as a slave within the *domus* of Aegeates, she has served her mistress; however, at the same time she has contributed to the destruction of the household by introducing and supporting Maximilla's contact with Andrew.

Generally, the consensus is that Euclia is a "bad girl"[42] or Maximilla's "evil twin."[43] However, this portrayal becomes more complex once one considers Euclia's role-set. First, as numerous scholars have discussed, one of the major roles performed by slaves, especially female slaves, is the

38. Rose, "Construction of Mistress and Slave," 45.

39. Glancy, "Mistress-Slave Dialectic," 77–80.

40. Schwartz, "From Bedroom to Courtroom," 267–311.

41. Solevag, *Birthing Salvation,* 166.

42. Ibid., 167.

43. Schwartz, "From Bedroom to Courtroom," 301.

sexual servicing of their masters and/or mistresses.[44] This idea is ubiquitous throughout the Roman Empire. Seneca notes, "Unchastity is a crime in the freeborn, a necessity for a slave, a duty for a freedman" (*Impudicita in ingenuo crimen est, in servo necessitas, in libero officium*; *Controversies* 4. Praef. 10; ed. and trans. Winterbottom). Plutarch recommends that a wife not be jealous of her husband's slave girl because "it is respect for her [the wife] which leads him to share his debauchery, licentiousness, and wantonness with another woman" (*Mor.* 140B; trans. Fowler). The poems of Martial, the writings of Musonius Rufus, and Petrolinus's *Satyricon* all contain numerous references to masters and mistresses engaged in sexual exploits with their slaves. Even the various Roman laws tended to define "adultery" only in terms of sexual intercourse between a *matrona* and a man who is not her husband. As Richlin explains, "A married man could legitimately have intercourse with any male who is not freeborn, or with any woman who did not have the status of *matrona* and was not engaged, married, or on concubinate and he could seek concubine(s) of either sex in his household."[45] Therefore, Euclia, with her nightly bed adventures with Aegeates is performing one of the roles expected/required of female slaves. However, Euclia performs this duty under a ruse, a veil of deceit. She assumes the role of mistress.

One of the most famous examples of slave girls pretending to be freeborn women is reported by Plutarch (*Cam.* 33; *Rom.* 29). The story is told as the basis for the Festival of Slave Girls (*ancillarum feriaei*). The Latin allies, after the Gallic sack of Rome in 390 BCE, demanded that the Romans send them their virgins and wives as a sign of submission. According to Plutarch, a slave girl proposed that slaves (*ancillae*) dressed as freeborn women be sent in the place of the honored women. The *ancillae*, given their status, lost no honor in bedding the Latin soldiers and, when the time was appropriate, they signaled the Romans to attack. The assumption behind the ruse was the idea of "distinctive dress marking off honorable free women from slave women."[46] In fact, it was codified into law, as Saller notes:

> This distinction in clothing was taken for granted in the real world, where jurists used it as a basis for their discussion of legal actions for insult (the insult being decreasingly significant depending on whether its victim was dressed as a matron, a slave woman, or a prostitute, *Digest* 47.10.15.15).[47]

44. Joshel, *Slavery in the Roman World*, 40, 151; Perry, *Gender*, 12–16.
45. Richlin, *Arguments with Silence*, 42.
46. Saller, "Symbols of Gender," 90.
47. Ibid.

Plutarch's story emphasizes that the *ancillae* assume the dress of freeborn women in order to protect the virgins and widows. After all, as female slaves they have no honor to lose. Maximilla dresses Euclia in her garments, not to protect her honour as a *matrona* because the sexual encounter is with her lawful husband; rather, the ruse is to avoid fulfilling her role as wife. Here, one may return to Plutarch. Plutarch's promotion of Augustus's conjugal ethics casts the sexual relationship between elite couples as a fellowship, and it is this vision of a marriage that dominates Aegeates' view of his relationship with his wife.[48] However, Maximilla frames marital relations in terms of lust, filth, etc.—the type of sex more appropriate between a man and a slave, or prostitute. Therefore, in disguising Euclia as the mistress of the house, Maximilla is the one who is not acting according to the social code inherent in her role as the mistress. Maximilla is the one offering her husband an *ancillae* in the guise of a freeborn woman and she does so with the understanding that Euclia/Maximilla will be used like a whore or slave, whereas the husband is the one who seeks his wife as part of the conjugal agreement to produce children and ensure the legacy of their family.

The paradox in Maximilla's behavior in reference to her request to Euclia appears even more bizarre when compared with the presentation of female slaves and elite wives in the comedies. The comedies of Plautus frequently portray the wife as the angry, unsuccessful rival in the competition with prostitutes, and the most feared of these prostitutes is the one within the *domus*. *Casina* centres on a wife's need to control the sexual use of the slave girl (*ancilla*). *Ancillae* cannot be too attractive; in fact, the unattractive Syrians or Egyptians are said to be the most suitable for hard work and maintaining the proper behavior of the *dominus* (*Mercator* 210–11, 395–417). Amy Richlin, notes that in "a fragment of Caecilus Statius's comedy *Plocium* (in Gellius, *Nocte. att.* 2.23.10) a husband complains that his wife has made him sell an *ancilla* she suspects of being her *paelex*—that is, of having sex with her husband—one who, in the common comic epithet, 'looked good enough to be free' (*facie haut inliberali*, in Gellius's paraphrase, *Nocte. att.* 2.23.8)."[49] Even the writers of comedy never portray a Roman *matrona* agreeing to the ongoing presence of a *paelex*; they certainly did not conceive of a *matrona* arranging for a *paelex*.

Euclia is behaving according to her role as a female slave; she is obedient to the instructions of Maximilla and she is sexually serving Aegeates. However, Maximilla is behaving counter to her role-set as a *matrona*; she is assuming the role of a pimp providing her husband with sexual release.

48. Jacobs, "'Her Own Proper Kinship,'" 37.
49. Richlin "Making Up a Woman," 190.

Rather than limiting her husband's engagement with the female slaves, she is actually supplying him with a *paelex,* usually the arch-enemy of the mistress of the house.

In addition, the manner in which this arrangement takes place is through disguise and trickery—the type of actions normally associated with slaves. Since slaves were viewed as articulate tools, there was the overarching paradox that these articulate tools, who should have no volition or will, actually maintained the household on numerous levels. This paradox results in a portrayal of slaves as loyal and subservient, enacting their owner's will, or as deceitful and cunning. In other words, slaves, because they have no status or position, are only able to act with deceit. Again, Plautus's comedies are filled with slaves in disguise or role-playing. Maximilla, through her ruse, assumes the behavior expected from deceitful slaves. As the kind of Roman *matrona* envisioned by Aegeates, Maximilla should be demonstrating her overall loyalty to the common household.[50] Even in comedies, the upper-class wife maintains her dignity; in fact, her "dramatic function" is as guardian of the economic and moral integrity of the household over against a transgressive husband.[51] Maximilla's behavior is counter to her role-set.[52]

As part of the common understanding of Euclia as the "bad slave," her demands for freedom, money, clothing, fine linen, and headbands are often cast as "blackmail." However, in setting up the ruse, Maximilla promised she would be "benefactor" for all of Euclia's needs. Therefore, a new set of role expectations are created. Eculia's demands then are the type of requests one would expect from a slave who has been specially tasked and whose relationship has changed. Slaves did receive gifts is in the performance of specific "additional" tasks or special services. In fact, this was incorporated within the institution of slavery. Slaves had *peculia.* According to the jurist Florentius, "a *peculium* is made up of anything a slave had been able to save by his own economies or has been given by a third party in return for meritorious services or has been allowed by his master to keep as his own" (*Digest* 15.1.39). The *peculium* was actually owned by the master; however, slaves used these resources to purchase clothes, tombstones, or their freedom.[53] Furthermore, *domina* could grant freedom without the consent of

---

50. Treggiari, *Roman Marriage,* 229–61.

51. Rei, "Villains, Wives and Slaves," 96.

52. There is also the pseudomeretrix; a woman of free status trapped in a brothel. The pseudomeretrix also asserts her moral and social superiority, and she rejects the typical behaviors of tricksters, such as disguise and role-play. See Rei, "Villains, Wives and Slaves," 97.

53. Joshel, *Slavery in the Roman World,* 128.

their husbands.[54] So, Euclia's behavior is within keeping with her role as a slave, and her requests/demands are appropriate.

Even Euclia's boasting is not totally foreign to her role-set. Again, returning to Plautus's comedies, fantasies about freedom and elevation of status are often part of the repertoire of the slave characters.[55] As Jacobs discusses, in the *Ephesian Tale*, the slaves Leukon and Rhode become wealthy landowners.[56] The point is not that slaves often obtained freedom and elite status; rather, it is expected that they would have those desires, and would, at least, strive for freedom and the status of freedman or freedwoman. In reference to the specific context of Euclia, female slaves could, through affection and devotion to their masters, obtain a higher status within the household or even freedom. As Matthew J. Perry notes,

> Roman authors and lawmakers condoned and supported long-term relationships between male owners and their female slaves, so long as they were conducted with respects to standards of social propriety. An owner could express increased esteem for his sexual partner by bestowing the title of concubine (*concubina*) upon her, although legal commentators asserted that women of this status really ought to be manumitted. The idea of the slave *concubine* established an apex of female slave status against which other individuals and relationship could be measured. Here, female slaves were closest to the standing of respectable free women.[57]

In addition, Perry comments that there is considerable inscriptional evidence that reveals "that manumissions 'for the sake of marriage' (*causa matrimonii*) were reasonably common."[58]

Euclia, with Maximilla as her benefactor, is granted freedom and she has some of the resources necessary to economically support herself. More important, as a freedwoman who is still fulfilling the request to "play the mistress," she has the opportunity to raise her status. Schwartz suggests that the reference to a period of eight months elapsing is a veiled reference to the conception of a child between Aegeates and Euclia.[59] The reference is perhaps

---

54. Elizabeth Leigh Gibson points to the "well-attested but admittedly confounding ability of women to manumit slaves without the consent of their husbands or oversight of a guardian" (*Manumission Inscriptions*, 131).

55. Richlin, "Talking to Slaves," 192–93.

56. Jacobs, "'Her Own Proper Kinship,'" 33–34.

57. Perry, *Gender*, 40.

58. Ibid., 55.

59. Schwartz, "From Bedroom to Courtroom," 301.

too veiled. However, Eculia's recent elevation to the status of freedwoman and her continuing sexual relationship with Aegeates does raise the potential not only for children, but for the acceptance of the children as more than slaves. While marriage with slaves and freedwomen is discouraged among the elite, the children of concubines have the possibility of a raised status in the *familia*. This is probably more so the case when a legitimate heir is not forthcoming. This expectation would then easily explain Euclia's decision to expose the ruse to the other slaves. Solevag is correct that Euclia's boasting can be read as "hubris";[60] however, it is not unexpected given her role-set.

Understanding Euclia's role-set also elaborates further Aegeates' violent punishment of the slave *(Pass. Andr. 22)*. First, her tortured confession would reveal Maximilla's betrayal of her role as an elite wife. Maximilla acted as a pimp supplying Aegeates with a *paelex*; she did so in a manner that was as deceitful as a slave and, in doing so, she risked the creation of a non-elite heir. After all, if the ruse was so successful, what would have prevented Maximilla from continuing the ruse to the point of passing off Euclia's child as her own? Euclia certainly would have seen the advantages for her status. This ruse challenged the honor of Aegeates; he was thoroughly duped by his wife. It was also a complete act of betrayal of the conjugal ethics and the stability of the *domus*.

In the *exemplum* literature, one of the ideals associated with wives is loyalty. The *exempla* show how loyal wives protected their husbands from betrayal by others and after such betrayal.[61] As Holt Parker notes, the *exempla* served to quell the anxiety produced through the addition of "outsiders" into the *domus*—specifically slaves and wives. The *exempla* are tales designed to show the code of behavior required and expected. According to the *exempla*, Maximilla has failed; she has betrayed her husband and the *familia*. In fact, one of the other set of *exempla* show the proper behavior of wives and slaves in reference to the suicide of the *dominus*. The basic assumption is that a Roman elite male prefers suicide to the loss of honor and, out of loyalty, wives and slaves assist in this goal. Instead, Maximilla's betray will result in Aegeates' loss of honor and, due to this loss, his suicide. According to the *exempla*, the wife always commits suicide herself to avoid any suspicion of disloyalty or adultery. Yet Maximilla survives.

The role-set of Iphidama and Euclia suggest that in reference to the direct destruction of Aegeates' household, it is an *ornatix* who brings the influence of Andrew into the *domus*, and then it is Maximilla's exploitation of Euclia that brings the final downfall. Andrew may provide the alternative

60. Solevag, *Birthing Salvation*, 167.
61. Parker, "Loyal Slaves and Loyal Wives," 170–75.

of a chaste 'spiritual' marriage; however, it is slaves and women, who actually bring about the fall of the house.

CONCLUSIONS

The key to understanding both soap operas and the *Passion of Andrew* is the social codes and conventions for familial life. The Roman household of Aegeates, as with most Roman households, is governed through the ideas of *concordia*, interlocking ideas of honor and shame, and layers of patronage and clientage. Almost all of these conventions are overturned by Maximilla in her desire to follow the ascetic life advocated by Andrew. Maximilla rejects her husband's pleas to adhere to *concordia*; she shames her husband and herself through the ruse of a "fake wife," and she places her client Euclia into a situation that results in Euclia's violent death. The main sphere of confrontation may be between Andrew and Aegeates; however, due to the actions of Maximilla and Iphidama, the internal structure of the home is already collapsing.

– 10 –

Manichaean Redaction of the
Secret Book of John

— Timothy Pettipiece —

THE DISCOVERY OF THE Nag Hammadi codices in 1945 was a game-changer in Early Christian Studies. They provided a wealth of intriguing and often bewildering texts in multiple genres and from multiple theological perspectives. Most were previously unknown. In the decades since, these texts have been studied primarily by those scholars interested in one of the various permutations of movements once lumped together as "gnostic," although outside of these specialized circles Nag Hammadi material has been relatively underexplored. Unfortunately, the main exception to this trend has been a somewhat myopic focus on the *Gospel of Thomas* (NHC II,2), largely due to the tendency of some scholars to treat it as a surrogate Q. Yet *Thomas* is only one artifact among a vast array of others and from the perspective of the presumed readership of the codices, was far from the most popular, existing as it does in only a single Coptic version. The codices contain two versions of the *Gospel of Truth* (I 3; XII,2), the *Gospel of the Egyptians* (III,2; IV,2) and *On the Origin of the World* (II 5; XIII,2) and there are no less than four versions of the *Secret Book of John* (=*Ap. John*)—two long (II,1; IV,1) and two short (III,1) including the Berlin Codex (BG 8502), which is closely related in terms of content and dialect to the Nag Hammadi manuscripts. In spite of its status as a relative "best seller," *Ap. John* has received far less attention.

Even less consideration has been paid to another large collection of Coptic texts from the same period: the Manichaean codices from Medinet Madi.[1] Though discovered in 1929, the editing and publication of these manuscripts has proceeded at a somewhat glacial pace, with much of the material still not widely accessible. This delay is in large part due to the extremely poor state of preservation of the texts as well as the stigma that still seems to be attached to Manichaean material in general, which is often seen as only marginally Christian at best. Ironically, what the Medinet Madi codices have demonstrated is the essentially Christian character of the movement and its founder, who regularly styled himself an "Apostle of Jesus Christ."[2] Thus, as the third largest corpus of ancient Coptic literature, the Manichaean material ought to be fully integrated into a holistic study of ancient Christianity.

Not surprisingly, the two bodies of texts have much in common. Physically both collections were written in similar "southern" Egyptian dialects (*L4* and *L6*)[3] and were produced sometime in the fourth century CE, likely in the vicinity of Lycopolis. Thematically, the Nag Hammadi and Medinet Madi codices preserve sources and traditions which have the most in common with one another. Few scholars, however, have ventured into comparative studies of the material;[4] much attention has been paid instead to delineating Valentinian, Sethian, Hermetic, and Platonic elements found within the Nag Hammadi corpus.

This study is part of a larger project to correct this lack of comparison between the two collections and to produce a "Manichaean reading" of the Nag Hammadi codices. As a launching point I will take the text which the codex compilers seem to have been most interested in—the *Secret Book of John*—and examine it through a Manichaean lens in order to determine what connections might have existed between the two bodies of early Christian literature. I will show that a close reading of the variant versions, *long* and *short*, of *Ap. John* reveals substantial evidence of both Manichaean reception and redaction.

1. For information on the discovery of these codices and their editing, see Robinson, *Manichaean Codices*; Funk, "Research on Manichaeism," 453–64; Gardner and Lieu, "From Narmouthis," 146–69; Schmidt and Polotsky, "Ein Mani-Fund," 4–90.

2. As evidenced in quotations from Mani's letters in *Cologne Mani Codex* 66, Augustine, *Haer.* 16, and now the Paris "Mani Seal" (see Gulácsi, "Crystal Seal of 'Mani'").

3. Funk, "Prolégomènes," 10–11; Funk, "Linguistic Aspect," 107–47.

4. Some exceptions being Rudolph, "Mani und die Gnosis," 191–200; Van Lindt, "Religious Terminology," 191–98; Mirecki, "Coptic Manichaean Psalm 278," 243–62; Stahl, "Derdekeas," 572–80; Funk, "Einer aus Tausend"; Coyle, "Gospel of Thomas in Manichaeism?"

GENDER-BENDING BARBELO

In the *short version* of *Ap. John*, after the lengthy evocation of the transcendent One, we learn that as he gazed at his own reflection in a pool of "living water," his "thought" (ЄⲚⲚⲞⲒⲀ) became actualized in the form of Barbelo(n) "the perfect aeon" (III 7.19 / BG 27.15). She is then androgynously identified (using the indefinite article) as "*a* first man" (ⲞⲨϨⲞⲨЄⲒⲦ ⲚⲢⲰⲘЄ)[5] and the "virginal spirit" (ⲠⲠⲚⲀ ⲚⲠⲀⲢⲐЄⲚⲒⲔⲞⲚ) (III 7.24 / BG 27.20). The *long version* adds: "she became the womb of everything, for she is prior to all of them, the Mother-Father (ⲦⲘⲎⲦⲢⲞⲠⲀⲦⲰⲢ), *the* First Man" (ⲠϢⲞⲢⲠ ⲚⲢⲰⲘЄ)" (II 5.5–7), using the definite article. While the designation "First Man" in the *short version* is rather striking in itself, the *long version's* alternate formulation—"*the* First Man" (ⲠϢⲞⲢⲠ ⲚⲢⲰⲘЄ)—using both the definite article and the ordinal term for "first," parallels in a rather specific fashion the form of the technical term used in Coptic Manichaean literature[6] to designate the envoy sent by the Father of Greatness to be devoured by the powers of darkness at the beginning of the cosmic drama.[7] It is this confrontation that initiates the mixture of Light and Darkness and leads to the creation of the cosmos. More than that, the figure of the First Man in Manichaean myth sometimes displays androgynous characteristics. For example, according to *Bema Psalm 223*, the Father sent forth his "strong son" (ϢⲎⲢЄ ⲚϪⲰⲢЄ) to counter the dark invasion. The son, however, produces someone called "his virgin" (ⲦЄϥⲠⲀⲢⲐЄⲚⲞⲤ), who, like the First Man, is equipped with "five powers" (ϯЄ ⲚϬⲀⲘ) in order to battle with the forces of darkness (*Psalm-Book* 10.6–9). Then, the psalmist records how First Man (here called the "watcher" [ⲠⲘⲀϨⲒⲀⲒⲦϥ]) reveals "his Maiden" to the dark powers, causing them to go mad with desire (*Psalm-Book* 10.10–14). This idea, also attested in a recently discovered Manichaean text from Kellis,[8] that it was a pair of beings who actually when out to meet the darkness, may reflect some very early stratum of early Manichaean discourse in which the principal beings of each evocation where conceived of as androgynous

---

5. The Coptic texts are cited from the synoptic edition by Waldstein and Wisse (*Apocryphon of John*) unless otherwise noted.

6. ⲠϢⲀⲢⲠ ⲚⲢⲰⲘЄ, *Psalm-Book* 1.26; 10.20; 22.16; 36.21; 85.4; 88.13; 118.3 etc; *Kephalaia* passim.

7. There is a similar instance in the *Gospel of the Egyptians*, where Adamas is called ⲠⲢⲰⲘЄ ⲠЄϨⲞⲨЄⲒⲦ in Codex III,2 49.9–10 and ⲠⲒϢⲰⲢⲠ ⲚⲢⲰⲘЄ in Codex IV,2 61.11.

8. In this Greek text, a feminine being addressed as πότνια ("lady") is depicted as clothing herself in the Five Elements and going out to meet the powers of darkness. See Gardner and Worp, "Leaves from a Manichaean Codex," 148–51.

pairs.[9] For those already familiar with Coptic Manichaean literature, such a reference is certainly remarkable. What is even more remarkable is that this androgynous "First Man" is then said to be represented by a series of five powers—a "pentad of aeons" derived from the Father.

Short Version (III,1) 9.3–8 / BG 29.8–14

ⲚⲀⲒ Ⲛ[Ⲉ Ⲡ]ϮⲞⲨ Ⲛ̄ⲀⲓⲰⲚ Ⲛ̄ⲦⲈ ⲠⲈⲒⲰⲦ ⲈⲦⲈ
[Ⲛ̄Ⲧ]ⲞϤ ⲠⲈ ⲠⲈϨⲞⲨⲈⲒⲦ Ⲛ̄ⲢⲰⲘⲈ Ⲧ̄ϨⲒⲔ[ⲰⲚ]
Ⲙ̄ⲠⲀϨⲞⲢⲀⲦⲞⲤ · ⲦⲀⲈⲒ ⲦⲈ ⲦⲂⲀⲢⲂⲎ[ⲖⲞⲚ] ⲘⲚ̄
ⲦⲈⲚⲚⲞⲒⲀ ⲘⲚ̄ ⲠⲰⲢ̄Ⲡ Ⲛ̄ⲤⲞⲞ[ⲨⲚ Ⲙ]Ⲛ̄
ⲦⲀ⳨ⲐⲀⲢⲤⲒⲀ ⲘⲚ̄ ⲠⲰⲚϨ Ⲛ̄Ϣ[Ⲁ ⲈⲚⲈ]Ϩ

Long Version (II,1) 6.2–7

Ⲧ[Ⲁ]Ï ⲦⲈ ⲦⲠⲈⲚⲦⲀⲤ Ⲛ̄ⲀⲒⲰⲚ Ⲛ̄ⲦⲈ ⲠⲒⲰⲦ [Ⲉ]ⲦⲈ
Ⲡ[ⲀÏ] ⲠⲈ ⲠϢⲞⲢⲠ Ⲛ̄ⲢⲰⲘⲈ Ⲑ︦ⲒⲔⲰⲚ
Ⲙ̄ⲠⲀϨⲞⲢⲀ[Ⲧ]ⲞⲤ Ⲙ̄ⲠⲚ̄Ⲁ̄ ⲦⲀÏ ⲦⲈ ⲦⲠⲢⲞⲚⲞⲒⲀ ·
ⲈⲦⲈ ⲦⲀÏ Ⲧ[Ⲉ] Ⲃ̄ⲀⲢⲂⲎⲖⲰ ⲀⲨⲰ ⲠⲘⲈⲈⲨⲈ ⲘⲚ̄
ⲦⲠⲢⲞⲚⲰⲤⲒⲤ ⲀⲨⲰ ⲦⲘⲚ̄ⲦⲦⲀⲦⲈⲔⲞ ⲀⲨⲰ
ⲠⲰⲚϨ [Ϣ]Ⲁ ⲈⲚⲈϨ · ⲀⲨⲰ ⲦⲘⲈ

These are the Five Aeons of the Father, which is the First Man, the image of the invisible one. This is Barbelon and Thought and Foreknowledge and Imperishability and Life eternal.

This is the pentad of Aeons of the Father, which is the First Man, the image of the invisible Spirit. This is Forethought—which is Barbelo—and Thought, and Foreknowledge and Imperishability and Life eternal and Truth.

This all seems very Manichaean. Indeed, I would say that the idea of a "First Man" accompanied by five powers is *characteristically* Manichaean and fits with the sort of theological patterning found especially in the Coptic *Kephalaia*.[10] The Manichaean First Man is often presented as being armed with five aspects, variously called *shekinahs*, light elements or intellectual powers, although the series of powers from *Ap. John* bares only a limited correspondence to the canonical Manichaean pentad.

Ap. John (Short Version)

1) Barbelon
2) Thought (ἔννοια)
3) Foreknowledge (πρόγνωσις)
4) Imperishability (ἀφθαρσία)
5) Eternal Life (*ἀθανασία?)

Manichaean Pentad

1) Mind (νοῦς)
2) Thought (ἔννοια)
3) Insight (φρόνησις)
4) Counsel (ἐνθύμησις)
5) Consideration (λογισμός)

Still, in both the *short* and *long* versions of *Ap. John* there seems to have been a deliberate (albeit imperfect) attempt to associate Barbelo with a pentadic "First Man," something that in itself is entirely incongruous with the Sethian cosmogony as expressed in related texts. Nowhere else is Barbelo referred to as "a/the First Man." In fact, Barbelo is more likely to be described as "Triple Male" and connected with Mother of the Father-Mother-Child

9. This is in fact confirmed by preliminary transcriptions of portions of Mani's *Living Gospel* from the Synaxeis Codex, in which First Man has a sister (*53–*56) (Wolf-Peter Funk, personal communication, July 2015).

10. See Pettipiece, *Pentadic Redaction*.

triad. Moreover, the original Sethian cosmogony[11] seems to suggest a numerological progression from *monad* (the One) to *triad* (Father/Invisible Spirit, Mother/Barbelo, Child/Autogenes) to *tetrad* (Four Luminaries) (see the *Gospel of the Egyptians*). Therefore, the presence of this pentadic First Man seems entirely out of place and suggests that the text has been interpolated—specifically by a Manichaean editor or scribe.

Interestingly, this redaction appears to be rather poorly executed. On the surface there does seem to be a desire to impose the idea of the five-fold "First Man," but there is an ambiguity in the text that appears to have confused the redactor of the *long version*. This stems from the fact that in the *short version* Barbelo is said to be *both* "Thought" (ἔννοια) (III 7.12 / BG 27.5) and "Forethought" (πρόνοια) (III 7.16 / BG 27.11). Moreover, she makes only three requests to the Father—for Foreknowledge, Imperishability, and Eternal life (III 7.5—8.23). As a result, there are really only four powers clustered in the *short version*: 1) Barbelo (Thought *and* Forethought), 2) Foreknowledge, 3) Imperishability, and 4) Eternal Life. This, in fact, would tend to fit with the proposed interpretation of Barbelo's name as "God in Four,"[12] and would set the stage for the appearance of the Four Luminaries, which seems to be the natural progression of the Sethian myth. But, in an effort to create a series of five, a redactor of the *short version* appears to have separated Barbelo as πρόνοια from ἔννοια to create an artificial pentad. The *long version*, for its part, seeks to make the pentad even more explicit[13] by adding "Truth" (ⲧⲙⲏⲉ < ἀληθεία) (II 5.11–34) to the series of powers called forth by Barbelo. This combined with the extraction of "Thought" already in the *short version* led the redactor of the *long version* into difficulty since there are now, in fact, six powers to be enumerated as the "pentad" of the First Man:

Short Version	*Long Version*
1) Barbelon	1) Forethought (πρόνοια)
2) Thought (ἔννοια)	2) Thought (ἔννοια)
3) Foreknowledge (πρόγνωσις)	3) Foreknowledge (πρόγνωσις)
4) Imperishability (ἀφθαρσία)	4) Imperishability (ἀφθαρσία)
5) Eternal Life (*ἀθανασία?)	5) Eternal Life (*ἀθανασία?)
	6) Truth (*ἀληθεία)

11. It is reasonable to assume that those figures in the Sethian corpus with Semitic names reveal the earliest strata of the cosmogony and its radical revision of Genesis.

12. Meyer, *Nag Hammadi Scriptures*, 110 n.17.

13. In Waldstein and Wisse's synoptic edition ⲡϯⲟⲩ ⲛⲁⲓⲱⲛ and ⲡⲙⲉϩϯ ⲛⲧⲉ ⲛⲓⲁⲓⲱⲛ of the *short versions* are both translated as "pentad," whereas only the *long version* has ⲧⲡⲉⲛⲧⲁⲥ ⲛⲁⲓⲱⲛ (*Apocryphon of John*, 38–39).

As a whole, this apparently clumsy redactional scheme seems designed to subordinate or absorb Barbelo to the pentadic First Man. This is a rather peculiar emphasis given the fact that Barbelo has so far been the main protagonist in the text and the so-called First Man virtually disappears from the subsequent narrative. As a result of this incongruity, it seems likely that a Manichaean hand has been at work. Remarkably, it would seem, on both versions of the text. The *short*, which Barc asserts is closest to the original,[14] may have received a somewhat *light* redaction, whereas in the *long* the Manichaean traces are far more evident (see below).

A LION-FACED LORD

After an elaborate series of emanations, *Ap. John* comes to one of its central episodes: the begetting of the demiurge by Wisdom (σοφία). Wisdom, we are told, wanted to bring forth a being like herself, but failed to get permission from her mother Spirit. As a result, she brought forth a monstrous offspring in the "form of a lion-faced serpent" (II 10.9 / III 15.11 / BG 37.21). Shocked by his grotesque appearance she hid him in a cloud and named him Yaldabaoth, the "Child of Chaos" (II 10.19 / III 15.22 / BG 38.14). In his arrogance, he began creating minions for himself in the lower realm where he could sit as Ruler (ἄρχων). The only other being aware of his existence is the "holy Spirit," the "Mother of the Living" (ΤΜΑΑΥ ΝΝΕΤΟΝϨ) (II 10.18).

As in the case of Barbelo and the First Man, here we are faced with a similar cluster of motifs with Manichaean connotations. According to *Kephalaia* ch. 6, the "King of Darkness," who like Yaldabaoth rules the lower-realm, is described in theriomorphic terms: "his head [is lion-faced, his] hands and feet are demon-[and devil-]faced, [his] shoulders are eagle-faced, while his belly [is dragon-faced,] (and) his tail is fish-faced" (*Keph.* 30.34—31.1). Such descriptions are not necessarily unique to Manichaean tradition since a very similar formulation is found in the Mandaean *Right Ginza* 280. Both of these easily could be dependent on an earlier prototype. We also have the reference to the Spirit as "Mother of the Living" (ΤΜΑΑΥ ΝΝΕΤΟΝϨ). This too is the exact form used in Coptic Manichaean texts to designate the Mother of Life.[15] Both the *long* and *short* versions from Nag Hammadi use this form, although the Berlin Codex reads "Life, the Mother of Everyone" (ΖΩΗ ΤΜΑΥ ΝΟΥΟΝ ΝΙΜ) (38.12–13). The title "Mother of Life" is used only later as a designation for Eve (II 23.24; III 30.14).

14. Barc and Funk, *Le Livre des secrets de Jean,* 5–6.

15. *Psalm-Book* 32.28; 36.21; 137.11; 144.17; 145.8; 147.72; 199.5; 201.2; *Keph.* 39.25; 40.1; 56.11.

More direct evidence of Manichaean editorial activity comes in the form of a gloss on the sub-rulers of Yaldabaoth's kingdom. Whereas the *short version* simply states that the demiurge placed "seven" powers (III 17.18, "kings" in the BG 41.13) to rule over the heavens and "five over the chaos of Hades" (III 17.19 / BG 41.14–15), the *long version* develops this description by saying:

ⲁⲩⲱ ⲁϥⲡⲱϣ ⲉϫⲱⲟⲩ ⲉⲃⲟⲗ ϩⲙ̄ ⲡⲉϥⲕⲱϩⲧ ⲙⲡⲉϥⲧⲛ̄ⲛⲉⲩ ⲇⲉ ⲉⲃⲟⲗ ϩⲛ̄ ⲧϭⲁⲙ ⲙ̄ⲡⲟⲩⲟⲉⲓⲛ ⲉⲛⲧⲁϥϫⲓⲧⲥ̄ ⲛ̄ⲧⲛ̄ ⲧⲉϥⲙⲁⲁⲩ ⲛ̄ⲧⲟϥ ⲅⲁⲣ ⲟⲩⲕⲁⲕⲉ ⲛ̄ⲁⲧⲥⲟⲟⲩⲛⲉ ⲡⲉ ⲡⲟⲩⲟⲉⲓⲛ ⲇⲉ ⲛ̄ⲧⲁⲣⲉϥⲧⲱϩ ⲙⲛ̄ ⲡⲕⲁⲕⲉ ⲁϥⲧⲣⲉⲡⲕⲁⲕⲉ ⲣ̄ ⲟⲩⲟⲉⲓⲛ ⲡⲕⲁⲕⲉ ⲇⲉ ⲛ̄ⲧⲁⲣⲉϥⲧⲱϩ ⲙⲛ̄ ⲡⲟⲩⲟⲉⲓⲛ ⲁϥϩⲧⲙ̄ⲧⲙ̄ ⲡⲟⲩⲟⲉⲓⲛ ⲁⲩⲱ ⲙ̄ⲡϥϣⲱⲡⲉ ⲛ̄ⲟⲩⲟⲉⲓⲛ ⲟⲩⲧⲉ ⲛ̄ⲕⲁⲕⲉ ⲁⲗⲗⲁ ⲁϥϣⲱⲡⲉ ⲉϥϣⲟⲡⲉ ⲡⲓⲁⲣⲭⲱⲛ ϭⲉ ⲉⲧϣⲟⲛⲉ ⲟⲩⲛ̄ⲧⲁϥ ⲙ̄ⲙⲁⲩ ⲙ̄ϣⲟⲙⲧ ⲛ̄ⲣⲁⲛ ⲡϣⲟⲣⲡ ⲛ̄ⲣⲁⲛ ⲡⲉ ⲓ̈ⲁⲗⲧⲁⲃⲁ[ⲱ]ⲑ ⲡⲙⲉϩⲥⲛⲁⲩ ⲡⲉ ⲥⲁⲕⲗⲁⲥ ⲡⲙⲉϩϣⲟⲙⲛⲧ ⲡⲉ ⲥⲁⲙⲁⲏⲗ

And he shared with them his fire, but he did not send forth from the power of the Light which he had received from his mother. For he is ignorant Darkness. And when the Light mixed with the Darkness, it made the darkness shine, and when the Darkness mixed with the Light it darkened the Light and it became neither Light nor Dark but dim. This Ruler who is weak has three names: the first name is Yaltabaoth, the second is Saklas, the third is Samael (II, 11.7–18).

This discussion of the "mixture" of Light and Dark is also a characteristically Manichaean concept, as is the harsh condemnation of the Ruler with a series of names that includes "Saklas," who is a key player in Manichaean tradition.[16] Moreover, this passage interrupts the narrative flow of the *short version* which continues with enumerating the seven heavenly rulers. The interpolation also pre-empts the climax of the treatise by repeating Yaldabaoth's proclamation: "I am God and there is no other god beside me." In the *short version* this dramatic indictment of the Jewish god only comes later (BG 44.14–15 / III lacuna). Also, while the *short version* places the five rulers "over the chaos of Hades" (ⲉϫⲙ ⲡⲉⲭⲁⲟⲥ ⲛⲁⲙⲏⲧⲉ) (BG 41.15 / III 17.19–20), the *long version* places them "over the depth of the Abyss" (ⲁⲭⲙ ⲡϣⲓⲕ ⲙⲡⲟⲩⲛ) (II 11.6). This may seem like a small detail, but "Abyss" (ⲛⲟⲩⲛ) is the standard term used in Coptic Manichaean sources to designate the lower-realm of Darkness.[17]

IMAGE AND LIKENESS

Later in the narrative, when Yaldabaoth hears a voice from the heavens, the *short version* of *Ap. John* relates that he and his powers saw an "image"

---

16. *Keph.* 138.2–3.

17. *Homilies* 35.19, 53.10, 78.17; *Keph.* 15.2, 29.29, 40.2, 41.19 etc; *Psalm-Book* 2.4, 3.24, 10.9, 73.23, 86.26; *Living Gospel* (Synaxeis *31?).

of the "holy, perfect one, the [first Man]" (ϨΟΥΕΙΤ ΝΡѠΜΕ) (BG 48.2 / III lacuna) in the water. As a result, he says to his powers: "Let [us create man] according to the image of God and according to *his* likeness" (III 22.4–6). The *long version*, however, includes an extensive gloss after the "First Man" (again using the alternate form ΠϢΟΡΠ ΝΡѠΜΕ) revealed his image:

ΑΥѠ ΑϤϹΤѠΤ ΤΗΡϤ Ñϭι ΠΑΙѠΝ	The whole aeon of the Chief Ruler
ΜΠΡѠΤΑΡΧѠΝ ΑΥѠ ΑΝϹΝ̄ΤΕ Μ̄ΠΝΟΥΝ	trembled and the foundations of the
ΑΥΚΙΜ ΑΥѠ ΕΒΟΛ ϨΙΤΝ̄ Μ̄ΜΟΥΕΙΟΟΥΕ ΝΑΪ	abyss shook. And of the waters which
ΕΤϢΟΟΠ ϨΙΧΝ̄ ΤϨΥΛΗ ΑϤΡ̄ Ο[ΥΟΕΙ]Ν Ñϭι	are above Matter, the underside was
ΠϹΑΜΠΙΤΝ̄ ΕΒΟΛ ϨΙΤΜ̄ ΠΟΥ[ѠΝϨ ΕΒ]ΟΛ	illuminated by the appearance of this
Ν̄ΤΕϤϨΙΚѠΝ ΤΑΪ ΕΝΤΑϹΟΥѠΝϨ[Ϲ ΑΥ]Ѡ	image which had been revealed. And
Ν̄ΤΑΡΟΥΕΙѠΡΜΕ Ñϭι ΝΕϪΟΥϹΙΑ ΤΗΡΟΥ ΑΥѠ	when all the authorities and the Chief
ΠΡѠΤΑΡΧѠΝ ΑΥΝΑΥ ΑΠΜΕΡΟϹ ΤΗΡϤ Μ̄ΠϹΑ	Ruler looked they saw the whole region
ΜΠΙΤΝΕ ΕΑϤΡ̄ΟΥΟΕΙΝ ΑΥѠ ΕΒΟΛ ϨΙΤΜ̄	below illuminated. And through the
ΠΟΥΟΕΙΝ ΑΥΝΑΥ ϨΡΑΪ ϨΜ̄ ΠΜΟΟΥ ΑΠΤΥΠΟϹ	Light they saw in the water the form of
Ν̄ΤϨΙΚѠΝ ΑΥѠ ΠΕΧΑϤ Ñ̄ΕϪΟΥϹΙΑ ΕΤϢΟΟΠ	the image. And he said to the authori-
ϢΑΡΟϤ ΧΕ ΑΜΗΕΙΝΕ Ν̄ΤΝ̄ΤΑΜΙΟ Ν̄ΟΥΡѠΜΕ	ties which attend him, "Come, let us
ΚΑΤΑ ΘΙΚѠΝ Μ̄ΠΝΟΥΤΕ ΑΥѠ ΚΑΤΑ ΠΝΕΙΝΕ	create a man according to the image of
ΧΕΚΑΑϹ ΑΡΕΤΕϤϨΙΚѠΝ ΝΑϢѠΠΕ ΝΑΝ	God and according to our likeness, that
Ν̄ΟΥΟΥΕΙΝ	his image may become a Light for us
	(II 14.25—15.4).

In the *long version's* account it is emphasized that the Ruler lives in the characteristically Manichaean lower-realm of "Matter." Therefore, he and his powers perceive the image shining through the waters above them. Once they perceive this light-image of the First Man they resolve to create man based not only on its likeness but on *their own* likeness as well. In the *Acts of Archelaus*, the same event is outlined as follows:

> Concerning Adam and how he was created, he says this, that the one who says: "Come let us make man in *our image* and like- ness" and following the form that we have seen, is a prince, who says this to his fellow princes, namely, "Come, give me some of the Light which we have received, and let us create following the form of ourselves, who are princes, and following that form we have seen, which is the First Man" (*Acts of Archelaus* 12).[18]

Similarly, the *Kephalaia* states that the evil powers "fashioned Adam and Eve in the flesh" (*Keph.* 56.23) when they "saw his image and formed their shapes after his likeness, who are Adam and Eve" (*Keph.* 133.14–15). Else- where it is said that "Saklas, chief of the demons, said, 'Come! Give me your light and I will make you an image after the likeness of the exalted one'" (*Keph.* 138.2–3). This detail, that the human form is a hybrid modeled on

18. Lieu, *Greek and Latin*, 49.

both light and dark paradigms, is central to the Manichaean revision of Genesis and is at the core of Manichaean anthropology. Therefore, we are faced with yet another instance of a scribal coloring to make the text seem more Manichaean in tone.

MISCELLANEOUS MODIFICATIONS

Pages 15.29—19.10 of the *long version* of *Ap. John* contains an extensive interpolated section seemingly derived from a work called the "Book of Zoroaster." In it, the parts of the body are associated with a vast array of demons with decidedly Semitic (or pseudo-Semitic) names. This sort of *melothesia* is found in Manichaean sources (such as *Keph.* ch. 70, "On the Body, that it was made to resemble the Cosmos"), though towards the end of the list we read that "the origin of the demons which are in the whole body is determined to be four—heat, cold, wetness, and dryness. And the mother of them all is Matter (ϨⲨⲖⲎ)" (II 18.2–5). In fact, the apparent addition of Matter to the list makes five demons rather than four. Another artificially imposed pentad like this could indicate a Manichaean redaction, although we find a rather striking parallel in the *Kephalaia* ch. 4 "On the Four Great Days, which have come from one another; along with the Four Nights":

ⲦⲘⲀϨϢⲀⲘⲦ[Ⲉ ⲚⲞⲨϢⲎ ⲠⲈ ⲠϮⲞⲨ] Ⲛ̅ⲔⲞⲤⲘⲞⲤ
Ⲛ̅ⲦⲤⲀⲢⲜ . . . . . . [ϨⲀⲨ]Ⲧ ⲘⲚ̅ ⲦϮⲈ ⲚⲤϨⲒⲘⲈ
ⲚⲈⲚⲦⲀⲨϪⲠⲀⲨ ⲀⲂⲀⲖ Ⲛ̅Ⲛ̅ϬⲀⲘ . . . ⲠⲈ ⲀⲨϨⲈⲒ̈Ⲉ
ⲀϪⲘ̅ ⲠⲔⲀϨ ⲈⲨⲞⲨⲀⲚϨ̅ ⲀⲂⲀⲖ ϨⲘ ⲠⲠⲈ
[ⲦϢⲞ]ⲨⲰⲨ Ⲙ̅Ⲛ̅ ⲠⲠⲈⲦⲀϬⲂⲈ ⲀϨ̅Ⲛ̅ ⲦⲤⲈⲦⲈ ⲘⲚ
ⲦϨⲎⲆⲞⲚⲎ [ⲈⲦⲞ]ⲨⲎ[Ϩ] Ⲛ̅ϨⲎⲦⲞⲨ ⲈⲦⲔⲒⲘ ⲀⲢⲀⲨ
ⲀϨⲞⲨⲚ ⲀⲚⲞⲨⲀⲢⲎⲨ [ⲦϨⲨ]Ⲗ[Ⲏ] ϨⲰⲤ
ⲦⲈⲚⲐⲨⲘⲎⲤⲒⲤ Ⲙ̅ⲠⲘⲞⲨ ⲈⲦⲈ ⲚⲦⲀⲤ ⲠⲈ
ⲦⲞⲨ[ⲘⲈⲨ] ⲦⲎⲢⲞⲨ

The third [Night is the Five] Worlds of Flesh . . . . . . [five(?) male] and the five female, those who are born of the powers . . . they fell upon the earth, while they are revealed in the dryness and cold, along with the fire and desire [which] dwells in them, which impel them towards one another. [Matter], however, is the Death-desire, which is [Mother] of them all (26.33—27.6)

As this passage shows, the association of dryness, cold, and fire (=heat) with Matter, the "Mother of them All" clearly seems to indicate a Manichaean adaptation.[19]

Another adaptation is found when in the *short version* the Mother petitions the Father to retrieve the power given to the ruler, the Father sends forth "Autogenes with his four lights" (III 24.2 / BG 51.9–10). In the *long version*, however, it is simply "five illuminators" (ϮⲞⲨ ⲘⲪⲰⲤⲦⲎⲢ) (II 19.19) that are sent forth. The modification is subtle. Even though Autogenes and

19. Van Lindt, "Religious Terminology," 196.

his four lights does add up to five, the redactor of the *long version* wants to make the pentad explicit and replaces Autogenes with "illuminator," a term Manichaeans associated with the Sun and Moon and with Mani himself. Also in the *short version*, when Christ explains to John who will be saved and deemed "worthy to enter these great lights" (III 33.7 / BG 65.8), the *long version* adapts this to "worthy of the greatness (ⲘⲚⲦⲚⲞϬ)" (II 25.26), another Manichaean technical term referring to the Father and his associates in the Light Realm.

Finally, when the *short version* describes the mating of the angels with the daughters of men (III 38.21—39.4), the *long version* adds that those deceived by their precious gifts died "without knowing the God of Truth (ⲠⲚⲞⲨⲦⲈ ⲚⲦⲘⲎⲈ)" (II 30.4)—the "God of Truth" being an epithet frequently applied to the Father of Greatness in the Manichaean *Psalm-Book* (36.7; 49.29; 57.31; 62.30; 75.7 etc.).

A MANICHAEAN EPILOGUE?

The *long version* of *Ap. John* contains a substantial expansion of the Savior's final discourse. As we might expect, this addition has several Manichaean characteristics. First of all, the Savior identifies himself with *pronoia* (II 30.12), a figure which, as we have already seen, the Manichaean redactor sought to assimilate to the First Man. Next he calls himself the "richness of the light" (ⲦⲘⲚⲦⲢⲘⲘⲀⲞ ⲘⲠⲞⲨⲞⲈⲒⲚ) (II 30.15). In the Manichaean *Psalm-Book* the First Man is called: "Our Father, the First Man. The Lord of Richness" (ⲠⲬⲀⲒⲤ ⲚⲦⲘⲚⲦⲢⲘⲘⲀⲞ) (137.17-18) and "rich" is a term that is often applied to beings in the light-realm, such as the "Twelve Rich Gods of Greatness" (*Keph.* 25.16). As *Kephalaia* ch. 50 states, three names can be applied to beings in the realm of light: god, rich one, and angel (125.25ff).

Then, the Savior describes how he has made three descents. First, we are told that, like the First Man, the Savior "went into the realm of darkness" (II 30.17), although the dark powers did not recognize him. Second, he "came from those belonging to the Light" (II 30.23) and again entered "into the middle of the Darkness and into Hades" (II 30.25-26) before fleeing to the "root of Light (II 30.30).[20] Then, he says, "I came forth yet a third time (II 30.32-33) as "the Light which exists in the Light" (ⲀⲚⲞⲔ ⲠⲈ ⲠⲞⲨⲞⲈⲒⲚ ⲈⲦϢⲞⲞⲠ ϨⲘ ⲠⲞⲨⲞⲈⲒⲚ) (II 30.33-34) so that "I might again enter" (ⲈⲈⲒⲚⲀⲂⲰⲔ) into the midst of Darkness. The Savior, we are told, entered the prison of the body, proclaiming "He who hears, may he get up from deep

20. Root (ⲚⲞⲨⲚⲈ) is one of the synonyms used in Coptic Manichaean texts for the principles of Light and Dark (cf. *Keph.* 35.3, etc.).

sleep" (II 31.4–6). These three descents appear to resemble three descents from the Manichaean cosmogony. More specifically, the three descents of the *third power* of the Manichaean trinity seem to be intended.

While Manichaean theology is known for its multiplicity of beings and divine powers, the entire system is rooted ultimately in a trinitarian scheme of Father-Mother-Child, which is also present in *Ap. John* at several points. As a result, many of the figures key to the cosmogony should be understood as diverse manifestations of the central triad. According to one of the best representations of the Manichaean myth recorded in Syriac by Theodore bar Khonai, in response to the hostility of the powers of darkness the Father of Greatness and the Mother of Life send forth the First Man to be devoured by the Darkness. Thus, the first descent of the Savior "into the realm of darkness." Next, in order to recover the light substance that had been consumed by the dark powers, the "second evocation" technically involves the Living Spirit being called forth to build the cosmos as a kind of light-filtering machine. In the "third evocation," however, the *son*-figure appears twice: once as the "Messenger" and once as Jesus. Like the image of the First Man earlier in *Ap. John*, the Messenger appears to the demons who then create Adam and Eve based on his image as a way to further ensnare light substance in the material prison of the body. Then, the *son* manifests a third time as "Jesus the Splendor," whom we are told "came to Adam, the innocent, and awoke him from the sleep of death, so that he might be delivered from many (evil) spirit(s)" (Theodore bar Khonai 317.16–17). After he receives this enlightening knowledge, Adam laments "Woe, woe to the one who formed my body and to the one who bound my soul and to the tyrants who have enslaved me" (Theodore bar Khonai 318.3–4).

It is possible then that the Manichaean redactor expanded the final discourse of the Savior as a way to re-enforce the equations which had already been made between Barbelo/*pronoia* and the First Man and to underscore the multiple ways in which the Savior is manifest in Manichaean cosmogony.[21] Such a reading, however, remains highly speculative.

IMPLICATIONS

As this study has shown, there does appear to be some grounds to connect *Ap. John* and Manichaean traditions. One the one hand, it seems likely that at some stage in the textual history of these versions a Manichaean redactor

---

21. Böhlig recognizes that in the Manichaean system, Jesus has been differentiated into multiple functions ("New Testament," 98). See also Franzmann, *Jesus in the Manichaean Writings*, 141.

was at work. Given the similarities in technical terms that we find evident in Coptic Manichaean sources it seems probable that the redactions were made to a Coptic version of the text rather than a Greek prototype. At the same time, there are key elements in the text, such as the Father-Mother-Child triad and some of the basic contours of the demiurgical myth, which surely predate any later editorial activity and probably influenced the formation of the Manichaean cosmogony itself. As a result, we are in the rather remarkable position of seeing a gnostic cosmogonic text being reworked by a representative of a later movement originally influenced by some of its core elements.

Such editorial activity should not be surprising given the fact that Manichaeans were a definite part of the Egyptian landscape in the fourth to fifth centuries CE. In fact, Lycopolis seems to have been one of the main centers of Manichaean activity,[22] as evidenced by the polemical treatise composed against them by Alexander, a local Platonist philosopher. As a result, Manichaeans would have inherited what Stroumsa calls the "dualistic and encratistic tendencies" of the Nile valley[23] and could have therefore formed part of the readership of the works found in the Nag Hammadi codices. Moreover, they may have served as a catalyzing force in the emergence of Egyptian monasticism, although we cannot know for certain.[24] What we do know, based on the material evidence of the manuscripts themselves, is that Manichaeans were involved in book production in Egypt. In fact, they have earned the distinction of having produced the largest (the *Psalm-Book*) and the smallest (*Cologne Mani Codex*) manuscripts surviving from late antiquity. It should not be surprising then to find them embedded within the early Coptic scribal culture of Upper Egypt—both overtly and possibly covertly as well. Stroumsa has argued also that a Manichaean "underground" existed in Egypt,[25] with some possibly taking refuge from state and ecclesiastical persecution in the monasteries. It is even reported, albeit in a late source, that bishop Timothy of Alexandria imposed a food-test to root out and expose Manichaeans among the Egyptian clergy.[26]

22. Stroumsa, "Manichaean Challenge," 308.

23. Ibid., 307–308.

24. Scholars are very divided on this question, which is frequently clouded by theological assumptions. On the one hand, some of those who have speculated about the Manichaean origin of monasticism in Egypt are driven by a more general antimonastic attitude that sees asceticism as "un-Christian" and a foreign element (Harmless, *Desert Christians*, 438–39). Others, however, tend to dismiss any possible connection as a way to insulate Egyptian monasticism from any "heretical" impurities.

25. Stroumsa, "Monachisme et 'marranisme,'" 313–14.

26. Eutychius in Gardner and Lieu, *Manichaean Texts*, 121.

As for the Nag Hammadi codices, ever since their discovery in the vicinity of Pachomian monastic settlements, many scholars have presumed that the texts have some connection to that environment, either as pious reading for heterodox monks or as a sort of heresiological reference library.[27] Others strongly disagree and, again, we may never know for certain. One has to ask, however, who else would have produced such books other than Christian scribes of some sort, probably monks (some of whom may have had Manichaean leanings)?

In closing, I would like to draw attention to the fact that the *long version* of *Ap. John* is found within Nag Hammadi Codex II.[28] This manuscript also contains the *Gospel of Thomas*, which Manichaeans appear to have made use of,[29] as well as *On the Origin of the World*, which Louis Painchaud has argued contains "une contamination manichéenne."[30] Note too that the *Book of Thomas* (NHC II,7), found in the same codex, presents Jesus predicting that what is sown "will hide in tombs of darkness,"[31] which evokes Manichaean terminology; similarly, *On the Origin of the World* ends with the statement that "light will [overcome the] darkness and banish it. The darkness will be like something that never was, and the source of darkness will be dissolved. Deficiency will be pulled out by its root (ΝΟΥΝΕ) and cast down into the darkness, and the Light will withdraw up to its root (ΝΟΥΝΕ)" (127.1–5). As such, the codex itself, or at least some of the writings it contains, may provide additional clues of Manichaean scribes at work.

27. Veilleux, "Monasticism and Gnosis," 284.

28. For a discussion of this see Pettipiece, "'Towards a Manichaean Reading,'" 43–54.

29. See Mirecki, "Coptic Manichaean Psalm 278," 243–62; Funk "'Einer aus tausend,'" 67–94; Coyle, "Gospel of Thomas in Manichaeism?" 75–91.

30. See Painchaud's translation of the text in Mahé and Poirier, eds., *Écrits gnostiques*, 436.

31. Layton, *Nag Hammadi Codex II,2–7*, 194–95.

– 11 –

"Cherries at Command"
Preaching the *Gospel of Pseudo-Matthew* in Anglo-Saxon England

— Brandon W. Hawk —

O then bespoke the babe,
within his mother's womb:
"Bow down then the tallest tree,
for my mother to have some."
Then bowed down the highest tree
unto his mother's hand:
Then she cried, "See, Joseph,
I have cherries at command."

—"THE CHERRY TREE CAROL"[1]

THESE LYRICS, FROM A traditional folk song known as "The Cherry Tree Carol," offer a useful introduction to the transmission of apocrypha across

---

1. Child, *English and Scottish Popular Ballads*, 2:1–6.

the centuries. This ballad relates Joseph's reluctance to pick cherries for his new, pregnant wife, and how the infant Jesus, still in the womb, commanded the trees to bend for his mother to pick their fruit. With evidence of its use in folk traditions from at least the fifteenth century, this song continues to hold a place in contemporary culture: it has been performed by a number of music icons, including Shirley Collins, Joan Baez, Peter, Paul and Mary, as well as, more recently, Sting and Annie Lennox. As may already be apparent (at least from my title), a closer look at this folk ballad reveals its origins in the *Gospel of Pseudo-Matthew* (BHL 5334–5342; CANT 51).[2] This particular apocryphon—consisting of a Latin adaptation of chs. 1–17 of the *Protevangelium of James* (BHG 1046; CANT 50) as well as an expansion of that account—contains a similar story about Jesus commanding palm trees to bend for Mary on the holy family's flight to Egypt. Of course, this carol is not the only persistent holdover from this apocryphon in popular music. For example, Christians still sing about the "ox and ass" at the nativity in songs like "What Child Is This?" and "Good Christian Men, Rejoice," despite the fact that this image appears nowhere in the canonical Gospels. Reasons for starting with these reflections on contemporary music are two-fold, since such examples demonstrate the endurance of Christian apocrypha across the centuries and directly intersect with the narrative subject of my paper.

Moving backward in time—to the tenth and eleventh centuries—in the rest of this essay, I examine uses of *Ps.-Mt.* for preaching and related media in late Anglo-Saxon England. Christian apocrypha enjoyed a prominent afterlife in the medieval period (and beyond), particularly as subjects for preaching; this is especially the case in early England.[3] In this study, I focus on versions of *Ps.-Mt.* in an Old English sermon designated Vercelli Homily 6 and a set of images in the Sacramentary of Robert of Jumièges, suggesting that these artifacts should be considered together as part of a larger media network of apocryphal narratives about Jesus' childhood circulating in late Anglo-Saxon England. This examination specifically addresses how visual media serve as translations of apocrypha, and therefore key contexts for the culture surrounding parallel narratives in Anglo-Saxon preaching texts. Adopting an interdisciplinary framework of transmission studies—encompassing book history, translations, and adaptations across media—allows for considering apocrypha beyond verbal representations, to encompass the many cultural currents that surrounded and affected Anglo-Saxons in their attitudes toward para-biblical narratives. Taken together, multimedia

2. References are to Gijsel, *Libri de nativitate Mariae*, 277–481 (forma textus P); translations are adapted from Ehrman and Pleše, eds. and trans., *Apocryphal Gospels*, 73–113.

3. For bibliographic overview, see Biggs, ed., *Apocrypha*.

witnesses to *Ps.-Mt.* further demonstrate how this apocryphon permeated Anglo-Saxon preaching contexts across a variety of porous social boundaries linked by common subjects. Just as apocrypha were preached in vernacular sermons to elites and commoners, ecclesiasts and laity, literate and illiterate, as well as men and women, these narratives appeared also in other media accessible to audiences across the spectrum of social strata.

MULTIMEDIA TRANSLATIONS

Various versions and translations of *Ps.-Mt.* survive from Anglo-Saxon England, particularly in relation to preaching.[4] Although this apocryphon circulated as early as the ninth century, English manuscript witnesses to the Latin text and revisions survive only from the late Anglo-Saxon period. A single independent witness, containing chs. 1 to 6:3, is extant in London, British Library, Cotton Nero E.i (s. $xi^{3/4}$, Worcester), as part of a legendary.[5] Two versions of the Carolingian revision known as the *Nativity of Mary* (*De Nativitate Mariae*; BHL 5343–5345; CANT 52) also exist:[6] in Durham, Cathedral Library A.III.29 (s. xi^{ex}, before 1096, Durham) and Salisbury, Cathedral Library 179 (s. xi^{ex}, Salisbury)—both included in copies of the *Homiliarium* of Paul the Deacon.[7] Finally, episodes from chs. 23 and 24 have close analogues in a Latin sermon on the Nativity of the Innocents (item 11) in a version of the *Homiliary of Saint-Père de Chartres* surviving in Cambridge, Pembroke College 25 (s. xi^{ex} or xi^2, Bury St. Edmunds).[8] The fact that all of these collections revolve around liturgical cycles is significant for their connections with preaching, made all the stronger by the fact that the versions included in homiliaries were explicitly stylized and intended as sermons. Furthermore, these types of collections also have strong ties with continental homiliaries, as the Anglo-Saxons looked to Carolingian models for their own sermon collections.[9] What these witnesses reveal, then, is that Anglo-Saxon sermons based on *Ps.-Mt.* are situated within a larger media network of early medieval uses of apocrypha for preaching purposes.

---

4. For summaries of scholarship, see Hall, "Gospel of Pseudo-Matthew"; and Clayton, "De Nativitate Mariae."

5. Gneuss and Lapidge, *Anglo-Saxon Manuscripts*, no. 344.

6. For an edition, see Beyers, *Libri de Nativitate Mariae*, 269–333.

7. Gneuss and Lapidge, *Anglo-Saxon Manuscripts*, nos. 222 and 753.

8. Ibid., no. 130. See Cross, *Cambridge Pembroke College MS. 25*, 22–23.

9. For overviews with further references, see Clayton, "Homiliaries and Preaching"; various essays in Kleist, *Old English Homily*; and Hill, "Ælfric and Haymo Revisited."

Old English translations of parts of *Ps.-Mt.* also demonstrate how Anglo-Saxons used this apocryphon for preaching. For example, a translation of chs. 1–12 exists as a sermon for the nativity of Mary, including the story of Anna and Joachim's infertility, the miraculous conception of Mary, her birth, and Mary's early life up to her doubting the miraculous conception of Jesus.[10] This sermon survives in three manuscripts: Cambridge, Corpus Christi College 367, Part II (s. xii, Worcester?); Oxford, Bodleian Library, Bodley 343 (s. xii[2], West Midlands); and Oxford, Bodleian Library, Hatton 114 (ca.1064–ca.1083, Worcester).[11] All three manuscripts represent Old English sermon collections, witnesses to the vibrant culture of vernacular preaching in early England. In these manuscript contexts, set alongside works of prominent preachers like Abbot Ælfric of Eynsham (ca.955–ca.1010) and Archbishop Wulfstan of York (d.1023), Old English translations of *Ps.-Mt.* as sermons also attest to the ways in which apocrypha had entered mainstream Anglo-Saxon Christianity.

The sermon known as Vercelli 6 appears in a collection of Old English preaching texts (both prose and poetry) surviving in Vercelli, Biblioteca Capitolare CXVII (s. x[2], SE England), more commonly referred to as the *Vercelli Book*.[12] This manuscript was compiled in the second half of the tenth century (likely 959–988 in Canterbury), although the precise origins and rationale behind the compilation remain unknown, as do the circumstances of its arrival in Vercelli, Italy.[13] The sermon designated Vercelli 6, intended for Christmas, focuses on Jesus' nativity and infancy as narrated in the canonical Gospel of Luke, with expansions from *Ps.-Mt.*[14] D. G. Scragg

10. See Clayton, *Apocryphal Gospels*, *passim*, with edition and translation at 164–90.

11. Ker, *Catalogue*, nos. 63, 310, and 331; and Gneuss and Lapidge, *Anglo-Saxon Manuscripts*, no. 638 (only on Hatton 114). See Clayton, *Apocryphal Gospels*, 153–63.

12. Ker, *Catalogue*, no. 394; and Gneuss and Lapidge, *Anglo-Saxon Manuscripts*, no. 941. Because of boundaries imposed around the prose and poetry of the *Vercelli Book* in modern scholarship, there is no edition of the full manuscript as it survives. For prose, see Scragg, *Vercelli Homilies*; and, for poetry, Krapp, *Vercelli Book*. For a recent assessment of the collection, addressing modern distinctions between prose and poetry, see Leneghan, "Teaching the Teachers." Scholarship on the collection is vast, but see recently Zacher, *Preaching the Converted*; and bibliography in Remley, "Vercelli Book and Its Texts."

13. For extended summaries of scholarship, see Zacher, *Preaching the Converted*, 3–29; and Leneghan, "Teaching the Teachers"; as well as Scragg's suggestions in *Vercelli Homilies*, xxxviii–ix; and "Vercelli Homilies and Kent."

14. References to the Vercelli sermons by line numbers are to Scragg, *Vercelli Homilies* (Vercelli 6 at 128–31). Readers and writers in medieval Western Europe (Anglo-Saxons in particular) had access to the Bible primarily through Jerome's translation, the Latin Vulgate; for this reason, unless otherwise noted, biblical references are

rightly observes the rarity of Old English Christmas sermons, since Vercelli homilies 5 and 6 are the only extant anonymous sermons on the subject[15]— a fact that points to the significance of Vercelli 6 as representative of how Anglo-Saxon authors used apocryphal elements to supplement the biblical story of the nativity.[16]

Even beyond translations undertaken for Old English preaching, Anglo-Saxon representations of apocryphal narratives are evident also in visual media. Scenes of the nativity and other episodes from Jesus' life often include details related not only to the canonical Gospels but also to para-biblical sources expanding on the basic narratives. Both Jessica Brantley and Thomas D. Hill have demonstrated how iconography can reveal possible sources for texts translating theological concepts, opening up ways of thinking more deeply about relationships between media.[17] Expanding these notions through an examination of media based on *Ps.-Mt.*, I pose possibilities for further understanding interactions between texts and images. Exploring this question reveals a series of analogues in visual media within the eleventh-century Sacramentary of Robert of Jumièges (Rouen, Bibliothèque Municipale 274 [Y.6]).[18] Considering these images and Vercelli 6 together as translations of *Ps.-Mt.* helps to situate their subjects within Anglo-Saxon mainstream religion. Indeed, as different media were accessible across different social classes, when taken together, these artifacts reveal the varieties of learned and popular discourses in which apocrypha circulated in late Anglo-Saxon England.

Surprisingly, methodological discussions of translation are not commonly addressed in scholarship about text-image relationships.[19] The inter-

---

to Weber, *Biblia sacra*; and translations are from *Holy Bible: Douay Version*.

15. Scragg, *Vercelli Homilies*, 109. Other versions of Vercelli 5 survive in Cambridge, Corpus Christi College 198 (s. xi) and Oxford, Bodleian Library, Bodley 340 and 342 (s. xi); see Ker, *Catalogue*, nos. 48 and 309; Gneuss and Lapidge, *Anglo-Saxon Manuscripts*, no. 64 and 569; and, for further details, Scragg, *Vercelli Homilies*, 108–10.

16. On liturgy and major Christian feasts like Christmas, see Bedingfield, *Dramatic Liturgy*.

17. Brantley, "Iconography"; and Hill, "Baby on the Stone."

18. Ker, *Catalgoue*, no. 377; Gneuss and Lapidge, *Anglo-Saxon Manuscripts*, no. 921; and Lucas and Lucas, *Anglo-Saxon Manuscripts*, 117–25. For an edition, see Wilson, ed., *Missal of Robert of Jumièges*, with illuminations printed as black and white plates 1–13.

19. The classic studies of text-image relationships are Mitchell, *Iconology*; and Mitchell, *Picture Theory*—though in neither is the notion of translation addressed. A related problem, Brantley observes, is that "Links between the visual and the narrative arts in the Anglo-Saxon period remain largely unexplored" ("Iconography," 43, n. 2, where some exceptions are cited); references in this chapter point to some further studies.

play between texts and images is well-trodden territory in scholarship, but, instead of "translation," scholars tend to employ terms such as "interchange" and "exchange," "transformation," "dynamic interaction," "appropriation," and, perhaps most often, "illustration"; when the term translation is used, it is often not accompanied by methodological explanation.[20] Adding to this muddled proliferation of vocabulary without elucidation, one recent critic describes an image as "translated" from text, but places the term within inverted commas without comment, as if the word stands as a surrogate for an undefined concept.[21] Similarly, extended discussions of translation rarely acknowledge the possibilities of this practice outside of a verbal medium, and only recently have scholars of translation studies begun to explore relationships across media.[22] These criticisms are not meant to challenge these contributions to scholarship, but to question the methodological assumptions for a significant subject that could benefit from further exploration.

This chapter rests on the assumption that translation occurs in and across all media. Marco Mostert poses the challenge of considering media representations in an interdisciplinary manner in the following way:

> Writing is a visual system representing speech, and because of its visuality, all writing is also image. This implies that every written text shares some of its aspects with images. Hence the metaphor of reading may be useful to refer to the search for meaning in images as it does for that in texts. This suggests that the historians of the image might try having a look at the questions posed by the historians of reading, so that these may be adapted to the study of images. If images can be regarded as symbols or representations to which different contemporary audiences ascribed different meanings, and if these meanings show a development over time, have a history, then the questions put by historians of reading seem, *mutatis mutandis*, if not identical then at least similar.[23]

Similarly, it is my hope that exploring theories of translation alongside work by those who study images will open up new assessments worth pursuing. From this perspective, the uses of apocryphal narratives in Anglo-Saxon

---

20. For recent examples, see esp. Hoffman, "Pathways of Portability"; Karkov, *Text and Picture*; Woodfin, "Officer and a Gentleman"; Robinson, "Arthur in Alhambra?"; and Smith, "Chivalric Narratives."

21. Smith, "Chivalric Narratives," 35.

22. For recent notable examples of these shifts, see Venuti, "Adaptation, Translation, Critique"; Zanoletti, "Marinetti and Buvoli"; and various essays in Wilson and Maher, *Words, Images and Performances*.

23. Mostert, "Reading Images and Texts," 6.

England—in both verbal and visual media—should lead to reconsidering notions of translations represented in a wider network of interrelations.

One claim in the following examination is that sermons and visual media are not so different in their adaptive translations of apocryphal gospels. Catherine E. Karkov has pointed out that visual translations (like sermons) refer to influences besides strictly textual sources, such as pictorial resonances.[24] If, as scholars have readily acknowledged, translation is a process contingent on complex contexts and influences, then associations that may not be apparent in a primary written source should be considered seriously. In this manner, it is useful to examine translations related to a common source (even those in different media) as analogous to each other. Thus, parallels open up differences as well as commonalities in adaptive translations, which may be understood as keys to cultural associations that resonate in and across media. When various materials are examined together as comparative projects of translation, it becomes apparent, as Brantley has pointed out, that they "represent related responses in different media."[25] In considering this issue, it is pertinent to remember that every translation is a specific, ideological representation of how the creator(s) perceived and used traditions from which the product was shaped. This reminder is particularly important for the present study, since various Anglo-Saxon media provide an understanding of not only the transmissions but also the receptions of apocrypha in Anglo-Saxon Christianity.

One common feature of representations in preaching and visual media based on *Ps.-Mt.* is how they emphasize Jesus' deeds rather than his teachings. In Christian tradition, Jesus' teachings are of course central, but Old English sermons based on apocrypha about his life do not use them as a basis; instead, they generally focus on narrating his actions. Similarly, artistic representations of Jesus' life depict scenes that emphasize narrative action—not surprisingly, since actions lend themselves to pictures more readily than words. By highlighting narrative actions in verbal and visual media, Anglo-Saxons acknowledged that Jesus' deeds are as significant for teaching Christian doctrine as his words, even when certain events are either not present or not related explicitly in the canonical Gospels.

Extended narratives surrounding Jesus' infancy miracles are wholly absent from biblical accounts, and the popularity of these traditions largely relies on details from apocryphal narratives. In other words, for medieval authors, apocryphal stories suitably embellish those in the canonical Gospels. These deeds are central to understanding Jesus' miraculous and divine

24. Karkov, *Text and Picture*, 17.
25. Brantley, "Iconography," 62.

nature as well as soteriological doctrines, making them, subsequently, central to Christian teaching. In fact, when considering the incarnational theology surrounding Jesus' life—especially for the nativity, crucifixion, and resurrection—the lines between Jesus' words and actions are blurred, since he is considered the Word of God. Jesus' words and actions are simultaneously representative of his transcendent character, entwined together as signifiers of his divinity. In this sense, messages relayed through his speeches are no different from messages relayed through his actions. Reflection upon translations of *Ps.-Mt.* in both verbal and visual media together reveals this convergence.

VERCELLI 6 AND JESUS' MIRACULOUS INFANCY

Apocryphal infancy gospels are not generally common in Anglo-Saxon England, but Vercelli 6 stands out as one of a few examples that do survive. This text includes an incipit (the only one in the *Vercelli Book*, though some items have titles) that states, "Incipit narrare miracula que facta fuerant ante aduentum Saluatoris Domini nostri Iesu Christi" ("We begin to narrate the miracles which had been done before the arrival of our Savior the Lord Jesus Christ"). Following this headnote, the sermon begins, "Her sagað ymb ðas mæran gewyrd þe to þyssum dæge gewearð, þætte ælmihtig dryhten sylfa þas world gesohte 7 þurh unwemme fæmnan on þas world acenned wæs, to þan þæt he eall manna cyn fram hellwara wite alysde 7 to heofona rices wuldre gefremede" (1–4: "Here we will tell about the famous event which happened on this day, that the Almighty Lord Himself sought this world and through an unspotted virgin he was born to this world, so that he freed all of mankind from the torments of hell and performed the glory of the kingdom of heaven"). In both theme and content, Vercelli 6 is intended for Christmas in its aims to center on the nativity and the salvific implications for that feast. For the impetus of the narrative, however, the sermon's author looked beyond only the canonical Gospels to a host of traditional materials suitable for translation at the occasion. Foremost among these sources is *Ps.-Mt.*, which is used along with the canonical Gospel of Luke and historiographical traditions.[26] In translating these sources, Vercelli 6 incorporates biblical and apocryphal materials synthetically, fusing together details about the nativity from a variety of sources rather than relying on a single text. In translating

---

26. Cf. excerpts from sources printed alongside Vercelli 6 in Scragg, *Vercelli Homilies*, 128–31, where Scragg relies on von Tischendorf's edition in *Evangelia Apocrypha*, 50–105.

these sources strategically, the author highlights the central theme of this sermon: Jesus' miraculous nature—in birth and childhood deeds.

Para-biblical details at the start of Vercelli 6 include a series of miracles purported to have occurred preceding Jesus' birth, some of which overlap with similar signs in Vercelli 5. As a contribution to source studies, James E. Cross offered the first detailed examination of these portents and linked them to Insular traditions derived from Roman writers such as Livy, Orosius, and Julius Obsequens.[27] Recently, Thomas N. Hall has provided an extensive treatment of the tradition in the early medieval period, and has demonstrated that such portents were widespread in biblical commentaries and homilies—especially those associated with Irish learning.[28] Hall's work thus complicates previous studies seeking to create clear source links.[29] The portents in the two Old English sermons may be catalogued as follows:[30]

> Golden ring(s) around the sun
> Roman emperor forgives all the people
> Slaves are restored to their masters (not in Vercelli 6)
> Peace throughout all the earth, no weapons
> Men are obliged to pay tribute to the emperor (not in Vercelli 6)
> Sun shines as brightly as in summer for seven nights before Nativity (not in Vercelli 5)
> Three wells flow with oil (not in Vercelli 5)

The effect that these miracles precipitate for the Christian audience is wonder, especially at the universal recognition of the coming birth of Jesus. These portents, in fact, have certain affinities with ancient oracular literature such as the *Sibylline Oracles* and other apocalyptica of Hellenistic Judaism and early Christianity,[31] particularly since astrological signs foretelling politico-religious changes were taken over by late antique and medieval his-

---

27. Cross, "Portents and Events."

28. Hall, "Portents."

29. The primary analogue compared by Cross is the *Catachesis Celtica*, a Hiberno-Latin florilegium of exegetical materials compiled sometime before the tenth century, although he notes that closer immediate sources must rest behind the Vercelli sermons. Atherton claims the *Catechesis* as variously a direct source, antecedent source, and one among multiple possible sources for Vercelli 5 and 6; see "Sources of Vercelli 5"; and "Sources of Vercelli 6"; cf. Zacher, *Preaching the Converted*, 20–21, who follows Atherton. A more circumspect assessment is provided by Wright, *Irish Tradition*, 80–81. Scragg prints the *Catechesis* in the critical apparatus for Vercelli 5, though he cautions, "It is not intended to suggest that the Latin text is a direct source" (*Vercelli Homilies*, 109 n. 1).

30. This list is indebted to Hall's extensive table in "Portents," 94–95.

31. See Collins, *Apocalyptic Imagination*, esp. 116–27.

toriographic writers.[32] Setting the scene for the nativity in Vercelli 6, these miracles point out the acknowledgment of Jesus' cosmic advent not only by the Roman emperor (forgiveness) and people (loyalty to the emperor) but also by the population of the whole earth (world-wide peace), the earth itself (wells springing forth oil), and even celestial bodies (the sun).

After enumerating these portents, the author of Vercelli 6 moves from the classically derived portents to the miraculous nativity itself. Here the narrative relates, "⁊ þa to þære sylfan niht ær morgensteorra upeode, dryhten wæs geboren on ðysne middangeard, ⁊ hine geborene englas onfengon ⁊ hine gebædon, ⁊ him wundorlico lof sungon ⁊ swa cwædon: 'Wuldor on heannesse Gode, ⁊ on eorðan sib mannum ðæs godan willan'" (55–58: "And then in that same night before the morning-star arose, the Lord was born on this earth, and angels bore Him, received Him, and prayed to Him, and sang praise to Him, and so said: 'Glory to God in the highest, and on earth peace to all men of good will'"). The recognizable words of praise are, ultimately, derived from Luke 2:14,[33] but this passage presents a translation from *Ps.-Mt.* 13:2: "Quae lux non defecit nec in die nec in nocte, quamdiu ibi Maria peperit masculum, quem circumdederunt nascentem angeli, et natum super pedes suos stantem adorauerunt eum dicentes: Gloria in excelsis deo et in terra pax hominibus bonae uoluntatis" ("This light did not diminish in day nor in night, until Mary brought forth a son, whom the angels surrounded at birth, and once he was born and standing on his feet, they worshiped him saying: 'Glory to God in the highest, and on earth peace to all men of good will'"). Rather than signaling a break from the canonical Gospel and the start of the translation of the apocryphon, the author incorporates a passage that blends the two sources. This is especially notable since the biblical *gloria* easily could have been used, especially considering that this passage from *Ps.-Mt.* comes from a chapter not otherwise incorporated into the Old English sermon. This transitional passage seems to indicate that for the author of Vercelli 6, traditions were blurred enough that preferring *Ps.-Mt.* raised no problems, and indeed allows a glimpse into the convergence

32. Astrological concerns run through much of the early Jewish pseudepigrapha, as discussed by Charlesworth, "Introduction." Astrological concerns were also of interest to early medieval authors; see Flint, *Rise of Magic*; and, more specifically, Williams, *Fiery Shapes*.

33. The Vulgate reads: "gloria in altissimis Deo et in terra pax in hominibus bonae voluntatis," while the apocryphal gospel gives variant readings: "gloria in excelsis Deo et in terra pax hominibus bonae voluntatis"; cf. Vercelli 5, lines 167–68: "'*Gloria in excelsis Deo.* Wuldor sie on heannessum Gode ⁊ sibb on eorðan þam mannum þe godne willan habbað." These variants represent Old Latin readings carried over into the apocryphon and the liturgy; see Sabatier, *Bibliorum sacrorum*, 3:267–68.

of canonical and apocryphal narratives for the author's ultimate purpose of narrating miraculous events.

For the most part, the rest of Vercelli 6 translates selections from *Ps.-Mt.* in order to narrate Herod's plot to kill all infants in the land, the holy family's flight into Egypt, and Jesus' miracles while there. Unfortunately, the manuscript—the sole witness to this sermon—is defective, and a leaf is missing after line 67. As Scragg notes, the author "presumably followed the source," which relates a number of miracles of the infant Jesus.[34] While not translating the entire source, the sermon's author selectively appropriates passages from *Ps.-Mt.*; when using this source, however, the author closely follows the Latin for rendering these selections into Old English. The Anglo-Saxon author's strategy, then, is to create an abridged translation, including only certain passages rather than the entire apocryphal story.

The selections from *Ps.-Mt.* in Vercelli 6 focus on two aspects of the narrative: Jesus' miracles and various scenes of veneration from Creation. Following on the cosmic miracles and veneration already present at Jesus' birth, the narrative relates Jesus subjugating dragons, other beasts, and a fruit tree,[35] as well as casting down pagan idols (71–73) and his veneration by a certain Afradisius in Egypt (74–80). This last episode serves as an example to highlight the ways in which Jesus' miracles and his veneration are handled in the text. When Jesus casts down idols in a pagan temple, Afradisius and his troops arrive to survey the scene, with the following response: "He eode to Marian þære fæmman, ⁊ he gebæd hælend þæt cild, ⁊ he spræc to eallum his werode, ⁊ cwæð: 'Þær ðe þis God ne wære, nænige þinga ura goda on hyra onyne gefeollon. ⁊ for þan us is þearf þæt we don swa ura god, þy læs his yrre ⁊ deaðes frecnes ofer us cume'" (78–80: "He [Afradisius] went to the Virgin Mary, and he prayed to the child Savior, and he spoke to all of his troop, and said: 'If this were not God, our gods would not for anything fall on their faces. And therefore it is necessary for us that we do as our gods, lest his ire and the danger of death overcome us'"). Just as the miracles testify to Jesus' sanctity, so too do the actions and words of Afradisius as a witness. All of this serves to extend the miracles surrounding the birth of the child Jesus, and to further demonstrate to the audience that he is Christ.

34. Scragg, *Vercelli Homilies*, 132.

35. The text breaks off at line 68 (the end of fol. 55v), with a tantalizing start to the scene with dragons: "Semninga þa uteodon of ðam scrafe manige dracan, þæt mitte ðe. . ." ("Then suddenly out of the cave went many dragons, so that when. . ."). The text picks up again (at line 69, the beginning of folio 56r) just as the holy family enters Egypt: "denum hy locedon on Egypta dune ⁊ hie wæron swiðe gefeonde" ("from the valley they looked on the hill of Egypt, and they were greatly rejoicing").

That these episodes are meant to demonstrate Jesus' miraculous personage is made most explicit in the final exhortation of the sermon, not drawn from any identified source. The author begins this exhortation, "Hwæt, we nu gehyrdon secgan hwylcnehwegu dæl ymb usses dryhtnes gebyrd, swylce eac ymb þa wundor þe he on his cildhade worhte. Utan we nu eorne tilian þæt we þe selran syn þonne we þylleca bysene usses dryhtnes beforan us reccan ⁊ rædan gehyrað" (86–89: "Lo, now we have heard told some portion about the birth of our Lord, likewise also about the wonders which he worked in his childhood. Let us now eagerly strive so that we are the better when we hear told and hear read such examples of our Lord before us"). About this sermon, Scragg mentions, "its conclusion is a more limited exhortation than is found in any piece [in the *Vercelli Book*] other than [homily] XXIII."[36] Notably, it is also a specific echo of the incipit at the start. Thus, the sermon is enclosed by a ring structure, drawing the audience in with promise of wonders (*miracula*), as well as the admonition that knowledge of these holy works (*wundor . . . worhte*) should help the audience to be spiritually better (*selran*). Reliance on *Ps.-Mt.* is not merely an exercise in translation, but a way to better help Anglo-Saxon audiences to know and meditate on holy miracles for the betterment of their piety.

VISUALIZING INFANCY MIRACLES

An appreciation for the importance and role of *Ps.-Mt.* in Vercelli 6 is further highlighted with examination of translations in other media. Previously, textual influences of this apocryphon have gained much attention, especially in relation to Marian devotion.[37] Yet, as with many Christian apocrypha in Anglo-Saxon culture, one aspect of this text's influence that has remained largely overlooked is its use in visual arts.[38] As I suggest in the following, the early eleventh-century Sacramentary of Robert of Jumièges contains a series of 13 illuminations, two of which portray iconography ultimately indebted to *Ps.-Mt.* Such identifications provide further circulation of these apocryphal traditions as well as expanded contexts for Vercelli 6 and related preaching texts based on this apocryphon.

---

36. Scragg, *Vercelli Homilies*, 127.

37. See Clayton, *Apocryphal Gospels*; and further references in Hall, "Gospel of Pseudo-Matthew."

38. To my knowledge, no overview or survey of apocrypha depicted in Anglo-Saxon visual arts exists. For a more general overview, see Cartlidge and Elliott, *Art and the Christian Apocrypha*.

The Sacramentary was compiled in the first quarter of the eleventh century (ca. 1014–ca. 1023), in the south of England, possibly at Christ Church, Canterbury (the location of its provenance before the mid-eleventh century). The book was later donated to the Abbey of Jumièges by the former abbot Robert Champart while he was bishop of London (1044–1051).[39] J. O. Westwood provided the earliest and most extensive formal descriptions of all of the illuminations together,[40] and some images have received subsequent individual attention, though without reference to *Ps.-Mt.*[41] Mary Clayton has claimed associations between Marian devotion and the Sacramentary, but she also does not directly link the images to *Ps.-Mt.*[42]

Figure 11.1: Sacramentary of Robert of Jumièges, folios 32v and 33r

I argue that translations of *Ps.-Mt.* in the Sacramentary are contained in a visual sequence across two illuminated pages (folios 32v and 33r) depicting events from Jesus' nativity and the flight into Egypt. In the following examination, I focus on three characteristics of these scenes: the ox and ass by Jesus' crib, a common motif in early medieval art; a midwife attending the Virgin Mary, a less common motif; and Jesus' childhood miracle with a

39. For summaries of scholarship, see Pfaff, "Massbooks," esp. 15–19; Pfaff, *Liturgy in Medieval England*; and Lucas and Lucas, *Anglo-Saxon Manuscripts*, 117–25.

40. Westwood, *Facsimiles*, 136–38.

41. See esp. Temple, *Anglo-Saxon Manuscripts*, no. 72; Turner, "Illuminated Manuscripts," no. 50; and, more recently, Karkov, *Art of Anglo-Saxon England*, 234–35; and Webster, *Anglo-Saxon Art*, 187–88.

42. Clayton, *Cult of the Virgin Mary*, 169–71.

palm tree, an uncommon image in Anglo-Saxon art. For its rarity among other Anglo-Saxon depictions, the last is the most notable and most significant for understanding this sequence as a series of episodes from *Ps.-Mt.* translated into images. Although not identified previously, this sequence in the Sacramentary is dependent (either directly or indirectly) on the apocryphal gospel and should be read as a translation of the narrative into visual art.[43] In this assessment, it is difficult, from an iconographic standpoint, to know whether these connections to *Ps.-Mt.* were the intentions of the artist, the director who oversaw the book's creation, or simply derived from models lying behind the imagery. Nonetheless, the Sacramentary represents how the apocryphal *Ps.-Mt.* became enmeshed in Anglo-Saxon media, even to the extent that its details were translated into visual depictions of Gospel events.

Figure 11.2: Sacramentary of Robert of Jumièges, folio 32v

43. Issues of "direct" and "indirect" influence echo the similar terms "immediate" and "antecedent" in source study; see Scragg, "Source Study"; and Wright, "Old English Homilies."

The first relevant illumination is a depiction of the nativity on folio 32v, which includes an angel overseeing the scene (in the upper register), a midwife attending the Virgin Mary (in the middle register), as well as an ox and ass at the side of the manger next to the child Jesus (in the lower register).[44] Little here is especially unique to early medieval depictions of the nativity, but it is significant that the midwife and the two animals are not included in any of the canonical Gospels, while they all appear in the nativity narrative of *Ps.-Mt.* Regarding the animals, the apocryphon relates the following:

> Tertia autem die natiuitatis domini egressa est Maria de spelunca et ingress est in stabulum et posuit puerum in praesepio, et bos et asinus genua flectentes adorauerunt eum. Tum adimpletum est quod dictum est per Esaiam prophetam dicentem: Agnouit bos possessorem suum et asinus praesepium domini sui. (Isa 1:3) Et ipse animalia in medio eum habentes incessanter adorabant eum. Tunc adimpletum est quod dictum Abacuc prophetam dicentem: In medio duorum animalium innotesceris. (Hab 3:2)[45]

> 14:1: On the third day after the Lord's birth, Mary left the cave and came into a stable, and she placed the child in a manger. And an ox and an ass bent their knees and worshiped him. Then was fulfilled what was spoken by Isaiah the prophet, who said, "The ox has recognized its owner and the ass the manger of its lord." These animals were around him, constantly worshiping him. Then was fulfilled what was spoken by Habakkuk the prophet, who said, "Between the two animals you will make yourself known."

It is clear that the purpose of this passage is to establish a typological relationship with the Old Testament prophets as an authenticating device for both Jesus' birth and the Gospel in which it was related. Regarding such associations, David R. Cartlidge and J. Keith Elliott observe, "A connecting of the old and new covenants stands out in virtually every scene of the Marian gospels."[46] As they further discuss, pictorial representations of the nativity

44. All images of the Sacramentary of Robert of Jumièges are used by permission of the Bibliothèque virtuelle des manuscrits médiévaux (http://bvmm.irht.cnrs.fr/), via a Creative Commons BY NC 3.0 license.

45. Both quotations correspond to the Old Latin; see Sabatier, *Bibliorum sacrorum*, 2:515 and 966. Cf. the Vulgate: "Cognovit bos possessorem suum et asinus praesepe domini sui" ("The ox knoweth his owner, and the ass his master's crib"); and "in medio annorum notum facies" ("In the midst of the years thou shalt make it known").

46. Cartlidge and Elliott, *Art and the Christian Apocrypha*, 23.

abound in medieval manuscripts, and the iconography consistently evokes these typological tropes for viewers.[47] Furthermore, for viewers familiar with *Ps.-Mt.*, the inclusion of the ox and ass in the lower register of the nativity illumination creates a symbolic link with the Marian subject just above the crib in the middle register of the same image.

A second passage from *Ps.-Mt.* serves as the source for the scene with Mary and her midwife in the middle register of the illumination. The apocryphon relates that after Mary had given birth in a cave, Joseph brings a midwife named Zahel, who inspects the Virgin and child, exclaiming, "Nulla pollutio sanguinis facta est in nascente, nullus dolor in pariente apparuit. Uirgo peperit et postquam peperit uirgo esse perdurat" (13:3: "No stain of blood can be found on the child, and no pain has appeared in the mother. A virgin has given birth and after giving birth she has remained a virgin"). Following this claim, an unconvinced midwife named Salome is brought to belief by inspecting the Virgin Mary herself—an episode not unlike that of the apostle Thomas in John 20:24–29. As a result of her unbelief, Salome suffers from a withered hand, which is later miraculously healed when she touches the infant Jesus. Consequently, Salome is often portrayed with a visibly disabled hand when she is present at the nativity.[48]

In his assessment of the Sacramentary, C. R. Dodwell gestures toward apocryphal traditions for the imagery of Mary and her midwife, linking it to the *Protevangelium of James* and identifying the midwife as Salome.[49] Similarly, Robert Deshman has examined the symbolic importance of the midwife in Byzantine and medieval iconography,[50] citing both the *Protevangelium* and *Ps.-Mt.* as examples of apocryphal details for the nativity in the *Benedictional of Æthelwold* (London, British Library, Additional 49598; ca. 971–ca. 984, Winchester), at folio 15v.[51] Casting doubt on the *Protevangelium* as source for these images, however, is the lack of substantial evidence for the circulation of this apocryphon in Anglo-Saxon England or generally in western Europe.[52] No complete Latin manuscript of the *Protevangelium* survives from the medieval period. The sole extant witness from Anglo-

47. On the influence of *Ps.-Mt.* on visual representations of the nativity, see ibid., 88–94.

48. See esp. Deshman, "Servants."

49. Dodwell, *Anglo-Saxon Gestures*, 106–109.

50. Deshman, "Servants"; and Deshman, *Benedictional of Æthelwold*, 18–19.

51. Gneuss and Lapidge, *Anglo-Saxon Manuscripts*, no. 301. See Prescott, *Benedictional of St Æthelwold*. For another relevant discussion of the nativity in the *Benedictional of Æthelwold*, see Hill, "Baby on the Stone," 73–75, with image at 74.

52. For a summary of scholarship, see Hall, "Protevangelium of James." On Latin manuscripts and possible wider circulation, see McNamara, *Apocrypha*, 37–40.

Saxon England appears in the Pembroke 25 *Homiliary of Saint-Père*, in a sermon for the nativity of Mary (item 51) that adapts chs. 1 to 8:1; yet this account relates only the lives of Anna and Joachim, Mary's birth, and her early life, not any of the episodes concerned with Jesus' birth and childhood.

Proposed correlations with the Greek *Protevangelium*, therefore, are often uncertain or likely mediated through other traditions such as the adaptive expansion in the Latin *Ps.-Mt.*, since it remained the more popular apocryphon throughout the medieval period. Given the known circulation and associations of *Ps.-Mt.* with a variety of other Anglo-Saxon media already discussed, and on the Continent in the early medieval period, the more probable conclusion is that the iconography of the Sacramentary relies on this apocryphon rather than the *Protevangelium*. The same conclusion may also be applied to the image in the *Benedictional of Æthelwold*, adding its nativity illumination to the network of media related to *Ps.-Mt.* in late Anglo-Saxon England. As for depictions of the midwife in the Sacramentary and *Benedictional*, both images lack signs of a crippled hand, and she uses both hands to prop up Mary's head with a pillow. Contrary to Dodwell's suggestion, the midwife in these nativity scenes is more likely the woman named Zahel, not the disabled Salome.[53]

53. Cf. Deshman's assessment of the nativity image in the Benedictional, in *Benedictional of Æthelwold*, 18–19.

Figure 11.3: Sacramentary of Robert of Jumièges, folio 33r

The other image in the Sacramentary related to *Ps.-Mt.* appears in the bottom register of the illumination on folio 33r, depicting the flight into Egypt. Westwood offers the following description: "The Virgin, seated on an ass, holds the Child in her lap, who stretches out its hands to Joseph leading the ass, and carrying the Virgin's distaff on his shoulder"[54]—but this explanation misses a major point. The flight into Egypt is, of course, well-attested in the Matt 2:13–23, though the inclusion of a tree in the Sacramentary illumination provides an unnoticed detail pointing toward a narrative not included

54. Westwood, *Facsimiles*, 136–37.

in any of the canonical Gospels. During the journey into Egypt as narrated in *Ps.-Mt.*, the holy family stop to rest under a palm where Mary desires the fruit from the tree, although she cannot reach it. The apocryphon continues:

> Tunc infantulus Iesus sedens in sinu matris suae uirginis excla-
> mauit ad palmam et dixit: Flectere, arbor, et de fructibus tuis
> refice matrem meam. Statim autem ad uocem eius inclinauit
> palma cacumen suum usque ad plantas Mariae, et colligentes ex
> ea fructus quos habebat omnes refecti sunt.

> 20:2: Then the young child Jesus, sitting in the lap of his mother,
> the virgin, cried out to the palm tree and said, "Bend down, O
> tree, and refresh my mother from your fruit." Immediately when
> he spoke, the palm tree bent its top down to Mary's feet. Every-
> one gathered the fruit in it and was refreshed.

I suggest that in the Sacramentary illustration, the child Jesus gestures not toward Joseph but toward the tree, pointing with his right hand and reaching with his left hand open. The tree, in turn, bends a branch toward Jesus, in comparison with the other more upright stalks in the middle and to the left.

Beyond relying on the same apocryphal gospel for details, both illu-minations in the Sacramentary appear on facing folios (32v–33r), depict-ing the same visual organization and architectural frames—suggesting that these images are most significantly understood as a narrative sequence read together. There is a noticeable trend in two earlier Anglo-Saxon depictions of similar narrative sequences: the *Benedictional of Æthelwold* and the Bou-logne Gospels (Boulogne, Bibliothèque Municipal 11; s. x/xi, St. Bertin).[55] While the Boulogne Gospels were produced in St. Bertin, they were deco-rated by an Anglo-Saxon artist, making both the *Benedictional* and the Boulogne Gospels witnesses to iconographic trends in England around the same time as (or just before) the production of the Sacramentary. Paral-lels with the nativity in the Sacramentary appear in both the *Benedictional* (folio 15v) and the Boulogne Gospels (folio 12r), as all three images contain the extra-biblical midwife and livestock. Unlike the Sacramentary, however, neither the *Benedictional of Æthelwold* nor the Boulogne Gospels contains a depiction of the flight into Egypt. Nonetheless, the framing of sequences in all three manuscripts helps to demonstrate that this was in style for Anglo-Saxon artists at the end of the tenth century and into the beginning of the eleventh.

---

55. For images of the Boulogne Gospels, see Ohlgren, *Anglo-Saxon Textual Illus-tration*, plates 5.1–28. On the relationships between these manuscripts, see esp. Temple, *Anglo-Saxon Manuscripts*, 23, 44, and 72.

The same framing design for the nativity and the flight into Egypt in the Sacramentary (in the first image above) also reinforces reading the two illuminations together as a visual narrative sequence: both borders consist of a floriated archway resting on two pillars, with towers at the top right and left corners and stylized falcons perched on the archway beside these towers. Furthermore, these two pages share other formal characteristics such as the same ground-line as well as tri-part structure to the registers. Framing devices across facing pages elsewhere in the Sacramentary also strengthen the reading of illuminations as sequential in this manuscript. For example, shared framing and formal elements appear for facing-page images of the journey and adoration of the Magi (folios 36v–37r), as well as the crucifixion and descent from the Cross (folios 71v–72r). In other words, these sequences show how images in the Sacramentary were designed as full-page pairs to be read together, as the book lay open.

The sequence concerning the Magi especially accentuates the visual relationships of reading across the pages of the Sacramentary. Here the motif of the city in the framing has returned, though with details distinct for joining these two folios together, and the ground-line of the two pages is again unified in the common registers. Furthermore, the two images contain the chiastic organization of enthroned royalty (Herod and Jesus) visited by the Magi at different points in the chronology of the Gospel. Like the images of the nativity and flight into Egypt, these depictions of the Magi highlight the significance of reading visual arts as translations that capture the drama of Christian narratives, as well as evidence for biblical and apocryphal details mingling together within the pages of a single book.

The sequence of narrative illuminations for the nativity and the flight into Egypt, like the translation of *Ps.-Mt.* in Vercelli 6, particularly highlights Jesus' miraculous nature, even as a child. In one sense, the depiction of the flight into Egypt in the Sacramentary preserves a portion of the apocryphal narrative (the tree's obedience to Jesus) otherwise lost from Vercelli 6. While damage to the *Vercelli Book* has precluded the survival of this episode in the Old English sermon (from which it was excised at some point), this part of *Ps.-Mt.* is attested in the Sacramentary's illuminations. The Sacramentary survives as a major witness for the general knowledge and circulation of episodes from *Ps.-Mt.* in Anglo-Saxon England. Like Vercelli 6, the illuminations also preserve an interest in the miracles of Jesus. The episodes of this apocryphon, as well as the translations in Vercelli 6 and the images of the Sacramentary, point to miracles as key to Jesus' life. Foremost among these miracles is the universal salvation of humanity through Jesus' crucifixion and resurrection. As Hill notes about this type of scene, "the iconographic program of the *Benedictional of Æthelwold* nativity scene and related illuminations associates the crib and the nativity with the passion and sacrifice of Jesus. The beginning and end of Jesus' earthly ministry are in effect conflated."[56] The nativity cannot help but evoke this progression, since in typological expectancy, Jesus' death and resurrection are the primary reasons for his birth in the first place.

Other than Jesus' childhood miracles, these illuminations also point forward to his future miracles. Most prominently, Jesus' miracle with the fruit tree points to his public miracles as an adult narrated in the canonical Gospels, especially the adoration that surrounds him. It even evokes Jesus' other botanical miracle: the cursing of the fig tree in Matthew 21:18–22 (cf. Mark 11:12–14, 20–25):

> mane autem revertens in civitatem esuriit et videns fici arborem unam secus viam venit ad eam et nihil invenit in ea nisi folia tantum et ait illi numquam ex te fructus nascatur in sempiternum et arefacta est continuo ficulnea et videntes discipuli mirati sunt dicentes quomodo continuo aruit respondens autem Iesus ait eis amen dico vobis si habueritis fidem et non haesitaveritis non solum de ficulnea facietis sed et si monti huic dixeritis tolle et iacta te in mare fiet et omnia quaecumque petieritis in oratione credentes accipietis

> And in the morning, returning into the city, he was hungry. And seeing a certain fig tree by the way side, he came to it and found nothing on it but leaves only. And he saith to it: "May no fruit grow on thee henceforward for ever. And immediately the fig tree withered away. And the disciples seeing it wondered, saying: How is it presently withered away? And Jesus answering, said to them: Amen, I say to you, if you shall have faith and stagger not, not only this of the fig tree shall you do, but also if you shall say to this mountain, Take up and cast thyself into the sea, it shall be done. And all things whatsoever you shall ask in prayer believing, you shall receive."

While the Gospel account leads to a moment of teaching—the expected response from Jesus as a rabbi to his disciples—the episode in *Ps.-Mt.* is one of several that diverge from this model. Instead, Jesus' power is on display, and this is taken over into both sermon and illumination in Vercelli 6 and in the Sacramentary.

There are also reasons to link the influences of *Ps.-Mt.* in the Sacramentary with the veneration of the Virgin Mary in Anglo-Saxon England. For medieval readers, this apocryphon was related to the rise of Marian

56. Hill, "Baby on the Stone," 75.

devotion, particularly from the ninth century onward, and possibly even at its inception.[57] In the introduction to his edition of *Ps.-Mt.*, Jan Gijsel suggests that the author of this apocryphon was a monk who was fascinated with the venerated depiction of Mary in the *Protevangelium of James*, and who used this potential in the hopes of promoting the expansion of Benedictine ideals. Connections with Marian devotion may be seen in adaptations of *Ps.-Mt.*, particularly the *Nativity of Mary*, which is often accompanied by an epistolary prologue spuriously attributed to Jerome.[58] This letter, purported to be a response to a request by Bishops Chromatius and Heliodorus for Jerome to translate the *Nativity of Mary*, begins: "Petitis a me ut uobis rescribam quid mihi de quodam libello uideatur qui de natiuitate sanctae Mariae a nonnullis habetur" ("You ask me to write to you my opinion of a certain book which some have concerning the birth of Saint Mary").[59] All of these texts related to *Ps.-Mt.* made an impact on Anglo-Saxon culture, in which the cult of the Virgin Mary developed strong roots by the late tenth century.

The popularity and significance of translations of *Ps.-Mt.* in Anglo-Saxon England are related also to the rise of the cult of Mary, which may be brought to bear on contextualizing the Sacramentary. Clayton claims that, "At the very end of the Anglo-Saxon period we find the first artistic reflections of the *Ps.-Mt.* legend," citing a troper containing supplemental liturgical texts for the Mass and Office from ca. 1050.[60] With the foregoing examination in mind, the details in the Sacramentary's miniatures allow for acknowledging an earlier date, in the first quarter of the eleventh century. While not noting the connection to *Ps.-Mt.*, Clayton does note the veneration afforded to the Virgin in the Sacramentary's visual art, particularly in the miniatures depicting the nativity and the ascension.[61] For instance, it is particularly noteworthy that "the angel's blessing is clearly directed at Mary" rather than the Christ child—a rare feature in Anglo-Saxon iconography for the nativity.[62] Other connections within the Sacramentary also add to these assessments. The two illuminations of the nativity and flight into Egypt closely follow the *temporale* entry for January 8, "Natale Domini ad Sanctam Mariam Maiorem," on folios 31r–31v. Part of the observation for this

57. On Marian devotion, see esp. Clayton, *Cult of the Virgin Mary*; and Clayton, *Apocryphal Gospels*; as well as Fulton, *From Judgment to Passion*; Gambero, *Mary in the Middle Ages*, esp. 74–80; and Rubin, *Mother of God*.

58. See Beyers, *Libri de Nativitate Mariae*, 272–77.

59. Beyers, *Libri de Nativitate Mariae*, 273, lines 1–3.

60. Clayton, *Cult of the Virgin Mary*, 172.

61. Ibid., 169–70.

62. Ibid., 170.

feast-day, as given in the Sacramentary, includes honoring "gloriosae sem-per uirginis maria genitricis dei et domini nostri iesu christi" (fol. 31v: "the glorious eternally virgin Mary, mother of our God and Lord Jesus Christ").[63] This entry certainly shares resonances with the declaration of Mary's per-petual virginity in Ps.-Mt. (a long-standing tradition),[64] and it is notable that even the child Jesus afforded veneration to Mary when he commanded the palm tree to yield its fruit for her refreshment.

Moreover, associations with Marian devotion are substantiated by the manuscript's early reception, since the donation inscription on folio 228r reads:[65]

> ego. Rotbertus abba gemmetesium prius postmodum uero sancte londoniorum sedis presul factus dederim librum hunc sancte Mariae in hoc michi comisso monachorum sancti Petri cenobio ad honorem sanctorum quorum hic mentio agitur et ob memoriale mei ut hic in perpetuum habeatur.

> I, Robert, former abbot of Jumièges, afterward made bishop of the holy See of London, give this book of Saint Mary to this community of the monks of Saint Peter having been entrusted to me, in honor of the saints, whose mention is made here, and as a memorial for me to be held here forever.

The Sacramentary images and the apocryphal narratives they translate thus evoke the significance of Marian veneration that developed from the very beginnings of Christianity. As a book specifically associated with Mary, the Sacramentary reflects the habits of the community to which it is given: they are meant to take the devotion between its covers and extend it into their world.

CONCLUSIONS

Understanding the Sacramentary as a close contemporary to audiences of Vercelli 6 allows for highlighting a number of features common to the two, as well as some key historical issues for considering late Anglo-Saxon Christian beliefs. As already noted, one commonality is that Jesus' deeds are key in these translations. But both artifacts also highlight ways in which the transmission and reception of Ps.-Mt. fit into Anglo-Saxon mainstream religion. Indeed, the Sacramentary shares a number of features important

63. Wilson, ed., *Missal of Robert of Jumièges*, 49.
64. Clayton, *Cult of the Virgin Mary*, 1–24.
65. Wilson, ed., *Missal of Robert of Jumièges*, 316.

for the contexts of preaching in late Anglo-Saxon England. After all, the intended use of the Sacramentary was in the mass itself. This resonates with connections to *Ps.-Mt.* already discussed, such as Latin and Old English sermons found in a range of Anglo-Saxon manuscripts. These media all speak to the fact that the circulation and use of this apocryphon in part was closely linked to liturgy and preaching. The images of Jesus' early life in the Sacramentary, therefore, are closely linked with Vercelli 6 not only because of common content but also through their inclusion among the necessary materials for Christian worship.

Also suggestive are the types of porous boundaries for preaching and belief exhibited when considering Anglo-Saxon sermons alongside the Sacramentary. While Latin and Old English sermons as well as the mass-book were created (and likely used) by elites in ecclesiastic or monastic communities, they illustrate the potential for a variety of people to be brought together in common belief and practice. Written in the vernacular, Old English sermons like Vercelli 6 (and other translations of *Ps.-Mt.*) were accessible to a wide range of audiences, lay and ecclesiastical. Similarly, the visual illuminations of the Sacramentary could have been just as accessible to a priest as to an elite layperson, even if nuances of understanding existed for different viewers. Furthermore, intriguing associations exist between Marian devotion and versions of *Ps.-Mt.* across media, in preaching texts as well as visual art, prompting consideration of audiences beyond ecclesiasts and elite laity. This facet of the apocryphon's afterlife is particularly relevant for the female religious who followed this cult, exposing porous boundaries between classes and genders. These cultural artifacts, then, demonstrate how a variety of social groups within Anglo-Saxon Christian communities were linked through a complex network of apocryphal media.

– 12 –

Apocrypha and Forgeries
Lessons from the "Lost Gospels" of
the Nineteenth Century

— Tony Burke —

THE CANONICAL GOSPEL OF John ends with the words: "There are also many other things that Jesus did; if every one of them were written down, I suppose that the world could not contain the books that could be written" (John 21:25). John's desire for brevity has not been shared by other Christians; in his own time, three others wrote a gospel of their own, and additional gospels soon followed, each one attributed to another apostle—a Gospel of Thomas, of Bartholomew, of James, of Judas, and even Mary Magdalene. Not long after, in fifth-century Egypt, a genre of literature flourished in which the authors claimed to have found lost gospel texts in a house in Jerusalem.[1] Non-Christians even joined in the creation of gospels. Jewish communities wrote and circulated the *Toledot Yeshu*, an anti-gospel portraying Jesus as a magician and a fraud. A Christian convert to Islam around 1300 wrote the *Gospel of Barnabas*, in which Jesus predicts the coming of Muhammad. Then, in the nineteenth century over a dozen new texts appeared, their translators often claiming to have discovered them in monastery libraries;

---

1. The genre of pseudo-apostolic memoirs was established independently by Hagen, "Ein anderer Kontext"; and Suciu, "Apocryphon Berolinense/Argentoratense."

however, their contents were clearly reflective of contemporary Christian interests.

Two other apocryphal texts, one published in the twentieth century, the other in the twenty-first, also suspiciously tap into the modern Western *Zeitgeist*. The first of these, the *Secret Gospel of Mark*, was published by Morton Smith (a scholar of some renown) in 1973.[2] He claimed to have found references to the text in a manuscript at the Mar Saba monastery in the Judean desert, but the manuscript has since disappeared. Those who think Smith forged the text have called it the "gay gospel" as it features a story in which a young man, smitten by Jesus, comes to Jesus one evening "wearing a linen cloth over his naked body," and spends the night with him, learning about the "mystery of the kingdom of God." The second text appeared in 2012 when Harvard scholar Karen L. King announced at a conference of Coptic scholars in Rome the existence of a fragment of a text in which Jesus says, at the start of a damaged sentence: "my wife." King's colleagues rushed to declare this *Gospel of Jesus' Wife* (as she called it) a forgery and criticized King for being easily duped.[3]

If these two texts are indeed modern "forgeries" then their creators were significantly more sophisticated in their efforts to deceive than the nineteenth-century publishers of "lost gospels."[4] Scholars similarly have to be more sophisticated in their efforts to prove them forgeries.[5] How did

2. In a scholarly monograph (Smith, *Clement of Alexandria*) and a popular-market book (Smith, *Secret Gospel*). The chief proponent of the theory that Smith created the text is Stephen Carlson (*Gospel Hoax*), and Smith's greatest champion is Scott Brown (*Mark's Other Gospel*). For an overview of the debate on the authenticity of the text see the introduction in Burke, ed., *Ancient Gospel*, 1–29.

3. King's initial report on the text appeared online, and soon followed a series of online articles and blog posts, for the most part arguing that the text is a modern, not ancient, production. King's paper ("'Jesus said to them'") was later published formally in a special issue of *Harvard Theological Review* dedicated to the text, along with several scientific reports on the papyrus, and an argument against its authenticity by Leo Depuydt ("Alleged Gospel"), followed by a response by King ("Response to Leo Depuydt"). Additional arguments for forgery are presented in the July 2015 issue of *New Testament Studies*; one of these articles—Robinson, "How a Papyrus Fragment Became a Sensation"—is particularly helpful for its documentation of the early online discussions of the text.

4. See the introduction to this volume, p. 1, on the use of the term "forgery," used here (as in the introduction) for a text written to deceive its intended readers as to its true origins.

5. The entry point for scholarship on modern apocrypha is Goodspeed, *Strange New Gospels*, supplemented in Goodspeed, *New Chapters*, 189–219, and fully updated as Goodpeed, *Modern Apocrypha*. Also integral is the work of Beskow, *Strange Tales*. Excerpts from some of the texts discussed here are given in Maffly-Kipp, *American Scriptures*. For more on the study of modern apocrypha see the introduction to this

earlier forgery critics determine that the nineteenth-century texts were modern, not ancient, apocrypha? What kind of investigations did they perform to reach certainty? What kind of evidence for the texts was expected of those who published them? And to what extent did they fail to produce it? These inquiries can be used to construct a "canon of evidence" with which to test the authenticity of "lost gospels," and which then can be applied to more-recent alleged forgeries, such as *Secret Mark* and *Jesus' Wife* (hereafter GJW), to see if they meet these expectations. If they do, then perhaps we need to take more seriously their publishers' and advocates' claims that they are indeed ancient Christian gospels.

MODERN APOCRYPHA AND THEIR CRITICS

Modern apocrypha come in two types: revealed texts, by which is meant a text dictated to its editor in the present day by a supernatural figure, whether Jesus or an angel; and what can be called "scholarly" apocrypha—texts said to have been found in one or more ancient manuscripts and, in most cases, are presented more as an object of study than for spiritual reflection. The following survey focuses on the second of these categories, as only these texts encroach upon the territory of biblical scholars, prompting them to challenge the veracity of the texts' origins and, ultimately, to accuse the editors/creators of forgery.

One of the earliest examples of modern apocrypha is the *Crucifixion of Jesus, by an Eyewitness*, which began its life as a work of speculative scholarship and only later was transformed into an apocryphon.[6] The *Crucifixion* first appeared in Leipzig in 1849, published by Christian Ernst Kollmann under the title *Enthüllungen über die wirkliche Todesart Jesu*. A sequel appeared later that same year called *Historische Enthüllungen über die wirklichen Ereignisse der Geburt und Jugend Jesu*, but it has not been translated into English.[7] The *Crucifixion* is a letter said to have been written seven years after the crucifixion by an Essene elder at Jerusalem to another elder living in Alexandria. Jesus is portrayed in the letter as an Essene monk, destined for that order since birth. His ministry and crucifixion are narrated; but here Jesus does not die, instead he revives and lingers for six months in concealment with his Essene brethren until his death. The text also says

---

volume and the chapter (ch. 13, below) on Jesus' journey to India by Bradley Rice.

6. Discussions in Goodspeed, *Strange New Gospels*, 31–41; Goodspeed, *Modern Apocrypha*, 20–27; Beskow, *Strange Tales*, 42–50.

7. In this sequel on the birth and childhood of Jesus, an Essene named Euphanias is said to be the real father of Jesus (see Beskow, *Strange Tales*, 46).

Jesus had an attachment to Mary of Bethany (identified here also as Mary Magdalene) but he refuses romantic entanglement with her because, as an Essene, he cannot marry. According to the German "translator," the text was preserved in Latin in a scroll found in a forgotten monastery library in Alexandria. Rescued from being destroyed by "orthodox fools," it became the property of a German brotherhood believing itself to be the last remnant of old Essene wisdom.[8] This brotherhood was a Masonic lodge and subsequent editions and translations are associated with lodges, including American editions published in 1907[9] and 1919.[10] Of course there is no evidence for the manuscript and the original Latin text (which is a peculiar language for a first-century Essene) has never been published.[11] According to the unnamed "German translator" (in reality, Kollmann), the manuscript was last seen in the possession of Freemasons in Germany.[12]

Shortly after its publication, the *Crucifixion* was proven by Johann Nepomuk Truelle to be plagiarized from Karl Heinrich Venturini's novel *Natürliche Geschichte des grossen Propheten von Nazareth* (*A Non-supernatural History of the Great Prophet of Nazareth*).[13] Venturini's novel was one of several efforts from the late eighteenth and early nineteenth century to apply rationalistic interpretation to the miracle stories of Jesus.[14] Initially unaware of this connection, Goodspeed naturally questioned the whereabouts of the manuscript:

8. Kollmann, *Enthüllungen über die wirkliche Todesart Jesu*, iii (English trans. in Kollmann, *Crucifixion*, 17).

9. Kollmann, *Crucifixion*; this edition features also the *Epistle of Lentulus* (pp. 25–27), the *Death Warrant of Jesus Christ* (pp. 29–31), and an essay on the "Order of Essees" (pp. 155–200).

10. Austin, ed., *Crucifixion*, translated from an 1851 Swedish edition by J. F. Sasberg published in 1880.

11. The Latin may be a translation from another language: see the remarks in Kollmann, *Enthüllungen über die wirkliche Todesart Jesu*, 71–72 (translated as Kollmann, *Crucifixion*, 133).

12. Kollmann, *Enthüllungen über die wirkliche Todesart Jesu*, iv (translated as Kollmann, *Crucifixion*, 18).

13. Truelle, *Die wichtigen historischen Enthüllungen*. A second refutation, by Richard Clemens (*Jesus von Nazareth*), appeared that same year. See also Schweitzer, *Quest*, 161–62; Jenkins, *Hidden Gospels*, 48; Beskow, *Strange Tales*, 47. Goodspeed acknowledges this connection in his 1956 revision (*Modern Apocrypha*, 26; references to Goodspeed's comments on the texts are from *Modern Apocrypha*, unless there are significant differences between the editions) but credits the text's exposure as a fraud to Dibelius, *Fresh Approach to the New Testament*, 93–94.

14. For a discussion of these fictional lives see Schweitzer, *Quest*, 38–47. Of them all, Venturini's "is plagiarised more freely than any other Life of Jesus, although practically unknown by name" (Schweitzer, *Quest*, 47).

The first inquiry scholarship would make would be for the Latin text. But the book before us gives us not a line of the Latin text, nor any hint of the present whereabouts of the manuscript itself—a matter of immense importance, if the supposed discovery is to be taken seriously. Yet the first translators of the work must first have copied the Latin text before they translated it; no one translates directly from an ancient manuscript without first copying its text. Nor have we any account of the size or date of the Latin parchment roll, or any hint of when it was found or of what has become of it . . . We have in short neither (1) the manuscript, nor (2) a photograph of it, nor (3) directions for finding it for ourselves in some definite city or library, nor (4) a copy of its Latin text; no recognized expert in Latin manuscripts has seen and examined it; and so we are thrown back upon what is called internal evidence: the impression of authenticity and antiquity made by the translated document itself.[15]

Goodspeed also noted a number of inconsistencies between the text and knowledge (in his day) of the Gospels, early Christianity, and the Essenes:

To recapitulate: the use of the Four Gospels, but no others; palpable blunders in the use even of them; inability to name any persons in the story except those mentioned in them; mistaken ideas about the Essenes; the introduction of the modern romantic interest; and the resolute rationalizing of the whole story, so alien to ancient modes of thought—these show at once that *The Crucifixion* is not the work of any eyewitness, as it professes to be, but of a nineteenth-century rationalist.[16]

Goodspeed could not have been more correct and Beskow makes up for Goodspeed's shortfalls by noting the text's connection to Venturini and placing the composition of the *Crucifixion* in the context of contemporary German rationalist enlightenment theology and German Masonic circles.[17] The contemporary concerns of the plagiarist can be seen most clearly in the "German translator's remarks," and it is interesting to see in them an indictment of canon formulators and some positive comments about Christian apocrypha:

Several efforts have been made already in past times to explain the myths of the gospel rationally, and, indeed, penetrating

15. Goodspeed, *Strange New Gospels*, 35–36. See also the problems presented in Beskow, *Strange Tales*, 44–46.

16. Goodspeed, *Modern Apocrypha*, 26–27.

17. Beskow, *Strange Tales*, 47–49.

minds have succeeded to give them the character of probability, but they could not be proved through any historical events, as the canonical dictators defined, what was authentical, only that which was serviceable to their canonical reign, and declared all such traditions to be apocryphical that will say not useful, which in reality were built on historical foundation, or were not written according to the desire of a holy seer for miracles. Even the Esseen letter that we have recorded above would by them have been considered apocryphical writing.[18]

The *Crucifixion* is an unequivocal case of plagiarism and fraud, and all that is really required of the investigator to discredit the text is to demonstrate its indebtedness to its source material. Nevertheless, the text remains useful in scholarship for its reflection of nineteenth-century theological trends and can contribute to discussions of the creation of ancient and medieval apocrypha, which similarly rework and recycle received material. In addition, despite its dubious origins, the *Crucifixion* remains influential in the Ahmadiyya movement, a branch of Islam that claims Jesus survived the crucifixion and died in northern India; the text continues to be printed and translated into new languages to serve the movement's mission activities.[19] Though the *Crucifixion* did not begin its existence as an ancient apocryphal text, nevertheless it functions today as one.

A similar transformation of fiction to apocryphon occurs in a text that appeared first in a pamphlet entitled *A Correct Transcript of Pilate's Court*, an account of the trial and death of Jesus reported to Emperor Tiberius by Pilate, published in 1879 by Rev. William Dennes Mahan, a Cumberland Presbyterian minister in Boonville, Missouri.[20] Mahan claimed to have been given the text by a German scholar named Henry C. Whydaman, who found it in a Latin manuscript in the Vatican Library. Later editions of the text include eight letters exchanged with Whydaman documenting their interaction.[21] The *Transcript* was soon republished several times and became a sensation in the media. One notable edition is that of George Sluter, who

18. Kollmann, *Crucifixion*, 137 (translated from Kollmann, *Enthüllungen über die wirkliche Todesart Jesu*, 73–74).

19. See Beskow, *Strange Tales*, 50. Beskow notes French and Swedish translations of the *Crucifixion* and its reuse in 1879 by Friedrich Clemens Gierke (writing as Friedrich Clemens) for his own apocryphal text, the *Ur-Gospel of the Essenes* (see Clemens, *Das fünfte Evangelium*).

20. Discussions in Goodspeed, *Strange New Gospels*, 42–62; Goodspeed, *Modern Apocrypha*, 28–44; Beskow, *Strange Tales*, 51–56; introduction and excerpts from two other *Archko Volume* texts in Maffly-Kipp, *American Scriptures*, 241–63.

21. Mahan, *Correct Transcript*, 36.

identified the text as the "true" Acts of Pilate.[22] Another edition, an 1880 reprint by William Overton Clough,[23] contains also the *Death Warrant of Jesus Christ* (see further below) and an assortment of Pilate Cycle texts taken from Alexander Walker's English apocrypha collection.[24] Most significant about Clough's edition, however, is that the English text of the *Transcript* (here called *Gesta Pilati*) is followed by what is said to be the original Latin.

Like some of the medieval Pilate Cycle texts, Pilate is presented in the *Transcript* as a wholly sympathetic character. He hears about Jesus and sees him one day as he is going by the place of Siloam. He describes Jesus as: "his hair and beard, of golden yellow, gave a celestial aspect. He appeared to be about thirty years old. Never have I seen a gentler or more serene countenance. What a difference between him and those listening."[25] Pilate is particularly pleased to hear Jesus give his "render unto Caesar" saying.[26] He decides to offer Jesus protection from his opponents, and when it looks like Jesus is in real danger, Pilate warns him to be more moderate in his criticisms of the powerful among the Jews. Pilate says to him, "Your words are those of a sage. I know not whether you have read Socrates and Plato; but this I do know, that there is in your discourses a majestic simplicity that elevates you far above these philosophers."[27] Alas Pilate cannot do much for Jesus, and when Passover comes, he fears for his own safety as Jews flood into the city from across the Empire. Soon the Pharisees, Herodians, and Sadducees conspire against Jesus, and Pilate cannot prevent his crucifixion. At Jesus' death, great portents happen; "So dreadful were the signs that were seen," Pilate says, "that Dionysius, the Areopagite, is reported to have exclaimed, 'Either the author of nature is suffering, or the universe is falling apart.'"[28] A few days after his death, Jesus' sepulchre is found empty and the disciples go out to preach his resurrection. Aside from the portents that attend Jesus' death, there is very little that is supernatural in the text; Jesus does not explicitly rise from death, his disciples merely believe he did so. The text is also somewhat anti-Semitic in its portrayal of the Jews and presents Pilate more sympathetically than even the heavily-revisionistic Pilate Cycle literature.

22. Sluter, ed., *Acta Pilati*, 6–7.

23. Clough, *Gesta Pilati*; English text, pp. 41–56; Latin, pp. 57–70.

24. Walker, *Apocryphal Gospels*.

25. Sluter, ed., *Acta Pilati*, 43.

26. Ibid., 44.

27. Ibid., 46.

28. Ibid., 54.

In 1884 Mahan published additional texts in a collection of documents called the *Archeological and the Historical Writings of the Sanhedrin and Talmuds of the Jews*, also known as the *Archko Volume*. It features the *Transcript* alongside 11 additional works said to have been found by Mahan in his travels to Rome and Constantinople, including interviews with the shepherds at Jesus' birth, Gamaliel's interview with Joseph and Mary, Caiphas's reports to the Sanhedrin, Eli's story of the Magi, Herod Antipater's defense before the Senate for the slaughter of the innocents, and Herod Antipas's defense before the senate. Mahan also expanded his *Transcription* by about 40 per cent after (he claimed) viewing the manuscript himself at the Vatican.

Though Mahan detailed his investigations and the scholars with whom he consulted about the texts, the names seem to have been false.[29] Mahan's publishing enterprise began to fall apart when it was discovered that "Eli's Story of the Magi" contained whole pages copied verbatim from General Lew Wallace's novel *Ben Hur* (published in 1880). Incensed by this theft, Wallace further investigated Mahan's claims and found that there was no knowledge among the American missions in Constantinople of Mahan visiting the city, and no record of the manuscripts that he claimed to have read at the Hagia Sophia mosque.[30] Another investigation of the Hagia Sophia by an American minister in 1898 also came up empty.[31] As it turns out, Mahan's *Transcript* also was plagiarized. It was copied, virtually verbatim, from a story written by French dramatician Joseph Méry called *Ponce Pilate à Vienne* published in 1837.[32] Méry said his tale was inspired by something he read in an old Latin manuscript, perhaps a copy of the ancient *Acts of Pilate*.[33] Mahan seems to have read Méry's story in an English translation from 1842, called *Pontius Pilate's Account of the Condemnation of Jesus Christ and his own Mental Suffering*, which transformed Méry's mention of his inspiration to a statement of origin: the edition is prefaced with a statement that the text came from a Latin manuscript found in a cave in Vienne, the place of Pilate's death in medieval tradition.[34] The 1842 edition was in turn transformed

29. Goodspeed, *Modern Apocrypha*, 31–32; Anderson, "Fraudulent," 46–47.

30. Wallace's investigations are discussed in his 1906 autobiography, but in a section written by his wife after his death (*Lew Wallace: An Autobiography*, 942–45; summarized in Goodspeed, *Modern Apocrypha*, 36–40). See Anderson, "Fraudulent," 49–51 for a synopsis of the relevant passages from Eli and *Ben Hur*.

31. Goodspeed, *Modern Apocrypha*, 40–41.

32. Collected also in Méry, *Les Nuits de Londres*, 2:173–227. The identification was made by Beskow, *Strange Tales*, 53–54.

33. Beskow, *Strange Tales*, 54.

34. Goodspeed, *Modern Apocrypha*, 42–43. Goodspeed provides additional publishing history of the 1842 text.

into an Arabic translation credited to Jerasimus Jared, bishop of Zahleh in Lebanon, first published in 1889 and then further translated into English by Beshara Shehadi in 1893.[35] Here the *Account* is here placed within an interview with an old friend of Pilate named Fabricius Albinus.

The investigation into the *Transcript* once again focused on its manuscript source. Mahan's chief opponent was James A. Quarles, who began in 1885 challenging Mahan's account of his travels and the various people he mentions consulting.[36] Quarles was first too to demonstrate Mahan's plagiarism of *Ben Hur*. In response to Quarles, Mahan said, "You are bound to admit that the items in the book cant do any harm even if it were faulce, but will cause many to read and reflect that otherwise would not. So the balance of good is in its favor, and as to the truth of its MSS I stand ready to defend them."[37] As a result of Quarles' efforts, Mahan was summoned before the New Lebanon presbytery in September 1885 to answer charges of falsehood and plagiarism. He was found guilty and suspended from ministry for a year; this was extended to an indefinite suspension when he published the *Archko Volume*.[38] Mahan was never able to establish the existence of manuscripts for any of his texts; which makes Clough's Latin text all the more mysterious. Goodspeed thought it had "a very modern sound,"[39] whereas Beskow is more unequivocal in saying, "there seems to be no doubt that the Latin fragments were fabricated by Clough."[40] The *Transcript* has remained popular regardless of its dubious origins and the thorough refutations; it has been printed and reprinted numerous times, both independently and as part of the *Archko Volume*. The text has been taken up also by the Ahmadiyya movement, and thus incorporated in an abbreviated form in Andreas Faber-Kaiser's 1978 book *Jesus Died in Kashmir*. Here the author says the *Transcript* was written in 32 CE; the original manuscript, he says, resides in the British museum and copies are available from the US Library of Congress.[41]

35. Shehadi, *Confession of Pontius Pilate*. Goodspeed treats the Arabic text in a separate chapter titled "The Confession of Pontius Pilate" (*Strange New Gospels*, 63–72; *Modern Gospels*, 45–49).

36. Quarles's efforts are described in Goodspeed, *Modern Gospels*, 36–39; Anderson, "Fraudulent," 51–52, 56.

37. Reproduced in Goodspeed, *Modern Gospels*, 37.

38. For a detailed account of Mahan's trials see Anderson, "Fraudulent," 51–54.

39. Goodspeed, *Modern Gospels*, 31.

40. Beskow, *Strange Tales*, 53.

41. Ibid., 52.

Yet another Pilate apocryphon, the *Death Warrant of Jesus Christ*, has a similarly convoluted pre-history.[42] In the middle of the nineteenth century a rumor was reported that the formal death warrant of Jesus had been found in Italy engraved on a copper plate. The text and the story of its discovery were publicized by an article in the French newspaper *Le Droit* in 1839.[43] According to the story, in 1810 (in some accounts, it was found originally in 1280 and then rediscovered in the nineteenth century) some people digging for Roman antiquities in the ancient city of Amitorum (now Aquila) in the Kingdom of Naples found a plate with a Hebrew inscription written by Pilate laying out the crimes of Jesus: "Jesus is a seducer, he is seditious, he is the enemy of the law," etc. and four witnesses are listed. The reverse side says, "A similar plate is sent to each tribe." After excavation (as the story goes) the plate was placed in an ebony box and preserved in the sacristy of the Carthusians, but a copy and translation was made by Dominique Vivant Denon, who brought it to France. The plate has since vanished, if it ever existed. The text actually was known several centuries earlier than *Le Droit*'s account. Beskow, drawing on work by Rudolf Berliner,[44] traces its origins to the sixteenth century during debates at the time about who was responsible for Jesus' death. One side of the debate was aided by a text found in Vienne, again, the legendary place of Pilate's death. Unfortunately, records of the time do not quote the text but the story of its discovery contains familiar elements: it was said to have been found in a box that had been unearthed and was written on parchment in Latin. In 1580 the text surfaced once again, this time in the vicinity of Amiternum, the birthplace of Pilate. Accounts say the text was written in Hebrew and was found in a ruined wall encased in three boxes: one of marble, one of iron, and the outermost of stone. This version, quoted in full (though in Italian), is longer than the one that circulated in the nineteenth century, beginning with a number of chronological markers and listing 15 witnesses, not four.[45] The longer version was widely disseminated in French, German, and Spanish throughout the seventeenth and eighteenth centuries, and was apparently shortened and recast as a copper-plate story in the nineteenth century. The author of the *Le Droit* article likely learned about the *Death Warrant* from a pamphlet of the time.

42. Discussions in Goodspeed, *Modern Apocrypha*, 92–96; Beskow, *Strange Tales*, 16–24.

43. The exact issue has not been determined but Beskow (*Strange Tales*, 112–13 n. 13) traces the publication back to a reprint of the same year in *Le Moniteur Universel*, 4 May 1839, p. 644. He notes also French and German printings of the text.

44. Berliner, "Urteil des Pilatus."

45. The differences are described in Beskow, *Strange Tales*, 20. Sutcliffe ("Apocryphal Form," 438–40) examines the chronological markers in detail.

Unaware of the Renaissance history of the text, Goodspeed investigated the *Death Warrant* using his skills as a biblical scholar. He points out a number of historical blunders: the plate could not be sent to "each tribe," since the tribal organization had long since broken down; Pilate is described as the "acting governor of Lower Galilee," not Judea; the date of the death warrant is anachronistically given as "March 25" (or March 27); three of the witnesses are surnamed "Robani," presumably a garbling of "Rabboni" but should read "Rabban," and the other is named "Capet," which Goodspeed says "is palpably French"; and the gate from which Jesus is to be led out is given as the otherwise-unknown "Gate of Struenus."[46] Goodspeed questions also the existence of the copper plate, declaring that "no competent scholar has ever reported seeing such a plate or published his transcription of one. Nor has any museum or institution claimed to possess such a plate."[47] Nevertheless, manuscripts of the text do exist, though they are relatively recent: Beskow mentions "a few contemporary manuscripts"[48] but only provides details for one in Italian from the seventeenth-century.[49] Also, the Latin text, said to be "from a manuscript in the possession of Mr. C. Havell, Reading," appears alongside an English translation in an 1851 broadsheet entitled "The Sentence of Condemnation as passed by Pontius Pilate against the Lord Jesus Christ, the Saviour of the World."[50] No stock can be placed in this evidence, however, since both examples antedate printed versions of the text.

Beskow appends to his discussion of the *Death Warrant* brief mention of another Passion-related text: the *Protocol of the Sanhedrin*.[51] The text recounts a meeting of the Sanhedrin where the guilt and punishment of Jesus are discussed. The twenty members of the council, which includes Joseph of Arimathea and Caiaphas, each express their opinions on Jesus. When pictured in art, they each hold large boards with their statements. The text seems to have originated around the same time as the *Death Warrant*, perhaps in Germany, and has been very popular in continental Europe, though no English versions are known. Beskow, for his part, is quite irenic

46. Goodspeed, *Modern Gospels*, 94–95; see also Sutcliffe, "Apocryphal Form," 440–41.

47. Goodspeed, *Modern Gospels*, 93. Beskow (*Strange Tales*, 21–22) speculates that a copper plate may have existed, perhaps even as the creation of Dominique Vivant Denon, whom Beskow describes as "a man strikingly free from scruples" (ibid., 21).

48. Beskow, *Strange Tales*, 19.

49. Printed in de Santos Otero, *Evangelios Apócrifos*, 532–35 and transcribed in Sutcliffe, "Apocryphal Form," 436–37.

50. Beskow, *Strange Tales*, 113 n. 15.

51. Ibid., 23–24, drawing upon Berliner, "Urteil des Pilatus."

about the text, saying "throughout its history it has never created any form of sensationalism, but has lived a quiet life as a popular apocryphal writing, in leaflets, broadsheets, and popular art."[52] He prefers to call it a "pious reconstruction" rather than a forgery, though the distinction between this text and other modern apocrypha is hardly clear.

Some modern apocrypha contain stories about the childhood of Jesus, but only one focuses entirely on that period of Jesus' life: *L'Évangile de la jeunesse de Notre-Seigneur Jésus-Christ d'après S. Pierre* published in 1894 by poet and dramatist Catulle Mendès.[53] The text, presented in Latin and French, is a compendium of stories found also in a number of ancient apocryphal infancy gospels—the *Protevangelium of James*, the *Infancy Gospel of Thomas*, the *Gospel of Pseudo-Matthew*, and the *Arabic Infancy Gospel*—along with several additional tales. It begins with a statement that the stories were dictated to the apostle Peter by Jesus' mother. An English translation of Mendès's text was made by Henry Copley Greene in 1904.[54] According to Mendès, and restated in the introduction to Greene's book written by English poet and essayist Alice Meynell, the manuscript for the text was said to have been found "in the ancient Abbey of Saint Wolfgang in the Salzkammergut" (Austria).[55] However, detailed examination of the Latin text determined that it was copied, at least partially, from a Latin translation of the *Arabic Infancy Gospel* made by Henry Sikes in the seventeenth century.[56]

It is entirely possible that Mendès came across a copy, maybe even a handwritten copy, of Sike's text, expanded and augmented by a Renaissance-era scribe; it is not unheard of for a published text to re-enter the manuscript tradition. But more likely, given Mendès's own creative endavours, the text is his own invention, and was created for the sake of whimsy; certainly the unique episodes in the gospel, which Meynell calls "the most lyrical," have a modern ring to them.[57] It was not that much earlier than Mendès's time that the line between history and fiction was difficult to determine in modern novels. For example, the initial 1764 edition of *The Castle of Otranto* by Horace Walpole was presented as a story from the Crusades found in an Italian manuscript printed at Naples in 1529. The manuscript, the preface states, "was found in the library of an ancient Catholic family in

52. Beskow, *Strange Tales*, 24.

53. The text is rarely mentioned in discussions of modern apocrypha. See the brief comments by James, *Apocryphal New Testament*, 89; Goodspeed, *Strange New Gospels*, 97–98; Beskow, *Strange Tales*, 6; and Charlesworth, *Authentic Apocrypha*, 55 n. 74.

54. Greene, *Gospel*.

55. The introduction is found in Greene, *Gospel*, 13–21.

56. James, *Apocryphal New Testament*, 89.

57. Greene, *Gospel*, 19.

the north of England" and was translated in the book by a certain William Marshal.[58] Walpole only admitted its real origins and his own authorship in subsequent editions. The same ambiguity is observed in several works by Daniel Defoe, author of *Robinson Crusoe*. His *A Journal of the Plague Year*, published in 1722, appears on the surface to be a non-fiction account of the Great Plague of London written in 1665.[59] Of course, even Defoe's and Walpole's audiences were not pleased with these deceptions. Meynell, for her part, may hint at knowledge of Mendès's deception and perhaps considered it forgivable given the relationship between apocrypha and the creative arts. She uses her introduction to note the use of apocryphal tales by Italian artists, such Giotto, Titian, Ghirlandajo, Raphael, and Tintoretto. "Every gallery in Europe," she writes, "every galley in America in which are old Italian paintings, of whatever century, has its illustrations of the Apocryphal Gospels. Those writings must have formed the lighter religious reading of the nations."[60] Meynell feels an attraction to the fairy-tale quality of the materials, though some material seems to have caused offense—the English edition places the gynecological examination of Salome (*Prot. Jas.* 20), "omitted from the text for reasons of taste," untranslated in an appendix.[61]

Perhaps the most well-known scholarly apocryphon is the *Life of Saint Issa*, published by Nicolas Notovitch (Nicolai Alexandrovitch Notovitch), first in French in 1894 and then quickly translated into other languages for multiple editions.[62] Notovitch was a Russian war correspondent who visited India and Tibet in 1887. According to his story,[63] contained in a travelogue encompassing almost 100 pages, he first heard of "very ancient memoirs, treating of the life of Christ" from a Lama at a Buddhist monastery in Ladak.[64] Though this particular monastery did not have copies of the memoirs, the Lama told Notovitch that others did, including Lass

58. See the discussion in Farrer, *Literary Forgeries*, 147–48; with brief mentions in Grafton, *Forgers and Critics*, 34; and Russett, *Fictions and Fakes*, 13–14.

59. See Russett, *Fictions and Fakes*, 14. Defoe was himself a victim of forgery in the numerous pamphlets falsely ascribed to him.

60. Greene, *Gospel*, 15.

61. Ibid., 270–71. It is not known if Mendès did the same; I was not able to obtain a copy of his edition.

62. Discussions in Goodspeed, *Strange New Gospels*, 10–24; Goodspeed, *Modern Apocrypha*, 28–44; Beskow, *Strange Tales*, 57–65; Beskow, "Modern Mystifications," 461–64; and Beskow, *Jesus i Kashmir*. Maffly-Kipp, *American Scriptures*, 290–319 reproduces the entire text. See also the chapter (ch. 13) by Bradley N. Rice in this volume.

63. Recounted in Notovitch, *Unknown Life of Jesus*, 13–97 (references are to the New York edition of 1894).

64. Ibid., 8.

where they "number many thousands."[65] In hopes of seeing these texts for himself, Notovitch journeyed on to Leh and finally to Himis, where he was taken in by the monks of a monastery after breaking his leg in a fall from horseback. There the Lama read to him stories and teachings of Issa, which is the Tibetan name for Jesus. With the help of a translator Notovitch took notes and, after returning home, published the text along with his narrative of its discovery.

Notovitch describes the text as "written in the form of isolated verses, which frequently bear no connection between each other."[66] His transcription is an attempt to present the narrative in some logical order. The text begins with a prologue stating that the stories were told by "merchants who have come from Israel" (1.5). Then Issa is born as an incarnation of the "Eternal Spirit" who has come to our world to teach "how we may reach a state of moral purity and separate the soul from its gross envelope, that it may attain the perfection necessary to enter the Kingdom of heaven which is immutable and where eternal happiness reigns" (4.4). Issa shows promise as a child but, to avoid marriage, he clandestinely leaves Jerusalem at the age of 13 in the company of merchants and travels to India. There he is told by the Brahmans and the Kshatriyas that he should not teach the Vaisyas and the Soudras; but Issa refuses their demand, believing "God the Father establishes no difference between his children, who are all equally dear to him" (5.11). Issa continues his teachings against the caste system and against idol worship and human sacrifice, journeying from India to Persia (chs. 5–8) before returning to Palestine at the age of 29 (9). There he acquires a large following from the Jews, who consider him their rightful king (10–13). This concerns the procurator Pilate, who imprisons Issa on false charges and crucifies him along with two criminals (14). The people continue to honor Issa at his tomb, so Pilate takes the body and buries it elsewhere; this just leads the people to believe that "the Supreme Judge" had taken away his body (14.7). The text ends with Issa's followers going out to preach about him (14.10–11).

Notovitch follows his gospel with commentary that tells more about the origins of the text along with details not found in the text itself. He says,

> The two manuscripts read to me by the lama of the Himis Convent, were compiled from divers copies written in the Thibetan tongue, translated from rolls belonging to the Lassa library and brought from India, Nepal, and Maghada two hundred years

65. Ibid., 51–52.
66. Ibid., 96

after Christ. These were placed in a convent standing on Mount Marbour, near Lassa, where the Dalai-Lama now resides.[67]

A few pages later Notovitch provides more details, saying the text was "recorded within three or four years after the death of Christ from the testimonies of eye witnesses."[68] Already his commentary shows the influence of the scholarship of his time, which involved itself in weighing evidence for the life of Jesus; it was also the heyday for interest in India.[69] The *Life of Saint Issa* is considered by Notovitch "more likely to bear the stamp of truth" than the NT Gospels, because it was written closer to the events, since the Evangelists "wrote at divers epochs, and so long a time after these events took place, that we can not be astonished if the facts have been altered or distorted."[70] Notovitch's Issa does not perform miracles nor rise from the grave. Pilate alone is culpable in Issa's death. But the most convincing connection between the text and contemporary scholarship is its treatment of Judas. The text does not mention Judas by name; it only discusses a paid informant at the trial (13.21). But Notovitch identifies him as Judas in the commentary and mentions "about ten years ago" reading an article on Judas in the German journal *Fremdenblatt* about Judas being Jesus' friend and that betraying him would help hasten the kingdom. Notovitch dismisses this "lucubration" in favor of what is revealed in his text.[71] Notovitch's commentary about Moses, mentioned in the text's prologue, similarly sounds affected by scholarship; in the text Moses is not an Israelite but an Egyptian prince who is taught by the Israelites and shows them favor. According to Notovitch, Moses wanted to have his own kingdom since his elder brother debarred him from the Egyptian throne, and naturalistic explanations are given for the plagues and the deaths of the Egyptian soldiers in the Red Sea.[72]

The *Life of Saint Issa* was very popular upon its publication; however, scholars immediately challenged Notovitch's claims. Notovitch himself relates troubles he encountered getting the book published, and even recounts an exchange with Ernest Renan, author of his own life of Christ,[73] over the work. He said Renan wanted his notes and offered to "report on them to the Academy" but Notovitch decided to publish it himself, worried that Renan

67. Ibid., 151.
68. Ibid., 153.
69. See Beskow, *Strange Tales*, 62.
70. Notovitch, *Unknown Life of Jesus*, 153.
71. Ibid., 180.
72. Ibid., 154–57.
73. Renan, *Vie de Jésus*.

would take credit for his work.[74] Friedrich Max Müller, an acknowledged expert on India, quickly attacked the book in an 1894 article in *The Nineteenth Century*.[75] Müller was hesitant at first to accuse Notovitch of fraud, thinking instead that he may have been duped. Still, he found problems in the story. Two things, he said, seemed impossible:

> The first, that the Jews from Palestine who come to India about 35 A.D. should have met the very people who had known Issa when he was a student at Benares; the second, that this Sûtra of Issa, composed in the first century of our era, should not have found a place either in the Kandjur or in the Tandjur (the collections of Tibetan literature).[76]

He wondered too why Jesus was given the name Issa but Pontius Pilate's name was unchanged.[77] Müller's critique alludes to recent discoveries, saying, "In these days of unexpected discoveries in Egypt and elsewhere, everything is possible,"[78] yet he remained skeptical. His article concludes with the reproduction of a letter dated 29 June 1894 that he received from an Englishwoman visiting Tibet.[79] In it she says she was at Himis monastery and enquired about Notovitch, but they knew nothing about him. There was also no life of Christ there.

Notovitch responded to these criticisms in a note "To the Publishers" in the first English translation of the book. He says the books could not be found in the catalogs because the material is "to be found scattered through more than one book without any title";[80] he says he had offered to take his critics with him to the monastery to verify the passages, but no one as yet had responded to the invitation.[81] Fortunately, other manuscripts, he says, are more readily accessible. He claims that a Roman Catholic cardinal had informed him that, "the Vatican Library possesses sixty-three complete or incomplete manuscripts in various Oriental languages referring to this matter, which have been brought to Rome by missionaries from India, China, Egypt and Arabia."[82] Notovitch's response to his critics includes also a defense of apocryphal texts:

74. Notovitch, *Unknown Life of Jesus*, 11.
75. Müller, "Alleged Sojourn."
76. Ibid., 519.
77. Ibid., 518.
78. Ibid., 521.
79. Ibid., 521–22.
80. Notovitch, *Unknown Life of Jesus*, 106.
81. Ibid., 108.
82. Ibid., 107.

Is it a new thing in the Christian world—a book that aims at completing the New Testament and throwing light on hitherto obscure points? The works known as apocryphas were so numerous in the sixteenth century that the Latin Council of Trent was forced to curtail and immense number of them so as to avoid controversies.[83]

He goes on to say that the Nicene Council "also reduced to a minimum the sum of transcendental truths."[84] Speculating further about the origins of his text, Notovitch mentions the apostles and asks, "Have these friends of Jesus, these familiar witnesses of his preaching and his martyrdom, written nothing?" Then, thinking about the exploits of Thomas in India recounted in the *Acts of Thomas*, he says his text "may have been actually spoken by St. Thomas."[85] Finally, Notovitch comments specifically about the discovery of apocryphal texts in his own time, saying, "May not this resurrection of books which have been buried under the dust of secular ages be the starting point of a new science which should be fertile in unforeseen and unimaginable results?"[86]

Notovitch's challenge to check his story was taken up a year later by J. Archibald Douglas, a teacher at the Government College of Agra. He traced Notovitch's path and visited the Lama at Himis. He interviewed the Lama about Notovitch's account,[87] and the Lama reportedly screamed "Lies, lies, nothing but lies!"[88] Furthermore, no one at the monastery remembered caring for a foreigner with a broken leg, though there was a report of a Russian gentleman named Notovitch who had been recently treated for a toothache at the Leh hospital; so Notovitch does seem to have been in the area.[89] Müller added a postscript to Douglas' article, apologizing for saying the Lamas may have duped him; he now fully believed Notovitch invented the text. In Goodspeed's survey of the text, he says that Notovitch should have "interested himself actively to secure copies and even photographs of the scattered portions which Notovitch said he had assembled."[90] Even after the publication, Notovitch "did not take the obvious and, most of us

---

83. Ibid., 111.

84. Ibid.

85. Ibid., 112–13.

86. Ibid., 113.

87. A transcript is given in Douglas, "Chief Lama," 671–72; and the complete documents are published in "Documents."

88. Douglas, "Chief Lama," 672.

89. Ibid., 669.

90. Goodspeed, *Modern Apocrypha*, 11.

would think, the unavoidable steps to substantiate his supposed discovery."[91] Other authors, such as H. Louis Fader,[92] have worked to prove the text is a modern composition, chiefly by discrediting Notovitch's discovery story, though Günter Grönbold refuted also a number of the text's claims (including Jesus' connection to the Essenes)[93] and Robert Aron also sought to show that the text's description of Jesus' education does not fit with knowledge of first-century Judaism.[94]

Despite the efforts of Notovitch's critics to discredit the *Life of Saint Issa*, people continue to romanticize about the notion that Jesus visited India. Ahmadiyya Islam considers the text authentic,[95] and the ideas were taken up by Elizabeth Clare Prophet, leader of the American-based Summit Lighthouse and the Church Universal and Triumphant, and then passed on to Levi Dowling in whose hands they were incorporated into the *Aquarian Gospel*.[96] Several authors of dubious academic credentials—including Fida Hassnain and Holger Kersten[97]—have written in support of Notovitch. Kersten's *Jesus Lived in India* is perhaps the best known of these efforts. The book attempts to substantiate Notovitch's story with appeal to a number of other witnesses to the mysterious manuscripts—including a certain Mrs. Hervey who is said to have described the texts in her book *The Adventures of a Lady in Tartary, Thibet, China and Kashmir* in 1853, and Lady Henrietta Merrick who mentions them in *In the World's Attick* in 1931.[98] But these claims cannot be found in the books mentioned.[99] In Notovitch's defense, Norbert Klatt has suggested that the author may have come across portions of the Bible that Heinrich August Jäschke had translated into Tibetan

91. Ibid., 12.

92. Fader, *Issa Tale*.

93. Grönbold, *Jesus in Indien*.

94. Aron, *Jesus of Nazareth*.

95. See Beskow, *Strange Tales*, 63–64; Beskow, *Modern Mystifications*, 460–63. Mirza Ghulam Ahmad, founder of the movement, published his complete Jesus legend, *Masih hindustan mein*, in 1899.

96. Maffly-Kipp, *American Scriptures*, 291. The *Aquarian Gospel* is discussed in Goodspeed, *Strange New Gospels*, 25–30; Goodspeed, *Modern Apocrypha*, 15–19; and Maffly-Kipp, *American Scriptures*, 378–406 (with excerpts).

97. Hassnain, *Search for the Historical Jesus*; Kersten, *Jesus Lived in India*. For a critical response to these works see Grönbold, *Jesus in Indien*.

98. Kersten, *Jesus Lived in India*, 15–17.

99. See Jacobs, *When Jesus Lived in India*, 188–89. Others who claimed to have seen the manuscripts are discussed pp. 13–15, 187–90, but none of these claims have been substantiated.

between 1857 and 1868.[100] Of course, Klatt's explanation does not account for the wealth of non-biblical information in the text.

Four additional "lost gospels" appeared early in the twentieth century. The first of these is the *Letter of Benan, the Egyptian Physician*.[101] The text was published in Berlin in 1910 by Ernst Edler von de Planitz, a writer of poems, novels, and stories. He claimed the text was found in a fifth-century Coptic papyrus roll found in a tomb in the ancient site of Memphis,[102] but the original letter was written in Greek in 83 CE. Von de Planitz apparently worked on the text for over 50 years, publishing five books with a translation, notes, and commentary. In the letter, Benan writes to Strato, once secretary of the emperor Tiberius, in response to Strato's request for information about Jesus. Benan says he met Jesus in Egypt, where he spent much of his life and became an adept in Egyptian priestly lore; Jesus did not come to Palestine until his late 20s. When nothing is heard from Jesus for three years, Benan goes to Palestine to investigate. He sees the three empty crosses on Calvary and witnesses the resurrection. Later Benan meets Paul in prison in Rome, and James and John in Jerusalem. Benan encounters all the important early Christian figures and is present at all the major events—he's the Forrest Gump of early Christianity. In 1919, Von der Planitz announced the discovery of a related Greek papyrus—housed in an unidentified "public museum"—containing a reference to "Jesus of Anu" (in Egypt). Carl Schmidt of Berlin called for Von der Planitze to publish the original texts; Von der Planitze responded in a published statement "with great assurance and much bitterness."[103] Schmidt then followed in 1921 with a full critique calling the *Letter of Benan* a fiction.[104] Goodspeed, for his part, points out a number of historical inconsistencies in the text along with examples of peculiar language (a jumble of Egyptian, Greek, Latin, and Hebrew, and phrases that have never been found in ancient Coptic writings).[105] In addition, errors in Egyptian names seem to derive from the works of a maverick Coptologist named Lauth who taught at the University of Munich when Von de Planitz was a student there. Goodspeed doubted the authen-

100. Klatt, *Jesus in Indien*, 74–75.

101. Discussions in Goodspeed, *Strange New Gospels*, 73–84; Goodspeed, *Modern Apocrypha*, 50–57.

102. Goodspeed provides additional details: "Its editor . . . stated that the roll had been bought in 1860, by an independent Munich scholar named Baron von Rabenau, from a native in the village of Mit Rahinê, on the site of the ancient Memphis. It had been found in a tomb at Sakkara" (*Modern Apocrypha*, 50).

103. Goodspeed, *Modern Apocrypha*, 53.

104. Schmidt, *Benanbrief*.

105. Goodspeed, *Modern Apocrypha*, 54–55.

ticity of the text for the same reasons adduced for the nineteenth-century
"lost gospels": no manuscript, no photograph, no transcript.[106]

Several elements already encountered in modern apocrypha—a journey to India, a relationship with Mary Magdalene, and teaching on reincarnation—appear again in the *Gospel of the Holy Twelve* (aka the *Gospel
of the Perfect Life*) published by the English clergyman Rev. Gideon Jasper
Ouseley at the turn of the century.[107] Ouseley was a writer of ten books on
vegetarianism and occult matters and founded a number of societies with
theosophical and vegetarian goals. Not surprisingly, then, his gospel features a vegetarian Jesus who preaches a diet of fruit and herbs; so, this Jesus
feeds the multitude not with five loaves and two fish, but with five melons.
Flowers spring up wherever Jesus walks, he speaks a language of birds and
beasts, and a lion lies down at his feet.

The various editions of the text provide conflicting discovery stories
for the gospel. In early editions, Ouseley claimed his text was an Aramaic
gospel older and more authentic than those of the New Testament. It was
revealed to him in English through spiritual communications from a group
of deceased luminaries, including a fourteenth-century Franciscan friar
named Placidus, the eighteenth-century theologian and mystic Emanuel
Swedenborg, John Wesley, and Theosophical Society members Anna Kings-
ford and Edward Maitland.[108] Technically, then, the *Gospel of the Holy Twelve*
is not a scholarly apocryphon. But, according to a 1956 English edition the
gospel was written by the apostle John during his imprisonment in Rome
around 70 CE and later it was taken by John to a Tibetan monastery. There
it was found by the friar Placidus (here living in the 1870s), who translated
it into Latin and brought it to Rome where it lay hidden away in the Vatican
Library.[109] The editors clearly have been influenced, in varying degrees, by
the turn-of-the-century gospel discoveries; this influence is stated explicitly
in the 1911 edition, where the unnamed writer of the preface identifies the
gospel as the lost *Gospel of the Hebrews* and likens the discovery of the text

106. Ibid., 55. See also the brief comments in Dibelius, *Fresh Approach to the New
Testament*, 94.

107. Discussion in Beskow, *Strange Tales*, 66–74. The book has a complicated publication history, summarized in ibid., 124 n. 83. A curious 1911 edition credited only to
"a Disciple of the Master" published by the United Templars' Society includes also the
Letter of Lentulus (p. ii) and an Epistle of Apollos to Hierasthenes, dated here to about
71 and 72 (p. 165–66).

108. The process of these communications are described in Disciple of the Master,
Gospel of the Holy Twelve (1911 ed.), vi–ix

109. Ouseley, *Gospel of the Holy Twelve* (1956 ed.), viewed online at http://www.
thenazareneway.com/origins_gh12.htm/ (n.p.). This account is also summarized by
Beskow (*Strange Tales*, 67) from an English edition published in 1972.

to the Old Syriac Gospels found by Agnes Smith Lewis at St. Catherine's Monastery and published only a year earlier.[110] The 1956 editors draw on the popular notion of apocryphal texts as containing "censored" but true teachings of Jesus:

> The reason this Gospel contains much that is in St. Matthew, St. Mark, St. Luke and St. John is because there were many Gospels written about this time containing the true teaching of Jesus, but this was the only one that escaped the pen of the 'correctors,' because they did not know of its existence. The other Gospels contained the teaching of Jesus about the avoidance of meat-eating and about the love for animals, but all this teaching was eliminated by the 'correctors.' "The Gospel of the Holy Twelve" is an authentic Gospel and should be accepted just as it is as the original teaching of Jesus.[111]

The mystical aspects of the text are then given context with appeal to another "lost gospel," the *Gospel of Thomas*:

> In all sacred mysteries, parables are used as garments for Truth that is hidden in its very expression. In one of the 'Sayings of Jesus'—as recorded in the Oxyrhynchus Papyri—we are told: "That which is hidden from thee shall be revealed to thee. For there is nothing hidden which shall not be made manifest, nor buried which shall not be raised." To those who hid "the key to knowledge" Jesus said "Ye entered not in yourselves and to them that were entering in ye opened not." Ultimately, "Truth itself is unutterable save by God to God."

And finally, Beskow describes German and Swiss editions which, influenced this time by Notovitch's discovery story, eliminate entirely the spiritual aspects of the gospel's discovery and state instead that Ouseley found the gospel on a journey in Tibet in 1881.[112]

The themes of the *Gospel of the Holy Twelve* carry over into the *Essene Gospel of Peace*, published by Edmond Bordeaux Szekely in 1937.[113] Szekely was the leader of a "biogenic" institute and published about 60 books, mainly about health food. The Jesus of his gospel teaches a Mother-Father theology: the heavenly father takes care of things that are spiritual, the earthly Mother

110. Disciple of the Master, *Gospel of the Holy Twelve* (1911 ed.), v–vii.

111. Ouseley, *Gospel of the Holy Twelve* (1956 ed.), n.p.

112. Described in Beskow, *Strange Tales*, 67; cf. Beskow's critique of this claim p. 73. Ouseley's gospel is mentioned by Young (*Is God a Vegetarian?*, 5–6) and dismissed as inauthentic based on Beskow's investigation.

113. Discussion in Beskow, *Strange Tales*, 81–91.

the body; one must cleanse the body of evil-smelling filth to be reborn to a fuller life. To aid in this process, Jesus provides the following instruction:

> Seek, therefore, a large trailing gourd, having a stalk the length of a man; take out its inwards and fill it with water from the river which the sun has warmed. Hang it upon a branch of a tree, and kneel upon the ground before the angel of water, and suffer the end of the stalk of the trailing gourd to enter your hinder parts, that the water may flow through all your bowels.[114]

Szekely says he discovered this useful text in two manuscripts—one in Old Slavonic in the National Library of Vienna, one in Aramaic in the secret archives of the Vatican—as well as some Hebrew fragments said to have once belonged to the Benedictine Monastery of Monte Cassino. Szekely produced a cottage industry of books related to the *Gospel of Peace*, one of which reveals in great detail the transmission of the text—it was among the apocryphal materials known to Jerome, from whom they made their way to Monte Cassino, and then to the Vatican, where they were discovered and translated by Szekely.[115] Beskow describes one particular volume that actually includes fifteen pages of nonvocalized Hebrew text but without translation. Drawing upon the expertise of Bo Lundén, Beskow says the text is "correct Hebrew of a postbiblical period, similar to that found in the Mishnah," but cautions readers that "having a Hebrew text is really not the same as possessing a Hebrew original."[116] As for the Vienna and Vatican manuscripts, they have not been published, nor has anyone ever seen them, and Szekely's name is not listed in the Vatican Library's visitor registry.[117]

Finally, we come to the *Gospel of Josephus*,[118] named for the Jewish writer of the first century. This text is little more than a harmony of the four canonical Gospels, presented as the lost original life of Jesus upon which they are based. It is said to have been found by Helena, the mother of Constantine, in a house near the temple of Jerusalem; it was later sold to some Jews who in turn sold it to the library of Alexandria. Many centuries later, Italian newspapers reported in 1927 that a certain Luigi Moccia found a third/fourth-century parchment Greek manuscript of the text under the false bottom of a wrought-iron chest which he had bought in an antique shop in Rome. The reports also said that Moccia had admitted the text was a

114. Quotation from the 1977 edition: Szekeley, *Gospel of Peace*, 17.

115. Recounted in Szekely, *Discovery of the Essene Gospel of Peace*.

116. Beskow, *Strange Tales*, 85–86.

117. Ibid., 84–85. See also Young, *Is God a Vegetarian?*, 5.

118. Discussions in Goodspeed, *New Chapters*, 196–201; Goodspeed, *Modern Apocrypha*, 76–80.

hoax created to stimulate faith, while others said it was to advertise a novel he intended to produce. But the story does not end there. In 1931 Salvatore Riggi of Schenectady New York contacted Edgar Goodspeed and said he had seven sheets of Moccia's Greek manuscript and he had translated it into Italian for his mission work. He also had an accompanying document in Latin with an endorsement of the gospel by Zosimus, the librarian of Alexandria. To Goodspeed the manuscript looked suspicious—it was carefully separated into words and paragraphs with modern punctuation, and was written on only one side of the paper. The paper was old, probably taken from flyleaves of old manuscripts, but the writing was recent.[119]

This survey of modern apocrypha comes to a close with two texts that claim to be continuations of the book of Acts. The *Twenty-ninth Chapter of Acts*,[120] published as a pamphlet by George J. Stevenson in London in 1871,[121] was reportedly found on a piece of paper tucked into an English edition of oriental traveler C. S. Sonnini's *Travels in Turkey and Greece*, originally published in 1799. The text was translated into French from a Greek manuscript found in the Archives at Constantinople, and presented to Sonnini by the Sultan Abdoul Achmet. The text substantiates the arguments of the British-Israel movement, which claims that the English peoples are descendants of the lost ten tribes of Israel. These ideas were given some support in works by British astronomer Charles Piazzi Smith in books published in 1864 and 1867. The text reports that Paul, left in Rome at the end of the canonical book of Acts, departs from the city for Spain and Britain, having heard that Israelites had escaped to Britain; he preaches in Britain and then moves on to Belgium and Switzerland and back toward Asia Minor. In one memorable episode, Paul predicts the seventh British census of 1861, which was a contributing factor to the beginnings of the British-Israel movement, and the building of St. Paul's cathedral:

> Behold, in the last days the God of peace shall dwell in the cities, and the inhabitants thereof shall be numbered; and in the seventh numbering of the people, their eyes shall be opened, and the glory of their inheritance shine forth before them. And nations shall come up to worship on the mount (i.e., Mount Lud) that testifies of the patience and long suffering of a servant of the Lord.[122]

119. Goodspeed, *Modern Apocrypha*, 77.

120. Discussions in Goodspeed, *Strange New Gospels*, 85–95; Goodspeed, *Modern Apocrypha*, 58–69.

121. A 2011 printing by The Covenant Publishing Company Ltd. credits "notes and comments" to T. G. Cole.

122. From v. 10, reproduced in Goodspeed, *Modern Apocrypha*, 62.

254 Fakes, Forgeries, and Fictions

Archaeologist John Ora Kinnaman, a defender of the text, stated in a 1940 article that the original manuscript can be found in the British Museum, cataloged as no. 3227-D9.[123] Goodspeed investigated Kinnaman's claim and determined that the catalog number is for a book: Stevenson's 1871 publication. Kinnaman also said that the text was found in the Coptic and Syriac versions of Acts, but it is not.[124] In his final thoughts on the authenticity of the text, Goodspeed concluded: "Neither the Greek manuscript, then, nor the English manuscript translation of it, nor the present possessor of either, nor the name of the scholar who translated the Greek text into English (for that Sonnini did this is a most improbable conjecture) can now be found."[125]

The second text purported to continue the story of Acts is the long-lost *Second Book of Acts*, published by Episcopal clergyman and doctor Kenneth Sylvan Guthrie in Medford Massachusetts in 1904. The text, claiming to "set forth the Blessed Mary's teachings about reincarnation,"[126] begins with a scene similar to the familiar deathbed gathering in the *Dormition of Mary*, with Paul and the other apostles assembling in Palestine at the bedside of the Virgin Mary. She instructs those gathered about reincarnation and declares who she was in her past lives. She then brings the apostles to the Mount of Olives, where Jesus appears and reveals to them his previous incarnations. In an odd twist, Mary and Jesus' past selves are all revealed to be famous couples (Noah and Yonah, Zarathustra and Parshandathah, Socrates and Eunike, Gautama Siddhartha and Yasodhara). Just to be clear: this is the Virgin Mary, not Mary Magdalene. Guthrie never gave any details about the source of this text: not the language in which it was composed, nor in what manuscripts or editions it may be found.

How did critics of these texts come to the conclusion that they were modern, not ancient documents? They considered the two usual categories of evidence pursued in the discipline: external and internal. By external is meant actual copies of the text in question and references to the text by ancient authorities. In almost all cases, the editors and publishers of these texts failed to present photographic copies of the manuscripts, nor even transcriptions in their original languages; also, when pressed they could not provide precise information about where the original manuscripts could be found. Furthermore, investigations into the stories of discovery of the texts revealed inconsistencies and falsifications; indeed, some of the texts have

123. Published in *The Defender* (Wichita, Kansas); see Goodspeed, *Modern Apocrypha*, 64.

124. Goodspeed, *Modern Apocrypha*, 66.

125. Ibid., 65.

126. Discussion in ibid., 97–101. Only 155 copies of the pamphlet were printed and it has not been reprinted since.

been shown to be plagiarized from works of fiction. The only exceptions are the *Gospel of Josephus*, with its apparently modern Greek writing on ancient paper, and the transcribed Hebrew fragments of the *Gospel of Peace*, likely also created by a modern writer. The *Transcript of Pilate's Court* and the *Childhood of Christ* appeared in Latin, but both texts were plagiarized from earlier published works. As for knowledge by ancient authorities, none of these texts are mentioned by ancient writers, though they sometimes bear similarities to ancient texts discovered in modern times, such as the *Acts of Pilate* and the *Dormition of Mary*.

In the absence of external evidence, scholars looked at internal indications of the texts' authenticity. Alas, all of these texts bear the marks of modern composition: they reflect the gaps in knowledge of first-century Judaism in the scholarship of the time and feature anachronistic depictions of Jesus and the early church, most often influenced by contemporary interests in such things as naturalistic explanations for the miracles and resurrection of Jesus, reincarnation, vegetarianism, and connections between Jesus' teachings and Eastern (i.e., Indian and Egyptian) thought (influenced by the work of the nineteenth-century Religionsgeschichtliche Schule). Also observable in the introductory comments and defense of these texts is an interest in the discoveries of legitimate ancient Christian and Jewish apocrypha and the impact such discoveries had on both scholarship and the wider public.[127] Kollman's afterword to the *Crucifixion of Jesus*, for example, is positive about the historical value of apocryphal texts for recovering the life of Jesus and is critical about the motives of the compilers of the canon;[128] similarly, Notovitch's defense of his *Life of Saint Issa* refers to recent archeological discoveries of long-forgotten texts and characterizes apocrypha as books that "[aim] at completing the New Testament and throwing light on hitherto obscure points."[129] The publication of "lost gospels" provided the creators of modern apocrypha with an audience for their work and lent their discovery stories the plausibility required for their texts to be accepted as genuine.

SECRET MARK AND JESUS' WIFE

The twentieth and twenty-first centuries saw only four arguments of forgery made about possibly-ancient apocryphal texts: Paul R. Coleman-Norton's "amusing *agraphon*" and the *Gospel of Judas*, both of which, for very

---

127. Note, in this regard, the comments in Jenkins, *Hidden Gospels*, 46.

128. Kollmann, *Enthüllungen über die wirkliche Todesart Jesu*, 73–74.

129. Notovitch, *Unknown Life of Jesus*, 111.

different reasons, can be dispensed with quickly, and *Sec. Mark* and GJW, which require more detailed discussion.

In a 1950 article for *Catholic Biblical Quarterly*, Coleman-Norton presented the Greek text of a saying of Jesus he found embedded in a fragment of the *Opus imperfectum in Matthaeum*, a collection of homilies on sections of Matthew otherwise known only in Latin.[130] Bruce Metzger, Coleman-Norton's primary critic, describes the discovery:

> At the conclusion of Matt 24:51, which in the canonical text refers to the judgment when "men will weep and gnash their teeth," the fragment continues with the question, raised by one of the disciples, how these things can be for persons who happen to be toothless. Whereupon Jesus replied, "Teeth will be provided."

Metzger argues that the saying is modern, not ancient, because Coleman-Norton was known to joke with his students about dentures being provided at the last judgment years before his alleged discovery of the Greek fragment, of which there is no material evidence.[131] Little mention of the text has been made since, except for some comparisons with Morton Smith's discovery of *Sec. Mark*.[132]

As for *Gos. Judas*, the accusation of forgery was made in a 2008 article by Richard J. Arthur and given support a few years later by Robert M. Price.[133] Price helpfully summarizes the Arthur article in three points: the text betrays an awareness of modern moral issues ("it seems to be editorializing on the priestly scandals of our time, as it depicts priests sleeping with women and 'sacrificing' children, this last perhaps pointing to abortion or molestation"), part of the gospel copies from the *Apocryphon (or Secret Book) of John* ("the impression one gets from reading it is of a patch transferred out of context, no longer making the sense it did in the original"), and it contains a scribal error found also in one of the extant copies of *Ap. John* from Nag

130. Coleman-Norton, "Amusing *Agraphon*."

131. Metzger, "Literary Forgeries," 3–4 (see also Metzger, *Reminiscences of an Octogenarian*, 136–39); discussed briefly in Grafton, *Forgers and Critics*, 4.

132. Carlson, *Gospel Hoax*, 17–20 notes the *agraphon* as an example of a suspicious find that reflects modern interests; Carlson, "Can the Academy," 303–304 mentions both *Sec. Mark* and the *agraphon* as texts that are demonstrably forgeries because the scholars who published them seemed aware of their contents before the discoveries. Evans, "Morton Smith," 78–81, 94–96 expands on this theory, providing evidence from Smith's works indicating this prior knowledge and showing both Smith and Coleman-Norton drew upon the novel *The Mystery of Mar Saba* in crafting the stories of their discoveries (for a rebuttal see Brown and Pantuck, "Craig Evans," 101–104).

133. Arthur, "Gospel of Judas"; Price, *Secret Scrolls*, 76–77, 181.

Hammadi (Price asks, "what are the chances that the scribe of *Judas* copied from another [i.e., non Nag-Hammadi] copy of *The Secret Book of John* that made the *very same goof in the very same spot?*").[134] Price accedes that the papyrus on which *Judas* is written is genuinely ancient (it was carbon-dated by the National Geographic Society to between 220 and 340 CE)[135] but the text is not. He goes on to declare that the forger is one of the members of the NGS team, but does not say which one (the team includes Rodolphe Kasser, Gregor Wurst, François Gaudard, Marvin Meyer, and Florence Darbre).[136] Arthur does not make this charge in the original paper, but he does say, "that our hoaxer is a member of the community of modern Coptic scholars who have special regard for Codex II as the first exemplar of the *Apocryphon of John* from Nag Hammadi to be published."[137] Arthur concludes the paper on a conciliatory note, despite the severity of the accusation:

> The *Gospel of Judas* is probably a hoax, and all the writings in it of recent authorship. These writings were prepared in our time, on some old papyrus leaves, probably from a palimpsest, without a binding. There is no cause for rebuke. One of our colleagues has created great excitement; he is a jolly fellow and has done us all a favor.[138]

Though no scholar, other than Price, has taken Arthur's theory seriously, it is surprising how much the forgery accusation is similar to the charges against *Sec. Mark* and GJW. In all three cases, the contents of the texts resonate with modern concerns (homosexuality for *Gos. Judas* and *Sec. Mark*; the marital status of Jesus for GJW), and all three have suspicious or at least questionable stories of discovery. In addition, the theories regarding the creation of the manuscript for both GJW and *Gos. Judas* involve authentic ancient papyrus and modern ink based on an ancient recipe. Of course, other details in each case contribute to the particular conclusions reached by scholars on authenticity but it is notable that, as with cases of Enlightenment-era forgery,[139] the investigations into the origins of these texts begin with objections to their contents.

The same surely can be said of *Sec. Mark*. This controversial text was discovered, as the story goes, in 1958 when American historian Morton Smith journeyed to the monastery of Mar Saba in the Judean desert to

134. Price, *Secret Scrolls*, 76–77.
135. Kasser and Wurst, *Gospel of Judas*, 183–85.
136. Price, *Secret Scrolls*, 181.
137. Arthur, "Gospel of Judas," 47.
138. Ibid.
139. See the introduction to this volume, pp. 3–9.

catalogue the library in the monastery's great tower. Smith found there a number of printed books and a handful of manuscripts. Smith noted that the blank pages of printed books often contained additional writing in Greek—a demonstration of how scarce paper was in the recent centuries of the monastery's history. The end-papers of one of these printed books, a 1646 edition of Isaac Voss's epistles of Ignatius, particularly attracted Smith's attention. In an apparent eighteenth-century hand there is a text that begins: "From the letters of the most holy Clement, the author of the *Stromateis*; to Theodore." Smith had chanced upon a previously unknown letter by Clement of Alexandria, a well-known early Christian writer whose other works were written between 175 and 215 CE. That alone would be a major discovery, but the writer of this *Letter to Theodore* mentions also the existence of a longer version of Mark current in his time. He provides two excerpts from this longer Mark, the largest is a story of Jesus raising a young man from death (reminiscent of the story of Lazarus from the Gospel of John) and then spending the night with him teaching him the mysteries of the kingdom of God.

Initially, Smith's peers trusted in his integrity and the authenticity of the *Letter to Theodore* was not in doubt. Early reactions focused on *Sec. Mark*, declaring it a typical second-century apocryphal gospel with its attendant expansion and combination of canonical traditions. The first scholar to question publicly the origins of the letter was Quentin Quesnell. In a 1975 article Quesnell declared that the text bore the characteristics of a hoax and therefore must be authenticated, and that this can be done only by personally examining the manuscript.[140] He was drawing upon Edgar Goodspeed's demand that anyone claiming to have found a new document must present the document itself.[141] Unlike the other publishers of modern apocrypha, Smith did actually take photographs of the text and published them in his commentary, but Quesnell considered Smith's photographs inadequate for the study of the text as they were mediocre in quality and had been cropped by the publisher for publication.[142] Quesnell placed the onus on Smith to produce the manuscript for forensic examination.[143] Smith's failure to do so looked suspicious to many and led to speculation that there was no manuscript at all (part of what Scott Brown has called the "folklore of forgery"

140. Quesnell, "Mar Saba," esp. 52; see also Quesnell, "Reply to Morton Smith," 201.

141. Quesnell, "Mar Saba," 48–49 and later restated in personal correspondence to Scott Brown, reproduced in Brown, *Mark's Other Gospel*, 34: "All the characteristics of a hoax were present; all the classic mistakes that popular summaries like Goodspeed's warn against were being made."

142. Quesnell, "Mar Saba," 51.

143. Quesnell, "Reply to Morton Smith," 200–201.

around the text).[144] Quesnell also remarked that the *Letter to Theodore* could have been created in recent times with the assistance of studies of Clement's style such as the Clement index published by Otto Stählin in 1936.[145]

The arguments for forgery were re-invigorated in 2005 in Stephen Carlson's *The Gospel Hoax*. Carlson put his legal skills as a patent attorney to the task of breaking the stalemate in the academy on the authenticity of the text. He concluded that Smith had "the means, motive, and opportunity" to create the text.[146] Carlson is careful to call *Sec. Mark* a hoax, not a forgery: "hoaxes are done with a different motive—to test the establishment, whether to expose flaws in the gatekeepers of authenticity, to exhibit one's skill and cunning, or to take pleasure in the failure of self-appointed experts to pass the test."[147] And these are precisely the motives Carlson ascribes to Smith. But what of the proof? Carlson demonstrates several indications of forgery observable in the handwriting of the manuscript, including forger's tremor, unnatural pen lifts, inconsistency of letter forms, and retouching of letters—all indicative of "drawn imitation of an eighteenth-century hand."[148] Carlson's arguments were very convincing. Many scholars who equivocated over the letter's authenticity now declared it a modern forgery; others already predisposed to dislike this "gay gospel" proclaimed loudly that Smith's forgery of the text had been proven.[149] Further evidence was provided just a few years later in Peter Jeffery's 2007 study *The Secret Gospel of Mark Unveiled*, which focuses on the apparent homoeroticism of the text. Jeffery identifies a number of double entendres—Jesus seizing the young man's "hand," the tomb as a closet[150]—that must be the product of a modern and, in Jeffery's words, "anguished soul."[151]

Subsequent scholarship on the text has shown, however, that *Sec. Mark* actually meets the expectations of proof for the discovery of ancient texts.[152] Smith acted entirely appropriately when cataloguing the manuscript: he found it in the library, photographed it, catalogued it (assigning it a specific number), and left it in the library where it belonged. It was not his

---

144. Brown, *Mark's Other Gospel*, 12.

145. Quesnell, "Mar Saba," 55.

146. Carlson, *Gospel Hoax*, 74.

147. Ibid., 78.

148. Ibid., 78–80.

149. See Burke, "Introduction," 13–14, in Burke, ed., *Ancient Gospel*.

150. Jeffery, *Secret Gospel*, 92–99.

151. Ibid., ix.

152. See particularly the defense of authenticity given in Hedrick, "*Secret Mark*."

responsibility to preserve the manuscript for future scholars.[153] But other scholars *have* seen it, though not recently, as the library seems to have lost it—likely intentionally, in order to discourage interest in the text.[154] With regards to Goodspeed's requirements (no manuscript, no photographs, no transcript), for *Sec. Mark* we have the manuscript (or at least its one-time existence is not in doubt), photographs, and transcript.[155] But could Smith have created the manuscript himself as some have claimed? Unlikely, as document examiners commissioned by *Biblical Archaeological Review* in 2009 have shown it was written by a native Greek writer;[156] also, Allan J. Pantuck has demonstrated that Smith did not have the ability to compose a text in Greek,[157] and superior photographs have surfaced, made by the librarian, showing that Carlson's so-called forger's tremor and pen lifts are just an illusion of the halftone black and white photographs published by Smith.[158] As for internal evidence, proponents of the authenticity of the text see no basis for the claim that *Sec. Mark* depicts a twentieth-century gay Jesus: the young man is not naked, as some have stated,[159] and the phrase "spend the night" may sound like a modern euphemism for sex, but it also shows up in the Gospel of Luke in a story where Jesus is urged to "spend the night" with two of his disciples (24:29).[160] To those who see homoeroticism in the text, *Sec. Mark* betrays its twentieth-century composition; but perhaps in a few decades it will be more clear that it is the *perception* of homoeroticism that is contemporary. Nevertheless, it remains possible that *Sec. Mark* is not an ancient document—it could have been created in the eighteenth-century by whoever copied the text into the back of the book found at the monastery; but it certainly was not created by Morton Smith.

The story of GJW begins in September 2012 when Harvard scholar Karen L. King delivered a paper on the text at the International Congress of Coptic Studies in Rome. The manuscript fragment came to her knowledge in 2010 when a private collector asked her for a translation. He acquired the manuscript in a batch of papyri in 1997 from a previous owner. It came with a handwritten note from a professor of Egyptology in Berlin, now deceased,

153. Against Quesnell, "Mar Saba," 49.

154. Ibid., 43.

155. Ibid., 55.

156. The reports of the two examiners, Agamemnon Tselikas and Venetia Anastasopoulou, are summarized in Hedrick, "*Secret Mark*," 33–38.

157. Pantuck, "Question of Ability."

158 As demonstrated in Viklund, "Tremors."

159. For example, Evans, *Fabricating Jesus*, 95.

160. As shown in Hedrick, "*Secret Mark*," 33.

calling the fragment the sole example of a text in which Jesus claims to have a wife. The text contains a question from the apostles about the worthiness of Mary (likely intended to be Mary Magdalene). Jesus responds, "My wife . . . she will be able to be my disciple." King submitted an article on the text to *Harvard Theological Review* and stated at the Rome colloquium that scientific testing of the manuscript was under way. In the meantime, a draft of her article was made available online.[161] King believed the manuscript was created in the fourth century,[162] but Coptic manuscripts are notoriously difficult to date. The fragment measures only 4 by 8 centimeters; the writing is splotchy and uneven but the calligraphy is consistent with other ancient Coptic manuscripts; the ink is faded, but the reverse side is even less preserved, with only a few words still visible.

Critics immediately pounced on the text. They said its contents were too good to be true; it fit too well the *Zeitgeist*, particularly after Dan Brown's novel *The Da Vinci Code* popularized the idea that Jesus was married to Mary Magdalene. Many commentators dismissed the text simply because Jesus was NOT married, though King never made any claim that the text was proof of anything about the historical Jesus. Within three days of King's announcement it was difficult to find anyone who supported its authenticity other than King and the experts she consulted to write her article. Arguments were made that the text was a mishmash of phrases from the *Gospel of Thomas*, but particularly suspicious is that the fragment reproduces a linebreak in the middle of one word from a particular critical edition of the gospel.[163] *Harvard Theological Review* finally published King's article in May of 2014 along with the results of the scientific studies of the manuscript. These studies demonstrate that the papyrus originated between 659 and 859 and the ink matches that of other papyri from the first to the eighth century; however, critics claimed the ink could be easily duplicated and the tests on the paper only demonstrated that the paper was old (a similar situation as found with the *Gospel of Josephus*). But most damning of all is the conclusions some have drawn from the image of a fragment of the Gospel of John published in King's article. This John fragment, also found among the papyri of the owner of GJW, has some alarming similarities to an authenticated

161. King, "'Jesus said to them'" (draft).

162. This date was given on the first page of the original draft of the article, but King revised the date to the eighth century in the published paper (see King, "'Jesus said to them,'" 33–37).

163. The argument was made initially by Francis Watson ("How a Fake Gospel-Fragment") and then developed by Andrew Bernhard ("Textual Evidence"). For further discussion of the reception of GJW in print and online scholarship, see the contributions to this volume by James McGrath (ch. 16) and Caroline Schroeder (ch. 15).

copy of John in Coptic found in 1923—it replicates every other line from a page of the published codex and for 17 lines the line breaks are identical; also the writing appears to be by the same hand as the GJW fragment. It would appear that the John fragment was copied from an image of the 1923 discovery perhaps found online; and if the John fragment is a forgery, critics argue, then so must be GJW.[164]

How well does GJW meet scholars' expectations for an authentic ancient text? As with *Sec. Mark*, a manuscript does exist, and this time not just in photographs, and it was made readily available for scholars to examine. We do not know what the name of the text was, since we have only a fragment, so it cannot be authenticated by looking for references to it by ancient authorities; however, the contents are similar to material from the *Gospel of Thomas*, indicating theological and literary kinship with an ancient document. The mention of a wife for Jesus is an indication of modern interests, but, as with *Sec. Mark*, care should be taken not to quickly dismiss a text simply because its portrayal of Jesus is not to one's liking. That said, the fragment's relationship to what appears to be a forged copy of the Gospel of John and the creator's apparent use of a modern critical edition of the *Gospel of Thomas* are our best indicators that GJW too is a forgery. Additionally, some sleuthing into the history of ownership of the text has shown that the documents that accompanied the papyrus also are fabricated.[165]

If *Sec. Mark* and GJW are "forgeries" then they are forgeries of a different order than the lost gospels of the nineteenth and early twentieth centuries. They both are supported by manuscripts that have been carefully catalogued, photographed, transcribed, and translated by reputable scholars. The texts have appeared in scholarly books and journals, not self-published in pamphlets or popular-market paperbacks. Also, they are far less transparently contemporary in their depictions of Jesus—yes, a gay Jesus and a married Jesus certainly capture the spirit of our times but these aspects of the texts are much more subtle than the Indian, Essene, or vegetarian Jesuses of the modern apocrypha. If the two texts are indeed forgeries, then they are very sophisticated, requiring rare skill to fabricate.

CONCLUSIONS

Many scholars in the field make a distinction between ancient apocrypha, written in the first three or four centuries, and apocryphal texts written

164. The argument was made by Christian Askeland, first online ("Jesus Had a Sister-in-Law"), and then in print as Askeland, "Lycopolitan Forgery."

165. See the discussion of the supporting documents in Bernhard, "Call for Closure."

thereafter. Apocrypha from late antiquity and the Middle Ages are often labeled hagiography, in part because the stories they tell culminate in the institution of festivals or the discovery of relics. While efforts are being made to draw these more-recent texts into the definition of "apocrypha," few scholars argue to broaden the definition even further to include the modern "lost gospels." Wilhelm Schneemelcher's comments on the modern texts are illustrative:

> ... the apocryphal texts generally, like the canonical Gospels, have their origin in the tradition of communities in which they arose. Most of them, despite their often clear theological tendencies, which are considerably different from those of the 'orthodox' literature, are based on older traditions of the communities. In contrast the modern fictions were cobbled together by individual authors from various motives (sensationalism, the quest for gain, hostility to the Church). This literature arose under quite different conditions, and is therefore not to be compared with the apocryphal gospels of the early centuries.[166]

The two great documenters of modern apocrypha, Goodspeed and Beskow, are similarly dismissive. Goodspeed says they have "baseless character," having been "dredged up from obscure depths mostly beyond the ken of educated people," and he only examined them to show that they were not "genuine documents of Christian antiquity."[167] Beskow is more irenic and occasionally excuses the texts as pious frauds. But when considering whether it is permissible to create new gospels for a modern age he says, "the Gospel forgeries are related to the real Gospels"—distinguished here as "documents of faith"—"just as false coins are to genuine coins: they are unoriginal imitations, more or less well done, and they pretend to be what they are not. Falseness cannot be a road towards creativity."[168]

But examined in comparison to ancient apocrypha, there really is little difference between the modern texts and other apocryphal texts created throughout Christian history. They all claim to be written either by an esteemed early Christian figure or their disciple, they all draw upon canonical Christian Scripture (variously reinterpreting and augmenting it), and they all seek to speak to contemporary situations in ways that canonical texts do not. If the modern texts are treated with contempt then scholars fall into the pattern of the ancient heresiologists, who declared texts outside of their own interests to be inauthentic, derivative, spurious, forged, false. Whatever

166. Schneemelcher, "General Introduction," 85.

167. Goodspeed, *Modern Apocrypha*, v.

168. Beskow, *Strange Tales*, 108.

the motives behind the creation of modern apocrypha—whimsy, lucre, to create support for theological or historical positions, to confound scholars—they are just as worthy of study as ancient apocrypha, as reflections of the interests, beliefs, practices, and knowledge of their time. They even inform the study of earlier apocrypha, because in them we can observe more clearly how apocrypha are created and how they are transformed over time, as well as how they continue to bring meaning to their readers even despite their dubious origins. Proof that Notovitch created his *Life of Saint Issa* is immaterial for the study of Ahmadiyya Islam, for example, just as evidence that a second-century presbyter from Asia Minor created the *Acts of Paul* is of little consequence for how the text functioned among encratites and Manicheans. Over time GJW also may tear free from its creator's intended purposes and scholars may be more inclined to see it too as a text reflecting the needs of a community who considers it meaningful.

In the meantime, cases like *Sec. Mark* and GJW, whether the texts are authentic or not, contribute to scholarship by forcing scholars to keep pace with forgers and learn new methods for determining the origins of the texts we study. As Anthony Grafton states, "criticism has been dependent for its development on the stimulus that forgers have provided."[169] And these texts have indeed led to re-evaluations of certain aspects of early Christianity—gospel development, the writings of Clement of Alexandria, baptism, homosexuality in the ancient world, the marital status of Jesus, the role of Mary Magdalene—and we have learned more about the vagaries of forging ancient ink and papyrus than we ever thought we would need to know. Hopefully, too, they have encouraged us to consider what it is about these texts that gave rise to accusations of forgery. We would do well to heed the words of Paul Baines, that "the discovery of forgery was never neutral,"[170] and ask what these accusations say about our own assumptions about antiquity, and how much the need to declare a text a forgery—or even "apocryphal"—is motivated not so much by a desire to understand its origins as by a distaste for its contents.

169. Grafton, *Forgers and Critics*, 123.
170. Baines, *House of Forgery*, 31.

– 13 –

The Apocryphal Tale of Jesus' Journey to India

Nicolas Notovitch and the *Life of Saint Issa* Revisited

— Bradley N. Rice —

THE LIFE OF SAINT ISSA (*Life Issa*) is undoubtedly the most famous and influential gospel forgery[1] of modern times. Published in 1894 as part of the *Unknown Life of Jesus Christ* by Nicolas Notovitch,[2] *Life Issa* tells how Jesus spent his "lost years" in India, learning the sacred teachings of Brahmins and Buddhists before returning to Palestine to begin his public ministry.[3] Notovitch claims to have discovered *Life Issa* while traveling in Kashmir and Ladakh in 1887. As the story goes, Notovitch had heard accounts of a certain "Issa" from Tibetan Buddhist monks and therefore went to the

1. Here I use "forgery" for any text written to deceive its intended readers about its true origins.

2. Originally published in French as *La vie inconnue de Jesus Christ*. *Life Issa* is found on pp. 153–228.

3. Accessible accounts of Notovitch and summaries of the *Unknown Life* may be found in Goodspeed, *Modern Apocrypha*, 3–14; Beskow, *Strange Tales*, 57–63; and Ehrman, *Forged*, 252–54. See also Grönbold, *Jesus in Indien*, 18–33; and Klatt, *Lebte Jesus in Indien?*, 46–50.

Hemis monastery so as to inquire further. Initially unable to gain access to the monastery, Notovitch was finally allowed inside after a bad fall from his horse had left him with a broken leg. While being nursed back to health by the monastery's lamas, Notovitch again inquired about Issa, and to his surprise the chief lama brought to his bedside two large Tibetan volumes containing *Life Issa*. The lama read aloud from them to Notovitch, and with the aid of an interpreter Notovitch was able to scribble down the account, later reworking the material to make it more presentable to the public. The result is the *Unknown Life of Jesus Christ*, containing both *Life Issa* as well as Notovitch's extraordinary tale of his "discovery."

Notovitch's *Unknown Life* was an immediate sensation. The book went through eight editions in Paris in 1894 alone;[4] within less than a year, English translations of the *Unknown Life* lined bookshelves on both sides of the Atlantic.[5] According to the press releases, the so-called "lost years" of Jesus had finally been found. Or had they? Within a matter of months, critical reviews of the *Unknown Life* appeared exposing the many inaccuracies of *Life Issa* and the improbabilities surrounding its existence. The renowned Indologist and Oxford professor Max Müller believed that Notovitch had been duped by the lamas at Hemis, famously saying that "[i]t is pleasanter to believe that Buddhist monks can at times be wags, than that M. Notovitch is a rogue."[6] Still others wondered whether Notovitch had even visited the Hemis monastery; and indeed he had not. J. Archibald Douglas demonstrated that a certain Russian by the name of Notovitch was apparently treated in the hospital at Leh after suffering not from a broken leg, but a toothache.[7]

In the end, the *Unknown Life of Christ* and its *Life Issa* turned out to be an elaborate hoax crafted by Notovitch himself. But why did he do it? And why should scholars of Christian apocrypha care about Notovitch and his tale? After all, Wilhelm Schneemelcher had the following to say about the *Unknown Life* and other similar modern apocrypha:

> Such works, in which fantasy, untruth, and ignorance (above all in the linguistic area) are combined, and which are in addition marked by anti-Church feeling, have nothing to do with historical research. In our context we must only raise the further

4. Thus Goodspeed, *Modern Apocrypha*, 3 n. 1.

5. There were at least three editions in the United States, all published in 1894 in translations by Crawford, Connelly and Landsberg, and Loranger; and one in Britain by Crispe in 1895.

6. Müller, "Alleged Sojourn," 521.

7. Douglas, "Chief Lama of Hemis."

question, whether these modern fictions are in any way to be compared with the apocryphal texts which are presented in this volume. Can we eventually show analogous motives for the origin of apocryphal gospels (e.g. the Infancy Gospels) and the modern Life of Jesus forgeries? This question must clearly be answered in the negative.[8]

Schneemelcher goes on to say that whereas ancient apocryphal gospels expand upon the New Testament narrative and are "always related to the Jesus who is spoken of in the canonical Gospels," such modern gospel forgeries do not do so in the same way; and even if early apocryphal gospels are not always "orthodox," they are certainly based in the traditions of their respective communities. He then continues: "In contrast the modern fictions were cobbled together by individual authors from various motives (sensationalism, the quest for gain, hostility to the Church). This literature thus arose under quite different conditions, and is therefore not to be compared with the apocryphal gospels of the early centuries."[9] To be sure, the landscape of Christian Apocrypha Studies has changed since Schneemelcher wrote. The temporal horizons have now been broadened to include many late antique and medieval apocrypha within their scope,[10] as may be seen in more recent CA collections such as *Écrits apocryphes chrétiens* (1997–2005), *Antike christliche Apokryphen* (2012),[11] and *New Testament Apocrypha: More Noncanonical Scriptures* (2016). But modern apocrypha continue to linger on the fringes. Even those scholarly books devoted to modern apocrypha, such as Goodspeed's *Modern Apocrypha* or Beskow's *Strange Tales about Jesus*, are more concerned to disprove their antiquity than to study them.[12]

8. Schneemelcher, "Gospels," 83–84.

9. Ibid., 84.

10. On the dissolution of the potential chronological limits of Christian apocrypha see especially Junod, "Apocryphes du Nouveau Testament"; and the discussions in Shoemaker, "Early Christian Apocryphal Literature," 528–32; Piovanelli, "What Is a Christian Apocryphal Text."

11. In this latest edition of the Hennecke-Schneemelcher collection, Schneemelcher's disdainful comments on modern apocrypha are replaced with a more cautious statement by Christoph Markschies ("Außerkanonische Evangelien," 352). Even here, however, modern apocrypha are said generally to relate only quite superficially ("meist nur sehr oberflächlich") to ancient Christian apocrypha.

12. Goodspeed is explicit on this point, and says that apocrypha have "for the most part been judged unworthy of serious consideration. And so they would be, but for the extravagant claims made by them . . . When increasing numbers of people are being misled by them, it is time to put our fastidiousness aside and state the facts . . . since in the study of early Christian literature we constantly seek to distinguish the genuine from the spurious, what is gathered here may at least serve as a footnote to its serious study" (*Modern Apocrypha*, vi). Beskow is generally more charitable, but still concludes

At least one way forward has been proposed by Pierluigi Piovanelli, who has urged that modern apocrypha ought not be so summarily dismissed by biblical scholars à la Schneemelcher.[13] Using the example of Levi Dowling's *Aquarian Gospel*, Piovanelli argues that we should try to understand this work as the product of a man who genuinely believed he had been commissioned by the goddess Visel to announce the coming of the "Aquarian Age." That is, the *Aquarian Gospel* cannot simply be discounted as the work of "a swindler, an adventurer looking for easy gains."[14] Even if other modern apocrypha turn out to be the work of "swindlers," it would be "unfair and inaccurate" to characterize all such texts that way.[15] But while Piovanelli has aptly demonstrated that the *Aquarian Gospel* is not simply the work of a swindler, might this not still be true of the *Unknown Life*? Beskow had written that "unlike most Gospel forgers, Notovitch had no ideological motive for writing his account of the life of Jesus" and that his primary purpose was "to arouse sensation."[16] However, a closer look at the life and times of Nicolas Notovitch reveals that the opposite is the case.

WHO WAS THIS MYSTERIOUS RUSSIAN?

Nicolas Alexandrovitch Notovitch was born in 1858 in the Crimean city of Kerch.[17] He attended university at St. Petersburg in the early 1870s, and seems to have studied literature, history, and politics. After entering the military in 1874, Notovitch was involved in a number of campaigns for the expansion of the Russian Empire, including the Russo-Turkish war of 1877–

---

toward the end of his work that "the Gospel forgeries are related to the real Gospels just as false coins are to genuine coins: they are unoriginal imitations, more or less well done, and they pretend to be what they are not. Falseness cannot be a road toward creativity" (*Strange Tales*, 109). See also Piovanelli's critique of Goodspeed and Beskow ("What Is a Christian Apocryphal Text," 33–34).

13. Piovanelli, "What Is a Christian Apocryphal Text," 31–40.

14. Ibid., 35. It is unclear whether Piovanelli sees in Notovitch just such a swindler; he also remarks that Dowling was "far from being an adventurer of the likes of the Russian journalist Nicolas Notovitch."

15. Ibid., 34.

16. Beskow, *Strange Tales*, 61–62.

17. By far the best modern resource on Notovitch's life is Klatt, *Jesus in Indien*, upon which my sketch is largely based. Klatt points out that the sources for Notovitch's life are quite few and generally derive from Notovitch's own writings. Even the bits of information on Notovitch in the Parisian *Dictionnaire national des contemporains* "gehen wahrscheinlich auf Notovitch selbst zurück und müssen daher kritisch gewertet werden" (Klatt, *Jesus in Indien*, 8). See also the entry on Notovitch in Curinier, ed., *Dictionnaire*, 3:274.

1878. Soon thereafter he embarked upon what would become an extremely productive literary career. In 1883 Notovitch acquired a post at the Russian newspaper *Novoye Vremya*, and it was as a correspondent of this paper that he would undertake his extensive travels throughout the East. Between 1883 and 1887 Notovitch was to be found in the Balkans, Caucasus, Central Asia, Persia, and India. He trekked through Kashmir and Ladakh in the autumn of 1887. After returning to Europe in 1889, Notovitch relocated to Paris and continued to work as a journalist, publishing articles in papers such as *Le Figaro*, *Le Journal*, and *La science française*. During this time he also published two important books on the Russian tsars: *L'empereur Alexandre III et son entourage* (1893) and *L'empereur Nicolas II et la politique russe* (1895).

While residing in Paris in 1894–1895, Notovitch was swept into the controversy surrounding publication of the *Unknown Life*. If the exposure of Notovitch as a fraud earned him the ire of scholars in Europe and North America, the consequences in his native Russia were still more severe: during a visit to St. Petersburg in 1895 he was arrested and exiled to Siberia. By Notovitch's own report, his literary conduct was deemed "dangerous for the state and for society."[18] Undeterred by his imprisonment, however, Notovitch continued to write. After his return in 1897, Notovitch mentioned having written a novel entitled *Un française en Sibérie*.[19] In the following year he published *L'Europe et l'Egypte* (1898), and the year after that he was received into the prestigious Société d'Histoire Diplomatique in Paris. In the years 1903–1904 Notovitch may have been living in London. This seems to be the backdrop for his next book, *La Russie et l'alliance anglaise* (1906).

After the Russian Revolution of 1905, Notovitch's footsteps become much harder to trace. According to Klatt, Notovitch may have returned to Russia, as a certain Nicolas Alexandrovitch Notovitch is listed as an editor and/or publisher in a catalogue of Russian newspapers from 1901–1916,[20] a Russian translation of *La Russie et l'alliance anglaise* appeared in 1907, and another Russian edition of the *Unknown Life* was published in 1906.[21] Was

18. As stated in the revised French edition of *Vie inconnue* published in 1900: "[L]a conduite littéraire de M. Notovitch [est] dangereuse pour l'État et pour la Société" (apud Klatt, *Jesus in Indien*, 25–26).

19. It is not clear whether this novel was ever published. The entry in the *Dictionnaire national* has "On annonce du même auteur [sc. Notovitch] une importante étude: *Un française en Sibérie*, d'après les mémoires d'une française mariée à un décembriste (révolutionnaire russe) et dont Alexandre Dumas avait parlé déjà dans son roman: *Un Maître d'armes*"). Is Notovitch here comparing himself to Dumas, who had published his *Mémoires d'un maître d'armes ou dix-huit mois à St. Pétersbourg* in 1840?

20. In *Bibliografiia periodicheskikh izdanii rossii: 1901–1916* (Leningrad, 1958), as reported in Klatt, *Jesus in Indien*, 39.

21. Klatt, *Jesus in Indien*, 38–39.

Notovitch working in St. Petersburg again? What would have motivated him to return to Russia during such turbulent times? Above all, why would a Russian journalist and political commentator write *Life Issa*? Perhaps the answers lie within the text itself.

THE *LIFE OF SAINT ISSA* AND THE LIFE OF NICOLAS NOTOVITCH

Life Issa consists of fourteen chapters of 244 verses.[22] It begins with a résumé of the message and untimely death of the prophet Issa, "the best of the sons of men" (1.1–5). *Life Issa* then looks back to the time of Moses, describing the enslavement of the Israelites in Egypt and the exodus led by "Mossa," who here actually lives to see the Israelites settle the promised land (2.1–19). Soon after, they forget the God of Israel and turn to magic (3.1–5), and later the Romans[23] invade Palestine and wreak utter destruction upon the land (3.6–12). Then, in a crucial moment of Israel's history, Issa is born (4.1–5) and begins to preach even as a child (4.5–9). At age 13, in order to escape being married off by his parents Issa joins a caravan for "Sindh" or India (4.10–13). He is welcomed by Jains after his arrival (5.1–2), and soon thereafter travels to the holy cities of India and spends six years learning to read the Vedas (5.3–5). During this time, however, Issa frequently comes into conflict with the Brahmins, insofar as he denies the divine origin of the Vedas and inveighs against the caste system (5.6–27). His life now in danger, Issa goes to "the country of the Gautamides, where the great buddha Sakyamuni was born" (6.1–2). Here he spends another six years, learning Pali and acquiring expertise in the Sutras (6.3–4). Issa is chosen by the Buddha to expound the scriptures, and therefore leaves the Himalayas and travels through various "pagan territories," continuing to preach (6.5—7.18). He even travels through Persia and preaches among the Zoroastrians (8.1–24).

This story of how Jesus spent his "lost years" with Brahmins and Buddhists in India is well known, but less familiar is how the story continues, after Issa returns to Palestine at age 29 (*Life Issa* 9–14). He preaches among the Israelites, but in so doing immediately arouses the suspicions of Pilate and the "chiefs of the towns" (9.1—10.2). Pilate wishes to have Issa arrested, but ultimately insists that the priests and "Hebrew elders" judge him instead

22. Here and throughout I have used the original 1894 French edition of the *Vie inconnue*. Translations are my own.

23. In 3.8 they are called "pagans from the country of Romeles" ("des païens . . . du pays de Romèles"), which Notovitch (*Vie inconnue*, 292) describes as the homeland of Romulus—i.e., Rome.

(10.2–3). Issa then goes to Jerusalem to preach, and engages there in discussions with the priests and elders (10.4–21) who turn out to be quite receptive to Issa's message (11.1–3). Dissatisfied, Pilate sends his subordinates to spy on Issa as Issa continues to preach in neighboring towns (11.4–15). Issa is interrogated by Pilate's spies (12.1–7), and even gives a longer, suspiciously progressive sermon on women (12.8–21). Issa continues to preach for another three years, with Pilate's spies shadowing him the entire time, though finding no reason to arrest him (13.1–2). But fearing an insurrection, Pilate has Issa arrested anyway, and orders one of his spies to fabricate charges against him (13.3). Issa is imprisoned, tortured, and brought to the tribunal (13.4–20). The priests and elders can find no reason to condemn Issa (13.20), so Pilate calls forth Issa's betrayer (presumably Judas) to bear witness against him (13.21). Issa pardons Judas, fully aware that the betrayal was not his design, and frankly condemns Pilate for his behavior (13.22). Pilate becomes enraged with Issa and condemns him to death (13.23).

What happens next is surprising. The Jewish authorities unambiguously absolve themselves of any involvement in Issa's crucifixion:

> After consulting amongst themselves, the judges said to Pilate: "We will not bring upon our heads the egregious sin of condemning an innocent man and acquitting criminals, something contrary to our laws. Do then what you please." Having said this, the priests and wise elders went out, washed their hands in a sacred vessel and said: "We are innocent of the death of this righteous man" (13.24–25).

Life Issa is explicit, therefore, that the responsibility for Jesus' crucifixion belongs to Pilate and not the Jews. This stands in remarkable contrast to the vast majority of ancient Christian narratives, from the Gospel of Mark to the *Acts of Pilate*, in which there is an increasing tendency to blame the Jews and exonerate Pilate.

What might have motivated Notovitch to paint such a different portrait of Jesus' final days? Notovitch professed to be a Christian, and his writings consistently reveal his enthusiasm for the Russian Orthodox Church.[24] At least one motive, however, emerges from the imperfect details of Notovitch's life. Somewhat surprisingly, it is Notovitch's lesser-known older brother who provides the first clue. An article published more than a century ago in the *Jewish Encyclopedia* reveals that Osip Notovitch (b. 1849) was the son

---

24. Notovitch even took care to defend his Russian Orthodoxy in the first British edition of the *Unknown Life*: "In the French journal, *La Paix*, I concisely affirmed my belief in the orthodox Russian religion, and I hold to that affirmation" (apud Klatt, *Jesus in Indien*, 13).

of a rabbi, though he became "a member of the Greek Church early in life."[25] Like his brother Nicolas, Osip was known to have written political essays; but he was also known to have defended Jews against anti-Semitic attacks when writing for the daily newspaper *Novosti*, which he edited from 1876 onwards. This means that Nicolas Notovitch was born a Jew.[26] It therefore also seems reasonable to suppose that the politically savvy Notovitch could not have been unaware of the severe situation facing Jews in late nineteenth-century Russia.

Shortly before Notovitch began working for *Novoye Vremya*, Tsar Alexander II was assassinated and his son Alexander III (r. 1881–1894) took the throne. In contrast to the liberal reforms of his father, Alexander III launched an intense policy of "Russification" in which the Russian Empire was to be united in nationality, language, and *religion*—by which he meant the Russian Orthodox Church.[27] Severe restrictions were placed upon Jews throughout the empire in ways ominously anticipating Nazi Germany. Jews could no longer own property outside the Pale of Settlement and could no longer do business on Christian holidays; the number of Jews that could attend school or become doctors was strictly controlled; edicts of expulsion were issued to Jews in Kiev and Moscow; and Jews were strictly prohibited from adopting Christian names. In the early years of Alexander III's reign, there were more than five million Jews living in Russia; after his reign had ended, nearly two million had fled.[28]

Clearly these were dark times for Jews in Russia. But whereas Osip Notovitch evidently took pains to protect Jews from rampant anti-Semitism Nicolas Notovitch publicly defended the Russian Orthodox Church. Notovitch ostensibly supported the goals and ideology of Alexander III, even referring to the tsar as the "shadow of the Orthodox God."[29] But with the intolerant and anti-Semitic policies of Alexander III, could Notovitch have publicly professed anything other than full devotion to the Orthodox Church? Notovitch does, of course, offer a very subtle defense of the Jews

25. Rosenthal and Waldstein, "Osip Konstantinovich Notovich," 341; see also Wininger, "Osip Konstantinovich Notovich," 547.

26. When Notovitch converted to Christianity is uncertain; see the discussion in Klatt, *Jesus in Indien*, 13–14.

27. Chapman, *Imperial Russia*, 123–24.

28. Ibid., 125–29; Löwe, *Antisemitismus*, 30–39.

29. Notovitch (*L'empereur Alexandre III*, 175) describes the Russian army as "pour la Russie l'ombre du Tsar bien-aimé qu'elle vénère et qui est lui-même l'ombre du Dieu orthodoxe qu'elle adore." As Klatt succinctly puts it, "Die vielen zeitgeschichtlichen Publikationen Nikolaus Notovitchs sind geprägt von einer glühenden Verehrung Rußlands und des autokratisch regierenden Zaren" (*Jesus in Indien*, 14).

in *L'empereur Alexandre III et son entourage*. Observing that several Russian diplomats have been "accused" of being Jews, Notovitch counters that their political incompetence is proof to the contrary, citing Benjamin Disraeli in England and Adolphe Crémieux in France as counterexamples.[30] But had Notovitch wished to provide a more sustained defense of the Jews, he could not have done so without seriously compromising his political and literary career. Perhaps, then, *Life Issa* provided just such an opportunity.[31]

THE APOCRYPHAL TALE OF JESUS' JOURNEY TO INDIA

If *Life Issa* was politically driven, then perhaps we can show "analogous motives" for the composition of modern apocrypha after all. Early Christian apocrypha belonging to the Pilate Cycle were politically motivated as well, and these texts also are considered forgeries.[32] If early Pilate apocrypha may be used to shed light on Jewish-Christian relations in antiquity, then why not also *Life Issa* to shed light on Jewish-Christian relations in late nineteenth-century imperial Russia?

Another respect in which *Life Issa* and other modern apocrypha should interest scholars is how they bear witness to the phenomenon of "apocryphicity" or the "apocryphal impulse"—that inexorable drive toward

30. "Leur incapacité notoire et la preuve du contraire. Le savoir-faire, la finesse, la souplesse, la rapidité dans la décision, l'habileté à se tirer d'un mauvais pas sont les qualités instinctives du juif" (Notovitch, *L'empereur Alexandre III*, 154). Notovitch further comments that "un juif diplomate doit se trouver maître de la situation partout où il se trouve. Partout et toujours il fait tête à l'orage et conserve de l'allure" (ibid., 154–55). Notovitch's engagement with Judaism *might* also be shown by a tract entitled *The Truth about the Jews* (Russ. *Pravda ob evreyakh*) published in Moscow in 1889. Although the contents of this book remain inaccessible outside of Russia, Klatt describes it as a critical engagement with Judaism that "deutlich macht, dass Notovitch sich offenbar auch innerlich von der Religion seiner Väter abgewandt hat" (*Jesus in Indien*, 18). This is assuming, of course, that Notovitch actually wrote the book. If *The Truth about the Jews* is as anti-Semitic as some sources seem to indicate, one wonders if this might not be a forgery written in Notovitch's name, perhaps written during the pogroms of the early 1880s.

31. Apparently *Life Issa* enjoyed a positive reception among some Jews in France. Ferdinand Gombault observes that one contemporary author had written in *La Vrai Parole* that "si je m'appelais le baron de Rothschild, j'acquerrais la propriété du livre de M. Notovitch, et le répandrais en une dizaine de millions d'exemplaires dans tous les pays chrétiens" ("Christianisme et Bouddhisme," *Revue de Lille* 22 (1910) 1010 [apud Klatt, *Jesus in Indien*, 72–73, n. 183]).

32. Most of these texts may be found in the collection of Ehrman and Pleše, *Apocryphal Gospels*, 419–585. For more on the motivations behind their composition, see Ehrman, *Forged*, 152–59.

the apocryphal in retelling the story of Christian origins. Piovanelli quite rightly points out that apocryphicity is just as lively today as it was in antiquity, as may be seen not only in modern texts such as the *Aquarian Gospel*, but also modern novels such as Nikos Kazantzakis' *Last Temptation of Christ* and its film adaptation by Martin Scorsese. These new apocryphal tales are not simply borne of the desire to tell an entertaining story, but reflect what we might call a "remythologization" of Christian origins. By this Piovanelli means, following the language of Jean-Claude Picard, the need of a community "to retell and to adapt, from one epoch to another one, the story of its origins."[33] In other words, the story of Jesus is retold in terms that are meaningful for the present.

I suggest that one such remythologization of Christian origins is what we may call the "Jesus in India narrative" (JiIN).[34] By this I mean a much larger apocryphal narrative that locates Jesus in India, of which Notovitch's *Unknown Life* is perhaps the most important representative. When Notovitch wrote in the late nineteenth century, the story of Jesus had just begun to be retold in ways that reimagined him as a traveler to the more distant East. British and French colonialism had opened up vast expanses of Asia to Europeans for the first time in history, revealing Buddhist texts which were thought to predate the New Testament and yet contained many of the same teachings as Jesus. Had one religion influenced the other? This was certainly the answer of some scholars.[35] It was the Jesus in India narrative, however, that offered the perfect solution to this dilemma: Jesus had in fact gone to the East and studied with Buddhists before returning to Palestine to preach. Thus, the story of Jesus' early years was "remythologized" to reconcile the teachings of both East and West.

The earliest traces of the JiIN are to be found, as it turns out, in a forgery: the so-called *Ezourvedam*.[36] This is a long dialogue between two Indian sages, in which the wise Chumantou (Sumantou) repeatedly criticizes his interlocutor, Biach (Vyāsa), for bringing ignorance, superstition, and idolatry to humankind. Chumantou insists that the teachings of the Vedas

33. Piovanelli, "What Is a Christian Apocryphal Text," 37; Picard, "Les chemins de la mythologie chrétienne," 259. Piovanelli further comments that "the apocryphal reinvention of the origins is, in my opinion, an almost universal phenomenon that can contribute to save a living tradition from the oblivion that is in store for it, constantly re-actualizing and re-legitimizing such a tradition as time goes by" ("What Is a Christian Apocryphal Text," 39).

34. I have adapted this abbreviation from Grönbold's "JiIL" (*Jesus-in-Indien-Legende*), preferring the term "narrative" to "legend" (see Grönbold, *Jesus in Indien*, 9).

35. E.g., Seydel, *Evangelium von Jesu*; Lillie, *Influence of Buddhism*.

36. On the *Ezourvedam* generally, see Ludo Rocher, *Ezourvedam*.

have been perverted from their original form, and thus the *Ezourvedam* was to serve as a corrective and offer the true meaning of the Vedas. Although it was supposed to have originally been written in Sanskrit, the *Ezourvedam* survives solely in a French translation that was used and popularized by none other than Voltaire, who is said to have received a copy of it in 1760 from a certain Laurent de Féderbe, Chevalier de Maudave. Voltaire was fascinated by the *Ezourvedam*'s apparent revelation of a form of Indian religion which was in essential agreement with and yet preceded Christianity.[37] Of course, only a few short years after Voltaire died the *Ezourvedam* was shown to be a forgery. It turned out to have been written by Catholic missionaries in Pondichéry, who had apparently begun the process of translating their own "Christian Vedas" into Sanskrit.[38] There is no little irony in the fact that one of Voltaire's weapons in his assault on Christianity turned out to be a Christian tract intended to win converts.

But though the *Ezourvedam* certainly hinted at some contact of Jesus with the East, it is only with the writings of Louis Jacolliot and François Laouenan that we find concrete indications that Jesus may actually have visited India. In his book *La Bible dans l'Inde: Vie de Iezeus Christna* (1869), Louis Jacolliot suggests that Jesus *must* have been studying in Egypt and perhaps also India, for it is the only way to explain the "moral revolution" that Jesus brought about.[39] For Jacolliot, ancient India was the source of the highest morality and spirituality, and if Jesus preached the same, he surely must have gone there.

A similar opinion was expressed several years later by François Laouenan, who had worked as a Catholic missionary at Pondichéry and published a massive work entitled *Du brahmanisme et de ses rapports avec le judaïsme et le christianisme*. Laouenan considered India the wellspring from which Egypt, Greece, and other civilizations have drawn their knowledge and culture.[40] Laouenan further reports what he learned about Jesus from

37. At a time when research on the Vedas had scarcely begun, Voltaire dated the text to some time before Alexander the Great.

38. Rocher (*Ezourvedam*, 65–66) suggests that even the name *Ezourvedam* may have been a coded way of referring to the "gospel" (*vedam*) of "Jesus" (*Ezour*, being another form of *Yezous*).

39. Jacolliot, *Bible dans l'Inde*, 348–49: "Puis, enfin, que fit-il de douze ans à trente ans? . . . [L]a vérité est que le Christ, pendant cette période de temps, étudia en Égypte, *peut-être même* dans l'Inde, les livres sacrés, réservés depuis des siècles aux initiés . . ." (italics mine).

40. "En un mot, les mages de l'Égypte, les sages de la Grèce, les philosophes et les législateurs de tous les peuples, Moïse et Jésus-Christ lui-même, seraient venus tour-à-tour apprendre à l'école des Brahmes les doctrines et les sciences qui étaient cultivées dans l'Inde depuis l'antiquité la plus reculée" (Laouenan, *Du brahmanisme et de ses*

a Protestant minister in Bangalore: Jesus' preaching had been borrowed (*empruntée*) from the other great religions, about which Jesus learned by sitting alongside a caravan route in Palestine.[41] According to others whom Laouenan encountered, Jesus had in fact gone to India and studied with the Brahmins.[42]

These early developments of the JiIN in the cultural context of the nineteenth century had clearly paved the way for Notovitch's *Unknown Life*. As part of this larger narrative, *Life Issa* provided the perfect climax: conclusive evidence that Jesus had been to India. It turned out, of course, to be a hoax, as did the *Ezourvedam*. But the story continued to be told. Just a few short years after Notovitch was unmasked as a fraud, a book appeared in Urdu entitled *Masih hindustan mein* ("Christ in India").[43] It was written by Mirza Ghulam Ahmad (1835–1908), the renowned founder of the Ahmadiyya Muslim Community. In his book Ahmad claims not only that Jesus survived the crucifixion, but also that he traveled to Kashmir to preach to the lost tribes of Israel and there died of old age.[44] His tomb is said to be found in Srinagar at *Roza Bal*, the "place of the tomb." Ahmad's *Masih hindustan mein* thus began to weave another important strand into the JiIN, which was now expanded to include both Jesus' youth *and* his old age.[45]

Although the *Unknown Life* seems to have had minimal impact upon Ahmad himself,[46] Notovitch's tale has been incorporated into the writings of Ahmadiyya Muslims, according to whom Jesus returned to India after his crucifixion precisely because he had spent his youth there.[47] In their

---

rapports, 1:ii).

41. Ibid., 1:7. Laouenan further comments that "l'Enfant Jésus entendait leurs récits et les questionnait; et c'est ainsi que Dieu lui fit connaître la vérité sur la morale et sur le dogme."

42. Ibid., 1:7–8. Incidentally, the fact that both Laouenan and Jacolliot had previously suggested that Jesus had some contact with India was not lost on the public in France, such that Notovitch was compelled to acknowledge their work in the 1900 French edition of the *Vie inconnue* (Klatt, *Jesus in Indien*, 66).

43. Mirza Ghulam Ahmad, *Masih hindustan mein.*

44. For more on Mirza Ghulam Ahmad's claims concerning Jesus, see Walter, *Ahmadīya Movement*, 90–94.

45. On this other important trajectory of the JiIN, see especially Beskow, *Jesus i Kashmir*; summarized in Beskow, *Strange Tales*, 63–64; and Beskow, "Modern Mystifications," 461–64.

46. According to Beskow, Ahmad knew about *Life Issa* as well as Max Müller's devastating criticism of it, "but he seems not to have understood the gravity of the latter, and his teaching is not consistent with Notovitch's story" ("Modern Mystifications," 462).

47. Among those supporting and expanding upon Ahmad's claims are Khwaja Nazir Ahmad, *Jesus in Heaven on Earth*; Kashmiri, *Christ in Kashmir*; and more recently

search for the footsteps of Jesus in India, popular authors such as Andreas Faber-Kaiser and Holger Kersten manage to weave together the strands woven by Notovitch and Ahmad into an even lengthier tapestry of Jesus' life embroidered with other apocryphal tales.[48] Faber-Kaiser, for instance, cites *A Correct Transcript of Pilate's Court*, another modern apocryphon that purports to be an account of the trial and death of Jesus made by Pilate for the emperor Tiberius.[49] The *Crucifixion of Jesus, by an Eyewitness*, telling how Jesus survived the crucifixion and was hidden away by Essenes, factors into Kersten's account of the Essenes and has been employed by the Ahmadiyya movement as well.[50] Faber-Kaiser's interpretation of the *Acts of Thomas* implies that Jesus lived to join the apostle Thomas in his missionary travels to India.[51] Even the Shroud of Turin is pressed into service to show that Jesus was not really dead when taken down from the cross.[52]

FROM MADAME BLAVATSKY TO EDGAR CAYCE: EXPLORING LOST APOCRYPHAL CONTINENTS

Thus the Jesus in India narrative, from the *Ezourvedam* to Kersten's *Jesus Lived in India*, illustrates an intricate web of apocryphicity that has not only supplied the "missing years" of Jesus' life between ages twelve and thirty, but has also added quite a few more years to his life after his apparent death. Use of the narrative by Ahmadiyya Muslims further shows how the JiIN may be employed even today by religious communities. Forgeries such as *Life Issa*

Hassnain, *Search for the Historical Jesus*; Hassnain and Dahan, *Fifth Gospel*.

48. Faber-Kaiser, *Jesus Died in Kashmir*; Kersten, *Jesus Lived in India*.

49. Faber-Kaiser, *Jesus Died in Kashmir*, 22–35. For overviews of the text, see Goodspeed, *Modern Apocrypha*, 28–44; Beskow, *Strange Tales*, 51–56.

50. Kersten, *Jesus Lived in India*, 98–109. For overviews of the text, see Goodspeed, *Modern Apocrypha*, 20–27; Beskow, *Strange Tales*, 42–50.

51. According to Faber-Kaiser, "Following Jesus's trail further east, we find traditions that he passed through the locality of Taxila, in Pakistan, not far from the border of Kashmir. According to the Apocryphal *Acta Thomae* ('Acts of Thomas'), Thomas was there for the wedding of a son of Gad, brother to King Gondafras, and, after the ceremonies had finished, '... Thomas left his place. The bridegroom then drew back the curtain that separated him from his bride, and saw Thomas, as he tought [*sic*], talking to her. Surprised, he asked him, 'How is it that you are here? Did I not see you leave?' And the Lord answered, "I am not Judas Thomas, but his brother"' (*Jesus Died in Kashmir*, 80; cf. *Acts Thom.* 11.2–5). The *Acts of Thomas* is also discussed in some detail by Kersten, *Jesus Lived in India*, 179–86.

52. Faber-Kaiser, *Jesus Died in Kashmir*, 28–35; Kersten, *Jesus Lived in India*, 131–169. For more on Kersten's understanding of the shroud, see Kersten and Gruber, *Jesus Conspiracy*.

and the *Crucifixion of Jesus, by an Eyewitness*, for instance, have come to have a nearly "canonical" status within the Ahmadiyya Community. This is not wholly unlike how many ancient Christian apocrypha, including not a few forgeries, held a similar significance for early Christian communities across the Mediterranean.

In North America and Europe, the JiIN has played a particularly important role in forms of religion commonly classed as "New Age." These are holistic, syncretistic, and usually "alternative" spiritualities that attempt to combine the insights of science and religion as well as the teachings of both East and West.[53] The religious philosophy known as "theosophy"[54] is perhaps the most important predecessor of this new spirituality. Its teachings are said to be based on the so-called *Book of Dzyan*, an obscure document that was discussed at length by Helena Blavatsky in her massive two-volume work *The Secret Doctrine*.[55] Blavatsky claims to have discovered the *Book of Dzyan* in a Himalayan cave while traveling in Tibet, and describes it as a collection of palm leaves written in an otherwise unknown language called Senzar.[56] Its language being inaccessible, Blavatsky was forced to rely on commentaries in Sanskrit, Tibetan, and Chinese in order to recover its contents.[57] As pieced together and translated from these commentaries, the *Book of Dzyan* is said to contain the esoteric doctrines of theosophy, which Blavatsky herself claims to have reproduced faithfully in the *Secret Doctrine*.

In the end, there was no *Book of Dzyan*; it was an invention by Blavatsky herself. Even her alleged travels in Tibet proved to have been plagiarized.[58] Blavatsky thus made the same move as Notovitch, fabricating both an "ancient" book as well as the tale of its discovery; and it may well be that Notovitch was partly inspired by Blavatsky's *Secret Doctrine*.[59] But unlike Notovitch's *Life Issa*, Blavatsky's insights were not based solely on a

---

53. This is my own tentative definition. On the many difficulties involved in defining the term "New Age," see Chryssides, "Defining the New Age"; Hanegraaff, *New Age Religion*. On the use of the JiIN in "New Age" spiritualities, see also the discussion by Joseph, "Jesus in India?," 180–83.

54. Hammer defines theosophy as the "vast panorama of esoteric cosmology and history presented in the theosophical literature" which "constitutes a myth purporting to definitively answer the basic questions regarding the origin, nature, and destiny of man" (*Claiming Knowledge*, 81).

55. Blavatksy, *Secret Doctrine*. On Blavatsky generally, see Cranston, *HPB*.

56. Blavatsky, *Secret Doctrine*, 1:1 and 1:37.

57. Ibid., 1:23. Elsewhere she states that the *Book of Dzyan* is to be found "scattered throughout hundreds and thousands of Sanskrit MSS" (1:xxiii).

58. Hammer, *Claiming Knowledge*, 131.

59. So, e.g., Beskow, *Strange Tales*, 62 (and 122 n. 73); Klatt, *Jesus in Indien*, 70–71; Fader, *Issa Tale*, 85–86.

lost book that could never be found. She allegedly communicated spiritually with gurus called *mahatmas* who continually provided her with knowledge and insight from a spiritual realm.[60] India and Tibet played an important role in this spiritual universe, for they were the homelands of the *mahatmas*. Sanskrit could still be called the "language of the gods"[61] and a trip to India was thought an allegorical representation of the first steps of an initiate into theosophy.[62] Tibet, on the other hand, was prized by Blavatsky for its relative inaccessibility, much like the *Book of Dzyan* itself.[63]

In some respects, Blavatsky set the stage for the reception of Notovitch and the JiIN into theosophy and "New Age" spirituality. If Indian and Tibetan wisdom could be acquired through spiritual channels, the JiIN need no longer be dependent on forgeries such as *Life Issa*. It could now be accessed by what would become known as the "Akashic records," a kind of spiritual or cosmic repository of all events and knowledge accessible only to the few.[64] Thus when Levi Dowling wrote his *Aquarian Gospel*, he claimed only to be discerning the ethereal vibrations of the ākāśa.[65] Any similarities to Notovitch's *Life Issa*—and there are many—would then only mean that Jesus' travels in the East are simply what actually happened, and potentially accessible by anyone in the ākāśa.

One of the more remarkable integrations of modern apocrypha and the JiIN into new spiritualities may be seen in Edgar Cayce. While in a trance, Cayce was said to be able not only to access the Akashic records, but also diagnose illnesses and describe past lives. In 1931 he founded the Association for Research and Enlightenment (A.R.E.) in order to disseminate his psychic "readings," and the organization continues even today with a renewed focus on spirituality and holistic healing.[66] With Cayce's readings we enter an astonishing universe of apocryphicity: Cayce combines not only existing modern apocrypha with his own apocryphal retellings, but

60. Hammer, *Claiming Knowledge*, 59–60.

61. Ibid., 124.

62. Blavatsky, *Isis Unveiled*, 1:19.

63. As Klatt puts it, Tibet was a land which "den Theosophen als das unzugängliche mystische Land gilt, aus dem geheimnisvolle Meister durch medialbegabte Menschen ihre Botschaften senden" (*Jesus in Indien*, 73).

64. Hanegraaff describes the Akashic records as a "universal memory of the Logos or world-soul" (*New Age Religion*, 255). On Blavatsky as the source of this concept, see Hammer, *Claiming Knowledge*, 125. We might think of it as a kind of "spiritual internet."

65. Piovanelli, "What Is a Christian Apocryphal Text," 35–36. Dowling called the ākāśa the "Book of God's Remembrance."

66. Hanegraaff, *New Age Religion*, 35–36. See also the website www.edgarcayce.org/.

also extends the JiIN into an even more distant past—to the lost continent of Atlantis.

According to Cayce, Jesus is the avatar of a divine wisdom that began in Atlantis, a civilization far more spiritually and technologically advanced than our own.[67] Before this "lost continent" was swallowed by the sea, a number of Atlanteans are said to have emigrated to Egypt.[68] Egypt is then depicted as the cradle of all monotheistic religions, especially Judaism.[69] At this point the Essenes enter the story, and these Cayce considers members of what he calls the "Great White Brotherhood," an ancient cult of divine wisdom going back to the Atlanteans. The Essenes are said to be their representatives in Palestine, though they also have a presence in Egypt.[70] According to Cayce, Jesus became the receptacle for this divine wisdom when Joseph and Mary had taken him to Egypt as a child. The readings are not consistent about the length of this Egyptian sojourn; it may have been two and a half years, four years, or five years.[71] There Jesus studied "eastern" records in Heliopolis along with John the Baptist, and was subsequently initiated into the Great White Brotherhood in the Pyramids of Giza.[72]

After Jesus' initiation into the Brotherhood and brief return to Palestine, he undertakes further travels to Persia and India. One reading gives the itinerary as follows:

> Here, after the period again of presentation at the Temple, when there were those questionings among the groups of the leaders, the entity was then sent again into Egypt for only a short period, and then into India, and then into what is now Persia. Hence in all the ways of the teachers the entity was trained. From Persia he was called to Judea at the death of Joseph, and then into Egypt for the completion of the preparation as a teacher. He was with John, the Messenger, during the portion of the training there in Egypt.[73]

67. Ibid., 310, 317; Furst, *Edgar Cayce's Story of Jesus*, 173.

68. Hammer, *Claiming Knowledge*, 108; Hanegraaff, *New Age Religion*, 310, 313.

69. Hammer, *Claiming Knowledge*, 114.

70. Hanegraaff, *New Age Religion*, 316. Cayce further located their headquarters at Mount Carmel and connected them to the prophet Elijah.

71. Readings [=R] 1010–17 and 5749–7; Furst, *Edgar Cayce's Story of Jesus*, 165, 167; Read, *Edgar Cayce on Jesus*, 63–64.

72. R 1010–17 and 2067; Furst, *Edgar Cayce's Story of Jesus*, 166, 171; Read, *Edgar Cayce on Jesus*, 71; Hanegraaff, *New Age Religion*, 313–14.

73. R 5749–7; Furst, *Edgar Cayce's Story of Jesus*, 167.

Again, the readings are not consistent. In other readings Jesus is said to have been sent first to Persia and later to India,[74] to have traveled between his twelfth and fifteenth or sixteenth year,[75] and to have spent at least three years in India.[76] He was in Persia when his father died, and in India when John the Baptist went to Egypt at age 17.[77] The names of his teachers in India, Persia, and Egypt are said to have been Kahijan, Junner, and Zar, respectively.[78] Cayce is also emphatic that Jesus spent far more time studying abroad than in Palestine: "The periods of study in Palestine were only at the time of His sojourn in the Temple or in Jerusalem during those periods when He was quoted by Luke as being among the Rabbi [sic], or teachers. His studies in Persia, India, and Egypt covered much greater periods."[79]

So does Cayce fill in Jesus' "missing years." Although it is certainly possible that Cayce was influenced by Notovitch's *Life Issa*, the vague references in his readings make it more likely that he has been influenced by the Jesus in India narrative as mediated by Dowling and others.[80] The prominence given to the Essenes here has no doubt been inspired by modern apocrypha such as the *Letter of Benan*[81] or the *Crucifixion of Jesus, by an Eyewitness.* Sometimes Cayce simply adds further details to the infancy story as told by Matthew and Luke. The Magi, for instance, are said to have come from the very three countries Jesus was to visit, and they are present at Jesus' dedication in the temple.[82] John the Baptist's mother Elizabeth is an Essene, and there is an additional appearance of the angel Gabriel after the child John leaps in Elizabeth's womb.[83]

74. R 1010–17; Furst, *Edgar Cayce's Story of Jesus*, 166.

75. R 2067–11; Furst, *Edgar Cayce's Story of Jesus*, 170.

76. Read, *Edgar Cayce on Jesus*, 70.

77. R 5749–7 and R 2067–11; Furst, *Edgar Cayce's Story of Jesus*, 167, 170; Read, *Edgar Cayce on Jesus*, 171.

78. R 5749–2; Furst, *Edgar Cayce's Story of Jesus*, 170.

79. R 2067; Furst, *Edgar Cayce's Story of Jesus*, 169.

80. When Cayce was once asked why the Bible had so little to say about Jesus' education, he responded that "There are some that have been forged manuscripts" (Furst, *Edgar Cayce's Story of Jesus*, 172). Might this have been a quiet nod to Notovitch?

81. On the *Letter of Benan* see Goodspeed, *Modern Apocrypha*, 50–57.

82. Read, *Edgar Cayce on Jesus*, 47, 52. Cf. Matt 2:1–2 and Luke 2:21–40.

83. Read, *Edgar Cayce on Jesus*, 35. Cf. Luke 1:5–8 and 1:41.

THE APOCRYPHAL IMPULSE
FROM THE FIRST CENTURY TO THE TWENTY-FIRST

From Notovitch to Cayce, the narrative process that unfolds in the JiIN is not unlike that seen in ancient Christian apocrypha in general and the infancy gospels in particular. The desire to fill in the missing years of Jesus' childhood, for example, is already seen in the Gospel of Matthew, which tells of Jesus' birth in Bethlehem, the visit of the Magi, and the flight of Jesus and his parents to Egypt. Luke expands the tale to include the birth of John the Baptist as well as Jesus' visit to the temple at age twelve. The *Protevangelium of James* expands the backstory offered by Luke to include further details on the birth and childhood of his mother Mary, while the *Infancy Gospel of Thomas* tells of the child Jesus' scandalous exploits before age twelve.[84] The *Gospel of Pseudo-Matthew* revises and expands on the *Protevangelium of James*, recounting additional adventures of the holy family in Egypt, in some manuscripts even integrating *Infancy Thomas*.[85] Infancy gospels such as the *Arabic Infancy Gospel* and *Armenian Infancy Gospel* only continue to add colorful threads to the already intricate tapestry of Jesus' childhood.[86]

But the ancient story of Jesus' life skips from the twelve-year-old Jesus in the temple to his ministry activities at age thirty. What was Jesus doing in his teens and twenties? Was he simply working as a carpenter in Galilee? Did he undertake any travels as a younger man? Perhaps it should come as no surprise that Jesus' story was ready for a new chapter. But following the Enlightenment and the advent of higher biblical criticism, Jesus' story could not quite be told as it had been in antiquity; sources and facts were now needed. Thus when Notovitch published his *Unknown Life*, he not only invented the story of Jesus' eastern travels but also the details of how *Life Issa* was found and how it related to contemporary scholarship. Similarly, when Ahmadiyya Muslims expanded the story of Jesus into a life lived well after the crucifixion, they could point to his tomb in Srinagar as evidence. As in antiquity, forgeries continue to be a part of this narrative process. We need only recall that the most popular infancy gospel in antiquity, the *Protevangelium of James*, claimed to have been written by none other than James, the brother of Jesus. So too the *Book of Dzyan* was forged by Helena

84. For texts, translations, and introductions see Ehrman and Pleše, *Apocryphal Gospels*, 3–71.

85. For discussion of the manuscripts, see Ehrman and Pleše, *Apocryphal Gospels*, 74–75; text and translation may be found on pp. 78–113.

86. A concise introduction to these and other infancy gospels may be found in Burke, *Secret Scriptures Revealed*, 52–54; on the *Armenian Infancy Gospel*, see now Terian, *Armenian Gospel of the Infancy*.

Blavatsky; the *Crucifixion of Jesus* was plagiarized from a German novel; the purportedly revealed *Aquarian Gospel* relied heavily on Notovitch's *Life Issa*. Even non-textual forgeries may come into play, such as the use of the Shroud of Turin by Faber-Kaiser and Kersten.

Even today, forgeries continue to play a role in the apocryphal retelling of Christian origins. The most famous forgery of this century is no doubt the *Gospel of Jesus' Wife*. To be sure, this gospel is not part of the JiIN sketched here. But it would be fair to say that it belongs to another remythologization of Jesus' story that makes him relevant to the twenty-first century: the marriage of Jesus and Mary Magdalene narrative. Apocryphal speculation on Jesus' marital status is surely the most widespread and seductive apocryphal story of our times. Were Jesus and Mary sexually involved? Did they get married and have children? And if so, do they have any living descendants? If all that begins to sound a little like *The Da Vinci Code*, it should. Dan Brown's bestselling novel is certainly one of the most important champions of this larger apocryphal narrative. Others would include the aforementioned *Last Temptation of Christ* by Kazantzakis, *The Holy Blood and the Holy Grail* by Baigent, Leigh, and Lincoln,[87] or the more recent *The Lost Gospel* by Wilson and Jacobovici.[88]

Like the JiIN, the Jesus and Mary Magdalene narrative is readily understandable within our own modern context. The publication of the Nag Hammadi writings together with the sexual revolution and civil rights movements of the 1960s and 1970s undoubtedly fueled the flame of this story. The publication of the *Gospel of Philip* revealed a Mary Magdalene who was in a special relationship with Jesus,[89] adding fresh brushstrokes to the striking portrait of Mary's apostleship seen in the *Gospel of Mary*.[90] In the wake of *The Da Vinci Code*, the idea that Jesus might have been married has contributed to a certain distrust of the Catholic Church, bound up with suspicions that the Vatican has hidden away earlier, more authentic gospels in a well-orchestrated conspiracy.[91] In the context of this larger apocryphal

87. Baigent, et al., *Holy Blood and the Holy Grail*. For a compelling discussion of this book and its relation to *The Da Vinci Code*, see Aaronovitch, *Voodoo Histories*, 187–218.

88. Jacobovici and Wilson, *Lost Gospel*.

89. For a reassessment of Jesus and Mary Magdalene's relationship in the *Gospel of Philip* in light of the *Gospel of Jesus' Wife*, see King, "Place of the *Gospel of Philip*."

90. On the discovery of the *Gospel of Mary* in the nineteenth century and its eventual publication in the 1950s, see King, *Gospel of Mary of Magdala*, 7–12.

91. In Brown's *The Da Vinci Code*, the fictional character Leigh Teabing scornfully remarks that "the Vatican, in keeping with their tradition of misinformation, tried very hard to suppress the release of these [sc. Nag Hammadi] scrolls" (p. 234). On the (mis) use of the *Gospel of Philip* and *Gospel of Mary* in *The Da Vinci Code* more generally, see Ehrman, *Truth and Fiction*, 175–79. Similar ideas are found in the film *Stigmata*,

284 Fakes, Forgeries, and Fictions

narrative, should we really be surprised that the *Gospel of Jesus' Wife* has appeared? Like Notovitch's *Unknown Life* long before, in our own time it seems not to take much to persuade a willing audience. Perhaps a better understanding of the larger apocryphal narratives surrounding texts like *Life Issa* or the *Gospel of Jesus' Wife* will offer us something of an Archimedean point from which we might assess alleged forgeries. As we continue to investigate these and other modern apocrypha in the years to come, perhaps the question ought not be "What do they say about Jesus" but "What do they say about us?"

---

which—among other things—features an Aramaic *Gospel of Thomas*. For an excellent discussion of the movie and its use of *Gos. Thom.*, see Painchaud, "Un évangile secret au Box Office."

– 14 –

Expanding the Apocryphal Corpus
Some "Novel" Suggestions

— Eric M. Vanden Eykel —

THE QUESTION OF WHICH texts should be included under the rubric "Christian apocrypha" is not new. One of the more common answers to it has been that the category should be restricted to works that were written with an eye toward achieving canonical status, but that for whatever reason, were ultimately not granted such status.[1] Aside from the historically problematic and somewhat arbitrary drawing of chronological boundaries, one of the chief issues with this definition is that it presumes a shared motive for the production of apocryphal texts: "making it" into the canon of Christian Scripture. Stephen Shoemaker captures the heart of the matter well: "[The] establishment of the New Testament canon as the literary and theological norms that define the apocrypha makes it difficult to understand the varied purpose and function of Christian apocrypha."[2] And if the history of modern exegesis has taught us anything, it is that gauging authorial intent is a notoriously sticky task.

While the definition noted above remains influential, it has not gone unchallenged. In a seminal 1983 article, for example, Éric Junod called for

---

1. See, e.g., the definition in Schneemelcher, "General Introduction," 9.
2. Shoemaker, "Between Scripture and Tradition," 493.

an expansion of the traditional boundaries. His oft-cited definition is as follows:

> [Christian apocrypha are] anonymous or pseudepigraphical texts of Christian origin which maintain a connection with the books of the New Testament as well as the Old Testament because they are devoted to events described or mentioned in these books, or because they are devoted to events that take place in the expansion of events described or mentioned in these books, because they focus on persons appearing in these books, or because their literary genre is related to those of the biblical writings.[3]

Junod's definition allows for the inclusion of apocryphal writings that post-date Athanasius's *39th Festal Letter* of 367 CE, which is typically cited as the earliest extant articulation of the New Testament canon. By removing the dating criterion from the equation, Junod effectively opens the floodgates so that any text 1) written anonymously or pseudepigraphically, 2) that originates from within a Christian circle, and 3) that is somehow "connected" with the Old and New Testaments becomes a legitimate object of inquiry for scholars of the Christian apocrypha. Many of the essays in the current volume exhibit the fruits of this more inclusive approach.

In this essay I aim to build on what is in my estimation a wholly positive trend by asking what it would look like to broaden our already-extended parameters even further. Specifically, what would it mean to remove the criterion that is currently keeping the remaining waters at bay, namely, that of anonymity/pseudepigraphy? I explore this question by means of four relatively recent novels: Christopher Moore's *Lamb: The Gospel According to Biff, Christ's Childhood Pal* (2002); Bruce W. Longenecker's *Lost Letters of Pergamum* (2003); Naomi Alderman's *The Liar's Gospel* (2012); and Colm Tóibín's *The Testament of Mary* (2012). In contrast to certain other "modern apocrypha" like the *Life of Saint Issa, A Correct Transcript of Pilate's Court*, and others, none of the works addressed here were penned with the goal of deceiving their audiences into thinking that they are ancient.[4] Though pseudonymous, their empirical authors are all known, and all were consciously written as works of Christian fiction. I chose these four not necessarily on the basis of literary merit (some are better than others), but

---

3. Junod, "Apocryphes du Nouveau Testament?" 409–14. ET cited in Shoemaker, "Between Scripture and Tradition," 495.

4. For other examples of modern apocrypha, see Goodspeed, *Modern Apocrypha*; Beskow, *Strange Tales*; and the chapters in this volume by Bradley N. Rice and Tony Burke.

because they are relatively current and because they correspond in many ways to their more "traditional" apocryphal cousins in terms of style, form, and content.

In what follows I address in turn each of the four books mentioned above in order to provide a broad overview of their contents and to highlight some of their more significant plot points. I also note instances where these texts seem to resonate with more ancient Christian literature (canonical and apocryphal). Each section includes a brief biography of the relevant author to help provide context.

LAMB: THE GOSPEL ACCORDING TO BIFF, CHRIST'S CHILDHOOD PAL (2002)

Christopher Moore is a comic fantasy author whose corpus includes a series of vampire novels, with such titles as *Bloodsucking Fiends: A Love Story* (1995), *You Suck: A Love Story* (2007), and *Bite Me: A Love Story* (2010). He explores some new ground in *Lamb: The Gospel according to Biff, Christ's Childhood Pal*, where he focuses on the life of Jesus (here Josh/Joshua) from age six until his crucifixion. The novel begins when the angel Raziel resurrects a man named Biff, one of Josh's lesser-known disciples. Biff is charged with writing a new gospel detailing the experiences that he and Josh had shared before he began his ministry. In order to ensure that his story remains true to what actually happened, Biff is imprisoned by Raziel in the Hyatt Regency St. Louis until he completes his task.[5]

Biff's antics and asides propel the narrative forward in a lively fashion. He describes himself as being deeply in love with Josh's mother (most people are, he says), and he claims to have invented the pencil, sarcasm, the cinnamon latte, and any joke that begins with "two Jews walked into a bar." The two Jews, of course, are him and Josh (*Lamb*, 68).[6] His first encounter with Josh is when they are both six years old and Biff sees Josh and his

---

5. As far as angels go, Raziel is not particularly bright. He is the one sent to announce Jesus' birth to the shepherds, for example, but he does not make it to the stable on time. In fact, he is about ten years late, and he ends up announcing Jesus' birth to Jesus and Biff. While Biff is working on his new gospel, Raziel watches television compulsively and becomes obsessed with Spider-Man, professional wrestling, and above all, soap operas. At one point he procures a copy of *Soap Opera Digest*, which he refers to as a book of prophecies.

6. Biff also recounts a conversation in which he and Josh disagree on the shape of the earth. Josh believes it is flat, and Biff believes that it is round. "When your best friend is the son of God," Biff remarks, "you get tired of losing every argument" (Moore, *Lamb*, 68).

siblings playing with a lizard. Their game involves battering and killing the
lizard with a rock so that Josh can bring it back to life by putting it into
his mouth (*Lamb*, 7–8). This initial scene seems to play off those canonical
stories in which Jesus cures by means of his mouth, or more specifically,
his saliva. For example, in the Gospel of Mark some residents of Bethsaida
bring a blind man to Jesus, and Jesus cures him by spitting into his eyes
(Mark 8:22–26). Something similar happens in the Johannine pericope of
the man born blind, when Jesus causes the man to see by means of mud
that he creates from his own saliva (John 9:1–7). Both stories imply that the
fluid generated by Jesus' mouth is, in some sense, miraculous and powerful.
The same is the case in *Lamb*, where Josh's mouth is the means by which the
perpetually murdered and resurrected lizard is given new life.

The way that Moore introduces Josh's character in *Lamb* is vaguely
reminiscent of the start of the *Infancy Gospel of Thomas*, where a five-year-
old Jesus creates a flock of clay sparrows and then, with a clap of his hands,
brings them to life and causes them to fly away (*Inf. Gos. Thom.* 2:2–4).
From this scene the reader gathers not only that Jesus has an innate ability
to give life, but that as a five-year-old he might have used this ability in a way
that we would expect a five-year-old to use it: as a means of play. From the
very beginning of his narrative, then, Moore depicts Josh as a profoundly
powerful character, but also as one whose behavior is in keeping with his
age.

Josh has a keen awareness in *Lamb* that he is the Messiah and Son of
God (two labels that Moore uses more-or-less interchangeably), but he only
comes to an awareness of what that means as he matures. When he is thirteen, he seeks out the rabbi Hillel in hopes that he might answer some questions about his identity, and Hillel advises that he look elsewhere: "Look,
kid, your mother says that some very wise men came to Bethlehem to see
you when you were born . . . Why don't you go see them? Ask them about
being the Messiah" (*Lamb*, 97). Josh sets out, and Biff goes with him. Their
journey lasts almost twenty years. They travel first to Kabul, where they
find Balthasar, a wealthy Ethiopian magician (*Lamb*, 109–97).[7] From him
Josh learns the tenets of Taoism—specifically, compassion, moderation, and
humility. Next they journey east to a monastery in proximity to the Great
Wall of China. Here they meet the second magus, a Buddhist monk named
Gaspar (*Lamb*, 201–55). He helps Josh attain enlightenment and trains him
in the ways of the Bodhisattva, which he frames in terms of loving one's

7. In this portion of the narrative Moore draws clearly from the "Jesus went East"
motif, a point he admits in the Afterword (so *Lamb*, 438–44).

neighbor. Finally, they encounter Melchior, a Hindu renouncer who teaches Jesus to perform miracles such as food multiplication (*Lamb*, 259–300).

Throughout *Lamb* Biff is portrayed as a bit of a sex addict, and while Josh is learning how to be the Messiah, Biff involves himself in more carnal pastimes. While they are staying with Balthasar he seduces several of the magus's concubines, and while they are with Melchior in India he obtains a copy of the *Kama Sutra* and devotes himself to mastering it. In many ways, Biff's lusty character provides balance to Josh's more restrained one. Josh is frequently curious about sex, especially when he is younger, but he does not allow himself to engage in it. Instead, he uses Biff as a type of research proxy. At one point Josh procures a prostitute for Biff so that he can describe what he's feeling as he's feeling it: "Do you feel sinful? Is it like Satan rubbing against you? Does it burn like fire?" (*Lamb*, 115). As Biff pretends that all this is simply his burden to bear, Josh remarks, "You're a good friend to suffer this for me . . . Greater love hath no man, than he lay down for his friend." Biff responds, "That's a good one, Josh. You should remember that one for later" (*Lamb*, 116). After they return home Josh begins his ministry and gathers his disciples. Moore depicts the disciples in a quite Markan fashion, with Josh at one point referring to them as "stupid little children" and "the dumbest sons of bitches on earth" (*Lamb*, 394).[8]

The tone of the narrative shifts in the final section, in the days leading up to Josh's execution. As Josh and his disciples arrive in Jerusalem, Josh knows that he is there to die, and he embraces this task. While he is dining with the disciples, he even recruits Judas to aid in his arrest: "'One of you will betray me this very night,' said Joshua. 'Won't you, Judas?'" (*Lamb*, 414).[9] The crucifixion scene in *Lamb* is particularly moving. Biff does everything that he can to stay close to his friend, going so far as to throw dice with the Roman soldiers at the foot of the cross (*Lamb*, 429–31). He is enraged when Josh dies, and he tracks Judas down and hangs him, even though he knew that Judas was only following orders. Biff then jumps off a cliff and kills himself (*Lamb*, 435). Biff's "gospel" ends here, abruptly, and the reader comes to the startling realization of why he never got around to writing his story.

8. Of course, this characterization may reflect also the sour attitude of the text's fictional author, who is thoroughly bewildered to discover that his *real* name (Levi son of Alphaeus) is mentioned only once in the canonical accounts of Jesus' life (in Mark 2:14–15).

9. The notion that Judas was simply following Jesus' orders when he went to betray him is found prominently in the *Gospel of Judas*, though because the English translation of this text was published in 2006, four years after *Lamb*, it is doubtful that this served as one of Moore's sources.

In the epilogue, Biff encounters a resurrected Mary Magdalene (Maggie) in the hallway of the hotel. As it turns out, she was also brought back to write her account of Josh. They walk away arm-in-arm, presumably to live happily ever after (*Lamb*, 436–37).

THE LOST LETTERS OF PERGAMUM (2003)

Bruce W. Longenecker is currently a professor of Biblical Studies and chair of the Department of Religion at Baylor University.[10] Of the authors surveyed here, he is the only biblical scholar. *The Lost Letters of Pergamum* is a fictional correspondence between a character named Antipas (of Rev 2:13 fame) and the author of the Gospel of Luke. In terms of genre, a collection such as this is not wholly unlike the *Epistles of Paul and Seneca* or the so-called *Abgar Correspondence*. The narrative, Longenecker writes, arises from one supposition, one fact, and one tradition.[11] The supposition is "that the Antipas mentioned in Revelation 2:13 had been named after Herod Antipas." The fact, which Longenecker bases entirely on the reference to Antipas in Revelation 2:13, is "that Antipas died as a martyr for Christ in Pergamum." The tradition, finally, is that of "Antipas' gruesome martyrdom." When these elements combine, Longenecker concludes, all that is left for the storyteller to do is "fill in the blanks."[12]

In the "editor's preface," a fictional and anonymous editor describes the discovery of a document cache in the ancient city of Pergamum. The documents are said to have survived the passage of time with only negligible decay, and were most likely written during a ten-month period in 92 CE.[13] The letters are organized into 14 "collections." The first two are correspondences between Antipas and Calpurnius of Ephesus, son of the recently deceased Theophilus (of Luke-Acts fame). In these early letters, Antipas self-identifies as a worshipper of "Zeus Olympios the Savior," and he writes to Calpurnius initially in order to invite him to a series of gladiatorial games in Pergamum. Calpurnius conveys a dislike of gladiatorial matches, but he accepts the invitation in order to perpetuate a healthy civic relationship between Ephesus and Pergamum (*Lost Letters*, 19–22).

The subject matter shifts in the second collection of letters, when Antipas inquires about the contents of Calpurnius's library, which he heard

---

10. When *The Lost Letters of Pergamum* was published Longenecker was a Senior Lecturer in New Testament Studies at St. Mary's College, University of St. Andrews.

11. Longenecker, *Lost Letters*, 9.

12. Ibid.

13. Ibid., 13–14.

about from the servant who delivered the initial letter. Specifically, he wonders whether it contains a copy of the Alexandrian recensions of the *Iliad*
and the *Odyssey*, and if so, he asks, would be possible for him to borrow
them. Calpurnius responds by saying that he does possess these works, that
they belonged to his recently-deceased father, Theophilus. At this point Calpurnius perceives an opportunity to evangelize, if subtly. He mentions Luke,
"a doctor and a scholar," whom Theophilus "commissioned . . . to write a
historical account of an intriguing man from Galilee and his followers"
(*Lost Letters*, 29). Luke will be passing through Pergamum in the spring, he
writes, and the suggestion is made that he and Antipas might "profit from
each other's interests" (*Lost Letters*, 29).

In the next collection of letters it is Luke, and not Calpurnius, who
writes back to Antipas. He explains that he is looking over Calpurnius's
house while he is away on family business (*Lost Letters*, 36). With his letter
to Antipas, Luke sends along a copy of the first volume of "the monograph"
that Theophilus had commissioned him to write. He suggests that Antipas
might appreciate it because of his own connections with Galilee.[14] Nearly
every collection of letters after this point centers in some way upon discussion of Luke's work. Antipas expresses his admiration for the way that
Luke situates the story of Jesus in the context of the Roman Empire, and
he asks about such things as Jesus' relationship to John the Baptist and the
Essenes (*Lost Letters*, 52, 62–64). Especially in the early stages of their correspondence Antipas does not shy away from sharing the rumors he has
heard about Christians: "They proclaim a different lord than the emperor
and promote a different empire than that of Rome," and "they frequently
stir up trouble and have the blame for ravaging Rome . . . with fire" (*Lost
Letters*, 41).

Antipas's criticisms disappear almost entirely once he visits a gathering
of Christians at the house of a man named Antonius in Pergamum. There
he is struck by the various social groups present and he expresses admiration for how well they all got along. Each time he visits, he brings the first
volume of Luke's monograph and treats those gathered to a public reading.
He closes one letter by admitting that he "[has] taken a curious interest in
them" (*Lost Letters*, 93). Luke guides Antipas's reading of his gospel, correcting any misunderstandings that arise, and from his letters it is clear that
his goal is to direct him toward a sort of conversion experience. As it turns
out, this is why he wanted Antipas to visit the group in Pergamum. "In my
experience," he writes, "the combination of the story of Jesus, a community

14. Antipas mentioned in a previous letter that he once owned land in Galilee and
had lived for a time in Tyre and Caesarea Maritima.

of love, and the moving of God's Spirit frequently results in new and surprising patterns of life, as you yourself have perhaps unwittingly experienced" (*Lost Letters*, 102).[15]

As their correspondence continues, this dynamic becomes more and more clear. One person in particular who spurs Antipas into a new form of life is a young girl named Nouna, with whom he becomes close. In one of the reading digests that he sends to Luke, Antipas describes the experience of playing with her. She creates a game in which she is supposed to be him and he is supposed to be her servant. "This was harmless fun," he says, but then he jokes with her that according to Jesus, what she had *actually* just done was put *him* in charge of the game that they were playing. Because, after all, "the last will be first," as in Luke 13:30 (*Lost Letters*, 138).

In the penultimate collection of letters Antipas describes growing tensions between the Christians in Antonius's house and the Pergamene authorities, the former being accused of "antisocial behavior" (*Lost Letters*, 163). Nouna's caretaker Demetrius, he writes, has been accused of atheism and is awaiting execution (*Lost Letters*, 165). Luke calls Antipas to a sort of conversion, noting that he has read and studied the story of Jesus and has grown to love the community of his followers. And with the political situation growing ever more dire, all of them, it would seem, face the possibility of martyrdom. Luke mentions the stories of Stephen and James from the "second volume" of his "monograph," and with them, the recently-exiled John (of Patmos) as examples of persons who came into tension with the governing authorities. Antipas must now choose whether he will be willing to endure a similar fate. "That decision," Luke writes, "is a matter for only you" (*Lost Letters*, 168). This final letter from Luke ends with a blessing: "May the grace of the Lord Jesus Christ be with you, to the eternal glory of the most high God" (*Lost Letters*, 169).

The last "collection" in the volume consists of a single letter from Antonius, who writes to inform Luke that Antipas has perished as a martyr. On the day when Demetrius was sentenced to be executed, Antipas gave a compelling speech in the arena in which he announced his "commitment to the empire of the God of Israel," and offered to die in Demetrius's place (*Lost Letters*, 176–77). The emperor honored his request, and Antipas was roasted

---

15. As their correspondence continues, Antipas describes his visits to at least one other gathering of Christians at the house of a man named Kalandion. At this gathering, he says, his reading of Luke 13–14 "was not well received," and sacrificial rituals were performed to Jesus and Asklepios (*Lost Letters*, 108–109). Scenes like this remind the reader of the great diversity present in early Christianity, of which Longenecker is keenly aware.

alive in the hollowed-out carcass of a bull (*Lost Letters*, 178).[16] The evening before his demise, Antipas paid a final visit to Nouna, and he charged Antonius with preserving his correspondence with Luke. At the end of the letter Antonius comments, "Diotis [one of Nouna's caretakers] has requested that I keep them until such time as they can be read to Nouna to enable her to know more of the man who died so that her adopted father might live" (*Lost Letters*, 180).

Throughout *The Lost Letters of Pergamum* the reader journeys with Antipas toward some sort of conversion experience. The details of this journey, particularly the centrality of the written word and the need for Antipas to make a "decision," almost certainly reflect the empirical author's Evangelical Protestant context. Similarly, the means by which Antipas's death is described exhibits a particular atonement theology of substitution: Antipas dies so that someone else will not have to, and in doing so, he imitates Jesus' own act of self-giving on the cross.

THE LIARS' GOSPEL (2012)

Naomi Alderman is a British author and professor of creative writing at Bath Spa University. In *The Liars' Gospel*, her third novel, she conveys four narratives centered on individual characters with some connection to Jesus (here Yehoshuah): Mary (his mother), Judas, Caiaphas, and Barabbas.[17] In all of these narratives Jesus is a relatively minor character, and in most cases he appears only in flashbacks. The work is bookended by a preface offering an interesting meditation on the nature of sacrifice mixed with an account of Pompey's siege of Jerusalem, and an epilogue recounting Titus's destruction of that city just over 100 years later.[18] Alderman situates her four perspectives on the person of Jesus between these two incidents.

16. Traditions of Antipas's death include reference to the so-called Sicilian Bull, a means of execution in which the condemned is placed inside a bronze bull and cooked over a fire.

17. Her first novel, *Disobedience,* was published in 2006 and has since been translated and published in ten languages. Her second, *The Lessons,* was published in 2010 and was met with mixed reviews. In *The Liars' Gospel* Alderman uses traditional Hebrew names for her characters. So: Jesus=Yehoshuah; Mary=Miryam; Judas=Iehuda from Qeriot; and Barabbas=Bar-Avo.

18. Alderman, *Liars' Gospel*, 3–10, 291–301.

294 Fakes, Forgeries, and Fictions

Miryam (Mary)

The first chapter begins when a man named Gidon arrives in Nazareth. He is discovered on a hillside by some herders, unconscious and at the point of death, and is brought into the city on a mule (*Liars' Gospel*, 13). When he regains consciousness he reveals that he had been searching for "the village of Yehoshuah the teacher" (*Liars' Gospel*, 15). Those gathered around him run to fetch Mary, and when she arrives he tells her that he is looking for the friends and family of Jesus in order "to meet and befriend them." Mary responds: "He was a traitor, a rabble-leader, a rebel, a liar and a pretender to the throne. We have tried to forget him here" (*Liars' Gospel*, 17).

Over the course of this chapter the narrator switches, without warning, between past and present, between Mary's experiences with Jesus before he was executed and her conversations with Gidon. She recalls her son as an inquisitive, charming, and reserved child who was drawn more to reading than to playing with other children (*Liars' Gospel*, 25). She remembers how he was uninterested in women, how tensions between him and his father, Joseph, led him to sojourn among the Essenes for a period of time, and how quick to anger he was after he returned. In one particularly heated episode, Jesus strikes his father on the face, nearly causing him to topple over. Mary recalls—somewhat regrettably, in retrospect—that in the moment she blamed Joseph for provoking Jesus instead of holding a grown man responsible for losing his temper and hitting another (*Liars' Gospel*, 27–28).

Mary also tells Gidon of how Joseph married another woman after giving her a contract of divorce: "He was angry with me. I disobeyed him too often. I was a stubborn wife, and people told him that I had disobeyed his wishes in . . . a certain matter. He put me away" (*Liars' Gospel*, 48). And finally, she recalls how Jesus' followers took his body after the crucifixion and would not tell her where it was. "Even in death," the narrator comments, "they would not give him back to her" (*Liars' Gospel*, 74). Many of these stories shock Gidon, who never met Jesus but considers himself one of his followers. He came to Nazareth to learn more about the man Jesus, or at least to receive confirmation of stories he had already heard; one could say that he leaves with far more than he bargained for.

Iehuda from Qeriot (Judas Iscariot)

In the second chapter the narrator's focus pans to Judas, who is wandering through the Jerusalem marketplace during Passover, not long after Jesus' execution. As he eavesdrops on a conversation between two women, one of them says that she heard he had died: "He threw himself from a rocky cliff onto a field of stones. Or I heard someone else say that some of the others threw him off" (*Liars' Gospel*, 80). Judas turns an oil lamp in his hands, and as he imagines throwing it to the floor and allowing its oil to spill forth, he is confronted by a memory of the woman who anointed Jesus so lavishly with expensive perfume (so Mark 14:3 par.). This episode serves as a sort of trigger for him throughout the chapter. Later it will become clear that this incident was the straw that broke the camel's back, so to speak, ultimately leading him to betray Jesus.

As Judas begins to reminisce about his time with Jesus, he does so fondly. The narrator refers to Jesus as "the man [Judas] loved best in all the world" (*Liars' Gospel*, 90). The two first meet in Judas's hometown, not long after the untimely death of Judas's wife. They talk about charity and care for the poor, about keeping the commandments, and about the nature of obedience (*Liars' Gospel*, 94–101). Judas becomes one of Jesus' first disciples. Time passes, and Jesus attracts more followers. At one point he charges them to go out to teach and to heal, and although they are reluctant, they go anyway. Judas makes his way to an unnamed village where he is presented with a crippled boy (*Liars' Gospel*, 111). He prays as he lays his hands on the boy's twisted leg, but nothing happens; the boy remains crippled. When he reconvenes with Jesus and the others, everyone shares tales of the healing they had performed. Judas wants to believe that they are lying, but he cannot escape the thought that he was simply not "favored" by God as the others were (*Liars' Gospel*, 115).

Judas becomes increasingly frustrated by the fact that an "inner circle" seems to have formed among the disciples and, more significantly, that he is not part of it (*Liars' Gospel*, 121). A major tipping point for him comes when all are gathered in a house and a woman approaches Jesus with a jar of perfumed oil and empties the contents onto his head. This upsets Judas not only because he saw it as wasteful and not in keeping with Jesus' character to accept such lavish treatment, but because the woman was clearly suffering from some sort of emotional or mental condition. The narrator describes her as speaking with a slurred voice, as smiling "lopsidedly" with "eyes rolled back in her head," and "breathing quickly" (*Liars' Gospel*, 124–25). As the contents of the jar are exhausted, the woman giggles and crushes the stone vessel with her hands, the blood mixing with the oil as it streams down onto Jesus (*Liars' Gospel*, 126).

Shortly after this event, Judas breaks with the group and journeys to the temple to turn Jesus in. There he prays to God: "I have returned to you. I am sorry for my absence." Without any hint that it is a hallucination, God responds to him, "You are welcome in my house, my beloved son" (*Liars'*

Gospel, 133). Here we find hints of that theme so prevalent in the *Gospel of Judas*, namely, that Judas's betrayal of Jesus was in some way part of a larger divine plan. As such, his actions are admirable, not despicable. After the crucifixion, toward the end of the chapter, the narrator comments in this vein: "The pious would like to believe that God does not speak to the sinners, that one has to earn the right to hear his His voice. The pious are wrong. God speaks to Judas of Qeriot just as he spoke to Yehoshuah of Natzaret" (*Liars' Gospel*, 149).

Caiaphas

Caiaphas's chapter begins not with Caiaphas *per se*, but with a brief reflection on the significance of the temple's location. "The Holy of Holies," the narrator comments, "is built on the navel of the world . . . The whole world is arranged in concentric circles around this spot" (*Liars' Gospel*, 153–54). This is followed by a description of the High Priest's yearly ritual in that space on Yom Kippur (*Liars' Gospel*, 154–55). Jesus is a minor character in this chapter, even more so than in the others. Much of this particular narrative is centered on Caiaphas's anxiety about his wife, whom he suspects of infidelity, and the question of whether he should allow Pilate to use temple funds in the building of an aqueduct.[19]

The first time Jesus is mentioned in this chapter he is referred to as "a madman they handed to the Prefect for Roman justice" (*Liars' Gospel*, 182). The narrator indicates that Caiaphas only encountered Jesus three times, and that "each time [he] seemed less impressive than the previous occasion" (*Liars' Gospel*, 182). The first encounter was in the courtyard of the temple, during the famous "Temple Tantrum" episode. The narrator describes this event, from Caiaphas's perspective, not primarily as an assault against the temple itself, but as one against worshippers and the merchants selling their wares. One "straggly-haired fellow of fifty," for example, loses his entire stock of olive oil when Jesus flips his table over. Jesus behaves, according to the narrator, "like a Roman soldier bent on destruction" (*Liars' Gospel*, 183). The second encounter is at Jesus' trial before the Sanhedrin, where Caiaphas seeks to hold Jesus accountable for his actions, but to do so in the least bloody way possible (*Liars' Gospel*, 187). The third is when Caiaphas hands Jesus over to Pilate, somewhat reluctantly, it would seem, to be executed on charges of blasphemy "against the sacred cult of Tiberius the Emperor" (*Liars' Gospel*, 189).

19. The so-called Aqueduct Riots mentioned by Josephus (in *J.W.* 2.175–177; *Ant.* 18.60–62) are described later in this chapter (Alderman, *Liars' Gospel*, 191–98).

Throughout this chapter Alderman presents Caiaphas as a character torn between religious/professional, political, and marital issues. His power struggles with Pilate over funding for the aqueduct runs alongside questions regarding the nature of his role as a priest in the temple. And underlying all of this is the issue of his wife's fidelity (or lack thereof), an issue that is never really resolved in the course of the chapter. She insists that she has been faithful, and even submits to a form of the so-called Ordeal of Bitter Water mentioned in Numbers 5:16–28 and described in various later sources (*Liars' Gospel*, 214–16; see e.g., *m. Sotah*; *Prot. Jas.* 16:4–8). The chapter ends as Caiaphas emerges from the Holy of Holies after making an incense offering on Yom Kippur, and the focus shifts away from his own concerns and toward the social significance of his priesthood: "His own experience of the moments is entirely irrelevant" (*Liars' Gospel*, 223).

Bar-Avo (Barabbas)

Alderman's final chapter centers on Barabbas. It begins with an episode from his youth in which Barabbas and his friends provoke some Roman soldiers and incite a riot. The experience clearly invigorates him; the narrator comments that "it [seemed] as far away from death as it is possible for any experience to be" (*Liars' Gospel*, 233). Barabbas is soon recruited by a Jewish resistance group, and he works his way up the ranks and finds himself in charge of a small company of fighters whose job is to stir the pot: "They make mischief, steal things where they can, riot and destroy property, telling themselves every time that, piece by piece, they are pulling Rome off their land" (*Liars' Gospel*, 239).

As time passes, Barabbas's role in the organization shifts from mischief-making to recruitment. Parallels between Jesus and Barabbas are numerous, almost to the point of tedium. Like Jesus in the Synoptic tradition (specifically, Mark 1:14–20 par.), Barabbas travels through Galilee and approaches fishermen in an attempt to rally them to his cause. "Come and follow me," he beckons, "follow me and free the country from tyranny" (*Liars' Gospel*, 245–46). The parallels between Barabbas and Jesus continue as he journeys to Jerusalem before Passover with his men, eats a meal with them, and attaches significance to the bread and wine they consume: "Just as we eat this bread and drink this wine, so we will devour the armies of Rome and drink sweet victory" (*Liars' Gospel*, 250). The following day, moreover, Barabbas is arrested by the Romans after one of his closest friends turns him in "for a handful of silver" (*Liars' Gospel*, 250).[20]

20. This friend is finally caught in the end and executed by hanging, but in a way

Barabbas wakes up in a cell next to Jesus, and throughout their conversation Jesus speaks cryptically and apocalyptically. "It is no accident that you and I are in this cell together," he remarks (*Liars' Gospel*, 255). Both are taken to see Pilate individually. With seemingly little effort, Barabbas manipulates Pilate into considering his release. It will actually work in Pilate's favor, Barabbas argues, as his men will suspect that he has turned against them and cooperated with Rome (*Liars' Gospel*, 262). Pilate brings him and Jesus before a crowd that (unbeknownst to Pilate) is constituted largely of Barabbas's own men; he gives the crowd a choice, and the cries for Barabbas drown out those for Jesus (*Liars' Gospel*, 262–66). Barabbas is released, and the narrator frames this "exchange" in terms of a sort of substitutionary atonement: "This is the man who will die in his place, whose death has brought life . . . He has lived his life in the exact opposite fashion to the way this Yehoshuah has lived and that is why he, Bar-Avo, lives and Yehoshuah will die" (*Liars' Gospel*, 268).

The chapter draws to a close when, many years after these events, Barabbas bursts into the chamber of High Priest Annas (here Ananus) the Younger. After a forceful discussion about Annas's collaboration with the Romans, Barabbas recalls the shouts of the crowd calling for his release and Jesus' execution. "Bar-Avo," the narrator comments, "does not play that Roman game. It is he who decides who will live and who will die." The chapter ends abruptly, as follows: "Bar-Avo puts the knife to Ananus's throat and bleeds him like a lamb" (*Liars' Gospel*, 290).[21]

THE TESTAMENT OF MARY (2012)

Weighing in at just under 81 pages, Colm Tóibín's *The Testament of Mary* is the shortest of the books surveyed here. Its brevity is deceptive, however, and its narrative is exceptionally dark. One reviewer comments: "Tóibín says he writes in a chair that's 'one of the most uncomfortable ever made,' one that 'causes pain in parts of the body you did not know existed.' It's not hard to imagine that *The Testament of Mary* would grow from time in that chair."[22] To be sure, there is nothing "easy" or "short" about this read.

The book is written from Mary's perspective as an elderly woman living alone in Ephesus. It begins with Mary's description of two mysterious men who visit her on a regular basis: "There is something hungry and rough in them, a brutality boiling in their blood, which I have seen before and can

---

that his death appears to be the result of suicide (*Liars' Gospel*, 269–70).

21. Josephus recounts the murder of Annas by Zealots in *J.W.* 4.318.

22. Pinsker, "*Testament of Mary.*"

smell as an animal that is being hunted can smell" (*Testament of Mary*, 1). In the course of the work it becomes clear through hints that Mary gives (e.g., "one was there with us until the end") that one of these figures is supposed to be the apostle John, but the other is never identified (*Testament of Mary*, 2). The two men visit Mary in order to record stories of her memories of Jesus, whom she never refers to by name. Her relationship with them is one of uncomfortable and profound tension. When one of them sits in what turns out to be her late husband's chair, for example, Mary pulls out a knife and threatens, "if either of you touch the chair again, if you so much as touch it, I will wait, I am waiting now, and I will come in the night, I will move as silently as the air itself moves, and you will not have time to make a sound. Do not think for a moment that I will not do this" (*Testament of Mary*, 16).

The visitors become frustrated at points because the stories Mary shares with them are stories that they have no interest in, or that are contrary to the accounts they are piecing together. One example is a tale that Mary tells near the start of the book of a mysterious man at the foot of her son's cross. He carried with him a bag of live rabbits and an angry, caged bird. One by one, she says, he removed the rabbits and fed them to the bird. She recalls the experience of watching the bird rip open the rabbits with its claws "a mild distraction from what was really going on" (*Testament of Mary*, 3). She does tell the men of a few miracles that she saw Jesus perform, specifically, the raising of Lazarus from the dead and the turning of water to wine at the wedding in Cana (*Testament of Mary*, 20–27, 30–40). She does not recount these stories with an admiration of her son's power, but with a longing for the son she had before he became powerful. There is a sense throughout the book that the more Jesus comes to be admired by those who follow him, the more distant he becomes to his mother, at least from her perspective.

Tóibín's portrait of Mary grates hard against more "traditional" characterizations of her as the pious and largely-passive Virgin. The men who visit her explain their belief that the death Jesus suffered has had profound significance for the salvation of all, and her response is wholly cynical: "When you say that he redeemed the world, I will say that it was not worth it" (*Testament of Mary*, 80). Here she speaks not as one who embraced or cooperated willingly in the alleged mission of her son, but as one who has suffered and who continues to suffer an unspeakable trauma. And in this way, Tóibín pushes the reader to consider the complexity of Mary's character as a mother who has witnessed the execution of her child and who is haunted and tormented by her memories of that scene and the alienation that preceded it.

METHODOLOGICAL CONSIDERATIONS
AND LINGERING QUESTIONS

The value of modern novels as instances of reception history is beyond dispute: each of them manifests a particular interpretation of texts and traditions at a particular point in time, and as such, they provide insight into
how their empirical authors interpret the story of Jesus and the origins of
Christianity, and they allow us to see examples of how culture impresses
itself on the literature of its day. Scholars of ancient literature in the distant
future will no doubt have a field day trying to figure them out. But is it
the case that these texts also have value not only as instances of reception
history, but as "primary sources" as well? At this point at least two central
questions need to be addressed, though not necessarily answered fully here.
The first concerns whether it is possible or even wise to consider modern
novels like the ones addressed above as examples of "Christian apocrypha."
The second is related to the first and is in many ways a more pressing one:
How might the inclusion of such novels in our study of apocryphal texts
benefit our understanding of the processes by which more ancient Christian
literature was produced and interpreted?

At the heart of the first question is the issue of the so-called slip-
pery slope. Could removing the criterion of anonymity/pseudepigraphy
from Junod's definition open the metaphorical floodgates to a point that
the waters become unmanageable? If we are willing to consider modern
novels as instances of Christian apocrypha, then what prevents us from
considering other, possibly non-textual media? What about paintings? Or
music? Or what about film? Could we imagine a situation wherein Denys
Arcand's *Jésus de Montréal* (1989) or Mel Gibson's *Passion of the Christ*
(2004) are listed alongside, say, the *Gospel of Peter* or the Ethiopian *Book
of the Rooster* as "Passion Gospels"? Or what about films that are not explicitly "religious" but have christological undertones? Matthew McEver, for
example, maintains that *Cool Hand Luke* (1967), *One Flew Over the Cuckoo's
Nest* (1975), *Dead Poets Society* (1989), and *Sling Blade* (1997) all depend
on a "messianic figure" formula that we find manifested clearly in the NT
Gospels. In all of these narratives, he suggests, "the central character is a
non-conformist or unlikely redeemer who transforms lives and ultimately
undergoes martyrdom."[23] Roland Boer, moreover, has argued for the presence of a number of christological themes in James Cameron's *Terminator*
and *Terminator II: Judgment Day.*[24]

23. McEver, "Messianic Figure in Film."
24. Boer, "Christological Slippage," 165–93.

Would an openness to modern novels as instances of Christian apocrypha also necessitate an openness to non-textual media? Or is it the case that the "text" criterion in Junod's definition has, for whatever reason, a more timeless quality than the others? And would it therefore be wise to draw the lines in such a way as to emphasize the "literature" component of Christian apocryphal literature? I do not pretend to have clear and firm answers to these questions at this point, but they will be critical ones to keep in mind as the conversation about adjusting and expanding boundaries of the apocryphal corpus continues.

There is also the crucial and in many ways more significant question of what scholars of Christian apocrypha stand to gain by including modern novels in their corpus of texts. From the perspective of a more traditional, author-centric exegetical methodology, the inclusion of these novels alongside ancient or medieval works is not as problematic as it is boring. What I mean by this is not that the novels themselves are boring, but that the questions we typically ask of more ancient texts are relatively vapid when applied to contemporary literature. We know precisely who wrote these novels, for example, and we know the contexts in which they were produced. We know where and by whom they were published, and it would be fairly painless to discover precisely how many copies were sent to which bookstores. In some cases we know why their authors wrote what they did and even what sources they used in composing their narratives, and we know this because the authors tell us in their prefaces or epilogues.[25] Indeed, for almost any question we can imagine, we know that the authors are (at least for now) only an e-mail or a phone call away. I am not convinced that a *purely* author-centric methodology is able to provide a compelling reason to read and study these novels as instances of Christian apocrypha.

When we move away from the author and the author's intentions as the terminal loci of meaning, however, and begin to rephrase the matter in terms of readers, we find ourselves on remarkably different ground. A fundamental and enduring insight of postmodern literary criticism is that readers play an active role in determining what a text "means," and that they do this in a variety of ways. One of the more common concepts used to illustrate this claim is that of "intertextuality," first defined in 1967 by the Bulgarian literary critic Julia Kristeva. "Any text," she argues, "is constructed as a mosaic of quotations; any text is the absorption and transformation of another."[26] Kristeva includes a text's reader in what she calls the "discursive

---

25. With Tóibín as the only exception, each of the authors surveyed above includes an excursus or epilogue with detailed notes about their sources.

26. So Kristeva, "Word, Dialogue and Novel," 66.

universe" of that text, so when a reader reads something, they make sense of what they are reading by forming connections between it and other things that they have read. She and others who have appropriated and adapted her methodology have argued that while the definition of this phenomenon is new, the phenomenon itself is not; this is how reading works, and it works this way regardless of whether you think it does.

Another way of stating this issue is to say that these novels can have a profound impact on how their intended readers understand other texts. I have seen this happen in my own classes when I have students read one of these novels (or others like them) and write up an assessment of what they have read. Students understand that what they are reading is historical fiction, yet in their final papers I often encounter curious claims about how these texts have affected how they understand this or that biblical character. "I never thought that Jesus could have been like this as a kid," remarked one student writing about *Lamb*. Another student commented after reading *The Testament of Mary*: "Now I have a better understanding of why Jesus' mother may have tried to stop him from preaching in the Gospel of Mark." In the same way that the infancy traditions in Matthew and Luke become conflated in the traditional nativity scene, many of my students conflate these more recent narratives with their more ancient counterparts.

As a biblical scholar trained in historical-critical exegesis, my first reaction to such claims is to say they are sorely misguided. We do not *know* what Jesus was like as a child, and just because a talented author writes an extremely compelling narrative from Mary's perspective, that does not mean he or she has accurately conveyed that perspective. But on the level of popular and actual reading practice, the conflation that I witness in my students' work is, in fact, more true to how *real* readers read and make sense of what they are reading. For the most part, real readers do not typically approach literature in a conscious effort to discern authorial intention or context; they read for a host of other reasons, including entertainment, relaxation, reflection, etc. And as they read, they often unconsciously form connections between the characters, themes, and plot points of whatever they are reading and the characters, themes, and plot points of what they have read in the past.

Authors can facilitate this process through literary allusion, though ultimately the connections that the reader is going to draw will be determined by *their* knowledge of other texts, not the author's. Christopher Moore, for example, can have the young Jesus remark to lusty Biff that "greater love hath no man, than he lay down for his friend," but the reference will be lost on the reader unfamiliar with the Gospel of John. A reader, on the other hand, might find resonances between *Lamb* and the *Gospel of Judas*, even if no such resonances were intended by Christopher Moore. And what reader of *The Testament of Mary*, even one who knows that the portrait painted there is a fictitious one, will approach other stories about Jesus' mother without the image of the traumatized victim at least somewhere in their mind. To reframe the concept of "meaning" in these terms is to affirm that every act of reading affects every act of reading that will come after it; texts begin to take on new shape as they are read and interpreted in light of other texts.

CONCLUSION

The question of how modern novels like the four outlined above might benefit our understanding of Christian literature is undeniably complex. While the move to redraw boundaries to accommodate more texts under the rubric "Christian apocrypha" is well underway, there remain a number of considerations to be taken into account before such modern works can be included as full siblings alongside their more ancient counterparts. In this essay I have argued that there is good reason for doing so, however, when we examine these texts from the perspective of their intended audiences. When we take seriously the ways in which intended readers seek—either consciously or unconsciously—to understand the texts that they read, and when we attend to the "sparks" that form between texts in this process of reading, we gain valuable insight into the process of reading and meaning production. And this, in turn, has the capacity to shine light on some of the dynamics at work in the apocryphal imagination throughout history.

– 15 –

Gender and the Academy Online

The Authentic Revelations
of the *Gospel of Jesus' Wife*

— Caroline T. Schroeder —

USUALLY I WRITE ABOUT dead people. Dead people cannot ostracize you, dead people cannot eviscerate you in another publication, dead people can be safer objects of inquiry than the living. This paper, however, analyzes the living—the way we as a field responded to the appearance of the *Gospel of Jesus' Wife* fragment (GJW) and what that says about Biblical Studies. In particular, I wish to look at issues of authenticity. The authenticity of the fragment itself lay at the center of the maelstrom. I seek to untangle more nebulous markers of authenticity as well. I argue that the debate about the authenticity of the document hinged in no small part on these *other* markers of authenticity (in addition to the traditional means of documenting an ancient text). First, GJW simultaneously exposed our society's privileging of "hard" scientific modes of inquiry to determine authenticity over traditional humanistic ones and the inadequacy of those scientific methods to provide the certainty we crave. Second, even our traditional humanist research methods proved unsatisfying in the absence of very particular political and ethical commitments—namely, transparency about provenance. Third, the debate demonstrated that deeply entrenched social markers of authenticity of individuals—status, gender, identity—affect the academic production of knowledge. Finally, the authentic revelations of this text include the deep conservatism of our field, which includes a distrust of digital scholarship and digital publishing (including the openness it enables).

The GJW affair has taught us at least as much, if not more, about how authenticity operates in the academy as about authenticating ancient manuscripts. Moreover, I argue, these two are not separate issues—debates about *personal* authenticity in academia's prestige economy directly influence scholarly work regarding the authenticity of *texts*. As scholarship becomes more digital, as our work is increasingly conducted online, our awareness of our own political and ideological commitments—and how they matter— becomes increasingly important.

When I use the terms "authentic" and "authenticity" in this essay, when I talk about the authenticity of the *fragment itself*, I do not mean authenticity in terms of authorship (i.e., is this really a Gospel written by "Jesus' Wife"?) or even if it is authentically from someone who knew Jesus, or even if it provides authentic evidence that Jesus had a wife. Scholarly consensus from the beginning dismissed this text as historical evidence that Jesus had a wife, or as a document ultimately originating from Jesus' own time. When I speak of the authenticity of the fragment, I use the benchmark set by Karen King: whether this is an ancient text, written down in this form at some point in late antiquity.

MARKERS OF AUTHENTICITY FOR THE MANUSCRIPT

At this point, the scholarly conversation over the authenticity of the fragment itself is well documented online and in published journals, and James McGrath's essay in this same volume speaks to the role of bloggers in this conversation. I also refer readers to Michael W. Grondin's three-part timeline for a concise history.[1] I am on record stating that I believe the piece to be a forgery, or at the very least, not an ancient witness to an ancient text.[2] So I do not seek to re-argue points against or in favor of the *fragment's* authenticity here; rather, I wish to highlight the principle criteria for determining authenticity and weigh *their* significance.

The primary means of determining the authenticity of GJW proved to be related to questions about transparency regarding the collection of documents to which it belonged and provenance. Other methods for testing

---

1. Grondin, "Question of Content"; Grondin, "Jesus' Wife Fragment 2014"; Grondin, "Jesus' Wife Fragment 2015."

2. Le Donne, "Interview with Schroeder."

and studying the fragment in isolation proved inconclusive at worst and unsatisfying at best. In this section, I seek to review the primary criteria used to measure the fragment's authenticity and explore what the success or failure of those criteria says about our field. The methods and markers I will examine include scientific testing, paleography, philology and close reading, linguistics, and provenance studies.

Scientific Testing

Early press coverage of GJW quickly zeroed in on two measures of determining authenticity: the credentials of the scholars involved, and the availability of scientific testing.[3] Regarding the latter methodology, the first articles in the *New York Times* and the *Smithsonian* stated that Karen King and her colleagues believed the document to be authentic, but that scientific tests of the papyrus had yet to be conducted. Ink and carbon-dating tests, they noted, could possibly confirm or call into question King's dating of the document. Other scholars (including myself) maintained that such tests could quite likely prove inconclusive: a smart forger could use a scrap of old papyrus and concoct ink that could fool such tests. Nonetheless, the question remained pressing. So pressing that in April 2014 *Harvard Theological Review* published alongside King's article about the fragment several other articles dedicated to tests and examinations of the manuscript to determine its authenticity. Of the seven articles and one response devoted to GJW in the issue, four were dedicated to "scientific testing": chemical testing of the ink, infrared microspectroscopy of the papyrus, and two reports on radiocarbon dating.[4] Although the scientists conducting the tests and writing the reports remained circumspect about their findings—maintaining that the results were not proof of the text's antiquity—nonetheless these scientific tests were marshaled in arguments defending the fragment's authenticity as a late-antique document. King's own article made use of these findings as key evidence for her assertions that accusations of forgery were unwarranted (e.g., "Current testing thus supports the conclusion that the papyrus and ink of GJW are ancient").[5] The Harvard University website devoted to GJW still proclaims (as of 12 June 2016) as a main headline that "Testing

3. Goodstein, "Historian Says"; Goodstein, "Fresh Doubts"; Goodstein, "Papyrus"; and Sabar, "Inside Story."

4. Azzarelli, Goods, and Swager, "Study of Two Papyrus Fragments"; Hodgins, "Accelerated Mass Spectrometry"; Tuross, "Accelerated Mass Spectrometry"; Yardley and Hagadorn, "Characterization."

5. King, "'Jesus said to them,'" 7–8, 33–34 (quotation from p. 8).

indicates 'Gospel of Jesus's Wife' Papyrus Fragment to be Ancient" and that "scientific testing of the papyrus and ink . . . demonstrated that the material is ancient."[6] Antiquity here serves as proxy for authenticity; no mention is made of the emerging consensus regarding forgery, nor of the fact that a document could be forged while simultaneously "passing" the tests.

Even into 2016, media coverage continued to ask whether "scientific" inquiry can trump the more "fuzzy" humanities methods; can we find a test that will prove once and for all that the document was written in antiquity?[7] Although these tests have produced conclusions about the fragment, they have proven inconclusive in terms of determining authenticity.

Paleography

Another methodology applied to the fragment was paleography, the study of manuscript production and ancient handwriting. Paleography is often used to date manuscripts, although the accuracy of this methodology has come into question recently by papyrologists such as Brent Nongbri.[8] Speculation about the possible forgery of the fragment arose in no small part due to questions about the handwriting. Soon after the announcement about the text, Alin Suciu and Hugo Lundhaug on Suciu's blog, as well as others on the *Evangelical Textual Criticism* blog, raised questions about the shapes and strokes of the letters.[9] They simply did not look ancient.

In her original draft article entitled, "'Jesus said to them, "My wife. . ."': A New Coptic Gospel Papyrus," published on Harvard University's website in September 2012, King anticipated questions about paleography, noting that she had consulted experts in papyrology and addressing questions raised by the anonymous peer reviewers based on paleography. I quote the relevant passages:

> In March, 2012, she transported the papyrus to the Institute for the Study of the Ancient World in New York, where it was viewed by the Institute's director and renowned papyrologist, Roger Bagnall and by AnneMarie Luijendijk (Princeton). Our lengthy discussion about the characteristics of the papyrus (detailed below) concluded with the judgement that the papyrus was very likely an authentic ancient text that could be dated on paleographical grounds to circa 4th c. C.E. On this basis, work

6. Beasley, "Testing."
7. Baden and Moss, "Why Scientists."
8. Nongbri, "Limits of Palaeographic Dating"; Nongbri, "Use and Abuse of P[52]."
9. Suciu and Lundhaug, "So-Called Gospel."

began in earnest on a critical edition, translation, and interpretation of the fragment.

In August, 2012, a version of the present article was submitted
to the *Harvard Theological Review* for consideration for publication. In the course of the normal external review process,
reviewers differed in their judgments about authenticity. One
accepted the fragment, but two raised questions, without yet
being entirely certain that it is a fake, and suggested review by
experienced Coptic papyrologists and testing of the chemical
composition of the ink. The third reviewer provided detailed
comments on a number of difficulties with the text's grammar
and paleography. Neither of the reviewers who questioned the
fragment's authenticity was aware that Bagnall had already seen
the actual fragment and judged it to be authentic. Their own
views were based on relatively low resolution photographs of
the fragment.[10]

I will return to this passage in a moment, when I address issues of authenticity in the academy, and particularly in the academic prestige economy, but
for now I wish to focus on paleography. King did her due diligence in this
area, consulting with Bagnall (a papyrologyist) and Luijendijk (a papyrolo-
gist with expertise in Coptic). Doubts about the fragment, however, were
raised immediately by the peer reviewers, and in her article King displays
transparency in acknowledging their questions, and determination in asserting nonetheless that the fragment is likely from the fourth century. This
original draft article set the stage for the paleographical debate that would
ensue for the next two years. Paleography alone could not be relied upon as
an "objective" measure of authenticity. Discussion continued on social media and in the blogosphere, with the handwriting on the fragment emerging
as a key source of doubt regarding its authenticity.[11]

The special issue of *HTR* focusing on GJW included one article devoted entirely to paleography. The piece was authored by one of the foremost
experts in Coptic papyrology, Malcolm Choat. Ultimately, it concluded that
elements of the fragment could be interpreted as pointing in the direction of
a forgery, while other elements evinced characteristics of ancient handwriting.[12] The evaluation was inconclusive. King's revised version of her draft
article was suitably updated to take this new research into account.

---

10. King, "'Jesus said to them'" (draft), 3–4.
11. Suciu and Lundhaug, "So-Called Gospel."
12. Choat, "Preliminary Paleographical Assessment."

Linguistics

Linguistic issues also arose as criteria for determining authenticity from the very beginning, but as with other methods, for the most part they pushed the evaluation in the direction of forgery. Leo Depuydt and Gesine Schenke Robinson immediately noted the grammatical problems with the text—errors that went beyond the possibility of a sloppy or under-educated ancient scribe.[13]

Slavomír Čéplö went so far as to conduct a computational study of the syntax of GJW back in 2012. Čéplö looked at the linguistic construction "peje-"—translated "(pronoun) said"—in GJW, and computed how many times the construction appears in the Sahidic versions of the Gospels of Matthew, Mark, Luke, John, and Thomas, and with what combinations of following words.[14] The results of his computational study are that the construction in GJW has no parallels in the other five texts, and that such a construction is not only awkward but exceedingly unlikely in the wild. Now granted, a more definitive study would include all of the Nag Hammadi corpus, but I think these five gospels proved to be a good sample. Čéplö thus confirmed the nature of the text as forgery; late antique Egyptians simply did not speak and write in the way presented in the new "gospel" fragment. Unfortunately, Čéplö's work was not really discussed much in the blogosphere, despite its importance (in my opinion).

Philology & Close Reading

The backbone of scholarly humanistic inquiry—philology and close reading—dominated early exploration of the fragment's authenticity. Everyone noted the similarity of the vocabulary in the fragment to the vocabulary of the *Gospel of Thomas*. For King, the shared vocabulary corroborated the document's ancient milieu; it fit quite nicely with other fourth-century Coptic documents found at Nag Hammadi.[15] For skeptics, philological close reading provided mounting evidence of forgery. And the closer the skeptics read, the higher that mountain of evidence grew. Francis Watson of Durham University posted a number of online essays on Mark Goodacre's blog and helped launch the argument that GJW was a forgery based

---

13. Depuydt is quoted in Farrior, "Divorcing Mrs. Jesus"; see Robinson's comment on Halton's blog post ("'Gospel of Jesus's Wife' Saga"), reposted as its own blog post: Robinson and Halton, "Gesine Robinson."

14. Čéplö, "Tahime."

15. King, "'Jesus said to them'" (draft), inter alia.

on snippets copied from the *Gospel of Thomas*.[16] What began with very basic
questions about vocabulary—such as, what is the likelihood of all these key
words (Mary, Jesus, wife, mother, disciple, gave-me-life) occurring in such
a small space?—soon turned to the realization by many that the fragment
copied direct phrases from the Coptic *Gospel of Thomas*. Ultimately this led
to Andrew Bernhard's and Mark Goodacre's discovery that the fragment
even reproduces a typographical error in Michael Grondin's online interlinear translation of the Coptic *Gospel of Thomas*.[17] Philology also helped
pound the final nail in the coffin for the fragment: Christian Askeland concluded that GJW was a forgery because it was copied by the same hand as
a fragment of the Gospel of John that accompanied GJW in the materials
presented to King by the manuscripts' owner, and the John fragment was
clearly a forgery—a copy of a Coptic version of John in Cambridge known
as the Qau codex.[18] Askeland's philological expertise led to this discovery;
he completed his dissertation on the Coptic Bible at Cambridge and published a book on the Coptic Gospel of John and was intimately familiar with
the Qau codex.

Provenance

While the traditional humanistic methodologies of philology and linguistics pointed us to a clear conclusion to the question of authenticity, one
other contributing factor must be mentioned: transparency about the fragment's ownership, collection history, and provenance. King agreed to keep
the name of the owner and some of the documentation about the fragment
and the rest of its collection private. Askeland was able to uncover the
fraudulent John manuscript that was in the same collection *only* because an
image of that papyrus was published online as part of the documentation
for the scientific testing results published in *HTR*. Only because additional
information about the collection was released could we arrive at our current
state of knowledge regarding the fragment.

    Roberta Mazza, a papyrologist at Manchester, has been outspoken
on issues of provenance for the past several years, weighing in not only
on this controversy but also regarding the Green collection of biblical papyri and private collections generally. Mazza maintains that holding back

16. See this revised version of a report first posted 20 September 2012: Watson,
"Fake Gospel-Fragment." For a full account of Watson's work on Goodacre's blog, see
Goodacre's roundup "Revised Versions of Francis Watson's Articles."

17. Bernhard, "Patchwork"

18. Askeland, "Jesus Had a Sister-in-Law."

information about an ancient object's provenance hinders scholarship and contributes to an unethical (and often illegal) antiquities market.[19] The war and political upheaval in the Middle East have resulted in a wave of un-provenanced, illegal antiquities for sale to predominantly wealthy Western buyers. Academics' responsibility, she argues, should be to eschew publication of private collections unless their provenance is assured and clearly documented. Doing otherwise feeds the antiquities market and undermines the production of knowledge at the heart of scholarship. Provenance and collection history lead scholars to important conclusions about the documents, and sometimes to matching fragmentary documents with their lost partner-fragments. In 2014 Mazza wrote:

> In presenting the results of research to peers and the public, academics use means of communication and follow rules that are centred on the values of trust and accountability. Good arguments in any scholarly discussion are based on a method that provides sources and data that not only proves the points, but is also reliable and verifiable . . .
>
> The lack of discussion on provenance, including acquisition history, is bad practice, and it is usually criticized by academics because it deprives the readers of important data for verifying the reliability of the arguments made in publications. It also goes against one of the principles of our profession, the advancement of scholarship and knowledge, because it denies the possibility to open (or exclude) further research on the above-mentioned manuscript's history and connections.
>
> Besides all this, to avoid discussion of provenance undermines trust: would you trust someone who conceals information?[20]

Mazza was not alone in calling on King to release all provenance information and collection history about the fragment. Certainly, if all of the collection had been released in 2012 when the existence of GJW was announced, we would have arrived at our current conclusions about the fragment far, far sooner. Moreover, Mazza's ethical and political questions about how our work with private, secret, or unprovenanced material might aid the antiquities markets have not received enough attention in Biblical Studies.

---

19. Like many of the participants in this scholarly conversations, Mazza publishes much of her work on these issues online, in her blog and on Twitter. Mazza has a collection of essays under the topic of "provenance" on her blog *Faces & Voices*: https://facesandvoices.wordpress.com/category/provenance/.

20. Mazza, "Provenance Issues."

She calls on us to reckon with the political and ethical consequences of our work—not an easy conversation, but a necessary one.

Mazza frames the current state of scholarship as one in which transparency and openness about provenance and collection history are the standards.

> For those who work with artefacts reliability and access to as many details as possible related to the ancient sources under scrutiny, often published for the first time, is particularly important. Images and other key-information are provided, including a clear discussion of the archaeological provenance and acquisition history of the object in question. In the case of papyrus editions, this has become the norm.[21]

I would argue, however, that this "norm" is still not as normative as we would like. In May 2015, the University of Virginia acquired a papyrus fragment.[22] The initial announcement made no mention of provenance; on Facebook I immediately raised the question of provenance and collection history. Brice Jones and Dorothy King e-mailed the university's library to inquire directly. As it turns out, the University of Virginia purchased the fragment without even thinking to ask for information about provenance—this in 2015, after controversies about the Sappho papyrus, Green collection, and GJW fragment, and after countless news stories about ISIS selling looted antiquities to support its war.[23]

Transparency about provenance and collection history, I would argue, is not as normative as it should be.[24] All of us working on papyri or Coptic literature have built our scholarly reputations on stolen or looted cultural heritage (and in Biblical Studies, exhibit A is Codex Sinaiticus.) Transparency is not currently a methodology but a political and ethical commitment. Ultimately, all the scholarly methodologies applied to GJW give us only a fraction of the information a political and ethical commitment to transparency could provide.

21. Ibid.

22. Whitesell, "Please Welcome P. Virginia 1."

23. Whitesell, "Problematic Provenance."

24. See also Robinson's mention of the *Gospel of Judas* as a similar cautionary tale in "How a Papyrus Fragment Became a Sensation."

Conclusions

Of all these potential markers of authenticity, the "fuzzy" humanities meth-ods have proven sharper than "hard science." Moreover, I would argue that scientific testing as a measure of authenticity has proven problematic in one important way: in directing our attention away from the most hu-man and political means of determining authenticity—i.e., disclosing full information about the collection and the provenance of the fragment. The scholarly community has expressed our disappointment about the paucity of information regarding the owner and the provenance of the collection. However, King promised the fragment's owner anonymity, thus putting her in a strange bind: questionable for agreeing to keep the owner's identity pri-vate but laudable for keeping her promise in the face of enormous pressure.[25]

Unless a legal non-disclosure agreement has been signed, in the face of competing ethical obligations, the scholar's primary obligation should be to transparency of knowledge in the field. There are two issues here: 1) the continued secrecy about the identity of the owner, especially when a fraud has possibly been perpetrated not only on our scholarly community, but on the general public; and 2) the pursuit of expensive scientific testing that diverts both financial resources and scholarly attention away from other pursuits. As I have argued, such transparency has *not* been the norm in the field, and I find myself forced to consider that were I in King's position, I too might have agreed to non-disclosure, as well, at that time. Now, however, we are past that point. One of the revelations of the GJW controversy is that in the academic production of knowledge, our political commitments matter as much as our methodological expertise. As we move forward as a schol-arly community, we need to apply self-scrutiny when we use the "pursuit of knowledge" to rationalize what we now know to be ethically murky work.

SCHOLARLY STATUS AND AUTHENTICITY

Equally important over the last three years, I argue, have been markers of authenticity that adhere to the participants in the conversation. Markers of authenticity in the academic prestige economy influenced the scholarly conversation in both predictable and surprising ways. In particular I am interested in the traditional peer review process compared to the digital publication cycle, the status markers of academics' physical and social

---

25. Andrew Bernhard ("Call for Closure"), who has called on King to release all the documents, has written: "I also respect that she has maintained her personal com-mitment not to (sic) the identity of the owner of the *Gospel of Jesus' Wife* for so long."

locations (both institutions and social networks), and gender. These markers of personal authenticity intersected and at times conflicted in interesting ways, with some actors in the GJW controversy privileging some measures of authenticity, and other actors privileging different measures. In particular, Harvard and King proceeded according to fairly traditional markers of personal and institutional authenticity, while in the blogging world and in social media, those markers held little weight. Gender, I will argue, cut across all of them.

The Traditional Publishing Cycle
vs. Digital Publishing/Blogging

King's research on the papyrus fragment followed a traditional model of scholarly production. The initial essay adhered to a predictable process of authentication. King, the author, worked on her edition, translation, and article, consulting with known experts in the field, and submitted her work for peer review by *HTR*. King then responded to criticisms levied in the peer reviews and the article was accepted for publication. This is a fairly traditional publication cycle, and although one might think that the referees' criticisms were rather serious, one cannot argue that the process was entirely flawed: King was transparent in her initial *HTR* pre-publication essay regarding the major criticisms of the referees.[26]

I want to compare the subsequent online modes of scholarship with this process. One might be tempted to argue that they existed in conflict, or that they represented two distinctive modes of scholarly inquiry: blogging/social media in a digital ecosystem compared to traditional scholarly peer review, versus a more "democratic" or unregulated free-for-all online. However, I posit that the digital conversation online represented a kind of telescoping of traditional scholarly publication practices. Research and scholarly conversations that would normally have taken years to unfold occurred over the course of weeks or months online. Although particular *actors* in this scholarly conversation occupied different social and physical locations, and disseminated their work in these different locations, nevertheless, the online work in some ways mimicked traditional scholarship, except that it operated at a speed heretofore unseen in Biblical Studies because it was not bound by administrative structures of traditional peer reviewed publishing. Blogs such as *Evangelical Textual Criticism* and Mark Goodacre's *NT Blog* published research on the fragment, and the online scholarly community functioned essentially as crowd-sourced peer review

26. King, "'Jesus said to them'" (draft), 3–4.

in comments on the blogs and in social media discussion about the blog posts on Facebook and Twitter.[27]

The work that Watson, Grondin, Robinson, Bernhard, Goodacre, and Askeland conducted was in many cases the quality of work one would expect from traditional peer-reviewed scholarship. In fact, much of this work was later revised into articles in the peer-reviewed journal *New Testament Studies* in 2015, of which Watson is the editor. The impact of their work, however, peaked long before the publication of the *NTS* volume; the publication process lent the articles a patina of official authenticity, but the argumentation within these pieces had already been accepted by the scholarly community as authentic.

Returning to King's publication cycle, as online scholarship accumulated, King chose to continue publishing in traditional modes. Rather than engage with the blogosphere and social media by publishing responses online on Harvard's *Gospel of Jesus' Wife* website or on the blogs (ETC, Goodacre's blog) and social media sites (Twitter and Facebook), King chose to follow the path of peer review. The 2012 *HTR* essay was pulled—by whom I do not know, whether by King, *HTR*, Harvard, or by mutual agreement—and King pursued the route of scientific testing and private consultation with experts. This research culminated in the *HTR* issue in 2014, at which point King's article "'Jesus said to them, "My wife. . .""" was finally officially published. Although King gave papers and talks on the fragment, and conducted media interviews with the *New York Times* and the *Smithsonian*, she chose not to engage on social media or blogs. The *HTR* issue addressed some of the concerns that had been raised online, but in the context of a traditional peer-reviewed journal article. Therefore, digital scholarship and traditional scholarship continued along somewhat parallel but separate tracks until this point.

One small adaptation to the new norms of digital scholarship ultimately led to the uncovering of the document as a fraud. When *HTR* published the articles on paleography, scientific testing, and King's own work, Harvard and King also released online the original reports and data from the ink and papyrus tests, including images of the aforementioned Gospel of John papyrus in the collection along with supplementary documentation. These materials appeared as a digital companion of sorts to the traditional journal release.

Since the *HTR* issue appeared, all of the significant analysis of the fragment has taken place on blogs, e-mail lists, and social media. As mentioned,

27. Note James McGrath's discussion of the speed and quality of this conversation in his contribution to this volume, below (ch. 16).

New Testament Studies published a recent issue with several articles arguing for forgery, almost all of which were once non-peer-reviewed, digital
publications. Thus, the traditional peer-reviewed record recapitulated the
original work of new media. One of the most remarkable turning points
that signaled the shift in the location of scholarly knowledge production
from the traditional to the digital occurred when renowned Coptologist
Stephen Emmel posted a pdf on Alin Suciu's blog, documenting all the reasons he believed GJW to be a forgery.[28] In format and style, Emmel's essay
resembled a traditional journal article, not a blog post or social media conversation; nonetheless, the fact that even Emmel, known for his cautious,
traditional peer-reviewed scholarship, entered the online conversation signaled that scholarly knowledge production had moved online.

Professional Status

The academic currency of peer review goes hand in hand with other aspects
of the academic prestige economy. Academic gossip has long held that the
status of the institution rubs off on the status of a scholar, with a somewhat
unofficial recognition that outstanding scholars may exist outside of elite institutions, but the reputation of an elite institution contributes further to the
reputation of its scholars. Recent work on the prestige economy of higher
education has revealed that the status of one's institution is indeed a factor
in determining the career trajectory of individual scholars. One particular
study of PhD programs has demonstrated that most hires at the most elite
universities—so-called "Research 1" universities—come from a pool of PhD
candidates at a few elite universities' graduate programs.[29] We all know that
the resources at elite institutions—research funding, lower teaching loads,
the ability to teach seminars in one's research area, etc.—also contribute to
the academic prestige economy; faculty at these institutions produce more
publications in part because they have more resources to do so.

During the GJW controversy, the status of most of the scholars producing new knowledge in online communities and the status of scholars
working in the traditional peer review realm were quite distinct. With the
exception of Mark Goodacre and Francis Watson, most of the bloggers and
participants on social media producing new knowledge about the fragment
were not established scholars at elite research universities.[30] Grondin and

28. Emmel, "Codicology."

29. Clauset, et al., "Systematic Inequality"; see also Oprisko, "Superpowers."

30. Candida Moss, as professor at the University of Notre Dame, is also quite
high status by traditional metrics. Moss's work significantly influenced the public

Bernhard are independent scholars, and Christian Askeland was teaching at the Kirchliche Hochschule Wuppertal, a very small theological school in Germany. James McGrath is at Butler. Anthony Le Donne, one of the editors of *The Jesus Blog* who blogged about the document and then wrote a book about it, was an adjunct instructor at the University of the Pacific for a time before moving to a tenure-track position at the United Theological Seminary.[31] Gesine Schenke Robinson also circulated criticisms of the GJW publication process over e-mail and blogs; Robinson is a well-known Coptologist with a contract position at Claremont Graduate University. The experts consulted for King's original article, on the other hand, most definitively came from the realm of the academic elite: tenured or tenure-track faculty at premier research universities. King consulted with Roger Bagnall of New York University, AnneMarie Luijendijk of Princeton, and Ariel Shisha Halevy of the Hebrew University of Jerusalem before going public.

Moreover, Harvard's stature as "Harvard" enabled the massive publicity machine that accompanied the original press release about the document: a front page *New York Times* article appeared the day after King's first presentation on the document at the International Association of Coptic Studies Congress. Reporters also swarmed the Congress the day after the presentation, putting microphones in front of bewildered scholars who had come to discuss their own latest arcane research. And a Smithsonian Channel documentary was arranged. The publicity roll-out for this fragment reflected the importance of Harvard as much as it did the fragment, possibly even more so. In all, the initial publicity surrounding the announcement of the fragment reflected the high status of the scholar, her institution, and her network.

New Media as a Platform for Knowledge Production

This division in status between the scholars writing online and those producing traditional peer-reviewed publications is not unique to Biblical Studies. Bonnie Stewart's work on academic social media has demonstrated that markers of authenticity on academic social media differ from those in traditional scholarship.

On social media (including academic circles on social media) authenticity is not measured using the same criteria as in the traditional academic

---

dissemination of GJW scholarship being produced online. In what follows, I examine the status of the scholars producing new knowledge about the fragment itself, rather than scholars producing knowledge about the controversy.

31. Le Donne, *Wife of Jesus*.

prestige economy. Social media participants judge authenticity by level of engagement, not traditional status markers. This holds true especially on so-called "academic Twitter," where Stewart's research has shown that the "the impression of capacity for meaningful contribution" to a conversation carries more weight than credentials such as university ranking or tenure status.[32] Stewart writes,

> How do scholars within open networks judge whether another scholar's signals are credible or worthy of engagement? . . . [they employ] complex logics of influence to assess the networked profiles and behaviors of peers and unknown entities. Significantly, these logics of influence depart from the codified terms of rank and bibliometric indexing on which conventional academic influence is judged. While some are numeric—participants recognized relatively large-scale accounts as a general signal of influence—recognizability and commonality are as important as or more important than quantifiable measures or credentials.[33]

Perceptions of engagement, shared interests, and shared viewpoints contribute to influence and status on social media.

Stewart's research on networked scholarship was vindicated in two ways during the GJW controversy. First, the logics of engagement and shared interests were at work on the *Evangelical Textual Criticism* blog, where Askeland published his research proving GJW was a forgery. The *Evangelical Textual Criticism* blog is a community that is exactly what it says it is: a site for Evangelical Christians with interests in text criticism to come together and discuss the Bible. A shared religious commitment is a key factor in this community's identity; the tagline reads, "A forum for people with knowledge of the Bible in its original languages to discuss its manuscripts and textual history from the perspective of historic evangelical theology." The vast majority of contributors to the blog are also male; of the 18 contributors currently listed on the website, only one is a woman.

When Askeland posted his "smoking gun" blog post, he originally titled it "Jesus's Wife had an ugly sister-in-law"; by sister-in-law he was referring to the aforementioned fragment of the Gospel of John in the same collection of materials as GJW. Eva Mroczek, Meredith Warren, and other feminist scholars began to question the title of Askeland's post. Mroczek stated that it "plays on old tropes that have long alienated and shamed women—not just scrutinizing them for their appearance, but allegorizing

32. Stewart, "Open to Influence."
33. Ibid., 287. The quotation is taken from the article's abstract.

them to make negative points." Additional comments were made in support of her initial post but some were removed by Askeland, who characterized them as "combative."[34] Some of the factors Stewart has identified as relevant for social networking and perceptions of authenticity online are operating here, in particular shared gender and religious identities. Askeland's status as a reputable Coptic scholar contributed to his authority in determining authenticity, but within this online community, so did his gender and religious commitments. Mroczek, Warren, and their allies (some of whom were men writing in support of the women scholars) were feminist outsiders and critics of evangelical Christian biblical interpretation. Noteworthy in this regard also is an e-mail sent by Brown University's Leo Depuydt to journalists and scholars stating his support of Askelend's findings and making serious accusations against King: "When is this papyrological pantomime, this Keystone Coptic, this academic farce, this philological burlesque finally going to stop? Is this academic misconduct or is this not academic misconduct?"[35]

Simultaneously on Twitter and Facebook, the views of scholars such as Alin Suciu, Hugo Lundhaug, Andrew Bernhard, Michael Grondin, Mark Goodacre, and myself gained traction. As I have noted already, with the exceptions of Watson and Goodacre, most of us commenting held low status positions in the academy. Yet our views were held in high regard, I would argue, either because we already had credibility on social media due to perceptions of "engagement and shared interest," or because the networked credibility of one scholar rubbed off on the others (e.g., Goodacre's reputation as a dynamic, responsive tweeter rubbed off on Grondin and Bernhard when he tweeted about their posts on his blog). Grondin and Bernhard also had reputations as digital scholars in Coptic due to their own websites, where Grondin's edition and translation of the *Gospel of Thomas* proved crucial in the argument that GJW was a forgery.

---

34. Mroczek, "Sexism," examines the discussion and reproduces some of the deleted comments.

35. The e-mail, dated 24 April 2014, was posted to Gregg W. Schwendner's blog *What's New in Papyrology* (http://papyrology.blogspot.ca/2014/04/christian-askeland-jesus-had-ugly.html/). Depuydt is similarly brusque in the final volley in an exchange with King that began with his own contribution to the *HTR* volume ("Alleged Gospel"), continued in King's response ("Response to Leo Depuydt"), and concluded with a further response by Depuydt posted on Mark Goodacre's *NT Blog* ("Papyrus Fragment"). In this last response, Depuydt marshals evidence to refute King's statement that Depuydt had made an "error of analysis" and in the process implies King is merely "a budding little grammarian" and concludes in a rather patronizing fashion with "So, my little friend, sleep soundly and dream sweetly because there has been no 'error of analysis'" (ibid., 4).

Two other social and digital media phenomena also deserve mention here. Candida Moss of Notre Dame published extensively in *The Daily Beast, CNN Belief Blog,* and *The Atlantic* about the GJW controversy.[36] Moss's writing brought a greater awareness to the general public of the scholarly conversations online. Without her work, arguably the world outside of "academic Twitter" would have little awareness of the contours of the scholarly controversy. Likewise, Eva Mroczek's article in *Religion Dispatches,* "'Gospel of Jesus' Wife' Less Durable than Sexism Surrounding It," earned quite a bit of attention. This piece likely had a substantial number of readers outside the Biblical Studies community and was widely shared and discussed by academics online.

The conversations on Twitter and Facebook contributed to the scholarly consensus on GJW's status as inauthentic, as a forgery. This coheres with Stewart's research on Twitter as a platform for the production of knowledge: scholarship produced in networked online communities is indeed scholarship. Scholars heavily invested in traditional markers of status in the academic prestige economy might dismiss digital platforms, but the scholars on networked media regard it as a legitimate and primary medium for knowledge production. Networked participatory scholarship takes multiple forms, including discovery:

> Participants appeared to carve out regular areas of discussion and investigation for which they become known, in their Twitter circles; peers would then send them links on those topics due to their expressed interests, and signal them into conversations in those areas, thereby extending participants' network reach and visibility. A majority of participants reported that this circulation of ideas and resources not only helped them build new knowledge and become aware of new literature in their fields, but also broadened their understanding of alternate viewpoints in their areas of expertise. Twitter was a site of learning and public scholarly contribution.[37]

Moreover, Twitter facilitates interdisciplinary work, because scholars encounter other modes of research online.[38] Finally, digital networks disproportionately engage scholars marked as lower status by various traditional academic criteria of authenticity; they comprise "a means by which women,

---

36. A few examples: Baden and Moss, "New Clues"; Baden and Moss, "Curious Case"; Moss, "Still as Big a Mystery."

37. Stewart, "In Abundance," 323

38. Ibid., 323.

minorities, and junior scholars could engage openly as public thinkers and experts," whereas senior scholars often eschew the platform.[39]

Gender

The last, but to my mind one of the most important, features of this debate has been gender. Although some of what I have had to say here may appear to be a critique of King, in particular, for choosing not to engage in the digital scholarly conversation, in fact her response (or lack of response) can be understood only when we examine gender as one of the primary markers of authenticity in the academy and in online scholarly communities. We can unpack gender's influence on the scholarly conversation by examining two ways gender operates as a marker of authenticity: women academics in Biblical Studies face pervasive, structural discrimination, and women encounter harassment online at a much higher rate than men.

Charles Haws of the Society of Biblical Literature has conducted several studies of demographic data available from the SBL and national surveys of student degree completion.[40] Women who earn undergraduate degrees in Religious Studies and Biblical Studies go on to complete PhDs at a lower rate than men. And although the raw ratio of women earning PhDs compared to men has increased since the 1990s, the data shows that fewer women than expected are completing their doctorates. In other words, despite an overall increase in women PhDs, the field exhibits a leaky pipeline. Haws took the data on the number of men and women earning Bachelors degrees in Religious Studies as a base cohort of people prepared to go on to graduate work in the field. Then he looked at PhD completion as a percentage of that cohort. The proportion of *prepared women* who go on to complete PhDs has *decreased* compared to *prepared men* who complete PhDs. Somewhere along the way over the past decade and a half, fewer women who are interested in Religious Studies and capable of doing graduate research in the field are completing doctorates compared to men. Women are being squeezed out of our field on a systematic basis.

Another data point on structural inequality involves publication. For two years, Ellen Muehlberger of the University of Michigan tracked the number of female authors in the *Review of Biblical Literature* (of both books and their reviewers), and the percentage of women contributors is consistently and significantly lower than the percentage of women in the Society.[41]

39. Ibid., 330.
40. Haws, "Women Earning Doctorates."
41. Muehlberger, "Review of Biblical Literature"; Muehlberger, "Thoughts after Two

Even the *Journal of Early Christian Studies*, whose senior editor was a self-identified feminist, in 2014 published only two articles by women; less than 10 percent of 2014 *JECS* article authors were women. In other words: even for women who have survived the leaky pipeline, their voices are marginal to the field.[42] For scholars of color, this problem is further magnified. Some of this data, such as the *JECS* statistics, shows that the problem cannot be conveniently blamed on the population of more politically or theologically conservative biblical scholars.

Women on social media and women scholars who publish or appear in interviews in popular media outlets experience also a high degree of harassment and discrimination in the digital realm. In 2014, Pew released a major study about online harassment and concluded that while "men are more likely to experience online harassment," women experience more severe and sustained abuse. Men are called names more frequently, but women online are more likely to experience stalking, sexual harassment, and physical threats. Forty percent of women who had been harassed online reported that it was "extremely or very upsetting," compared to only 17% of men.[43] The sexism and trolling that Classics scholar Mary Beard experiences provides the clearest example of this phenomenon in academia. In one of the most egregious episodes, television critic A. A. Gill opined that Beard was too old and ugly to be on television. Beard, of course, fought back, charging him with clear and blatant misogyny.[44] Beard's response, however, did not end the torrent of sexist abuse sent her way; writers on the Internet continued to disparage her for her age, appearance, clothing, and style of speaking.[45] Beard's encounters with her sexist detractors in the media, on blogs, and on Twitter have been documented in a 2014 profile in the *New Yorker*. Beard fights back on social media (by retweeting and responding to even some of her most craven trolls), and in private, by e-mailing and messaging her detractors. The *New Yorker* profile reveals the amount of labor a high-profile woman academic on social media expends simply in combating misogyny. This time and the emotional labor constitute expenditures not faced by male academics, or at least not to such a degree.

The risks are high for women academics to engage their critics online. The costs run even higher—their emotional equilibrium, their productivity

---

Years."

42. For an explanation of how institutional sexism affects the individual academic, see Bond, "Sexism and NT Scholarship."

43. Duggan, "Online Harassment."

44. Rojas, "Mary Beard."

45. Gill's column in the *Spectator* provides just one example. A Google search will uncover many more, such as Liddle, "It's Not Misogyny."

derailed. These two factors combined (sexism in the academy and online harassment) create a climate that encourages women not to engage in public scholarship, especially in popular online media venues, such as blogs and social media. The risks and costs for women of color run even higher, as Tressie McMillan Cottom has documented in her article, "'Who do you think you are?': When Marginality Meets Academic Microcelebrity"; McMillan Cottom cites the substantial harassment and threats against several Black women academics, including history of Christianity professor Dr. Anthea Butler.[46]

The Responsibilities of Universities

Finally, I wish to note how academic institutions affect these personal markers of authenticity. In the case of the GJW fragment, Harvard leveraged its status and reputation in order to "signal boost" King's scholarship on the manuscript. However, after Askeland and others raised questions about the manuscript's authenticity, King and Harvard both became silent, reacting to virtually none of the news circulating on Facebook, Twitter, and blogs about the manuscript. Harvard also did not publish the *HTR* article as originally planned. King was left in a bit of a lurch: on the forefront in the media about this controversial topic, yet unable to publish her work in *HTR*.

Tressie McMillan Cottom has written about higher education institutions' desire for their faculty to produce public, accessible scholarship, and their simultaneous discouragement of such work. In her blog post, "Everything but the Burden," McMillan Cottom charges that institutions essentially fatten up their faculty before throwing them to the wolves. Public scholarship, media appearances, and public engagement bring prestige and accolades to an institution. They also bring controversy. McMillan Cottom writes, "Basically, the scale of current media is so beyond anything academia can grasp that those with agendas get a leg up on pulling the levers of universities' inherent conservativism." When the inherent conservatism of the university kicks in, the public academic feels vulnerable and censured.[47] The stakes are higher for women and especially women of color than other faculty. And as Anthony Le Donne noted in his book, the online outrage machine was primed to react due to the very title given the papyrus. Writing about his participation on a panel I organized at the University of the Pacific, Le Donne reflects, "What I learned from this experience is that the topic of 'the wife of Jesus' brings a host of expectations with it. This topic has

---

46. McMillan Cottom, "'Who Do You Think You Are?'"

47. Ibid.; see also McMillan Cottom, "Everything but the Burden."

been sold as a scandal for so long that people can't help but be scandalized by it."[48]

Harvard bears no small amount of responsibility in this controversy—for winding it up and exposing King to the resulting maelstrom. As Eva Mroczek observed, King was subject to derogatory remarks about her appearance and her character.[49] Although I do not know what happened at Harvard, I submit that Harvard did King a disservice by not publishing the *HTR* article right away alongside the work of some of the critics, by not releasing the collection history and provenance information, by neither encouraging King to participate in the online digital scholarship about the fragment nor providing some mechanism for other university representatives to engage (and then supporting those who did), and by not addressing the ongoing social media conversation on the official Harvard GJW website and on social media itself.

From an outsider's perspective, it appears that Harvard did protect King in the ways McMillan Cottom argues all institutions must: by providing resources to deal with the wave of inquiries, academic freedom protections, and generally not throwing King under the bus (as arguably other institutions have done to their controversial faculty). However, Harvard protected its professor at a price, the price of privileging a model of academic knowledge production based on scarcity rather than one based on openness and abundance.[50]

CONCLUSION: CEDING THE TERRITORY

Bonnie Stewart's research suggests that scholarship will increasingly happen online, including in social media circles, because scholars find these venues useful and productive.[51] The groups of scholars who are practicing online scholarship do not always line up with the metrics of traditional academic credentialing. Research is happening online. In this case, it grew primarily on social media and on blogs, particularly on a more conservative, Evangelical blog, but that was not the only location: on Facebook and Twitter, scholars who did not identify as Evangelical exchanged theories about the

48. Le Donne, *Wife of Jesus*, x.

49. Mroczek, "Sexism."

50. Here I take language from Stewart's analysis of online networked scholarly practices ("In Abundance").

51. Stewart ("In Abundance") does note that academics on Twitter have expressed concerns that institutions and other pressures are beginning to constrain the networked participatory scholarship they value.

document. Academics who dismiss social media and digital publishing do so at their own peril—especially scholars who dismiss the conservatism or tone of the blogs. To dismiss this work is to cede the territory of future scholarly conversation. The transformation of blog posts into the *New Testament Studies* issue on GJW proves that the landscape is shifting, and that the digital production of knowledge bears fruit in the more traditional academic publishing pipeline. For women scholars, the territory can be a treacherous one, but I would argue that that is all the more reason for self-identified feminist, progressive scholars of early Christianity and the New Testament to engage online and support their female colleagues online, especially senior scholars. To leave this responsibility to women themselves or to early career scholars is unethical and does not contribute to the growth of knowledge in our field.

Finally, digital scholarship is pushing back against the habits of secrecy, seclusion, and private ownership upon which humanities scholarship is currently built: the scholar working in isolation until "ready" to present his/her work to the world, the anonymous peer review system, and mystery and dread about where many of our sources—especially in Coptic—come from. Many of us have made our names studying colonized and/or stolen material. I know I will never look at newly-published and newly-discovered manuscripts in the same way again, and many of my colleagues have shared with me the same sentiment.

The digital, of course, is not synonymous with openness. In *The Immanent Frame*, Kathryn Lofton argues that the digital is often "a place to hide." She presses, "We may see the Internet as an openness, an availability, a potential divulgence of privacy and overexposure of self. But what if it all is just song and dance relative to its basic proposition, namely that none of us never ever get to know what is really going on?"[52] Lofton has a point: digital records are easily confused, altered, and used to misdirect. The digital, as I have argued here, is also a place to bully, a place to force someone (especially a woman) into hiding. We delude ourselves, however, if we believe that the pillars of traditional academic work do not also frequently obscure "what is really going on." The leaky PhD pipeline and our field's publication records show that the traditional apparatus of the academic prestige economy has hidden quite a bit from our view. At this moment, I argue, to hide *from* the digital is to cede the territory to others who will then shape the contours of our field without us.

52. Lofton, "Digital."

– 16 –

Slow Scholarship
Do Bloggers Rush in Where Jesus' Wife Would Fear to Tread?

— James F. McGrath —

WE LIVE IN AN era in which information flows quickly, sometimes *too* quickly. *Christianity Today* recently featured an article about the problem of Christians sharing fake news stories that came to their attention and were accepted uncritically.[1] But the issue is not limited to religious communities. I know a self-proclaimed skeptic who almost daily posts things on Facebook that are satire, but which he mistakes for real news. International news agencies have repeated "news" featured in the satirical newsmagazine the *Onion*. Academics are not immune from this: there are few if any of us whose information-literacy skills are so well-honed that we could never find ourselves mistaking satire for factual reporting, falling for a hoax, or getting "rickrolled." This chapter explores how this ever-quickening pace of information flow impacts scholars and the work we do, using the case of the *Gospel of Jesus' Wife* (GJW) as the primary example.

There have been reactions of protest to the ever-quickening pace of life; the "slow food movement" is one example. But despite the echo in the title, this chapter is not advocating a slow scholarship movement; rather,

1. Stetzer, "Embarrassing Week."

326

it seeks to evaluate whether there is a point beyond which any increase in *pace* will result in a corresponding loss of *scholarly rigor*. Even less will this chapter advocate for a *print* scholarship movement. I do not prefer physical papers (which slowly inch their way along in manila envelopes through campus mail) to e-mails. I do not long for the days when I had to make a trip to a library, use a card catalogue to try to find an item, and hopefully find it on the shelf, just in order to check a reference. I delight at the fact that I live in an era when I can often use Google to track down in seconds a piece of information that might in the past have involved a literal slow boat to China.

I believe that GJW provides a very interesting and important test case for some of the new ways we are approaching scholarship and scholarly interaction for a number of reasons. Perhaps most significantly, the majority of bloggers appear to be right, and some were right all along, that this papyrus fragment was indeed a modern forgery. Bloggers have been at the forefront of reporting on the topic, seeking to pass along accurate information to media outlets, and engaging in scholarly discussion about the papyrus fragment. The GJW case appears to vindicate biblioblogging as an approach to scholarship. So why is this essay voicing concerns and advising caution, even as the activity of blogging is moving further from the margins into the heart of the mainstream?

The case of GJW most certainly does provide evidence for the positive contribution of bloggers and blogging in the academy. But it is possible to draw that conclusion too quickly, and on the basis of insufficient evidence, even as some bloggers had done in the case of GJW's authenticity. They may have been proven right in the long term. But the crucial point which must be made emphatically in this context is that it is not the rightness of conclusions which defines scholarship, but the *methods* whereby those right conclusions are drawn. When Philolaus the Pythagorean supposed that the Earth moved around a central fire, because of the hierarchical relationship of fire to other elements in his system of thought, he was in a sense right that the Earth was not the stationary center of things, and right again that something hot was at the center. But he was not right about these things *for the right reasons*.[2] I am concerned that some bloggers *happened to turn out to be right*, after having made up their minds prematurely, before the evidence became available, and the arguments made about that evidence justified the conclusions that they drew.

---

2. On Philolaus's astronomical system, and the assumptions that led to it, see Huffman, "Philolaus."

In other words, under a tongue-in-cheek title (of the sort you would probably expect from a blogger), this chapter addresses the nature of scholarly methods and scholarly epistemology, and asks what remains the same and what is different between the traditional print approach to scholarship and the new avenues opened to us through blogging. While there is reason for concern and caution, there is also reason for excitement at ways that blogging and other forms of online interaction can make our work not only quicker, but also more accurate, and ultimately more accessible. But I would argue that our blogging is only in genuine service of the academy and the public when we make sure that we blog as scholars, making our points in appropriate scholarly ways.

Let me elaborate in more detail with specific examples from the case of GJW.[3] A good place to begin is with an outline sketch of the timeline whereby the news broke, the bloggers responded, and conclusions were drawn, as this information conveys very clearly the pace with which news travels and discussion unfolds in the biblioblogosphere. It was September 18, 2012 when Karen King made her presentation about the Coptic papyrus fragment that depicts Jesus saying "My wife. . ."[4] Once the news broke, bloggers like Mark Goodacre said what could be said safely at that stage, indicating that the text (1) did not tell us anything about the historical Jesus, and that (2) while there was reason to be cautious if not indeed suspicious, sometimes genuine discoveries have included things some would consider sensational.[5] One thing that blogs allow us to do is to be very precise about the timing of posts. In this case, Goodacre posted on his blog at 1:31am on September 19; clearly he was trying to get a balanced statement on the subject onto his blog as quickly as possible, even if that meant burning the midnight oil and beyond.

Yet even earlier, at some point on the very same day the news broke, a blogger named Jim West had already dismissed the fragment as "rubbish" because of its unknown provenance.[6] Ironically, he wrote the following about the statements by scholars that were being reported in the media: "In short, what it shows is that even now, when people should know better, they still are more than willing to say more than can honestly and confidently be

---

3. A useful timeline is maintained by Michael Grondin at *Question of Content*; Grondin, "Jesus' Wife Fragment 2014"; and Grondin, "Jesus' Wife Fragment 2015."

4. The existence of the text was announced more widely in *Harvard Magazine* ("New Gospel"); see also the Harvard Divinity School *Gospel of Jesus' Wife* website http://gospelofjesuswife.hds.harvard.edu/.

5. Goodacre, "Gospel of Jesus' Wife."

6. West, "No, People."

said." Surely his own confidence at this very early stage itself represents a willingness to "say more than can honestly and confidently be said"?

By the evening of September 19, Nicole Winfield of the Associated Press had interviewed two papyrologists who both expressed doubts about the fragment's authenticity.[7] On September 19 and 20, Tom Verenna posted twice on his blog, the first post indicating that GJW looked like a forgery, the second still inclining in that direction, but noting the still very good reasons to not jump to that conclusion on the basis of evidence currently available.[8] On September 21, Francis Watson posted two pdfs on Mark Goodacre's blog, arguing that the work is most likely a forgery.[9] Rafael Rodriguez in turn blogged about Watson's article, under the title "A Verdict is In."[10] By the end of the day, Andrew Brown was declaring the matter settled in the *Guardian*, even while getting key details incorrect in his reporting.[11]

Also on September 21, I joined the discussion, pointing out that Watson's arguments about the derivative character of the work applied equally well to authentic gospels. I stressed that Watson's comparison of GJW to the *Secret Gospel of Mark* simply presumed the inauthenticity of the latter, and so hurt his case in the eyes of those who do not share his assumption.[12] On September 27, Timo Panaanen provided me with a pdf to host on my blog space, which showed that the same method Watson had applied to GJW, purportedly showing it to be a forgery, could be applied with the same results to a verifiably authentic ancient papyrus.[13] The argument whereby the most influential case had been made for inauthenticity at this stage was clearly flawed, as the evidence surveyed, while compatible with forgery, most certainly did not prove it in any meaningful sense. Nonetheless, by the end of the month, the Vatican as well as various Evangelical Christian apologetics blogs were claiming with confidence that the text is a fake.[14]

Let me stop my overview of the unfolding online reporting—on scholars' blogs and in the media—to focus in on this one particular moment. Within *three days* (and in some cases significantly less), there were scholars

---

7. Other than on the Internet Archive, one of the few places where this press release can still be found online is Jim West's blog; see West, "And Now the Motive."

8. Verenna, "'Wife of Jesus' Fragment"; Verenna, "Two Days Later."

9. Watson, "Fake Gospel-Fragment"; Watson, "Introduction and Summary."

10. Rodriguez, "Verdict Is In." He had not taken this view when he first shared the news about the papyrus the day before: Rodriguez, "Gospel of Jesus' Wife."

11. Brown, "Fake, Claims Expert"; Mark Goodacre pointed out some of the errors in an update to his post sharing Watson's article ("Fake Gospel-Fragment").

12. McGrath, "Is the Gospel of Jesus' Wife a Fake?"

13. Paananen, "Another 'Fake.'"

14. O'Leary, "Fragment Is a Fake."

who felt that they were in a position to comment with confidence on a question pertaining to a papyrus which had not been subjected to scientific testing, which they had not studied in person, and about which experts in papyrology had expressed a range of opinions. They did so on the basis of what I hope we can agree are problematic arguments. The fact that the writing on the papyrus was not that of professional quality does not tell us about its antiquity or recent production. Nor does the presence of grammatical and other errors. Those of us who study ancient artifacts, such as magic bowls from Mesopotamia, know that there were people throughout history who had learned enough writing to produce and sell such objects to others, but whose writing on the bowls ranged from meaningless combinations of letters to awkwardly and inaccurately-copied versions of the compositions of others. One might call these "forgeries"—and to his credit, Watson acknowledged in his article that GJW could have been an *ancient* forgery rather than a modern one, but his article nonetheless ran together those two possibilities, which scholars of antiquity ought to keep separate, and should want to ensure that the wider public can also keep separate. To my knowledge, no scholar was suggesting that GJW was an early work that might answer the historical question of whether Jesus was married. The only question was whether the papyrus might provide evidence of what some people believed in later centuries about Jesus and his wife. A work like the *Gospel of Philip*, which depicts Jesus and Mary Magdalene as kissing frequently on the [lacuna] (63.35–36), can be categorized as an "ancient forgery" in the sense that it is a work from a later time, pretending to be written by an individual named Philip who had lived earlier. But ancient forgeries are of great value to historians and scholars for the things they tell us about the people who forged them and the context in which they considered it worth doing so. And so even to risk giving the impression that the choice was between the work being a historically authentic account of the life of a married Jesus or a forgery (ancient or modern), which is thus of little or no value, is to fail to accurately convey scholarly nuance in what is communicated. And while the press has a notorious history of being resistant to such nuance and precision, it is crucial that we try to convey it nevertheless.

Blogs would later present evidence that seems to demonstrate beyond reasonable doubt that GJW is indeed a forgery. But the fact that subsequent evidence and study demonstrated this does not justify the premature assertion, based on inadequate evidence and unconvincing arguments, that the matter had already been settled. It is arguable that Galileo Galilei did harm to his own case (as well as that of others) for heliocentrism when he claimed that the tides provided proof of the Earth's rotation. His critics correctly saw the problems with this claim, and this affected their impression of his overall case.[15] The fact that he used bad arguments in his case for a conclusion that nevertheless proved to be correct, and had a tendency to belittle and insult those who disagreed with him, certainly makes Galileo a historical example from which bloggers ought to learn, prone as we are to both these shortcomings. And so the issue is not merely procedural but also practical. If we jump too hastily to conclusions, bolstered by flawed arguments, it may undermine the credibility of our views—and may continue to do so even later, when other, better evidence and arguments shows that our initial hunch was correct all along.

Would anything have been lost if scholars in those first few days had consistently emphasized that forgery was a *real possibility*; that scientific testing needed to be done but that, even if the papyrus and the ink were ancient, such testing would not exclude the possibility of forgery; and that even if the text was an authentic ancient fragment, it was one from long after the time of Jesus and thus told us about beliefs in those times, and not about Jesus himself? And was anything gained by jumping to a conclusion so hastily, before the evidence justified it? My own view is that because scholarship is characterized by rigorous methods, it is to our credit when we openly acknowledge that certain views we hold are hunches, and that we still await the results of further investigation to show whether or not our instincts are as good as our methods. It will also make it easier to change our minds if further evidence comes to light which should lead us to do so.

It is worth listing the bloggers of whom I am aware who commented even briefly on this matter within those first few days after the news about the papyrus broke, since it gives a sense of the impressive speed and collaborative attention in the response of scholars and of others who regularly read and engage with scholars' blogs. They are: Paul Barford, Allan Bevere, Mike Bird, John Byron, Stephen Carlson, Steve Caruso, Jim Davila, April DeConick, Bart Ehrman, Jeffrey Garcia, Mark Goodacre, Chuck Grantham, Larry Hurtado, Ferrell Jenkins, Dirk Jongkind, Brian LePort, Timo Paananen, Stephen Prothero, Rafael Rodriguez, Gavin Rumney, Ken Schenck, James Tabor, Tom Verenna, Dan Wallace, Joel Watts, Jim West, and Ben Witherington.[16] While not all of the above are scholars or even students in a relevant field, the list still features an impressive number of names of not merely scholars, but *well-known* scholars with an international reputation. All of the aforementioned individuals commented within a week of the news breaking, and used blogs to do so. Surely this is a noteworthy mo-

---

15. See further Shea, "Galileo's Claim," 111–27; Finocchiaro, *Routledge Guidebook*, 215–56.

16. McGrath, "Is the Gospel of Jesus' Wife a Fake?"

ment in the history of scholarship, whatever one may think of the specific conclusions drawn or points made.

Returning to our survey of the unfolding events, on October 11, Andrew Bernhard posted a pdf article with the title "How The Gospel of Jesus's Wife Might Have Been Forged: A Tentative Proposal."[17] On October 16, making reference to Bernhard's article, Andrew Brown wrote on the subject in *The Guardian* once again, declaring that "It's been fairly clear for weeks that the papyrus fragment known as the 'gospel of Jesus's wife' was a modern fake."[18] I want to highlight the contrast between these two online publications. Note Bernhard's tentativeness—emphasized in the title—despite having very insightful evidence and arguments which would be vindicated later.[19] Also to be noted is what Bernhard had to say about the *process* of how this matter was handled through online venues. Bernhard told *Live Science* that the involvement of the Internet in the release of information and scholarly interaction was a significant step forward: "My personal opinion is that Karen King and *Harvard Theological Review* have significantly improved the traditional peer review process by utilizing the Internet. In fact, this could potentially be a watershed moment in the history of scholarship where the academic process becomes more open and transparent."[20] This claim too seems to have been vindicated. It would take two to three years for these matters to be addressed in the traditional print format of scholarly journals.[21] Even then, many of us have read the articles in *Harvard Theological Review* and *New Testament Studies* online. And the print articles were in almost every instance interacting with the earlier online discussion; in some cases they were simply more developed versions of those online articles and blog posts.

There is a longstanding precedent in other fields to this approach of academic discussion beginning online in a similar manner to what we have documented here.[22] In physics and other fields of science, drafts of work have been shared on the online repository arXiv (or its predecessor) since

17. Bernhard, "Tentative Proposal."

18. Brown, "Very Modern Fake."

19. Bernhard, "Patchwork"; see also Bernhard, "Patchwork (Recap)" and additional discussion in Askeland, "Grondin's Interlinear."

20. Brynner, "Authenticity Tests."

21. See the April 2014 *HTR* issue and the July 2015 *NTS* issue. See also Baden and Moss, "Curious Case"; Pattengale, "Hoax Fell Apart."

22. Anne Mahoney recently wrote, "Classicists can take digital humanities (DH) for granted. We are all familiar with projects like the TLG, Perseus, the Bibliotheca Neo-Latina, and even BMCR itself" (Review of Klein, *Interdisciplining*).

the early 1990s.[23] These are not peer reviewed (although there is oversight of submissions to ensure relevance), and the appearance online of pre-publication copies of works apparently does not prevent subsequent publication in print. Indeed, it is arguable that the feedback received on drafts plays an important role in the quality of the finalized published versions—or whether the research is continued at all. In January of this year, that site celebrated the posting of its *millionth* paper.[24] The closest we have had in our fields is arguably the academic conference—and the parallel is even closer for some of us who, for a good many years now, have participated in sessions for which digital copies of papers have been circulated in advance, allowing for them to be read and not merely heard, and for them to be reflected on, facilitating not only more but better discussion and feedback.[25]

The digital dissemination of scholarship is connected to another aspect of this topic, since an online source is thought to have been used by the person who forged GJW. Andrew Bernhard, in his article in *NTS*, acknowledged that each suspicious detail could have a legitimate plausible explanation in an authentic text, and that it is the combination of these features that makes it most likely that GJW is a forgery: "No genuinely ancient writing would be likely to compress so many suspicious textual features into just eight short, partial lines of text. GJW is better understood as a modern forgery that contains numerous indications of its recent origin: all five notable textual features can be explained well as the result of a forger's dependence on 'Grondin's Interlinear.'"[26] If online discussion played a decisive role in the case for the work being a forgery, online material may also have played a crucial role *in the forgery itself.*

Michael Grondin's website has been very useful to scholars, and so it is also worth noting that Grondin is a computer programmer with an interest in the *Gospel of Thomas* but has no degrees that relate directly to the study of that text.[27] The Internet, it has been said, democratizes knowledge—anyone can create a blog or website on any topic they wish. Some have decried this as creating a free-for-all in which expertise counts for nothing. Yet far from representing a departure from historic scholarship, this shift is actually a return to something that was commonplace in earlier eras. The proliferation of experts in crowded research areas has, in recent decades, tended to

23. Ginsparg, "Twenty Years Ago."

24. Noorden, "arXiv Preprint Server."

25. The conference that led to the production of the present volume is itself an example of this procedure being followed.

26. Bernhard, "Textual Evidence," 354.

27. See Grondin's website for more information: http://gospel-thomas.net/s_persnl.htm.

marginalize those outside the academy, with very few exceptions. But we are all presumably aware of some famous instances of crucial work done by people who would be dismissed as amateurs in our time. For instance, would Darwin even be given a hearing by modern biologists given that he only earned an undergraduate degree, and even then in theology rather than biology?[28] And arguably the most important work on the Mandaeans in the twentieth century was undertaken by Ethel Stephana Drower, who was an autodidact in the relevant fields. But living in Iraq, she made friends with the Mandaeans and acquired the most important collection of Mandaean manuscripts for the Bodleian Library in Oxford, wrote what is still the go-to survey of the Mandaeans, published the only translations in English of a number of Mandaean texts, and published articles and reviews in mainstream scholarly journals. Today such an "independent scholar" might find it much harder to get a hearing, perhaps because the Internet has made us more aware of how many cranks there are around, but also because there are so many scholars *within* the academy vying for spots in publications and conferences that there is less room for anyone else. Nonetheless, in the case of GJW, and also in discussion of *Secret Mark*, we have seen the important role played not only by professional academics who blog, but also people whose interest in ancient religious texts is not connected directly to their qualifications or profession.[29]

Another point that is relevant in the consideration of this new approach to scholarship online is the penchant for online articles and blog posts, even those with substantial scholarly content, to contain snide or offensive remarks which would be unlikely to make it into a peer-reviewed print journal article—or even be included in a submission to such a venue. For instance, the conclusion of Francis Watson's online article reads:

> The Jesus of the Secret Gospel [of Mark] likes to consort naked with young men at night, while seeming hostile to women. By contrast, the new gospel fragment has Jesus speak

---

28. Jump ("Watson and Crick") suggests that even Watson and Crick, who had relevant qualifications and who famously proposed the double helix structure of DNA, would have found it hard to get that idea published if they were seeking to do so in our time.

29. Another oddity related to blogs and publications on this topic is when I was cited in an article on GJW by David Kim ("Reconsidering"). The bibliography has a link under my name to Francis Watson's pdf article hosted on Mark Goodacre's blog! Errors happen in print scholarship as well as electronic, but it is worth mentioning that the blog format—in which there can be guest posts and hosted articles—may make confusion of this sort more common. Also noteworthy is the small amount of print publications cited in Kim's bibliography.

disconcertingly of "my wife." Has this new heterosexual Jesus been created to complement Smith's homosexual one?[30]

I am not sure which is more problematic: the homophobic mischaracterization of what *Secret Mark* depicts, or the suggestion that merely by depicting Jesus as heterosexual (which apparently is disconcerting), GJW might be offering a deliberate counterpart to *Secret Mark*. Arguably worse still, Christian Askeland, in a blog post that offered what many of us consider the decisive evidence that GJW was a forgery (showing as it did that the Lycopolitan Gospel of John text which accompanied it was written in the same hand and follows the line breaks of a print edition) managed to distract from the substantive matters by referring to the text as the "ugly sister" of Jesus' wife.[31] The title of the post was eventually changed as a result of feedback, but the matter still drew attention.[32]

But let us set aside matters such as the casual tone of most blogs, which one can also find in conference papers (which, as I have already said, I consider the closest historic analogue in our field to substantive blog posts), and return once again to the most crucial point, which is not the speed at which scholarship moved in the case of GJW, so much as the speed with which particular scholarly proposals came to be treated as definitive, not only by the media, but by other scholars. In the traditional workings of scholarship, the appearance of a new article would typically mark either the beginning of a conversation or its continuation, and only very rarely its definitive end, and that after much consideration of its merits. We are aware that our work as academics moves constantly between two poles, that of consensus-building and consensus-challenging. We seek to break new ground, but we know that our points of agreement as an academic community are more likely to be correct, and the correctness or otherwise of our new proposals must be evaluated by the scholarly guild as a whole.

And so let me pose the question in epistemological terms: at what point if any could we appropriately say that we *knew* that GJW is a modern forgery? When I ask about our *knowledge*, I mean in the sense that our scholarly conclusion was adequately justified. The epistemology of scholarship has been a focus of significant discussion in recent years, in particular in relation to the Digital Humanities.[33] If we set the bar too high, then perhaps even now we do not yet *know with absolute certainty* that GJW is a

30. Watson, "Fake Gospel-Fragment."

31. Askeland, "Jesus Had a Sister-in-Law."

32. See Mroczek, "Sexism."

33. See for instance Schon, "Knowing-in-action"; Cecire, "Introduction"; Ramsay and Rockwell, "Developing Things"; Kitchin, "Big Data"; Liu, "Theses."

forgery. It seems extremely likely based on current evidence, to be sure, but how likely does it need to be for us to speak of *knowledge*? And is input from a significantly larger number of experts necessary before we can be not just confident but, for all intents and purposes, certain?

Consensus-building takes time. As we teach students to inquire into the scholarly consensus as a starting point for their own research, the question arises as to where is best to look in order to find out what the consensus of experts is on a particular matter. To what extent do scholarly blogs give the public a clear sense of the scholarly consensus on any given topic? If those scholars who happen to blog also tend to have views that are a minority stance in the guild, could that lead to misperception by readers outside of the field? To give but one example, I sometimes get the sense that skepticism about the classic four-source solution to the Synoptic Problem (the Q hypothesis) is more common in the biblioblogosphere than in the academy more generally. To the extent that not all scholars blog, will those who do blog have an undue influence in shaping the impression amongst the media and the general public of what scholars think?

This ought not to concern us too much. The bigger issue is how to convey to the public that attempts to further knowledge, whether on blogs or in peer-reviewed articles, will often be seeking to challenge a consensus. Reading just one publication, whether it be a blog post or a peer-reviewed article, in many instances will not convey a sense of what the scholarly consensus is. In seeking to distinguish scholarship from other voices online, we have rightly pointed to peer review as distinctive of the scholarly enterprise. But it seems that, in turn, we also need to make clear that peer review does not guarantee that the viewpoint expressed or conclusions drawn are correct; that judgment requires the further steps of discussion, evaluation, response, counterargument, and consensus-building that are also key features of the scholarly endeavor.

Since that process is so crucial, we may take delight in the possibility that blogs and other online forums may speed things up considerably. When it comes to the process of academic publication and dialogue, there is nothing inherently positive about taking a long time. No-one, I am sure, thinks that the lengthy process and tedious delays before the Dead Sea Scrolls finally became available is preferable to the process around GJW. I am not advocating for us to move more slowly, but to move as quickly as we can while still being *careful*. Nor has print scholarship always moved at a snail's pace. For example, after the publication of E. P. Sanders' seminal work *Paul and Palestinian Judaism*, four reviews by major scholars appeared within the following year, and many scholars seemed to be aware very quickly that a landmark publication had taken place.[34] It might be interesting to speculate as to what this example might have looked like if it happened now, in our Internet era. Would Sanders' 600+ pages have worked as a series of blog posts? If Sanders had blogged on his points while working on the book, his posts certainly would have appeared over time as they were written, rather than all at once. And with blog posts one does not usually go back and polish a previous post; instead, one writes a new one, and the effect of such rewriting on the persuasiveness of one's arguments has not, to my knowledge, been studied. If the entire argument of the book had appeared in a series of blog posts, would it have seemed as persuasive? And how might the reviews have impacted things, if they too had appeared on blogs? Presumably there would have been interaction throughout the series, but would the interactions, and the reactions of the scholarly community as well as of religious groups, have been the same?

Turning to another example, what might have unfolded in the blogosphere if Codex Sinaiticus had been discovered in our time? Larry Hurtado mentioned Constantine Simonides on his blog in connection with the discussions of GJW.[35] Simonides, a famous forger, claimed to have forged Codex Sinaiticus, which Tischendorf discovered at St. Catherine's Monastery in the nineteenth century. Lest this seem too speculative an undertaking, I would point out that, unbeknownst to most academics, debates continue on blogs between Christian apologists about the authenticity of Codex Sinaiticus to this very day, with the case for its inauthenticity championed in particular by members of the King James Only movement.[36] If the matter were not something considered to be long settled among scholars, but was something that appeared as breaking news, how might scholarly bloggers have reacted to this sensational find, which was followed in turn by a confession from a renowned forger that he had produced the artifact? I will not try to apply to the methods used by bloggers in analyzing GJW to Sinaiticus in detail—it is not, at any rate, a precisely parallel situation. But I suspect that some of us might have considered the sensational character of the find, coupled with the confession of the forger, to settle the matter. It would be worth looking closely at precisely what persuaded scholars of the authenticity of Codex Sinaiticus, and what would be involved in the same kind of evidence being found persuasive in the context of online discussion and interaction today, whether about GJW or something else.

34. See the reviews by Dahl, Sandmel, Caird, and Jacob Neusner.
35. Hurtado, "Master Hoaxer."
36. Pack, "Codex Sinaiticus."

What about *Secret Mark*? In this case, we have Stephen Carlson, a blogger who has also published a book on that specific subject.[37] And so this is not a purely theoretical case, but one in which we can ask about the role of blogging in relation to print scholarship. In this instance, however, there is far, far less agreement among scholars about the question of forgery vs. authenticity than in the case of Sinaiticus. A Google search for "Secret Gospel of Mark" turns up many blogs among the first two pages of results, with a mix of arguments for authenticity and inauthenticity—perhaps representing quite well the lay of the scholarly land on this topic. It would be another interesting thought experiment, to consider how the situation might be similar or different if the news about the discovery of *Secret Mark* broke for the first time in the present day. We would surely have accusations of forgery, but perhaps the matter might have been resolved more satisfactorily if Morton Smith himself had had the opportunity to write a guest blog post responding to Stephen Carlson's accusations, as well as those of others.

Looking at this case, another issue arises related to blogging and online scholarship: the penchant of online scholarship to later disappear from the Internet. Andrew Bernhard's name has been mentioned already in connection with GJW, but he also at one point had materials online related to *Secret Mark*. His current website, however, does not include those pages, and the Internet Archive suggests they disappeared from the web in the late 1990s.[38] Blogs and other web pages are notorious for being ephemeral, but residual copies of materials that have since been updated and improved continue to be accessible, if one knows where to look for them. Scholarship depends on our ability to access work that was done previously and to build upon it. If finding print copies of articles and books is much more tedious and time-consuming than accessing them online, the ease and speed of access to blog posts and online pdfs will not be an advantage if those things disappear from the web completely, unobtainable even through interlibrary loan.

Blogging is simply a *format* of online publication, which can serve to make available anything from pictures of cats to scholarly arguments. The same things can be found in print, although much less frequently are they found side-by-side in the same publication. But the fact that hobbies and humor may appear on blogs alongside reflections on ongoing research and commentary on breaking news about archaeological finds has, for some of us, created a genuine sense of getting to know one another as people via the Internet. Given the penchant for rancor and insult in online venues,

37. Carlson, *Gospel Hoax*.

38. For those who may be interested, the materials are accessible via the Internet Archive at https://web.archive.org/web/19981205133918/http://www.teleport.com/~cabern/andrew/translations/secret_mark.html/.

the potential benefit of something that leads us to recognize one another—and thus hopefully treat one another—as real human beings, offsets, in my mind, the potential disadvantages of the mixing of frivolity and scholarship on blogs and other social media.

In conclusion, I want to very briefly propose that scholars who maintain an online presence ought to work together to determine how best to achieve the aim of preserving scholarly rigor while coupling it with the greater speed possible through the harnessing of current and future technology. The following elements seem to me to be of particular importance and urgency:

1. More participation: One of the strengths of the academy is that it has participants around the world, who all look in some standard places for the research carried out by others. To have that strength as part of online scholarship, we need a much larger number of scholars involved in blogging, present on social media, and participating in the scholarly process online.

2. More caution: A day or two, in my opinion, is unlikely to ever be an appropriate amount of time in which to draw a definitive conclusion about a serious subject. But even when drawing a tentative conclusion, we need to be aware that media reports are often inaccurate, photographs do not always give an accurate impression of artifacts, and that in other ways we may not yet have access to the information that we need. And, to the extent that we comment day-by-day as things unfold, we need to be an example in our willingness to change our minds as newly-available evidence makes a compelling case for our doing so.

3. More openness and accessibility: To the extent that we can make our publications available online, not just on blogs but institutional repositories and open-access peer-reviewed journals, we can allow interaction not just with blog posts but with full-fledged articles online.

Blogging and online publication and interaction have already had a transformative impact on scholarship, and I am excited about the many ways that technology will enhance what we do in the future, in ways that we have yet to imagine. In the meantime, I hope that we can work together to make sure that rather than imposing an arbitrary speed limit on scholarship which does nothing but slow us down, we can move quickly but collaboratively. We have more insight together than we do alone. By drawing conclusions too quickly as individuals, and by hearing only select voices (whether by choice or because other scholars are not participating in online discussion), we risk losing that which gives scholarship its strength. The good news is that none of those things is a necessary part of blogging and online interaction. And so all it should take in order for us to preserve the historic strengths of scholarship and combine them with the greater speed that the Internet makes possible, is for us to make a concerted effort to do so. We have not always seen that happen, but we can surely find examples to show how similar shortcomings have been evidenced in the past in print scholarship too. The academy is what academics make it, and I for one am more thrilled than worried by the positive things we have seen as academics have come together and joined forces to investigate and expose a forgery, across wide distances of geography as well as ideology, in ways that could not be achieved as easily, as quickly, or as effectively in the past. It is my hope that the next time a major discovery—authentic or forged—makes headlines, we will see a response that includes all the positive elements in the response to GJW, while surpassing what we achieved in that instance in terms of caution, scholarly interaction, accuracy of reporting, judiciousness, and effectiveness in conveying our scholarly insights to the media and to the wider public.

– 17 –

Jesus' Wife, the Media, and *The Da Vinci Code*

— Mark Goodacre —

It is now beyond reasonable doubt that the *Gospel of Jesus' Wife* (GJW) is a modern forgery. Articles in the July 2015 issue of *New Testament Studies*[1] crystallized and carried forward arguments that had been appearing in blogs and other online venues for many months, arguments that made it clear that GJW could not have come from antiquity.[2] Under such circumstances, attention inevitably turns away from the ancient historical context at first thought to shed light on the fragment,[3] and instead focuses on the contemporary context that helps to make sense of the reaction to it.[4]

---

1. *NTS* 61/3 (July 2015). This issue of *New Testament Studies* was essentially a response to the volume of *Harvard Theological Review* that was devoted to the fragment, *HTR* 107/2 (April 2014). The key article in the latter is King, "'Jesus said to them.'"

2. For the blog response, see the many posts gathered under *NT Blog*: Gospel of Jesus' Wife (http://ntweblog.blogspot.com/search/label/Gospel of Jesus Wife/), which also provides a live history of the discussion. See too James McGrath's chapter in this volume (ch. 16).

3. See especially King, "'Jesus said to them,'" 149–52. By the "fragment," here and throughout, I am referring to GJW and not simply the papyrus scrap that it was written on. The papyrus itself appears to date from the eighth century. On the material issues, see Krutzsch and Rabin, "Material Criteria."

4. In her most recent comment on the fragment, Karen King (in the Queries and Comments section of *BAR* 41/5 [Sept./Oct. 2015]) notes that "So far the academic response to the Gospel of Jesus' Wife fragment has been almost solely concerned with questions of forgery, but little with interpretation of its meaning—either in antiquity *or*

When GJW was announced in the media, journalists found it difficult to resist associating it with Dan Brown's 2003 novel *The Da Vinci Code*, even if the association often took place in contexts that attempted to generate some degree of distance between the new fragment and the recent fiction. *The Boston Globe*, for example, one of the three newspapers granted special access to the news about the fragment in September 2012,[5] wrote:

> The notion that Jesus may have been married, considered heretical by the Catholic church, has long captivated artists and conspiracy theorists. The success of Dan Brown's 2003 international best-seller, "The Da Vinci Code," which posits that the Catholic church covered up the marriage and progeny of Jesus and Mary Magdalene, testifies to its potency in the popular imagination.[6]

The New York Times similarly concluded its article announcing the discovery with an allusion to the plot of Brown's novel:

> The notion that Jesus had a wife was the central conceit of the best seller and movie "The Da Vinci Code." But Dr. King said she wants nothing to do with the code or its author: "At least, don't say this proves Dan Brown was right."[7]

For many in the media, the association between the newly published fragment and *The Da Vinci Code* was instant and irresistible. Journalists were quick to draw attention to the parallel. It became part of the story, an all-too-rare example of history imitating popular culture. The popularity of *The Da Vinci Code* was providing the ideal cultural context for the enthusiastic reception of GJW.[8]

Since some academics might be inclined to underestimate the role played by popular culture on the media reception of scholarly claims, it is worth remembering the huge impact made by *The Da Vinci Code*. Its commercial success was massive. In its year of release, 2003, it was only

---

today" (8, italics added). The present piece is an attempt at looking at the contemporary cultural context of the reception of GJW.

5. The other two were the *New York Times* and *Harvard Magazine*. The *Smithsonian* also carried a special feature in association with the (then) forthcoming documentary. See further below.

6. Wangsness, "Historian's Finding."

7. Goodstein, "Historian Says."

8. The striking match was not lost on Dan Brown's official publicists, who declared on his website that "New scientific evidence further supports the premise of *The Da Vinci Code*" (*The Official Website of Dan Brown: News* [http://www.danbrown.com/news]).

outsold by *Harry Potter and the Order of the Phoenix*,[9] and the 2006 film adaptation directed by Ron Howard had a worldwide theatrical box office of $767.8 million.[10] Public interest in *The Da Vinci Code* was so great that several academics wrote books to help readers to navigate their way through the claims made in and around it, not least of which was the claim that Jesus was married to Mary Magdalene. By 2005, there were already four major scholarly refutations of the book's claims,[11] all of them highly sceptical of the idea that Jesus was married to Mary.

When GJW emerged in 2012, it did so against the backdrop of the *Da Vinci Code* phenomenon. But while news reports attempted to generate interest in the new fragment by appealing to *The Da Vinci Code*, these appeals often functioned to create some distance from Dan Brown's novel. Readers were being reassured that this is a serious scholarly claim and not sensationalism. The journalists, and the academics they are quoting, mention *The Da Vinci Code* in order to express their intellectual superiority to those who struggle to distinguish history from fiction. Thus *The Guardian*, for example, quoted Oxford professor Diarmaid MacCulloch's disdainful remark: "If this is genuine, it is fantastically interesting and the first reference to Jesus and wife, but it was almost certainly written in the context of an early debate on the position of women in the church. It certainly doesn't give carte blanche to the likes of Dan Brown and the idiots who think like him."[12]

The journalists' concern was that the new fragment might be met with the kind of instant dismissal that regularly greets the sensationalist books and television documentaries. Anxiety over sensationalism is explicit in the *Smithsonian* magazine article that acted as a companion piece to the (then) forthcoming Smithsonian Channel documentary. Ariel Sabar cautioned readers: "But Dan Brown fans, be warned: King makes no claim for its usefulness as biography. The text was probably composed in Greek a century or so after Jesus' crucifixion, then copied into Coptic some two centuries later. As evidence that the real-life Jesus was married, the fragment is scarcely more dispositive than Brown's controversial 2003 novel, *The Da Vinci Code*."[13] In the same context, Sabar notes that Karen King

9. Minzesheimer, "'Code' Deciphers Interest." Minzesheimer writes that "nine months after publication, there are 4.5 million copies in print."

10. For detailed breakdown of figures for the *Da Vinci Code* movie, see *The Numbers*, "The Da Vinci Code" (http://www.the-numbers.com/movie/Da-Vinci-Code-The).

11. Bock, *Breaking the Da Vinci Code*; Ehrman, *Truth and Fiction*; Price, *Da Vinci Fraud*; and Witherington, *Gospel Code*.

12. Bates, "Did Jesus Christ Really Have a Wife?"

13. Sabar, "Inside Story." This online article is an earlier and slightly different version of what was later published as Sabar, "Gospel according to King." The partial

shared this kind of instant reaction: "'My reaction is, This is highly likely to be a forgery,' King recalled of her first impressions. 'That's kind of what we have these days: Jesus' tomb, James's Ossuary.' She was referring to two recent 'discoveries,' announced with great fanfare, that were later exposed as hoaxes or, at best, wishful thinking. 'OK, Jesus married? I thought, Yeah, yeah, yeah.'"[14] Yet while some journalists and academics were attempting to place some distance between themselves and the *Da Vinci Code* generation, it soon became clear that others were using the fragment as confirmation of sensationalist views.[15] To this extent, GJW was appealing directly to those for whom *The Da Vinci Code* was more than mere fiction. Filmmaker Simcha Jacobovici had argued in a 2007 documentary that the lost family tomb of Jesus had been found, and that it contained the ossuaries of both Jesus and his wife, Mary Magdalene. The tomb was located in Talpiyot, a suburb of east Jerusalem, first excavated in 1980 and subsequently covered over when an apartment block had been built. The documentary had backing from James Cameron, director of films like *Titanic* (1997), and its thesis was that the concatenation of names found on the ossuaries in the tomb bore so striking a resemblance to names connected with Jesus' family, that it is highly probable that this is the lost family tomb of Jesus.[16] For Jacobovici, GJW provided dramatic confirmation of his documentary's claims.[17] One of the elements that makes Jacobovici's case so striking is his clear admiration for Dan Brown's novel, which he frequently references in a favourable way.[18]

---

quotation is on p. 76.

14. Sabar, "Inside Story"; and Sabar, "Gospel," 80. King's quoted reaction is to sensationalist "discoveries" rather than to the content of GJW. As early as 2003, she had suggested, "It is true that from early on the possibility had existed that Mary Magdalene might emerge from the speculative fray as Jesus' wife and lover" (*Gospel of Mary of Magdala*, 152–53). See further King, "Place of the *Gospel of Philip*."

15. The terms "sensational," "sensationalism," and "sensational claims" are used here descriptively rather than polemically. Simcha Jacobovici himself uses these terms in relation to *The Da Vinci Code*. See Jacobovici and Tabor, *Jesus Discovery*, 33, 46 and 129.

16. *The Lost Tomb of Jesus* (Discovery Channel, 4 March 2007). The associated book is Jacobovici and Pellegrino, *Jesus Family Tomb*. The website is *The Jesus Family Tomb* (http://www.jesusfamilytomb.com/). For assessments of the case, see Tabor, "Tombs at Talpiot"; Goodacre, "Jesus Discovery?"; and Rollston, "Talpiyot (Jerusalem) Tombs."

17. See especially Jacobovici and Wilson, *Lost Gospel*, 294–98.

18. For a discussion of Simcha Jacobovici's fascination with *The Da Vinci Code* and his conceptualizing of his own work as a "real life" version of *The Da Vinci Code*, see Goodacre, "Da Vinci Code and the Talpiot Tomb." Note, for example, Jacobovici's comments, in the video *The Lost Tomb of Jesus and "The Da Vinci Code"* (https://www.youtube.com/watch?v=6WWeB7OMtfI/): "So in a sense the *Da Vinci Code* has laid the

In the post-*Da Vinci Code* culture, Jacobovici was able to appeal to Jesus' marriage to Mary Magdalene as a cultural given,[19] a piece of information known and shared by the audience.[20] There is a clear contrast here with the coverage of the same find in the British media in 1996, when Jesus' marriage was not popular currency, and the news story made little impact.[21]

This cultural climate in which Jesus' marriage to Mary Magdalene is regarded as a natural, expected element in the discussion of Christian origins is a recent phenomenon. There is a clear contrast between popular cultural expectations in the post-*Da Vinci Code* world and the expectations before it. In 1988, for example, there was some controversy over Martin Scorsese's *Last Temptation of Christ*, a film based on the 1953 book by Nikos Kazantzakis, in which Jesus is a tortured, anxious, self-critical character on a journey that involves the conversion of Mary Magdalene, a prostitute who is aligned with the woman taken in adultery from John 8. The controversy centers on the hallucination that takes up the last 35 minutes of screen time, in which Jesus is beckoned to come down from the cross by a young girl (British actress Juliette Caton) to see the life that he could be leading, including a sexual relationship with Mary Magdalene.

At this point, in 1988 (and still less 1953), the idea of a marriage between Jesus and Mary Magdalene had not yet taken root. It is still an outlandish idea, something that is only countenanced in a controversial narrative in which viewers are allowed to hear Jesus' thoughts and to see his fantasies. *The Last Temptation* imagines Jesus' sexual relationship with Mary, and her conception of a child with him, but it is a temptation that

---

groundwork for this investigation in my film and the book . . . *The Da Vinci Code* is fiction, thrilling fiction. This is thrilling reality."

19. For example: "In the post–*Da Vinci Code* era, the idea that Jesus had a wife and children is part of the popular imagination. There is also no question that secret societies have subscribed to this belief for centuries, if not millennia" (Jacobovici and Pellegrino, *Jesus Family Tomb*, 207).

20. There is a difference between *The Jesus Family Tomb* and the subsequent book, *The Jesus Discovery*, cowritten with James Tabor. Tabor was initially skeptical of the idea of Jesus' marriage to Mary Magdalene (46) but later came to accept it and argue in favour of it (129–58).

21. The Talpiyot Tomb was discussed in a BBC 1 documentary, *Heart of the Matter: The Body in Question*, broadcast on 7 April 1996 (on Easter Day), and in an associated feature in *The Sunday Times* a week earlier (Bakewell, "Tomb That Dare Not Speak Its Mind"). Bakewell has to explain the potential relationship between Jesus and Mary Magdalene: "The second Mary was not a problem. There is, as Chris [Chris Mann, the director of the documentary] was well aware, a reference in the Gnostic gospel of Philip, a text from the beginning of the Christian era found in Egypt in 1945." This is not, in 1996, an element in received popular opinion.

Jesus ultimately rejects.[22] *The Last Temptation* is not making a historical claim about Jesus' marriage. It is attempting to make a theological statement about the nature of Jesus' humanity. In late twentieth-century historical fiction, Jesus of Nazareth is not yet married to Mary Magdalene, and having sex with her is something that only takes place in his mind's temptation.

At this point, the storyteller's interest is still focused on the old Western tradition that Mary Magdalene was a repentant prostitute.[23] It is a motif that is present in practically all the English language Jesus films of the twentieth century, including *King of Kings* (dir. Nicholas Ray, 1961), *The Greatest Story Ever Told* (dir. George Stevens, 1965), and *Jesus of Nazareth* (dir. Franco Zeffirelli, 1977).[24] Mary Magdalene is harmonized with the woman of Luke 7:36–50, and sometimes also the woman caught in adultery of John 7:53—8:11. Moreover, Andrew Lloyd-Webber and Tim Rice's *Jesus Christ Superstar*, the film version of which was released in 1973 (dir. Norman Jewison), plays with the difficult sexual dynamics in the relationship between Jesus and the former prostitute Mary Magdalene, making Mary a star, and giving the viewer access to her inner turmoil.[25] The premise of Mary's predicament is that she is not in any kind of romantic relationship with Jesus, still less a marriage.

Even as recently as the turn of the millennium, the idea of a married Jesus was uncommon in mainstream popular culture. In the American television miniseries *Jesus* (dir. Roger Young, 1999), for example, Jesus (Jeremy Sisto) rejects the idea of marriage and its pre–*Da Vinci Code* pedigree is witnessed by the fact that the very question is discussed in relation to Jesus' attraction to Mary of Bethany (Stefania Rocca) rather than Mary Magdalene (Debra Messing), who in this film is still depicted as a prostitute. And in *The Passion of the Christ* (dir. Mel Gibson, 2004), there is a last gasp for the idea that Mary Magdalene (Monica Bellucci) was the woman caught in adultery from John 7:53—8:11.[26]

22. Moreover, although Mary Magdalene conceives a child, she dies before it is born, and Jesus goes on to have a family with Mary and Martha.

23. The literature on the history of perceptions of Mary Magdalene is massive, but see especially King, *Gospel of Mary of Magdala*; Brock, *Mary Magdalene*; Schaberg, *Resurrection of Mary Magdalene*; and de Boer, *Gospel of Mary*. These books all made a major contribution in changing perceptions of Mary Magdalene, especially among academics, but it is *The Da Vinci Code* that provided the engine for a change in perceptions about her in popular culture.

24. *Godspell* (dir. David Greene, 1973) would be an exception but Mary Magdalene does not feature in the film.

25. The songs that develop the character and her relationship with Jesus are "What's the Buzz?," "Strange Thing, Mystifying," and "Everything's Alright."

26. *The Passion of the Christ* was released in the USA on 25 February 2004. Filming

There were, of course, precedents for the idea of a marriage between Jesus and Mary. Dan Brown did not invent the idea but drew on elements on the fringes of pseudo-historical scholarship of the late twentieth century, most obviously the conspiracy-laden *The Holy Blood and the Holy Grail*.[27] The key point, however, is that the idea only entered mainstream popular culture in the wake of the unprecedented success of *The Da Vinci Code* in 2003. It is *The Da Vinci Code* that gives GJW its frisson, its cultural significance, its media clout.

The fact that GJW is so congenial to the cultural context into which it was introduced in 2012 does not demonstrate that the fragment is a forgery. Sometimes history has an uncanny way of imitating art, as when the Titanic sank in 1912 in tragic, coincidental imitation of the 1898 novella *The Wreck of the Titan*, in which a ship called the "Titan" sinks in the North Atlantic Ocean after hitting an iceberg.[28] Or more recently, the *Gospel of Judas* emerged onto the scene after Judas, like Mary Magdalene, had become a figure of huge interest in popular culture.[29] It could be the case, in principle, that GJW was this kind of discovery—a matter of remarkable, fortuitous timing. To press this point, though, would be to miss the significance of the ideal cultural context that the popular love of *The Da Vinci Code* provides.

GJW successfully functions as a fragment that apparently provides confirmation for an idea that has enormous popular appeal: the idea that Jesus was married to Mary Magdalene.[30] It is an idea that has had major cultural capital only in recent history, since Dan Brown's novel was published in 2003. Popular culture's obsession with *The Da Vinci Code* provided the ideal context for the reception of GJW. Since it seems clear, on other

took place in 2003, and the writing of the screenplay (by Mel Gibson and Benedict Fitzgerald) predated that, so this is still in the pre-*Da Vinci Code* period.

27. Baigent, et al., *Holy Blood and the Holy Grail*. See too the earlier sensationalist investigation, Donovan Joyce's *Jesus Scroll*, in which Jesus survives the crucifixion, marries Mary Magdalene, fathers a child with her, and dies at the age of eighty at Masada. I am grateful also to Janet Spittler for pointing out, in a response to this paper at the York Symposium, that Jesus' marriage is a common trope in Mormon literature. See her chapter below.

28. Robertson, *Wreck of the Titan*. For a discussion of life imitating fiction in connection to another contentious gospel, the *Secret Gospel of Mark*, see Pantuck, "Solving the Mysterion," and Francis Watson's response, "Beyond Reasonable Doubt," 5.

29. Kasser and Wurst, eds., *Gospel of Judas*. Nevertheless, the reception of the *Gospel of Judas* is instructive in that it is arguable that the popular cultural rehabilitation of the character of Judas, which is rife in popular literature and films, influenced the cultural reception of the gospel, at first to provide ancient justification for a reconsideration of Judas's reputation.

30. GJW does not, of course, identify Mary as "Magdalene" but in the post-*Da Vinci Code* culture, others were quick to supply the name.

grounds, that the fragment is of modern origin, perhaps its creator was also a fan of Dan Brown.

– 18 –

Responses to Mark Goodacre, James McGrath, and Caroline Schroeder on the *Gospel of Jesus' Wife*

— Janet E. Spittler —

RESPONSE TO MARK GOODACRE

MARK GOODACRE POINTS TO the enormous role that Dan Brown's novel *The Da Vinci Code* and Ron Howard's film adaptation have played in at least the media's representation of the significance of the *Gospel of Jesus' Wife* (GJW), and I heartily agree: *The Da Vinci Code*'s role can hardly be overestimated. I agree with Goodacre, moreover, that "popular culture's obsession with *The Da Vinci Code* provided the ideal context for the reception of GJW" (p. 347 above) and share his suspicion that the forger had *The Da Vinci Code* in mind when producing the fragment.[1] In response, however, I hope to both

---

1. Like Goodacre and (as far as I can tell) the majority of New Testament scholars, I have been convinced by the evidence and arguments pointing towards forgery. I suspect Goodacre's final comment on GJW ("perhaps its creator was also a fan of Dan Brown," p. 348 above) is in some respect tongue-in-cheek, but—if Goodacre is correct that GJW was composed with *The Da Vinci Code* in mind—it is fair to ask what the forger's particular attitude towards the novel and the notions therein is, and what his/her purpose in creating the forgery was. Is s/he a "fan"? Was the purpose of the forgery to lend credence to an idea the forger approved of? Or does s/he disapprove of the notion of Jesus' marriage and/or Mary Magdalene's prominence in the early church? Could the forgery have been designed to be uncovered, intended as a device to

349

broaden and narrow Goodacre's focus: 1) broadening to include America's long history with the notion of (and controversy concerning) a married Jesus (substantially longer than Goodacre's account indicates), and 2) narrowing to look at a particular aspect of *The Da Vinci Code*—that is, the way it constructs the significance of Jesus' marriage vis-à-vis feminism—as the primary "contribution" of the novel to our collective reaction to GJW.

Broadening the Focus: Jesus' Wife in America

America's history with the notion of a married Jesus reaches back a good bit further than the 1990s or even the last half of the twentieth century—well before the publication of *The Da Vinci Code* and Kazantzakis' *The Last Temptation of Christ*. The idea is found in mid-nineteenth-century Mormon circles, where a married Jesus, while never an official part of Latter-day Saints doctrine, was a commonly held notion.[2]

The notion is evident as early as the 1840s, when Brigham Young seemed to understand Mary Magdalene as the wife of Jesus in a reference to the resurrection appearance in John 20: "she fell right down at his feet—every woman will come right to her husband's feet same as Mary."[3] In 1853, Jedediah Grant, an LDS apostle and mayor of Salt Lake City, claimed that Jesus was persecuted and ultimately crucified for his polygamy: "The grand reason why the Gentiles and philosophers of his school persecuted Jesus Christ, was, because he had so many wives: there were Elizabeth, and Mary, and a host of others that followed him."[4] Also in 1853, Orson Pratt

---

embarrass a prominent feminist scholar? Or did the forger simply have the popularity of *The Da Vinci Code* in mind, hoping to capitalize (literally) on its success by selling a forged papyrus that seemed to tie in to the novel's content? Cf. Christian Askeland's suspicions, note 53 below; see also Baden and Moss, "Curious Case."

2. In this section I am indebted to Turner, *Mormon Jesus,* especially pp. 217–46, as well as verbal and e-mail exchanges with Kathleen Flake (Richard Lyman Bushman Chair of Mormon Studies at the University of Virginia).

3. Brigham Young discourse of 27 December 1847, Box 1, Folder 61, GCM; quoted from Turner, *Mormon Jesus,* 230.

4. Jedediah Grant discourse of 7 August 1853, transcript by George D. Watt, in CR 100 317, Church History Library; this discourse was also published in Young, *Journal of Discourses,* 1:341–49, here 345; cited in Turner, *Mormon Jesus,* 231. Interestingly, Grant here claims to be quoting Celsus, whom he identifies as both a physician and a philosopher. As Anthony Le Donne has noted, Grant here confuses (or, perhaps better, conflates) the second-century philosopher Celsus (against whose *The True Word* Origen later wrote) and the first-century physician Aulus Cornelius Celsus (whose work *De medicina* is extant) (see Le Donne, *Wife of Jesus,* 76–79). Watt's transcript of the discourse perhaps reflects some of the confusion, when Celsus is identified as "a physician in the age of the apostles," the last phrase being crossed out and replaced with the

published a long essay titled "Celestial Marriage," offered in 12 monthly installments in *The Seer*. In the eleventh installment, Pratt finally takes up the notion of a married Jesus: "Now let us enquire whether there are any intimations in Scripture concerning the wives of Jesus."

Pratt is circumspect, but points (as Brigham Young did) to the resurrection appearances for traces of Jesus' marital status:

> The Evangelists do not particularly speak of the marriage of Jesus; but this is not to be wondered at, for St. John says: 'There are also many other things which Jesus did, the which, if they should be written every one, I suppose that even the world itself could not contain the books that should be written.' (John 21:25.) One thing is certain, that there were several holy women that greatly loved Jesus—such as Mary, and Martha her sister, and Mary Magdalene; and Jesus greatly loved them, and associated with them much; and when He arose from the dead, instead of first showing Himself to His chosen witnesses, the Apostles, He appeared first to these women, or at least to one of them—namely, Mary Magdalene. Now it would be very natural for a husband in the resurrection to appear first to his own dear wives, and afterwards show himself to his other friends. If all the acts of Jesus were written, we no doubt should learn that these beloved women were his wives.[5]

Pratt goes on to cite Psalm 45:8–9, translated as "All thy garments smell of myrrh, and aloes, and cassia: when thou comest out of the ivory palaces, where they have made thee glad, Kings' daughters were among thine honorable WIVES."[6] Pratt argues that this verse refers to "the Son of God and His Wives," pointing to the previous two verses (Ps 45:7–8) and their interpretation as referring to Jesus in Hebrews 1:8–9, concluding, "Let it be remembered, then, that the Son of God is expressly represented as having 'honorable Wives.'"[7]

---

superscript "first century" (CR 100 317, Church History Library).

5. Pratt, "Celestial Marriage," 10:159.

6. Ibid., italics original.

7. Ibid., 160. Pratt then notes that his translation differs from the King James Version: "King James' translators were not willing that this passage should have a literal translation, according to the former English rendering, lest it should give countenance to Polygamy; therefore they altered the translation to honorable *women* instead of *wives*; but any person acquainted with the original can see that the first translators have given the true rendering of that passage."

Further, Pratt takes up the parable of the ten bridesmaids in Matthew 25:1–13, arguing that the five wise virgins are not wedding guests, but "females who are to be married to the Bridegroom." He concludes:

> Are not these five wise virgins the 'honorable Wives' which the Psalmist represents the Son of God as having taken from among kings' daughters? From the passage in the forty-fifth Psalm, it will be seen that the great Messiah who was the founder of the Christian religion, was a Polygamist, as well as the Patriarch Jacob and the prophet David from whom He descended according to the flesh. Paul says concerning Jesus, 'Verily he took not on him the nature of angels; but he took on him the seed of Abraham.' (Heb. 2:16.) Abraham the Polygamist being a friend of God, the Messiah chose to take upon himself his seed; and by marrying many honorable wives himself, show to all future generations that he approbated the plurality of Wives under the dispensations in which His Polygamist ancestors lived.[8]

In the final installment of the essay, Pratt includes the married Christ as one of 15 "questions for the consideration of such of our readers as may be opposed to the plurality system":

> If polygamy is to be considered sinful under the gospel dispensation, why did David speak of the honorable wives of the son of God himself and so particularly describe one of His Queens.

8. Pratt, "Celestial Marriage," 11:172. Pratt's essay on marriage is a fascinating read for scholars of the New Testament. Among his most interesting arguments for polygamy is a rather ingenious interpretation of 1 Tim 3 in combination with 1 Cor 7. Pratt takes the command that deacons and bishops be married to "only one wife" as taking for granted the existence (and desirability) of a plurality of wives; Pratt understands the limitation to one wife to reflect Paul's quite practical understanding of the demands of polygamy (also at play, according to Pratt, in 1 Cor 7): "Paul knew this to be the general disposition of mankind, and he knew that there were but a very few men to be found who would sacrifice houses and lands, wives and children, and everything else of an earthly nature for the sake of the gospel, therefore, he no doubt wrote his instructions to Timothy to select those among the church members who had but one wife, as they would be much more free from care than those who had several wives and children depending on them for their support." ("Celestial Marriage," 5:74). Further, Pratt notes the contradiction between 1 Cor 7:8 ("To the unmarried and widows I say that it is well for them to remain unmarried as I am") and 1 Tim 5:14 ("I would have younger widows marry"), explaining that in Corinth, where "divisions, contentions, fornications, brother going to law with brother, and various other evils existed," Paul feared that few faithful might marry "wicked companions that would lead them away to destruction," and thus, under those circumstances, felt that the avoidance of marriage altogether was preferable. Elsewhere, however, "where such evils did not exist, it was his will that they should marry" (ibid.).

Would Christ sanction a sinful institution by his own practice? and then command his disciples to follow him?[9]

A third early LDS leader, Orson Hyde, focused specifically on the question of whether Jesus was married in a sermon delivered at the Tabernacle on 6 October 1854 (printed in *The Deseret* on 19 October). Like Young, he points to Mary's interactions with the resurrected Jesus in John 20, this time making the lexical argument that the terms used by Mary to refer to and address Jesus in this passage are in fact terms used by a wife of her husband. He concludes: "Is there not here manifested the affections of a wife. Where will you find a family so nearly allied by the ties of common religion?"[10] Hyde anticipates objection: "'Well,' you say, 'that appears rather plausible, but I want a little more evidence, I want you to find where it says the Savior was actually married.'"[11] Hyde claims that there is such a passage, which he will read aloud "or you might not believe my words were I to say that there is indeed such a scripture."[12] He then reads John 2:1–11, the wedding at Cana, in the King James Version. Much like Orson Pratt, Hyde suggests that the original meaning of the passage had been obscured by translation and, perhaps, editing:

> Gentleman, that is as plain as the translators or different councils over this scripture, dare allow it to go to the world; but the thing is there; it is told; Jesus was the bridegroom at the marriage of Cana in Galilee, and he told them what to do. Now there was actually a marriage; and if Jesus was not the bridegroom on that occasion, please tell who was. If any man can show this, and prove that it was not the Savior of the world, then I will acknowledge I am in error.[13]

9. Pratt, "Celestial Marriage," 12:190.

10. Hyde, "Lecture, Tabernacle," 1. Hyde bases this argument on common English usage of the term "master," noting, "In England we frequently hear the wife say 'where is my master?' She did not mean a tyrant, but as Sarah called her husband Lord, she designated hers by the word master." Hyde—who interestingly claims to have memorized the Bible in English, German and Hebrew, but not Greek—understands Mary's reference to Jesus in 20:13 ("Lord" in the KJV and Hyde's quotation) and her address in 20:16 ("Rabboni, which is to say, Master" in KJV and Hyde's quotation) as equivalent to the English wife's "master" with reference to husband.

11. Ibid. Note that this is a sermon, delivered at the Tabernacle: does Hyde expect objections from within the Mormon congregation, or does the "you" here refer to an imagined outsider?

12. Ibid.

13. Ibid.

Moreover, Hyde continues, Jesus' marriage produced offspring, and their descendants may well survive to this day:

> We say it was Jesus Christ who was married; to be bro't into the relation whereby he could see his seed, before he was crucified . . . I do not despise to be called a son of Abraham, if he had a dozen wives; or to be called a brother, a son, a child of the Savior if he had Mary, and Martha, and several others, as wives; and tho' he did cast seven devils out of one of them, it is all the same to me.[14]

Particularly notable in comparison with the *The Da Vinci Code*[15] are Hyde's speculations about Jesus' children:

> I shall say here, that before the Savior died, he looked upon his own natural children, as we look upon ours; he saw his seed and immediately afterwards, he was cut off from the earth; but who shall declare his generation? They had no father to hold them in honorable remembrance; they passed into the shades of obscurity, never to be exposed to mortal eye as the seed of the blessed one. For no doubt had they been exposed to the eye of the world, those infants might have shared the same fate as the children in Jerusalem in the days of Herod, when all the children were ordered to be slain under such an age, with the hopes of slaying the infant Savior. They might have suffered by the hand of the assassin, as the sons of many kings have done who were heirs apparent to the thrones of their fathers.[16]

After Hyde spoke, Brigham Young (then President of the LDS) gave a response, fully approving of its content ("I do not wish to eradicate any items from the lecture Elder Hyde has given us this evening"), but quibbling with his interpretation of 1 Tim 3.[17]

---

14. Ibid.

15. See Brown, *Da Vinci Code*, 274–77. The character Leigh Teabing explains, "Mary Magdalene was pregnant at the time of the crucifixion. For the safety of Christ's unborn child, she had no choice but to flee the Holy Land. With the help of Jesus' trusted uncle, Joseph of Arimathea, Mary Magdalene secretly traveled to France, then known as Gaul. There she found safe refuge in the Jewish community. It was here in France that she gave birth to a daughter. Her name was Sarah" (275).

16. Hyde, "Lecture, Tabernacle," 1.

17. Young, "Remarks by President Brigham Young," 2, cited by Turner, *Mormon Jesus*, 233. Hyde had argued, much like Pratt, that 1 Tim 3 restricts bishops and deacons to one wife (while implicitly acknowledging the desirability of more); Young takes 1 Tim 3 differently: "Instead of my believing for a moment that Paul wished to signify to Timothy that he must select a man to fill the office of a bishop that would have but *one*

Anti-Mormon Response

The sermons on Jesus' marital status were not just read by members of the LDS community: these and other items printed in *The Deseret* were frequently reprinted, excerpted, and responded to in East Coast newspapers. Washington's *The Globe* printed extended excerpts from Hyde's sermon; *The New York Times* printed a response under the title "Mormon Shamelessness," railing against the "disgustingly obscene and blasphemous" speeches of the "Elders that rule over Utah." Referring to the recent printing of Hyde's and Young's discourses in *The Deseret*, the uncredited editor writes:

> On the 6th of October [Orson Hyde] delivered an address in the Mormon Tabernacle, in which the low depravity of the sect is more openly evident than in any other published document we have seen which originated there. He argues the right of the plurality of wives, from the patriarchal habit and the *example of Christ*. He shamelessly attempts to prove that Jesus was the bridegroom at Cana.[18]

John Hanson Beadle, harsh critic of the Latter-day Saints and author of *Polygamy: or, The Mysteries and Crimes of Mormonism*, was similarly scandalized by Hyde's interpretation of John 2:1–11, which he refers to as "clear as mud": "Orson Hyde took for his specialty the case of Christ, and proved to his own satisfaction that the Saviour had five wives, including Martha and Mary."[19]

After the Latter-day Saints' official rejection of polygamy in the 1890 Manifesto, references to a married Jesus by leaders of the church rather abruptly halted,[20] though echoes remained. In 1912, for example, Charles

---

wife, I believe directly the reverse; but his advice to Timothy amounts simply to this: It would not be wise for you to ordain a man to the office of a bishop unless he has a *wife*; you must not ordain a *single* or *unmarried* man to that calling."

18. "Mormon Shamelessness."

19. Beadle, *Polygamy*, 304. Note the full title of the work: *Polygamy: or, the Mysteries and Crimes of Mormonism, being a Full and Authentic History of Polygamy and the Mormon Sect from its origin to the present time, with a complete analysis of Mormon society and theocracy and an exposé of the secret rites and ceremonies of the Latter-day Saints*. Cf. Folk, *Mormon Monster*, 114 and 234; Oswalt, *Pen Pictures of Mormonism*, 77. See also discussion by Mason, *Mormon Menace*, 102–26.

20. Thus, for example, James Talmage's 1915 tome *Jesus the Christ* discusses the wedding at Cana (pp. 144–47) and Jesus' resurrection appearance to Mary Magdalene (pp. 678–83) with no hint that the wedding might have been Jesus' own or that Mary might have been his wife. See discussion in Turner, *Mormon Jesus*, 236–37. On the complicated situation vis-à-vis polygamy left in the wake of the 1890 Manifesto, see Flake, *Politics*, 56–81, 130–35.

W. Penrose published in a Mormon periodical a list of "peculiar questions, evidently prompted by persons who desired to provoke controversy rather than to obtain information," along with brief responses. Several of the questions have to do with plural marriage; the second is: "Do you believe that Jesus was married?" to which Penrose replies, "We do not know anything about Jesus Christ being married. The Church has no authoritative declaration on the subject."[21] Relative silence from LDS members on the possibility of a married Jesus follows, though in 1948 the excommunicated fundamentalist Joseph White Musser published (in the journal that he edited) an article entitled "Did Jesus Marry, and Did He Live the Patriarchal Law?" in which he argues that Jesus had married Martha and Mary at Cana, and later Mary Magdalene.

Regardless of official LDS statements—or, rather, the lack thereof—on the marital status of Jesus, reference to the married Jesus by Evangelical anti-Mormon "countercult" writers continued unabated through the twentieth century.[22] According to J. B. Haws, there was a notable uptick in Evangelical anti-Mormon propaganda in the 1980s. While nineteenth-century anti-polygamy (and anti-Mormon) campaigns had been steered by Protestant leaders, "what had largely been a sectarian conflict bubbled to the surface of national consciousness, and Christian warnings about the Mormon 'cult' swayed opinions among new audiences *outside* of the religious community."[23] Particularly influential was Ed Decker's 1982 expensively produced anti-Mormon "documentary" *The God Makers*, which, in an easily excerptible animated short presented within the film as a summary of LDS teachings, refers to Pratt's claim that Jesus was married to Mary, Martha, and Mary Magdalene.[24] The film, which was originally distributed primarily through screenings before Evangelical Christian audiences, reached an enormous audience; according to contemporary media reports, "the movie was being shown to 'about 1,000 audiences a month,' often to 'standing-room only crowds.'"[25] The film's *Nachleben* has also been significant: sections of the animated short are shown, for example, in Bill Maher's 2008 film *Religulous*, and the short has been posted many times over on YouTube. One version, uploaded in October 2008, has since been viewed upwards of

---

21. Penrose, "Peculiar Questions," 1042. See discussion in Turner, *Mormon Jesus*, 236–37.

22. See, for example, van Baalen, *Chaos of Cults*, 139; Sanders, *Heresies*, 112–13; Hoekema, *Four Major Cults*, 56. See discussion in Turner, *Mormon Jesus*, 241–42.

23. Haws, *Mormon Image*, 100.

24. On the broad impact of *The God Makers* in American perceptions of the LDS, see Haws, *Mormon Image*, 112–25.

25. Ibid., 115.

900,000 times.[26] Similar anti-Mormon material, including reference to the married Jesus, continues to be produced in various Evangelical circles; the multiple publications of Richard Abanes are a good example.[27]

William Phipps, Ogden Kraut, and the Married Jesus

Interestingly, the arguments first articulated by Grant, Pratt, and Hyde also turn up in a few non-LDS sources, most prominently two articles and two books by New Testament scholar William Phipps.[28] Phipps, a professor of Religion and Philosophy at a Presbyterian liberal arts college in Pennsylvania, first published a short piece in 1968 on the plausibility of either Jesus or Paul having been married. His arguments—primarily based on the notion that Jesus' "marital outlook corresponded to that of other devout Jews" (marriage being the norm) and on the interpretation of the term *agamos* in 1 Cor 7:8 (which Phipps takes as "widower")—are not particularly persuasive.[29] But they did, according to Phipps's own account, elicit a "voluminous and overwhelmingly negative response," which led him to develop his ideas in two monographs.[30]

26. The clip is titled "What Mormons Really Believe" (online: https://www.youtube.com/watch?v=3HSlbuli7HM/) and is excerpted such that a more credulous viewer might take it to be an official LDS production.

27. E.g., Abanes, *Inside Today's Mormonism*, 239–41.

28. Another example, cited by Phipps, is Columbia University professor of English John Erskine, one of the early proponents of the "Great Books" movement. In 1945, Erskine published a work titled *The Human Life of Jesus*. He writes, "It has been suggested also that . . . [Jesus] was moved by the hopes and ambitions proper to mankind—love, marriage, parenthood—and that in equal measure he suffered disappointment or bereavement. There is no basis in fact for these theories any more than for the fancy that he traveled through the East, yet just because man's normal emotional life is near to us all, it does not seem improbable that he did fall in love and had some experience of parenthood. Here I try to choose my words carefully, not to start unworthy thoughts or to seem to invent for the Saviour any acquaintance with cheap romance. But reading his words carefully as I have done all my life, I long ago had the impression that he understood women well indeed, with the special understanding of a man who has been hurt by one of them . . . I think he early met someone who charmed but who was unworthy, someone he idealized, and by whom he was cruelly disillusioned" (ibid., 27). I admit I am rather at a loss as to which sayings of Jesus Erskine has in mind here; in any case, Erskine concludes "whether, as some people would like to believe, he ever married and had a son, is an irrelevant question" (ibid., 28), but without noting the identity of these "people."

29. Phipps, "Did Jesus or Paul Marry?"

30. Phipps, *Was Jesus Married?*, 2.

There is no indication in the initial article that Phipps was aware of the matter of a married Jesus within Mormon circles, but he would soon become acquainted. In 1969, fundamentalist Ogden Kraut picked up Phipps's arguments, citing them with enthusiasm in his essay "Jesus was Married."[31] Kraut writes:

> Jesus lived through a constant barrage of attacks against his birth, character, authority, law and doctrine. Yet if He had lived a celibate life, that alone would have given his enemies their greatest advantage to dispute His claims, for it was against the traditional and scriptural law for a Rabbi to remain single. Jesus could only have avoided this pitfall by obeying the Rabbinical law of marriage.[32]

Kraut also points to apocryphal texts as evidence of a married Jesus. Either confusing or conflating Qumran and Nag Hammadi, Kraut writes: "Recent manuscripts found in Qumran and other excavations have introduced further information to substantiate Christ's marriage. In The Gospel According to Thomas there are significant references to the marriage of Jesus . . . and in another apocryphal manuscript called the Gospel of Philip."[33] Kraut then quotes the *Gospel of Thomas* logia 22 and 114 (from A. Guillaumont's 1959 translation), and the *Gospel of Philip* sections 32 and 35 (from R. McL. Wilson's 1962 translation).

Phipps, in turn, cites Orson Hyde in his 1970 monograph *Was Jesus Married?*[34] and cites both Kraut and Hyde in an article for *Dialogue: A Journal of Mormon Thought*. Notably, Phipps now reports (seemingly with appreciation) Hyde's suggestion that the wedding at Cana was Jesus' own. Moreover, he takes up the fact that Hyde had done missionary work among Jews in Palestine as evidence that he and Hyde were ultimately driven by the same basic observation:

> That cultural association doubtless made [Hyde] more aware than most Christians that marriage in traditional Judaism—either single or plural—was prerequisite to righteous manhood. Since Jesus was addressed as "Rabbi" and was a devout Jew, he would in all probability have married.[35]

31. See discussion in Turner, *Mormon Jesus*, 240–42.

32. Kraut, *Jesus Was Married*, ch. 3.

33. Ibid., ch. 4.

34. Phipps, *Was Jesus Married?*, 9–10.

35. Phipps, "Case for a Married Jesus," 44. Phipps's arguments (in both articles and both monographs on the topic) are largely anti-Catholic, ultimately arriving at a new version of the familiar nineteenth-century American Protestant position, which

Further, Phipps goes beyond the canonical New Testament material discussed in his initial article to include the *Gospel of Philip*—first raised as evidence of a married Jesus (as far as I can tell) by Ogden Kraut—as well as the *Gospel of Mary* and the *Pistis Sophia*.[36]

In an interesting turn, we find Charles A. Davis, a prominent English theologian and Roman Catholic priest, citing Phipps's *Was Jesus Married?* in a 1971 article in *The Observer*.[37] Davis, who in 1966 had left the priesthood to marry, was very much a public figure; he announced his departure—not just from the priesthood but also from the Catholic Church—quite vocally, offering an essay of explanation, which was condensed and reprinted in a wide variety of publications.[38] Davis is not entirely persuaded by Phipps's arguments, and criticizes what he sees as "[Phipps's] strong personal views" that "are so clearly present and operative from the outset."[39] Nevertheless, Davis writes as follows:

> The wife of Jesus might have died before his ministry, so that he began his public life as a widower. His wife might have remained in Nazareth, possibly hostile to her husband's mission and preaching. The Gospels report such hostility on the part of Jesus's brothers and the inhabitants of Nazareth. The recently discovered 'Gospel of Philip', a second-century work, which some scholars think can be used as an independent historical witness, gives Mary Magdalene as the wife of Jesus. Perhaps Jesus, like the prophet Hosea, had to endure an unfaithful wife and draw her back by the constancy of his own love.

---

took a majority of Catholic doctrine (and other theological developments of the preceding millennia) as "Platonizing" accretions to an otherwise pure original Christianity. Thus, in this article, Phipps explains: "Sexual asceticism was found in early Greek philosophy and it became increasingly prominent in the Hellenistic age . . . In the Roman era an extreme ethic was popular among eclectic philosophers who drew on the earlier asceticism of Pythagoreanism, Platonism, and Cynic-Stoicism. Philosophers such as Cicero, Philo, Plotinus and Porphyry—all scathing in their denunciation of physical pleasure—had a powerful impact on what came to be known as the Christian ethic. This ascetic tendency among philosophers, coupled with the popular veneration for virginity in cults of the Mediterranean area, partially eclipsed the biblical belief in the sanctity of the physical" (ibid., 47). On the tracing and critique of "Platonizing" elements of early Christianity in nineteenth-century America, see Smith, "On the Origin of Origins," in *Drudgery Divine*, 1–35.

36. Phipps, *Was Jesus Married?*, 135–38. Note John P. Meier's extended and thoughtful response to Phipps's work in *A Marginal Jew*, 332–45.

37. Davis, "Was Jesus Married?"

38. See, for example, Davis, "Priest Explains Why he Left Church."

39. Davis, "Was Jesus Married?"

As for children, the marriage might well have been child-
less. Or the children may have remained unbelievers and never
become disciples. In that case, having no part of place in the
Christian Church, they would not have been mentioned in the
gospels or Christian literature. All this is playing with hypotheses, but I am merely showing that the silence of the Gospels on
Jesus's marriage does not prove his celibacy.[40]

In yet another twist, Davis's article was introduced as evidence for the de-
fense at the 2006 trial in which Michael Baigent and Richard Leigh accused
Dan Brown of plagiarizing their non-fiction (so-to-speak) work *Holy Blood,
Holy Grail*.[41] As Goodacre has noted, *Holy Blood, Holy Grail* was, by Dan
Brown's admission, a primary source in the composition of *The Da Vinci
Code*.[42] But what were Baigent and Leigh's sources for the notion of a mar-
ried Jesus? They cite the works of two authors who argue for a married Jesus:
the *Observer* article by Charles Davis and the second monograph of William
Phipps—that is, one of the works Phipps wrote after his acquaintance with
the arguments of Orson Hyde and Ogden Kraut.[43]

The Da Vinci Code and the Latter-day Saints

It may be helpful, now, to remember the specific evidence for Jesus' marriage to Mary Magdalene according to *The Da Vinci Code*. The big reveal
takes place in chapter 58; the mystery is unveiled to the reader as Leigh
Teabing explains it to the novel's heroine, Sophie. As the book's title suggests,

40. Ibid.

41. See Smith, "Rebel Theologian."

42. Note that the name of Brown's clever professor ("Leigh Teabing") is a reference to the *Holy Blood, Holy Grail* authors' last names (Teabing being an anagram of
Baigent).

43. See Baigent, et al., *Holy Blood, Holy Grail*, ch. 12, nn. 10 and 11. Notably, the
authors first quote Géza Vermès's *Jesus the Jew* as writing, "'There is complete silence
in the Gospels concerning the marital status of Jesus . . . Such a state of affairs is sufficiently unusual in ancient Jewry to prompt further enquiry.'" The full quotation from
Vermès reads, "There is complete silence in the Gospels concerning the marital status
of Jesus. No wife accompanies him in his public career, or, for that matter, stays at home,
as the wives of his followers were expected to do. Such a state of affairs is sufficiently
unusual in ancient Jewry to prompt further enquiry, for the Hebrew Bible, though it
prescribes temporary sexual abstinence in certain circumstances, never orders a life of
total celibacy" (*Jesus the Jew*, 99). The unusual "state of affairs" is "Jesus' apparent voluntary embrace of celibacy" (ibid., 101); what Vermès attempts to understand through
enquiry is *not* (as Baigent et al. lead their reader to believe) whether or not Jesus was
married, but why he made the (unusual in his context) choice to be celibate.

Leonardo da Vinci was aware of Jesus' marriage and thus painted Jesus and Mary Magdalene together (along with a host of visual clues evident to "symbologists" such as Professor Robert Langdon, the novel's hero) in his Last Supper. But, as Teabing tells Sophie, the source of this information is not Leonardo, rather "the marriage of Jesus and Mary Magdalene is part of the historical record."[44] The evidence he then rehearses is: 1) Jesus was Jewish, and "according to Jewish custom, celibacy was condemned, and the obligation for a Jewish father was to find a suitable wife for his son. If Jesus were not married, at least one of the Bible's gospels would have mentioned it and offered some explanation for his unnatural state of bachelorhood"; and 2) The *Gospel of Philip* and the *Gospel of Mary* indicate Mary Magdalene as Jesus' spouse.[45] Granted, there are many works of both fiction and non-fiction (the latter including both scholarship and pseudo-scholarship) that speculate on the sexuality and marital status of Jesus that have not been surveyed here.[46] Tracking down all the links and making determinations of literary or other dependency is a Herculean task—and one for another scholar, one whose field of expertise is in the twentieth century. That said, what digging I have done indicates that while Brown does not take over all the lines of argumentation found in LDS authors (e.g., Brown makes no reference to the wedding at Cana as Jesus' own), the two basic pieces of "historical" evidence cited seem to be drawn (perhaps via *Holy Blood, Holy Grail*) from William Phipps—but specifically the work he produced after entering into conversation with the work of Orson Hyde and Ogden Kraut.

We come full circle when we consider contemporary Mormon responses to *The Da Vinci Code*. The connection of the ideas presented in the novel and the film to LDS history, if not official doctrine, was not lost on the LDS leadership. Thus, ahead of the film's release at Cannes in 2006, LDS spokesman Dale Bills released the following statement: "The belief that Christ was married has never been official Church doctrine. It is neither sanctioned nor taught by the Church. While it is true that a few Church leaders in the mid-1800s expressed their opinions on the matter, it was not then, and is not now, Church doctrine."[47] On quite the other end of the spectrum of responses, we find amateur historian Vern Swanson, who, in the wake of *The Da Vinci Code*, published *Dynasty of the Holy Grail: Mor-*

44. Brown, *Da Vinci Code*, 265.

45. Ibid., 264–67.

46. In addition to the titles mentioned within *The Da Vinci Code* itself (273–74), we might note Joyce, *Jesus Scroll* (cited by Goodacre) as well as *Da Vinci Legacy* and *Daughter of God*, both by Lewis Perdue, who—like the authors of *Holy Blood, Holy Grail*—unsuccessfully sued Dan Brown's publisher for plagiarism.

47. See "Claims of a Married Jesus."

monism's Sacred Bloodline, which argues that Joseph Smith was the direct descendant of Jesus and Mary Magdalene. According to an article about Swanson in *The Deseret News,* "while the book takes an LDS point of view and includes statements by early church leaders that Christ may have been married, it doesn't stray from a recent church statement that a married Christ is not official LDS doctrine."[48] A particularly interesting response to *The Da Vinci Code* is *What Da Vinci Didn't Know: An LDS Perspective,* a book written for a popular audience by three Brigham Young University professors: Richard Neitzel Holzapfel, Andrew C. Skinner, and Thomas A. Wayment.[49] After laying out the numerous historical problems with the novel's claims, the authors conclude:

> On the issue of what the historical record tells us about the subject, we admit that the New Testament record is virtually silent on the marital status of both Jesus and Mary Magdalene. Restoration scripture provides little additional information on this subject. However, we are left with little doubt that several of the leaders of the Church in the early part of this dispensation believed and taught that Jesus was married. We do not need to explain or defend them.[50]

At the end of the day, the LDS perspective is remarkably similar to the various responses published by biblical scholars ranging from Evangelical to agnostic in response to Dan Brown's novel.[51] *What Da Vinci Didn't Know* is notable, if anything, for its more measured and decidedly *not* polemical tone.

Again, while I agree with Goodacre that *The Da Vinci Code* provides the most immediate context for the GJW, and that the news media in particular proved utterly incapable of setting the novel and film aside when reporting on the GJW, the notion of a married Jesus has a much wider history in American religiosity, specifically in both Mormon thought and anti-Mormon propaganda. This history is, as we have seen, the immediate source of the ideas found in *The Da Vinci Code,* but also the broader source of the fury and controversy: various types of American Christians have been

48. Hardy, "Book Takes On 'Da Vinci.'" Notably, this article quotes Swanson as saying, "I've never known a Mormon, with the exception of a couple, who didn't believe Christ wasn't married."

49. Holzapfel et al., *What Da Vinci Didn't Know.*

50. Ibid., 50.

51. In its treatment of the historical implausibility of theories put forward by characters in *The Da Vinci Code,* Holzapfel et al.'s book is very much in line with the scholarly/popular response cited by Goodacre: Bock, *Breaking the Da Vinci Code*; Ehrman, *Truth and Fiction*; Price, *Da Vinci Fraud*; and Witherington, *Gospel Code.*

scandalized by—and, in the case of the anti-Mormon propaganda, have attempted to scandalize others with—the notion of a married Jesus for over 150 years.

Narrowing the Focus:
What the Feminist Woman Has Always Wanted—To Get Married!

There is one element of the GJW controversy that I *do* think *The DaVinci Code* can lay exclusive claim to: the idea that a married Jesus is an inherently feminist notion. This idea has clearly circulated in popular media accounts and the blogosphere (in headlines such as "Tiny Papyrus Fragment on 'Jesus' Wife' Leveraged to Push Feminist Agenda"[52]), but also lurks in scholarly discussions of GJW.[53] To be sure, self-identified feminist scholars (including, as noted by Goodacre, Karen King, Ann Graham Brock, Jane Schaberg,[54] April DeConick, and Esther de Boer) have paid significant attention to texts like the *Gospel of Mary* and the *Gospel of Philip* as evidence of the role of women (historical and metaphorical) in various strands of early Christianity. Karen

52. Bauer, "Tiny Papyrus Fragment."

53. For example, consider the following comment by Christian Askeland on his own post—in which he identifies what has widely been recognized as the crucial piece of evidence pointing towards forgery—on the *Evangelical Textual Criticism* blog: "The issue here is that a forger is playing off of hyperfeminist sensibilities, forging a 'Gospel of Jesus's Wife' and forging accompanying paperwork describing the fragment as said gospel. To me, seems highly likely that this was even given intentionally to King, who has specialized in women in apocryphal literature, and who is at Harvard, epicenter of American biblical gender studies. I did not bring in the gender issue here, the forger did and King swallowed it whole" ("Jesus Had a Sister-in-Law"). On the one hand, Askeland clearly implies that a feminist scholar would *want* GJW to be authentic, so much so that his/her judgment might be clouded. The less obvious point, however, is Askeland's assumption that the inclusion of a wife for Jesus is somehow a logical or obvious choice for a forger attempting to deceive a feminist—as if a married Jesus were exactly what feminists were hoping for. On the broader role of sexism in the discussion of GJW, see Mroczek, "Sexism." See also Baden and Moss, "Curious Case."

54. Schaberg—in a chapter titled "Mary Magdalene as Successor to Jesus"—writes, "The threatening thought appears: that Mary Magdalene can be considered a—or the—founder of Christianity, if one wants to use such a term; that she was 'a creator of the Christian belief in the resurrection,' and has a better claim than Paul to the title 'the first great interpreter of Jesus'" (*Resurrection of Mary Magdalene*, 303). While Dan Brown's character Leigh Teabing associates the notion of Mary Magdalene as Jesus' wife with her role as successor and leader of the young church, for Schaberg the potential status as "successor" has nothing to do with a sexual or marital relationship with Jesus. Later in the chapter Schaberg writes: "In this book, I let lie the issue of the sexuality of Mary Magdalene, in that I let it remain ambiguous whether or not she and Jesus were lovers" (ibid., 352).

King's published discussions of GJW place the fragment in that context. But nowhere in this scholarship will you find the idea that a married Jesus, or Mary Magdalene specifically as the wife of Jesus, is feminist *per se*. For the popularization of that idea, we have to turn to Dan Brown.

And so let us return to chapter 58 of *The Da Vinci Code*, the scene where Teabing reveals the big mystery to Sophie—that Mary Magdalene was married to Jesus and had a child—while Professor Langdon condescendingly smiles, nods, and mansplains.[55] Given the gendered nature of much of the controversy surrounding GJW (as noted by Schroeder and to be discussed below), I do not think it is out of place to point out that the whole chapter reads like a long-form mansplanation, narrated by an omniscient mansplainer.[56] The narrative is moved along with transitional sentences such as the following: "Sophie was certain she had missed something"; "Sophie turned to Langdon for help" [saying] 'I'm lost.' Langdon smiled"; "Uncertain, Sophie made her way closer . . ."; "Sophie was mesmerized"; "Sophie was trying to keep up"; "Sophie was speechless"; "Sophie was starting to feel overwhelmed"; "Sophie found herself again glancing at Langdon, who again nodded"; and "Sophie stood transfixed."[57] Teabing and Langdon are so knowledgeable. Sophie is very impressed.

Leaving aside the absurdly sexist construction of the scene, this is the moment where Teabing reveals to Sophie that Jesus had intended that his wife, not Peter, should inherit leadership of the Christian church after his death. Teabing concludes, "Jesus was the original feminist."[58] Granted, in the novel it is not just that Jesus was married to Mary Magdalene that makes him a feminist; it is that he wants her to lead the young church. But that point is, I think, pretty well elided in the popular response to the novel and film, such that in what Goodacre calls the "post-DaVinci Code world" a

55. "Mansplain," a portmanteau of "man" and "explain," entered our lexicon (quite literally as one of Oxford's "words of the year") only recently. Rebecca Solnit is largely credited with the first long-form articulation of the concept in her essay "Men Explain Things to Me," though she never uses the term itself. In short, "mansplaining" is when a man explains something to a woman, utterly confident that he knows what he is talking about, and equally confident that she requires and will benefit from his explanation. See, for example, Rothman, "Cultural History of Mansplaining."

56. By "omniscient mansplainer" I mean to indicate that this section of the narrative proceeds according to what I take to be a mansplainer's point of view—that is, the men (Teabing and Langdon) are wise and knowing experts who benevolently condescend to explain things to the wide-eyed woman (Sophie), who is eager to understand but desperately needs their help.

57. Brown, *Da Vinci Code*, 261–70 and *passim*.

58. Ibid., 268.

married Jesus—bizarrely—now equals feminism, and the "feminist agenda" must include a wife for Jesus.

This is perhaps a good moment to point to one aspect of Phipps's work not discussed above—that is, the "sex-positive" (to use a more contemporary term) nature of his arguments for a married Jesus. For Phipps, the notion of a celibate Jesus has, at a minimum, contributed to negative views of sexuality within traditional Christianity, above all Roman Catholicism. To the extent that such negative views of sexuality have had particularly negative effects for women, Phipps's sex-positive, married Jesus might be seen (and I suspect Phipps did see it) as a feminist notion.[59]

This is certainly the tack taken by John Shelby Spong (the Episcopal Bishop of Newark until his retirement in 2000), who takes up the question of Jesus' marital status in his book *Born of a Woman*. In a chapter titled "Suppose Jesus were Married," Spong writes, "the negativity that surrounds the idea that Jesus might have been married . . . reflects the residue of that deep Christian negativity toward women that still infects the church."[60] And further:

> Why is there still a continuing sense, ranging from disease to revulsion, that arises in us when we hear the suggestion that Jesus might have been married? I suggest that far more than any of us realize we are subconsciously victimized by the historic negativity toward women that has been a major gift of the Christian church to the world. So pervasive is this negativity that unconsciously we still regard holy matrimony to be less than the ideal, and we still operate out of an understanding of women that defines them as the source of sin, the polluter of otherwise moral men. For only in the service of this attitude would we greet with fear and negativity the suggestion that Jesus was married.[61]

Spong does not refer to Mormon sources, nor does Phipps (or Davis, Hyde or Kraut) appear in his bibliography. Instead he takes as his jumping-off point *Jesus Christ Superstar*, *Godspell*, and *The Last Temptation of Christ*, which he

---

59. Phipps's "sex positivity" is also a bit homophobic and sexist in his clear objections to an "effeminate" Jesus; he writes that "although some of the artistic and cultic expressions of Christianity do suggest that Jesus was effeminate, there is no biblical basis for this assumption" (*Was Jesus Married?*, 8) and ultimately describes Jesus as a "red-blooded male" (ibid., 190). In this respect, too, Phipps represents a bit of a throwback to late nineteenth- and early twentieth-century debates on Jesus, specifically a rejection of "effeminate" images. For a discussion of the masculinization of Jesus in this era, see Prothero, *American Jesus*, 87–94.

60. Spong, *Born of a Woman*, 188.

61. Ibid., 197.

describes as the most recent instances of a longstanding "undercurrent that linked Jesus with Mary Magdalene in a romantic way."[62] Nevertheless, the arguments he presents (including, for example, his interpretation of Cana as Jesus' own wedding) closely parallel arguments first presented by Hyde and Phipps.

Whether or not one thinks of "sex positivity" as a part of contemporary feminism, I hasten to point out that the early Christian texts in which women play the most prominent roles (i.e., the *Acts of John*, *Acts of Andrew*, *Acts of Paul*, and *Acts of Thomas*) are decidedly not sex-positive. And, over the past few millennia, marriage has not exactly been the clear path to self-actualization for most women.[63] Here, I would give Karen King the last word: "Why do we feel the need to re-sexualize Mary? We've gotten rid of the myth of the prostitute. Now there's this move to see her as wife and mother. Why isn't it adequate to see her as disciple and perhaps apostle?"[64]

RESPONSE TO JAMES MCGRATH

Turning now to James McGrath's paper, I begin by stating how helpful I found his timeline of online events to be, especially as someone who "checked in" on the blogs during that week in 2012, but was not exactly glued to the screen. I think that McGrath is dead-on in his assessment of the great benefits and potential of online scholarship and the fact that other fields in the humanities are already doing a much better job of taking advantage of those benefits; I also agree entirely on his suggestions for what would make online scholarship much, much better: more participation, more caution, and more transparency and accessibility. Exactly.

I would, however, push back on several other points. First is his characterization of several online comments regarding gender and sexuality as a reflection of the "casual tone of most blogs" (p. 335 above). I think he is right, to the extent that expressions of misogyny and homophobia are indeed usually quite casual. I would point out, further, that the very casualness with which misogyny and homophobia are expressed in our field is pretty indicative of the scale of our problem. While he did not comment explicitly, I am sure that McGrath is well aware that in his list of early bloggers on GJW, one of those bloggers is not like the others: April DeConick

62. Ibid., 187.

63. This statement hardly requires a footnote, but I will take the opportunity to cite my own mother, Joan Leland Spittler, who has explained her decision to enter a convent in 1958 with: "I didn't want to get married. I wanted to go to graduate school."

64. Karen King as quoted by Darman, "Inconvenient Woman."

is the only female on the list of 27. That makes the ratio of male to female contributors to the *Evangelical Textual Criticism* blog, noted by Schroeder as 17 to 1, look pretty good. It is pretty clear to me that when we call for "more participation" in online scholarship, the one group that we probably *do not need more of* is (white)[65] men. And so if we truly are interested in greater participation, the question really has to be: why are Bible bloggers mostly just men?

"Trolls. Trepidation. Time."

This leads me to the only point where I really disagree with McGrath—or agree, but not in the sense that McGrath intends his comments. He writes:

> The fact that hobbies and humor may appear alongside reflections on ongoing research and commentary on breaking news about archaeological finds has, for some of us, created a genuine sense of getting to know one another as people via the internet. Given the penchant for rancor and insult in online venues, the potential benefit of something that leads us to recognize one another—and thus hopefully treat one another—as real human beings offsets, in my mind, the potential disadvantages of the mixing of frivolity and scholarship on blogs and other social media. (pp. 338–39 above)

To the extent that I learn from blogs that my colleagues are really into sci-fi or are fans of Swedish pop music, I agree. But just as frequently what I learn from blogs is that some of my colleagues are bigots. On several of the more popular Bible blogs, the "humor" that is mixed in is sometimes straight-up misogyny, homophobia, and racism. And because of the "community" aspect in the Bible blogging world (the way in which Bible bloggers of various stripes link to each others' blogs and are otherwise connected by social media) the whole pool—speaking only for myself here—feels tainted by what a minority of Bible bloggers are putting out there. In other words, the very thing that makes the Bible blogosphere an attractive and comfortable space for McGrath makes it less hospitable for women.

---

65. While I am primarily addressing the issue of gender inclusiveness here, I want to underscore our field's desperate lack of racial and ethnic diversity. According to the latest Society of Biblical Literature statistics, only 3.4 percent of the members of our primary professional organization are African Americans, 2.3 percent are Asian Americans, and 1.7 percent are Latina/o. Moreover, as Schroeder has noted, issues of online harassment (discussed below) are substantially amplified for women of color.

And make no mistake: the Internet is an inhospitable place for women. The clearest piece of evidence for this is undoubtedly the online rape threat phenomenon—something with which all women with any online presence are familiar. Readers of this essay may or may not be familiar with "Gamergate,"[66] a term that refers, in part, to a harassment campaign against Anita Sarkeesian, a cultural critic who has analyzed misogynistic tropes in video games—but there are many examples much closer to our home in the academy. In her essay, Caroline Schroeder points us toward the experiences of Mary Beard, who maintains a lively Twitter account and whose blog, A Don's Life, is hosted by the *Times Literary Supplement.*[67] In a 2014 lecture at the British Museum (titled "Oh Do Shut Up Dear!"), she described some of the venom with which her blogging and tweeting is met: "It doesn't much matter what line of argument you take as a woman. If you venture into traditional male territory, the abuse comes anyway. It's not what you say that prompts it—it's the fact that you are saying it . . . 'Shut up you bitch' is a fairly common refrain . . . [along with a] predictable menu of rape, bombing, murder, and so forth."[68] In the same lecture, Beard read the following tweet threat: "I'm going to cut off your head and rape it."

This sort of harassment is not limited to scholars who regularly appear on television, as Mary Beard does. In a blog post titled "Trolls at My Door," Liv Ingeborg Lied, a scholar who blogs on Old Testament pseudepigrapha and its use in Late Antiquity and the Middle Ages, categorizes the "responses" she receives via social media:

1. Responses that in various ways call for my attention, but not as a scholar. Some respondents ask, quite discretely, if they can be in touch with me privately or have my phone number. Others share pictures of themselves dressed in army uniforms. Curiously, I receive these army uniform messages again and again, each time from a different respondent.

2. At times I receive messages of a far more aggressive kind. These are the messages I would categorize as trolling, defined elsewhere as "recreational abuse." Out of concern for

66. For those unfamiliar with Gamergate, see Dewey, "Only Guide to Gamergate."

67. http://timesonline.typepad.com/dons_life/.

68. Quoted from Mead, "Troll Slayer." While Beard has famously (and publicly) engaged many of her online trolls, and this "troll taming" has been widely praised (for example, Ellis-Petersen, "Mary Beard"), others have noted that Beard's engagement approach hardly works for everyone. In a *Guardian* opinion piece, Hadley Freeman ("'How to Tame Your Troll'") contrasts the coverage of Beard's "troll taming" with the threats directed at Anita Sarkeesian, which were so violent and credible that she was forced to leave her home.

the fainthearted I will not summarize them here, but simply share one short quote to illustrate their general contents and style. That first troll knocking at my door back in 2013 claimed, among other things, that I "obviously needed to be ****** by a real man." No need to go into detail—you get the picture.[69]

I cannot help emphasizing it: there is a Venn diagram to be drawn, with one circle representing "people who visit blogs on Old Testament pseudepigrapha and its late antique reception" and another circle representing "people who make online rape threats," and *those circles overlap.*

Of course, it is not just rape threats that discourage women from blogging. Blogger and historian of American religious history Kelly Baker describes her experiences in a blog post titled "The Men Who Email Me," writing:

> The men who email me tell me that I'm wrong. I've made the wrong argument. I've missed the essential issue or the salient details. I've made errors and mistakes. I didn't use data. I used too much data. They assert that gender is not as big of an issue as I make it out to be or that I don't realize how hard it is to be a man. They assert that I can never be anything but wrong. The men who email me claim that I don't know anything about higher education, religious studies, labor, gender, or any other topic I've ever written an essay about. They ignore my credentials in favor of assuming my incompetency . . . The men who email me sometimes start with a compliment about how much they "enjoyed" my essay. They then proceed to send me their own writing on the subject and tell me to "please include it" next time because they are experts on the topic. They are *the* experts. How did I not know that? They are just remedying the situation and improving my knowledge.[70]

And this sort of response, too, has a clear chilling effect. Baker describes her choice *not* to write an essay for online publication—an essay that had already been pitched to editors and accepted—as follows:

> What I couldn't face was a dumpster fire in my inbox. I weighed the impact of the essay's possible reception against my mental well-being. I killed an essay because I knew I wouldn't be able to manage the nasty responses. Some weeks, I can ignore what

---

69. Lied, "Trolls at My Door."
70. Baker, "Men Who Email Me."

the men who email me say. Last week was not one of those. My
essay died a quiet death, and my inbox remained uneventful.[71]

I have no doubt that male bloggers, too, experience "dumpster fires" in their
e-mail inboxes. But there is good research to back up the mountain of anecdotal evidence suggesting that women face far more serious and far more
disturbing online abuse than men do.[72]

My own conversations with other women who *should* be blogging (that
is, women who are reading blogs and are otherwise engaged in social media) but are not, indicates that the decision not to blog is based, unsurpris-
ingly, on a combination of factors. One friend summarized her reasoning
with: "Trolls. Trepidation. Time."—and I hear variations on this sentiment
echoed by almost every female scholar I speak with about blogging. We
do not want to deal with trolls; we are hesitant to subject our ideas to the
scrutiny of the "men who email us"; and, faced with those disincentives,
who wants to spend the time?—especially on a product that will not "count"
for tenure and promotion review.

This last factor, time, is yet another area in which gender plays a role.
There is now substantial data indicating that women do a disproportionate
amount of service work within American universities.[73] While this phenomenon is no doubt driven by what I would characterize as a very positive
impulse—that is, the desire to create gender parity in the day-to-day admin-
istration and governance of the university—it creates a burden on women
faculty that, ironically, has detrimental effects on our careers (most notably
slowing our progress to promotion). Women are frequently counseled to
"just say no" to service requests, but as Karen Pyke has shown, the overall
deficit of women in higher education combined with the desire to increase
gender diversity on committees results in women receiving far more and
far more persistent requests for service, and these requests generally come
earlier in women's careers. Alongside the data, Pyke illustrates the phenomenon with her own experience on the University of California Riverside
Academic Senate's Committee on Committees. She writes:

> It was customary practice for COC members to pressure women
> faculty who initially rejected a service request to reconsider, un-
> derscoring the committee's need for a woman. I do not recall a
> time when the committee issued a repeated request to a man

71. Ibid.

72. See, for example, the 2014 Pew study (cited by Schroeder) which revealed that,
while men are more likely to experience online harassment, women were more likely to
experience serious, damaging abuse (Duggan, "Online Harassment").

73. See, for example, Pyke, "Faculty Gender Inequity."

faculty member who said no, because men were not in short supply. Hence, men faculty and administrators are better able to control their service labor by saying no than can women faculty, who must say no more often, and repeatedly, while also ignoring any obligation they feel to represent women on campus.[74]

I suspect many of my women colleagues will recognize their own experiences here; I certainly do. The phenomenon seems to be at play in the Society of Biblical Literature, where 23.9% of members, but 41.3% of Annual Meeting program chairs, are women.[75]

To reiterate, I view efforts towards gender diversity in academic leadership roles as a very positive movement; I am as desperate to avoid the "all male panel" or "all male committee" as the rest of you, and have on many occasions pressured women colleagues to participate. I am part of the problem! So are you. That is the nature of institutional and structural barriers. So, yes, I agree with McGrath that blogging is generally a good thing that would benefit from more and broader participation. I worry, however, that the obstacles to that broader participation are rather more intractable than McGrath acknowledges.

RESPONSE TO CAROLINE SCHROEDER

I very much like the analysis of the GJW controversy as a group of multilayered and intersecting markers of authenticity; this elegant description of the real significance of GJW within our field is, to my mind, dead on. In what follows I will respond to parts one and two of her paper in reverse order.

Schroeder and McGrath seem to be on the same page in regarding digital and traditional scholarship as doing, actually, pretty similar work. McGrath has pointed to speed as a primary difference; in part one of her essay, Schroeder raises the element of professional status. That Bible bloggers and other social-media participants are *not*, by and large, authenticated by their status as established scholars at elite universities but through things like "level of engagement," "shared interests" and "shared viewpoints" seems to me to be an important point. This is clearly a very positive aspect of digital scholarship: I hope we are all aware that positions at elite universities are attained by equal measures (at best!) of luck and merit, and generally alongside a heaping portion of privilege. And, as someone once said, "to those who have, more will be given." The academic job market and the American

74. Ibid., 88.

75. I am very grateful to Charles Haws, Society of Biblical Literature Director of Programs, for assembling this data for me.

university system's increased reliance on contingent faculty have ensured that many top-notch researchers are either doing 4–4 loads at teaching colleges, or have accepted the "independent scholar" designation and are making a living by various other means—which may well leave more time for research than a 4–4 load. Moreover—and this is by no means to disparage Roger Bagnall, AnneMarie Luijendijk, or their respective institutions—the GJW episode has offered us clear evidence that the blogging community, made up largely of scholars from less prestigious institutions, is very much capable of doing *more persuasive work* than scholars from our most elite universities.

But, as Schroeder has indicated, the gender issue cuts through all of this at an odd angle. That women academics in Biblical Studies face structural discrimination is obvious; the raw numbers are clear evidence of that. In addition to Haws's valuable research on the "leaky pipeline" of women entering the field,[76] I would note that female membership in the Society of Biblical Literature (currently at 23.9%, as noted above) has made virtually no gains over the last decade.[77] I will admit that I have generally associated the continued existence of gender imbalance in our field—such that we lag behind sister fields like Classics—with the fact that conservative Christianities are such prominent feeders to Biblical Studies programs. Much of the data Schroeder cites (e.g., Muehlberger's Review of Biblical Literature Parity project, and data concerning journals like *JECS*) is good evidence that there are more—and more complicated—factors at play. I would point out, though, that one place where women in our field *have* reached some degree of parity is precisely at those elite research universities (e.g., Elisabeth Schüssler Fiorenza, Karen King, and Laura Nasrallah at Harvard; Adela Yarbro Collins at Yale; Elizabeth Clark at Duke; Margaret Mitchell at Chicago, etc.). In other words, there is a disturbing disconnect whereby digital scholarship has indeed fostered a degree of democratization and the breakdown of meaningless markers of academic prestige, but has not had similar success in breaking down gendered barriers—and, in fact, may well be pushing us in the opposite direction.

In response to part 1 of Schroeder's essay, I want to amplify her comments on the ethical dimensions of transparency as regards the provenance and all available information about the ancient materials with which we work. And, of course, I feel compelled to confess how easy it is to ignore

---

76. Charles Haws's study of the "leaky pipeline," cited by Schroeder, is particularly disturbing in its conclusion that the leak has gotten worse, not better, over the past fifteen years—a time period that, to my dismay, lines up precisely with my own participation as graduate student and junior professor in the field.

77. See membership data here: https://www.sbl-site.org/SBLDashboard.aspx/.

such concerns. When I saw the announcement that the University of Virginia (my own employer) had acquired its first papyrus, I eagerly hurried off to special collections, thinking only of transcribing the text (maybe it was actually more interesting than it sounded!) and of its possible use in training graduate students. I would like to say that I "assumed" the acquisitions librarians had done due diligence in establishing the papyrus's provenance, but the truth is that whether or not due diligence had been done never even crossed my mind—not until, that is, I saw Schroeder and Brice Jones raising the question on social media.

I also want to underscore the point that throughout this controversy, as Schroeder puts it, "the 'fuzzy' humanities methods have proven sharper than 'hard science'" (p. 313 above). To the degree that there is a positive message to be derived from the GJW episode, I think that is it: we, scholars of early Christianity—well trained in ancient languages, immersed in the literature and material culture of the time and place we study, working transparently and collaboratively, and submitting our work to peer review, whether traditional or crowd-sourced online—are simply better at this than scientists with carbon dating tests. And I suspect that will continue to be the case, probably for a very long time.

CONCLUSION

When asked to serve as respondent in a session on GJW, I did not expect sexism and other forms of discrimination to be the thread that connected the three essays (or, rather, *my response to* the three essays: only Schroeder's essay deals with these issues explicitly). But as so many, beginning with Karen King, have pointed out: GJW tells us nothing about the historical Jesus. And as has become increasingly clear: GJW tells us nothing about early Christianity. GJW does, however, tell us something about ourselves—about both our moment in religious history and our moment as an academic field. I generally try to avoid the overused phrase "a perfect storm," but given the role that best-selling books and mediocre movies have played in the controversy surrounding our tiny papyrus fragment, it might just be appropriate here: GJW has stirred up a perfect storm in Biblical Studies, pulling in, whipping up, spinning around, and spitting out all that is good, bad, and ugly about us.

Bibliography

Aageson, James W. *Paul, the Pastoral Epistles, and the Early Church*. Library of Pauline Studies. Grand Rapids: Baker Academic, 2007.

Aaronovitch, David. *Voodoo Histories: The Role of the Conspiracy Theory in Shaping Modern History*. London: Cape, 2009.

Abanes, Richard. *Inside Today's Mormonism: Understanding Latter-day Saints in Light of Biblical Truth*. Eugene, OR: Harvest House, 2004.

Ahmad, Khwaja Nazir. *Jesus in Heaven on Earth*. Woking, UK: Woking Muslim Mission & Literary Trust, 1952.

Ahmad, Mirza Ghulam. *Masih hindustan mein*. Qadian, India: Islam International, 1899.

Alderman, Naomi. *The Liars' Gospel*. New York: Back Bay, 2012.

Allegro, John Marco. *The Shapira Affair: The Mystery of a Nineteenth-Century Discovery of a Dead Sea Manuscript: A Forgery of the Oldest Bible in the World?* New York: Doubleday, 1965.

Allen, Charlotte. "Jesus' Wife? The Final Debunking." *Weekly Standard* (posted 4 July 2016). http://www.weeklystandard.com/jesus-wife/article/2002985/.

Amann, Émile. *Le Protévangile de Jacques le Mineur et ses remaniements latins. Introduction, textes, traduction et commentaire*. Paris: Letouzey, 1910.

Anderson, Gary A. "The Cosmic Mountain: Eden and Its Early Interpreters in Syriac Christianity." In *Genesis 1–3 in the History of Exegesis: Intrigue in the Garden*, edited by Gregory Allen Robbins, 187–224. Studies in Women and Religion 27. Lewiston, NY: Mellen, 1988.

Anderson, Richard Lloyd. "The Fraudulent Archko Volume." *BYU Studies* 15/1 (1975) 43–64

Armstrong, Jonathan J. "Victorinus of Pettau as the Author of the Muratorian Fragment." *VC* 62 (2008) 1–34.

Aron, Robert. *Jesus of Nazareth: The Hidden Years*. New York: Morrow, 1962.

Arthur, Richard J. "The Gospel of Judas: Is It a Hoax?" *Journal of Unification Studies* 9 (2008) 35–47.

Ashwin-Siejkowski, Piotr. *Clement of Alexandria: A Project of Christian Perfection*. T. & T. Clark Theology. London: T. & T. Clark, 2008.

Askeland, Christian. "The Gospel of Jesus Wife and Grondin's Interlinear." *Evangelical Textual Criticism* (posted 29 August 2015). http://www.evangelicaltextualcriticism.blogspot.com/2015/08/the-gospel-of-jesus-wife-and-grondins.html/.

————. "Jesus Had a Sister-in-Law." *Evangelical Textual Criticism* (posted 24 April 2004, originally titled "Jesus Had an Ugly Sister-in-Law"). http://evangelicaltextualcriticism.blogspot.de/2014/04/jesus-had-ugly-sister-in-law.html/.

————. "A Lycopolitan Forgery of John's Gospel." *NTS* 61/3 (2015) 314–34.

————. "More on the Gospel of Jesus' Wife and Walter Fritz." *Evangelical Textual Criticism* (posted 16 June 2016). http://evangelicaltextualcriticism.blogspot.ca/2016/06/more-on-gospel-of-jesus-wife-and-walter.html/.

Atherton, M. "The Sources of Vercelli 5 (Cameron B.3.2.1)." *Fontes Anglo-Saxonici: A Register of Written Sources Used by Anglo-Saxon Authors.* 1996. http://fontes.english.ox.ac.uk/.

————. "The Sources of Vercelli 6 (Cameron B.3.4.10)." *Fontes Anglo-Saxonici: A Register of Written Sources Used by Anglo-Saxon Authors.* 1996. http://fontes.english.ox.ac.uk/.

Azzarelli, Joseph M., et al. "Study of Two Papyrus Fragments with Fourier Transform Infrared Microspectroscopy." *HTR* 107 (2014) 165.

Baalen, Jan Karel van. *The Chaos of Cults: A Study in Present-Day Isms.* Grand Rapids: Eerdmans, 1947.

Baden, Joel, and Candida R. Moss. "New Clues Cast Doubt on 'Gospel of Jesus' Wife.'" *CNN Belief Blog* (posted 29 April 2014). http://religion.blogs.cnn.com/2014/04/29/new-evidence-casts-doubt-on-gospel-of-jesus-wife/.

————. "The Curious Case of Jesus' Wife." *Atlantic*, December 2014, 80. http://www.theatlantic.com/magazine/archive/2014/12/the-curious-case-of-jesuss-wife/382227/.

————. "Why Scientists and Scholars Can't Get Their Facts Straight." *Atlantic* (posted 10 September 2015). http://www.theatlantic.com/technology/archive/2015/09/why-scientists-and-scholars-cant-get-their-facts-straight/404254/.

Baigent, Michael, et al. *The Holy Blood and the Holy Grail.* New York: Bantam Dell, 1982.

Baines, Paul. *The House of Forgery in Eighteenth-Century Britain.* Aldershot, UK: Ashgate, 1999.

Baker, Kelly. "The Men Who Email Me." *Cold Takes* (posted 27 April 2016). http://www.kellyjbaker.com/the-men-who-email-me/.

Bakewell, Joan. "The Tomb That Dare not Speak Its Mind: An Archaeological Discovery in Israel Challenges the Very Basis of Christianity." *Sunday Times*, 31 March 1996, 1.

Banning, Joop van, ed. *Opus Imperfectum in Matthaeum. Praefatio.* CCSL 87b. Turnhout: Brepols, 1988.

Barc, Bernard, and Wolf-Peter Funk, eds. and trans. *Le Livre des secrets de Jean, Recension brève (NH III,1 BG,2).* BCNH Textes 35. Leuven: Peeters, 2012.

Barnes, Timothy D. "'Another Shall Gird Thee': Probative Evidence for the Death of Peter." In *Peter in Early Christianity*, edited by Helen K. Bond and Larry W. Hurtado, 76–95. Grand Rapids: Eerdmans, 2015.

Barrier, Jeremy W. *The Acts of Paul and Thecla: A Critical Introduction and Commentary.* WUNT 2/270. Tübingen: Mohr/Siebeck, 2009.

Bates, Stephen. "Did Jesus Christ Really Have a Wife?" *Guardian* (posted 19 September 2012). http://www.theguardian.com/world/2012/sep/19/jesus-christ-really-have-wife/.

Bauer, Rick. "Tiny Papyrus Fragment on 'Jesus' Wife' Leveraged to Push Feminist Agenda." *Hark* (blog). *Denver Post* (posted 12 September 2012). http://blogs. denverpost.com/hark/2012/09/21/tiny-papyrus-fragment-jesus-wife-leveraged-fit-feminist-agenda/1203/.

Baum, Armin. *Pseudepigraphie und literarische Fälschung im frühen Christentum.* WUNT 2/313. Tübingen: Mohr/Siebeck, 2001.

Baumeister, Theofried. "Die Rolle des Petrus in gnostischen Texten." In *Acts of the Second International Congress of Coptic Studies*, edited by Tito Orlandi and Frederick Wisse, 3–12. Rome: C.I.M., 1985.

Beadle, John H. *Polygamy: or, the Mysteries and Crimes of Mormonism.* Philadelphia: National Publishing, 1882.

Beal, Timothy. "Reception History and Beyond: Toward the Cultural History of Scriptures." *BibInt* 19 (2011) 357–72.

Beasley, Jonathan. "Testing Indicates 'Gospel of Jesus's Wife' Papyrus Fragment to Be Ancient." *The Gospel of Jesus's Wife* (posted 10 April 2014). http://gospelofjesusswife. hds.harvard.edu/testing-indicates-gospel-jesuss-wife-papyrus-fragment-be-ancient/.

Bedingfield, M. Bradford. *The Dramatic Liturgy of Anglo-Saxon England.* Anglo-Saxon Studies 1. Woodbridge, UK: Boydell, 2002.

Beker, J. Christiaan. *Heirs of Paul: Paul's Legacy in the New Testament and in the Church Today.* Grand Rapids: Eerdmans, 1996.

Bell, H. Idris and T. C. Skeat, eds. *Fragments of an Unknown Gospel and Other Early Christian Papyri.* London: Trustees of the British Museum, 1935.

Bell, Sinclair. "Role Models in the Roman World." In *Role Models in the Roman World: Identity and Assimilation*, edited by Sinclair Bell and Inge Lyse Hansen, 1–39. MAAR Supplementary Volume 7. Ann Arbor: University of Michigan Press, 2008.

Berding, Kenneth. *Polycarp and Paul: An Analysis of Their Literary & Theological Relationship in Light of Polycarp's Use of Biblical & Extra-Biblical Literature.* SVC 62. Leiden: Brill, 2002.

———. "Polycarp's Use of *1 Clement*: An Assumption Reconsidered." *JECS* 19 (2011) 127–39.

Berger, Samuel. *Histoire de la Vulgate pendant les premiers siècles du Moyen-Age.* Paris: Hachette, 1893

Berliner, Rudolf. "Urteil des Pilatus." *Die christliche Kunst* 30 (1933/1934) 128–47.

Bernhard, Andrew. "The Gospel of Jesus' Wife: A Call for Closure." *NT Blog* (posted 24 August 2015). http://ntweblog.blogspot.com/2015/08/the-gospel-of-jesus-wife-call-for.html/.

———. "The Gospel of Jesus' Wife: 'Patchwork' Forgery in Coptic . . . and English." *NT Blog* (posted 28 August 2015). http://ntweblog.blogspot.com/2015/08/the-gospel-of-jesus-wife-patchwork.html/.

———. "The Gospel of Jesus' Wife: 'Patchwork' Forgery in Coptic . . . and English (Recap)." *NT Blog* (posted 29 August 2015). http://ntweblog.blogspot.ca/2015/08/the-gospel-of-jesus-wife-patchwork_29.html/.

———. "The Gospel of Jesus' Wife: Textual Evidence of Modern Forgery." *NTS* 61 (2015) 335–55.

———. "How The Gospel of Jesus's Wife Might Have Been Forged: A Tentative Proposal." *Gospels.net* (posted 11 October 2012). Pages 1–15. http://www.gospels. net/gjw/mighthavebeenforged.pdf/.

————, ed. and trans. *Other Early Christian Gospels: A Critical Edition of the Surviving Greek Manuscripts*. T. & T. Clark Library of Biblical Studies. Library of New Testament Studies 315. Studies in New Testament Greek. London: T. & T. Clark, 2007.

Berry, George R. "Priests and Levites." *JBL* 42 (1923) 227–38.

Beskow, Per. *Jesus i Kashmir: Historien om en legend*. Stockholm: Proprius, 1981.

————. "Modern Mystifications of Jesus." In *The Blackwell Companion to Jesus*, edited by Delbert Burkett, 458–73. Blackwell Companions to Religion. Malden, MA: Wiley-Blackwell, 2011

————. *Strange Tales about Jesus: A Survey of Unfamiliar Gospels*. Rev. ed. Philadelphia: Fortress, 1983. Swedish editions: *Fynd och fusk i bibelns värld: Om vår tids Jesus-apokryfer* [Discoveries and cheats in the biblical world: The Jesus apocrypha of our time]. 1979; rev. in 2005 as *Fynd och fusk: Falsarier och mystifikationer omkring Jesus* [Discoveries and cheats: Forgeries and mystifications about Jesus].

Beyers, Rita, ed. *Libri de Nativitate Mariae: Libellus de Nativitate Sanctae Mariae, Textus et Commentarius*. CCSA 10. Turnhout: Brepols, 1997.

Bickell, Gustav, ed. "Das Nichtkanonische Evangelien-Fragment." In *Mittheilungen aus der Sammlung der Papyrus Erzherzog Rainer* 1.3–4, 53–61. Vienna: Hof- und Staatsdruckerei, 1887.

————, ed. "Ein Papyrusfragment eines nichtkanonischen Evangeliums." *ZKT* 9 (1885) 498–504.

Biggs, Frederick M., ed. *Sources of Anglo-Saxon Literary Culture: The Apocrypha*. Instrumenta Anglistica Mediaevalia 1. Kalamazoo: Medieval Institute Publications, 2006.

Blavatsky, Helena Petrovna. *Isis Unveiled: A Master-Key to the Mysteries of Ancient and Modern Science and Theology*. 6th ed. New York: Bouton, 1877.

————. *The Secret Doctrine: The Synthesis of Science, Religion, and Philosophy*. 2 vols. London: Theosophical Publishing, 1888.

Blossom, Stefaniw. "Becoming Men, Staying Women: Gender Ambivalence in Christian Apocryphal Texts and Contexts." *Feminist Theology* 18/3 (2010) 341–55.

Bock, Darrell. *Breaking the Da Vinci Code: Answers to the Questions Everyone's Asking*. Nashville: Nelson, 2004.

Boer, Esther de. *The Gospel of Mary: Beyond a Gnostic and a Biblical Mary Magdalene*. JSNTSup 260. London: T. & T. Clark, 2004.

Boer, Martinus de. "Images of Paul in the Post-Apostolic Period." *CBQ* 42 (1980) 359–80.

Boer, Roland. "Christological Slippage and Ideological Structures in Schwarzenegger's *Terminator*." *Semeia* 69–70 (1995) 165–93.

Böhlig, Alexander. "The New Testament and the Concept of the Manichaean Myth." In *The New Testament and Gnosis: Essays in Honour of Robert McL. Wilson*, edited by Alastair Logan and Alexander J. M. Wedderburn, 90–104. Edinburgh: T. & T. Clark, 1983.

Bond, Helen. "Helen Bond on Sexism and NT Scholarship." *The Jesus Blog* (posted 10 December 2014). http://historicaljesusresearch.blogspot.ca/2014/12/helen-bond-on-sexism-and-nt-scholarship.html/.

Bouriant, Urbain. *Fragments du texte grec du livre d'Enoch et de quelques écrits attribués à Saint Pierre*. Paris: Leroux, 1892.

Bovon, François. *New Testament and Christian Apocrypha: Collected Studies II*, edited by Glenn E. Snyder. WUNT 237. Tübingen: Mohr/Siebeck, 2009.

Bovon, François et al., eds. *Écrits apocryphes chrétiens*. 2 vols. Bibliothèque de la Pléiade 442 and 516. Paris: Gallimard, 1997–2005.

Bowles, Kate. "Soap Opera: 'No End of Story, Ever.'" In *The Australian TV Book*, edited by Graeme Turner and Stuart Cunningham, 117–29. St. Leonards, NSW: Allen & Unwin, 2000.

Bradley, Keith R. *Slavery and Society at Rome*. Key Themes in Ancient History. Cambridge: Cambridge University Press, 1994.

Brankaer, Johanna, and Hans-Gebhard Bethge, ed. and trans. "Der Brief des Petrus an Philippus." In *Codex Tchacos: Texte und Analysen*, 5–80. TU 161. Berlin: de Gruyter, 2007.

Brantley, Jessica. "The Iconography of the Utrecht Psalter and the Old English *Descent into Hell*." *Anglo-Saxon England* 28 (1999) 43–63.

Brashler, James A., trans. "Apocalypse of Peter: Text, Translation, and Notes." In *Nag Hammadi Codex VII*, edited by Birger A. Pearson, 201–47. NHMS 30. Leiden: Brill, 1996.

———. "The Coptic Apocalypse of Peter: A Genre Analysis and Interpretation." PhD diss., Claremont Graduate School, 1977.

Brock, Ann Graham. *Mary Magdalene, The First Apostle: The Struggle for Authority.* HTS 51. Cambridge: Harvard University Press, 2003.

Brown, Andrew. "The Gospel of Jesus's Wife: A Very Modern Fake." *Guardian* (posted 16 October 2012). http://www.theguardian.com/commentisfree/belief/2012/oct/16/gospel-jesus-wife-modern-fake-typo/.

———. "Gospel of Jesus's Wife Is Fake, Claims Expert." *Guardian* (posted 21 September 2012). http://www.theguardian.com/world/2012/sep/21/gospel-jesus-wife-forgery/.

Brown, Dan. *The Da Vinci Code*. New York: Doubleday, 2003.

Brown, Peter. *The Body and Society: Men, Women and Sexual Renunciation in Early Christianity*. Lectures on the History of Religions n.s. 13. New York: Columbia University Press, 1988.

Brown, Scott G. "Behind the Seven Veils, I." In *Ancient Gospel or Modern Forgery? The Secret Gospel of Mark in Debate*, edited by Tony Burke, 247–83. Eugene, OR: Cascade Books, 2013.

———. "The *Letter to Theodore*: Stephen Carlson's Case against Clement's Authorship." *JECS* 16 (2008) 535–72.

———. *Mark's Other Gospel: Rethinking Morton Smith's Controversial Discovery*. ESCJ 15. Waterloo, ON: Wilfrid Laurier University Press, 2005.

———. "The Mystical Gospel of Mark (Part One)." *Fourth R* 25/6 (2012) 5–10.

———. "The Mystical Gospel of Mark (Part Two)." *Fourth R* 26/1 (2013) 5–7, 18–22, 24.

Brown, Scott G., and Allan J. Pantuck. "Craig Evans and the Secret Gospel of Mark: Exploring the Grounds for Doubt." In *Ancient Gospel or Modern Forgery? The Secret Gospel of Mark in Debate*, edited by Tony Burke, 101–34. Eugene, OR: Cascade Books, 2013.

Brox, Norbert. *Falsche Verfasserangaben: zur Erklärung der frühchristlichen Pseudepigraphie*. SBS 79. Stuttgart: KBW, 1975.

Brunsdon, Charlotte. "'Crossroads': Notes on Soap Opera." *Screen* 22/4 (1981) 32–37.

Brynner, Jeanna. "'Gospel of Jesus' Wife' Faces Authenticity Tests." *Live Science* (posted 19 October 2012). http://www.livescience.com/24139-gospel-of-jesus-wife-faces-authenticity-tests.html/.

Bucur, Bogdan G. *Angelomorphic Pneumatology: Clement of Alexandria and Other Early Christian Witnesses.* VCSup 95. Leiden: Brill, 2009.

———. "The Divine Face and the Angels of the Face: Jewish Apocalyptic Themes in Early Christology and Pneumatology." In *Apocalyptic Thought in Early Christianity*, edited by Robert J. Daly, 143–53. Holy Cross Studies in Patristic Theology and History. Grand Rapids: Baker Academic, 2009.

Burke, Tony, ed. *Ancient Gospel or Modern Forgery? The Secret Gospel of Mark in Debate.* Eugene, OR: Cascade Books, 2013.

———, ed. *Forbidden Texts on the Western Frontier: The Christian Apocrypha in North American Perspectives.* Eugene, OR: Cascade Books, 2015.

———. "Introduction." In *Ancient Gospel or Modern Forgery? The Secret Gospel of Mark in Debate*, edited by Tony Burke, 1–29. Eugene, OR: Cascade Books, 2013.

———. *Secret Scriptures Revealed: A New Introduction to the Christian Apocrypha.* Grand Rapids: Eerdmans, 2013.

Burke, Tony, and Brent Landau, eds. *New Testament Apocrypha: More Noncanonical Scriptures.* Vol. 1. Grand Rapids: Eerdmans, 2016.

Burrus, Virginia. *Chastity as Autonomy: Women in the Stories of the Apocryphal Acts.* Studies in Women and Religion 23. Lewiston, NY: Mellen, 1987.

———. "Chastity as Autonomy: Women in the Stories of the Apocryphal Acts." *Semeia* 38 (1986) 101–17.

Caird, George B. Review of *Paul and Palestinian Judaism*, by E. P. Sanders. *JTS* 29 (1978) 538–43.

Carlson, Stephen C. "Can the Academy Protect Itself from One of Its Own? The Case of *Secret Mark*." In *Ancient Gospel or Modern Forgery? The Secret Gospel of Mark in Debate*, edited by Tony Burke, 299–307. Eugene, OR: Cascade Books, 2013.

———. *The Gospel Hoax: Morton Smith's Invention of Secret Mark.* Waco, TX: Baylor University Press, 2005.

Cartlidge, David R., and J. Keith Elliott. *Art and the Christian Apocrypha.* London: Routledge, 2001.

Castelli, Elizabeth A. *Martyrdom and Memory: Early Christian Culture Making.* Gender, Theory, and Religion. New York: Columbia University Press, 2004.

Cecire, Natalia. "Introduction: Theory and the Virtues of Digital Humanities." *Journal of Digital Humanities* 1/1 (2011). http://journalofdigitalhumanities.org/1-1/introduction-theory-and-the-virtues-of-digital-humanities-by-natalia-cecire/.

Čéplö, Slavomír. "Tahime." *Bulbulistan* (posted 30 September 2012). http://blog.bulbul.sk/2012/09/tahime.html#more/.

Chambers, Sir Edmund Kerchever. *The History and Motives of Literary Forgeries: Being the Chancellor's English Essay for 1891.* 1891. Reprint, New York: Burt Franklin, 1970.

Chapman, Tim. *Imperial Russia 1801–1905.* London: Routledge, 2001.

Charlesworth, James H. *Authentic Apocrypha: False and Genuine Christian Apocrypha.* The Dead Sea Scrolls & Christian Origins Library 2. North Richland Hills, TX: BIBAL, 1998.

———. "Introduction for the General Reader." In *The Old Testament Pseudepigrapha*, edited by James H. Charlesworth, 1:xxxiii–iv. 2 vols. Garden City, NY: Doubleday, 1983.

Charlier, Philippe. Review of *The Chemical Muse*, by David C. A. Hillman. *Bryn Mawr Classical Review* (posted 29 December 2008). http://bmcr.brynmawr. edu/2008/2008-12-29.html/.

Child, Francis James, ed. *The English and Scottish Popular Ballads*. 5 vols. New York: Houghton Mifflin, 1882.

Choat, Malcolm. "The Gospel of Jesus's Wife: A Preliminary Paleographical Assessment." *HTR* 107/2 (2014) 160–62.

———. "Lessons from the 'Gospel of Jesus' Wife' Affair." *Marks of Authenticity* (posted 19 June 2016). https://markersofauthenticity.wordpress.com/2016/06/19/lessons-from-the-gospel-of-jesus-wife-affair/.

Chryssides, George D. "Defining the New Age." In *Handbook of New Age*, edited by Daren Kemp and James R. Lewis, 5–24. Brill Handbooks on Contemporary Religion 1. Leiden: Brill, 2007.

Cicero. *The Speeches: pro Caelio; de Provinciis Consularibus; pro Balbo*. Translated by Robert Gardner. LCL 447. Cambridge: Harvard University Press, 1958.

"Claims of a Married Jesus Aren't LDS Church Doctrine." *Deseret News* (posted 17 May 2006). http://www.deseretnews.com/article/635208289/Claims-of-a-married-Jesus-arent-LDS-Church-doctrine.html?pg=all.

Clark, Gillian. *Women in Late Antiquity: Pagan and Christian Lifestyles*. New York: Oxford University Press, 1996.

Clauset, Aaron et al. "Systematic Inequality and Hierarchy in Faculty Hiring Networks." *Science Advances* 1/1 (2015) 1–6. http://advances.sciencemag.org/content/1/1/ e1400005.full/.

Clayton, Mary. *The Apocryphal Gospels of Mary in Anglo-Saxon England*. Cambridge Studies in Anglo-Saxon England 26. Cambridge: Cambridge University Press, 1998.

———. *The Cult of the Virgin Mary in Anglo-Saxon England*. Cambridge Studies in Anglo-Saxon England 2. Cambridge: Cambridge University Press, 1990.

———. "Homiliaries and Preaching in Anglo-Saxon England." In *Old English Prose: Basic Readings*, edited by Paul E. Szarmach, 151–98. Garland Reference Library of the Humanities 1447. Basic Readings in Anglo-Saxon England 5. New York: Garland, 2000.

———. "De Nativitate Mariae." In *Sources of Anglo-Saxon Literary Culture: The Apocrypha*, edited by Frederick M. Biggs, 25–26. Instrumenta Anglistica Mediaevalia 1. Kalamazoo: Medieval Institute Publications, 2006.

Clemens, Friedrich. *Das fünfte Evangelium, oder, Das Urevangelium der Essäer*. Crossen a. d. Oder: Wrose, 1879.

Clemens, Richard. *Jesus von Nazareth, oder, Das Evangelium und die evangelische Geschichte im Geiste und Bewusstsein der Gegenwart: zugleich zum ergänzenden Verständniss der beiden Schriften, "Wichtige historische Enthüllungen über die wirkliche Todesart Jesu" und "Historische Enthüllungen über die wirklichen Ereignisse der Geburt und Jugend Jesu" (Leipzig, 1849)*. Stuttgart: Scheible, 1850.

Clement of Alexandria. *The Excerpta ex Theodoto of Clement of Alexandria*. Translated by Robert Pierce Casey. London: Christophers, 1934.

————. *Exhortation to the Greeks, The Rich Man's Salvation, and the Fragment of an Address Entitled "To the Newly Baptized."* Translated by George William Butterworth. LCL 92. London: Heinemann, 1919.

————. *Paedagogus.* Translated by William Wilson. In *The Ante-Nicene Fathers,* vol. 2, edited by Alexander Roberts and James Donaldson, 209–98. 10 vols. 1885. Reprint, Peabody, MA: Hendrickson, 1994.

————. *Paedagogus.* Edited by Miroslav Marcovich. VCSup 61. Leiden: Brill, 2002.

————. *Stromateis.* Translated by William Wilson. In *The Ante-Nicene Fathers,* vol. 2, edited by Alexander Roberts and James Donaldson, 299–568. 10 vols. 1885. Reprint, Peabody, MA: Hendrickson, 1994.

Clough, William Overton, ed. *Gesta Pilati; or the Reports, Letters and Acts of Pontius Pilate.* Indianapolis: Robert Douglass, 1880.

Coleman, Christopher B. *The Treatise of Lorenzo Valla on the Donation of Constantine. Text and Translation into English.* New York: Russell & Russell, 1922.

Coleman-Norton, Paul R. "An Amusing *Agraphon.*" *CBQ* 12 (1950) 439–49.

Collins, John J. *The Apocalyptic Imagination: An Introduction to Jewish Apocalyptic Literature.* 2nd ed. Grand Rapids: Eerdmans, 1998.

Cooper, Kate. *The Virgin and the Bride: Idealized Womanhood in Late Antiquity.* Cambridge: Harvard University Press, 1996.

Cornford, Francis Macdonald. *Plato's Theory of Knowledge: The Theaetetus and the Sophist of Plato.* London: Routledge and Kegan Paul, 1935.

Cotterill, Joseph M. *Modern Criticism and Clement's Epistles to Virgins: (first printed, 1752) or their Greek version, newly discovered in Antiochus Palaestinensis; with appendix containing newly found versions of fragments attributed to Melito.* Edinburgh: T. & T. Clark, 1884.

————. *Peregrinus Proteus: An Investigation into Certain Relations Subsisting Between De Morte Peregrini, the Two Epistles of Clement to the Corinthians, the Epistle to Diognetus, the Bibliotheca of Photius, and Other Writings.* Edinburgh: T. & T. Clark, 1879.

Coyle, J. Kevin. "The Gospel of Thomas in Manichaeism?" In *Colloque international L'Évangile selon Thomas et les textes de Nag Hammadi, Québec, 29–31 mai 2003,* edited by Louis Painchaud and Paul-Hubert Poirier, 75–91. Québec: Les Presses de l'Université Laval / Leuven: Peeters, 2007.

Cranston, Sylvia L. *HPB: The Extraordinary Life and Influence of Helena Blavatsky, Founder of the Modern Theosophical Movement.* New York: Putnam, 1993.

Cross, James E., ed. *Cambridge Pembroke College MS. 25: A Carolingian Sermonary Used by Anglo-Saxon Preachers.* King's College London Medieval Studies 1. Exeter: King's College London, 1987.

————. "Portents and Events at Christ's Birth: Comments on Vercelli V & VI and the Old English Martyrology." *Anglo-Saxon England* 2 (1973) 209–20.

Curinier, C. E., ed. *Dictionnaire national des contemporains.* 6 vols. Paris: Office général d'édition, de librairie et d'imprimerie, 1899–1919.

Dahl, Nils A. Review of *Paul and Palestinian Judaism,* by E. P. Sanders. *RSR* 4 (1978) 153–58.

Daniélou, Jean. *A History of Early Christian Doctrine before the Council of Nicaea,* vol. 2, *Gospel Message and Hellenistic Culture.* Edited and translated by John Austin Baker. Philadelphia: Westminster, 1973.

Daniels, Jon. "The Egerton Gospel: Its Place in Early Christianity." PhD diss., Claremont Graduate School, 1989.

D'Anna, Alberto. "The New Testament and the Third Epistle to the Corinthians." In *Christian Apocrypha: Receptions of the New Testament in Ancient Christian Apocrypha*, edited by Jean-Michel Roessli and Tobias Nicklas, 133–48. Novum Testamentum Patristicum 26. Göttingen: Vandenhoek & Ruprecht, 2014.

Darman, Jonathan. "An Inconvenient Woman." *Newsweek*, 28 May 2006, 38. http://www.newsweek.com/inconvenient-woman-110341/.

Davies, Stevan L. *The Revolt of the Widows: The Social World of the Apocryphal Acts*. Carbondale: Southern Illinois University Press, 1980.

———. "Women, Tertullian, and the *Acts of Paul*." *Semeia* 38 (1986) 139–43.

Davila, James R. "Ritual in the Jewish Pseudepigrapha." In *Anthropology and Biblical Studies: Avenues of Approach*, edited by Louise J. Lawrence and Mario I. Aguilar, 158–83. Leiden: Deo, 2004.

Davis, Charles. "Priest Explains Why He Left Church." *Milwaukee Journal*, 7 January 1967, 4.

———. "Was Jesus Married?" *Observer*, 28 March 1971, U06.

De Bruyne, Donatien. "Un quatrième manuscrit latin de la correspondence apocryphe de Saint Paul avec les Corinthiens." *RBén* 45 (1933) 189–95.

Delisle, Léopold. "Cujas déchiffreur de papyrus." In *Mélanges offerts à M. Émile Chatelain*, edited by Émile Chatelain, 486–91. Paris: Librarie ancienne H. Champion, 1910.

Den Dulk, Matthijs. "I Permit No Woman to Teach Except for Thecla: The Curious Case of the Pastoral Epistles and the Acts of Paul Reconsidered." *NovT* 54 (2012) 176–203.

Depuydt, Leo. "The Alleged Gospel of Jesus's Wife: Assessment and Evaluation of Authenticity." *HTR* 107 (2014) 172–89.

———. "The Papyrus Fragment and the Crocodile: When Discerning a Blunder Is Itself a. . ." *NT Blog* (posted 16 April 2014). Pages 1–4. http://markgoodacre.org/Depuydt.pdf/.

Deshman, Robert. "Servants of the Mother of God in Byzantine and Medieval Art." *Word & Image* 5 (1989) 36–42.

———. *The Benedictional of Æthelwold*. Studies in Manuscript Illumination 9. Princeton: Princeton University Press, 1995.

Desjardins, Michel "Apocalypse of Peter: Introduction to VII,3." In *Nag Hammadi Codex VII*, edited by Birger A. Pearson, 201–16. NHMS 30. Leiden: Brill, 1996.

Dewey, Caitlin. "The Only Guide to Gamergate You Will Ever Need to Read." *Washington Post* (posted 14 October 2014). https://www.washingtonpost.com/news/the-intersect/wp/2014/10/14/the-only-guide-to-gamergate-you-will-ever-need-to-read/.

Dibelius, Martin. *A Fresh Approach to the New Testament and Early Christian Literature*. International Library of Christian Knowledge. London: Nicholson & Watson, 1936.

Dodwell, C. Reginald. *Anglo-Saxon Gestures and the Roman Stage*. Cambridge Studies in Anglo-Saxon England 28. Cambridge: Cambridge University Press, 2000.

Donaldson, James. *A Critical History of Christian Literature and Doctrine from the Death of the Apostles to the Nicene Council*. 2 vols. London: Macmillan, 1864–1866.

Donelson, Lewis R. *Pseudepigraphy and Ethical Argument in the Pastoral Epistles*. HUT 22. Tübingen: Mohr/Siebeck, 1986.

Douglas, J. Archibald. "The Chief Lama of Hemis on the Alleged Unknown Life of Christ." *Nineteenth Century* 39 (1896) 667–78.

―――. "Documents Prove Notovitch Swindle!" *Orientalische Bibliographie* 10 (1896) 111.

Downs, David J. "Justification, Good Works, and Creation in Clement of Rome's Appropriation of Romans 5–6." *NTS* 59 (2013) 415–32.

Duggan, Maeve. "Online Harassment." *Pew Research Center's Internet & American Life Project* (posted 22 October 2014). Pages 1–8. http://www.pewinternet.org/2014/10/22/online-harassment/.

Dunn, Geoffrey D. *Tertullian*. The Early Church Fathers. London: Routledge, 2004.

Dunn, Peter W. "*The Acts of Paul* and the Pauline Legacy in the Second Century." PhD diss., Cambridge University, 1996.

Dweck, Yaacob. *The Scandal of Kabbalah: Leon Modena, Jewish Mysticism, Early Modern Venice*. Princeton: Princeton University Press, 2011.

Eastman, David L., ed. and trans. *The Ancient Martyrdom Accounts of Peter and Paul*. WGRW 39. Atlanta: SBL, 2015.

Ehrman, Bart D. *Forged: Writing in the Name of God; Why the Bible's Authors Are Not Who We Think They Are*. New York: HarperOne, 2011.

―――. *Forgery and Counterforgery: The Use of Literary Deceit in Early Christian Polemics*. New York: Oxford University Press, 2013.

―――, ed. and trans. "The Martyrdom of Polycarp." In *The Apostolic Fathers*, vol. 1 edited by Bart D. Ehrman, 355–401. 2 vols. LCL 24. Cambridge: Harvard University Press, 2003.

―――. *The Orthodox Corruption of Scripture: The Effect of Early Christological Controversies on the Text of the New Testament*. New York: Oxford University Press, 1993.

―――. *Truth and Fiction in "The Da Vinci Code": A Historian Reveals What We Really Know about Jesus, Mary Magdalene, and Constantine*. Oxford: Oxford University Press, 2004.

Ehrman, Bart D., and Mark A. Plunkett. "The Angel and the Agony: The Textual Problem of Luke 22:43–44." *CBQ* 45 (1983) 401–16.

Ehrman, Bart D., and Zlatko Pleše, eds. and trans. *The Apocryphal Gospels: Texts and Translations*. Oxford: Oxford University Press, 2011.

Elliott, J. Keith, ed. and trans. *The Apocryphal New Testament*. Rev. ed. Oxford: Oxford University Press, 1999.

―――. *Codex Sinaiticus and the Simonides Affair: An Examination of the Nineteenth-Century Claim that Codex Sinaiticus Was Not an Ancient Manuscript*. Thessaloniki: Patriarchikon Idryma Paterikōn Meletōn, 1982.

Ellis-Petersen, Hannah. "Mary Beard Reveals She Befriended Twitter Trolls Following Online Abuse." *Guardian* (posted 27 August 2014). http://www.theguardian.com/books/2014/aug/27/mary-beard-befriends-twitter-trolls-online-abuse/.

Emmel, Stephen. "The Codicology of the New Coptic (Lycopolitan) Gospel of John Fragment (and Its Relevance for Assessing the Genuineness of the Recently Published Coptic 'Gospel of Jesus' Wife' Fragment) [2014]." *Alin Suciu* (posted 22 June 2014). http://alinsuciu.com/2014/06/22/guest-post-stephen-emmel-the-codicology-of-the-new-coptic-lycopolitan-gospel-of-john-fragment-and-its-relevance-for-assessing-the-genuineness-of-the-recently-published-coptic-go-2/.

Epp, Eldon Jay. "The Multivalence of the Term 'Original Text' in New Testament Textual Criticism." *HTR* 92 (1999) 245–81.

Erskine, John. *The Human Life of Jesus*. New York: Morrow, 1945.

Evans, Craig A. *Fabricating Jesus: How Modern Scholars Distort the Gospels*. Downers Grove, IL: InterVarsity, 2006.

———. "Morton Smith and the *Secret Gospel of Mark*: Exploring the Grounds for Doubt." In *Ancient Gospel or Modern Forgery? The Secret Gospel of Mark in Debate*, edited by Tony Burke, 75–134. Eugene, OR: Cascade Books, 2013.

Faber-Kaiser, Andreas. *Jesus Died in Kashmir: Jesus, Moses and the Ten Lost Tribes of Israel*. London: Gordon & Cremonesi, 1977.

Fader, H. Louis. *The Issa Tale That Will not Die: Nicolas Notovitch and His Fraudulent Gospel*. Lanham, MD: University Press of America, 2003.

Farrell, Anne Mary. "Plato's Use of Eleusinian Mystery Motifs." PhD diss., University of Texas at Austin, 1999.

Farrer, James A. *Literary Forgeries*. London: Longmans, Green, 1907.

Farrior, Mary-Evelyn. "Divorcing Mrs. Jesus." *The College Hill Independent* (posted 5 October 2012). http://www.theindy.org/a/131/.

Ferguson, Everett. "Canon Muratori: Date and Provenance." *StPatr* 17 (1982) 677–83.

Fewster, Gregory P. "'Can I Have Your Autograph?' On Thinking about Pauline Authorship and Pseudepigraphy." *BSOR* 43/3 (2014) 30–39.

Finkelberg, Margalit. "Plato's Language of Love and the Female." *HTR* 90 (1997) 231–61.

Finocchiaro, Maurice A. *The Routledge Guidebook to Galileo's Dialogue*. New York: Routledge–Taylor & Francis, 2013.

Flake, Kathleen. *The Politics of American Religious Identity: The Seating of Senator Reed Smoot, Mormon Apostle*. Chapel Hill: University of North Carolina Press, 2004.

Flint, Valerie I. J. *The Rise of Magic in Early Medieval Europe*. Princeton, NJ: Princeton University Press, 1991.

Folk, Edgar Estes. *The Mormon Monster: or, The Story of Mormonism with a Full Discussion of the Subject of Polygamy*. Chicago: Revell, 1900.

Foster, Paul. "The *Epistle to Diognetus*." In *The Writings of the Apostolic Fathers*, edited by Paul Foster, 147–56. London: T. & T. Clark, 2007.

———. "The Epistles of Ignatius of Antioch and the Writings that Later Formed the New Testament." In *The New Testament and the Apostolic Fathers*, vol. 1, *Reception of the New Testament in the Apostolic Fathers*, edited by Andrew F. Gregory and Christopher M. Tuckett, 159–86. 2 vols. Oxford: Oxford University Press, 2005.

———, ed. and trans. *The Gospel of Peter: Introduction, Critical Edition and Commentary*. TENTS 4. Leiden: Brill, 2010.

Franzmann, Majella. *Jesus in the Manichaean Writings*. London: T. & T. Clark, 2003.

Freemaan, Hadley. "'How To Tame Your Troll' Only Really Works If You're Mary Beard." *Guardian* (posted 29 August 2014). http://www.theguardian.com/commentisfree/2014/aug/29/tame-troll-mary-beard-online-abuse/.

Fulton, Rachel. *From Judgment to Passion: Devotion to Christ and the Virgin Mary, 800–1200*. New York: Columbia University Press, 2002.

Funk, Robert et al., eds. *The Five Gospels: What Did Jesus Really Say?* San Francisco: HarperOne, 1996.

Funk, Wolf-Peter. "Einer aus Tausend, zwei aus Zehntausend: Zitate aus dem Thomasevangelium in den koptischen Manichaica." In *For the Children, Perfect Instruction:*

Studies in Honor of Hans-Martin Schenke, edited by Hans-Gebhard Bethge, et al., 67–94. NHMS 54. Leiden: Brill, 2002.

———. "The Linguistic Aspect of Classifying the Nag Hammadi Codices." In *Les Textes de Nag Hammadi et le problème de leur classification: Actes du colloque tenu à Québec du 15 au 19 septembre 1993*, edited by Louise Painchaud and Anne Pasquier, 107–47. Bibliothèque copte de Nag Hammadi. Section "Etudes" 3. Leuven: Peeters, 1995.

———. "Prolégomènes à une grammaire du copte manichéen." *EPHE Livret-Annuaire* 15 (1999–2000) 10–11.

———. "Research on Manichaeism in Egypt: 1988–1996." In *Ägypten und Nubien in spätantiker und christlicher Zeit: Akten des 6. Internationalen Koptologenkongresses (Münster, 20.–26. Juli 1996)*, edited by Stephen Emmel et al., 453–64. Sprachen und Kulturen des Christlichen Orients 6. Wiesbaden: Reichert, 1999.

Furst, Jeffrey. *Edgar Cayce's Story of Jesus.* New York: Coward-McCann, 1969.

Gambero, Luigi. *Mary in the Middle Ages: The Blessed Virgin Mary in the Thought of Medieval Latin Theologians.* San Francisco: Ignatius, 2005.

Gardner, Iain, and Klaas Worp. "Leaves from a Manichaean Codex." *ZPE* 117 (1997) 148–51.

Gardner, Iain, and Samuel N. C. Lieu. "From Narmouthis (Medinet Madi) to Kellis (Ismant El-Kharab): Manichaean Documents from Roman Egypt." *JRS* 86 (1996) 146–69.

———. eds. *Manichaean Texts from the Roman Empire.* Cambridge: Cambridge University Press, 2004.

Gathercole, Simon. *The Gospel of Thomas: Introduction and Commentary.* TENTS 11. Leiden: Brill, 2014.

Gero, Stephen. "The Infancy Gospel of Thomas: A Study of the Textual and literary Problems." *NovT* 13 (1971) 46–80.

Gibson, Elizabeth Leigh. *Manumission Inscriptions of the Bosporus Kingdom.* TSAJ 75. Tübingen: Mohr/Siebeck, 1999.

Gieschen, Charles A. "Baptismal Praxis and Mystical Experience in the Book of Revelation." In *Paradise Now: Essays on Early Jewish and Christian Mysticism*, edited by April D. DeConick, 341–54. SBLSymS 11. Atlanta: SBL, 2006.

Gijsel, Jan, ed. *Libri de Nativitate Mariae: Pseudo-Matthaei Evangelium, Textus et Commentarius.* CCSA 9. Turnhout: Brepols, 1997.

Ginsparg, Paul. "It Was Twenty Years Ago Today . . ." *arXiv.org* (revised 13 September 2011). http://arxiv.org/abs/1108.2700/.

Glancy, Jennifer A. "The Mistress-Slave Dialectic: Paradoxes of Slavery in Three LXX Narratives." *JSOT* 72 (1996) 71–87.

Gneuss, Helmut, and Michael Lapidge. *Anglo-Saxon Manuscripts: A Bibliographical Handlist of Manuscripts and Manuscript Fragments Written or Owned in England up to 1100.* Toronto Anglo-Saxon Series 15. Toronto: University of Toronto Press, 2014.

Goodacre, Mark. "The Da Vinci Code and the Talpiot Tomb." *NT Blog* (posted 9 March 2012). http://ntweblog.blogspot.com/2012/03/da-vinci-code-and-talpiot-tomb.html/.

———. "The Gospel of Jesus' Wife." *NT Blog* (posted 19 September 2012). http://ntweblog.blogspot.com/2012/09/the-gospel-of-jesus-wife.html/.

————. "Gospel of Jesus' Wife: Last Chapter Round-Up." *NT Blog* (posted 20 June 2016). http://ntweblog.blogspot.ca/2016/06/gospel-of-jesus-wife-last-chapter-round. html/.

————. "The Jesus Discovery? The Sceptic's Perspective." *Bible and Interpretation* (posted April 2013). http://www.bibleinterp.com/articles/2013/goo378026.shtml/.

————. "Revised Versions of Francis Watson's Articles on the Jesus Wife Fragment." *NT Blog* (posted 27 September 2012). http://www.ntweblog.blogspot.de/2012/09/ revised-versions-of-francis-watsons.html/.

Goodenough, Erwin R. *By Light, Light: The Mystic Gospel of Hellenistic Judaism*. 1935. Reprinted, Amsterdam: Philo, 1969.

Goodspeed, Edgar J. *Modern Apocrypha and Famous "Biblical" Hoaxes*. Grand Rapids: Baker, 1956.

————. *New Chapters in New Testament Study*. New York: Macmillan, 1937.

————. *Strange New Gospels*. Chicago: Chicago University Press, 1931. (This was expanded as *Modern Apocrypha*, above.)

Goodstein, Laurie. "Fresh Doubts Raised about Papyrus Scrap Known as 'Gospel of Jesus' Wife.'" *New York Times*, 4 May 2014, A17. http://www.nytimes.com/ 2014/05/05/us/fresh-doubts-raised-about-papyrus-scrap-known-as-gospel-of-jesuss-wife.html/.

————. "Historian Says Piece of Papyrus Refers to Jesus' Wife." *New York Times*, 18 September 2012, A1. http://www.nytimes.com/2012/09/19/us/historian-says-piece-of-papyrus-refers-to-jesus-wife.html/.

————. "Papyrus Referring to Jesus' Wife Is More Likely Ancient Than Fake, Scientists Say." *New York Times*, 10 April 2014, A12. http://www.nytimes.com/2014/04/10/ science/scrap-of-papyrus-referring-to-jesus-wife-is-likely-to-be-ancient-scientists-say.html/.

Grafton, Anthony. *Forgers and Critics: Creativity and Duplicity in Western Scholarship*. Princeton: Princeton University Press, 1990.

Gregory, Andrew F. "*1 Clement*: An Introduction." *ExpTim* 117 (2006) 227–28.

————. "*1 Clement* and the Writings That Later Formed the New Testament." In *The New Testament and the Apostolic Fathers*, vol. 1, *The Reception of the New Testament in the Apostolic Fathers*, edited by Andrew F. Gregory and Christopher M. Tuckett, 129–57. 2 vols. Oxford: Oxford University Press, 2005.

Gregory, Andrew F., and Christopher Tuckett. "Series Preface." In *Gospel Fragments*, by Thomas J. Kraus, et al., v–xi. Oxford Early Christian Gospel Texts. Oxford: Oxford University Press, 2009.

Grenfell, Bernard P. and Arthur S. Hunt, eds. and trans. *New Sayings of Jesus and Fragment of a Lost Gospel from Oxyrhynchus*. London: Frowde, 1904.

————. *The Oxyrhynchus Papyri*. vols. 1 and 4. London: Egypt Exploration Fund, 1893 and 1904.

Grönbold, Günter. *Jesus in Indien: Das Ende einer Legende*. Munich: Kösel, 1985.

Grondin, Michael W. "The Jesus' Wife Fragment 2014." *Gospel of Thomas Resource Center* (posted 23 April 2014). http://gospel-thomas.net/x_gjw2.html/.

————. "The Jesus' Wife Fragment 2015." *Gospel of Thomas Resource Center* (posted 30 June 2015). http://gospel-thomas.net/x_gjw3.html/.

————. "The Jesus' Wife Fragment 2016: The End of a Hoax." *Gospel of Thomas Resource Center* (posted 7 July 2016). http://www.gospel-thomas.net/x_gjw4.htm.

————. "A Question of Content: How I Saw the Internet Furor over the Jesus' Wife Fragment." *Gospel of Thomas Resource Center* (posted 10 October 2012). http://gospel-thomas.net/x_gjw.htm/.

Guerra-Doce, Elisa. "Psychoactive Substances in Prehistoric Times: Examining the Archaeological Evidence." *Time and Mind* 8 (2015) 91–112.

Gulácsi, Zsuzsanna. "The Crystal Seal of 'Mani, the Apostle of Jesus Christ' in the Bibliothèque Nationale de France." In *Manichaean Texts in Syriac: First Editions, New Editions and Studies*, edited by Nils A. Pedersen and John M. Larsen, 245–67. Corpus Fontium Manichaeorum. Series Turcica 1. Turnhout: Brepols, 2013.

Guthrie, Kenneth Sylvan. *The Long-Lost Second Book of Acts, Setting Forth the Blessed Mary's Teachings about Reincarnation*. Medford, MA: Prophet Publishing House, 1904.

Hagen, Joost L. "Ein anderer Kontext für die Berliner und Straßburger 'Evangelien-fragmente.' Das 'Evangelium des Erlösers' und andere 'Apostelevangelien' in der koptischen Literatur." In *Jesus in apokryphen Evangelienüberlieferungen. Beiträge zu außerkanonischen Jesusüberlieferungen aus verschiedenen Sprach- und Kulturtraditionen*, edited by Jörg Frey and Jens Schröter, 339–71. WUNT 254. Tübingen: Mohr/Siebeck, 2010.

Hagner, Donald A. *The Use of the Old and New Testament in Clement of Rome*. NovTSup 34. Leiden: Brill, 1973.

Hahneman, Geoffrey Mark. *The Muratorian Fragment and the Development of the Canon*. Oxford Theological Monographs. Oxford: Clarendon, 1992.

Haines-Eitzen, Kim. *Guardians of Letters: Literacy, Power, and the Transmitters of Early Christian Literature*. Oxford: Oxford University Press, 2000.

Hall, Thomas N. "Gospel of Pseudo-Matthew." In *Sources of Anglo-Saxon Literary Culture: The Apocrypha*, edited by Frederick M. Biggs, 23–25. Instrumenta Anglistica Mediaevalia 1. Kalamazoo, MI: Medieval Institute Publications, 2006.

————. "The Portents at Christ's Birth in Vercelli Homilies V and VI: Some Analogues from Medieval Sermons and Biblical Commentaries." In *New Readings in the Vercelli Book*, edited by Samantha Zacher and Andy Orchard, 62–97. Toronto Anglo-Saxon Series 4. Toronto: University of Toronto Press, 2009.

————. "Protevangelium of James." In *Sources of Anglo-Saxon Literary Culture: The Apocrypha*, edited by Frederick M. Biggs, 21–23. Instrumenta Anglistica Mediae-valia 1. Kalamazoo, MI: Medieval Institute Publications, 2006.

Halton, Charles. "Reflections on the 'Gospel of Jesus's Wife' Saga." *Charles Halton* (posted 26 September 2012). http://charleshalton.com/?p=2211/.

Hammer, Olav. *Claiming Knowledge: Strategies of Epistemology from Theosophy to the New Age*. SHR 90. Leiden: Brill, 2004.

Hanegraaff, Wouter J. *New Age Religion and Western Culture: Esotericism in the Mirror of Secular Thought*. SHR 72. Leiden: Brill, 1996.

Hardy, Rodger L. "Book Takes on 'Da Vinci' from an LDS Perspective." *Deseret News*, 15 June 2006, 1.

Harmless, William. *Desert Christians: An Introduction to the Literature of Early Monasticism*. Oxford: Oxford University Press, 2004.

Harnack, Adolf von. *Die Pfaff'schen Irenäus-Fragmente als fälschungen Pfaffs*. TU n.s. 5.3. Leipzig: Hinrichs, 1900.

Harrill, J. Albert. "The Domestic Enemy: A Moral Polarity of Household Slaves in Early Christian Apologies and Martyrdom." In *Early Christian Families in Context: An*

Interdisciplinary Dialogue, edited by David L. Balch and Carolyn Osiek, 231–54. Grand Rapids: Eerdmans, 2003.

Hartenstein, Judith. *Die Zweite Lehre: Erscheinungen des Auferstandenen als Rahmen-zählungen frühchristlicher Dialoge*. TU 146. Berlin: Akademie, 2000.

Hartog, Paul. *Polycarp and the New Testament: The Occasion, Rhetoric, Theme, and Unity of the* Epistle to the Philippians *and Its Allusions to New Testament Literature*. WUNT 2/134 Tübingen: Mohr/Siebeck, 2002.

Hassnain, Fida M. *A Search for the Historical Jesus*. Bath, UK: Gateway, 1994.

Hassnain, Fida and Dahan Levi. *The Fifth Gospel: New Evidence from the Tibetan, Sanskrit, Arabic, Persian and Urdu Sources about the Historical Life of Jesus Christ*. Revised and edited by Ahtisham Fida. Nevada City, CA: Blue Dolphin, 2006.

Havelaar, Henriette, trans. "Die Apokalypse des Petrus." In *Nag Hammadi Deutsch. 2. Band: NHC V,2–XIII,1, BG 1 und 4*, edited by Hans-Martin Schenke, et al., 591–600. GCS N.F. 12. Berlin: de Gruyter, 2003.

———, ed. and trans. *The Coptic Apocalypse of Peter (Nag Hammadi-Codex VII,3)*. TUGAL 144. Berlin: Akademie, 1999.

Haws, Charles G. "Women Earning Doctorates in the Field of Religion/Religious Studies." *Charles G. Haws* (posted 9 October 2014). https://public.tableau.com/s/profile/cghaws#!/vizhome/degrees1987–2013/Story1/.

Haws, John B. *The Mormon Image in the American Mind: Fifty Years of Public Perception*. Oxford: Oxford University Press, 2013.

Hedrick, Charles W. "*Secret Mark*: Moving on from Stalemate." In *Ancient Gospel or Modern Forgery? The Secret Gospel of Mark in Debate*, edited by Tony Burke, 30–66. Eugene, OR: Cascade Books, 2013.

Hilhorst, Anthony. "The Mountain of Transfiguration in the New Testament and in Later Tradition." In *The Land of Israel in Bible, History, and Theology: Studies in Honour of Ed Noort*, 317–38. Vetus Testamentum Supplements 124. Leiden: Brill, 2009.

———. "Tertullian on the Acts of Paul." In *The Apocryphal Acts of Paul and Thecla*, edited by Jan N. Bremmer, 150–63. Studies on the Apocryphal Acts of the Apostles 2. Kampen: Kok Pharos, 1996.

Hill, Joyce. "Ælfric and Haymo Revisited." In *Intertexts: Studies in Anglo-Saxon Culture Presented to Paul E. Szarmach*, edited by Virginia Blanton and Helene Scheck, 331–47. MRTS 334. Tempe: Arizona Center for Medieval and Renaissance Studies, 2008.

Hill, Thomas D. "The Baby on the Stone: Nativity as Sacrifice (The Old English *Christ III*, 1414–1425)." In *Intertexts: Studies in Anglo-Saxon Culture Presented to Paul E. Szarmach*, edited by Virginia Blanton and Helene Scheck, 69–77. MRTS 334. Tempe: Arizona Center for Medieval and Renaissance Studies, 2008.

Hillman, David C. A. *The Chemical Muse: Drug Use and the Roots of Western Civilization*. New York: St. Martin's, 2008.

Hodges, Horace J. Review of Dan Merkur, *The Mystery of Manna*. *Review of Biblical Literature* 4 (2002) 170–73.

Hodgins, Gregory. "Accelerated Mass Spectrometry Radiocarbon Determination of Papyrus Samples." *HTR* 107 (2014) 166–69.

Hoekema, Anthony A. *The Four Major Cults*. Grand Rapids: Eerdmans, 1963.

Hoffman, Eva R. "Pathways of Portability: Islamic and Christian Interchange from the Tenth to the Twelfth Century." *Art History* 24 (2001) 17–50.

Holmes, Michael W. "Polycarp and Paul." In *Paul and the Second Century*, edited by Michael F. Bird and Joseph R. Dodson, 57–69. LNTS 412. London: T. & T. Clark, 2011.

———. "Polycarp's *Letter to the Philippians* and the Writings that Later Formed the New Testament." In *The New Testament and the Apostolic Fathers*, vol. 1, *The Reception of the New Testament in the Apostolic Fathers*, edited by Andrew F. Gregory and Christopher M. Tuckett, 187–227. 2 vols. Oxford: Oxford University Press, 2005.

The Holy Bible: Douay Version Translated from the Latin Vulgate. London: Catholic Truth Society, 1956.

Holzapfel, Richard N. et al. *What Da Vinci Didn't Know: An LDS Perspective*. Salt Lake City: Deseret, 2006.

Horst, Pieter W. van der. "Silent Prayer in Antiquity." *Numen* 41 (1994) 1–25.

Hovhanessian, Vahan. *Third Corinthians: Reclaiming Paul for Christian Orthodoxy*. StBibLit 18. New York: Lang, 2000.

Huffman, Carl. "Philolaus." *Stanford Encyclopedia of Philosophy* (Summer 2012 edition). Edited by Edward N. Zalta. http://plato.stanford.edu/archives/sum2012/entries/philolaus/.

Hurtado, Larry W. *Earliest Christian Artifacts: Manuscripts and Christian Origins*. Grand Rapids: Eerdmans, 2006.

———. "A Master Hoaxer: Constantine Simonides." *Larry Hurtado's Blog* (posted 29 April 2014). https://larryhurtado.wordpress.com/2014/04/29/a-master-hoaxer-constantine-simonides/.

Hyde, Orson. "Lecture, Tabernacle, Oct. 6 1854, 6 p.m." *Deseret News*, 19 October 1854, 1.

Itter, Andrew C. *Esoteric Teaching in the* Stromateis *of Clement of Alexandria*. VCSup 97. Leiden: Brill, 2009.

Jackson, Howard M. "Why the Youth Shed His Cloak and Fled Naked: The Meaning and Purpose of Mark 14:51–52." *JBL* 116 (1997) 273–89.

Jacobovici, Simcha. "Underwear Blogger." *Simcha Jacobovici Television* (posted 28 August 2013). http://www.simchajtv.com/underwear-blogger/.

Jacobovici, Simcha, and Charles Pellegrino. *The Jesus Family Tomb: The Evidence behind the Discovery No One Wanted to Find*. San Francisco: HarperSanFrancisco, 2007.

Jacobovici, Simcha, and James Tabor. *The Jesus Discovery: The New Archaeological Find That Reveals the Birth of Christianity*. New York: Simon & Schuster, 2012.

Jacobovici, Simcha, and Barrie A. Wilson. *The Lost Gospel: Decoding the Ancient Text That Reveals Jesus' Marriage to Mary the Magdalene*. New York: Pegasus, 2014.

Jacobs, Alan. *When Jesus Lived in India: The Quest for the Aquarian Gospel; The Mystery of the Missing Years*. London: Watkins, 2010.

Jacobs, Andrew S. "'Her Own Proper Kinship': Marriage, Class and Women in the Apocryphal Acts of the Apostles." In *A Feminist Companion to the New Testament Apocryphal*, edited by Amy-Jill Levine with Maria Mayo Robbins, 18–46. FCNTECW 11. Cleveland: Pilgrim, 2006.

Jacolliot, Louis. *La Bible dans l'Inde: Vie de Iezeus Christna*. Paris: Librairie Internationale, 1869.

James, Montague Rhodes, ed. and trans. *The Apocryphal New Testament: Being the Apocryphal Gospels, Acts, Epistles, and Apocalypses, with Other Narratives and Fragments Newly Translated*. Oxford: Clarendon, 1924. Corr. ed., 1953.

————. "A Mare's Nest from Missouri." *Guardian Church Newspaper*, 14 March 1900, 403–404.

Jarus, Owen. "Gospel of Jesus's Wife Likely a Fake, Bizarre Backstory Suggests." *Live Science* (posted 17 June 2016). http://www.livescience.com/55110-gospel-of-jesus-wife-a-fake.html/.

————. "Origins of 'Gospel of Jesus's Wife' Begin to Emerge." *Live Science* (posted 24 August 2015). http://www.livescience.com/51954-gospel-of-jesus-wife-origins.html/.

Jeffery, Peter. *The Secret Gospel of Mark Unveiled: Imagined Rituals of Sex, Death, and Madness in a Biblical Forgery*. New Haven: Yale University Press, 2007.

Jenkins, Philip. *Hidden Gospels: How the Search for Jesus Lost Its Way*. Oxford: Oxford University Press, 2001.

————. *The Many Faces of Christ: The Thousand-Year Story of the Survival and Influence of the Lost Gospels*. New York: Basic Books, 2015.

Jerome, Saint. *Lives of Illustrious Men*. Translated by Ernest Cushing Richardson. In *A Select Library of Nicene and Post-Nicene Fathers of the Christian Church*. Translated into English with Prolegomena and Explanatory Notes. 2nd ser. Vol. 3, *Theodoret, Jerome, Gennadius, and Rufinus: Historical Writings*, edited by Philip Schaff and Henry Wace, 524–613. 14 vols. New York: Christian Literature Company, 1892.

————. *Gli uomini illustri. De viris illustribus*. Edited by Aldo Ceresa-Gastaldo. Biblioteca patristica 12. Florence: Nardini, 1988.

Jewett, Robert. *A Chronology of Paul's Life*. Philadelphia: Fortress, 1979.

Jones, Brice C. "The Bodmer 'Miscellaneous' Codex and the Crosby-Schøyen Codex Ms 193: A New Proposal." *JGRChJ* 8 (2011) 9–20.

————. *New Testament Texts on Greek Amulets from Late Antiquity*. LNTS 554. London: Bloomsbury, 2016.

Jones, Christopher. "The Jesus' Wife Papyrus in the History of Forgery." *NTS* 61 (2015) 368–78.

Jones, Jeremiah. *A New and Full Method of Settling the Canonical Authority of the New Testament*. 2 vols. London: Printed for J. Clark and R. Hett at the Bible and Crown in the Poultrey near Cheapside, 1726.

Joseph, Simon J. "Jesus in India? Transgressing Social and Religious Boundaries." *JAAR* 80 (2012) 161–99.

Joshel, Sandra R. *Slavery in the Roman World*. Cambridge Introduction to Roman Civilization. Cambridge: Cambridge University Press, 2010.

Joyce, Donovan. *The Jesus Scroll*. New York: Dial, 1973.

Jump, Paul. "Watson and Crick Rejected?" *Inside Higher Ed* (posted 6 August 2015). https://www.insidehighered.com/news/2015/08/06/journal-article-speculates-crick-and-watson-would-have-difficulty-today-publishing/.

Junod, Éric. "Apocryphes du Nouveau Testament ou apocryphes chrétiens anciens? Remarques sur la désignation d'un corpus et indications bibliographiques sur instruments de travail récents." *ETR* 59 (1983) 409–21.

Kaestli, Jean-Daniel. "Mapping an Unexplored Second Century Apocryphal Gospel: The Liber de Nativitate Salvatoris (CANT 53)." In *Infancy Gospels: Stories and Identities*, edited by Claire Clivaz et al., 506–33. WUNT 281. Tübingen: Mohr/Siebeck, 2011.

Kaler, Michael. "The Letter of Peter to Philip and Its Message of Gnostic Revelation and Christian Unity." *VC* 63 (2009) 264–95.

————. "Towards an Expanded Understanding of Nag Hammadi Paulinism." *SR* 33 (2004) 301–17.

Karkov, Catherine E. *The Art of Anglo-Saxon England*. Woodbridge, UK: Boydell, 2011.

————. *Text and Picture in Anglo-Saxon England: Narrative Strategies in the Junius 11 Manuscript*. Cambridge Studies in Anglo-Saxon England 31. Cambridge: Cambridge University Press, 2001.

Kashmiri, Aziz. *Christ in Kashmir*. Srinagar, India: Roshni, 1973.

Kasser, Rodolphe and Gregor Wurst, eds. *The Gospel of Judas: Together with the Letter of Peter to Philip, James, and a Book of Allogenes from Codex Tchacos*. Critical ed. Washington DC: National Geographic Society, 2007.

Kaye, John. *Some Account of the Writings and Opinions of Clement of Alexandria*. London: Gilbert & Rivington, 1835.

Kazantzakis, Nikos. *The Last Temptation of Christ*. Translated by Peter A. Bien. New York: Simon & Schuster, 1960.

Keener, Craig S. *Acts: An Exegetical Commentary*, vol. 1, *Introduction and 1:1—2:47*. 4 vols. Grand Rapids: Baker Academic, 2012.

Keith, Chris. "'In My Own Hand': Grapho-Literacy and the Apostle Paul." *Biblica* 89 (2008) 39–58.

————. *Jesus' Literacy: Scribal Culture and the Teacher from Galilee*. LNTS 413. London: T. & T. Clark, 2011.

Ker, Neil R. *Catalogue of Manuscripts Containing Anglo-Saxon*. Oxford: Clarendon, 1957.

Kersten, Holger. *Jesus Lived in India*. Shaftesbury, UK: Element, 1986. Translated from *Jesus Lebte in Indien*. Munich: Droemer Knaur, 1983.

Kersten, Holger, and Elmar R. Gruber. *The Jesus Conspiracy: The Turin Shroud and the Truth about the Resurrection*. Shaftesbury, UK: Element, 1994.

Kim, David W. "Reconsidering the Gospel of Jesus' Wife: An Imperfect Forgery or Another Polemical Gnostic Fragment." *RelStTh* 34/1 (2015) 19–40.

King, Karen L. *The Gospel of Mary of Magdala: Jesus and the First Woman Apostle*. Santa Rosa, CA: Polebridge, 2003.

————. "'Jesus said to them, "My wife. . ."': A New Coptic Gospel Papyrus." (Pre-Publication Draft). Pages 1–52. Originally posted 20 September 2012. http://www.gospel-thomas.net/King_JesusSaidToThem_draft_0917.pdf/.

————. "'Jesus said to them, "My wife . . ."': A New Coptic Papyrus Fragment." *HTR* 107 (2014) 131–59.

————. "Martyrdom and Its Discontents in the Tchacos Codex." In *Codex Judas Papers: Proceedings of the International Congress on the Tchacos Codex Held at Rice University, Houston, Texas, March 13–16, 2008*, edited by April D. De Conick, 23–42. NHMS 71. Leiden: Brill, 2009.

————. "The Place of the *Gospel of Philip* in the Context of Early Christian Claims about Jesus' Marital Status." *NTS* 59 (2013) 565–87.

————. "Response to Leo Depuydt, 'The Alleged Gospel of Jesus's Wife: Assessment and Evaluation of Authenticity.'" *HTR* 107 (2014) 190–93.

Kitchin, Rob. "Big Data, New Epistemologies and Paradigm Shifts." *Big Data and Society*. April-June 2014. Pages 1–12. http://journals.sagepub.com/doi/full/10.1177/2053951714528481.

Kivistö, Sari. "Crime and Its Punishment: Alfonso Ceccarelli's False Chronicles." In *Past and Present in Medieval Chronicles*, edited by Mari Isaho, 148–75. Collegium:

Studies across Disciplines in the Humanities and Social Sciences 17. Helsinki: Collegium for Advanced Studies, 2015.

Klatt, Norbert. *Jesus in Indien: Nikolaus Alexandrovitch Notovitchs "Unbekanntes Leben Jesu," sein Leben und seine Indienreise.* Orientierungen und Berichte 13. Stuttgart: Evangelische Zentralstelle für Weltanschauungsfragen, 1986. 2nd ed. Göttingen: Klatt, 2011. http://www.klatt-verlag.de/wp-content/uploads/2014/06/notovitch.pdf/.

———. *Lebte Jesus in Indien?: Eine religionsgeschichtliche Klärung.* Göttingen: Wallstein, 1988.

Kleist, Aaron J., ed. *The Old English Homily: Precedent, Practice, and Appropriation.* Turnhout: Brepols, 2007.

Klijn, Albertus F. J. "The Apocryphal Correspondence between Paul and the Corinthians." *VC* 17 (1963) 2–23.

Kloppenborg, John S. "Literate Media in Early Christ Groups: The Creation of a Christian Book Culture." *JECS* 22 (2014) 21–59.

Koester, Helmut. *Ancient Christian Gospels: Their History and Development.* London: SCM, 1990.

———. *From Jesus to the Gospels: Interpreting the New Testament in Its Context.* Minneapolis: Fortress, 2007.

Kollmann, Christian Ernst. *The Crucifixion by an Eye-Witness.* Translated from the German by T. K. Supplemental Harmonic Series 2. Chicago: Indo-American Book Co., 1907

———. *The Crucifixion and the Resurrection of Jesus by an Eye-Witness.* Translated from the Swedish edition of J. S. Sasberg by the Fellows of the Theosophical Society. Edited by Benjamin Fish Austin. 1880. Los Angeles: Austin Publishing Co., 1919.

———. *Historische Enthüllungen über die wirklichen Ereignisse der Geburt und Jugend Jesu.* Leipzig: Christian Ernst Kollmann, 1849.

———. *Wichtige historische Enthüllungen über die wirkliche Todesart Jesu.* Leipzig: Kollmann, 1849.

Koschorke, Klaus. *Die Polemik der Gnostiker gegen das kirchlichen Christentum: Unter besonderer Berücksichtigung der Nag-Hammadi-Traktate "Apokalypse des Petrus" (NHC VII,3) und "Testimonium Veritatis" (NHC IX,3).* NHS 12. Leiden: Brill, 1978.

Kovacs, Judith L. "Concealment and Gnostic Exegesis: Clement of Alexandria's Interpretation of the Tabernacle." *StPatr* 31 (1997) 414–37.

Krapp, George Philip, ed. *The Vercelli Book.* Anglo-Saxon Poetic Records 2. New York: Columbia University Press, 1932.

Kraus, Thomas J. "The Fayum Gospel." In *The Non-Canonical Gospels*, edited by Paul Foster, 150–56. London: T. & T. Clark, 2008.

———. "Introduction." In *Gospel Fragments*, edited by Thomas J. Kraus, et al., 1–8. Oxford: Oxford University Press, 2009.

———, ed. and trans. "Other Gospel Fragments." In *Gospel Fragments*, by Thomas J. Kraus, et al., 219–97. Oxford Early Christian Gospel Texts. Oxford: Oxford University Press, 2009.

———, ed. "P.Vindob. G 2325: The So-Called Fayûm-Gospel—Re-edition and Some Critical Conclusions." In *Ad fontes: Original Manuscripts and Their Significance for Studying Early Christianity—Selected Essays*, 69–94. TENT 3. Leiden: Brill, 2007.

———, trans. "Das sogenannte Faijumfragment (P.Vindob. G. 2325)." In *Antike christliche Apokryphen in deutscher Übersetzung*, vol. 1, *Evangelien und Verwandtes*,

edited by Christoph Markschies and Jens Schröter, 375–76. Tübingen: Mohr/
Siebeck, 2012.

Kraus, Thomas J., and Tobias Nicklas, ed. and trans. *Das Petrusevangelium und die Petrusapokalypse: Die griechischen Fragmente mid deutscher und englischer Übersetzung*. GCS 11. Berlin: de Gruyter, 2004.

Kraus, Thomas J., et al., eds. and trans. "The 'Unknown Gospel' on *Papyrus Egerton* 2 (+*Papyrus Cologne* 225)." In *Gospel Fragments*, by Thomas J. Kraus, et al., 9–120. Oxford Early Christian Gospel Texts. Oxford: Oxford University Press, 2009.

Kraut, Ogden. *Jesus Was Married*. Salt Lake City: Ogden Kraut, 1969.

Kristeva, Julia. "Word, Dialogue and Novel." In *Desire in Language: A Semiotic Approach to Literature and Art*, edited by Leon S. Roudiez, 64–91. European Perspectives. New York: Columbia University Press, 1980. Originally published as "Bakhtine, le mort, le dialogue et le roman." *Critique* 23 (1967) 438–65.

Kruger, Michael J. *The Gospel of the Savior: An Analysis of P.Oxy. 840 and Its Place in the Gospel Traditions of Early Christianity*. TENTS 1. Leiden: Brill, 2005.

———, ed. and trans. "Papyrus Oxyrhynchus 840." In *Gospel Fragments*, by Thomas J. Kraus, et al., 121–215. Oxford Early Christian Gospel Texts. Oxford: Oxford University Press, 2009.

———. "Papyrus Oxyrhynchus 840." In *The Non-Canonical Gospels*, edited by Paul Foster, 157–70. London: T. & T. Clark, 2008.

Krutzsch, Myriam, and Ira Rabin. "Material Criteria and Their Clues for Dating." *NTS* 61 (2015) 356–67.

Kuhn, Annette. "Women's Genres." *Screen* 25/1 (1984) 18–29.

Landau, Brent, trans. *Revelation of the Magi: The Lost Tale of the Wise Men's Journey to Bethlehem*. San Francisco: HarperOne, 2010.

———. "The Revelation of the Magi: A New Summary and Introduction." In *New Testament Apocrypha: More Noncanonical Scriptures*, vol. 1, edited by Tony Burke and Brent Landau, 19–38. Grand Rapids: Eerdmans, 2016.

———, ed. and trans. "The Sages and the Star-Child: An Introduction to the Revelation of the Magi, An Ancient Christian Apocryphon." ThD diss., Harvard Divinity School, 2008.

Landau, Brent, and Stanley E. Porter, trans. "Papyrus Oxyrhynchus 210: A New Translation and Introduction." In *New Testament Apocrypha: More Noncanonical Scriptures*, vol. 1, edited by Tony Burke and Brent Landau, 109–24. Grand Rapids: Eerdmans, 2016.

Laouenan, François. *Du brahmanisme et de ses rapports avec le judaïsme et le christianisme*. 2 vols. Pondichéry: Imprimerie de la mission catholique, 1884–1885.

Lawson, Scott. "Jesus' Wife Evidence Led to Venice." *North Port Sun* (posted 24 June 2016). http://yoursun.com/sunnews/venice/venicenews/11187325-696/story.html. csp/.

Layton, Bentley, ed. "The Book of Thomas." In *Nag Hammadi Codex II,2–7 Together with XIII,2*, Brit. Lib. Or. 4926(1), and P. Oxy. 1, 654, 655*, edited by Bentley Layton, 1:171–205. 2 vols. NHS 20, 21. Leiden: Brill, 1989.

Le Boulluec, Alain. "La Lettre sur l'Évangile secret' de Marc et le *Quis dives salvetur?* de Clément d'Alexandrie." *Apocrypha* 7 (1996) 27–41.

Le Donne, Anthony. "The Jesus Blog: Interview with Caroline T. Schroeder Re: Jesus' Wife Fragment." *The Jesus Blog* (posted 25 April 2014). http://historicaljesusresearch. blogspot.ca/2014/04/interview-with-caroline-t-schroeder-re.html/.

————. *The Wife of Jesus: Ancient Texts and Modern Scandals.* London: Oneworld, 2013.

Leibowitz, Yeshayahu. *Judaism, Human Values, and the Jewish State.* Edited by Eliezer Goldman. Cambridge: Harvard University Press, 1992.

Leneghan, Francis. "Teaching the Teachers: The Vercelli Book and the Mixed Life." *English Studies* 94 (2013) 627–58.

Lenglet du Fresnoy, Nicolas. *A New Method for Studying History, Geography and Chronology.* Translated by Richard Rawlinson. 2 vols. London: Davis, 1730. Originally published as *Méthode pour étudier l'histoire.* Bruxelles: Aux dépens de la Compagnie, 1714.

Lentz, John Clayton. *Luke's Portrait of Paul.* SNTSMS 77. Cambridge: Cambridge University Press, 1993.

León, Moses de. *Sefer Mishkan ha-Edut.* Edited by Avishai Bar Asher. Los Angeles: Cherub, 2013.

Levine, Joseph M. "'Et Tu Brute?' History and Forgery in 18th-century England." In *Fakes and Frauds: Varieties of Deception in Print and Manuscript,* edited by Robin Myers and Michael Harris, 71–97. Winchester: St. Paul's Bibliographies, 1989.

Liddle, Rod. "It's Not Misogyny, Professor Beard. It's You." *Spectator,* 26 January 2013, 17. http://www.spectator.co.uk/2013/01/its-not-misogyny-professor-beard-its-you.

Lied, Liv Ingeborg. "Trolls at My Door: Reflections on the Occasion of the International Women's Day 2015 (8 March)." *Religion—Manuscripts—Media Culture Blog* (posted 6 March 2015). http://livlied.blogspot.ca/2015/03/trolls-at-my-door-reflections-on.html/.

Lieu, Judith M. "The Battle for Paul in the Second Century." *ITQ* 75.1 (2010) 3–14.

Lieu, Samuel N. C. *Greek and Latin Sources on Manichaean Cosmogony and Ethics.* Corpus Fontium Manichaeorum, Series Subsidia 6. Turnhout: Brepols, 2010.

Lightfoot, Joseph B., ed. and trans. *The Apostolic Fathers,* part 1: *S Clement of Rome. A Revised Text with Introductions, Notes, Dissertations, and Translations.* London: Macmillan, 1890.

Lilla, Salvatore R. C. *Clement of Alexandria: A Study in Christian Platonism and Gnosticism.* Oxford: Oxford University Press, 1971.

Lillie, Arthur. *The Influence of Buddhism on Primitive Christianity.* New York: Scribner, 1893.

Lindt, Paul van. "The Religious Terminology of the Nag Hammadi Texts in Manichaean Literature." In *The Nag Hammadi Texts in the History of Religions,* edited by Søren Giversen, et al., 191–98. Historisk-filosofiske skrifter 26. Copenhagen: Reitzel, 2002.

Liu, Alan. "Theses on the Epistemology of the Digital: Advice For the Cambridge Centre for Digital Knowledge." *Alan Liu* (posted 14 August 2014). http://liu.english.ucsb. edu/theses-on-the-epistemology-of-the-digital-page/.

Lofton, Kathryn. "The Digital Is a Place to Hide." *The Immanent Frame: Secularism, Religion, and the Public Square* (posted 7 January 2015). http://blogs.ssrc.org/ tif/2015/01/07/the-digital-is-a-place-to-hide/.

Longenecker, Bruce W. *The Lost Letters of Pergamum: A Story from the New Testament World.* Grand Rapids: Baker Academic, 2003.

Love, Harold. *Attributing Authorship: An Introduction*. Cambridge: Cambridge University Press, 2002.

Löwe, Heinz-Dietrich. *Antisemitismus und reaktionäre Utopie: Russischer Konservatismus im Kampf gegen den Wandel von Staat und Gesellschaft*. Historische Perspektiven 13. Hamburg: Hoffmann & Campe, 1978.

Lucas, Peter J., and Angela M. Lucas. *Anglo-Saxon Manuscripts in Microfiche Facsimile*, vol. 18, *Manuscripts in France*. 25 vols. MRTS 381. Tempe: Arizona Center for Medieval and Renaissance Studies, 2012.

Luck, Georg. Review of *The Road to Eleusis*, by R. Gordon Wasson et al. *AJP* 122 (2001) 135–38.

Lührmann, Dieter, and Egbert Schlarb, eds. *Fragmente Apokryph gewordener Evangelien in Griechischer und Lateinischer Sprache*. Marburger theologische Studien 59. Marburg: Elwert, 2000.

Luttikhuizen, Gerard P. "The Apocryphal Correspondence with the Corinthians and Paul." In *The Apocryphal Acts of Paul and Thecla*, edited by Jan Bremmer, 75–91. Apocryphal Acts of the Apostles 2. Kampen: Pharos, 1996.

———. *Gnostic Revisions of Genesis Stories and Early Jesus Traditions*. NHMS 58. Leiden: Brill, 2006.

———. "The Suffering Jesus and the Invulnerable Christ in the Gnostic *Apocalypse of Peter*." In *The Apocalypse of Peter*, edited by Jan N. Bremmer and István Czachesz, 187–99. Studies on Early Christian Apocrypha 7. Leuven: Peeters, 2003.

———. "The Letter of Peter to Philip and the New Testament." In *Nag Hammadi and Gnosis: Papers Read at the First International Congress of Coptology (Cairo, December, 1976)*, edited by Robert M. Wilson, 96–102. NHMS 14 Leiden: Brill, 1978.

MacDonald, Dennis R., ed. and trans. *The Acts of Andrew and the Acts of Andrew and Matthias in the City of the Cannibals*. SBLTT 33. Christian Apocrypha 1. Atlanta: Scholars, 1990.

———. *The Legend and the Apostle: The Battle for Paul in Story and Canon*. Philadelphia: Westminster, 1983.

Mackay, Thomas W. "Response [to S. Davies]." *Semeia* 38 (1986) 145–49.

Maffly-Kipp, Laurie F., ed. *American Scriptures: An Anthology of Sacred Writings*. Penguin Classics. New York: Penguin, 2010.

Mahan, William Dennes. *A Correct Transcript of Pilate's Court: As Taken from Tiberius Caesar's records in the Vatican at Rome, giving a correct account of the apprehension, trial and crucifixion of Jesus of Nazareth*. St. Louis: Perrin & Smith, 1875.

Mahoney, Anne. Review of *Interdisciplining Digital Humanities: Boundary Work in an Emerging Field*, by Julie Thompson Klein. *Bryn Mawr Classical Review* (2015. 08.44). http://bmcr.brynmawr.edu/2015/2015-08-44.html/.

Marguerat, Daniel. *Paul in Acts and Paul in His Letters*. WUNT 310. Tübingen: Mohr/Siebeck, 2013.

Marjanen, Antti. "The Suffering of One Who Is a Stranger to Suffering: The Crucifixion of Jesus in the Letter of Peter to Philip." In *Fair Play: Diversity and Conflicts in Early Christianity: Essays in Honour of Heikki Raisenen*, edited by Ismo Dunderberg, et al., 487–98. NovTSup 103. Leiden: Brill, 2001.

Markschies, Christoph. "Außerkanonische Evangelien." In *Antike christliche Apokryphen in deutscher Übersetzung*, vol. 1, *Evangelien und Verwandtes*, edited by Christoph Markschies and Jens Schröter, 343–52. Tübingen: Mohr/Siebeck, 2012.

Markschies, Christoph, and Jens Schröter, eds. *Antike christliche Apokryphen in deutsch-er Übersetzung*, vol.. 1, *Evangelien und Verwandtes*. Tübingen: Mohr/ Siebeck, 2012.

Marshall, John W. "Misunderstanding the New Paul: Marcion's Transformation of the *Sonderzeit* Paul." *JECS* 20/1 (2012) 1–29.

————. "When You Make the Inside Like the Outside: Pseudepigraphy and Ethos." In *Rhetoric, Ethics, and Moral Persuasion in Biblical Discourse*, edited by Thomas H. Olbricht and Anders Eriksson, 88–102. Emory Studies in Early Christianity 11. New York: T. & T. Clark, 2005.

Martial. *Epigrams*. Translated by Walter C. A. Ker. 2 vols. LCL 94. Cambridge: Harvard University Press, 1979.

Mason, Patrick. *The Mormon Menace: Violence and Anti-Mormonism in the Postbellum South*. Oxford: Oxford University Press, 2011.

Matt, Daniel C., trans. *Zohar: Pritzker Edition*. 10 vols. to date. Stanford: Stanford University Press, 2004–2016.

Matthews, Christopher. *Philip: Apostle and Evangelist. Configurations of a Tradition*. NovTSup 105. Leiden: Brill, 2002.

Mayeda, Goro. *Das Leben-Jesu-Fragment Papyrus Egerton 2 und seine Stellung in der urchristlichen Literaturgeschichte*. Bern: Haupt, 1946.

Mazza, Roberta. "The Jesus's Wife Fragment: End of Story?" *Faces & Voices* (posted 17 June 2016). https://facesandvoices.wordpress.com/2016/06/17/the-jesus-wife-fragment-end-of-story/.

————. "Provenance Issues: Some Thoughts—Part 1." *Faces & Voices* (posted 6 December 2014). https://facesandvoices.wordpress.com/2014/12/06/provenance-issues-some-thoughts-part-1/.

McEver, Matthew. "The Messianic Figure in Film: Christology beyond the Biblical Epic." *Journal of Religion and Film* 2 (1998). https://www.unomaha.edu/jrf/McEverMessiah.htm/.

McGrath, James F. "Is the Gospel of Jesus' Wife a Fake?" *Exploring Our Matrix* (posted 21 September 2012). http://www.patheos.com/blogs/exploringourmatrix/2012/09/is-the-gospel-of-jesus-wife-a-fake.html/.

McLean, B. Hudson. *The Cursed Christ: Mediterranean Expulsion Rituals and Pauline Soteriology*. JSNTSup 126. Sheffield: Sheffield Academic, 1996.

McMillan Cottom, Tressie. "Everything but the Burden: Publics, Public Scholarship, and Institutions." *Tressiemc* (posted 12 May 2015). http://tressiemc.com/2015/05/12/everything-but-the-burden-publics-public-scholarship-and-institutions/.

————. "'Who Do You Think You Are?': When Marginality Meets Academic Microcelebrity." *Ada: A Journal of Gender, New Media, and Technology* 7 (2015). http://adanewmedia.org/2015/04/issue7-mcmillancottom/.

McNamara, Martin. *The Apocrypha in the Irish Church*. Dublin: Dublin Institute for Advanced Studies, 1974.

Mead, Rebecca. "The Troll Slayer: A Cambridge Classicist Takes on Her Sexist Detractors." *New Yorker*, 1 September 2014, 30–36. http://www.newyorker.com/magazine/2014/09/01/troll-slayer/.

Meier, John P. *A Marginal Jew: Rethinking the Historical Jesus*, vol. 1, *The Roots of the Problem and the Person*. 5 vols. New York: Doubleday, 1991.

Mendès, Catulle. *L'Évangile de la jeunesse de Notre-Seigneur Jésus-Christ d'après S. Pierre*. Paris: Armand Colin, 1894.

————. *The Gospel of the Childhood of Our Lord Jesus Christ.* Translated by Henry Copley Greene. London: Burns & Oates, 1904.

Merkur, Dan. *The Mystery of Manna: The Psychedelic Sacrament of the Bible.* Rochester, VT: Park Street, 2000.

————. "The Visionary Practices of Jewish Apocalyptists." In *Psychology and the Bible: A New Way to Read the Scriptures,* vol. 2, *From Genesis to Apocalyptic Vision,* edited by J. Harold Ellens, 317–47. Praeger Perspectives. Westport, CT: Praeger, 2004. Originally published in *The Psychoanalytic Study of Society,* vol. 14, *Essays in Honor of Paul Parin,* edited by L. Bryce Boyer and Simon A. Grolnick, 119–48. Hillsdale, NJ: Analytic Press, 1989.

Merlin, Mark D. "Archaeological Evidence for the Tradition of Psychoactive Plant Use in the Old World." *Economic Botany* 57 (2003) 295–323.

Méry, Joseph. *Les Nuits de Londres.* 2 vols. Paris: Dumont, 1840.

Merz, Annette. *Die fiktive Selbstauslegung des Paulus.* NTOA 52. Göttingen: Vandenhoeck & Ruprecht, 2004.

————. "The Fictitious Self-Exposition of Paul: How Might Intertextual Theory Suggest a Reformulation of the Hermeneutics of Pseudepigraphy." In *The Intertextuality of the Epistles: Explorations of Theory and Practice,* edited by Thomas L. Brodie, et al., 113–32. New Testament Monographs 16. Sheffield: Sheffield Phoenix, 2006.

Metzger, Bruce M. "Literary Forgeries and Canonical Pseudepigrapha." *JBL* 91 (1972) 3–24. Reprinted in Metzger, *New Testament Studies: Philological, Versional, and Patristic,* 1–22. NTTS 10. Leiden: Brill, 1980.

————. *Reminiscences of an Octogenarian.* Peabody, MA: Hendrickson, 1997.

Meyer, Marvin W., ed. *The Nag Hammadi Scriptures.* New York: HarperOne, 2007.

————, trans. "The Letter of Peter to Philip." In *The Nag Hammadi Scriptures: The International Edition,* edited by Marvin Meyer et al., 585–93. New York: HarperOne, 2007.

————, trans. "The Revelation of Peter." In *The Nag Hammadi Scriptures: The International Edition,* edited by Marvin Meyer, 487–97. New York: HarperOne, 2007.

————. *Secret Gospels: Essays on Thomas and the Secret Gospel of Mark.* Harrisburg: Trinity, 2003.

Meyer, Marvin, and François Gaudard, ed. and trans. "The Letter of Peter to Philip." In *The Gospel of Judas: Together with the Letter of Peter to Philip, James, and a Book of Allogenes from Codex Tchacos,* edited by Rodolphe Kasser and Gregor Wurst, 79–114. Critical ed. Washington DC: National Geographic, 2007.

Minzesheimer, Bob. "'Code' Deciphers Interest in Religious History." *USA Today,* 11 December 2003, 21. http://usatoday30.usatoday.com/life/books/news/2003-12-11-da-vinci-code_x.htm/.

Mirecki, Paul Allan. "Coptic Manichaean Psalm 278 and the Gospel of Thomas 37." In *Manichaica Selecta: Studies Presented to Professor Julien Ries,* edited by Alois van Tongerloo and Søren Giversen, 243–62. Manichaean Studies 1. Turnhout: Brepols, 1991.

Mitchell, Margaret M. "Corrective Composition, Corrective Exegesis: The Teaching of Prayer in 1 Tim 2,1–15." In *1 Timothy Reconsidered,* edited by Karl Paul Donfried, 41–62. Colloquium Oecumenicum Paulinum 18. Leuven: Peeters, 2008.

————. "New Testament Envoys in the Context of Greco-Roman Diplomatic and Epistolary Conventions: The Example of Timothy and Titus." *JBL* 111/4 (1992) 641–62.

Mitchell, W. J. T. *Iconology: Image, Text, Ideoology*. Chicago: University of Chicago Press, 1986.

———. *Picture Theory: Essays on Verbal and Visual Representation*. Chicago: University of Chicago Press, 1994.

Modleski, Tania. *Loving with a Vengeance: Mass Produced Fantasies for Women*. Hamden, CT: Shoe String, 1982.

———. "The Search for Tomorrow in Today's Soap Operas." *Film Quarterly* 33.1 (1979) 12–21.

Moore, Christopher. *Lamb: The Gospel according to Biff, Christ's Childhood Pal*. New York: HarperCollins, 2002.

"Mormon Shamelessness." *New York Daily Times*, 27 December 1854, 4.

Moss, Candida R. *Ancient Christian Martyrdom: Diverse Practices, Theologies, and Traditions*. ABRL. New Haven: Yale University Press, 2012.

———. "The 'Gospel of Jesus's Wife' is Still as Big a Mystery as Ever." *The Daily Beast* (posted 13 April 2014). http://www.thedailybeast.com/articles/2014/04/13/the-gospel-of-jesus-s-wife-is-still-as-big-as-mystery-as-ever.html/.

Mostert, Marco. "Reading Images and Texts: Some Preliminary Observations Instead of an Introduction." In *Reading Images and Texts: Medieval Images and Texts as Forms of Communication*, edited by Mariëlle Hegeman and Marco Mostert, 1–7. Utrecht Studies in Medieval Literacy 8. Turnhout: Brepols, 2005.

Mount, Christopher. *Pauline Christianity: Luke-Acts and the Legacy of Paul*. NovTSup 104. Leiden: Brill, 2002.

Mroczek, Eva. "'Gospel of Jesus' Wife' Less Durable Than Sexism Surrounding It." *Religion Dispatches* (posted 6 May 2014). http://religiondispatches.org/gospel-of-jesus-wife-less-durable-than-sexism-surrounding-it/.

Muehlberger, Ellen. "Review of Biblical Literature Parity Project." 17 April 2015. https://docs.google.com/spreadsheets/d/1jpw5yFzCNpc3pcFPQfV5csI4cYHProt yBIwhdzUzcMo/.

———. "Thoughts after Two Years." 17 April 2015. https://docs.google.com/document/d/1D7ODzxsOX1Z1jMdTUCDjBuOFKDnMsRij6yfl_MW5LB4/edit?usp=drive_web&usp=embed_facebook.

Müller, Max. "The Alleged Sojourn of Christ in India." *Nineteenth Century* 36 (1894) 515–21.

Musurillo, Herbert A., ed. and trans. *The Acts of the Christian Martyrs: Introduction, Texts and Translations*. OECT. Oxford: Clarendon, 1972.

Myers, Jody. "Kabbalah at the Turn of the 21st Century." In *Jewish Mysticism and Kabbalah: New Insights and Scholarship*, edited by Frederick E. Greenspahn, 175–90. Jewish Studies in the 21st Century. New York: New York University Press, 2011.

Neander, Michael. *Catechesis Martini Lutheri parua, Graecolatina, postremum recognita*. 3rd ed. Basel: Ioannis Oporini, 1567.

Neubauer, Adolf. "The Bahir and the Zohar." *JQR* 4 (1892) 357–68.

Neusner, Jacob. Review of *Paul and Palestinian Judaism*, by E. P. Sanders. *HR* 18 (1978) 177–91.

"A New Gospel Revealed." *Harvard Magazine*, 18 September 2012. harvardmagazine.com/2012/09/new-gospel.

Nicklas, Tobias. "'Gnostic' Perspectives on Peter." In *Peter in Early Christianity*, edited by Helen K. Bond and Larry W. Hurtado, 196–221. Grand Rapids: Eerdmans, 2015.

———. "Papyrus Egerton 2." In *The Non-Canonical Gospels*, edited by Paul Foster, 139–49. London: T. & T. Clark, 2008.

———, trans. "PSI X 1200bis." In *Antike christliche Apokryphen in deutscher Übersetzung*, vol. 1, *Evangelien und Verwandtes*, edited by Christoph Markschies and Jens Schröter, 379. Tübingen: Mohr/Siebeck, 2012.

Nogueira, Sebastiana Maria Silva. "Tertuliano e os Atos de Paulo e Tecla." In *Apocrificidade: O Cristianismo Primitivo para além do Cânon*, edited by Paulo Augusto de Souza Nogueira, 101–19. São Paulo: Fonte, 2015.

Nongbri, Brent. "The Limits of Palaeographic Dating of Literary Papyri: Some Observations on the Date and Provenance of P.Bodmer II (P^{66})." *MH* 71 (2014) 1–35.

———. "The Use and Abuse of P^{52}: Papyrological Pitfalls in the Dating of the Fourth Gospel." *HTR* 98 (2005) 23–48.

Noorden, Richard van. "The arXiv Preprint Server Hits 1 Million Articles." *Nature* (posted 30 December 2014). http://www.nature.com/news/the-arxiv-preprint-server-hits-1-million-articles-1.16643/.

Norelli, Enrico. *Papia di Hierapolis. Esposizione degli oracoli del Signore. I frammenti.* Letture cristiane del primo millennio 36. Milan: Paoline, 2005.

Norris, Richard A., Jr. "Irenaeus' Use of Paul in His Polemic against the Gnostics." In *Paul and the Legacies of Paul*, edited by William S. Babcock, 79–98. Dallas: Southern Methodist University Press, 1990.

Notovitch, Nicolas. *L'empereur Alexandre III et son entourage.* 2nd ed. Paris: Paul Ollendorff, 1893.

———. *L'empereur Nicolas II et la politique russe.* Paris: Ollendorff, 1895.

———. *L'Europe et l'Égypte.* Paris: Ollendorff, 1898.

———. *Pravda ob evreyakh* [The truth about the Jews]. Moscow: Kushnerev, 1889.

———. *La Russie et l'alliance anglaise: Étude historique et politique.* Paris: Pion-Nourrit, 1906.

———. *La vie inconnue de Jésus Christ.* Paris: Ollendorff, 1894.

———. *The Unknown Life of Christ.* Translated by F. Marion Crawford. NY: Macmillan, 1894.

———. *The Unknown Life of Christ: With Maps and Fourteen Illustrations.* Translated by Violet Crispe. London: Hutchinson, 1895.

———. *The Unknown Life of Jesus Christ.* Translated by Alexina Loranger. Chicago: Rand, McNally, 1894.

———. *The Unknown Life of Jesus Christ, from Buddhistic Records.* Translated by J. H. Connelly and L. Landsberg. New York: Dillingham, 1894.

Oden, Thomas C., ed., and James A. Kellerman, trans. *Incomplete Commentary on Matthew (Opus Imperfectum).* 2 vols. Ancient Christian Texts. Downers Grove, IL: IVP Academic, 2010.

Ohlgren, Thomas H. *Anglo-Saxon Textual Illustration: Photographs of Sixteen Manuscripts with Descriptions and Index.* Kalamazoo: Medieval Institute Publications, 1992.

O'Leary, Naomi. "'Gospel of Jesus' Wife' Fragment is a Fake, Vatican Says." *Reuters* (posted 28 September 2012). http://www.reuters.com/article/us-religion-jesuswife-idUSBRE88R0NT20120928/.

Oprisko, Robert. "Superpowers: The American Academic Elite." *Georgetown Public Policy Review* (posted 21 September 2010). http://gppreview.com/2012/12/03/superpowers-the-american-academic-elite/.

Os, Bos van. "The Role of the Apostles in the *Letter of Peter to Philip*." *Annali di storia dell'esegesi* 29 (2012) 155–60.

Oswalt, Martin L. *Pen Pictures of Mormonism.* Philadelphia: American Baptist Publication Society, 1889.

Ouseley, Gideon Jasper. *The Gospel of the Holy Twelve: known also as the Gospel of the Perfect Life*, translated from the Aramaic. 1901. New ed., London: Watkins, 1956.

————. *The Gospel of the Holy Twelve: Known also as The Gospel of the Perfect Life. Translated and Edited by a Disciple of the Master.* Paris: Order of At-One-Ment and United Templars' Society, 1911.

Otero, Aurelio de Santos, ed. and trans. *Los Evangelios Apócrifos.* 2nd ed. Madrid: La Editorial Catolica, 1963.

Paananen, Timo S. "Another 'Fake' Or Just a Problem of Method? What Francis Watson's Analysis Does to Papyrus Köln 255." *Exploring Our Matrix* (posted 27 September 2012). http://www.patheos.com/blogs/exploringourmatrix/2012/09/timo-s-paananen-on-methods-of-forgery-detection-and-the-gospel-of-jesus-wife.html/.

Pack, Christine. "'Is *Codex Sinaiticus* a Modern Forgery?' A Landmark Debate between Dr. James White and Chris Pinto." *Sola Sisters* (posted 12 December 2013). http://www.solasisters.com/2013/12/is-codex-sinaiticus-modern-forgery.html/.

Pagels, Elaine. "Gnostic and Orthodox Views of Christ's Passion: Paradigms for the Christian's Response to Persecution." In *The Rediscovery of Gnosticism*, vol. 1, *The School of Valentinus*, edited by Bentley Layton, 262–83. 2 vols. SHR 41.1. Leiden: Brill, 1980.

Painchaud, Louis, trans. "Écrit sans titre (NH II,5 ; XIII, 2)." In *Écrits gnostiques: La bibliothèque de Nag Hammadi*, edited by Jean-Pierre Mahé and Paul-Hubert Poirier, 400–65. Bibliothèque de la Pléiade 538. Paris: Gallimard, 2007.

————. "Un évangile secret au Box Office." *LeFil* (posted 7 October 7 1999). http://www.scom.ulaval.ca/Au.fil.des.evenements/1999/10.07/stigmates.html/.

Pantuck, Allan J. "A Question of Ability: What Did He Know and When Did He Know it? Further Excavations from the Morton Smith Archives." In *Ancient Gospel or Modern Forgery? The Secret Gospel of Mark in Debate*, edited by Tony Burke, 184–211. Eugene, OR: Cascade Books, 2013.

————. "Solving the *Mysterion* of Morton Smith and the Secret Gospel of Mark." *Biblical Archaeology Review Scholar's Study* (posted 20 February 2011). http://www.bib-arch.org/scholars-study/secret-mark-handwriting-response-pantuck.pdf/.

Parker, David C. *The Living Text of the Gospels.* Cambridge: Cambridge University Press, 1997.

Parker, Holt. "Loyal Slaves and Loyal Wives: The Crisis of the Outsider-Within and Roman Exemplum Literature." In *Women and Slaves in Greco-Roman Culture*, edited by Sandra Joshel and Sheila Murnaghan, 157–78. London: Routledge, 1998.

Pasquali, Giorgio. *Storia della tradizione e critica del testo.* 2nd ed. Florence: Le Lettere, 1971.

Pattengale, Jerry. "How the 'Jesus' Wife' Hoax Fell Apart." *Wall Street Journal* (posted 1 May 2014). http://www.wsj.com/articles/SB10001424052702304178104579535 540828090438/.

Penrose, Charles W. "Peculiar Questions Answered Briefly." *Improvement Era* 15/11 (September 1912) 1042–46.

Perdue, Lewis. *The Da Vinci Legacy*. New York: Forge, 2004.

———. *Daughter of God*. New York: Forge, 2001.

Perkins, Judith. *The Suffering Self: Pain and Narrative Representation in the Early Christian Era*. London: Routledge, 1995.

Perkins, Pheme. *The Gnostic Dialogue: The Early Church and the Crisis of Gnosticism*. Theological Inquiries. New York: Paulist, 1980.

———. "Peter, Witness and Martyr." In *Peter: Apostle for the Whole Church*, 131–49. Studies on Personalities of the New Testament. Columbia: University of South Carolina Press, 1994.

Perry, Matthew J. *Gender, Manumission and the Roman Freedwoman*. Cambridge: Cambridge University Press, 2013.

Pervo, Richard I., ed. and trans. *The Acts of Paul: A New Translation with Introduction and Commentary*. Eugene, OR: Cascade Books, 2014.

———. *The Making of Paul: Constructions of the Apostle in Early Christianity*. Minneapolis: Fortress, 2010.

Pettipiece, Timothy. *Pentadic Redaction in the Manichaean Kephalaia*. NHMS 66. Leiden: Brill, 2009.

———. "Publicity or Perish: The Sad Finale of the Gospel of Jesus' Wife Saga." *Thoughts of Future Pasts* (posted 17 June 2016). http://thoughtsoffuturepasts.blogspot.ca/2016/06/publicity-or-perish-sad-finale-of_17.html/.

———. "Towards a Manichaean Reading of the Nag Hammadi Codices." *JCSCS* 3–4 (2012) 43–54.

Pfaff, Richard W. *The Liturgy in Medieval England: A History*. Cambridge: Cambridge University Press, 2009.

———. "Massbooks: Sacramentaries and Missals." In *The Liturgical Books of Anglo-Saxon England*, edited by Richard W. Pfaff, 7–34. Old English Newsletter Subsidia 23. Kalamazoo: Medieval Institute Publications, 1995.

Phillips, Thomas E. *Paul, His Letters, and Acts*. Library of Pauline Studies. Peabody, MA: Hendrickson, 2009.

Philo. *The Works of Philo Complete and Unabridged: New Updated Version*. Translated by C. D. Yonge. Peabody, MA: Hendrickson, 1993.

Phipps, William. "The Case for a Married Jesus." *Dialogue: A Journal of Mormon Thought* 7/4 (1972) 44–49.

———. "Did Jesus or Paul Marry?" *JES* 5 (1968) 741–44.

———. *The Sexuality of Jesus*. New York: Harper & Row, 1973.

———. *Was Jesus Married? The Distortion of Sexuality in the Christian Tradition*. New York: Harper & Row, 1970.

Picard, Jean-Claude. *Le continent apocryphe: Essai sur les littératures apocryphes juive et chrétienne*. Instrumenta Patristica et Mediaevalia 36. Turnhout: Brepols, 1999.

———. "Les chemins de la mythologie chrétienne." In *Le continent apocryphe: Essai sur les littératures apocryphes juive et chrétienne*, 247–64. Instrumenta patristica 36. Turnhout: Brepols, 1999.

Pinsker, Joe. "*The Testament of Mary* Isn't Really About Jesus' Mother at All." *Atlantic* (posted 9 October 2013). http://www.theatlantic.com/entertainment/archive/2013/10/-i-the-testament-of-mary-i-isnt-really-about-jesus-mother-at-all/280421/.

Piovanelli, Pierluigi. "The Miraculous Discovery of the Hidden Manuscript, or The Paratextual Function of the Prologue to the *Apocalypse of Paul*." In *The Visio Pauli and the Gnostic Apocalypse of Paul*, edited by Jan N. Bremmer and Istvan Czachesz, 23–49. Studies on Early Christian Apocrypha 9. Leuven: Peeters, 2007.

———. "Qu'est-ce qu'un 'écrit apocryphe chrétien', et comment ça marche? Quelques suggestions pour une herméneutique apocryphe." In *Pierre Geoltrain, ou comment "faire l'histoire" des religions. Le chantier des "origines," les méthodes du doute, et la conversation contemporaine entre disciplines*, edited by Simon C. Mimouni and Isabelle Ullern-Weité, 171–84. Bibliothèque de l'École des hautes études, Sciences religieuses 128. Turnhout: Brepols, 2006.

———. "What Is a Christian Apocryphal Text and How Does It Work? Some Observations on Apocryphal Hermeneutics." *NedTT* 59 (2005) 31–40.

Plato. *The Collected Dialogues of Plato*. Edited and translated by Edith Hamilton and Huntington Cairns. Bollingen Series 71. Princeton: Princeton University Press, 1963.

———. *Lysis; Symposium; Gorgias*. Translated by Walter R. M. Lamb. LCL 166. Cambridge: Harvard University Press, 1925.

Plautus. *Casina*. Edited and translated by Wolfgang de Melo. In *Casina, The Casket Comedy. Curculia. Epidus. The Two Menaeshmuses*, 3–122. LCL 61. Cambridge: Harvard University Press, 2011.

———. *Mercator*. Edited and translated by Wolfgang de Melo. In *The Merchant, The Braggart Soldier, The Ghost, The Persian*, 3–129. LCL 163. Cambridge: Harvard University Press, 2011.

Pliny. *Natural History. Books 1–2*. Translated by Harris Rackham. LCL 330. Cambridge: Harvard University Press, 1938.

Plutarch. *Moralia*. Translated by Harold North Fowler. 17 vols. in 18 bks. LCL 321. Harvard: Harvard University Press, 1936.

Polycarp. *Polycarp's Epistle to the Philippians and the Martyrdom of Polycarp: Introduction, Text, and Commentary*. Edited by Paul Hartog. Oxford Apostolic Fathers. Oxford: Oxford University Press, 2013.

Ponder, Ross. P., trans. "Papyrus Oxyrhynchus 5072: A New Translation and Introduction." In *New Testament Apocrypha: More Noncanonical Scriptures*, vol. 1, edited by Tony Burke and Brent Landau, 125–39. Grand Rapids: Eerdmans, 2016.

Porter, Stanley E. "Apocryphal Gospels and the Text of the New Testament before A.D. 200." In *The New Testament Text in Early Christianity/Le texte du Nouveau Testament au début du christianisme*, edited by Christian-B. Amphoux and J. Keith Elliott, 235–59. Histoire du texte biblique 6. Lausanne: Editions du Zèbre, 2003.

———. "Early Apocryphal Gospels and the New Testament Text." In *The Early Text of the New Testament*, edited by Charles E. Hill and Michael J. Kruger, 350–69. Oxford: Oxford University Press, 2012.

———. "The Greek Apocryphal Gospels Papyri: The Need for a Critical Edition." In *Akten des 21. Internationalen Papyrologenkongresses, Berlin 1995*, vol. 2, edited by Bärbel Kramer et al., 795–803. 2 vols. APF Beiheft 3. Stuttgart: Teubner, 1997.

———. *How We Got the New Testament: Text, Transmission, Translation.* Acadia Studies in Bible and Theology. Grand Rapids: Baker Academic, 2013.

———, trans. "Der Papyrus Oxyrhynchus II 210 (P.Oxy. II 210)." In *Antike christliche Apokryphen in deutscher Übersetzung,* vol. 1.1, *Evangelien und Verwandtes,* edited by Christoph Markschies and Jens Schröter, 387–89. Tübingen: Mohr/Siebeck, 2012.

———. *The Paul of Acts: Essays in Literary Criticism, Rhetoric, and Theology.* WUNT 115. Tübingen: Mohr/Siebeck, 1999.

———, ed. and trans. "POxy II 210 as an Apocryphal Gospel and the Development of Egyptian Christianity." In *Atti del XXII Congresso Internazionale di Papirologia, Firenze 1998,* edited by Isabella Andorlini et al., 1095–1108. Florence: Istituto Papirologico "G. Vitelli," 2001.

———. "Recent Efforts to Reconstruct Early Christianity on the Basis of Its Papyrological Evidence." In *Christian Origins and Greco-Roman Culture: Social and Literary Contexts for the New Testament,* edited by Stanley E. Porter and Andrew W. Pitts, 71–84. TENTS 9. Leiden: Brill, 2013.

———. "What Do We Know and How Do We Know It? Reconstructing Early Christianity from Its Manuscripts." In *Christian Origins and Greco-Roman Culture: Social and Literary Contexts for the New Testament,* edited by Stanley E. Porter and Andrew W. Pitts, 95–134. TENTS 9. Leiden: Brill, 2013.

Porter, Stanley E., and Wendy J. Porter. *New Testament Greek Papyri and Parchments: New Editions: Texts, Plates.* 2 vols. Mitteilungen aus der Papyrussammlung der Österreichischen Nationalbibliothek. Papyrus Erzherzog Rainer. Neue Ser., 29/30. Berlin: de Gruyter, 2008.

———, trans. "Rylands Apokryphes Evangelium (?) (P.Ryl. III 464)." In *Antike christliche Apokryphen in deutscher Übersetzung,* vol. 1, *Evangelien und Verwandtes,* edited by Christoph Markschies and Jens Schröter, 377–78. Tübingen: Mohr/Siebeck, 2012.

Postel, Guillaume. *Protevangelion, de seu de natalibus Iesu Christi et ipsius matris Virginis Mariae sermo historicus divi Iacobi Minoris. Evagelica historia quam scripsit B. Marcus. Vita Marei evangelistae collecta per Theodorum Bibliandrum.* Basel: Oporini, 1552.

Pratt, Orson. "Celestial Marriage." *Seer* 1.1–12 (January 1853–December 1853).

Prescott, Andrew, ed. *The Benedictional of St Æthelwold: A Masterpiece of Anglo-Saxon Art, A Facsimile.* London: British Library, 2001.

Press, Michael. "'The Lying Pen of Scribes': A Nineteenth-Century Dead Sea Scroll." *Appendix: Futures of the Past* 2.3 (July 2014) 144–52. http://theappendix.net/issues/2014/7/the-lying-pen-of-the-scribes-a-nineteenth-century-dead-sea-scroll/.

Price, Robert M. *The Da Vinci Fraud: Why the Truth Is Stranger Than Fiction.* Amherst, NY: Prometheus, 2005.

———. *Secret Scrolls: Revelations from the Lost Gospel Novels.* Eugene, OR: Wipf & Stock, 2011.

Prieur, Jean-Marc, ed. *Acta Andreae.* 2 vols. CCSA 5–6. Turnhout: Brepols, 1989.

Prothero, Stephen. *American Jesus: How the Son of God Became a National Icon.* New York: Farrar, Straus & Giroux, 2004.

Pyke, Karen. "Faculty Gender Inequity and the 'Just Say No to Service' Fairy Tale." In *Disrupting the Culture of Silence: Confronting Gender Inequality and Making*

Change in Higher Education, edited by Kristine De Welde and Andi Stepnick, 83–95. Sterling, VA: Stylus, 2014.

Quesnell, Quentin. "The Mar Saba Clementine: A Question of Evidence." *CBQ* 37 (1975) 48–67.

————. "A Reply to Morton Smith." *CBQ* 38 (1976) 200–203.

Rabinowicz, Oskar K. "The Shapira Scroll: A Nineteenth-century Forgery." *JQR* 56/1 (1965) 1–21.

Ramsay, Stephen, and Geoffrey Rockwell. "Developing Things: Notes toward an Epistemology of Building in the Digital Humanities." In *Debates in the Digital Humanities*, edited by Matthew K. Gold, 75–84. Minneapolis: University of Minnesota Press, 2012.

Read, Anne. *Edgar Cayce on Jesus and His Church.* New York: Warner, 1970.

Reale, Giovanni. *A History of Ancient Philosophy II: Plato and Aristotle.* Edited and translated by John R. Catan. Albany: State University of New York Press, 1990.

Rei, Annalisa. "Villains, Wives and Slaves in the Comedies of Plautus." In *Women and Slaves in Classical Culture*, edited by Sandra R. Joshel and Sheila Murnaghan, 94–111. London: Routledge, 1998.

Reinink, Gerrit J. "Das Land 'Seiris' [*Shir*] und das Volk der Serer in jüdischen und christlichen Traditionen." *JSJ* 6 (1975) 72–85.

Remley, Paul G. "The Vercelli Book and Its Texts: A Guide to Scholarship." In *New Readings in the Vercelli Book*, edited by Samantha Zacher and Andy Orchard, 318–416. Toronto Anglo-Saxon Series 4. Toronto: University of Toronto Press, 2009.

Renan, Ernest *Vie de Jésus.* Paris: Calmann-Lévy, 1863.

Reynolds, Leighton D., and Nigel G. Wilson. *Scribes and Scholars.* 3rd ed. Oxford: Clarendon, 1991.

Richards, E. Randolph. *The Secretary in the Letters of Paul.* WUNT 2/42. Tübingen: Mohr/Siebeck, 1991.

Richards, William A. *Difference and Distance in Post-Pauline Christianity: An Epistolary Analysis of the Pastorals.* StBibLit 44. New York: Lang, 2002.

Richlin, Amy. *Arguments with Silence: Writing the History of Roman Women.* Ann Arbor: University of Michigan Press, 2014.

————. "Making Up a Woman: The Face of Roman Gender." In *Arguments with Silence: Writing the History of Roman Women*, 166–96. Ann Arbor: University of Michigan Press, 2014.

————. "Talking to Slaves in the Plautine Audience." *Classical Antiquity* 33 (2014) 174–226.

Riesner, Rainer. *Paul's Early Period: Chronology, Mission Strategy, Theology.* Grand Rapids: Eerdmans, 1998.

Rist, Martin. "III Corinthians as a Pseudepigraphic Refutation of Marcionism." *Iliff Review* 26/3 (1969) 49–58.

Robertson, Morgan. *The Wreck of the Titan: Or Futility.* 1898. Reprinted, Rahway, NJ: Quinn & Boden, 1912.

Robinson, Cynthia. "Arthur in Alhambra? Narrative and Nasrid Courtly Self-Fashioning in The Hall of Justice Ceiling Paintings." *Medieval Encounters* 14 (2008) 164–98.

Robinson, Gesine Schenke. "How a Papyrus Fragment Became a Sensation." *NTS* 61 (2015) 379–94.

Robinson, Gesine Schenke, and Charles Halton. "Gesine Robinson on the 'Jesus Wife' Fragment." *Charles Halton* (posted 26 September 2012). http://awilum. com/?p=2216/.

Robinson, James M. *The Manichaean Codices of Medinet Madi.* Eugene, OR: Cascade Books, 2013.

Rocher, Ludo. *Ezourvedam: A French Veda of the Eighteenth Century.* University of Pennsylvania Studies on South Asia 1. Philadelphia: Benjamins, 1984.

Rodriguez, Raphael. "The Gospel of Jesus' Wife." *Verily Verily* (posted 20 September 2012). http://thinkinginpublic.blogspot.com/2012/09/the-gospel-of-jesus-wife. html/.

―――. "A Verdict Is In." *Verily Verily* (posted 21 September 2012). http://thinkinginpublic.blogspot.com/2012/09/a-verdict-is-in.html/.

Roessli, Jean-Michel. "North American Approaches to the Study of the Christian Apocrypha on the World Stage." In *Forbidden Texts on the Western Frontier: The Christian Apocrypha in North American Perspectives*, edited by Tony Burke, 19–57. Eugene, OR: Cascade Books, 2015.

Rojas, John-Paul Ford. "Mary Beard Hits Back at AA Gill after He Brands Her 'Too Ugly for Television.'" *Telegraph* (posted 24 April 2012). http://www.telegraph.co.uk/news/picturegalleries/celebritynews/9223149/Mary-Beard-hits-back-at-AA-Gill-after-he-brands-her-too-ugly-for-television.html/.

Rollston, Christopher A. "The Talpiyot (Jerusalem) Tombs: Some Sober Methodological Reflections on the Epigraphic Materials." *Bible and Interpretation* (posted April 2013). Pages 1–22. http://www.bibleinterp.com/articles/2013/rol378025.shtml/.

Roose, Hanna. "'A Letter as by Us': Intentional Ambiguity in 2 Thessalonians 2." *JSNT* 29 (2006) 107–24.

―――. "2 Thessalonians as Pseudepigraphic 'Reading Instruction' for 1 Thessalonians: Methodolgical Implications and Exemplary Illustration of an Intertextual Concept." In *The Intertextuality of the Epistles*, edited by Thomas L. Brodie, et al., 133–51. New Testament Monographs 16. Sheffield: Sheffield Phoenix, 2006.

Rordorf, Willy. "Tertullien et les *Actes de Paul* (à propos de *bapt.* 17,5)." In *Hommage à René Braun*, vol.. 2, *Autour de Tertullien*, edited by Jean Granarolo and Michèle Biraud, 153–60. 2 vols. Publication de la Faculté des lettres et sciences humaines de Nice 56. Nice: Faculté des lettres et sciences humaines de Nice, 1990. Reprinted in Willy Rordorf, *Lex orandi, lex credendi: Gesammelte Aufsätze zum 60. Geburtstag*, 475–84. Paradosis 36. Freiburg: Universitätsverlag, 1993.

Rose, Marice E. "The Construction of Mistress and Slave Relationship in Late Antique Art." *Woman's Art Journal* 29/2 (2008) 41–49.

Rosenmeyer, Patricia A. *Ancient Epistolary Fictions: The Letter in Greek Literature.* Cambridge: Cambridge University Press, 2001.

Rosenthal, Herman and A. S. Waldstein. "Osip Konstantinovich Notovich." *JE* 9 (1905) 341.

Rothman, Lily. "A Cultural History of Mansplaining." *Atlantic* (posted 1 November 2012). http://www.theatlantic.com/sexes/archive/2012/11/a-cultural-history-of-mansplaining/264380/.

Royse, James R. *Scribal Habits in Early Greek New Testament Papyri.* NTTSD 36. Leiden: Brill, 2008.

Rubin, Miri. *Mother of God: A History of the Virgin Mary.* New Haven: Yale University Press, 2009.

Ruck, Carl A. P. *Sacred Mushrooms of the Goddess: Secrets of Eleusis.* Oakland: Ronin, 2006.

Ruck, Carl A. P., et al. *The Apples of Apollo: Pagan and Christian Mysteries of the Eucharist.* Durham, NC: Carolina Academic, 2000.

Ruck, Carl A. P., et al. "Entheogens." *Journal of Psychoactive Drugs* 11 (1979) 145–46.

Ruck, Carl A. P., et al. *Mushrooms, Myth, and Mithras: The Drug Cult That Civilized Europe.* San Francisco: City Lights, 2009.

Rudolph, Kurt. "The Baptist Sects." In *CHJ* 3:471–500, 1135–39.

———. "Mani und die Gnosis." In *Manichaean Studies: Proceedings of the First International Conference on Manichaeism,* edited by Peter Bryder, 191–200. Lund Studies in African and Asian Religions 1. Lund: Plus Ultra, 1988.

Russett, Margaret. *Fictions and Fakes: Forging Romantic Authenticity, 1760–1845.* Cambridge: Cambridge University Press, 2006.

Sabar, Ariel. "The Inside Story of a Controversial New Text about Jesus." *Smithsonian* (posted 17 September 2012). http://www.smithsonianmag.com/history/the-inside-story-of-a-controversial-new-text-about-jesus-41078791/. Later published as "The Gospel according to King." *Smithsonian Magazine,* November 2012, 74–83.

———. "Karen King Responds to 'The Unbelievable Tale of Jesus's Wife.'" *Atlantic: Politics & Policy Daily* (posted 16 June 2016). http://www.theatlantic.com/politics/archive/2016/06/karen-king-responds-to-the-unbelievable-tale-of-jesus-wife/487484/.

———. "The Unbelievable Tale of Jesus's Wife." *Atlantic,* July/August 2016, 64–78. http://www.theatlantic.com/magazine/archive/2016/07/the-unbelievable-tale-of-jesus-wife/485573/.

Sabatier, Pierre, ed. *Bibliorum Sacrorum Latinae Versiones Antiquae, Seu Vetus Italica.* 3 vols. Rheims: Reginald Florentain, 1743.

Sagnard, François. *La gnose valentinienne et le témoignage de Saint Irénée.* Paris: Librairie Philosophique J. Vrin, 1947.

Saller, Richard P. "*Familia, Domus,* and the Roman Concept of the Family." *Phoenix* 38 (1994) 336–55.

———. "Symbols of Gender and Status in the Roman Household." In *Women and Slaves in Classical Culture,* edited by Sandra R. Joshel and Sheila Murnaghan, 87–93. London: Routledge, 1998.

Sanders, J. Oswald. *Heresies Ancient and Modern.* London: Marshall, Morgan & Scott, 1948.

Sandmel, Samuel. Review of *Paul and Palestinian Judaism,* by E. P. Sanders. *RSR* 4 (1978) 158–60.

Schaberg, Jane. *The Resurrection of Mary Magdalene: Legends, Apocrypha, and the Christian Testament.* New York: Continuum, 2002.

Schaper, Rüdiger. *Die Odyssee des Fälschers: Die Abenteuerliche Geschichte des Konstantin Simonides.* Munich: Siedler, 2011.

Schefer, Christina. "Rhetoric as Part of an Initiation into the Mysteries: A New Interpretation of the Platonic *Phaedrus.*" In *Plato as Author: The Rhetoric of Philosophy,* edited by Ann N. Michelini, 175–96. Cincinnati Classical Studies n.s. 8. Leiden: Brill, 2003.

408   Bibliography

Schmidt, Carl, ed. *Acta Pauli: Aus der Heidelberger koptischen Payrushandschrift Nr. 1.* 1904. 2nd enlarged ed. Leipzig: Hinrichs, 1905. Reprinted, Hildescheim: Olms, 1965.

———. *Der Benanbrief, eine moderne Leben-Jesu-Faelschung des Herrn Ernst Edler von der Planitz.* TU, new series, 44. Leipzig: Hinrichs, 1921.

Schmidt, Carl, and Hans-Jakob Polotsky. "Ein Mani-Fund in Ägypten." *SPAW* (1933) 4–90.

Schmidt, Carl, with Wilhelm Schubart, eds. *Act Pauli: Nach dem Papyrus der Hamburger Staats- und Universitäs-Bibliothek.* Hamburg: Augustin, 1936.

Schnabel, Eckhard J. "The Muratorian Fragment: The State of Research." *JETS* 57 (2014) 239–53.

Schneemelcher, Wilhelm, trans. "Acts of Paul." In *New Testament Apocrypha,* vol. 2, *Writings Relating to the Apostles; Apocalypses and Related Subjects,* edited by Wilhelm Schneemelcher, 213–70. Translated by Robert McL. Wilson. 2 vols. Louisville: Westminster John Knox, 1992.

———. "General Introduction." In *New Testament Apocrypha,* vol. 1, *Gospels and Related Writings,* edited by Wilhelm Schneemelcher, 9–75. Translated by R. McL. Wilson. 2 vols. Louisville: Westminster John Knox, 1991.

———. "Gospels: Non-Biblical Material about Jesus." In *New Testament Apocrypha,* vol. 1, *Gospels and Related Writings,* edited by Wilhelm Schneemelcher, 77–87. Translated by R. McL. Wilson. 2 vols. Louisville: Westminster John Knox, 1991.

———, ed. *New Testament Apocrypha.* Translated by R. McL. Wilson. 2 vols. Louisville: Westminster John Knox, 1991–1992. Originally published as *Neutestamentliche Apokryphen in deutscher Übersetzung.* 6th ed. 2 vols. Tübingen: Mohr/Siebeck, 1990.

Schoedel, William R. "Scripture and the Seventy-Two Heavens of the First Apocalypse of James." *NovT* 12 (1970) 118–29.

Schoenborn, Ulrich. *Diverbium Salutis. Literarische Struktur und theologische Intention des gnostischen Dialogs am Beispiel der koptischen "Apocalypse des Petrus."* SUNT 19. Göttingen: Vandenhoeck & Ruprecht, 1995.

Scholem, Gershom. *Major Trends in Jewish Mysticism.* Rev. ed. New York: Schocken, 1995.

Scholten, Clemens. *Martyrium und Sophiamythos im Gnostizismus nach den Texten von Nag Hammadi.* JAC 14. Münster: Aschendorff, 1987.

Schon, Donald A. "Knowing-in-action: The New Scholarship Requires a New Epistemology." *Change* 27/6 (1995) 26–34.

Schroeder, Caroline T. "More on Social Networks and Provenance." *Early Christian Monasticism in the Digital Age* (posted 23 June 2016). http://earlymonasticism.org/2016/06/16/social-networks/.

———. "On Institutional Responsibilities and on Gender: Final thoughts on the G of Jesus Wife." *Early Christian Monasticism in the Digital Age* (posted 23 June 2016). http://earlymonasticism.org/2016/06/23/on-institutional-responsibilities-and-on-gender-final-thoughts-on-the-g-of-jesus-wife/.

———. "Provenance Provenance Provenance." *Early Christian Monasticism in the Digital Age* (posted 16 June 2016). http://earlymonasticism.org/2016/06/16/provenance-provenance-provenance/.

Schwartz, Saundra. "From Bedroom to Courtroom: The Adultery Type-Scene in the *Acts of Andrew.*" In *Mapping Gender in Ancient Religious Discourses,* edited by

Todd Penner and Caroline Vander Stichele, 267–311. BibIntSer 84. Leiden: Brill, 2007.

Schweitzer, Albert. *The Quest of the Historical Jesus: A Critical Study of its Progress from Reimarus to Wrede*. 3rd ed. London: Black, 1954.

Scragg, Donald G. "Source Study." In *Reading Old English Texts*, edited by Katherine O'Brien O'Keeffe, 39–58. Cambridge: Cambridge University Press, 1997.

———. "The Vercelli Homilies and Kent." In *Intertexts: Studies in Anglo-Saxon Culture Presented to Paul E. Szarmach*, edited by Virginia Blanton and Helene Scheck, 369–80. MRTS 24. Tempe: Arizona Center for Medieval and Renaissance Studies, 2008.

———, ed. *The Vercelli Homilies and Related Texts*. Early English Texts Society, Original Series 300. Oxford: Oxford University Press, 1992.

Seneca. *Declamations*, vol. 1, *Controversiae Books 1–6*. Edited and translated by Michael Winterbottom. LCL 463. Cambridge: Harvard University Press, 1974.

Seydel, Rudolf. *Das Evangelium von Jesu in seinen Verhältnissen zu Buddha-Sage und Buddha-Lehre: Mit fortlaufender Rücksicht auf andere Religionskreise*. Leipzig: Breitkopf & Härtel, 1882.

Shanon, Benny. *The Antipodes of the Mind: Charting the Phenomenology of the Ayahuasca Experience*. Oxford: Oxford University Press, 2003.

Shea, William R. J. "Galileo's Claim to Fame: The Proof That the Earth Moves from the Evidence of the Tides." *British Journal for the History of Science* 5/2 (1970) 111–27.

Shehadi, Beshara. *The Confession of Pontius Pilate: First written, as alleged, in Latin, by Fabricius Albinus, a playmate of Pilate; translated into Arabic by Jerasimus Jared, late Bishop of Zahleh, in Lebanon*. Sydney: Booth, 1893.

Shoemaker, Stephen J. "Between Scripture and Tradition: The Marian Apocrypha of Early Christianity." In *The Reception and Interpretation of the Bible in Late Antiquity: Proceedings of the Montréal Colloquium in Honour of Charles Kannengiesser, 11–13 October 2006*, edited by Lorenzo DiTommaso and Lucian Turcescu, 491–510. Bible in Ancient Christianity 6. Leiden: Brill, 2006.

———. "Early Christian Apocryphal Literature." In *Oxford Handbook of Early Christian Studies*, edited by Susan Ashbrook Harvey and David G. Hunter, 521–48. Oxford: Oxford University Press, 2008.

Silverstein, Theodore. "The Date of the 'Apocalypse of Paul.'" *MS* 24 (1962) 335–48.

Simcox, William Henry. Review of *Peregrinus Proteus* by Joseph M. Cotterill. *The Academy* 15 (1879) 204–205.

Simonides, Constantin. *Fac-similes of Certain Portions of the Gospel of St. Matthew, and of the Epistles of Ss. James & Jude: Written on Papyrus in the First Century and Preserved in the Egyptian Museum of Joseph Mayer*. London: Trübner, 1861.

Sluter, George, ed. *The Acta Pilati: Important Testimony of Pontius Pilate, Recently Discovered*, by William Dennes Mahan. Shelbyville, IN: Robins, 1879.

Smith, David. "Rebel theologian surfaces at heart of Da Vinci case." *Guardian* (posted 4 March 2006). http://www.theguardian.com/uk/2006/mar/05/books.danbrown/.

Smith, Jonathan Z. *Drudgery Divine. On the Comparison of Early Christianity and the Religions of Late Antiquity*. Chicago: University of Chicago Press, 1990.

Smith, Kathryn A. "Chivalric Narratives and Devotional Experience in the Taymouth Hours." In *Negotiating Secular and Sacred in Medieval Art: Christian, Islamic, and Buddhist*, edited by Alicia Walker and Amanda Luyster, 17–54. Farnham, UK: Ashgate, 2009.

Smith, Morton. *Clement of Alexandria and a Secret Gospel of Mark.* Cambridge: Harvard University Press, 1973.

———. *The Secret Gospel: The Discovery and Interpretation of the Secret Gospel according to Mark.* New York: Harper & Row, 1973. Reprinted, Clearlake, CA: Dawn Horse, 1982.

Smith, Terence V. *Petrine Controversies in Early Christianity.* WUNT 2/15. Tübingen: Mohr/Siebeck, 1985.

Snyder, Glenn E. *Acts of Paul: The Formation of a Pauline Corpus.* WUNT 2/352. Tübingen: Mohr/Siebeck, 2013.

Solevag, Anna Rebecca. *Birthing Salvation: Gender and Class in Early Christian Childbearing Discourse.* BibIntSer 121. Leiden: Brill, 2013.

Solnit, Rebecca. *Men Explain Things to Me.* 2nd ed. Chicago: Haymarket, 2014.

Sozomen. "The Ecclesiastical History of Sozomen, Comprising a History of the Church, from A.D. 323 to A.D. 425." Translated by Chester D. Hartranft. In *A Select Library of Nicene and Post-Nicene Fathers of the Christian Church, Second Series, Translated into English with Prolegomena and Explanatory Notes,* vol. 2, *Socrates, Sozomenus: Church Histories,* edited by Philip Schaff and Henry Wace, 179–427. 14 vols. New York: The Christian Literature Company, 1890.

———. *Histoire ecclésiastique, livres VI–IX.* Translated by Guy Sabbah, Laurent Angliviel de la Beaumelle, André-Jean Festugière and Bernard Grillet. SC 516. Paris: Cerf, 2008.

Sparrow, Gerald. *The Great Forgers.* London: Long, 1963.

Speyer, Wolfgang. *Die literarische Fälschung im heidnischen und christlichen Altertum.* Handbuch der Altertumswissenschaft 1.2. Munich: Beck 1971.

Spong, John Shelby. *Born of a Woman: A Bishop Rethinks the Birth of Jesus.* New York: HarperCollins, 1992.

Stahl, Christel. "Derdekeas in the *Paraphrase of Shem,* NHC VII,I and the Manichaean Figure of Jesus, Two Interesting Paralells." In *Studia Manichaica IV, Internationaler Kongress zum Manichäismus,* edited by Ronald E. Emmerick, et al., 572–80. Berlin: Akademie, 1997.

Stetzer, Ed. "An Embarrassing Week for Christians Sharing Fake News." *Christianity Today* (posted 13 July 2015). http://www.christianitytoday.com/edstetzer/2015/july/embarrassing-week-for-christians-sharing-fake-news.html/.

Stewart, Bonnie E. "In Abundance: Networked Participatory Practices as Scholarship." *International Review of Research in Open and Distributed Learning* 16/3 (2015) 318–40. http://www.irrodl.org/index.php/irrodl/article/view/2158.

———. "Open to Influence: What Counts as Academic Influence in Scholarly Networked Twitter Participation." *Learning, Media and Technology* 40/3 (2015) 287–309.

Strawbridge, Jenn. "'A Preacher of the Truth': The Apostle Paul and Irenaeus." Paper presented at the Annual Meeting of the Society of Biblical Literature, Atlanta, GA, 22 November 2015.

Stroumsa, Gedaliahu. "Manichaean Challenge to Egyptian Christianity." In *The Roots of Egyptian Christianity,* edited by Birger A. Pearson and James E. Goehring, 307–19. Studies in Antiquity and Christianity. Philadelphia: Fortress, 1986.

———. "Monachisme et 'marranisme' chez les Manichéens d'Égypte." *Numen* 29 (1983) 184–201. Reprinted in Stroumsa, *Savoir et salut. Traditions juives et tentations dualistes dans le christianisme ancien*, 299–14. Patrimoines. Paris: Cerf, 1992.

Sturtevant, Edgar H. *Introduction to Linguistic Science*. New Haven: Yale University Press, 1947.

Suciu, Alin. "Apocryphon Berolinense/Argentoratense (Previously Known as the Gospel of the Savior). Reedition of P. Berol. 22220, Strasbourg Copte 5–7 and Qasr el-Wizz Codex ff. 12v–17r with Introduction and Commentary." PhD diss., Université Laval, 2013.

Suciu, Alin, and Hugo Lundhaug. "On the So-Called Gospel of Jesus's Wife: Some Preliminary Thoughts by Hugo Lundhaug and Alin Suciu." *Alin Suciu* (posted 26 September 2012). http://alinsuciu.com/2012/09/26/on-the-so-called-gospel-of-jesuss-wife-some-preliminary-thoughts-by-hugo-lundhaug-and-alin-suciu/.

Sundberg, Albert C., Jr. "Canon Muratori: A Fourth-Century List." *HTR* 66 (1973) 1–41.

Sutcliffe, Edmund F. "An Apocryphal Form of Pilate's Verdict." *CBQ* 9 (1947) 436–41.

Swanson, Vern G. *Dynasty of the Holy Grail: Mormonism's Sacred Bloodline*. Springville, UT: Cedar Fort, 2006.

Syme, Ronald. *Emperors and Biography: Studies in the "Historia Augusta."* Oxford: Carendon, 1971.

Szekely, Edmund Bordeaux. *The Discovery of the Essene Gospel of Peace: The Essenes and the Vatican*. San Diego: Academy, 1975.

———. *Essene Gospel of Peace*. Book One. San Diego: Academy, 1977. Originally published as Edmond Bordeaux Szekeley and Purcell Weaver, trans. *The Gospel of Peace of Jesus Christ by the Disciple John*. Ashington, Rochford, Essex: C. W. Daniel Company Ltd. and Leatherhead, Surrey: Bureaus of Cosmotherapy, Lawrence Weave House, 1937.

Tabor, James. "The Tombs at Talpiot: Overview of 'The Jesus Discovery.'" *Bible and Interpretation* (April 2013). Pages 1–33. http://www.bibleinterp.com/articles/2013/tab378024.shtml/.

Tajra, Harry W. *The Martyrdom of St. Paul: Historical and Judicial Contexts, Traditions, and Legends*. WUNT 2/67. Tübingen: Mohr/Siebeck, 1994.

Talmage, James. *Jesus the Christ: A Study of Messiah and His Mission according to the Holy Scriptures both Ancient and Modern*. Salt Lake City: Deseret News, 1915.

Temple, Elżbieta. *Anglo-Saxon Manuscripts, 900–1066*. A Survey of Manuscripts Illuminated in the British Isles 2. London: Miller, 1976.

Terian, Abraham, trans. *The Armenian Gospel of the Infancy: With Three Early Versions of the Protevangelium of James*. Oxford: Oxford University Press, 2008.

Tertullian. *Adversus Marcionem*. Translated by Ernest Evans. 2 vols. OECT. Oxford: Clarendon, 1972.

———. *On Baptism*. Translated by Sidney Thelwall. In *The Ante-Nicene Fathers*, vol. 3, edited by Alexander Roberts and James Donaldson, 669–79. 10 vols. 1885. Reprinted, Peabody, MA: Hendrickson, 1994.

———. *Tertullian's Homily on Baptism: The Text Edited with an Introduction, Translation and Commentary*. Edited by Ernest Evans. London: SPCK, 1964.

———. *Traité du baptême*. Edited by François Refoulé. 2nd ed. SC 35. Paris: Cerf, 2002.

Testuz, Michel, ed. *Papyrus Bodmer X–XII*. Cologne: Bibliotheca Bodmeriana, 1959.

Tischendorf, Constantin von. *Evangelia Apocrypha*. 2nd ed. Leipzig: Mendelssohn, 1876. Reprinted, Hildesheim: Olms, 1966.

Tite, Philip L. "Voluntary Martyrdom and Gnosticism." *JECS* 23 (2015) 27–54.

Tóibín, Colm. *The Testament of Mary*. New York: Scribner, 2012.

Toepel, Alexander, trans. "The Apocryphon of Seth." In *Old Testament Pseudepigrapha: More Non-Canonical Scriptures*, vol. 1, edited by Richard Bauckham, et al., 33–39. Grand Rapids: Eerdmans, 2013.

Tóth, Péter. "Way Out of the Tunnel? Three Hundred Years of Research on the Apocrypha: A Preliminary Approach." In *Retelling the Bible: Literary, Historical and Social Contexts*, edited by Lucie Dolezalová and Tamás Visi, 45–84. Frankfurt: Lang, 2011.

Tregelles, Samuel Prideaux, ed. and trans. *Canon Muratorianus, the Earliest Catalogue of the Books of the New Testament*. Oxford: Clarendon, 1867.

Treggiari, Susan. *Roman Marriage: Iusti Coniuges from the Time of Cicero to the Time of Ulpian*. Oxford: Clarendon, 1991.

Truelle, Johann Nepomuk. *Die wichtigen historischen Enthüllungen über Geburt und Todesart Jesu (bei Chr. Ernst Kollmann) sind ein: "Literarischer Betrug."* Regensburg: Manz, 1850.

Turner, Derek H. "Illuminated Manuscripts." In *The Golden Age of Anglo-Saxon Art, 966–1066*, edited by Janet Backhouse, D. H. Turner, and Leslie Webster, 46–87. London: British Museum Publications, 1984.

Turner, John G. *The Mormon Jesus: A Biography*. Cambridge: Belknap, 2016.

Tuross, Noreen. "Accelerated Mass Spectrometry Radiocarbon Determination of Papyrus Samples." *HTR* 107 (2014) 170–71.

Veilleux, Armand. "Monasticism and Gnosis in Egypt." In *The Roots of Egyptian Christianity*, edited by Birger A. Pearson and James E. Goehring, 271–306. Studies in Antiquity and Christianity. Philadelphia: Fortress, 1986.

Venuti, Lawrence. "Adaptation, Translation, Critique." *Journal of Visual Culture* 6 (2007) 25–43.

Verenna, Thomas. "Two Days Later: Another Evaluation of the 'Jesus Wife' Papyrus." *Musings of Thomas Verenna* (posted 20 September 2012). https://tomverenna. wordpress.com/2012/09/20/two-days-later-another-evaluation-of-the-jesus-wife-papyrus/.

———. "The 'Wife of Jesus' Fragment a Day Later: Some Concerns about Authenticity." *Musings of Thomas Verenna* (posted 19 September 2012). https://tomverenna. wordpress.com/2012/09/19/the-wife-of-jesus-fragment-a-day-later-some-concerns-about-authenticity/.

Vermès, Géza. *Jesus the Jew: A Historian's Reading of the Gospels*. Minneapolis: Fortress, 1981.

Viklund, Roger. "Tremors, or Just an Optical Illusion? A Further Evaluation of Carlson's Handwriting Analysis." *Jesus granskad* (posted 12 December 2009). http://www. jesusgranskad.se/theodore2.htm/.

Voss, Isaac. *Epistulae genuinae S. Ignatii Martyris*. Amsterdam: J. Blaeu, 1646.

Waldstein, Michael, and Frederik Wisse, eds. *The Apocryphon of John: Synopsis of Nag Hammadi Codices II,1; III,1; and IV,1 with BG 8592,2*. Leiden: Brill, 1995.

Walker, Alexander, ed. and trans. *Apocryphal Gospels, Acts and Revelations*. The Ante-Nicene Christian Library 16. Edinburgh: T. & T. Clark, 1873.

Wallace, Lew. *Lew Wallace: An Autobiography*. 2 vols. New York: Harper & Row, 1906.

Walter, Howard A. *The Ahmadīya Movement*. Religious Life of India. New York: Oxford University Press, 1918.

Walters, J. Edward. "Evidence for Citations of *3 Corinthians* and Their Influence in the Demonstrations of Aphrahat." *VC* 67 (2013) 248–62.

Wangsness, Lisa. "Historian's Finding Hints That Jesus Was Married." *Boston Globe* (posted 18 September 2012). http://www.bostonglobe.com/metro/2012/09/18/harvard-professor-identifies-scrap-papyrus-suggesting-some-early-christians-believed-jesus-was-married/VzqcRBAfiDRVFL9nWt4iTN/story.html/.

———. "'Jesus's Wife' Papyrus Likely Fake, Scholar Says." *Boston Globe* (posted 18 June 2016). https://www.bostonglobe.com/metro/2016/06/17/the-gospel-jesus-wife-fake/qvl3Vf3EXY8cJ31pqTQoOJ/story.html/.

Warren, Meredith J. C. "'My Heart Poured Forth Understanding': *4 Ezra*'s Fiery Cup as Hierophagic Consumption." *SR* 44 (2015) 1–14.

Wasserman, Tommy. "Papyrus 72 and the Bodmer Miscellaneous Codex." *NTS* 51 (2005) 137–54.

Wasson, R. Gordon. *Soma: Divine Mushroom of Immortality.* New York: Harcourt, Brace, Jovanovich, 1968.

Watson, Francis. "Beyond Reasonable Doubt: A Response to Allan J. Pantuck." *Biblical Archaeology Review Scholar's Study* (posted 2011). Pages 1–8. http://www.bib-arch.org/scholars-study/secret-mark-handwriting-response-watson.asp.

———. "The *Gospel of Jesus' Wife*: How a Fake Gospel-Fragment Was Composed." *NT Blog* (posted 26 September 2012). Pages 1–8. http://markgoodacre.org/Watson.pdf/.

———. "The *Gospel of Jesus' Wife*: How a Fake Gospel-Fragment Was Composed: Introduction and Summary." *NT Blog* (posted 27 September 2012). Pages 1–4. http://markgoodacre.org/Watson2.pdf/.

———. *Gospel Writing: A Canonical Perspective.* Grand Rapids: Eerdmans, 2013.

Wayment, Thomas. *The Text of the New Testament Apocrypha (100–400 CE).* London: Bloomsbury, 2013.

Weber, Robert, ed. *Biblia Sacra Iuxta Vulgatam Versionem.* 4th ed. Stuttgart: Deutsche Bibelgesellschaft, 2005.

Webster, Leslie. *Anglo-Saxon Art: A New History.* Cornell Paperbacks. Ithaca, NY: Cornell University Press, 2012.

West, Jim. "And Now the Motive for the Announcement of the 'Jesus' Wife' Fragment May Be Coming to Light." *Zwingli Redivivus* (posted 19 September 2012). https://zwingliusredivivus.wordpress.com/2012/09/19/and-now-the-motive-for-the-announcement-of-the-jesus-wife-fragment-may-be-coming-to-light/.

———. "No, People, a 4th Century Scrap Doesn't Prove Jesus Had a Wife." *Zwingli Redivivus* (posted 18 September 2012). https://zwingliusredivivus.wordpress.com/2012/09/18/no-people-a-4th-century-scrap-doesnt-prove-jesus-had-a-wife/.

Westwood, John O. *Facsimiles of the Ornaments of Anglo-Saxon and Irish Manuscripts.* London: Quaritch, 1868.

White, Benjamin L. "How to Read a Book: Irenaeus and the Pastoral Epistles Reconsidered." *VC* 65 (2011) 125–49.

———. "Reclaiming Paul? Reconfiguration as Reclamation in *3 Corinthians*." *JECS* 17/4 (2009) 497–523.

———. *Remembering Paul: Ancient and Modern Contests over the Image of the Apostle.* Oxford: Oxford University Press, 2014.

White, John L. "Saint Paul and the Apostolic Letter Tradition." *CBQ* 45 (1983) 433–44.

Whitesell, David. "This Just In: Please Welcome P. Virginia 1!" *Notes from Under Grounds* (posted 14 May 2015). http://smallnotes.library.virginia.edu/2015/05/14/this-just-in-please-welcome-p-virginia-1/.

———. "This Just In: Problematic Provenance." *Notes from Under Grounds* (posted 5 June 2015). smallnotes.library.virginia.edu/2015/06/05/this-just-in-problematic-provenance/.

Williams, Mark. *Fiery Shapes: Celestial Portents and Astrology in Ireland and Wales, 700–1700.* Oxford: Oxford University Press, 2010.

Willoughby, Harold R. *Pagan Regeneration: A Study of Mystery Initiations in the Graeco-Roman World.* 1929. Reprinted, Chicago: Chicago University Press, 1960.

Wilson, Henry A., ed. *The Missal of Robert of Jumièges.* Henry Bradshaw Society 11. London: Henry Bradshaw Society, 1896.

Wilson, Rita, and Brigid Maher, eds. *Words, Images and Performances in Translation.* New York: Continuum, 2012.

Wininger, Salomon. "Osip Konstantinovich Notovich." In *Große Jüdische National-Biographie: Ein Nachschlagewerk für das jüdische Volk und dessen Freunde,* vol. 4, edited by Salomon Wininger, 547. 7 vols. Cernăuți: Orient, 1929–1936.

Wisse, Frederick, trans. "The Letter of Peter to Philip." In *Nag Hammadi Codex VIII,* edited by John H. Sieber, 227–51. NHMS 31. Leiden: Brill, 1991.

Witakowski, Witold. *The Syriac Chronicle of Pseudo-Dionysius of Tel-Mahre: A Study in the History of Historiography.* Uppsala: Uppsala University Press, 1987.

Witherington, Ben, III. *The Gospel Code: Novel Claims about Jesus, Mary Magdalene, and Da Vinci.* Downers Grove, IL: InterVarsity, 2004.

Woodfin, Warren T. "An Officer and a Gentleman: Transformations in the Iconography of a Warrior Saint." *DOP* 60 (2006) 111–42.

Wright, Charles D. "Old English Homilies and Latin Sources." In *The Old English Homily: Precedent, Practice, and Appropriation,* edited by Aaron J. Kleist, 15–66. Turnhout: Brepols, 2007.

———. *The Irish Tradition in Old English Literature.* Cambridge Studies in Anglo-Saxon England 6. Cambridge: Cambridge University Press, 1993.

Yardley, James T., and Alexis Hagadorn. "Characterization of the Chemical Nature of the Black Ink in the Manuscript of The Gospel of Jesus's Wife through Micro-Raman Spectroscopy." *HTR* 107 (2014) 162–64.

Young, Brigham. *Journal of Discourses.* 26 vols. Liverpool: Richards, 1854.

———. "Remarks by President Brigham Young, after Elder Hyde had Lectured on the Marriage Relations, Oct. 6 1854." *Deseret News,* 26 October 1854, 2.

Young, Richard Alan. *Is God a Vegetarian? Christianity, Vegetarianism, and Animal Rights.* La Salle, IL: Open Court, 1998.

Zacher, Samantha. *Preaching the Converted: The Style and Rhetoric of the Vercelli Homilies.* Toronto Anglo-Saxon Series 1. Toronto: University of Toronto Press, 2009.

Zacher, Samantha, and Andy Orchard, eds. *New Readings in the Vercelli Book.* Toronto Anglo-Saxon Series 4. Toronto: University of Toronto Press, 2009.

Zanoletti, Margherita. "Marinetti and Buvoli: A Translation Studies Approach to Italian Art and Culture." In *Shaping an Identity: Adapting, Rewriting and Remaking Italian Literature,* edited by Pamela Arancibia et al., 175–91. Media and Education Studies 63. New York: Legas, 2012.

Zeller, Eduard. *Plato and the Older Academy.* Translated by Sarah Frances Alleyne and Alfred Goodwin. London: Longmans, Green, 1888.

Ancient Texts Index

Subject Index

Modern Authors Index

Aageson, James W., 154, 173
Aaronovitch, David, 283
Abanes, Richard, 357
Ahmad, Khwaja Nazir, 276
Ahmad, Mirza Ghulam, 276–77
Alderman, Naomi, 20, 293–98
Allen, Charlotte, 29
Allegro, John Marco, 8, 91
Amann, Émile, 10
Anastasopoulou, Venetia, 260
Anderson, Gary A., 86
Anderson, Richard L., 238–39
Armstrong, Jonathan J., 159
Aron, Robert, 248
Arthur, Richard J., 20, 256–57
Ashwin-Siejkowski, Piotr, 98, 102, 116
Askeland, Christian, 26–27, 28, 262,
    310, 315, 317, 318–19, 323, 332,
    335, 350, 363
Atherton, M., 215
Augustin, Antonio, 4
Austin, John, 234
Azzarelli, Joseph M., 306

Baalen, Jan Karel van, 356
Baden, Joel, 307, 320, 332, 350, 363
Bagnall, Roger S., 307–308, 317, 372
Baigent, Michael, 283, 347, 360–61
Baines, Paul, 5, 6, 8, 264
Baker, Kelly, 369
Bakewell, Joan, 345
Banning, Joop van, 82
Bar Asher, Avishai, 59
Barc, Bernard, 199
Barnes, Timothy D., 54, 142

Barrier, Jeremy W., 53
Bates, Stephen, 343
Bauer, Rick, 363
Baum, Armin, 44
Baumeister, Theofried, 143
Beadle, John H., 355
Beal, Timothy, 164
Beard, Mary, 322, 368
Beasley, Jonathan, 307
Bedingfield, M. Bradford, 211
Beker, Johan C., 154,
Bell, Sinclair, 67, 184
Bentley, Richard, 5, 6
Berding, Kenneth, 158, 160
Berger, Samuel, 9
Berliner, Rudolf, 240
Bernhard, Andrew, 63, 70, 261, 262,
    310, 313, 315, 317, 319, 332–33,
    338
Berry, George R., 119
Beskow, Per, 10, 13–14, 15, 232–36,
    238–39, 241–43, 245, 248,
    250–52, 263, 265, 267–68, 276,
    277–78, 286
Beyers, Rita, 209, 228
Bickell, Gustav, 61, 64
Biggs, Frederick M., 208
Blavatsky, Helena P., 278–79
Blossom, Stefaniw, 180
Bock, Darrell, 343, 362
Boer, Esther de, 346, 363
Boer, Martinus de, 154
Boer, Roland, 300
Böhlig, Alexander, 204
Bond, Helen K., 322

Made in United States
Orlando, FL
18 December 2024

56066546R00286